Reading Street

Grade 5,

Inventors a

DATE DUE

MAY 0 1 2013			
NOV 1 8 2014			

Demco, Inc. 38-293

D1472460

PEARSON
Scott Foresman

scottforesman.com

Editorial Offices: Glenview, Illinois • Parsippany, New Jersey • New York, New York
Sales Offices: Boston, Massachusetts • Duluth, Georgia • Glenview, Illinois
Coppell, Texas • Sacramento, California • Mesa, Arizona

We dedicate Reading Street to
Peter Jovanovich.

His wisdom, courage,
and passion for education
are an inspiration to us all.

Accelerated Reader®

Cover Greg Newbold

About the Cover Artist
Award-winning artist Greg Newbold began drawing and painting at age three—and never stopped. His illustrated books for children include *Spring Song* and *Winter Lullaby*. Mr. Newbold also does illustrations for magazines, motion pictures, and food products, such as catsup and jelly. He creates his illustrations in a studio next to his house, snuggled in the Rocky Mountains of Utah.

ISBN-13: 978-0-328-24387-7

ISBN-10:   0-328-24387-6

Copyright © 2008 Pearson Education, Inc.

All Rights Reserved. Printed in the United States of America. This publication is protected by Copyright, and permission should be obtained from the publisher prior to any prohibited reproduction, storage in a retrieval system, or transmission in any form by any means, electronic, mechanical, photocopying, recording, or likewise. For information regarding permission(s), write to: Permissions Department, Scott Foresman, 1900 East Lake Avenue, Glenview, Illinois 60025.

Many of the designations used by manufacturers and sellers to distinguish their products are claimed as trademarks. Where those designations appear in this book, and Scott Foresman was aware of a trademark claim, the designations have been printed with initial capitals and in cases of multiple usage have also been marked with either ® or ™ where they first appear.

2 3 4 5 6 7 8 9 10 11 V063 16 15 14 13 12 11 10 09 08 07
CC:N1

Reading STREET

Where the Love of Reading Begins

Reading Street Program Authors

Peter Afflerbach, Ph.D.
Professor, Department of
Curriculum and Instruction
University of Maryland at
College Park

Camille L.Z. Blachowicz, Ph.D.
Professor of Education
National-Louis University

Candy Dawson Boyd, Ph.D.
Professor, School of Education
Saint Mary's College of California

Wendy Cheyney, Ed.D.
Professor of Special Education
and Literacy, Florida
International University

Connie Juel, Ph.D.
Professor of Education, School of
Education, Stanford University

Edward J. Kame'enui, Ph.D.
Professor and Director, Institute for
the Development of Educational
Achievement, University of Oregon

Donald J. Leu, Ph.D.
John and Maria Neag Endowed
Chair in Literacy and Technology
University of Connecticut

Jeanne R. Paratore, Ed.D.
Associate Professor of Education
Department of Literacy
and Language Development
Boston University

P. David Pearson, Ph.D.
Professor and Dean,
Graduate School of Education
University of California, Berkeley

Sam L. Sebesta, Ed.D.
Professor Emeritus,
College of Education,
University of Washington, Seattle

Deborah Simmons, Ph.D.
Professor, College of Education
and Human Development
Texas A&M University
(Not pictured)

Sharon Vaughn, Ph.D.
H.E. Hartfelder/Southland
Corporation Regents Professor
University of Texas

Susan Watts-Taffe, Ph.D.
Independent Literacy Researcher
Cincinnati, Ohio

Karen Kring Wixson, Ph.D.
Professor of Education
University of Michigan

Components

Student Editions (1–6)

Teacher's Editions (PreK–6)

Assessment
Assessment Handbook (K–6)
Baseline Group Tests (K–6)
DIBELS™ Assessments (K–6)
ExamView® Test Generator CD-ROM (2–6)
Fresh Reads for Differentiated
Test Practice (1–6)
Online Success Tracker™ (K–6)*
Selection Tests Teacher's Manual (1–6)
Unit and End-of-Year
Benchmark Tests (K–6)

Leveled Readers
Concept Literacy Leveled Readers (K–1)
Independent Leveled Readers (K)
Kindergarten Student Readers (K)
Leveled Reader Teaching Guides (K–6)
Leveled Readers (1–6)
Listen to Me Readers (K)
Online Leveled Reader Database (K–6)*
Take-Home Leveled Readers (K–6)

Trade Books and Big Books
Big Books (PreK–2)
Read Aloud Trade Books (PreK–K)
Sing with Me Big Book (1–2)
Trade Book Library (1–6)

Decodable Readers
Decodable Readers (K–3)
Strategic Intervention
Decodable Readers (1–2)
Take-Home Decodable Readers (K–3)

Phonics and Word Study
Alphabet Cards in English and Spanish
(PreK–K)
Alphabet Chart in English and Spanish
(PreK–K)
Animal ABCs Activity Guide (K)
Finger Tracing Cards (PreK–K)
Patterns Book (PreK–K)
Phonics Activities CD-ROM (PreK–2)*
Phonics Activities Mats (K)
Phonics and Spelling Practice Book (1–3)
Phonics and Word-Building Board and Letters
(PreK–3)
Phonics Songs and Rhymes Audio CD (K–2)
Phonics Songs and Rhymes Flip Chart (K–2)
Picture Word Cards (PreK–K)
Plastic Letter Tiles (K)
Sound-Spelling Cards and Wall Charts (1–2)
Strategies for Word Analysis (4–6)
Word Study and Spelling Practice Book (4–6)

Language Arts
Daily Fix-It Transparencies (K–6)
Grammar & Writing Book and
Teacher's Annotated Edition, The (1–6)
Grammar and Writing Practice Book
and Teacher's Manual (1–6)
Grammar Transparencies (1–6)
Six-Trait Writing Posters (1–6)
Writing Kit (1–6)
Writing Rubrics and Anchor Papers (1–6)
Writing Transparencies (1–6)

Practice and Additional Resources
AlphaBuddy Bear Puppet (K)
Alphasaurus Annie Puppet (PreK)
Amazing Words Posters (K–2)
Centers Survival Kit (PreK–6)
Graphic Organizer Book (2–6)
Graphic Organizer Flip Chart (K–1)
High-Frequency Word Cards (K)
Kindergarten Review (1)
Practice Book and Teacher's Manual (K–6)
Read Aloud Anthology (PreK–2)
Readers' Theater Anthology (K–6)
Research into Practice (K–6)

Retelling Cards (K–6)
Scott Foresman Research Base (K–6)
Skill Transparencies (2–6)
Songs and Rhymes Flip Chart (PreK)
Talk with Me, Sing with Me Chart (PreK–K)
Tested Vocabulary Cards (1–6)
Vocabulary Transparencies (1–2)
Welcome to Reading Street (PreK–1)

ELL
ELL and Transition Handbook (PreK–6)
ELL Comprehensive Kit (1–6)
ELL Posters (K–6)
ELL Readers (1–6)
ELL Teaching Guides (1–6)
Ten Important Sentences (1–6)

Digital Components
AudioText CDs (PreK–6)
Background Building Audio CDs (3–6)
ExamView® Test Generator
CD-ROM (2–6)
Online Lesson Planner (K–6)
Online New Literacies Activities (1–6)*
Online Professional Development (1–6)
Online Story Sort (K–6)*
Online Student Editions (1–6)*
Online Success Tracker™ (K–6)*
Online Teacher's Editions (PreK–6)
Phonics Activities CD-ROM (PreK–2)*
Phonics Songs and Rhymes
Audio CD (K–2)
Sing with Me/Background Building
Audio CDs (PreK–2)
Songs and Rhymes Audio CD (PreK)

My Sidewalks Early Reading Intervention (K)

My Sidewalks Intensive Reading Intervention (Levels A–E)

Reading Street for the Guided Reading Teacher (1–6)

v

Unit 3

Inventors and Artists

Unit Opener. 260a
Unit 3 Skills Overview 260c
Unit 3 Monitor Progress. 260e
Grouping for AYP 260g
Theme Launch 260
Unit 3 Inquiry Project 261
Unit 3 Concept Development 261a

Wings for the King. 262a–287l
by Anne Sroda

Social Studies in Reading
**Becky Schroeder:
Enlightened Thinker** 282

Leonardo's Horse 288a–315l
by Jean Fritz

Social Studies in Reading
Humans with Wings. 312

**The Dinosaurs of
Waterhouse Hawkins** 316a–345l
by Barbara Kerley

Science in Reading
A Model Scientist 340

Mahalia Jackson. 346a–363l
by Julius Lester

Poetry
Perfect Harmony. 360

**Special Effects in Film
and Television** 364a–383l
by Jake Hamilton

Reading Online
Searching for Animation. 380

Unit 3 Concept Wrap-Up 384a
Unit 3 Reading Poetry 384
Unit 3 Wrap-Up. 388
Glossary. 389a
ELL Glossary 389e

Writing and Assessment WA1–WA18

Leveled Resources LR1–LR48

Differentiated Instruction . . . . . . DI•1–DI•60

Teacher Resources TR1–TR42

Unit 4

Adapting

Unit Opener. 390a
Unit 4 Skills Overview 390c
Unit 4 Monitor Progress. 390e
Grouping for AYP 390g
Theme Launch 390
Unit 4 Inquiry Project 391
Unit 4 Concept Development 391a

Weslandia 392a–411l
by Paul Fleischman

Poetry
Under the Back Porch/Keziah 410

Stretching Ourselves. 412a–435l
by Alden R. Carter

Science in Reading
Helpful Tools 434

Exploding Ants 436a–457l
by Joanne Settel

Science in Reading
**The Creature from the Adapting
Lagoon** 454

The Stormi Giovanni Club . . . 458a–483l
by Lydia R. Diamond

Social Studies in Reading
Think Dress Codes Are a Drag?. . . 480

The Gymnast 484a–503l
by Gary Soto

Reading Online
All About Gymnastics 500

Unit 4 Concept Wrap-Up 504a
Unit 4 Reading Poetry 504
Unit 4 Wrap-Up. 508
Glossary. 509a
ELL Glossary 509e

Writing and Assessment WA1–WA18

Leveled Resources LR1–LR48

Differentiated Instruction . . . . . . DI•1–DI•60

Teacher Resources TR1–TR42

Unit 5

Adventurers

Unit Opener 510a
Unit 5 Skills Overview 510c
Unit 5 Monitor Progress 510e
Grouping for AYP 510g
Theme Launch 510
Unit 5 Inquiry Project 511
Unit 5 Concept Development 511a

The Three-Century Woman . . 512a–535l
by Richard Peck

Short Story
Understanding the
Banana-Mobile 532

The Unsinkable Wreck of
the R.M.S. Titanic 536a–559l
by Robert D. Ballard and Rick Archbold

Social Studies in Reading
Shipwreck Season 554

Talk with an Astronaut 560a–581l
Interview

Reading Online
Women Astronauts 578

Journey to the Center of
the Earth 582a–603l
by Jules Verne

Science in Reading
Crust, Mantle, Core 600

Ghost Towns of
the American West 604a–625l
by Raymond Bial

Social Studies in Reading
Dame Shirley Goes to
the Gold Rush 622

Unit 5 Concept Wrap-Up 626a
Unit 5 Reading Poetry 626
Unit 5 Wrap-Up 630
Glossary 631a
ELL Glossary 631e

Writing and Assessment WA1–WA18

Leveled Resources LR1–LR48

Differentiated Instruction ...... DI•1–DI•60

Teacher Resources TR1–TR42

Unit 6

The Unexpected

Unit Opener 632a
Unit 6 Skills Overview 632c
Unit 6 Monitor Progress 632e
Grouping for AYP 632g
Theme Launch 632
Unit 6 Inquiry Project 633
Unit 6 Concept Development 633a

At the Beach 634a–653l
by Lulu Delacre

Folk Literature
The Eagle and the Bat 652

The Mystery of
Saint Matthew Island 654a–673l
by Susan E. Quinlan

Science in Reading
Get the Lead Out 670

King Midas and
the Golden Touch 674a–699l
by Charlotte Craft

Poetry
Jimmy Jet and His TV Set 698

The Hindenburg 700a–725l
by Patrick O'Brien

Reading Online
Earthquakes and
Primary Sources 722

Sweet Music in Harlem 726a–753l
by Debbie A. Taylor

Social Studies in Reading
Author's Note 750

Unit 6 Concept Wrap-Up 754a
Unit 6 Reading Poetry 754
Unit 6 Wrap-Up 758
Glossary 759a
ELL Glossary 759e

Writing and Assessment WA1–WA18

Leveled Resources LR1–LR48

Differentiated Instruction ...... DI•1–DI•60

Teacher Resources TR1–TR42

Unit 1
Meeting Challenges

Unit Opener 16a
Unit 1 Skills Overview 16c
Unit 1 Monitor Progress 16e
Grouping for AYP 16g
Theme Launch 16
Unit 1 Inquiry Project 17
Unit 1 Concept Development 17a

Frindle 18a–41l
by Andrew Clements
Fantasy
Punctuation Takes a Vacation 36

Thunder Rose 42a–67l
by Jerdine Nolen
Science in Reading
Measuring Tornadoes 66

Island of the Blue Dolphins . . . 68a–89l
by Scott O'Dell
Science in Reading
Seven Survival Questions 86

Satchel Paige 90a–111l
by Lesa Cline-Ransome
Social Studies in Reading
The Girls of Summer 110

Shutting Out the Sky 112a–133l
by Deborah Hopkinson
Reading Online
The Immigrant Experience 130

Unit 1 Concept Wrap-Up 134a
Unit 1 Reading Poetry 134
Unit 1 Wrap-Up 138
Genre/Author Studies 139a
Author/Illustrator Biographies 139c
Glossary 139q
ELL Glossary 139u

Writing and Assessment WA1–WA18

Leveled Resources LR1–LR48

Differentiated Instruction . . DI•1–DI•60

Teacher Resources TR1–TR42

Unit 2
Doing the Right Thing

Unit Opener 140a
Unit 2 Skills Overview 140c
Unit 2 Monitor Progress 140e
Grouping for AYP 140g
Theme Launch 140
Unit 2 Inquiry Project 141
Unit 2 Concept Development 141a

Inside Out 142a–161l
by Francisco Jiménez
Social Studies in Reading
Random Acts of Kindness 160

Passage to Freedom 162a–185l
by Ken Mochizuki
Social Studies in Reading
I Wanted My Mother 180

The Ch'i-lin Purse 186a–207l
by Linda Fang
Folk Literature
The Lion and the Mouse 206

**Jane Goodall's 10 Ways
to Help Save Wildlife** 208a–229l
by Jane Goodall
Science in Reading
**Why Some Animals Are
Considered Bad or Scary** 226

**The Midnight Ride of
Paul Revere** 230a–253l
by Henry Wadsworth Longfellow
Reading Online
Revolutionary War Women 250

Unit 2 Concept Wrap-Up 254a
Unit 2 Reading Poetry 254
Unit 2 Wrap-Up 258
Glossary 259a
ELL Glossary 259e

Writing and Assessment WA1–WA18

Leveled Resources LR1–LR48

Differentiated Instruction . . . . . . DI•1–DI•60

Teacher Resources TR1–TR42

Inventors and Artists

What do people gain from the work of inventors and artists?

Wings for the King

An inventor lifts a king's spirits.

PLAY

connect to SCIENCE

Paired Selection

Becky Schroeder: Enlightened Thinker

NARRATIVE NONFICTION

Leonardo's Horse

A genius gives the world his dream.

BIOGRAPHY

connect to SOCIAL STUDIES

Paired Selection

Humans with Wings

NARRATIVE NONFICTION

The Dinosaurs of Waterhouse Hawkins

A scientist makes dinosaurs into art.

BIOGRAPHY

connect to SCIENCE

Paired Selection

A Model Scientist

INTERVIEW

Mahalia Jackson

Singers put soul into music.

EXPOSITORY NONFICTION

connect to SOCIAL STUDIES

Paired Selection

Perfect Harmony

POETRY

Special Effects in Film and Television

Artists make the fantastic seem real.

EXPOSITORY NONFICTION

connect to SOCIAL STUDIES

Paired Selection

Searching for Animation

SEARCH ENGINES

Unit 3
Skills Overview

266–287
Wings for the King/ Becky Schroeder: Enlightened Thinker   PLAY

How do inventors inspire our imaginations?

292–315
Leonardo's Horse/ Humans with Wings   BIOGRAPHY

How do artists inspire future generations?

		Wings for the King/ Becky Schroeder: Enlightened Thinker	Leonardo's Horse/ Humans with Wings
Reading	**Comprehension**	T ⊙ **Skill** Author's Purpose ⊙ **Strategy** Story Structure T REVIEW **Skill** Cause and Effect	T ⊙ **Skill** Main Idea ⊙ **Strategy** Summarize T REVIEW **Skill** Fact and Opinion
	Vocabulary	T ⊙ **Strategy** Context Clues	T ⊙ **Strategy** Word Structure
	Fluency	Tone of Voice	Tempo and Rate
Word Work	**Spelling and Phonics**	Schwa	Compound Words
Oral Language	**Speaking/Listening/ Viewing**	Play Review Listen to Audio CD	Newscast Analyze a Painting
Language Arts	**Grammar, Usage, and Mechanics**	T Past, Present, and Future Tenses	T Principal Parts of Regular Verbs
	Weekly Writing	Skit Writing Trait: Conventions	Question/Answer Essay Writing Trait: Focus/Ideas
	Unit Process Writing	Compare and Contrast Essay	Compare and Contrast Essay
	Research and Study Skills	Advertisement	Skim and Scan
Integrate Science and Social Studies Standards		Science: Inventors, Scientific Method, Insects	Time for SOCIAL STUDIES: The Renaissance, Humanities, Culture

⊙ Target Skill   T Tested Skill

 **Big Idea** *What do people gain from the work of inventors and artists?*

WEEK 3	WEEK 4	WEEK 5
320–345 **The Dinosaurs of Waterhouse Hawkins/ A Model Scientist** BIOGRAPHY *How can paleontologists help us understand the past?*	350–363 **Mahalia Jackson/ Perfect Harmony** EXPOSITORY NONFICTION *How does an artist use music to inspire others?*	368–383 **Special Effects in Film and Television/ Searching for Animation** EXPOSITORY NONFICTION *How do artists create special effects to entertain us?*
T ⊙ **Skill** Fact and Opinion ⊙ **Strategy** Predict **T** REVIEW **Skill** Main Idea	**T** ⊙ **Skill** Main Idea ⊙ **Strategy** Graphic Organizers **T** REVIEW **Skill** Fact and Opinion	**T** ⊙ **Skill** Graphic Sources ⊙ **Strategy** Prior Knowledge **T** REVIEW **Skill** Author's Purpose
T ⊙ **Strategy** Context Clues	**T** ⊙ **Strategy** Context Clues	**T** ⊙ **Strategy** Word Structure
Phrasing	Tempo and Rate	Tempo and Rate
Consonant Sounds /j/, /ks/, /sk/, and /s/	One Consonant or Two	Prefixes *un-, de-, dis-*
Introduction Listen to Audio CD	Oral Presentation Listen to Music	Advertisement Analyze Media
T Principal Parts of Irregular Verbs	**T** Troublesome Verbs	**T** Prepositions and Prepositional Phrases
Feature Story Writing Trait: Organization/Paragraphs	Description Writing Trait: Word Choice	Expository Writing Writing Trait: Sentences
Compare and Contrast Essay	Compare and Contrast Essay	Compare and Contrast Essay
Schedule	Technology: Card Catalog/Library Database	Graphics/Symbols
Time for **Science** Fossils, Dinosaurs, Paleontology, Extinction	*Time for* **SOCIAL STUDIES** U.S. History, Contributions of African Americans, 20th Century Culture	*Time for* **SOCIAL STUDIES** Careers, Technology, Entertainment Industry

Unit 3
Monitor Progress

Predictors of Reading Success		WEEK 1	WEEK 2	WEEK 3	WEEK 4
WCPM	**Fluency**	Tone of Voice 115–122 WCPM	Tempo and Rate 115–122 WCPM	Phrasing 115–122 WCPM	Tempo and Rate 115–122 WCPM
Vocabulary	**Vocabulary/ Concept Development** (assessed informally)	experiment suggested theory	canvas charcoal easel Norman Rockwell	fossils paleontologists sandstone	beat blended time
	Lesson Vocabulary	**Strategy** Context Clues admiringly permit scoundrel subject worthless	**Strategy** Word Structure achieved architect bronze cannon depressed fashioned midst philosopher rival	**Strategy** Context Clues erected foundations mold occasion proportion tidied workshop	**Strategy** Context Clues appreciate barber choir released religious slavery teenager
Retelling	**Text Comprehension**	**Skill** Author's Purpose **Strategy** Story Structure	**Skill** Main Idea **Strategy** Summarize	**Skill** Fact and Opinion **Strategy** Predict	**Skill** Main Idea **Strategy** Graphic Organizers

⚙ Make Data–Driven Decisions

Data Management	Classroom Management
• Assess	• Monitor Progress
• Diagnose	• Group
• Prescribe	• Differentiate Instruction
• Disaggregate	• Inform Parents

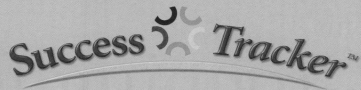

ONLINE CLASSROOM

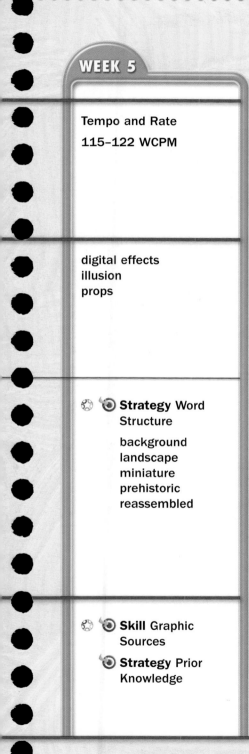

WEEK 5

Tempo and Rate
115–122 WCPM

digital effects
illusion
props

⚙ 🌐 **Strategy** Word
Structure

background
landscape
miniature
prehistoric
reassembled

⚙ 🌐 **Skill** Graphic
Sources

🌐 **Strategy** Prior
Knowledge

⚙ Manage Data

- Assign the Unit 3 Benchmark Test for students to take online.
- SuccessTracker records results and generates reports by school, grade, classroom, or student.
- Use reports to disaggregate and aggregate Unit 3 skills and standards data to monitor progress.
- Based on class lists created to support the categories important for AYP (gender, ethnicity, migrant education, English proficiency, disabilities, economic status), reports let you track adequate yearly progress every six weeks.

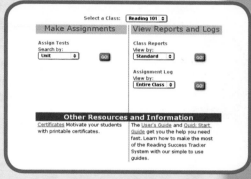

⚙ Group

- Use results from Unit 3 Benchmark Tests taken online through SuccessTracker to regroup students.
- Reports in SuccessTracker suggest appropriate groups for students based on test results.

⚙ Individualize Instruction

- Tests are correlated to Unit 3 tested skills and standards so that prescriptions for individual teaching and learning plans can be created.
- Individualized prescriptions target instruction and accelerate student progress toward learning outcome goals.
- Prescriptions include resources to reteach Unit 3 skills and standards.

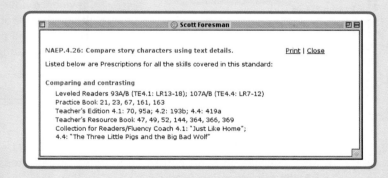

Unit 3
Grouping for AYP

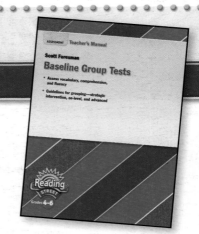

Diagnose and Differentiate

Diagnose
To make initial grouping decisions, use the Baseline Group Test or another initial placement test. Depending on students' ability levels, you may have more than one of each group.

Differentiate

If... student performance is	**Below-Level**	**then...** use the regular instruction and the daily Strategic Intervention lessons, pp. DI·2–DI·50.
If... student performance is	**On-Level**	**then...** use the regular instruction for On-Level learners throughout each selection.
If... student performance is	**Advanced**	**then...** use the regular instruction and the daily instruction for Advanced learners, pp. DI·3–DI·51.

Group Time

On-Level

- Explicit instructional routines teach core skills and strategies.
- Independent activities provide practice for core skills and extension and enrichment options.
- Leveled readers (LR1–45) provide additional reading and practice with core skills and vocabulary.

Strategic Intervention

- Daily Strategic Intervention lessons provide more intensive instruction, more scaffolding, more practice with critical skills, and more opportunities to respond.
- Reteach lessons (DI·52–DI·56) provide additional instructional opportunities with target skills.
- Leveled reader instruction (LR1–45) builds background for the main selection and provides practice with target skills and vocabulary.

Advanced

- Daily Advanced Lessons provide compacted instruction for accelerated learning, options for investigative work, and challenging reading content.
- Leveled readers (LR1–45) provide additional reading tied to lesson concepts.

Additional opportunities to differentiate instruction:
- Reteach Lessons, pp. DI·52–DI·56
- Leveled Reader Instruction and Leveled Practice, LR1–45
- My Sidewalks on Scott Foresman Reading Street Intensive Reading Intervention Program

MY SIDEWALKS ON
SCOTT FORESMAN
READING STREET
Intensive Reading Intervention

4–Step Plan for Assessment

1. **Diagnose and Differentiate**
2. **Monitor Progress**
3. **Assess and Regroup**
4. **Summative Assessment**

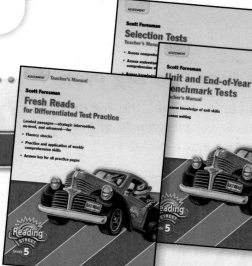

Monitor Progress

STEP 2

- **Guiding comprehension questions** and skill and strategy instruction during reading
- **Monitor Progress boxes** to check comprehension and vocabulary
- **Weekly Assessments** on Day 3 for comprehension, Day 4 for fluency, and Day 5 for vocabulary
- **Practice Book** pages at point of use
- **Weekly Selection Tests** or **Fresh Reads for Differentiated Test Practice**

Assess and Regroup

STEP 3

- **Days 3, 4, and 5 Assessments** Record results of weekly Days 3, 4, and 5 assessments in retelling, fluency, and vocabulary (pp. WA16–WA17) to track student progress.
- **Unit 3 Benchmark Test** Administer this test to check mastery of unit skills.
- Use weekly assessment information, Unit Benchmark Test performance, and the Unit 3 Assess and Regroup (p. WA18) to make regrouping decisions. See the time line below.

YOU ARE HERE
Begin Unit 3

SCOTT FORESMAN ASSESSMENT

Group Baseline Group Test

Week | 1 ... 5 ... 10 ... 15 ... 20 ... 25 ... 30

- Assess (Week 5)
- Regroup Units 1 and 2 (Week 10)
- Regroup Unit 3 (p. WA18) (Week 15)
- Regroup Unit 4 (Week 20)
- Regroup Unit 5 (Week 25)
- Assess (Week 30)

END OF YEAR

OUTSIDE ASSESSMENT

Initial placement ——→ Outside assessment for regrouping ——→ Outside assessment for regrouping

Outside assessments (e.g., DIBELS) may recommend regrouping at other times during the year.

Summative Assessment

STEP 4

- **Benchmark Assessment** Use to measure a student's mastery of each unit's skills.
- **End-of-Year Benchmark Assessment** Use to measure a student's mastery of program skills covered in all six units.

Unit 3
Theme Launch

Discuss the Big Idea

As a class, discuss the Big Idea question, *What do people gain from the work of inventors and artists?*

Explain that inventors and artists are important people because they add so much to our world. They can use their talents to inspire, entertain, and enrich people's lives.

Ask students to think of inventions that have made their lives better or artwork that has influenced them in some way.

A good example of an invention that has enriched people's lives is the Internet. It allows us to communicate quickly with people all over the world. It also gives us easy access to information and services.

Theme and Concept Connections

Weekly lesson concepts help students connect the reading selections and the unit theme. Theme-related activities throughout the week provide opportunities to explore the relationships among the selections, the lesson concepts, and the unit theme.

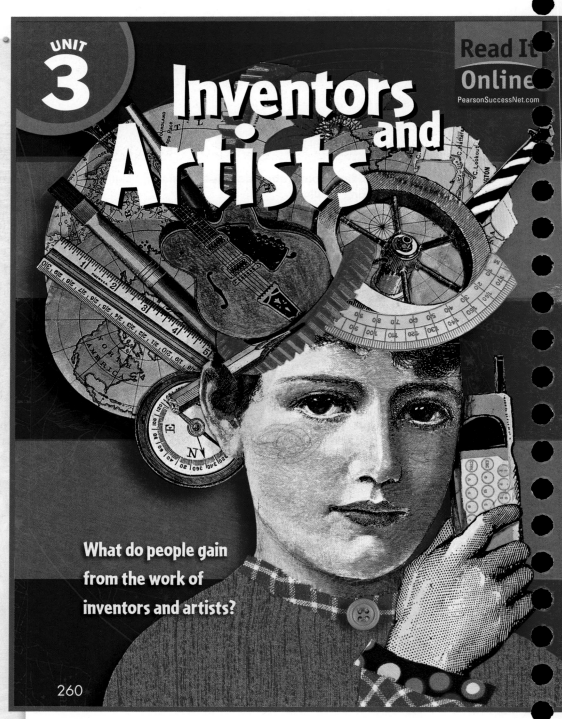

UNIT 3

Read It Online
PearsonSuccessNet.com

Inventors and Artists

What do people gain from the work of inventors and artists?

260

CONNECTING CULTURES

Use the following selections to help students explore the powerful impact art can have on others.

The Dinosaurs of Waterhouse Hawkins Have students discuss people's reactions to the dinosaurs that Waterhouse built. They can also tell about art they have seen or made that evoked strong feelings.

Mahalia Jackson Have students discuss how music can help people deal with difficult situations. They can also tell about songs they like to sing or listen to when they feel "the blues."

Wings for the King

An inventor lifts a king's spirits.

PLAY

connect to SCIENCE

Paired Selection

Becky Schroeder: Enlightened Thinker

NARRATIVE NONFICTION

Leonardo's Horse

A genius gives the world his dream.

BIOGRAPHY

connect to SOCIAL STUDIES

Paired Selection

Humans with Wings

NARRATIVE NONFICTION

The Dinosaurs of Waterhouse Hawkins

A scientist makes dinosaurs into art.

BIOGRAPHY

connect to SCIENCE

Paired Selection

A Model Scientist

INTERVIEW

Mahalia Jackson

Singers put soul into music.

EXPOSITORY NONFICTION

connect to SOCIAL STUDIES

Paired Selection

Perfect Harmony

POETRY

Special Effects in Film and Television

Artists make the fantastic seem real.

EXPOSITORY NONFICTION

connect to SOCIAL STUDIES

Paired Selection

Searching for Animation

SEARCH ENGINES

261

Unit Inquiry Project

Inventors and Artists

In the unit inquiry project, students each choose an inventor or artist and research his or her life and contributions. They may use print or online resources as available.

The project assessment rubric can be found on p. 384a. Discuss the rubric's expectations before students begin the project. Rubric 4 3 2 1

PROJECT TIMETABLE

WEEK	ACTIVITY/SKILL CONNECTION
1	**IDENTIFY QUESTIONS** Each student chooses an inventor or artist and browses a few Web sites or print reference materials to develop an inquiry question about this person and his or her contributions.
2	**NAVIGATE/SEARCH** Students conduct effective information searches and look for text and images that can help them answer their questions.
3	**ANALYZE** Students explore Web sites or print materials. They analyze the information they have found to determine whether or not it will be useful to them. Students print or take notes on valid information.
4	**SYNTHESIZE** Students combine relevant information they've collected from different sources to develop answers to their inquiry questions from Week 1.
	ASSESSMENT OPTIONS
5	**COMMUNICATE** Students contribute to a class display showing information about the people they researched and the inventions or works of art they created. Students may also write brief biographies of the people they researched and create them into a class book.

Unit 3

Inventors and Artists

CONCEPT QUESTION

What do people gain from the work of inventors and artists?

Expand the Concept

How do inventors inspire our imaginations?

Connect the Concept

Develop Language
experiment, suggested, theory

Teach Content
The First Flight
Scientific Process
Insects

Writing
Skit

Internet Inquiry
Inventions

Literature

TIME FOR Science

Expand the Concept

How do artists inspire future generations?

Connect the Concept

Develop Language
canvas, charcoal, easel, Norman Rockwell

Teach Content
The Renaissance
The Medici Family
Da Vinci's Inventions

Writing
Question/Answer Essay

Internet Inquiry
Artists and Their Legacies

Literature

TIME FOR SOCIAL STUDIES

Expand the Concept

How can paleontologists help us understand the past?

Connect the Concept

Develop Language
fossils, paleontologists, sandstone

Teach Content
Dinosaur Extinction
Fossils
Crystal Palace
Paleontology

Writing
Feature Story

Internet Inquiry
Dinosaurs

Literature

TIME FOR Science

Expand the Concept

How does an artist use music to inspire others?

Connect the Concept

Develop Language
beat, blended, time

Teach Content
Roots of Blues Music
Blues Artists
Boy's Choir of Harlem

Writing
Description

Internet Inquiry
Music and Musicians

Literature

TIME FOR SOCIAL STUDIES

Expand the Concept

How do artists create special effects to entertain us?

Connect the Concept

Develop Language
digital effects, illusion, props

Teach Content
Careers
Blue Screen Technology

Writing
Expository Writing

Internet Inquiry
Special Effects

Literature

TIME FOR SOCIAL STUDIES

Illinois

Planning Guide for Performance Descriptors

Wings for the King

Reading Street Teacher's Edition pages | **Grade 5 English Language Arts Performance Descriptors**

Oral Language

Speaking/Listening Build Concept Vocabulary: 262l, 273, 279, 287c
Read Aloud: 262m

1B.Stage E.10. Read age-appropriate material aloud with fluency and accuracy.

4B.Stage E.10. Contribute meaningfully to small and large group discussions by following accepted guidelines for verbal interaction (e.g., appropriate volume and rate; courteous, turn-taking behavior; respectful, relevant responses; appropriate language and vocabulary).

Word Work

Schwa: 287i–287j

1A.Stage E.1. Use a combination of word analysis and vocabulary strategies (e.g., word patterns, structural analyses) within context to identify unknown words.

Reading

Comprehension Author's Purpose: 262–263, 266–279, 282–287, 287b
Story Structure: 262–263, 266–279, 282–287

Vocabulary Lesson Vocabulary: 264b, 273, 279, 282
Context Clues: 264–265, 275, 287c

Fluency Model Tone of Voice: 262l–262m, 287a

Self-Selected Reading: LR1–9, TR16–17

Literature Genre—Drama: 266
Reader Response: 280

1A.Stage E.1. Use a combination of word analysis and vocabulary strategies (e.g., word patterns, structural analyses) within context to identify unknown words.

1C.Stage E.4. Compare the content and organization (e.g., themes, topics, text structure, story elements) of various selections.

1C.Stage E.6. Select reading strategies for text appropriate to the reader's purpose.

1C.Stage E.9. Explain how authors and illustrators use text and art to express their ideas (e.g., points of view, design hues, metaphors).

4B.Stage E.6. Use appropriate verbal and nonverbal communication elements (e.g., appropriate space, body language, pleasant tone, rate, volume).

Language Arts

Writing Skit: 287g–287h

Six-Trait Writing Conventions: 281, 287g–287h

Grammar, Usage, and Mechanics Past, Present, and Future Tenses: 287e–287f

Research/Study Advertisement: 287l

Technology New Literacies: 287k

3C.Stage E.3. Write creatively for a specified purpose and audience (e.g., short story, poetry, directions, song, friendly letter).

3C.Stage E.4. Use available technology to design, produce, and present compositions and multimedia works.

4B.Stage E.5. Use appropriate grammar, word choice, and pacing.

5A.Stage E.1. Generate questions of interest and narrow the focus of research.

Unit Skills

Writing Compare and Contrast Essay: WA2–9
Poetry: 384–387
Project/Wrap-Up: 388–389

2B.Stage E.4. Compare ideas from texts representing a variety of times and cultures.

3C.Stage E.3. Write creatively for a specified purpose and audience (e.g., short story, poetry, directions, song, friendly letter).

5A.Stage E.4. Compare (with limited support) information from a variety of sources.

This Week's Leveled Readers

Below-Level

1C.Stage E.9. Explain how authors and illustrators use text and art to express their ideas (e.g., points of view, design hues, metaphors).

2A.Stage E.8. Identify ways in which fiction and nonfiction works are organized differently.

Nonfiction

On-Level

1C.Stage E.9. Explain how authors and illustrators use text and art to express their ideas (e.g., points of view, design hues, metaphors).

2A.Stage E.2. Identify literary elements and techniques in literary genres and tell how they affect the story.

Nonfiction

Advanced

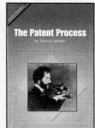

1B.Stage E.7. Identify structure of nonfiction text to improve comprehension.

1C.Stage E.9. Explain how authors and illustrators use text and art to express their ideas (e.g., points of view, design hues, metaphors).

Nonfiction

Content-Area Illinois Performance Descriptors in This Lesson

Social Studies

15D.Stage E.1. Explain the benefits of exchanging with the use of money.

15D.Stage E.3. Predict how people's lives would be different if they did not trade with others for goods and services they use.

17D.Stage E.2. Analyze how customs and traditions of people from different parts of the world change over time.

18A.Stage E.1. Describe how culture is shared through music, art, and literature throughout the world over time.

Science

11A.Stage E.2. Conduct scientific inquiry investigation: observing safety precautions and following procedural steps accurately over multiple trials.

11A.Stage E.3. Collect qualitative and quantitative data from investigation.

Math

7B.Stage E.3. Estimate the perimeter, area, and/or volume of regular and irregular shapes and objects.

Illinois!

NATIVE AMERICANS OF ILLINOIS
The Kickapoo

The Kickapoo are related to the Sauk and Fox peoples. The Kickapoo began moving into Illinois in the mid- to late 1700s. Skilled warriors, the Kickapoo often made raids as far away as Georgia in the east and Mexico in the south. They moved between summer and winter homes, growing crops such as corn, squash, and beans in the summer and hunting in the winter.

Students can . . .
Research the Kickapoo and write a chronology of them. Have students include a description of where the Kickapoo live today.

A SPECIAL ILLINOIS PLACE
Starved Rock State Park

Starved Rock State Park is located on the south side of the Illinois River, near Utica. The park is best known for its unique rock formations. In early spring melting snow and rain create waterfalls at the heads of eighteen sandstone canyons. The thick forests include black oak, white oak, red cedar, and white pine trees, and visitors can see a variety of colorful wildflowers as well. The park is home to animals such as raccoons, deer, rabbits, and many kinds of birds.

Students can . . .
Find out more about the natural features at Starved Rock State Park and create a visitor's guide to the park.

ILLINOIS FUN FACTS
Did You Know?

- One of the first colleges in Illinois was Rock Spring Seminary, which was established in 1827.

- Flooding in 1937 forced the citizens of Shawneetown, in southern Illinois, to move their town. After the flood the state began to move the town's buildings four miles to the west.

- The mascot of the sports teams at Southern Illinois University is a saluki. The saluki is a breed of hunting dog that originated in Egypt.

Students can . . .
Create a new mascot for Southern Illinois University using Illinois heritage as inspiration.

Unit 3
Inventors and Artists

CONCEPT QUESTION
What do people gain from the work of inventors and artists?

Week 1

How do inventors inspire our imaginations?

Week 2

How do artists inspire future generations?

Week 3

How can paleontologists help us understand the past?

Week 4

How does an artist use music to inspire others?

Week 5

How do artists create special effects to entertain us?

EXPAND THE CONCEPT
How do inventors inspire our imaginations?

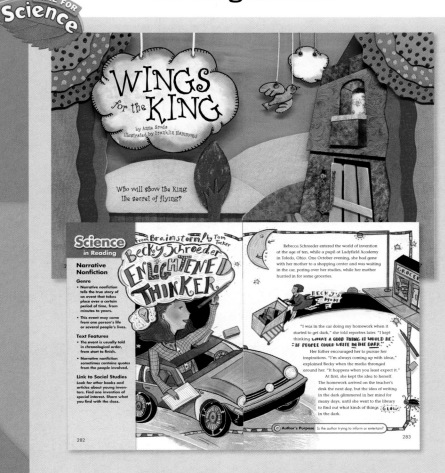

CONNECT THE CONCEPT

▶ **Build Background**
experiment, suggested, theory

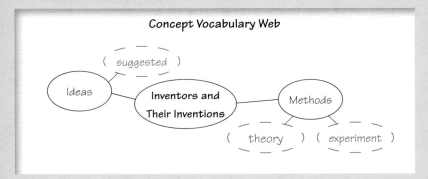

Concept Vocabulary Web

▶ **Science Content**
The First Flight, Scientific Process, Insects

▶ **Writing**
Skit

▶ **Internet Inquiry**
Inventions

Preview Your Week

How do inventors inspire our imaginations?

WINGS for the KING

by Anne Sroda
illustrated by Franklin Hammond

Who will show the King the secret of flying?

Genre A **play** is a story written to be acted out for an audience. As you read, imagine the actors speaking the lines and acting out the action.

Student Edition pages 266–279

Audio CD

Genre Play

⊙ **Vocabulary Strategy** Context Clues

⊙ **Comprehension Skill** Author's Purpose

⊙ **Comprehension Strategy** Story Structure

Paired Selection

Reading Across Texts
Compare Characters

Genre
Narrative Nonfiction

Text Features
Order of Events
Quotes
Title and Illustrations

Science in Reading

Narrative Nonfiction

Genre
- Narrative nonfiction tells the true story of an event that takes place over a certain period of time, from minutes to years.
- This event may come from one person's life or several people's lives.

Text Features
- The event is usually told in chronological order, from start to finish.
- Narrative nonfiction sometimes contains quotes from the people involved.

Link to Social Studies
Look for other books and articles about young inventors. Find one invention of special interest. Share what you find with the class.

From Brainstorm! *by Tom Tucker*

Becky Schroeder ENLIGHTENED THINKER

Rebecca Schroeder entered the world of invention at the age of ten, while a pupil at Ladyfield Academy in Toledo, Ohio. One October evening, she had gone with her mother to a shopping center and was waiting in the car, poring over her studies, while her mother hurried in for some groceries.

"I was in the car doing my homework when it started to get dark," she told reporters later. "I kept thinking *WHAT A GOOD THING IT WOULD BE IF PEOPLE COULD WRITE IN THE DARK*."

Her father encouraged her to pursue her inspirations. "I'm always coming up with ideas," explained Becky when the media thronged around her. "It happens when you least expect it."

At first, she kept the idea to herself. The homework arrived on the teacher's desk the next day, but the idea of writing in the dark glimmered in her mind for many days, until she went to the library to find out what kinds of things GLOW in the dark.

ⓒ **Author's Purpose** Is the author trying to inform or entertain?

Student Edition pages 282–287

Audio CD

Read It
ONLINE
PearsonSuccessNet.com

- **Student Edition**
- **Leveled Readers**

Integrate Science Standards

- **Inventors**
- **Scientific Method**
- **Insects**

Leveled Readers

⭐ **Skill** Author's Purpose

⭐ **Strategy** Story Structure

Lesson Vocabulary

Below-Level

On-Level

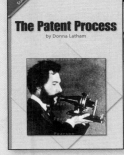

Advanced

ELL Reader

- Concept Vocabulary
- Text Support
- Language Enrichment

Scientific Methods in Action
by D. Michael Kim

Illustrated by Bruce Day

✓ **Read**

Wings for the King,
pp. 266–279

"Becky Schroeder: Enlightened Thinker,"
pp. 282–287

Leveled Readers

Below-Level — Support Concepts

On-Level — Develop Concepts

Advanced — Extend Concepts / Science Extension Activity

ELL Reader

✓ **Build Concept Vocabulary**
Inventors and Their Inventions, pp. 262l–262m

✓ **Teach Science Concepts**
The First Flight, p. 269
Scientific Method, p. 275
Insects, p. 283

✓ **Explore Science Center**
Be an Inventor!, p. 262k

Weekly Plan

READING

45-90 minutes

TARGET SKILLS OF THE WEEK

Comprehension Skill
Author's Purpose

Comprehension Strategy
Story Structure

Vocabulary Strategy
Context Clues

DAY 1
PAGES 262l-264b, 287a, 287e-287k

Oral Language

QUESTION OF THE WEEK *How do inventors inspire our imaginations?*

Read Aloud: "What's the Big Idea Ben Franklin?" 262m
Build Concepts, 262l

Comprehension/Vocabulary

Comprehension Skill/Strategy Lesson, 262–263

Author's Purpose **T**

Story Structure

Build Background, 264a

Introduce Lesson Vocabulary, 264b
admiringly, permit, scoundrel, subject, worthless **T**

Read Leveled Readers

Grouping Options 262f–262g

Fluency

Model Tone of Voice, 262l–262m, 287a

DAY 2
PAGES 264-273, 287a, 287e-287k

Oral Language

QUESTION OF THE DAY *Why does the King wish to fly so much?*

Comprehension/Vocabulary

Vocabulary Strategy Lesson, 264–265

Context Clues **T**

Read *Wings for the King*, 266–273

Grouping Options
262f–262g

Author's Purpose **T**

Story Structure **T**

REVIEW Cause and Effect **T**

Develop Vocabulary

Fluency

Choral Reading, 287a

LANGUAGE ARTS

30-60 minutes

Trait of the Week

Conventions

Grammar, 287e
Introduce Past, Present, and Future Tenses **T**

Writing Workshop, 287g
Introduce Skit
Model the Trait of the Week: Conventions

Spelling, 287i
Pretest for Schwa

Internet Inquiry, 287k
Identify Questions

Grammar, 287e
Develop Past, Present, and Future Tenses **T**

Writing Workshop, 287g
Improve Writing with Use Powerful Verbs

Spelling, 287i
Teach the Generalization

Internet Inquiry, 287k
Navigate/Search

DAILY WRITING ACTIVITIES

Day 1 Write to Read, 262

Day 2 Words to Write, 265
Strategy Response Log, 266, 273

DAILY SCIENCE CONNECTIONS

Day 1 Inventors and Their Inventions Concept Web, 262l

Day 2 Time for Science: The First Flight, 269
Revisit the Inventors and Their Inventions Concept Web, 273

DAILY SUCCESS PREDICTORS
for Adequate Yearly Progress

Monitor Progress and Corrective Feedback

Vocabulary

Check Vocabulary, *262l*

RESOURCES FOR THE WEEK

- Practice Book, *pp. 101–110*
- Word Study and Spelling Practice Book, *pp. 41–44*
- Grammar and Writing Practice Book, *pp. 41–44*

- Selection Test, *pp. 41–44*
- Fresh Reads for Differentiated Test Practice, *pp. 61–66*
- The Grammar and Writing Book, *pp. 110–115*

Grouping Options for Differentiated Instruction

Turn the page for the small group lesson plan.

DAY 3   PAGES 274–281, 287a, 287e–287k

Oral Language

QUESTION OF THE DAY   *How is reading a book like taking a journey?*

Comprehension/Vocabulary

Read *Wings for the King,* 274–280

Grouping Options 262f–262g

- Author's Purpose **T**
- Story Structure
- Context Clues **T**
- Develop Vocabulary

Reader Response

Selection Test

Fluency

Model Tone of Voice, 287a

Grammar, 287f
Apply Past, Present, and Future Tenses in Writing **T**

Writing Workshop, 281, 287h
Write Now
Prewrite and Draft

Spelling, 287j
Connect Spelling to Writing

Internet Inquiry, 287k
Analyze Sources

Day 3   Strategy Response Log, 278
Look Back and Write, 280

Day 3   Time for Science: Scientific Process, 275
Revisit the Inventors and Their Inventions
Concept Web, 279

DAY 4   PAGES 282–287a, 287e–287k

Oral Language

QUESTION OF THE DAY   *What abilities or personal qualities do you think make a person a great inventor?*

Comprehension/Vocabulary

Read "Becky Schroeder: Enlightened Thinker," 282–287

Grouping Options 262f–262g

Narrative Nonfiction/
Text Features

Reading Across Texts

Content-Area Vocabulary

Fluency

Partner Reading, 287a

Grammar, 287f
Practice Past, Present, and Future Tenses for Standardized Tests **T**

Writing Workshop, 287h
Draft, Revise, and Publish

Spelling, 287j
Provide a Strategy

Internet Inquiry, 287k
Synthesize Information

Day 4   Writing Across Texts, 287

Day 4   Time for Science: Insects, 283

DAY 5   PAGES 287a–287l

Oral Language

QUESTION OF THE WEEK   *To wrap up the week, revisit the Day 1 question.*

Build Concept Vocabulary, 287c

Fluency

Read Leveled Readers

Grouping Options 262f–262g

Assess Reading Rate, 287a

Comprehension/Vocabulary

- Reteach Author's Purpose, 287b **T**
- Metaphor, 287b
- Review Context Clues, 287c **T**

Speaking and Listening, 287d
Play Review
Listen to Audio CD

Grammar, 287f
Cumulative Review

Writing Workshop, 287h
Connect to Unit Writing

Spelling, 287j
Posttest for Schwa

Internet Inquiry, 287k
Communicate Results

Research/Study Skills, 287l
Advertisement

Day 5   Metaphor, 287b

Day 5   Revisit the Inventors and Their Inventions
Concept Web, 287c

KEY ◉ = Target Skill   **T** = Tested Skill

Comprehension   Check Retelling, *280*

Fluency   Check Fluency WCPM, *287a*

Vocabulary   Check Vocabulary, *287c*

SUCCESS PREDICTOR

Small Group Plan *for Differentiated Instruction*

Daily Plan
AT A GLANCE

Reading

Whole Group
- Oral Language
- Comprehension/Vocabulary

Group Time

Differentiated Instruction

Meet with small groups to provide:
- Skill Support
- Reading Support
- Fluency Practice

Read

This week's lessons for daily group time can be found behind the Differentiated Instruction (DI) tab on pp. DI·2–DI·11.

Whole Group
- Fluency

Language Arts
- Grammar
- Writing
- Spelling
- Research/Inquiry
- Speaking/Listening/Viewing

Use *My Sidewalks on Reading Street* for Tier III intensive reading intervention.

DAY 1

On-Level	Strategic Intervention	Advanced
Teacher-Led *Page DI·3*	**Teacher-Led** *Page DI·2*	**Teacher-Led** *Page DI·3*
• Develop Concept Vocabulary • **Read** On-Level Reader *The Story of Flight*	• **Reinforce** Concepts • **Read** Below-Level Reader *What a Great Idea!*	• **Read** Advanced Reader *The Patent Process* • Independent Extension Activity

(i) Independent Activities

While you meet with small groups, have the rest of the class...

- Visit the Reading/Library Center
- Listen to the Background Building Audio
- Finish Write to Read, p. 262
- Complete Practice Book pp. 103–104
- Visit Cross-Curricular Centers

DAY 2

On-Level	Strategic Intervention	Advanced
Teacher-Led *Pages 268–273*	**Teacher-Led** *Page DI·4*	**Teacher-Led** *Page DI·5*
• **Read** *Wings for the King*	• Practice Lesson Vocabulary • Read Multisyllabic Words • **Read** or Listen to *Wings for the King*	• Extend Vocabulary • **Read** *Wings for the King*

(i) Independent Activities

While you meet with small groups, have the rest of the class...

- Visit the Reading/Library Center
- Listen to the AudioText for *Wings for the King*
- Finish Words to Write, p. 265
- Complete Practice Book pp. 105–106
- Write in their Strategy Response Logs, pp. 266, 273
- Visit Cross-Curricular Centers
- Work on inquiry projects

DAY 3

On-Level	Strategic Intervention	Advanced
Teacher-Led *Pages 274–279*	**Teacher-Led** *Page DI·6*	**Teacher-Led** *Page DI·7*
• **Read** *Wings for the King*	• Practice Author's Purpose and Story Structure • **Read** or Listen to *Wings for the King*	• Extend Author's Purpose and Story Structure • **Read** *Wings for the King*

(i) Independent Activities

While you meet with small groups, have the rest of the class...

- Visit the Reading/Library Center
- Listen to the AudioText for *Wings for the King*
- Write in their Strategy Response Logs, p. 278
- Finish Look Back and Write, p. 280
- Complete Practice Book p. 107
- Visit Cross-Curricular Centers
- Work on inquiry projects

① Begin with whole class skill and strategy instruction.

② Meet with small groups to provide differentiated instruction.

③ Gather the whole class back together for fluency and language arts.

DAY 4

On-Level
Teacher-Led
Pages 282–287

- **Read** "Becky Schroeder: Enlightened Thinker"

Strategic Intervention
Teacher-Led
Page DI · 8

- Practice Retelling
- **Read** or Listen to "Becky Schroeder: Enlightened Thinker"

Advanced
Teacher-Led
Page DI · 9

- **Read** "Becky Schroeder: Enlightened Thinker"
- Genre Study

(i) Independent Activities

While you meet with small groups, have the rest of the class...

- Visit the Reading/Library Center
- Listen to the AudioText for "Becky Schroeder: Enlightened Thinker"
- Visit the Writing/Vocabulary Center
- Finish Writing Across Texts, p. 287
- Visit Cross-Curricular Centers
- Work on inquiry projects

DAY 5

On-Level
Teacher-Led
Page DI · 11

- **Reread** Leveled Reader *The Story of Flight*
- Retell *The Story of Flight*

Strategic Intervention
Teacher-Led
Page DI · 10

- **Reread** Leveled Reader *What a Great Idea!*
- Retell *What a Great Idea!*

Advanced
Teacher-Led
Page DI · 11

- **Reread** Leveled Reader *The Patent Process*
- Share Extension Activity

(i) Independent Activities

While you meet with small groups, have the rest of the class...

- Visit the Reading/Library Center
- Complete Practice Book pp. 108–110
- Visit Cross-Curricular Centers
- Work on inquiry projects

Grouping Place English language learners in the groups that correspond to their reading abilities in English.

Use the appropriate Leveled Reader or other text at students' instructional level.

TiP Send home the appropriate Multilingual Summary of the main selection on Day 1.

Take It to the NET™ ONLINE
PearsonSuccessNet.com

Deborah Simmons and Edward Kame'enui
For a review of research on effective vocabulary instruction, see the article "Vocabulary Acquisition" by S. K. Baker and Scott Foresman authors Deborah Simmons and Edward Kame'enui.

TEACHER TALK

Reapeated reading is a method for building fluency in which a student reads a short passage repeatedly until reaching a predetermined level of fluency.

Be sure to schedule time for students to work on the unit inquiry project "Inventors and Artists." This week students choose inventors or artists and develop inquiry questions.

Looking Ahead

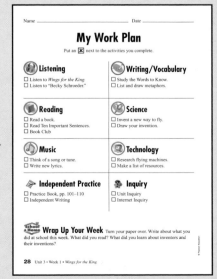

▲ **Group-Time Survival Guide**
p. 28, Weekly Contract

Wings for the King **262g**

☑ Customize Your Plan *by Strand*

ORAL LANGUAGE

Concept Development

How do inventors inspire our imaginations?

CONCEPT VOCABULARY

experiment   suggested   theory

BUILD

☐ **Question of the Week** Introduce and discuss the question of the week. This week students will read a variety of texts and work on projects related to the concept *inventors and their inventions*. Post the question for students to refer to throughout the week. **DAY 1** *262d*

☐ **Read Aloud** Read aloud "What's the Big Idea Ben Franklin?" Then begin a web to build concepts and concept vocabulary related to this week's lesson and the unit theme, Inventors and Artists. Introduce the concept words *experiment, suggested,* and *theory* and have students place them on the web. Display the web for use throughout the week. **DAY 1** *262l-262m*

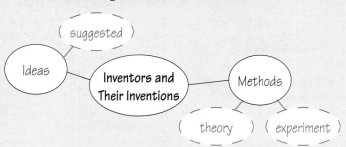

DEVELOP

☐ **Question of the Day** Use the prompts from the Weekly Plan to engage students in conversations related to this week's reading and the unit theme. **EVERY DAY** *262d-262e*

☐ **Concept Vocabulary Web** Revisit the Inventors and Their Inventions Concept Web and encourage students to add concept words from their reading and life experiences. **DAY 2** *273,* **DAY 3** *279*

CONNECT

☐ **Looking Back/Moving Forward** Revisit the Inventors and Their Inventions Concept Web and discuss how it relates to this week's lesson and the unit theme. Then make connections to next week's lesson. **DAY 5** *287c*

CHECK

☐ **Concept Vocabulary Web** Use the Inventors and Their Inventions Concept Web to check students' understanding of the concept vocabulary words *experiment, suggested,* and *theory*. **DAY 1** *262l,* **DAY 5** *287c*

VOCABULARY

STRATEGY CONTEXT CLUES Some words have more than one meaning. Use the words and sentences around the word with multiple meanings to figure out which meaning the author is using.

LESSON VOCABULARY

admiringly   subject
permit   worthless
scoundrel

TEACH

☐ **Words to Know** Give students the opportunity to tell what they already know about this week's lesson vocabulary words. Then discuss word meaning. **DAY 1** *264b*

☐ **Vocabulary Strategy Lesson** Use the vocabulary strategy lesson in the Student Edition to introduce and model this week's strategy, *context clues.* **DAY 2** *264-265*

Vocabulary Strategy Lesson

PRACTICE/APPLY

☐ **Leveled Text** Read the lesson vocabulary in the context of leveled text. **DAY 1** *LR1-LR9*

Leveled Readers

☐ **Words in Context** Read the lesson vocabulary and apply *context clues* in the context of *Wings for the King.* **DAY 2** *266-273,* **DAY 3** *274-280*

☐ **Writing/Vocabulary Center** List other metaphors comparing books or reading to something else, like *"Books are the best wings of all."* **ANY DAY** *262k*

Main Selection—Drama

☐ **Homework** Practice Book pp. 104, 105. **DAY 1** *264b,* **DAY 2** *265*

☐ **Word Play** Have students work with partners to make a list of words from *Wings for the King* that rhyme with other words. Have them list as many rhymes as possible for each of the words and then use some of them to write a rhyming poem based on the play. **ANY DAY** *287c*

ASSESS

☐ **Selection Test** Use the Selection Test to determine students' understanding of the lesson vocabulary words. **DAY 3**

RETEACH/REVIEW

☐ **Reteach Lesson** If necessary, use this lesson to reteach and review *context clues.* **DAY 5** *287c*

COMPREHENSION

SKILL AUTHOR'S PURPOSE The author's purpose is the reason or reasons an author has for writing. The purpose may change during a selection, but most selections have one main purpose. An author may write to persuade you, to inform you, to entertain you, or to express ideas or feelings.

STRATEGY STORY STRUCTURE Story structure is how a fictional story or article is put together. Paying close attention to the story structure may help you figure out the author's purpose for writing the selection.

TEACH

☐ **Skill/Strategy Lesson** Use the skill/strategy lesson in the Student Edition to introduce and model *author's purpose* and *story structure*. **DAY 1** *262-263*

Skill/Strategy Lesson

☐ **Extend Skills** Teach metaphors. **ANY DAY** *287b*

PRACTICE/APPLY

☐ **Leveled Text** Apply *author's purpose* and *story structure* to read leveled text. **DAY 1** *LR1-LR9*

Leveled Readers

☐ **Skills and Strategies in Context** Read *Wings for the King,* using the Guiding Comprehension questions to apply *author's purpose* and *story structure*. **DAY 2** *266-273,* **DAY 3** *274-280*

Main Selection—Drama

☐ **Skills and Strategies in Context** Read "Becky Schroeder: Enlightened Thinker," guiding students as they apply *author's purpose* and *story structure*. Then have students discuss and write across texts. **DAY 4** *282-287*

☐ **Homework** Practice Book pp. 103, 107, 108. **DAY 1** *263* **DAY 3** *279,* **DAY 5** *287b*

Paired Selection—Nonfiction

☐ **Fresh Reads for Differentiated Test Practice** Have students practice *author's purpose* with a new passage. **DAY 3**

ASSESS

☐ **Selection Test** Determine students' understanding of the selection and their use of *author's purpose*. **DAY 3**

☐ **Retell** Have students retell *Wings for the King*. **DAY 3** *280-281*

RETEACH/REVIEW

☐ **Reteach Lesson** If necessary, reteach and review *author's purpose*. **DAY 5** *287b*

FLUENCY

SKILL TONE OF VOICE Adjusting your tone of voice gives you the ability to show different emotions as you read. Emotions such as desperation or suspense are easily conveyed through a changing tone of voice.

TEACH

☐ **Read Aloud** Model fluent reading by rereading "What's the Big Idea Ben Franklin?" Focus on this week's fluency skill, tone of voice. **DAY 1** *262l-262m, 287a*

PRACTICE/APPLY

☐ **Choral Reading** Read aloud selected paragraphs from *Wings for the King,* emphasizing the changing inflections in your voice. Then practice as a class, doing three choral readings of the selected paragraphs. **DAY 2** *287a,* **DAY 3** *287a*

☐ **Partner Reading** Have partners practice reading aloud, reading with changing inflections to reflect different characters' emotions, and offering each other feedback. As students reread, monitor their progress toward their individual fluency goals. **DAY 4** *287a*

☐ **Listening Center** Have students follow along with the AudioText for this week's selections. **ANY DAY** *262j*

☐ **Reading/Library Center** Have students reread a selection of their choice. **ANY DAY** *262j*

☐ **Fluency Coach** Have students use Fluency Coach to listen to fluent readings or practice reading on their own. **ANY DAY**

ASSESS

☐ **Check Fluency** WCPM Do a one-minute timed reading, paying special attention to this week's skill—tone of voice. Provide feedback for each student. **DAY 5** *287a*

☑ Customize Your Plan *by Strand*

GRAMMAR

SKILL PAST, PRESENT, AND FUTURE TENSES The *tense* of a verb shows when something happens. Verbs in the *present tense* show action that happens now. Verbs in the *past tense* show action that has already happened. Verbs in the *future tense* show action that will happen.

TEACH

❑ **Grammar Transparency 11** Use Grammar Transparency 11, to teach past, present, and future tenses. **DAY 1** *287e*

Grammar Transparency 11

PRACTICE/APPLY

❑ **Develop the Concept** Review the concept of past, present, and future tenses and provide guided practice. **DAY 2** *287e*

❑ **Apply to Writing** Have students review something they have written and apply past, present, and future tenses. **DAY 3** *287f*

❑ **Test Preparation** Examine common errors in past, present, and future tenses to prepare for standardized tests. **DAY 4** *287f*

❑ **Homework** Grammar and Writing Practice Book pp. 41–43. **DAY 2** *287e*, **DAY 3** *287f*, **DAY 4** *287f*

ASSESS

❑ **Cumulative Review** Use Grammar and Writing Practice Book p. 44. **DAY 5** *287f*

RETEACH/REVIEW

❑ **Daily Fix-It** Have students find and correct errors in grammar, spelling, and punctuation. **EVERY DAY** *287e-287f.*

❑ **The Grammar and Writing Book** Use pp. 110–113 of The Grammar and Writing Book to extend instruction for past, present, and future tenses. **ANY DAY**

The Grammar and Writing Book

WRITING

Trait of the Week

CONVENTIONS Conventions are rules for written language. Conventions are signals that writers use to make the meaning clear to readers and the style of writing consistent.

TEACH

❑ **Writing Transparency 11A** Use the model to introduce and discuss the Trait of the Week. **DAY 1** *287g*

❑ **Writing Transparency 11B** Use the transparency to show students how using powerful verbs can improve their writing. **DAY 2** *287g*

Writing Transparency 11A   **Writing Transparency 11B**

PRACTICE/APPLY

❑ **Write Now** Examine the model on Student Edition p. 281. Then have students write their own skit. **DAY 3** *281, 287h*, **DAY 4** *287h*

> **Prompt** *Wings for the King* tells about a character who gains valuable knowledge. Think about a lesson that you believe is important for people to know. Now write a skit that shows a character learning that lesson.

Write Now p. 281

❑ **Writing/Vocabulary Center** List other metaphors comparing books or reading to something else, like "*Books* are the best *wings* of all." **ANY DAY** *262k*

ASSESS

❑ **Writing Trait Rubric** Use the rubric to evaluate students' writing. **DAY 4** *287h*

RETEACH/REVIEW

❑ **The Grammar and Writing Book** Use pp. 110–115 of The Grammar and Writing Book to extend instruction for past, present, and future tenses, using powerful verbs, and skits. **ANY DAY**

The Grammar and Writing Book

SPELLING

GENERALIZATION SCHWA In many words, the schwa in an unaccented syllable gives no clue to its spelling: *jewel, factory, garage, tropical.* Any vowel can stand for the schwa sound.

TEACH

❑ **Pretest** Give the pretest for words with schwa. Guide students in self-correcting their pretests and correcting any misspellings. **DAY 1** *287i*

❑ **Think and Practice** Connect spelling to the phonics generalization for the schwa sound. **DAY 2** *287i*

PRACTICE/APPLY

❑ **Connect to Writing** Have students use spelling words to write dialogue. Then review frequently misspelled words: *Christmas, beautiful, probably.* **DAY 3** *287j*

❑ **Homework** Word Study and Spelling Practice Book pp. 41–44. **EVERY DAY**

RETEACH/REVIEW

❑ **Review** Review spelling words to prepare for the posttest. Then provide students with a spelling strategy—secret pronunciations. **DAY 4** *287j*

ASSESS

❑ **Posttest** Use dictation sentences to give the posttest for words with schwa. **DAY 5** *287j*

Spelling Words

1. jewel*
2. kingdom*
3. gasoline
4. factory
5. garage
6. tropical
7. pajamas
8. estimate
9. tomorrow
10. humidity
11. Chicago
12. bulletin
13. carnival
14. illustrate
15. elegant
16. census
17. terrific
18. celebrate
19. operate
20. celery

Challenge Words

21. rehearsal
22. salamander
23. prominent
24. significant
25. parakeet

*Word from the selection

RESEARCH AND INQUIRY

❑ **Internet Inquiry** Have students conduct an Internet inquiry on inventors and inventions. **EVERY DAY** *287k*

❑ **Advertisement** Review the persuasive techniques used in advertisements and how to recognize propaganda in advertisements. **DAY 5** *287l*

❑ **Unit Inquiry** Allow time for students to choose inventors or artists and develop inquiry questions. **ANY DAY** *261*

SPEAKING AND LISTENING

❑ **Play Review** Have students review *Wings for the King*. Students can focus on their opinions of the play along with details to support these opinions. **DAY 5** *287d*

❑ **Listening to Audio CD** Have students listen to the AudioText of *Wings for the King* and answer questions. **DAY 5** *287d*

Resources for
Differentiated Instruction

LEVELED READERS

▶ **Comprehension**
- **Skill** Author's Purpose
- **Strategy** Story Structure

▶ **Lesson Vocabulary**
- **Context Clues**

subject   permit   scoundrel   admiringly   worthless

▶ **Science Standards**
- **Inventors**
- **Scientific Method**
- **Insects**

Leveled Reader Database ONLINE

PearsonSuccessNet.com

Use the Online Database of over 600 books to
- Download and print additional copies of this week's leveled readers.
- Listen to the readers being read online.
- Search for more titles focused on this week's skills, topic, and content.

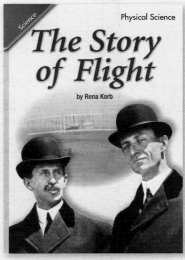

Physical Science

The Story of Flight
by Rena Korb

On-Level Reader

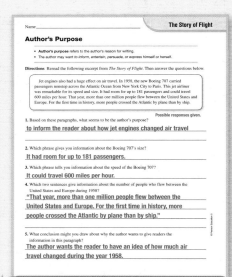

Name_____ The Story of Flight

Author's Purpose
- **Author's purpose** refers to the author's reason for writing.
- The author may want to inform, entertain, persuade, or express himself or herself.

Directions Reread the following excerpt from *The Story of Flight*. Then answer the questions below.

> Jet engines also had a huge effect on air travel. In 1958, the new Boeing 707 carried passengers nonstop across the Atlantic Ocean from New York City to Paris. This jet airliner was remarkable for its speed and size. It had room for up to 181 passengers and could travel 600 miles per hour. That year, more than one million people flew between the United States and Europe. For the first time in history, more people crossed the Atlantic by plane than by ship.

Possible responses given.

1. Based on these paragraphs, what seems to be the author's purpose?
to inform the reader about how jet engines changed air travel

2. Which phrase gives you information about the Boeing 707's size?
It had room for up to 181 passengers.

3. Which phrase tells you information about the speed of the Boeing 707?
It could travel 600 miles per hour.

4. Which two sentences give information about the number of people who flew between the United States and Europe during 1958?
"That year, more than one million people flew between the United States and Europe. For the first time in history, more people crossed the Atlantic by plane than by ship."

5. What conclusion might you draw about why the author wants to give readers the information in this paragraph?
The author wants the reader to have an idea of how much air travel changed during the year 1958.

On-Level Practice TE p. LR5

Name_____ The Story of Flight

Vocabulary
Directions Write a sentence using each of the vocabulary words. Try to make them relate to airplanes and flight.

Check the Words You Know
__admiringly __permit __scoundrels __subject __worthless

Possible responses given.

1. **The passengers looked *admiringly* at the shiny jumbo jet.**

2. **The pilot did not *permit* passengers to unfasten their seat belts.**

3. **Only *scoundrels* would try to sit in your airplane seat.**

4. **The King's loyal *subject* tried to design a way for people to fly.**

5. **Early designs for airplanes were sometimes found to be *worthless*.**

Directions Draw a line from the vocabulary word to its definition.
6. admiringly — to make possible or allow
7. permit — having no value
8. scoundrels — a person who lives under a king's or queen's rule
9. subject — with respect and awe
10. worthless — dishonest people

On-Level Practice TE p. LR6

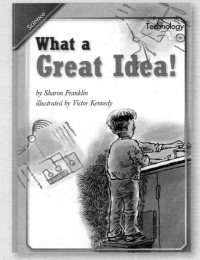

Technology

What a Great Idea!
by Sharon Franklin
illustrated by Victor Kennedy

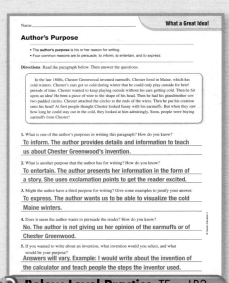

Below-Level Reader

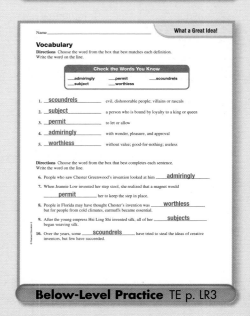

Name_____ What a Great Idea!

Author's Purpose
- The **author's purpose** is his or her reason for writing.
- Four common reasons are to persuade, to inform, to entertain, and to express.

Directions Read the paragraph below. Then answer the questions.

> In the late 1800s, Chester Greenwood invented earmuffs. Chester lived in Maine, which has cold winters. Chester's ears got so cold during winter that he could only play outside for brief periods of time. Chester wanted to keep playing outside without his ears getting cold. Then he hit upon an idea! He bent a piece of wire to the shape of his head. Then he had his grandmother sew two padded circles. Chester attached the circles to the ends of the wires. Then he put his creation onto his head! At first people thought Chester looked funny with his earmuffs. But when they saw how long he could stay out in the cold, they looked at him admiringly. Soon, people were buying earmuffs from Chester!

1. What is one of the author's purposes in writing this paragraph? How do you know?
To inform. The author provides details and information to teach us about Chester Greenwood's invention.

2. What is another purpose that the author has for writing? How do you know?
To entertain. The author presents her information in the form of a story. She uses exclamation points to get the reader excited.

3. Might the author have a third purpose for writing? Give some examples to justify your answer.
To express. The author wants us to be able to visualize the cold Maine winters.

4. Does it seem the author wants to persuade the reader? How do you know?
No. The author is not giving us her opinion of the earmuffs or of Chester Greenwood.

5. If you wanted to write about an invention, what invention would you select, and what would be your purpose?
Answers will vary. Example: I would write about the invention of the calculator and teach people the steps the inventor used.

Below-Level Practice TE p. LR2

Name_____ What a Great Idea!

Vocabulary
Directions Choose the word from the box that best matches each definition. Write the word on the line.

Check the Words You Know
__admiringly __permit __scoundrels
__subject __worthless

1. **scoundrels** _____ evil, dishonorable people; villains or rascals
2. **subject** _____ a person who is bound by loyalty to a king or queen
3. **permit** _____ to let or allow
4. **admiringly** _____ with wonder, pleasure, and approval
5. **worthless** _____ without value; good-for-nothing; useless

Directions Choose the word from the box that best completes each sentence. Write the word on the line.

6. People who saw Chester Greenwood's invention looked at him __**admiringly**__
7. When Jeannie Low invented her step stool, she realized that a magnet would __**permit**__ her to keep the step in place.
8. People in Florida may have thought Chester's invention was __**worthless**__ but for people from cold climates, earmuffs became essential.
9. After the young empress Hsi Ling Shi invented silk, all of her __**subjects**__ began weaving silk.
10. Over the years, some __**scoundrels**__ have tried to steal the ideas of creative inventors, but few have succeeded.

Below-Level Practice TE p. LR3

Advanced

The Patent Process
by Donna Latham

Advanced Reader

Name _____ **The Patent Process**

Author's Purpose

- **Author's purpose** refers to what the author is trying to accomplish.
- The author may want to inform, entertain, persuade, or express himself or herself.

Directions Reread the following excerpt from *The Patent Process*. Then answer the questions.

> On July 31, 1790, President George Washington signed the first United States patent. It went to Samuel Hopkins of Philadelphia, Pennsylvania, who had developed a method for mixing potash and pearl ash to be used for making soap.
>
> George Washington isn't the only United States president linked to the first patents. Thomas Jefferson, who became President in 1801, examined the very first patent applications while serving on the original three-person patent board . . . According to the United States Patent and Trademark Office, it now takes about 6,500 people to do the job that three people once did!

1. Based on these paragraphs, what seems to be the author's purpose? Possible responses given.
to inform the reader about the relationship of early presidents to
the development of the patent process

2. Which sentence tells you information about the person who earned the first United States patent?
It went to Samuel Hopkins of Philadelphia, who had developed a
method for making soap.

3. Which sentence tells about the president who was involved in granting the first United States patent?
On July 31, 1790, George Washington signed the first U.S. patent.

4. What kind of comparison is made between how patents were processed during Jefferson's time and how they are processed today?
Jefferson and his board used only three people. Today it takes
about 6,500 people.

5. What conclusion might you draw about why the author wants to give readers the information in this paragraph?
The author wants the reader to have an appreciation for the
early development of the patent process.

Advanced Practice TE p. LR8

Name _____ **The Patent Process**

Vocabulary
Directions Write a paragraph about an inventor and his or her invention. It can be imaginary. Use all of the vocabulary words.

Check the Words You Know

___clients	___eligible	___exclusive rights
___intellectual property	___notary	___patent
___patent attorney	___patentee	___provisional patent

Possible response given: Jackie Morante hoped she would be
able to find a lot of *clients* who would buy her new invention.
She had managed to get *exclusive rights* to a new pancake
flipper. She thought she would attract customers by saying
that the first one hundred buyers were *eligible* to get two for
the price of one. But first she had to apply for a *patent*. She
sketched her design on a piece of paper and went to a *notary*
to make it official. Then she found a *patent attorney* to guide
her through the process. A few months later, she was given
a *provisional patent*, so she started making infomercials to
sell it on television. By the end of the year she was an official
patentee, and the flipper was her *intellectual property*. Her
pancake flippers were selling like crazy.

Advanced Practice TE p. LR9

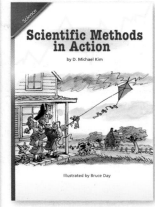

ELL Reader

ELL Poster 11

Teacher's Edition Notes

ELL notes throughout this lesson support instruction and reference additional resources at point of use.

Teaching Guide pp. 71–77, 232–233

- Multilingual summaries of the main selection
- Comprehension lesson
- Vocabulary strategies and word cards
- ELL Reader 5.3.1 lesson

ELL and Transition Handbook

Ten Important Sentences

- Key ideas from every selection in the Student Edition
- Activities to build sentence power

More Reading

Readers' Theater Anthology

- Fluency practice
- Five scripts to build fluency
- Poetry for oral interpretation

Leveled Trade Books

- Extended reading tied to the unit concept
- Lessons in the Trade Book Library Teaching Guide

School + Home

Homework

- Family Times Newsletter
- ELL Multilingual Selection Summaries

Take-Home Books

- Leveled Readers

Cross-Curricular Centers

Listen to the Selections

MATERIALS `SINGLES`
CD player, headphones, AudioText CD, student book

LISTEN TO LITERATURE Listen to *Wings for the King* and "Becky Schroeder: Enlightened Thinker" as you follow or read along in your book. Listen to identify the author's purpose in each selection.

If there is anything you don't understand, you can listen again to any section.

Read It Again!

MATERIALS `SINGLES` `PAIRS` `GROUPS`
Collection of books for self-selected reading, student book, reading logs

Select a book you have already read. Record the title of the book in your reading log. You may want to read with a partner.

Choose from the following:

- Leveled Readers
- ELL Readers
- Stories Written by Classmates
- Books from the Library
- *Wings for the King*

TEN IMPORTANT SENTENCES Read the Ten Important Sentences for *Wings for the King*. Then locate the sentences in the student book.

BOOK CLUB Gather as a group and read aloud together, taking turns playing the various parts. Discuss how the stage directions help you to understand the action of the play. Read other plays and get together with a group to share your favorites.

Write a Theme Song

MATERIALS `SINGLES` `GROUPS`
Paper, pencil

Create a theme song for *Wings for the King*.

1. Think of a song or tune that has a good melody. It should be easy to sing like *Mary Had a Little Lamb* or *Twinkle, Twinkle, Little Star*.
2. Write new lyrics for the song or tune that tell about *Wings for the King*.
3. Practice your theme song as a group.

EARLY FINISHERS Make up a pantomine to accompany your theme song.

Flying Along
The Endless Sky
Royal Wings

Scott Foresman Reading Street Centers Survival Kit
Use the *Wings for the King* materials from the Reading Street
Centers Survival Kit to organize this week's centers.

Writing/ Vocabulary

Science

Technology

Write a Metaphor

MATERIALS   SINGLES
Writing materials

In *Wings for the King*, Isaac tells the king that books are the best wings of all. The comparison of books to wings is a metaphor.

1. Make a list of other metaphors comparing books, or reading, to something else.
2. Draw a picture of one of your metaphors.

EARLY FINISHERS Write a pun or joke based on your metaphor.

A book is like a...

Be an Inventor!

MATERIALS   SINGLES
Writing and art materials   PAIRS

Invent a new and different way for humans to fly.

1. Draw a picture of your invention.
2. Label its parts.

EARLY FINISHERS With a partner come up with a clever name for your invention. Write a paragraph explaining how it works.

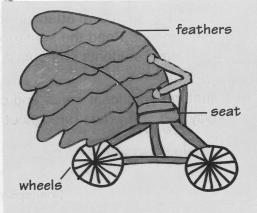

feathers

seat

wheels

Research Flight

MATERIALS   SINGLES
Internet access, writing materials, index cards

Log on to the Internet to research human flight.

1. Follow classroom rules for using a student-friendly search engine to find more information about the development of flying machines.
2. Make or print out a list of five different resources you found.
3. Highlight the two resources on your list which have the most valuable information.

EARLY FINISHERS Make a time line of important dates in aviation history.

Search Engine

flying machines

Important Events in Flight

1. 1903, Wright bros. fly

2. 1948, first jet flight

3.

ALL CENTERS

Tech Files ONLINE

To learn more about the history of flight, students can use a student-friendly search engine and the keywords *aviation history* to search the Internet. Be sure to follow classroom Internet rules.

ELL

Build Background Use ELL Poster 11 to build background and vocabulary for the lesson concept of inventions.

▲ **ELL Poster** 11

Build Background

ACTIVATE PRIOR KNOWLEDGE

BEGIN A KWL CHART about inventors.

- Give students two to three minutes to write as many things as they can about inventors, including who they are, what they do, what they are like, and so on.
- Give students two minutes to write three questions they would like to find out about inventors. Record questions on the KWL chart. Add a question of your own.
- Tell students that, as they read, they should look for the answers to their questions and note any new information to add to the chart.

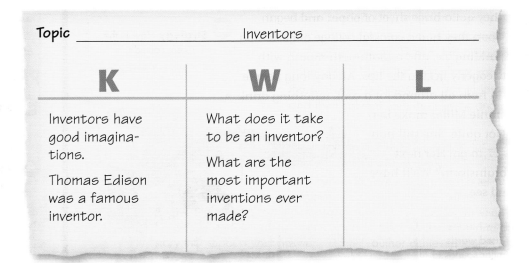

Topic _____ Inventors

K	W	L
Inventors have good imaginations. Thomas Edison was a famous inventor.	What does it take to be an inventor? What are the most important inventions ever made?	

▲ **Graphic Organizer** 4

BACKGROUND BUILDING AUDIO This week's audio explores flight. After students listen, discuss what they learned. What information did they find most surprising?

 **Background Building Audio**

Introduce Vocabulary

VOCABULARY CHART

Create a three-column chart with the headings *Word*, *Meaning*, and *Sentence*.

Word	Meaning	Sentence
admiringly	with wonder	Tom looked admiringly at his big brother.
permit	allow	My parents permit me to stay up until 9:00 p.m.
scoundrel		
subject		
worthless		

▲ **Graphic Organizer** 26

Read aloud the lesson vocabulary, asking students to raise their hands when they hear a familiar word. Have students record meanings and write sample sentences. When they come to a multiple-meaning word, students should record all the meanings they know and then predict which meaning will be used in the selection. ***Activate Prior Knowledge***

Invite students to share their work. Point out that in the list of this week's words they'll see the suffixes *-less* and *-ly*. Explain that *-less* means "without" and *-ly* means "with." Have students suggest other words with these suffixes and then tell the meaning of each. ***Suffixes***

As a class, return to students' charts after they finish reading to confirm their predictions.

Use the Multisyllabic Word Routine on p. DI·1 to help students read multisyllabic words.

Lesson Vocabulary

WORDS TO KNOW

T admiringly with wonder, pleasure, and approval

T permit to let; allow

T scoundrel an evil, dishonorable person

T subject person under the power, control, or influence of another

T worthless without value; good-for-nothing; useless

MORE WORDS TO KNOW

parapet a low wall at the edge of a balcony, roof, or bridge

reproachfully with disapproval

T = Tested Word

Vocabulary

Directions Choose the word from the box that best matches each definition. Write the word on the line.

worthless	1. without value	
admiringly	2. to look upon with approval	**Check the Words You Know**
scoundrel	3. rascals	___admiringly
permit	4. to allow	___permit
subject	5. a person under the power of someone else	___scoundrel ___subject ___worthless

Directions Choose the word from the box that best completes each sentence. Write the word on the line to the left.

admiringly	6. Henry Ford looked _____ at his Model T.
worthless	7. Ford's experiments were not _____, because he learned from them.
subject	8. After Ford built the first horseless carriage, he was the _____ of many news stories.
scoundrels	9. Untrustworthy _____ tried to sell a fake Model T for an outrageous price.
permit	10. The price of the first Model Ts did not _____ the average American to buy them.

Write a Newspaper Article
On a separate piece of paper, write a newspaper article about an imaginary new invention. Describe one or two failures the inventor experienced before he or she was successful.
Newspaper articles should include words from the vocabulary list and details about a new invention, real or imagined.

School + Home Home Activity Your child identified and used vocabulary from *Wings for the King*. Choose items in the room where you and your child are sitting. Describe each item. See if your child can guess what you are describing based on the clues you offer.

▲ **Practice Book** p. 104

Prereading Strategies

GENRE STUDY

Play

Wings for the King is a play. Explain that like a novel or a short story, a play tells a story but it is written to be acted out for an audience. Explain to students that plays have many unique literary elements such as acts, scenes, stage directions, and speech tags.

PREVIEW AND PREDICT

Have students look at the title, illustrations, and other external story structure features like the cast of characters, speech tags, and stage directions. Ask students to predict what the play is about. Have students use lesson vocabulary words when forming their predictions.

Strategy Response Log

Graphic Organizer Based on their previous discussion, have students begin a story sequence chart. Students will update their charts in the Strategy Response Log activity on p. 273.

WINGS for the KING

by Anne Sroda
illustrated by Franklin Hammond

Who will show the King the secret of flying?

Genre

A **play** is a story written to be acted out for an audience. As you read, imagine the actors speaking the lines and acting out the action.

266

ELL

Access Content Preview the play by pointing out the list of characters and the scene headings. Point out that spoken text is written in regular type and actions, or stage directions, are written in italics within parentheses. Invite students to point to an action in italics and perform it.

Consider having students read the selection summary in English or in students' home languages. See the Multilingual Summaries in the ELL Teaching Guide, pp. 75–77.

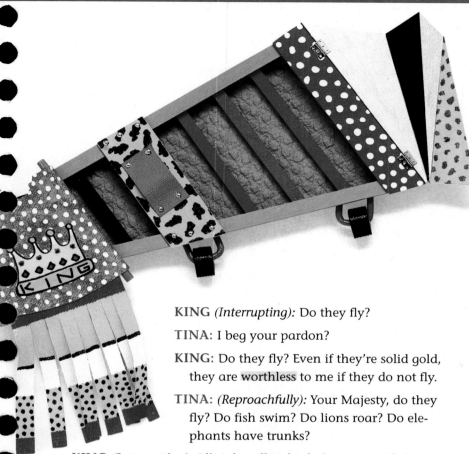

KING *(Interrupting):* Do they fly?

TINA: I beg your pardon?

KING: Do they fly? Even if they're solid gold, they are worthless to me if they do not fly.

TINA: *(Reproachfully):* Your Majesty, do they fly? Do fish swim? Do lions roar? Do elephants have trunks?

KING *(Interrupting):* All right, all right, let's get on with it. How do I wear them?

TINA: Oh, it's very simple, Your Majesty. Put your arms through here and hold onto these. *(She helps KING put on wings.)*

KING *(Running about stage, flapping wings):* These are wonderful wings! I just know they will work. *(He jumps up and down.)* Look! I feel lighter already! I shall take off from the parapet! *(He runs off.)*

QUEEN *(Calling after him):* Please be careful!

271

Cause and Effect REVIEW

TEACH

- Clue words often signal a cause and effect relationship.
- Clue words aren't always included. Sometimes a reader has to infer the relationship.

Think Aloud **MODEL** The events that happen in the first few pages of this play are the result of the King feeling bored and wanting to fly. So, I'll say the King's boredom is a cause and the effect is his subjects rush to make him wings.

PRACTICE AND ASSESS

- Have students write a sentence about a cause-effect relationship in the play using one of the clue words: *because*, *so*, or *since*.
- To assess, use Practice Book p. 106.

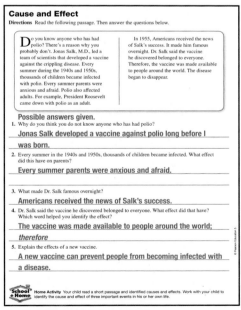

Cause and Effect

Directions Read the following passage. Then answer the questions below.

Do you know anyone who has had polio? There's a reason why you probably don't. Jonas Salk, M.D., led a team of scientists that developed a vaccine against the crippling disease. Every summer during the 1940s and 1950s, thousands of children became infected with polio. Every summer parents were anxious and afraid. Polio also affected adults. For example, President Roosevelt came down with polio as an adult.

In 1955, Americans received the news of Salk's success. It made him famous overnight. Dr. Salk said the vaccine he discovered belonged to everyone. Therefore, the vaccine was made available to people around the world. The disease began to disappear.

Possible answers given.

1. Why do you think you do not know anyone who has had polio?
Jonas Salk developed a vaccine against polio long before I was born.

2. Every summer in the 1940s and 1950s, thousands of children became infected. What effect did this have on parents?
Every summer parents were anxious and afraid.

3. What made Dr. Salk famous overnight?
Americans received the news of Salk's success.

4. Dr. Salk said the vaccine he discovered belonged to everyone. What effect did that have? Which word helped you identify the effect?
The vaccine was made available to people around the world; therefore

5. Explain the effects of a new vaccine.
A new vaccine can prevent people from becoming infected with a disease.

School + Home Home Activity Your child read a short passage and identified causes and effects. Work with your child to identify the cause and effect of three important events in his or her own life.

▲ **Practice Book** p. 106

Guiding Comprehension

6 🎯 **Story Structure • Critical**

How do the stage directions add to the play's humor?

Possible: The stage directions let you know this play is not serious. The stage direction has the King limping, with his wings broken and crown askew. This makes the scene seem light-hearted.

7 Dialogue • Critical

What does the Queen's dialogue tell you about her personality?

Possible response: You can tell from what she says that she is nervous and worries a lot. She worries for the King's safety.

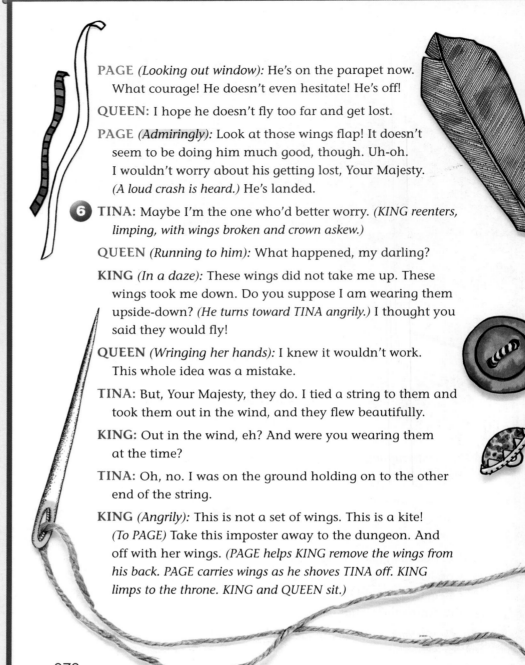

PAGE *(Looking out window):* He's on the parapet now. What courage! He doesn't even hesitate! He's off!

QUEEN: I hope he doesn't fly too far and get lost.

PAGE *(Admiringly):* Look at those wings flap! It doesn't seem to be doing him much good, though. Uh-oh. I wouldn't worry about his getting lost, Your Majesty. *(A loud crash is heard.)* He's landed.

6 **TINA:** Maybe I'm the one who'd better worry. *(KING reenters, limping, with wings broken and crown askew.)*

QUEEN *(Running to him):* What happened, my darling?

KING *(In a daze):* These wings did not take me up. These wings took me down. Do you suppose I am wearing them upside-down? *(He turns toward TINA angrily.)* I thought you said they would fly!

QUEEN *(Wringing her hands):* I knew it wouldn't work. This whole idea was a mistake.

TINA: But, Your Majesty, they do. I tied a string to them and took them out in the wind, and they flew beautifully.

KING: Out in the wind, eh? And were you wearing them at the time?

TINA: Oh, no. I was on the ground holding on to the other end of the string.

KING *(Angrily):* This is not a set of wings. This is a kite! *(To PAGE)* Take this imposter away to the dungeon. And off with her wings. *(PAGE helps KING remove the wings from his back. PAGE carries wings as he shoves TINA off. KING limps to the throne. KING and QUEEN sit.)*

272

Build Background Point out that the Heli-Cap-Ter on p. 273 is a play on the word *helicopter*. The Heli-Cap-Ter has rotors and propellers like a helicopter.

QUEEN: My beloved, will you please give up this dangerous business before you get yourself killed?

KING: Don't be absurd. Flying is no more dangerous than anything else. I could fall off a horse, you know.

QUEEN: Yes, but you would be a great deal closer to the ground.

KING: Balderdash! *(PAGE enters and blows horn, still off-key. KING covers his ears.)*

PAGE: Sire, may I present your loyal subject, Geraldine F. Kronmiller, and her *(Sighs)* wings. *(GERALDINE F. KRONMILLER enters, carrying a hat with a propeller attached.)*

GERALDINE *(Bowing):* Your Highness, I offer you my ingenious invention, the Heli-Cap-Ter. *(She holds hat forward.)*

KING *(Skeptically):* The Heli-Cap-Ter, eh. How does it work?

GERALDINE: Well, Sire, these things on top are called rotors. You wind the rotors to the left as far as they will go, and release them.

KING: And that's all there is to it?

GERALDINE: That's all, Your Highness. The spinning rotors lift you, and you tilt your head in the direction you want to go. Then, as the rotors wind down, they lower you gently back to the ground.

KING: Gently?

GERALDINE: Gently.

QUEEN *(Worried; to KING):* Don't do it. It doesn't look safe to me. **7**

KING: My dear, a child's hobbyhorse doesn't look safe to you. *(He removes his crown, crosses to GERALDINE, takes hat and puts it on.)* Just wind it up and let it go?

GERALDINE: That's all, Your Highness, except for one thing.

273

 STRATEGY SELF-CHECK

Story Structure

Ask students to identify the author's purpose. Remind them to use story structure to help identify the author's purpose.

SELF-CHECK

Students can ask themselves these questions to assess their ability to use the skill and strategy.

- Do I understand how the play is organized?
- Does it help me better understand the author's purpose for writing?

Monitor Progress
 **Author's Purpose**

If... students have difficulty using story structure to understand author's purpose,	**then...** revisit the skill lesson on pp. 262–263. Reteach as necessary.

 *Strategy Response Log*

Update Graphic Organizer Have students update sections of their story sequence charts. (See p. 266.) They should continue to fill in the chart as they read the rest of the play.

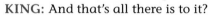

Develop Vocabulary

PRACTICE LESSON VOCABULARY

Students orally respond *yes* or *no* to each question and provide a reason.

1. Does the King *permit* visitors? *(Yes; he allows several visitors.)*

2. Is Geraldine Kronmiller a royal *subject*? *(Yes; she is a citizen in the kingdom.)*

3. Are Tina Applewhite's wings *worthless* when it comes to flying? *(Yes; they are too heavy to fly.)*

BUILD CONCEPT VOCABULARY

Review previous concept words with students. Ask if students have come across any words today in their reading or elsewhere that they would like to add to the Inventors and Their Inventions Concept Web, such as *courage* and *hesitate*.

If you want to teach this selection in two sessions, stop here.

Guiding Comprehension

If you are teaching the selection in two days, discuss the author's purpose and review the vocabulary.

8 **Compare and Contrast • Inferential**

Compare Tina's and Geraldine's inventions.

They both are creative and they both are designed to help the King fly. But, neither invention is practical nor do they work.

9 **Cause and Effect • Inferential**

What effect do you think the two failed inventions will have on the King?

Possible response: He will get frustrated and angry. But I don't think he will give up.

10 **Vocabulary • Context Clues**

Use context clues to determine the meaning of *skip* at the end of p. 275.

Clues: "before he can blow, King motions for him to stop" and "Let's just skip the fanfare." Meaning: pass over.

Monitor Progress	
Context Clues	
If... students have difficulty using context for the meaning of *skip*,	**then...** use the vocabulary strategy instruction on p. 275.

DAY 3 Grouping Options

Reading

Whole Group Discuss the Question of the Day.

Group Time Differentiated Instruction
 Read *Wings for the King.* See pp. 262h–262i for the small group lesson plan.

Whole Group Discuss the Reader Response questions on p. 280. Then use p. 287a.

Language Arts
Use pp. 287e–287k.

KING *(Interrupting):* Just a minute, my good woman. Tell me, have you tried the Heli-Cap-Ter yourself? I mean, really tried it?

GERALDINE: Oh, yes. Yes, indeed. It works. I guarantee it.

KING: That's good enough for me. *(He runs out.)*

GERALDINE: But Your Highness, wait!

274

ELL

Access Content Repeat the Page's exclamation, "How dauntless is Our Majesty!" Explain that *dauntless* means bold or not intimidated. Ask students if they agree with the Page that the King is dauntless.

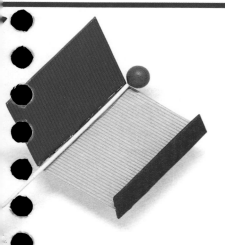

PAGE *(Looking out "window"):* How dauntless is Our Majesty! There he goes! *(Pauses)* There he goes—down. *(Loud crash is heard.)*

GERALDINE: But the Heli-Cap-Ter works! It's been laboratory tested. *(KING reenters, without Heli-Cap-Ter.)* **8**

QUEEN *(Running up to KING):* My poor baby! Didn't it work?

KING: Oh, it worked, all right. The Heli-Cap-Ter went up, up, up. *(He points up.)* But I went down, down, down. *(He points down.)*

GERALDINE: Does this mean I'm not going to get the bag of gold?

KING *(Angrily):* Take her to the dungeon! *(PAGE grabs GERALDINE's arm and leads her off. KING limps to throne, puts crown back on and sits, as does QUEEN.)* **9**

QUEEN: My dear, I hate to say I told you so, but. . . .

KING *(Interrupting):* If you hate to say it, then don't say it.

QUEEN *(Haughtily):* Well. *(PAGE enters and raises horn to his lips, but before he can blow, KING motions for him to stop.)*

KING: Please. Let's just skip the fanfare. What have you got now? **10**

275

Scientific Process

TIME FOR Science

The scientific process is the foundation for all science experiments, activities, and investigations. There are four key steps in the scientific process:

1. Identify the problem or question.
2. Form a hypothesis, or an educated guess, and propose an experiment to explain it.
3. Test the hypothesis and evaluate the data.
4. Draw conclusions and develop a new problem.
   Most science investigations result in more questions, as well as answers. A hypothesis proved true over time is a called a theory.

Context Clues

TEACH

- Remind students that some words have more than one meaning. Explain that context clues are words or information in the text that can help determine the correct meaning for the story.

- Read aloud the dialogue at the bottom of p. 275. Then model how to use context clues to determine the meaning of *skip*.

Think Aloud **MODEL** I read the last set of stage directions at the end of p. 275. It says that when the Page went to blow on his horn, the King stopped him. Then I read the King's next line: "Let's just skip the fanfare." Using these clues, I can determine that *skip* in this context means to pass over, not the other meaning of *skip* which is to leap or jump.

PRACTICE AND ASSESS

Have students use context to determine the spelling and meaning of these multiple-meaning words from p. 270 and p. 271: *subject* and *trunks*. *(subject: a person under the power or control of another; trunks: the long snouts of elephants)*

EXTEND SKILLS

Dialogue

Dialogue is the conversation between two or more characters. Dialogue reveals characters' thoughts, feelings, and motivations. It also helps show relationships between or among characters. In a play, the dialogue includes speech tags that identify the name of the character speaking and appear before the words the character speaks.

Guiding Comprehension

11 Predict • Inferential

Why do you think Isaac Summerville brought books to the King? What do the books symbolize?

Possible response: He wants to teach the King that reading is like flying, because they take you places you've never been before.

The books symbolize imagination and learning. By reading, one can imagine visiting far off places and learning about new cultures.

12 🔄 Author's Purpose • Critical

Explain what you think the author's purpose is on pp. 276–277.

Possible response: To express how exciting reading is; to show that reading is an adventure that takes the reader anywhere he or she wants to go.

Monitor Progress
🔄 Author's Purpose

If... students have difficulty identifying the author's purpose,	then... use the skill and strategy instruction on p. 277.

PAGE (*Lowering horn and clearing throat*): Sire, may I present your loyal subject, Isaac Summerville, and his . . . wings? (*ISAAC SUMMERVILLE enters, carrying an armload of at least eight books.*)

ISAAC (*Bowing awkwardly*)*:* Your Majesties, may I present the best wings of all! (*Holds out books*)

KING: Funny, those don't look like wings. How do you wear them?

ISAAC: You don't wear them, Your Majesty, you look at them. They are called books.

KING: Oh, I see. They're magic. You look at them, say a few words like abracadabra or fiddle-dee-faddle, and they take you wherever you want to go.

276

ELL

Extend Language Write *present* on the board and explain that it means "to introduce." Ask students if they know a word for *gift* that is spelled the same, but pronounced differently *(present).* Explain that words that are spelled the same with different pronunciations and meanings are called homographs.

ISAAC: Well, not exactly.

KING *(Losing patience):* Well, then how do they work?

ISAAC: Permit me. *(He crosses to KING and hands him a book.)* Open it. *(KING opens book.)*

KING: Here's a picture. *(Reads)* The pyramids of Egypt. So that's what they look like! *(QUEEN looks over his shoulder as he turns pages.)*

QUEEN: Look, my dear, a picture of Paris. There's the River Seine.

KING: What a good picture! I feel as if I'm really there.

ISAAC: Now you see what I mean. Books are wings to the land of knowledge. And they are also wings to the land of fun. Look at these. *(He gives three books to QUEEN. She opens one. KING looks over her shoulder.)*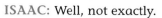

QUEEN: Why, it's a story about a little girl and a talking rabbit! It's called *Alice's Adventures in Wonderland.*

KING *(Scratching his head):* Wonderland. Is that north or south of here?

ISAAC: It's not north or south. Or east or west either. The only way you can visit Wonderland is by reading that book.

KING: Let's see the rest of these. *(He takes the rest of the books from ISAAC and looks at the titles.)* Hm-m-m. Here's one that will take me to China, and another about Africa.

QUEEN *(Taking another book from pile and leafing through it):* I could go to Switzerland with Heidi. I've always wanted to see the Alps.

KING: This is very exciting, indeed. *(Pauses thoughtfully)* But I had hoped to discover something.

277

⊙ SKILLS ⟷ STRATEGIES IN CONTEXT

Author's Purpose Story Structure

TEACH

Have students reread pp. 276–277. Ask them to think about why the author had books presented to the King instead of wings. Explain the author uses books (real, concrete objects) as symbols to represent imagination and learning (abstract or not concrete). Discuss with students other symbols, such as the American Flag and what it may represent (freedom, democracy). Help students support their responses with clues from the text structure.

Think Aloud **MODEL** Some parts of this page are funny, but I notice the dialogue and the stage directions aren't as silly or funny as on earlier pages. I read some of the stage directions on these two pages and they are more serious and straightforward. I think this shows the author is trying to express two important ideas. One, that reading is exciting and adventurous, and two, that books are symbolic for imagination and learning.

PRACTICE AND ASSESS

As students read p. 278, have them write a brief description of the author's purpose at the end of the play. Have them also describe how elements of story structure help support author's purpose. *(Possible response: The author's purpose at the end of the play is to express that reading is fun and exciting. The stage directions and the dialogue aren't as funny as they were at the beginning.)*

Guiding Comprehension

13 **Vocabulary • Multiple-Meaning Words**
Point out that the word *page* has multiple meanings. Ask students to use context clues to contrast the meaning of *page* in the second line of p. 278 with the character called Page.

The word *page* on p. 278 refers to a page in a book because Isaac is talking about reading. The character, Page, is a young person who is the King's attendant.

14 **Compare and Contrast • Critical**
Text to Self **Describe a time when you read something that took you on a journey to the "land of knowledge."**

Answers will vary but responses should describe a time students learned something from reading.

Strategy Response Log

Summarize When students finish reading the selection, provide this prompt: Imagine that your family has asked you to tell them about *Wings for the King*. Summarize the play in four or five sentences.

---

13 ISAAC: Reading is discovering, Your Highness. There's something new on every page.

KING (*Still looking at the titles*): Wait a minute! Here's a book called *The Principles of Aeronautics*. (*Calls*) Page! Take this book down to the dungeon. Make sure those two ~~scoundrels~~ read it, and then let them go free.

PAGE (*Crossing and taking book*): Yes, Sire.

KING (*Reaching beside his throne to get the bag of gold; to ISAAC*): Here, my good man, take your bag of gold. You have earned it. With books around, I don't think I'll ever be bored again.

ISAAC (*Taking gold and bowing*): I thank you, Your Highness.

KING: Now, both of you leave us alone so we can do some reading. (*ISAAC bows again and exits. PAGE bows and exits.*)

KING (*To QUEEN*): All right, my jewel, where do you want to go?

QUEEN: I can't decide. (*She looks at two open books in her lap.*) Should I visit the land of Oz with Dorothy in *The Wizard of Oz* or Never-Never Land with Peter Pan and Wendy?

KING (*Eagerly*): Never-Never Land! I would choose that one.

QUEEN: You'd like it, my darling. It's about a boy who really can fly. His name is Peter Pan.

KING: That sounds perfect!

QUEEN: All right. You read *Peter Pan* (*She hands him a book.*), I'll read *The Wizard of Oz*, and then we'll trade.

KING: Good idea! (*He opens the book.*) Well, bon voyage, your Highness. Have a nice trip.

QUEEN: You, too, Your Highness. I'm so glad we found out about books.

14 KING: So am I. It's the only way to fly! (*Both bury their noses in books as the curtain falls.*)

278

ELL

Access Content Read aloud the book title "Principles of Aeronautics." Explain that aeronautics refers to the science of aircraft navigation or flying. Ask students why the King wants to give this book to the two people in the dungeon.

RESEARCH/STUDY SKILLS

Advertisement

TEACH

OBJECTIVES

- Understand persuasive techniques used in advertisements.
- Recognize propaganda in advertisements.

Display advertisements from a variety of sources, such as magazines, newspapers, catalogues, and the Internet. Discuss the advertisements with students and the types of methods used in each to persuade consumers. During your discussion, define these advertising techniques.

- The purpose of an **advertisement** is to sell goods or services. Advertisers use many propaganda techniques to sell products.
- **Loaded words** affect the consumer by creating certain emotions or making value judgments.
- A **slogan** can have catchy words that appeal to people's emotions rather than logic. It is easily remembered.
- A **generality** is a vague statement. It doesn't give specific details or supporting facts and evidence.
- A **bandwagon statement** claims that a lot of people are buying the product. Bandwagon means "everyone else is doing it."
- A **testimonial** is an endorsement of a product from a celebrity or well-known person.

Provide students with sample advertisements. As they examine their ads, have them identify the persuasive techniques used. Then ask:

1. **What techniques are used in the advertisement?** *(Responses will vary, but students should use definitions above to describe techniques.)*

2. **Who is the target audience for the advertisement? How do you know?** *(Possible response: It's meant for children. I can tell because it shows children in the ad and it talks about impressing your friends at school.)*

3. **Do you think the techniques used are effective? Explain.** *(Possible response: Yes, because everyone wants to fit in at school and the ad tells students that if they have the product they will fit in.)*

Classified Section

Sale! Sale! Sale!

Valley View Estates, the finest neighborhood in Valley View Township, is holding a multi-family garage sale on Saturday, from 7 a.m. to 11 a.m. There will be bargains galore, and treasures for everyone. Arrive early for the best prices and selection. The whole town will be there with you!

ASSESS

Check that students can recognize propaganda techniques used in advertisements, and are able to make critical judgments about a product despite those techniques.

For more practice or to assess students, use Practice Book pp. 109–110.

▲ **Practice Book** p. 109

▲ **Practice Book** p. 110

Assessment Checkpoints *for the Week*

Selection Assessment

Use pp. 41–44 of Selection Tests to check:

   Selection Understanding

Comprehension Skill *Author's Purpose*

Selection Vocabulary
admiringly
permit
scoundrel
subject
worthless

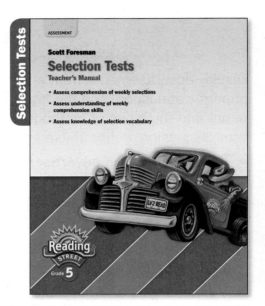

Leveled Assessment

On-Level

Strategic Intervention

Advanced

Use pp. 61–66 of Fresh Reads for Differentiated Test Practice to check:

 Comprehension Skill *Author's Purpose*

 REVIEW Comprehension Skill
Cause and Effect

 Fluency *Words Correct Per Minute*

Managing Assessment

Use Assessment Handbook for:

 Observation Checklists

 Record-Keeping Forms

 Portfolio Assessment

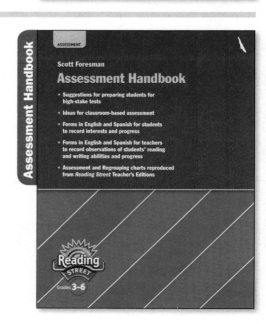

Illinois

Planning Guide for Performance Descriptors

Leonardo's Horse

Reading Street Teacher's Edition pages	Grade 5 English Language Arts Performance Descriptors
Oral Language **Speaking/Listening** Build Concept Vocabulary: 288l, 303, 309, 315c Read Aloud: 288m **Viewing** Analyze a Painting: 315d	**1A.Stage E.6.** Determine the meaning of a word in context when the word has multiple meanings. **1B.Stage E.10.** Read age-appropriate material aloud with fluency and accuracy. **5B.Stage E.1.** Analyze information from primary print and non-print sources.
Word Work Compound Words: 315i–315j	**1A.Stage E.1.** Use a combination of word analysis and vocabulary strategies (e.g., word patterns, structural analyses) within context to identify unknown words.
Reading **Comprehension** Main Idea: 288–289, 292–309, 312–315, 315b Summarize: 288–289, 292–309, 312–315 **Vocabulary** Lesson Vocabulary: 290b, 303, 309, 312 Word Structure: 290–291, 297, 305, 315c **Fluency** Model Tempo and Rate: 288l–288m, 315a **Self-Selected Reading:** LR10–18, TR16–17 **Literature** Genre—Biography: 292 Reader Response: 310	**1A.Stage E.1.** Use a combination of word analysis and vocabulary strategies (e.g., word patterns, structural analyses) within context to identify unknown words. **2A.Stage E.8.** Identify ways in which fiction and nonfiction works are organized differently. **2B.Stage E.3.** Analyze and remedy difficulties in comprehension (e.g., questioning, rephrasing, analyzing). **2B.Stage E.6.** Read a wide range of nonfiction (e.g., books, newspapers, magazines, textbooks, visual media). **4A.Stage E.4.** Separate main ideas from supporting facts and details. **4B.Stage E.3.** Use details to elaborate and develop main ideas for purposes of informing, entertaining, and persuading. **4B.Stage E.6.** Use appropriate verbal and nonverbal communication elements (e.g., appropriate space, body language, pleasant tone, rate, volume).
Language Arts **Writing** Question/Answer Essay: 315g–315h **Six-Trait Writing** Focus/Ideas: 311, 315g–315h **Grammar, Usage, and Mechanics** Principal Parts of Regular Verbs: 315e–315f **Research/Study** Skim and Scan: 315l **Technology** New Literacies: 315k	**2B.Stage E.3.** Analyze and remedy difficulties in comprehension (e.g., questioning, rephrasing, analyzing). **3C.Stage E.4.** Use available technology to design, produce, and present compositions and multimedia works. **4B.Stage E.5.** Use appropriate grammar, word choice, and pacing. **5C.Stage E.4.** Revise/edit the work.
Unit Skills **Writing** Compare and Contrast Essay: WA2–9 **Poetry:** 384–387 **Project/Wrap-Up:** 388–389	**2B.Stage E.4.** Compare ideas from texts representing a variety of times and cultures. **3C.Stage E.3.** Write creatively for a specified purpose and audience (e.g., short story, poetry, directions, song, friendly letter). **5A.Stage E.4.** Compare (with limited support) information from a variety of sources.

This Week's Leveled Readers

Below-Level

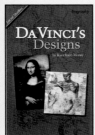

Biography

1B.Stage E.1. Set a purpose for reading and adjust as necessary before and during reading.

4A.Stage E.4. Separate main ideas from supporting facts and details.

On-Level

Nonfiction

1B.Stage E.4. Make judgments based on prior knowledge during reading.

4A.Stage E.4. Separate main ideas from supporting facts and details.

Advanced

Nonfiction

2B.Stage E.5. Make inferences and draw conclusions about contexts, events, character, and settings.

4A.Stage E.4. Separate main ideas from supporting facts and details.

Content-Area Illinois Performance Descriptors in This Lesson

Science

11A.Stage E.6. Communicate analysis and conclusions from investigation.

11B.Stage E.5. Communicate design findings: selecting graphs and charts that effectively report the data; preparing oral and written investigation conclusions; generating alternative design modifications which can be tested from original investigated question.

12C.Stage E.2. Apply scientific inquiries or technological designs to distinguish the properties of matter.

13B.Stage E.3. Investigate the interactions of societal decisions in science and technology innovations and discoveries.

Social Studies

18A.Stage E.1. Describe how culture is shared through music, art, and literature throughout the world over time.

18A.Stage E.2. Describe how an artistic tradition has been changed by technology (e.g., photography, music).

18C.Stage E.3. Identify historically significant people who affected social life or institutions.

Math

7B.Stage E.3. Estimate the perimeter, area, and/or volume of regular and irregular shapes and objects.

Illinois!

A FAMOUS ILLINOISAN
John A. Logan

John A. Logan (1826–1886), born in Jackson County, served as a general in the Union army during the Civil War. After the war he helped found the Grand Army of the Republic (GAR), a group of Union army veterans. In 1868, as head of the GAR, Logan proposed establishing a national holiday in the United States to remember those who died in defense of their country. The holiday is now called Memorial Day.

Students can . . .
Learn more about John Logan and write a short biography about his life.

A SPECIAL ILLINOIS PLACE
Glessner House Museum

In 1885 architect Henry Hobson Richardson designed the Glessner House, which was owned by John and Frances Glessner. Located on Prairie Avenue in Chicago, the house was made a national historic landmark in 1976. Today the Glessner House Museum has more than six thousand artifacts, many previously owned by the Glessners. In addition to its collections, the museum offers lectures and other public events.

Students can . . .
Find out about other national historic landmarks in Illinois. Have them use an outline map to locate the cities where the landmarks can be found.

ILLINOIS FUN FACTS
Did You Know?

• The first Memorial Day observance in Illinois occurred on April 29, 1866, at Woodlawn Cemetery in Carbondale.

• Moline gets its name from the French word *moulin*, which means "mill."

• Artist Pablo Picasso's fifty-foot sculpture in Chicago's Daley Plaza weighs 162 tons but cost taxpayers nothing; out of kindness, Picasso refused payment.

Students can . . .
Design and create a piece of art that represents their community. Have them share their creation with the class and explain how their piece of art reflects the community.

Unit 3
Inventors and Artists

CONCEPT QUESTION
What do people gain from the work of inventors and artists?

Week 1

How do inventors inspire our imaginations?

Week 2

How do artists inspire future generations?

Week 3

How can paleontologists help us understand the past?

Week 4

How does an artist use music to inspire others?

Week 5

How do artists create special effects to entertain us?

EXPAND THE CONCEPT
How do artists inspire future generations?

CONNECT THE CONCEPT

▶ **Build Background**
canvas, charcoal, easel, Norman Rockwell

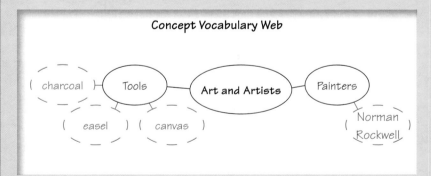

Concept Vocabulary Web

▶ **Social Studies Content**
The Renaissance, The Medici Family, Da Vinci's Inventions

▶ **Writing**
Question/Answer Essay

▶ **Internet Inquiry**
Artists and Their Legacies

Preview Your Week

How do artists inspire future generations?

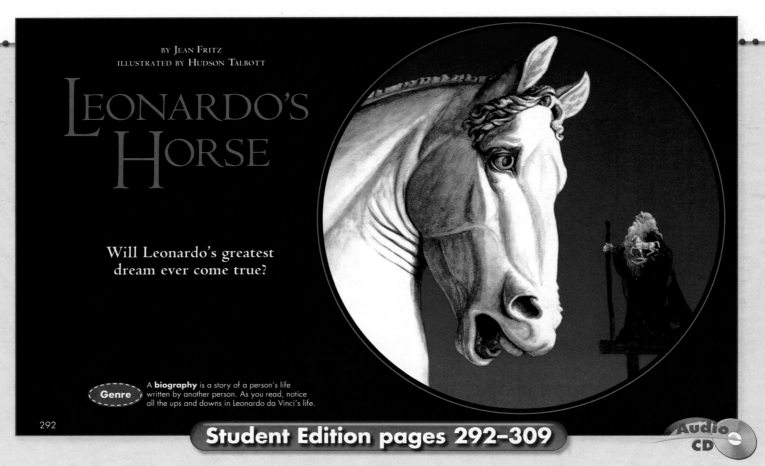

BY JEAN FRITZ
ILLUSTRATED BY HUDSON TALBOTT

LEONARDO'S HORSE

Will Leonardo's greatest dream ever come true?

Genre A **biography** is a story of a person's life written by another person. As you read, notice all the ups and downs in Leonardo da Vinci's life.

292

Student Edition pages 292–309

Audio CD

Genre	Biography
Vocabulary Strategy	Word Structure
Comprehension Skill	Main Idea
Comprehension Strategy	Summarize

Paired Selection

SOCIAL STUDIES

Reading Across Texts
List Triumphs and Tragedies

Genre
Narrative Nonfiction

Text Features
Time Line
Order of Events
Illustrations

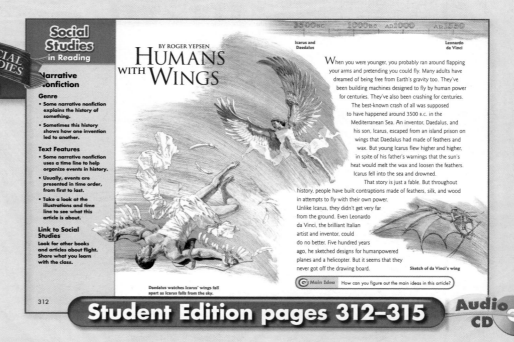

Social Studies in Reading

Narrative Nonfiction

Genre
• Some narrative nonfiction explains the history of something.
• Sometimes this history shows how one invention led to another.

Text Features
• Some narrative nonfiction uses a time line to help organize events in history.
• Usually, events are presented in time order, from first to last.
• Take a look at the illustrations and time line to see what this article is about.

Link to Social Studies
Look for other books and articles about flight. Share what you learn with the class.

BY ROGER YEPSEN
HUMANS WITH WINGS

When you were younger, you probably ran around flapping your arms and pretending you could fly. Many adults have dreamed of being free from Earth's gravity too. They've been building machines designed to fly by human power for centuries. They've also been crashing for centuries. The best-known crash of all was supposed to have happened around 3500 B.C. in the Mediterranean Sea. An inventor, Daedalus, and his son, Icarus, escaped from an island prison on wings that Daedalus had made of feathers and wax. But young Icarus flew higher and higher, in spite of his father's warnings that the sun's heat would melt the wax and loosen the feathers. Icarus fell into the sea and drowned.

That story is just a fable. But throughout history, people have built contraptions made of feathers, silk, and wood in attempts to fly with their own power. Unlike Icarus, they didn't get very far from the ground. Even Leonardo da Vinci, the brilliant Italian artist and inventor, could do no better. Five hundred years ago, he sketched designs for humanpowered planes and a helicopter. But it seems that they never got off the drawing board.

Sketch of da Vinci's wing

Main Idea How can you figure out the main ideas in this article?

Daedalus watches Icarus' wings fall apart as Icarus falls from the sky.

312

Student Edition pages 312–315

Audio CD

Read It
ONLINE
PearsonSuccessNet.com

- Student Edition
- Leveled Readers

Leveled Readers

Skill Main Idea

Strategy Summarize

Lesson Vocabulary

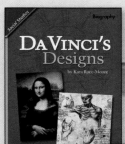

Below-Level

On-Level

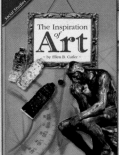

Advanced

ELL Reader

- Concept Vocabulary
- Text Support
- Language Enrichment

Integrate Social Studies Standards

- The Renaissance
- Humanities
- Culture

✓ **Read**

Leonardo's Horse,
pp. 292–309

"Humans with Wings,"
pp. 312–315

Leveled Readers

Below-Level **On-Level** **Advanced**

- Support Concepts
- Develop Concepts
- Extend Concepts
- Social Studies Extension Activity

ELL Reader

✓ **Build Concept Vocabulary**
Art and Artists, pp. 288l–288m

✓ **Teach Social Studies Concepts**
The Renaissance, p. 297
The Medici Family, p. 299
da Vinci's Inventions, p. 307

✓ **Explore Social Studies Center**
Think About Inventions,
p. 288k

Weekly Plan

READING

45–90 minutes

TARGET SKILLS OF THE WEEK

Comprehension Skill
Main Idea

Comprehension Strategy
Summarize

Vocabulary Strategy
Word Structure

DAY 1
PAGES 288l–290b, 315a, 315e–315k

Oral Language

QUESTION OF THE WEEK *How do artists inspire future generations?*

Read Aloud: "Norman Rockwell," 288m
Build Concepts, 288l

Comprehension/Vocabulary

Comprehension Skill/Strategy Lesson, 288–289
   Main Idea and Details **T**
   Summarize
Build Background, 290a
Introduce Lesson Vocabulary, 290b
achieved, architect, bronze, cannon, depressed, fashioned, midst, philosopher, rival **T**

Read Leveled Readers

Grouping Options 288f–288g

Fluency

Model Tempo and Rate, 288l–288m, 315a

DAY 2
PAGES 290–303, 315a, 315e–315k

Oral Language

QUESTION OF THE DAY *Why was da Vinci so driven to build the bronze horse?*

Comprehension/Vocabulary

Vocabulary Strategy Lesson, 290–291
   Word Structure **T**

Read *Leonardo's Horse,* 292–303

Grouping Options 288f–288g

   Main Idea and Details **T**
   Summarize
   Word Structure **T**
   REVIEW Fact and Opinion **T**
   Develop Vocabulary

Fluency

Echo Reading, 315a

LANGUAGE ARTS

30–60 minutes

Trait of the Week

Focus/Ideas

Grammar, 315e
Introduce Principal Parts of Regular Verbs **T**

Writing Workshop, 315g
Introduce Question/Answer Essay
Model the Trait of the Week: Focus/Ideas

Spelling, 315i
Pretest for Compound Words

Internet Inquiry, 315k
Identify Questions

Grammar, 315e
Develop Principal Parts of Regular Verbs **T**

Writing Workshop, 315g
Improve Writing with Stick to the Topic

Spelling, 315i
Teach the Generalization

Internet Inquiry, 315k
Navigate/Search

DAILY WRITING ACTIVITIES

Day 1 Write to Read, 288

Day 2 Words to Write, 291
Strategy Response Log, 292, 303

DAILY SOCIAL STUDIES CONNECTIONS

Day 1 Art and Artists Concept Web, 288l

Day 2 Time for Social Studies: The Renaissance, 297; The Medici Family, 299
Revisit the Art and Artists Concept Web, 303

DAILY SUCCESS PREDICTORS
for Adequate Yearly Progress

Monitor Progress and Corrective Feedback

Vocabulary Check Vocabulary, *288l*

RESOURCES FOR THE WEEK

- Practice Book, *pp. 111–120*
- Word Study and Spelling Practice Book, *pp. 45–48*
- Grammar and Writing Practice Book, *pp. 45–48*

- Selection Test, *pp. 45–48*
- Fresh Reads for Differentiated Test Practice, *pp. 67–72*
- The Grammar and Writing Book, *pp. 116–121*

Grouping Options for Differentiated Instruction

Turn the page for the small group lesson plan.

DAY 3 — PAGES 304–311, 315a, 315e–315k

Oral Language

QUESTION OF THE DAY *Why do you think so many people wanted to see da Vinci's horse completed?*

Comprehension/Vocabulary

Read *Leonardo's Horse, 304–310*

Grouping Options 288f–288g

- Main Idea **T**
- Summarize
- Word Structure **T**
- Develop Vocabulary

Reader Response

Selection Test

Fluency

Model Tempo and Rate, 315a

Grammar, 315f
Apply Principal Parts of Regular Verbs in Writing **T**

Writing Workshop, 311, 315h
Write Now
Prewrite and Draft

Spelling, 315j
Connect Spelling to Writing

Internet Inquiry, 315k
Analyze Sources

Day 3   Strategy Response Log, 308
Look Back and Write, 310

Day 3   Time for Social Studies: da Vinci's Inventions, 307
Revisit the Art and Artists Concept Web, 309

DAY 4 — PAGES 312–315a, 315e–315k

Oral Language

QUESTION OF THE DAY *What role do artists and art play in your life and in our society?*

Comprehension/Vocabulary

Read *"Humans with Wings," 312–315*

Grouping Options 288f–288g

Narrative Nonfiction/
Text Features

Reading Across Texts

Content-Area Vocabulary

Fluency

Partner Reading, 315a

Grammar, 315f
Practice Principal Parts of Regular Verbs for Standardized Tests **T**

Writing Workshop, 315h
Draft, Revise, and Publish

Spelling, 315j
Provide a Strategy

Internet Inquiry, 315k
Synthesize Information

Day 4   Writing Across Texts, 315

Day 4   Social Studies Center: Think About Inventions, 288k

DAY 5 — PAGES 315a–315l

Oral Language

QUESTION OF THE WEEK *To wrap up the week, revisit the Day 1 question.*

Build Concept Vocabulary, 315c

Fluency

Read Leveled Readers

Grouping Options 288f–288g

Assess Reading Rate, 315a

Comprehension/Vocabulary

- Reteach Main Idea, 315b **T**
- Illustrator's Craft, 315b
- Review Word Structure, 315c **T**

Speaking and Viewing, 315d
Newscast
Analyze a Painting

Grammar, 315f
Cumulative Review

Writing Workshop, 315h
Connect to Unit Writing

Spelling, 315j
Posttest for Compound Words

Internet Inquiry, 315k
Communicate Results

Research/Study Skills, 315l
Skim and Scan

Day 5   Illustrator's Craft, 315b

Day 5   Revisit the Art and Artists Concept Web, 315c

KEY ⊙ = Target Skill   **T** = Tested Skill

Comprehension — Check Retelling, *310*

Fluency — Check Fluency WCPM, *315a*

Vocabulary — Check Vocabulary, *315c*

SUCCESS PREDICTOR

Small Group Plan *for Differentiated Instruction*

Daily Plan
AT A GLANCE

Reading
Whole Group
- Oral Language
- Comprehension/Vocabulary

Group Time
Differentiated Instruction
Meet with small groups to provide:
- Skill Support
- Reading Support
- Fluency Practice

Read

This week's lessons for daily group time can be found behind the Differentiated Instruction (DI) tab on pp. DI·12–DI·21.

Whole Group
- Fluency

Language Arts
- Grammar
- Writing
- Spelling
- Research/Inquiry
- Speaking/Listening/Viewing

Use *My Sidewalks on Reading Street* for Tier III intensive reading intervention.

DAY 1

On-Level	Strategic Intervention	Advanced
Teacher-Led *Page DI · 13*	**Teacher-Led** *Page DI · 12*	**Teacher-Led** *Page DI · 13*
• Develop Concept Vocabulary • **Read** On-Level Reader *Michelangelo and The Italian Renaissance*	• Reinforce Concepts • **Read** Below-Level Reader *Da Vinci's Designs*	• **Read** Advanced Reader *The Inspiration of Art* • Independent Extension Activity

(i) **Independent Activities**
While you meet with small groups, have the rest of the class...

- Visit the Reading/Library Center
- Listen to the Background Building Audio
- Finish Write to Read, p. 288
- Complete Practice Book pp. 113–114
- Visit Cross-Curricular Centers

DAY 2

On-Level	Strategic Intervention	Advanced
Teacher-Led *Pages 294–303*	**Teacher-Led** *Page DI · 14*	**Teacher-Led** *Page DI · 15*
• **Read** *Leonardo's Horse*	• Practice Lesson Vocabulary • Read Multisyllabic Words • **Read** or Listen to *Leonardo's Horse*	• Extend Vocabulary • **Read** *Leonardo's Horse*

(i) **Independent Activities**
While you meet with small groups, have the rest of the class...

- Visit the Reading/Library Center
- Listen to the AudioText for *Leonardo's Horse*
- Finish Words to Write, p. 291
- Complete Practice Book pp. 115–116
- Write in their Strategy Response Logs, pp. 292, 303
- Visit Cross-Curricular Centers
- Work on inquiry projects

DAY 3

On-Level	Strategic Intervention	Advanced
Teacher-Led *Pages 304–309*	**Teacher-Led** *Page DI · 16*	**Teacher-Led** *Page DI · 17*
• **Read** *Leonardo's Horse*	• Practice Main Idea and Summarize • **Read** or Listen to *Leonardo's Horse*	• Extend Main Idea and Summarize • **Read** *Leonardo's Horse*

(i) **Independent Activities**
While you meet with small groups, have the rest of the class...

- Visit the Reading/Library Center
- Listen to the AudioText for *Leonardo's Horse*
- Write in their Strategy Response Logs, p. 308
- Finish Look Back and Write, p. 310
- Complete Practice Book p. 117
- Visit Cross-Curricular Centers
- Work on inquiry projects

① Begin with whole class skill and strategy instruction.

② Meet with small groups to provide differentiated instruction.

③ Gather the whole class back together for fluency and language arts.

DAY 4

On-Level

Teacher-Led
Pages 312–315
• **Read** "Humans with Wings"

Strategic Intervention

Teacher-Led
Page DI · 18
• Practice Retelling
• **Read** or Listen to "Humans with Wings"

Advanced

Teacher-Led
Page DI · 19
• **Read** "Humans with Wings"
• Genre Study

(i) Independent Activities

While you meet with small groups, have the rest of the class...

• Visit the Reading/Library Center
• Listen to the AudioText for "Humans with Wings"
• Visit the Writing/Vocabulary Center
• Finish Writing Across Texts, p. 315
• Visit Cross-Curricular Centers
• Work on inquiry projects

DAY 5

On-Level

Teacher-Led
Page DI · 21
• **Reread** Leveled Reader *Michelangelo and The Italian Renaissance*
• Retell *Michelangelo and The Italian Renaissance*

Strategic Intervention

Teacher-Led
Page DI · 20
• **Reread** Leveled Reader *Da Vinci's Designs*
• Retell *Da Vinci's Designs*

Advanced

Teacher-Led
Page DI · 21
• **Reread** Leveled Reader *The Inspiration of Art*
• Share Extension Activity

(i) Independent Activities

While you meet with small groups, have the rest of the class...

• Visit the Reading/Library Center
• Complete Practice Book pp. 118–120
• Visit Cross-Curricular Centers
• Work on inquiry projects

Grouping Place English language learners in the groups that correspond to their reading abilities in English.

Use the appropriate Leveled Reader or other text at students' instructional level.

TiP Send home the appropriate Multilingual Summary of the main selection on Day 1.

Take It to the NET ONLINE
PearsonSuccessNet.com

Sharon Vaughn
For ideas on grouping, see the article "Reading Instruction Grouping for Students with Reading Difficulties" by Scott Foresman author Sharon Vaughn and others.

TEACHER TALK

Skimming is quickly reading a text (or titles and sample sentences) to get the main ideas. **Scanning** is moving one's eyes down the page, looking for specific words and phrases.

Be sure to schedule time for students to work on the unit inquiry project "Inventors and Artists." This week students conduct searches for information that answers their inquiry questions about inventors and artists.

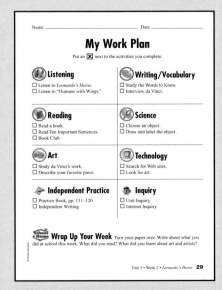

▲ **Group-Time Survival Guide**
p. 29, Weekly Contract

Leonardo's Horse **288g**

Customize Your Plan *by Strand*

ORAL LANGUAGE

SOCIAL STUDIES

Concept Development

How do artists inspire future generations?

CONCEPT VOCABULARY

canvas   charcoal   easel   Norman Rockwell

BUILD

☐ **Question of the Week** Introduce and discuss the question of the week. This week students will read a variety of texts and work on projects related to the concept *art and artists*. Post the question for students to refer to throughout the week. **DAY 1** *288d*

☐ **Read Aloud** Read aloud "Norman Rockwell." Then begin a web to build concepts and concept vocabulary related to this week's lesson and the unit theme, Inventors and Artists. Introduce the concept words *canvas, charcoal, easel,* and *Norman Rockwell* and have students place them on the web. Display the web for use throughout the week. **DAY 1** *288l-288m*

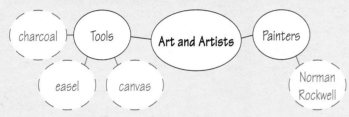

DEVELOP

☐ **Question of the Day** Use the prompts from the Weekly Plan to engage students in conversations related to this week's reading and the unit theme. **EVERY DAY** *288d-288e*

☐ **Concept Vocabulary Web** Revisit the Art and Artists Concept Web and encourage students to add concept words from their reading and life experiences. **DAY 2** *303,* **DAY 3** *309*

CONNECT

☐ **Looking Back/Moving Forward** Revisit the Art and Artists Concept Web and discuss how it relates to this week's lesson and the unit theme. Then make connections to next week's lesson. **DAY 5** *315c*

CHECK

☐ **Concept Vocabulary Web** Use the Art and Artists Concept Web to check students' understanding of the concept vocabulary words *canvas, charcoal, easel,* and *Norman Rockwell*. **DAY 1** *288l,* **DAY 5** *315c*

VOCABULARY

⟳ **STRATEGY WORD STRUCTURE** When you see an unfamiliar word, sometimes you can check if there is a familiar root within it. Greek and Latin roots are used in many English words. Using a root can help you figure out the meaning of an unknown word.

LESSON VOCABULARY

achieved	fashioned
architect	midst
bronze	philosopher
cannon	rival
depressed	

TEACH

☐ **Words to Know** Give students the opportunity to tell what they already know about this week's lesson vocabulary words. Then discuss word meaning. **DAY 1** *290b*

☐ **Vocabulary Strategy Lesson** Use the vocabulary strategy lesson in the Student Edition to introduce and model this week's strategy, *word structure.* **DAY 2** *290-291*

Vocabulary Strategy Lesson

PRACTICE/APPLY

☐ **Leveled Text** Read the lesson vocabulary in the context of leveled text. **DAY 1** *LR10-LR18*

☐ **Words in Context** Read the lesson vocabulary and apply *word structure* in the context of *Leonardo's Horse.* **DAY 2** *292-303,* **DAY 3** *304-310*

Leveled Readers

☐ **Writing/Vocabulary Center** Make a list of five questions you would ask in an interview with Leonardo da Vinci. **ANY DAY** *288k*

Main Selection—Nonfiction

☐ **Homework** Practice Book pp. 114–115. **DAY 1** *290b,* **DAY 2** *291*

☐ **Word Play** Discuss how words have denotations and connotations. Have students work with partners to select a word from *Leonardo's Horse,* record the word's denotation, and write a plus (+), zero (0), or minus (–) to indicate whether the word has a positive, neutral, or negative connotation. **ANY DAY** *315c*

ASSESS

☐ **Selection Test** Use the Selection Test to determine students' understanding of the lesson vocabulary words. **DAY 3**

RETEACH/REVIEW

☐ **Reteach Lesson** If necessary, use this lesson to reteach and review *word structure.* **DAY 5** *315c*

❶ Use assessment data to determine your instructional focus.

❷ Preview this week's instruction by strand.

❸ Choose instructional activities that meet the needs of your classroom.

COMPREHENSION

SKILL MAIN IDEA AND DETAILS The *main idea* is the most important idea about a paragraph, passage, or article. *Details* are small pieces of information that tell more about the main idea.

STRATEGY SUMMARIZE Summarizing is a short retelling of a portion of the text that includes the main ideas and leaves out unimportant details.

TEACH

❑ **Skill/Strategy Lesson** Use the skill/strategy lesson in the Student Edition to introduce and model *main idea and details* and *summarize.* **DAY 1** *288-289*

❑ **Extend Skills** Teach illustrator's craft. **ANY DAY** *315b*

Skill/Strategy Lesson

PRACTICE/APPLY

❑ **Leveled Text** Apply *main idea and details* and *summarize* to read leveled text. **DAY 1** *LR10-LR18*

❑ **Skills and Strategies in Context** Read *Leonardo's Horse,* using the Guiding Comprehension questions to apply *main idea and details* and *summarize.* **DAY 2** *292-303,* **DAY 3** *304-310*

Leveled Readers

❑ **Skills and Strategies in Context** Read "Humans with Wings," guiding students as they apply *main idea and details* and *summarize.* Then have students discuss and write across texts. **DAY 4** *312-315*

Main Selection—Nonfiction

❑ **Homework** Practice Book pp. 113, 117, 118. **DAY 1** *289,* **DAY 3** *309,* **DAY 5** *315b*

Paired Selection—Nonfiction

❑ **Fresh Reads for Differentiated Test Practice** Have students practice *main idea and details* with a new passage. **DAY 3**

ASSESS

❑ **Selection Test** Determine students' understanding of the selection and their use of *main idea and details.* **DAY 3**

❑ **Retell** Have students retell *Leonardo's Horse.* **DAY 3** *310-311*

RETEACH/REVIEW

❑ **Reteach Lesson** If necessary, reteach and review *main idea and details.* **DAY 5** *315b*

FLUENCY

SKILL TEMPO AND RATE Reading with appropriate tempo means that you take breaths at appropriate times and pause at punctuation. Reading with an appropriate rate means that you do not read too fast or too slow.

TEACH

❑ **Read Aloud** Model fluent reading by rereading "Norman Rockwell." Focus on this week's fluency skill, tempo and rate. **DAY 1** *288l-288m, 315a*

PRACTICE/APPLY

❑ **Echo Reading** Read aloud selected paragraphs from *Leonardo's Horse,* modeling appropriate reading rate and tempo. Have students practice, doing three echo readings of the selected paragraphs. **DAY 2** *315a,* **DAY 3** *315a*

❑ **Partner Reading** Have partners practice reading aloud, using appropriate tempo and rate, and offering each other feedback. As students reread, monitor their progress toward their individual fluency goals. **DAY 4** *315a*

❑ **Listening Center** Have students follow along with the AudioText for this week's selections. **ANY DAY** *288j*

❑ **Reading/Library Center** Have students reread a selection of their choice. **ANY DAY** *288j*

❑ **Fluency Coach** Have students use Fluency Coach to listen to fluent readings or practice reading on their own. **ANY DAY**

ASSESS

❑ **Check Fluency WCPM** Do a one-minute timed reading, paying special attention to this week's skill—tempo and rate. Provide feedback for each student. **DAY 5** *315a*

☑ Customize Your Plan *by Strand*

GRAMMAR

SKILL PRINCIPAL PARTS OF REGULAR VERBS A verb's tenses are formed from its *principal parts* (four basic forms). The principal parts of a verb are the present, present participle, past, and past participle.

TEACH

❑ **Grammar Transparency 12** Use Grammar Transparency 12 to teach the principal parts of regular verbs. **DAY 1** *315e*

Grammar Transparency 12

PRACTICE/APPLY

❑ **Develop the Concept** Review the concept of principal parts of regular verbs and provide guided practice. **DAY 2** *315e*

❑ **Apply to Writing** Have students review something they have written and apply principal parts of regular verbs. **DAY 3** *315f*

❑ **Test Preparation** Examine common errors in principal parts of regular verbs to prepare for standardized tests. **DAY 4** *315f*

❑ **Homework** Grammar and Writing Practice Book pp. 45–47. **DAY 2** *315e*, **DAY 3** *315f*, **DAY 4** *315f*

ASSESS

❑ **Cumulative Review** Use Grammar and Writing Practice Book p. 48. **DAY 5** *315f*

RETEACH/REVIEW

❑ **Daily Fix-It** Have students find and correct errors in grammar, spelling, and punctuation. **EVERY DAY** *315e–315f*

❑ **The Grammar and Writing Book** Use pp. 116–119 of The Grammar and Writing Book to extend instruction for principal parts of regular verbs. **ANY DAY**

The Grammar and Writing Book

WRITING

Trait of the Week

FOCUS/IDEAS Good writers focus on a main idea and develop this idea with strong supporting details. Having a purpose—whether it is to inform, to persuade, or to entertain—helps keep focus on the main idea.

TEACH

❑ **Writing Transparency 12A** Use the model to introduce and discuss the Trait of the Week. **DAY 1** *315g*

❑ **Writing Transparency 12B** Use the transparency to show students how sticking to the topic can improve their writing. **DAY 2** *315g*

Writing Transparency 12A **Writing Transparency 12B**

PRACTICE/APPLY

❑ **Write Now** Examine the model on Student Edition p. 311. Then have students write their own question/answer essay. **DAY 3** *311, 315h*, **DAY 4** *315h*

Prompt *Leonardo's Horse* describes some of Leonardo da Vinci's inventions. Think about modern inventions. Which recent invention changed people's lives most? Write an essay answering that question.

Write Now p. 311

❑ **Writing/Vocabulary Center** Make a list of five questions you would ask in an interview with Leonardo da Vinci. **ANY DAY** *288k*

ASSESS

❑ **Writing Trait Rubric** Use the rubric to evaluate students' writing. **DAY 4** *315h*

RETEACH/REVIEW

❑ **The Grammar and Writing Book** Use pp. 116–121 of The Grammar and Writing Book to extend instruction for principal parts of regular verbs, sticking to the topic, and question/answer essays. **ANY DAY**

The Grammar and Writing Book

❶ Use assessment data to determine your instructional focus.

❷ Preview this week's instruction by strand.

❸ Choose instructional activities that meet the needs of your classroom.

SPELLING

GENERALIZATION COMPOUND WORDS A compound word is smaller words joined together. Keep all the letters when spelling compounds: *water + proof = waterproof*. To decode a compound word, divide it and sound out each smaller word.

TEACH

❑ **Pretest** Give the pretest for compound words. Guide students in self-correcting their pretests and correcting any misspellings. DAY 1 *315i*

❑ **Think and Practice** Connect spelling to the phonics generalization for compound words. DAY 2 *315i*

PRACTICE/APPLY

❑ **Connect to Writing** Have students use spelling words to write questions. Then review frequently misspelled words: *something, everybody, everyone.* DAY 3 *315j*

❑ **Homework** Word Study and Spelling Practice Book pp. 45–48. **EVERY DAY**

RETEACH/REVIEW

❑ **Review** Review spelling words to prepare for the posttest. Then provide students with a spelling strategy—divide and conquer. DAY 4 *315j*

ASSESS

❑ **Posttest** Use dictation sentences to give the posttest for compound words. DAY 5 *315j*

Spelling Words

1. waterproof
2. teaspoon
3. grasshopper
4. homesick
5. barefoot
6. courthouse
7. earthquake
8. rowboat
9. scrapbook
10. countryside*
11. lightweight*
12. fishhook
13. spotlight
14. blindfold
15. whirlpool
16. tablespoon
17. greenhouse
18. postcard
19. hummingbird
20. thumbtack

Challenge Words

21. sledgehammer
22. brokenhearted
23. chalkboard
24. straightforward
25. granddaughter

*Word from the selection

RESEARCH AND INQUIRY

❑ **Internet Inquiry** Have students conduct an Internet inquiry on artists and their artistic and cultural legacies. **EVERY DAY** *315k*

❑ **Skim and Scan** Review how to skim and scan text and discuss how students can use this strategy to determine important information contained in a text. DAY 5 *315l*

❑ **Unit Inquiry** Allow time for students to conduct searches for information that answers their inquiry questions about inventors and artists. **ANY DAY** *261*

SPEAKING AND VIEWING

❑ **Newscast** Have students use information from the selection to create a newscast about the unveiling of Leonardo's horse in 1999. DAY 5 *315d*

❑ **Analyze a Painting** Have students analyze a painting that captures the spirit of the Renaissance and answer questions. DAY 5 *315d*

Resources for
Differentiated Instruction

LEVELED READERS

▶ **Comprehension**
- ◎ **Skill** Main Idea
- ◎ **Strategy** Summarize

▶ **Lesson Vocabulary**
- ◎ Word Structure

achieved
architect
bronze
cannon
depressed
fashioned
midst
philosopher
rival

▶ **Social Studies Standards**
- The Renaissance
- Humanities
- Culture

Leveled Reader Database
ONLINE

PearsonSuccessNet.com

Use the Online Database of over 600 books to
- **Download and print additional copies of this week's leveled readers.**
- **Listen to the readers being read online.**
- **Search for more titles focused on this week's skills, topic, and content.**

On-Level Reader

On-Level

Social Studies

Michelangelo and the Italian Renaissance
by Liz Murray

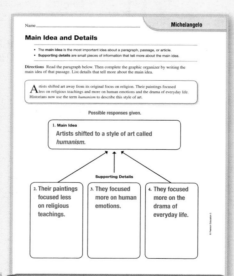

Name _____   Michelangelo

Main Idea and Details
- The **main idea** is the most important idea about a paragraph, passage, or article.
- **Supporting details** are small pieces of information that tell more about the main idea.

Directions Read the paragraph below. Then complete the graphic organizer by writing the main idea of that passage. List details that tell more about the main idea.

Artists shifted art away from its original focus on religion. Their paintings focused less on religious teachings and more on human emotions and the drama of everyday life. Historians now use the term *humanism* to describe this style of art.

Possible responses given.

1. **Main Idea**
Artists shifted to a style of art called *humanism*.

Supporting Details

2. Their paintings focused less on religious teachings.
3. They focused more on human emotions.
4. They focused more on the drama of everyday life.

◎ **On-Level Practice** TE p. LR14

Name _____   Michelangelo

Vocabulary
Directions Draw a line from each word to its definition.

Check the Words You Know
___achieved   ___architect   ___bronze
___cannon   ___depressed   ___fashioned
___midst   ___philosopher ___rival

1. achieved — gloomy
2. architect — person who tries to understand the nature of reality
3. bronze — formed
4. cannon — accomplished
5. depressed — the middle of
6. fashioned — competitor
7. midst — person who designs buildings
8. philosopher — alloy of copper and tin
9. rival — big gun

Directions Write a sentence for each of the following words: *architect, fashioned, midst, philosopher, rival.*

10. Sentences will vary. _____
11. _____
12. _____
13. _____
14. _____

◎ **On-Level Practice** TE p. LR15

Strategic Intervention

Social Studies   Biography

DAVINCI'S Designs
by Kara Race-Moore

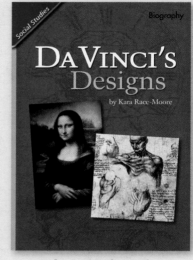

Below-Level Reader

Name _____   Da Vinci's Designs

Main Idea and Details
- The **main idea** is the most important idea about a paragraph, passage, or article.
- **Supporting details** are small pieces of information that tell more about the main idea.

Directions Read the paragraph below. Then complete the graphic organizer by writing the main idea of the passage. List details that tell more about the main idea.

Da Vinci was fascinated by the idea of flying. He thought he would become even more famous if he could find a way for humans to fly. To unlock the secret of flight, da Vinci studied wind currents and the flight patterns of flying creatures. He studied the wings of bats and birds, making many drawings of their shapes and bone structures.

Possible responses given.

1. **Main Idea**
Da Vinci tried to learn the secret of flying.

Supporting Details

2. studied wings of bats and birds
3. studied wind currents
4. studied flight patterns

◎ **Below-Level Practice** TE p. LR11

Name _____   Da Vinci's Designs

Vocabulary
Directions Use the vocabulary words in the box to fill in the blanks in the sentences below.

Check the Words You Know
___achieved   ___architect   ___bronze
___cannon   ___depressed   ___fashioned
___midst   ___philosopher ___rival

1. He was in the **midst** of reading his book when the phone rang.
2. The **rival** soccer team was ready to score.
3. She **achieved** a high score on her test.
4. The **architect** included a winding staircase in his design.
5. The **cannon** at the bicentennial celebration sounded like thunder.
6. The student liked to observe the world around her and asked so many questions that they called her a **philosopher**.
7. He **fashioned** a ramp so the old dog could get into the truck.
8. The American runner won the **bronze** medal at the Olympics.
9. The rain made the kids feel **depressed**.

Directions Choose three of the vocabulary words. Write a sentence of your own using each one.

10. Sentences will vary. _____
11. _____
12. _____

◎ **Below-Level Practice** TE p. LR12

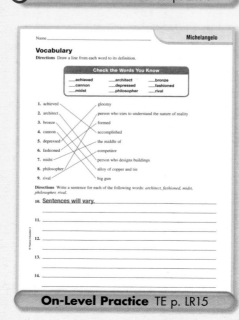

Advanced

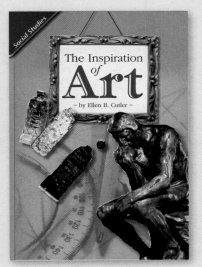

Advanced Reader

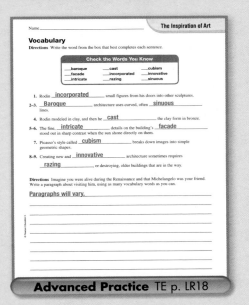

Advanced Practice TE p. LR17

Advanced Practice TE p. LR18

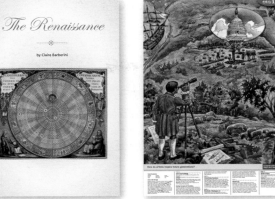

ELL Reader

ELL Poster 12

Teacher's Edition Notes

ELL notes throughout this lesson support instruction and reference additional resources at point of use.

**Teaching Guide
pp. 78–84, 234–235**

- Multilingual summaries of the main selection
- Comprehension lesson
- Vocabulary strategies and word cards
- ELL Reader 5.3.2 lesson

ELL and Transition Handbook

Ten Important Sentences

- Key ideas from every selection in the Student Edition
- Activities to build sentence power

More Reading

Readers' Theater Anthology
- Fluency practice
- Five scripts to build fluency
- Poetry for oral interpretation

Leveled Trade Books

Below-Level

Advanced

On-Level

- Extended reading tied to the unit concept
- Lessons in the Trade Book Library Teaching Guide

School + Home

Homework
- Family Times Newsletter
- ELL Multilingual Selection Summaries

Take-Home Books
- Leveled Readers

Cross-Curricular Centers

Listening

Listen to the *Selections*

MATERIALS `SINGLES`
CD player, headphones, AudioText CD, student book

LISTEN TO LITERATURE Listen to *Leonardo's Horse* and "Humans with Wings" as you follow or read along in your book. Listen for the main idea about Leonardo da Vinci's dream.

If there is anything you don't understand, you can listen again to any section.

Reading/Library

Read It Again!

MATERIALS `SINGLES` `PAIRS` `GROUPS`
Collection of books for self-selected reading, reading logs, student book

Select a book you have already read. Record the title of the book in your reading log. You may want to read with a partner.

Choose from the following:

- **Leveled Readers**
- **ELL Readers**
- **Stories Written by Classmates**
- **Books from the Library**
- *Leonardo's Horse*

TEN IMPORTANT SENTENCES
Read the Ten Important Sentences for *Leonardo's Horse*. Then locate the sentences in the student book.

BOOK CLUB Discuss how the illustrations in *Leonardo's Horse* help you to better understand Leonardo's life and work. Read other books about Leonardo da Vinci, or look at pictures of his artwork and inventions. Get together with a group to share your favorites.

Art

Explore Art

MATERIALS `SINGLES`
Writing and art materials, books on Leonardo da Vinci, Internet access

Use books and Internet resources to find out more about the artwork of Leonardo da Vinci.

1. **Study pictures of Leonardo's work. Choose a painting, sculpture, or drawing that you like best.**
2. **Write a paragraph describing the piece of art and explain why you like it.**

EARLY FINISHERS Sketch or draw a reproduction of your favorite piece of da Vinci artwork.

Leonardo da Vinci

Leonardo da Vinci painted the <u>Mona Lisa</u>. I like this painting because...

Scott Foresman Reading Street Centers Survival Kit
Use the *Leonardo's Horse* materials from the Reading Street
Centers Survival Kit to organize this week's centers.

 **Writing/ Vocabulary**

 Science

 Technology

Interview *da Vinci*

MATERIALS `SINGLES`
Writing materials, student
book, books about da Vinci

Imagine that you are going to interview Leonardo da Vinci.

1. **Look back through the selection to find something about da Vinci or his works that you have more questions about.**
2. **Make a list of five questions that you would like to ask da Vinci in an interview.**

EARLY FINISHERS Use research materials and what you have learned about da Vinci to make up answers that you think he might have given.

Think About Inventions

MATERIALS `SINGLES`
Writing and art materials,
student book

Be a science detective!

1. **Choose an object pictured on p. 296 in *Leonardo's Horse*.**
2. **Draw a picture of it and label it.**
3. **Give the object a name.**

EARLY FINISHERS Write a paragraph describing what you think the object does and what it might have been used for.

Quadra-decahedron

Visit a *Virtual Museum*

MATERIALS `SINGLES` `PAIRS`
Internet access, writing
materials

Conduct a search for images of Renaissance art.

1. **Follow classroom rules for searching the Internet. Use a student-friendly search engine to search for art museum Web sites.**
2. **Look for artwork from the Renaissance period.**

EARLY FINISHERS Make a list of the Web sites you thought were the best. Compare with a partner.

ALL CENTERS

Concept Vocabulary

canvas strong cloth with a coarse weave made of cotton, flax, or hemp used for painting

charcoal a black, brittle form of carbon used for drawing made by partly burning wood in the absence of air

easel a stand for holding a picture

Norman Rockwell a popular 20th century American painter

Monitor Progress

Check Vocabulary

If...	then... review the
students are unable to place words on the web,	lesson concept. Place the words on the web and provide additional words for practice, such as *props* and *projector.*

SUCCESS PREDICTOR

DAY 1 Grouping Options

Reading
Whole Group
Introduce and discuss the Question of the Week. Then use pp. 288l–290b.

Group Time
Differentiated Instruction
Read this week's Leveled Readers. See pp. 288h–288i for the small group lesson plan.

Whole Group
Use p. 315a.

Language Arts
Use pp. 315e–315k.

Build Concepts

FLUENCY

MODEL TEMPO AND RATE As you read "Norman Rockwell," model how to read a string of sentences that describe a series of sequential events with an even tempo. You can do this effectively with the first paragraph, which describes Rockwell's first use of photography, or the third paragraph, which describes the process he used to incorporate photography into his art.

LISTENING COMPREHENSION

After reading "Norman Rockwell," use the following questions to assess listening comprehension.

1. **What is the main idea of this selection?** (Possible response: In the 1930s, Norman Rockwell began using photography to enhance his painting.) **Main Idea**

2. **How did the photographs help him?** (Possible responses: They provided him more details and angles from which to see a scene; he didn't have to keep a live model in his studio for days.) **Details**

BUILD CONCEPT VOCABULARY

Start a web to build concepts and vocabulary related to this week's lesson and the unit theme.

- Draw the Art and Artists Concept Web.

- Read the sentence with the name *Norman Rockwell* again. Ask students to pronounce *Norman Rockwell* and discuss who he was.

- Place *Norman Rockwell* in an oval attached to *Painters.* Explain that *Norman Rockwell* is related to this concept. Read the sentences in which *easel, charcoal,* and *canvas* appear. Have students pronounce the words, place them on the web, and provide reasons.

- Brainstorm additional words and categories for the web. Keep the web on display and add words throughout the week.

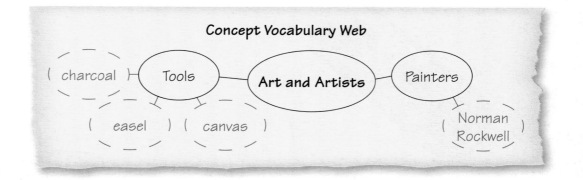

Concept Vocabulary Web

Norman Rockwell

by Beverly Gherman

During his career, Norman Rockwell became one of the best-known artists in the country. He was especially popular for his covers for the magazine Saturday Evening Post*. In this excerpt, Rockwell is reluctantly moving from using live models to a new technology.*

By the mid-1930s, [Norman Rockwell] noticed that his covers were all done from the same angles because he always drew from his easel. Maybe he should try photography after all. He set up the scene for his model, arranged the props, and hired a photographer to take hundreds of shots. He discovered that it made a tremendous difference. Photographs provided him many more angles and details all at once, and he didn't have to keep a model for days when that person needed to be back on the farm or in the classroom.

Once the photographs were developed, he spread them out all over the floor and chose the ones he liked the best. Then he made a few small pencil sketches to organize his material. At last he was ready to do a full-size charcoal drawing.

He transferred the charcoal layout to a canvas, either by tracing it with special tracing paper or by using a projector…to enlarge the image onto a canvas that might be four feet tall.

At last he was ready to start working in color. He was always nervous that he would get tense and spoil the painting, but it rarely happened. The final painting could take a few days or a few weeks, depending upon how complicated the picture was.

When he was beginning his career, people always called him "the kid with the camera eye" because he captured a scene so accurately. Now he added the actual camera lens to his own good eye, and the combination made his work richer and even more interesting.

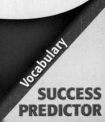

BEFORE READING

 SKILLS ⬌ STRATEGIES IN CONTEXT

Main Idea
Summarize

OBJECTIVES

- Determine main idea and identify details.
- Use main ideas and details to summarize.

Skills Trace
Main Idea

Introduce/Teach	TE: 5.3 288–289, 346–347; 5.6 654–655
Practice	Practice Book: 113, 117, 118, 126, 133, 137, 138, 156, 216, 263, 267, 268, 286
Reteach/Review	TE: 5.3 315b, 325, 335, 363b, DI-53, DI-55; 5.4 401; 5.5 545; 5.6 673b, 711, 717, DI-53
Test	Selection Test: 45–48, 53–56, 105–108; Benchmark Test: Unit 3

INTRODUCE

Write the topic *Renaissance Art* and add details: *Arts and artists flourished in Italy during the Renaissance. The wealthy Medici family supported many artists with money during the 1600s. Leonardo da Vinci, Donatello, and Michelangelo are just three such artists. Their paintings, architecture, and sculpture can still be found throughout Italy.* Ask students if the main idea is stated or unstated *(stated),* and what it is. *(Arts and artists flourished in Italy during the Renaissance.)*

Have students read the information on p. 288. Explain the following:

- Main ideas provide the most important information about a topic and help you summarize as you read.
- Sometimes main ideas are stated; other times readers have to figure them out.

Use Skill Transparency 12 to teach main idea and summarize.

Comprehension

Skill
Main Idea and Details

Strategy
Summarize

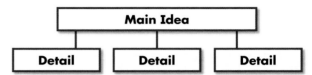 ## Main Idea
and Details

- The main idea is the most important idea about a topic. Details are small pieces of information that tell more about the main idea.

- Sometimes the author states the main idea of a paragraph or an entire article in a single sentence at the beginning, middle, or end. Other times the author leaves the main idea unstated, so readers must put it into their own words.

Main Idea		
Detail	Detail	Detail

Strategy: Summarize

Active readers summarize to help them understand the most important information they read. Summarizing can help you find the main idea of a selection. Writing a summary can help you organize the information.

Write to Read

1. Read "Bronze." Make a graphic organizer like the one above to show the main idea and the details that support it.

2. Use information from your graphic organizer to help you write a summary of "Bronze."

288

Strategic Intervention

Main Idea In "Bronze," the title states the topic, which is broader than a main idea. The main ideas develop the topic by explaining why bronze was and continues to be a good sculpting material. To help students develop the main idea graphic organizer on p. 288, work with them to determine the main idea of each paragraph. Then have them work in pairs to add supporting details for each main idea.

ELL

Access Content

Beginning/Intermediate For a Picture It! lesson on main idea and details, see ELL Teaching Guide, pp. 78–79.

Advanced Before students read "Bronze," have a volunteer read the first sentence aloud. Ask students to think about the opening sentence and the title of the selection to help them determine the main idea.

Bronze

People have used bronze for thousands of years to make many things. Bronze is a soft metal made from copper and tin. It cannot be hammered or bent, so it is not a good material for making tools. However, in molten or liquid form it can be shaped into things such as statues, pots, and bowls.

> **1** **Skill** Notice the first sentence of this paragraph, telling basically what it is all about.

Thousands of years ago, bronze was shaped using the "lost-wax method." In this method, a model was made using plaster or clay. Then it was coated in wax followed by another layer of plaster or clay. When heated, the wax melted away, leaving a space. The bronze was melted and poured into the space. When it cooled, the plaster or clay was taken off. Using this method, only one item could be made from the model.

> **2** **Strategy** This is a good place to summarize. What two or three most important ideas have you read so far?

In time, molds were formed out of other materials, such as wood. A wooden mold could be used again and again. It was pressed into sand, and when it was removed, the impression was left in the sand. Bronze was poured into the sand. Later, it was removed, and the surface was smoothed.

> **3** **Skill** Did one sentence seem to tell what this article was basically about? Hint: Look early on in the article.

Bronze is still used today. You may even have some items made from bronze in your home!

> **4** **Strategy** How will summarizing help you remember important ideas?

289

Available as **Skill Transparency** 12

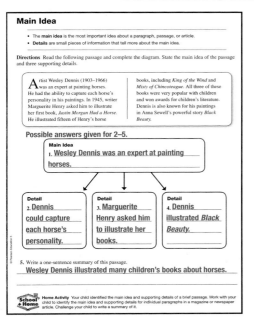

TEACH

1 **SKILL** Use paragraph 2 to model how to determine the main idea.

> **Think Aloud** **MODEL** The first sentence in paragraph 2 mentions a method for shaping bronze. The rest of the sentences in this paragraph provide details about this method. Since the first sentence tells what the paragraph is all about, it is the main idea.

2 **STRATEGY** Summarize the article so far.

> **Think Aloud** **MODEL** This is a good place to summarize because I've read about a few important ideas. They are: When melted, bronze can be shaped into many things. The "lost-wax method" is one way of making bronze things.

PRACTICE AND ASSESS

3 **SKILL** Main idea: For thousands of years, people have used bronze to make many things.

4 **STRATEGY** Answers will vary but should include the idea that summaries reflect understanding of the main ideas.

WRITE Have students complete steps 1 and 2 of the Write to Read activity. You might consider using this as a whole-class activity.

Monitor Progress

↻ Main Idea

If... students are unable to complete **Write to Read** on p. 288,	**then...** use Practice Book p. 113 to provide additional practice.

Tech Files
ONLINE

Have students type the keywords *Leonardo da Vinci* into a student-friendly search engine for background information about the famous inventor, scientist, and artist. Be sure to follow classroom guidelines for using the Internet.

ELL

Build Background Use ELL Poster 12 to build background and develop vocabulary about the influence of the Renaissance on art and artists.

▲ **ELL Poster** 12

Build Background

ACTIVATE PRIOR KNOWLEDGE

BEGIN A KWL CHART about Leonardo da Vinci.

• Give students two to three minutes to write as many things as they can about Leonardo da Vinci. Prompt them with categories from the Concept Web from p. 288l. Record what students know on the KWL chart.

• Give students two minutes to write three questions they would like to answer about Leonardo da Vinci. Record questions in the second column of the chart. Add a question of your own.

• Tell students that, as they read, they should look for the answers to their questions and note any new information to add to the chart.

K	W	L
Leonardo da Vinci is a famous scientist.	What is Leonardo's Horse?	
Leonardo da Vinci painted the Mona Lisa.	What other things did Leonardo invent?	

▲ **Graphic Organizer** 4

BACKGROUND BUILDING AUDIO This week's audio explores Italy at the time of Leonardo da Vinci. After students listen, discuss what they found most interesting and what they found most surprising about the times.

Background Building Audio

Introduce Vocabulary

WORD RATING CHART

Create word rating charts using the categories *Know*, *Have Seen*, and *Don't Know*.

Word Rating Chart

Word	Know	Have Seen	Don't Know
achieved		✓	
architect			✓
bronze		✓	
cannon	✓		
depressed			
fashioned		✓	
midst			✓
philosopher			✓
rival	✓		

▲ **Graphic Organizer** 5

Read each word to students and have them place it in one of the three columns: *Know* (know and can use); *Have Seen* (have seen or heard the word; don't know meaning); *Don't Know* (don't know the word).

Activate Prior Knowledge

Have students share where they may have seen some of these words. Point out that some of this week's words relate to social studies and a specific period in time called the Renaissance *(philosopher, architect, rebirth)*. (For additional practice with Content Area Vocabulary, see p. 315c.)

Content Area Vocabulary

Check charts with students at the end of the week and have them make changes to their ratings.

Use the Multisyllabic Word Routine on p. DI·1 to help students read multisyllabic words.

Lesson Vocabulary

WORDS TO KNOW

T achieved carried out to a successful end

T architect person who designs and makes plans for buildings

T bronze a dark yellow-brown alloy of copper and tin

T cannon a big gun, especially one mounted on a base or wheels

T depressed gloomy; sad

T fashioned made, shaped, or formed

T midst in the middle of

T philosopher a person who attempts to discover and understand the basic nature of knowledge and reality

T rival a person who wants and tries to get the same thing as another or one who tries to equal or do better than another; competitor

MORE WORDS TO KNOW

rebirth a new birth; being born again

Renaissance the great revival of art and learning in Europe during the 1300–1500s

togas loose, outer garments worn in public by citizens of ancient Rome

T = Tested Word

Vocabulary

Directions Choose the word from the box that best matches each definition. Write the word on the line.

cannon	1. a big gun mounted on a base or wheels
architect	2. a person who designs and makes plans for buildings
fashioned	3. made, shaped, or done
philosopher	4. a person who studies the basic nature of knowledge and reality
rival	5. a person who wants and tries to get the same thing as another or tries to do better than another

Check the Words You Know
___achieved
___architect
___bronze
___cannon
___depressed
___fashioned
___midst
___philosopher
___rival

Directions Choose the word from the box that best fits in each sentence. Write the word on the line shown to the left.

bronze	6. The horse's yellow-brown coat was so rich and shiny it looked like it was made from ___.
achieved	7. Working together on their books about horses, Wesley Dennis and Marguerite Henry ___ great success.
rival	8. Amelia was known as the best artist in school, but her ___ Lily was trying to outdo her with a new painting.
midst	9. The wild pony did not like being fenced in. It was happier in the ___ of the wide open fields.
depressed	10. Julia felt ___ when she had to leave the ranch at the end of the summer.

Write a Journal Entry
On a separate sheet of paper write a journal entry describing an animal you have drawn. Use as many vocabulary words as you can. Include a drawing if possible.

Journal entries should describe an animal the student has drawn and include words from the vocabulary list. It may also include a drawing.

Home Activity Your child identified and used vocabulary words from *Leonardo's Horse*. Read a story or nonfiction article with your child. Have your child point out unfamiliar words. Work together to figure out the meaning of each word by using other words that are near it.

▲ **Practice Book** p. 114

Vocabulary Strategy

OBJECTIVE

Use word structure to determine word meaning.

INTRODUCE

Discuss the strategy for Greek and Latin roots using the steps on p. 284.

TEACH

- Have students read "They Called It the Renaissance," paying attention to how vocabulary is used.
- Model using word structure to determine the meaning of *philosopher*.

Think Aloud **MODEL** I see the Greek root *philo-*, which means "loving," in the word *philosopher*. Another word I know with the same root word is *philosophy*, which is "the study of life." A philosopher must be "one who loves the study of life and ideas."

Words to Know

depressed
achieved
philosopher
architect
fashioned
midst
bronze
cannon
rival

Remember

Try the strategy. Then, if you need more help, use your glossary or dictionary.

Vocabulary Strategy
for Greek and Latin Roots

Word Structure Many words in English are based on Greek and Latin roots. For example, *bio-* means "life." It is found in words such as *biography* and *biology*. When you see a longer word you cannot read, look for a root that can help you figure out the word's meaning.

1. Look at the unfamiliar word. Try to identify a root word within it.
2. Think of words you know where this same root appears.
3. What does the root mean in these words?
4. Try the meaning in the unfamiliar word and see if it makes sense in the sentence.

As you read "They Called It the Renaissance," look for Greek and Latin roots to help you figure out the meanings of unknown words. (Hint: The Greek root *arch-* means "chief, ruler." The Greek root *philo-* means "loving.")

290

DAY 2 Grouping Options

Reading
Whole Group Discuss the Question of the Day. Then use pp. 290–293.

Group Time Differentiated Instruction
Read *Leonardo's Horse.* See pp. 288h–288i for the small group lesson plan.

Whole Group Use p. 315a.

Language Arts
Use pp. 315e–315k.

Strategic Intervention

Word Structure List some Greek or Latin roots, for example, *bio-*, *arch-* and *philo-*, on the board. Review the meaning of each root.

ELL

Access Content Use ELL Poster 12 to preteach vocabulary. Choose from the following to meet language proficiency levels.

Beginning Point to the word *philosopher* in the third paragraph on p. 291. Point out that the root *philo-* means "loving," and that *sophia* means "wisdom." Ask students the meaning of *philosopher*.

Intermediate Ask students for equivalent words in their home languages for the words *philosopher* and *rival*. Point out that these words have Spanish cognates: *filósofo* and *rival*.

Advanced Teach the lesson on pp. 290–291. Have students return to the word rating chart and make appropriate changes to their ratings.

Resources for home-language words may include parents, bilingual staff members, bilingual dictionaries, or online translation sources.

They Called It the RENAISSANCE

The Middle Ages ran from about A.D. 500 to about 1450. This was a time that might have depressed anyone. People in Europe looked back at the past instead of forward to the future.

But by 1450, people had stopped thinking only about the past and started looking ahead to what might be achieved in the future. This new age was known as the Renaissance.

Inventors started coming up with exciting new inventions. The title philosopher became important again, as thinkers explored new ways to enrich people's lives. The architect became an important figure as beautiful new buildings took shape in cities and towns across Europe. Artists fashioned powerful sculptures and painted vivid paintings that looked natural and real.

In the midst of all this growth and change, of course, there was still fighting. Art was the glory of the age, but war was the harsh reality. Bronze might be used to make a beautiful statue or a deadly cannon. People were sailing off to find new lands. A nation might become a rival of another nation, fighting for land in the Americas. In so many ways, people in the Renaissance were preparing for the modern world.

Words to Write

Leonardo da Vinci did many things during the Renaissance. Look at the illustrations in *Leonardo's Horse*. Write a paragraph about what you think he might have achieved. Use as many of the words from the Words to Know list as you can.

291

PRACTICE AND ASSESS

- Have students use their knowledge of Greek and Latin roots to find the meaning of *architect* in paragraph 3.
- Point out that if students don't know the meaning of a root word, they may need to refer to a dictionary or thesaurus for help.
- If you began a word rating chart (p. 284b), have students recheck their ratings.
- Have students complete Practice Book p. 115.

WRITE Writing should include vocabulary words that describe Leonardo da Vinci and his accomplishments in art and science.

Monitor Progress

Word Structure

| If... students need more practice with the lesson vocabulary, | then... use Tested Vocabulary Cards. |

Vocabulary · Word Structure

- Many words in English are based on Greek and Latin roots. Sometimes you can use Greek and Latin roots to figure out the meaning of an unfamiliar word.
- The root *bio–* means "life," *arch–* means "chief or ruler," and *philo–* means "loving." These roots all come from the Greek language.

Directions Read the following passage. Then answer the questions below.

The great Renaissance artist Raphael achieved fame during his lifetime. He was respected as an architect. He designed two churches in Rome, but he is more known for his painting than for his architecture. One of his most famous paintings is called *The School of Athens.* It shows the philosopher as a hero. The Greek philosophers Plato and Aristotle are at the center of the painting. They are standing in the midst of other great philosophers from ancient times.

Raphael had many students in his studio. They helped him complete his larger works. Raphael was a well-loved teacher, and some of the students thought of others students as rivals. After Raphael's death, however, his students worked together to complete many important works started by their teacher. The biographer Giorgio Vasari called Raphael "the prince of painters."

1. The Greek root *arch–* means "chief or ruler." The Greek word *tekton* means "builder." What do these tell you about the meaning of *architect*?
   An architect can be a chief builder.

2. The Greek root *philo–* means "loving." The Greek word *sophia* means "knowledge, learning." What do these tell you about the meaning of *philosopher*?
   A philosopher can be a person who loves knowledge.

3. The Greek root *bio–* means "life." The Greek word *graphia* means "record." What do these tell you about the meaning of *biographer*?
   It means "a person who makes a record of someone's life."

4. The Latin word *studium* means "to study." What does this tell you about the meaning of *studio*?
   A studio can be a place to study.

5. Write as many words as you can think of that use the roots *arch–*, *philo–*, and *bio–*. If you cannot think of any words on your own, use the dictionary for help.
   Check students' answers for accuracy.

Home Activity Your child identified Greek and Latin roots to understand unfamiliar words in a passage. Read a passage with your child and see if you can find words with Greek or Latin roots. First, identify the root. Then think of other words with the same root to figure out its meaning.

▲ **Practice Book** p. 115

Prereading Strategies

- Identify main idea and supporting details to improve comprehension.
- Summarize to identify main idea.

GENRE STUDY

Biography

Leonardo's Horse is a biography. Explain that a biography is a story of a real person's life written by another person.

PREVIEW AND PREDICT

Have students preview the selection title and illustrations and identify the subject of this biography. Have students use selection vocabulary words as they talk about what they expect to learn.

Strategy Response Log

Ask Questions Have students generate two questions about Leonardo da Vinci and his dream. Students will answer their questions in the Strategy Response Log activity on p. 303.

BY JEAN FRITZ
ILLUSTRATED BY HUDSON TALBOTT

LEONARDO'S HORSE

Will Leonardo's greatest dream ever come true?

 Genre A **biography** is a story of a person's life written by another person. As you read, notice all the ups and downs in Leonardo da Vinci's life.

292

 ELL

Access Content Take students on a picture walk, pointing out Vinci, the town Leonardo was from (p. 295), his drawings and inventions (p. 296), items Leonardo thought of making (pp. 298–299), the drawings of horses he made in preparation for his gigantic sculpture (p. 301), and his most famous painting, the *Mona Lisa* (p. 306).

Consider having students read the selection summary in English or in students' home languages. See the Multilingual Summaries in the ELL Teaching Guide, pp. 82–84.

293

SET PURPOSE

Read the first page of the selection aloud to students. Have them consider their preview discussion and tell what they hope to find out as they read.

Remind students to look for main ideas and supporting details as they read.

STRATEGY RECALL

Students have now used these before-reading strategies:

- preview the selection to be aware of its genre, features, and possible content;
- activate prior knowledge about that content and what to expect of that genre;
- make predictions;
- set a purpose for reading.

Remind students that, as they read, they should monitor their own comprehension. If they realize something does not make sense, they can regain their comprehension by using fix-up strategies they have learned, such as:

- use phonics and word structure to decode new words;
- use context clues or a dictionary to figure out meanings of new words;
- adjust their reading rate—slow down for difficult text, speed up for easy or familiar text, or skim and scan just for specific information;
- reread parts of the text;
- read on (continue to read for clarification);
- use text features such as headings, subheadings, charts, illustrations, and so on as visual aids to comprehension;
- make a graphic organizer or a semantic organizer to aid comprehension;
- use reference sources, such as an encyclopedia, dictionary, thesaurus, or synonym finder;
- use another person, such as a teacher, a peer, a librarian, or an outside expert, as a resource.

After reading, students will use these strategies:

- summarize or retell the text;
- answer questions they or others pose;
- reflect to make new information become part of their prior knowledge.

Audio CD AudioText

Guiding Comprehension

1  **Main Idea • Inferential**

What is the main idea of p. 295? Name one detail that supports the main idea.

Main Idea: It was apparent that the young Leonardo da Vinci would grow up to be an artist. Detail: He examined everything and studied art.

Monitor Progress

 Main Idea

If... students are unable to determine the main idea,	**then...** use the skill and strategy instruction on p. 295.

2 **Literary Elements • Inferential**

How would you characterize the young Leonardo da Vinci?

Possible answers: inquisitive, curious, artistic

Tech Files
ONLINE

Students who have access to the Internet can type the keywords *Leonardo da Vinci biography* into a student-friendly search engine to learn more about da Vinci's childhood. Students should follow classroom rules when conducting a search.

294

ELL

Extend Language Point to the word *landscape*. Tell students that a landscape is a view of an area of land. A landscape is also the term used for a picture or painting of that view. Ask them to point to the landscape on pp. 294–295 and tell what it is illustrating.

ANYONE who watched the young Leonardo wander the countryside around his home in Vinci might have guessed that he would be an artist. He stopped to examine everything. He looked at the landscape as if he were memorizing it. So it was no surprise when his father took him as a young teenager to Florence to study art.

1

2

295

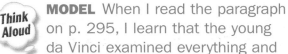
SKILLS ↔ STRATEGIES IN CONTEXT

Main Idea

TEACH

- Remind students that a main idea makes an important point about the selection's topic.
- Supporting details are smaller pieces of information that develop the main idea.
- Model finding the main idea on p. 295.

Think Aloud **MODEL** When I read the paragraph on p. 295, I learn that the young da Vinci examined everything and drew pictures from memory. When I look at the illustration, I see a boy on a horse drawing a picture. Together, this information helps me figure out the main idea: that the young Leonardo da Vinci will likely grow up to be an artist.

PRACTICE AND ASSESS

Have students reread p. 295 and find one additional detail that supports the idea that Leonardo da Vinci will grow up to be an artist. *(He could practically memorize the landscape; he went to study art in Florence.)*

Guiding Comprehension

③ Author's Purpose • Critical

Question the Author **Why do you think the author tells you that da Vinci was different from other boys his age?**

Possible answer: The author wants you to know that Leonardo was a bit unusual and more creative than other boys his age.

④ 🔊 Vocabulary • Word Structure

The Greek root *astro-* in the word *astronomer* means "star." What does an *astronomer* do?

An *astronomer* is a scientist who studies the stars.

Monitor Progress	
🔊 **Word Structure**	
If... students have difficulty using word structure to figure out the meaning of *astronomer*,	**then...** use the vocabulary strategy instruction on p. 297.

296

ELL

Activate Prior Knowledge Reread aloud the sentence "He was an engineer, an architect, a musician, a philosopher, an astronomer." List the professions on the board. Ask students to tell what they know about each of them. Provide any missing information.

In November 1493, he had completed the clay model—twenty-four feet high. It was shown off at one of the duke's special occasions, and it was a sensation. **10** **11**

303

Develop Vocabulary

PRACTICE LESSON VOCABULARY

Students orally respond *true* or *false* to each statement and provide a reason for any false statements.

1. An *architect* studies the stars. *(False; an architect designs.)*
2. A *philosopher* loves to think and ask questions. *(True)*
3. *Achieved* means to have been disappointed about something. *(False; achieved means to be successful.)*

BUILD CONCEPT VOCABULARY

Review previous concept words with students. Ask if students have met any words today in their reading or elsewhere that they would like to add to the Art and Artists Concept Web, such as *measured* and *casting*.

🎯 STRATEGY SELF-CHECK

Summarize

Ask students to identify the main ideas in the selection so far. Remind them to use the summarizing strategy when a main idea isn't contained in a single paragraph. *(Possible responses: Leonardo was a talented artist and inventor who wanted to build a bronze horse. He studied real horses and statues of horses in order to make a realistic clay model.)*

Students can use the main ideas to write a summary of the selection so far. Have them check that their summaries include the most important ideas in the selection.

SELF-CHECK

Students can ask themselves these questions to assess their ability to use the skill and strategy.

- Did I identify main ideas as I read *Leonardo's Horse*?
- Was I able to locate supporting details?
- How did this help me to summarize?

Monitor Progress
🎯 **Main Idea**

If... students have difficulty recognizing main ideas or writing summaries,	then... use the revisit the skill lesson on pp. 288–289. Reteach as necessary.

Strategy Response Log

Answer Questions Have students answer the two questions they asked at the beginning of the selection. (See p. 292.) Have them ask another question they expect to answer by reading the rest of the selection.

If you want to teach this selection in two sessions, stop here.

Guiding Comprehension

If you are teaching this selection in two days, discuss the main ideas so far and review the vocabulary.

12 🎯 **Vocabulary • Word Structure**

What is the meaning of the word *invade* on p. 304?

Invade means to enter with force.

Monitor Progress
🎯 Word Structure

If... students are unable to use word structure to figure out the meaning of *invade*,	**then...** use the vocabulary strategy instruction on p. 305.

13 **Predict • Critical**

Do you think Leonardo will continue working on his horse?

Answers will vary. Some students will predict that Leonardo will continue because the horse was his greatest dream. Others will say no because it would be difficult to start all over again.

DAY 3 Grouping Options

Reading
Whole Group Discuss the Question of the Day.

Group Time Differentiated Instruction
Read *Leonardo's Horse.* See pp. 288h–288i for the small group lesson plan.

Whole Group Discuss the Reader Response questions on p. 310. Then use p. 315a.

Language Arts
Use pp. 315e–315k.

But Leonardo seemed to be in no hurry to start casting. Perhaps he wasn't sure how he'd do it. Besides, he was planning a new project.

Later, in 1498, there were rumors that the French were **12** preparing to invade Milan, and the duke wanted to be ready. And there was all the metal that Leonardo had collected. Just what the duke needed. So he sent it off to be made into cannon. Well, this is war, Leonardo reasoned. What else could they do?

When the French came in 1499, Leonardo and the duke fled. But the horse couldn't leave. There he was when the French arrived. The archers laughed. Never would they find as perfect a target, they said. Pulling back the strings on their bows, they let their arrows fly. Ping! Ping! Ping! The horse sagged. Ping!

Then it rained. And the horse became smaller and smaller. **13** At last it was nothing but a pile of mud stuck with arrows.

304

ELL

Access Content Point to the word *archers*. Tell students that an *archer* is a person who shoots with a bow and arrow. Explain that the sport of shooting with a bow and arrow is called *archery*.

 VOCABULARY STRATEGY

Word Structure

TEACH

- Remind students that knowing Greek and Latin roots can help them understand the meanings of unfamiliar words.
- The Greek or Latin root is often explained at the end of a dictionary entry.
- Model using a dictionary or thesaurus and Latin roots to determine the meaning of *invade* on p. 304.

Think Aloud **MODEL** I'm not sure what *invade* means, so I'll look it up in a dictionary. I see that *invade* means "to enter with force." It comes from the Latin *in* and *vadere*, meaning "to go, or walk in." Understanding word structure helps me remember the definition of *invade*.

PRACTICE AND ASSESS

Have students use a dictionary to determine the Latin roots of the word *prepare*. Have them explain how this helps them remember the meaning of the word.

305

Guiding Comprehension

14 **Character • Critical**

Michelangelo taunted Leonardo for not finishing the bronze horse. Why do you think he might have done that?

Possible response: Michelangelo was Leonardo's rival and this was one way to hurt him.

15 **Main Idea • Inferential**

What is the main idea of p. 306?

Main idea: Despite all his achievements, Leonardo da Vinci was depressed because he never completed his horse.

Monitor Progress
🎯 **Main Idea**

If... students are unable to determine the main idea on p. 306,	then... use the skill and strategy instruction on p. 307.

Leonardo went back to inventing and painting, but he never forgot his horse.

He still wanted to invent a flying machine. But he still couldn't do it.

His greatest disappointment, however, was his horse.

As Leonardo became older, his hair turned white and grew down to his shoulders. His beard reached to his waist.

And he became depressed. What had he achieved? he asked himself. He complained to his notebook: "Tell me," he asked, "if anything has been achieved by me. Tell me. Tell me." It was especially hard when his rival, Michelangelo, taunted him.

"You," Michelangelo said, "who made a model of a horse you could never cast in bronze and which you

14 gave up, to your shame."

In his notebook Leonardo mourned, "I have wasted my hours."

On May 2, 1519, Leonardo da Vinci died. It was said

15 that even on his deathbed, Leonardo wept for his horse.

306

ELL

Access Content Reread aloud the sentence "His greatest disappointment, however, was his horse." Explain that a disappointment is a feeling of not having fulfilled one's hopes. Ask students why they think this was Leonardo's greatest disappointment.

307

Main Idea
Summarize

TEACH

Reread p. 306. Have students identify key words to find the main idea on this page. *(greatest disappointment, depressed, shame, mourned, wasted)* Use this information to model how to summarize the important points.

 MODEL Now that I know the main ideas, I can use this information to summarize the key points on the page and put them into my own words. My summary is that Leonardo da Vinci died feeling sad and disappointed that he never made the bronze horse.

PRACTICE AND ASSESS

Have students work in pairs to find the main ideas on p. 308. Have them write summaries that include these ideas. To assess, make sure that summaries include the main ideas on the page and are written in student's own words.

Time for
SOCIAL STUDIES

da Vinci's Inventions

Leonardo da Vinci is well-known for his paintings of the *Mona Lisa* and *The Last Supper*. But, as this selection points out, da Vinci was much more than an artist. He studied many different fields of science, including astronomy, botany, geology, and anatomy. He sketched out his ideas and inventions in notebooks, which were published 400 years after his death. Some of his inventions include flying machines, cannons, scissors, and the parachute.

EXTEND SKILLS

Diary/Journal

Point out that a diary is an individual's daily record of events. A diary may also be called a journal, or in the case of Leonardo da Vinci, a notebook. Diaries and journals provide insights into the thoughts and feelings of the people who write them. The author tells us that da Vinci wrote in his notebook about the bronze horse and his inability to complete it. Ask students to tell why they think the author included this information and what it tells them about da Vinci.

Guiding Comprehension

16 **Text Structure • Inferential**

The text on p. 308 is set in italics and commonly referred to as an *afterword*. Why do you think the author included this information?

The author included this text to tell what happened after Leonardo's death.

17 **Summarize • Critical**

Text to Self **Describe a time that, like Leonardo da Vinci, you were disappointed for being unable to accomplish something that was important to you.**

Possible response: His story reminds me of the time I didn't make the soccer team.

Strategy Response Log

Summarize When students finish reading the selection, provide this prompt: How would you summarize *Leonardo's Horse* for a friend interested in learning about Leonardo da Vinci and his bronze horse? Write four or five sentences to explain the important points of the selection.

In 1977 Charles Dent, an American and a big fan of Leonardo, saw a magazine article about him. When he read that Leonardo died grieving for his horse, Charles said, "Let's give Leonardo his horse."

But Charles Dent died before work was finished. Later, a sculptor from New York City, Nina Akamu, carried on with Charles's dream. Many people contributed money to help her finish. Finally, on September 10, 1999, in Milan, Italy, in front of huge crowds, the
16 *horse was unveiled.*

308

ELL

Access Content Reread aloud the phrase "the horse was unveiled." Tell students that *unveil* literally means to remove a veil (a piece of thin material) to reveal something. This term is also used when something new is being announced. Ask a volunteer to act out unveiling an object.

At last Leonardo's horse was home. **17**

309

Summarize

Have students identify the main ideas from the selection and determine the main idea for the entire selection. Students can use the main ideas to write a summary. Use Practice Book p. 117.

SELF-CHECK

Students can ask themselves these questions to assess understanding of the selection.

- Did I accurately identify the main idea for the selection?
- Does my summary include the most important points from the article?

Monitor Progress

Main Idea

If... students have difficulty recognizing main ideas or writing a summary,	**then...** use the Reteach lesson on p. 315b.

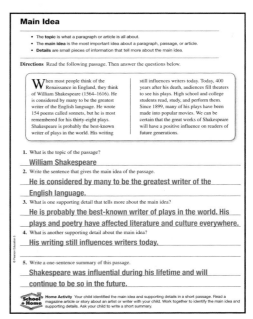

▲ **Practice Book** p. 117

Develop Vocabulary

PRACTICE LESSON VOCABULARY

Have students briefly orally respond to each question.

1. **What would be more valuable: a *bronze* or a clay horse?** *(bronze)*
2. **Who was Leonardo's *rival*?** *(Michelangelo)*
3. **Why was Leonardo *depressed*?** *(He failed to build his bronze horse.)*
4. **In warfare, would a bridge or a *cannon* be more useful?** *(cannon)*

BUILD CONCEPT VOCABULARY

Review previous concept words with students. Ask if students have come across any words today in their reading or elsewhere that they would like to add to the Art and Artists Concept Web such as *unveiled.*

Reader Response

Open for Discussion **Personal Response**

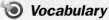

MODEL First, I'd think about all of Leonardo's achievements, such as his many inventions and paintings. Then, I'd put myself in his shoes and think about how I would feel if I were Leonardo.

Comprehension Check **Critical Response**

1. Responses will vary, but they could include details such as Leonardo's eating no meat and juggling. ***Author's Purpose***

2. Possible response: Despite his achievements, Leonardo died thinking he was a failure. ***Main Idea***

3. Responses should include Leonardo's early years in Florence, his being chosen to build a bronze horse, his attempts at building it, and his later years. ***Summarize***

4. Leonardo was also an inventor, engineer, musician, astronomer, and painter. ***Vocabulary***

Look Back and Write For test practice, assign a 10–15 minute time limit. For assessment, see the Scoring Rubric at the right.

Retell

Have students retell *Leonardo's Horse*.

Monitor Progress
Check Retelling Rubric 4 3 2 1

If... students have difficulty retelling the selection,	**then...** use the Retelling Cards and the Scoring Rubric for Retelling on p. 311 to assist fluent retelling.

SUCCESS PREDICTOR

Check Retelling Point to each illustration and make sure that students understand the words used to describe Leonardo's inventions. Encourage students to use the illustrations for help in writing their retellings. Let students listen to other retellings before attempting their own. For more ideas on assessing students' retellings, see the ELL and Transition Handbook.

Reader Response

Open for Discussion Remember that Leonardo da Vinci died mourning the things he had left unfinished. If he could glance over your shoulder and read about himself now, what would he say?

1. Jean Fritz's biographies put the reader right there alongside the subject of the book. Identify examples that seem to put you right there, beside Leonardo. **Think Like an Author**

2. What is Jean Fritz's main idea in this selection? She shows how Leonardo was brilliant, but what else does she show about his character, about the kind of person he was? Look back at page 298 to answer the question. **Main Idea and Details**

3. Look back through the selection and think about the major events. Discuss which events you would use to summarize Leonardo's life. **Summarize**

4. The words *architect* and *philosopher* describe two of Leonardo's talents. What other talents were mentioned in the selection? **Vocabulary**

Look Back and Write
Leonardo da Vinci was a man of many talents. To prove this, write a list of his accomplishments, beginning with the professions that are mentioned on page 297.

Meet author **Jean Fritz on page 762.**

310

Scoring Rubric **Look Back and Write**

Top-Score Response A top-score response will list Leonardo da Vinci's accomplishments as an artist, engineer, architect, musician, philosopher, and astronomer and will identify specific projects or achievements from the selection.

Example of a Top-Score Response Leonardo da Vinci was a famous artist who created statues like a giant horse and paintings such as the *Mona Lisa.* He was also an engineer who made one-of-a-kind bridges, cannons, and chariots. As a court musician, he sang and played instruments. He also juggled, asked riddles, and made plays. Leonardo was also an architect, astronomer, and philosopher.

For additional rubrics, see p. WA10.

Illinois

Planning Guide for Performance Descriptors

The Dinosaurs of Waterhouse Hawkins

Reading Street Teacher's Edition pages

Grade 5 English Language Arts Performance Descriptors

Oral Language

Speaking/Listening Build Concept Vocabulary: 316l, 327, 337, 345c
Read Aloud: 316m

1B.Stage E.10. Read age-appropriate material aloud with fluency and accuracy.

4B.Stage E.10. Contribute meaningfully to small and large group discussions by following accepted guidelines for verbal interaction (e.g., appropriate volume and rate; courteous, turn-taking behavior; respectful, relevant responses; appropriate language and vocabulary).

Word Work

Consonant Sounds /j/, /ks/, /sk/, and /s/: 345i–345j

1A.Stage E.1. Use a combination of word analysis and vocabulary strategies (e.g., word patterns, structural analyses) within context to identify unknown words.

Reading

Comprehension Fact and Opinion: 316–317, 320–337, 340–345, 345b
Predict: 316–317, 320–337, 340–345

Vocabulary Lesson Vocabulary: 318b, 327, 337, 340
Context Clues: 318–319, 331, 345c

Fluency Model Phrasing: 316l–316m, 345a

Self-Selected Reading: LR19–27, TR16–17

Literature Genre—Biography: 320
Reader Response: 338

1B.Stage E.9. Apply self-monitoring and self-correcting strategies continuously to clarify understanding during reading.

1B.Stage E.10. Read age-appropriate material aloud with fluency and accuracy.

1C.Stage E.3. Identify evidence for inferences and interpretations based on text combined with prior knowledge.

1C.Stage E.6. Select reading strategies for text appropriate to the reader's purpose.

2A.Stage E.2. Identify literary elements and techniques in literary genres and tell how they affect the story.

2A.Stage E.3. Predict how the story might be different if the author changed literary elements or techniques.

Language Arts

Writing Feature Story: 345g–345h

Six-Trait Writing Organization/Paragraphs: 339, 345g–345h

Grammar, Usage, and Mechanics Principal Parts of Irregular Verbs: 345e–345f

Research/Study Schedule: 345l

Technology New Literacies: 345k

3A.Stage E.1. Write paragraphs that include a variety of sentence types (i.e., declarative, interrogative, exclamatory, imperative).

3C.Stage E.4. Use available technology to design, produce, and present compositions and multimedia works.

4B.Stage E.5. Use appropriate grammar, word choice, and pacing.

5A.Stage E.5. Arrange information in an orderly manner.

Unit Skills

Writing Compare and Contrast Essay: WA2–9

Poetry: 384–387

Project/Wrap-Up: 388–389

1B.Stage E.7. Identify structure (e.g., description, compare, cause/effect, sequence) of nonfiction text to improve comprehension.

3C.Stage E.3. Write creatively for a specified purpose and audience (e.g., short story, poetry, directions, song, friendly letter).

This Week's Leveled Readers

Below-Level

Nonfiction

1C.Stage E.2. Ask open-ended questions.

1C.Stage E.3. Identify evidence for inferences and interpretations based on text combined with prior knowledge.

On-Level

Nonfiction

1C.Stage E.3. Identify evidence for inferences and interpretations based on text combined with prior knowledge.

1C.Stage E.5. Recognize similarities/differences of varying styles or points of view.

Advanced

Nonfiction

1C.Stage E.3. Identify evidence for inferences and interpretations based on text combined with prior knowledge.

2A.Stage E.5. Make inferences about character traits and check text for verification.

Content-Area Illinois Performance Descriptors in This Lesson

Science

11A.Stage E.1. Construct an inquiry hypothesis that can be investigated.

11A.Stage E.3. Collect qualitative and quantitative data from investigation: using available technologies; determining the necessary required precision; validating data for accuracy.

11B.Stage E.1. Identify an innovative technological design from ordinary surroundings or circumstances.

13A.Stage E.1. Apply appropriate principles of safety.

13B.Stage E.3. Investigate the interactions of societal decisions in science and technology innovations and discoveries.

Social Studies

16A.Stage E.1. Explain how life changed or stayed the same in a region or place using two historic maps that depict different times in that region or place.

16A.Stage E.2. Describe trends during a time period using political, economic, environmental, and social data from appropriate graphs or charts.

17A.Stage E.2. Create thematic maps and graphs of the students' local community, Illinois, United States, and the world using data and a variety of symbols and colors.

Illinois!

NATIVE AMERICANS OF ILLINOIS
The Fox

The Fox people came to Illinois from northeastern Wisconsin in the 1700s. They built permanent villages, and the women grew crops including corn and squash. After the crops were harvested many Fox left the village to participate in group bison hunts during the winter months. The Fox had a leader and a council of elders, but the entire group made important decisions together.

Students can . . .
Learn more about how Native Americans grew crops and write a short, illustrated report about their findings.

A SPECIAL ILLINOIS PLACE
Adler Planetarium and Astronomy Museum

The Adler Planetarium and Astronomy Museum in Chicago was the first planetarium built in the United States. Opened on May 12, 1930, the planetarium was named after its founder, Max Adler, a prominent Chicago businessperson. Today visitors can explore collections of astronomical instruments and participate in interactive adventures.

Students can . . .
Suppose they are astronomers who have discovered a new planet. Have them draw a picture of the planet, name it, and write a brief description.

ILLINOIS FUN FACTS
Did You Know?

- For about 200 of its 475 miles, the Wabash River forms the southeastern border of Illinois.

- The area of what is now Illinois was originally part of the Northwest Territory of the United States, created by the Northwest Ordinance.

- Held in August each year, the Chicago Air and Water Show is the oldest and largest free-admission show of its kind in the United States.

Students can . . .
Research the types of aircraft and watercraft that appear in the Chicago Air and Water Show. Choose one craft and make a fact card. Put the craft's picture on the front and write information about it on the back.

Unit 3
Inventors and Artists

CONCEPT QUESTION
What do people gain from the work of inventors and artists?

EXPAND THE CONCEPT

How can paleontologists help us understand the past?

Week 1
How do inventors inspire our imaginations?

Week 2
How do artists inspire future generations?

Week 3
How can paleontologists help us understand the past?

Week 4
How does an artist use music to inspire others?

Week 5
How do artists create special effects to entertain us?

CONNECT THE CONCEPT

▶ **Build Background**
fossils, paleontologists, sandstone

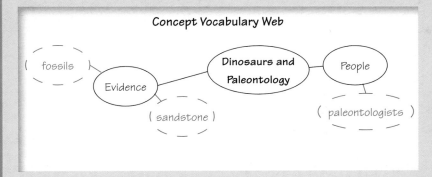

Concept Vocabulary Web

fossils — Evidence — Dinosaurs and Paleontology — People — (paleontologists)
(sandstone)

▶ **Science Content**
Dinosaur Extinction, Fossils, Crystal Palace, Paleontology

▶ **Writing**
Feature Story

▶ **Internet Inquiry**
Dinosaurs

Preview Your Week

How can paleontologists help us understand the past?

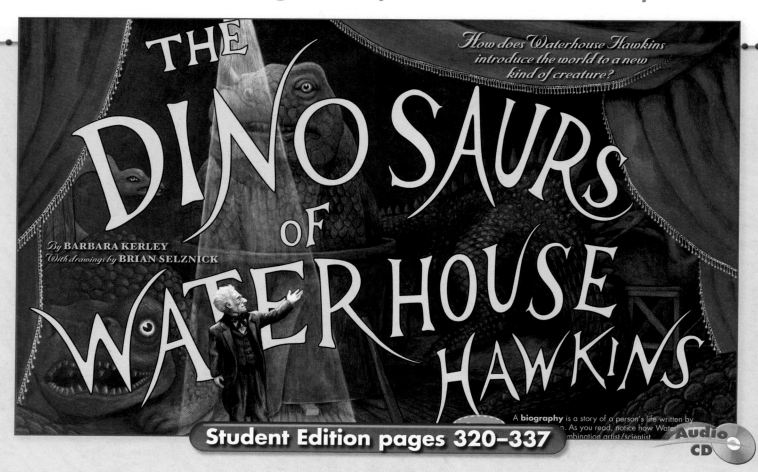

How does Waterhouse Hawkins introduce the world to a new kind of creature?

THE DINOSAURS OF WATERHOUSE HAWKINS

By BARBARA KERLEY
With drawings by BRIAN SELZNICK

A **biography** is a story of a person's life written by another. As you read, notice how Waterhouse Hawkins... combination artist/scientist...

Student Edition pages 320–337

Audio CD

Genre Biography
Vocabulary Strategy Context Clues
Comprehension Skill Fact and Opinion
Comprehension Strategy Predict

Paired Selection

Reading Across Texts
Verify Information
by Making Notations

Genre
Interview

Text Features
Introduction of Interviewee
Question-and-Answer Format

Science in Reading

Interview

Genre
- In an interview, the interviewer asks questions and the subject answers them.
- Interviews are often found in magazines and newspapers.

Text Features
- The interview first introduces the subject, or the person being interviewed.
- An interview gives the actual words spoken by the subject and interviewer.
- Preview the questions in bold type. What do they tell you about the interview?

Link to Science
Research how scientists use other kinds of models in their work, such as computer models. Explain to a classmate what you have learned.

A Model SCIENTIST
FROM OWL MAGAZINE

Meet Garfield Minott. He's been making dinosaur models since he was seven years old. Back then, he made dinosaurs just for fun. Today, his passion for the prehistoric has turned into a cool and unusual dinosaur job.

Q: OWL: What exactly do you do?
A: Garfield: I'm a paleo-artist. I bring dinosaurs back to life!

Q: How do you do that?
A: I build real-life models of the dinosaurs scientists discover. My models help dinosaur scientists to gain a better understanding of these incredible creatures. I get bags of bones shipped to me from scientists, and I use these bones to plan my models. When it comes to learning about dino bones, nothing beats the real thing!

Q: What can you tell from a simple bone?
A: Lots of stuff! If you took all the muscles off of a bone, you'd be left with marks on the bone called "scarring." These marks tell me how the muscles were attached. Then, I can tell how the skin formed around the muscles. As I build up, layer after layer from the inside out, I can bring an animal back to life!

Q: How do you make your models?
A: Once I've researched in books and bones, I make a rough drawing. Then, I make a skeleton of the body out of welded steel. Next, I start layering on the muscles, which are made out of clay. When that's done, I start on the skin. If the dinosaur had scales, then I make the scales and layer them on one at a time. This could take three to five weeks. I want my dinosaur models to look as close as possible to the real thing.

340

Predict What will this be about? How quickly will you read it?

Student Edition pages 340–345

Audio CD

Read It ONLINE
PearsonSuccessNet.com
- Student Edition
- Leveled Readers

TIME FOR Science

Leveled Readers

🔵 **Skill** Fact and Opinion

🔵 **Strategy** Predict

Lesson Vocabulary

Paleontology: Digging for Dinosaurs and More
by Laura Johnson

Below-Level

SEARCHING FOR DINOSAURS ~ by Anne Cambal ~

On-Level

What's New with Dinosaur Fossils?
by Laura Johnson

Advanced

ELL Reader

DINOSAUR TIME LINE
by Carl Escobedo
Illustrated by Gary Torrisi

- Concept Vocabulary
- Text Support
- Language Enrichment

Integrate Science Standards

- **Fossils**
- **Dinosaurs**
- **Paleontology**
- **Extinction**

✓ **Read**

The Dinosaurs of Waterhouse Hawkins, pp. 320–337

"A Model Scientist," pp. 340–345

Leveled Readers

Below-Level
- Support Concepts

On-Level
- Develop Concepts

Advanced
- Extend Concepts
- Science Extension Activity

ELL Reader

✓ **Build Concept Vocabulary**
Dinosaurs and Paleontology, pp. 316l–316m

✓ **Teach Science Concepts**
Dinosaur Extinction, p. 325
Fossils, p. 331
Crystal Palace, p. 335
Paleontology, p. 345

✓ **Explore Science Center**
Compare Information, p. 316k

The Dinosaurs of Waterhouse Hawkins **316c**

Weekly Plan

READING

45–90 minutes

TARGET SKILLS OF THE WEEK

Comprehension Skill
Fact and Opinion

Comprehension Strategy
Predict

Vocabulary Strategy
Context Clues

DAY 1
PAGES 316l–318b, 345a, 345e–345k

Oral Language

QUESTION OF THE WEEK *How can paleontologists help us understand the past?*

Read Aloud: "Graveyards of the Dinosaurs," 316m
Build Concepts, 316l

Comprehension/Vocabulary

Comprehension Skill/Strategy Lesson, 316–317

Fact and Opinion **T**

Predict

Build Background, 318a

Introduce Lesson Vocabulary, 318b
erected, foundations, mold, occasion, proportion, tidied, workshop **T**

Read Leveled Readers

Grouping Options 316f–316g

Fluency

Model Phrasing, 316l–316m, 345a

DAY 2
PAGES 318–327, 345a, 345e–345k

Oral Language

QUESTION OF THE DAY *Why did Waterhouse want to build dinosaurs?*

Comprehension/Vocabulary

Vocabulary Strategy Lesson, 318–319

Context Clues **T**

Read *The Dinosaurs of Waterhouse Hawkins,* 320–327

Grouping Options 316f–316g

Fact and Opinion **T**

Predict

REVIEW Main Idea **T**

Develop Vocabulary

Fluency

Echo Reading, 345a

LANGUAGE ARTS

30–60 minutes

Trait of the Week

Organization/Paragraphs

DAY 1

Grammar, 345e
Introduce Principal Parts of Irregular Verbs **T**

Writing Workshop, 345g
Introduce Feature Story
Model the Trait of the Week:
   Organization/Paragraphs

Spelling, 345i
Pretest for Consonant Sounds /j/, /ks/, /sk/, and /s/

Internet Inquiry, 345k
Identify Questions

DAY 2

Grammar, 345e
Develop Principal Parts of Irregular Verbs **T**

Writing Workshop, 345g
Improve Writing with Paragraph Structure

Spelling, 345i
Teach the Generalization

Internet Inquiry, 345k
Navigate/Search

DAILY WRITING ACTIVITIES

Day 1 Write to Read, 316

Day 2 Words to Write, 319
Strategy Response Log, 320, 327

DAILY SCIENCE CONNECTIONS

Day 1 Dinosaurs and Paleontology Concept Web, 316l

Day 2 Time for Science: Dinosaur Extinction, 325
Revisit the Dinosaurs and Paleontology Concept Web, 327

DAILY SUCCESS PREDICTORS
for Adequate Yearly Progress

Monitor Progress and Corrective Feedback

Vocabulary   Check Vocabulary, *316l*

RESOURCES FOR THE WEEK

- Practice Book, *pp. 121–130*
- Word Study and Spelling Practice Book, *pp. 49–52*
- Grammar and Writing Practice Book, *pp. 49–52*
- Selection Test, *pp. 49–52*
- Fresh Reads for Differentiated Test Practice, *pp. 73–78*
- The Grammar and Writing Book, *pp. 122–127*

Grouping Options for Differentiated Instruction
Turn the page for the small group lesson plan.

DAY 3 PAGES 328-339, 345a, 345e-345k

Oral Language

QUESTION OF THE DAY *Why do you think the public was so excited to see Waterhouse's dinosaur exhibit?*

Comprehension/Vocabulary

Read *The Dinosaurs of Waterhouse Hawkins,* 328–338

Grouping Options 316f–316g

- Fact and Opinion **T**
- Predict
- Context Clues **T**
- **REVIEW** Main Idea **T**

Develop Vocabulary

Reader Response
Selection Test

Fluency

Model Phrasing, 345a

Grammar, 345f
Apply Principal Parts of Irregular Verbs in Writing **T**

Writing Workshop, 339, 345h
Write Now
Prewrite and Draft

Spelling, 345j
Connect Spelling to Writing

Internet Inquiry, 345k
Analyze Sources

Day 3 Strategy Response Log, 336
Look Back and Write, 338

Day 3 Time for Science: Fossils, 331; Crystal Palace, 335; Revisit the Dinosaurs and Paleontology Concept Web, 337

DAY 4 PAGES 340-345a, 345e-345k

Oral Language

QUESTION OF THE DAY *What might paleontologists learn about the dinosaurs that might be helpful in today's world?*

Comprehension/Vocabulary

Read "A Model Scientist," 340–345

Grouping Options 316f–316g

Interview/Text Features
Reading Across Texts
Content-Area Vocabulary

Fluency

Partner Reading, 345a

Grammar, 345f
Practice Principal Parts of Irregular Verbs for Standardized Tests **T**

Writing Workshop, 345h
Draft, Revise, and Publish

Spelling, 345j
Provide a Strategy

Internet Inquiry, 345k
Synthesize Information

Day 4 Writing Across Texts, 345

Day 4 Time for Science: Paleontology, 345

DAY 5 PAGES 345a-345l

Oral Language

QUESTION OF THE WEEK *To wrap up the week, revisit the Day 1 question.*
Build Concept Vocabulary, 345c

Fluency

Read Leveled Readers

Grouping Options 316f–316g

Assess Reading Rate, 345a

Comprehension/Vocabulary

- Reteach Fact and Opinion, 345b **T**
- Steps in a Process, 345b
- Review Context Clues, 345c **T**

Speaking and Listening, 345d
Introduction
Listen to Audio CD

Grammar, 345f
Cumulative Review

Writing Workshop, 345h
Connect to Unit Writing

Spelling, 345j
Posttest for Consonant Sounds /j/, /ks/, /sk/, and /s/

Internet Inquiry, 345k
Communicate Results

Research/Study Skills, 345l
Schedule

Day 5 Steps in a Process, 345b

Day 5 Revisit the Dinosaurs and Paleontology Concept Web, 345c

KEY = Target Skill **T** = Tested Skill

Comprehension — Check Retelling, *338*

Fluency — Check Fluency WCPM, *345a*

Vocabulary — Check Vocabulary, *345c*

SUCCESS PREDICTOR

Small Group Plan *for Differentiated Instruction*

Daily Plan AT A GLANCE

Reading
Whole Group
- Oral Language
- Comprehension/Vocabulary

Group Time
Differentiated Instruction

Meet with small groups to provide:
- Skill Support
- Reading Support
- Fluency Practice

Read

This week's lessons for daily group time can be found behind the Differentiated Instruction (DI) tab on pp. DI·22–DI·31.

Whole Group
- Fluency

Language Arts
- Grammar
- Writing
- Spelling
- Research/Inquiry
- Speaking/Listening/Viewing

Use My Sidewalks on Reading Street for Tier III intensive reading intervention.

DAY 1

On-Level
Teacher-Led
Page DI · 23
- Develop Concept Vocabulary
- **Read** On-Level Reader *Searching for Dinosaurs*

Strategic Intervention
Teacher-Led
Page DI · 22
- Reinforce Concepts
- **Read** Below-Level Reader *Paleontology: Digging for Dinosaurs and More*

Advanced
Teacher-Led
Page DI · 23
- **Read** Advanced Reader *What's New with Dinosaur Fossils?*
- Independent Extension Activity

(i) Independent Activities
While you meet with small groups, have the rest of the class...
- Visit the Reading/Library Center
- Listen to the Background Building Audio
- Finish Write to Read, p. 316
- Complete Practice Book pp. 123–124
- Visit Cross-Curricular Centers

DAY 2

On-Level
Teacher-Led
Pages 322–337
- **Read** *The Dinosaurs of Waterhouse Hawkins*

Strategic Intervention
Teacher-Led
Page DI · 24
- Practice Lesson Vocabulary
- Read Multisyllabic Words
- **Read** or Listen to *The Dinosaurs of Waterhouse Hawkins*

Advanced
Teacher-Led
Page DI · 25
- Extend Vocabulary
- **Read** *The Dinosaurs of Waterhouse Hawkins*

(i) Independent Activities
While you meet with small groups, have the rest of the class...
- Visit the Reading/Library Center
- Listen to the AudioText for *The Dinosaurs of Waterhouse Hawkins*
- Finish Words to Write, p. 319
- Complete Practice Book pp. 125–126
- Write in their Strategy Response Logs, pp. 320, 327
- Visit Cross-Curricular Centers
- Work on inquiry projects

DAY 3

On-Level
Teacher-Led
Pages 328–337
- **Read** *The Dinosaurs of Waterhouse Hawkins*

Strategic Intervention
Teacher-Led
Page DI · 26
- Practice Fact and Opinion, and Predict
- **Read** or Listen to *The Dinosaurs of Waterhouse Hawkins*

Advanced
Teacher-Led
Page DI · 27
- Extend Fact and Opinion and Predict
- **Read** *The Dinosaurs of Waterhouse Hawkins*

(i) Independent Activities
While you meet with small groups, have the rest of the class...
- Visit the Reading/Library Center
- Listen to the AudioText for *The Dinosaurs of Waterhouse Hawkins*
- Write in their Strategy Response Logs, p. 336
- Finish Look Back and Write, p. 338
- Complete Practice Book p. 127
- Visit Cross-Curricular Centers
- Work on inquiry projects

① Begin with whole class skill and strategy instruction.

② Meet with small groups to provide differentiated instruction.

③ Gather the whole class back together for fluency and language arts.

DAY 4

On-Level	Strategic Intervention	Advanced
Teacher-Led *Pages 340–345*	**Teacher-Led** *Page DI · 28*	**Teacher-Led** *Page DI · 29*
• **Read** "A Model Scientist"	• Practice Retelling • **Read** or Listen to "A Model Scientist"	• **Read** "A Model Scientist" • Genre Study

(i) Independent Activities

While you meet with small groups, have the rest of the class...

- Visit the Reading/Library Center
- Listen to the AudioText for "A Model Scientist"
- Visit the Writing/Vocabulary Center
- Finish Writing Across Texts, p. 345
- Visit Cross-Curricular Centers
- Work on inquiry projects

DAY 5

On-Level	Strategic Intervention	Advanced
Teacher-Led *Page DI · 31*	**Teacher-Led** *Page DI · 30*	**Teacher-Led** *Page DI · 31*
• **Reread** Leveled Reader *Searching for Dinosaurs* • Retell *Searching for Dinosaurs*	• **Reread** Leveled Reader *Paleontology: Digging for Dinosaurs and More* • Retell *Paleontology: Digging for Dinosaurs and More*	• **Reread** Leveled Reader *What's New with Dinosaur Fossils?* • Share Extension Activity

(i) Independent Activities

While you meet with small groups, have the rest of the class...

- Visit the Reading/Library Center
- Complete Practice Book pp. 128–130
- Visit Cross-Curricular Centers
- Work on inquiry projects

ELL

Grouping Place English language learners in the groups that correspond to their reading abilities in English.

Use the appropriate Leveled Reader or other text at students' instructional level.

TIP Send home the appropriate Multilingual Summary of the main selection on Day 1.

Take It to the NET ONLINE
PearsonSuccessNet.com

Peter Afflerbach
For research on prediction strategies, see the article "The Influence of Prior Knowledge and Text Genre on ... Prediction Strategies" by Scott Foresman author Peter Afflerbach.

TEACHER TALK

Guided reading is a technique in which students read instructional-level text while the teacher uses prompts and questions to support and monitor comprehension.

Looking Ahead ➤

Be sure to schedule time for students to work on the unit inquiry project "Inventors and Artists." This week students analyze the information they have found about inventors and artists.

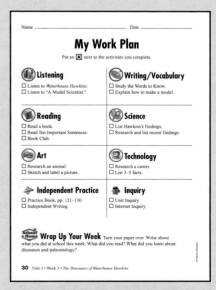

▲ **Group-Time Survival Guide** p. 30, Weekly Contract

☑ Customize Your Plan *by Strand*

ORAL LANGUAGE

 Science

Concept Development

How can paleontologists help us understand the past?

CONCEPT VOCABULARY

fossils   paleontologists   sandstone

BUILD

☐ **Question of the Week** Introduce and discuss the question of the week. This week students will read a variety of texts and work on projects related to the concept *dinosaurs and paleontology*. Post the question for students to refer to throughout the week. **DAY 1** *316d*

☐ **Read Aloud** Read aloud "Graveyards of the Dinosaurs." Then begin a web to build concepts and concept vocabulary related to this week's lesson and the unit theme, Inventors and Artists. Introduce the concept words *fossils, paleontologists,* and *sandstone* and have students place them on the web. Display the web for use throughout the week. **DAY 1** *316l–316m*

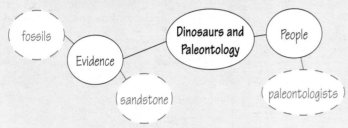

DEVELOP

☐ **Question of the Day** Use the prompts from the Weekly Plan to engage students in conversations related to this week's reading and the unit theme. **EVERY DAY** *316d–316e*

☐ **Concept Vocabulary Web** Revisit the Dinosaurs and Paleontology Concept Web and encourage students to add concept words from their reading and life experiences. **DAY 2** *327*, **DAY 3** *337*

CONNECT

☐ **Looking Back/Moving Forward** Revisit the Dinosaurs and Paleontology Concept Web and discuss how it relates to this week's lesson and the unit theme. Then make connections to next week's lesson. **DAY 5** *345c*

CHECK

☐ **Concept Vocabulary Web** Use the Dinosaurs and Paleontology Concept Web to check students' understanding of the concept vocabulary words *fossils, paleontologists,* and *sandstone*. **DAY 1** *316l*, **DAY 5** *345c*

VOCABULARY

⟳ **STRATEGY CONTEXT CLUES**
Sometimes an unfamiliar word is a homonym. Homonyms are words with the same spelling but different histories and meanings. You can use context to help figure out its meaning. The words and sentences around the homonym can offer clues.

LESSON VOCABULARY

erected   proportion
foundations   tidied
mold   workshop
occasion

TEACH

☐ **Words to Know** Give students the opportunity to tell what they already know about this week's lesson vocabulary words. Then discuss word meaning. **DAY 1** *318b*

☐ **Vocabulary Strategy Lesson** Use the vocabulary strategy lesson in the Student Edition to introduce and model this week's strategy, *context clues*. **DAY 2** *318–319*

Vocabulary Strategy Lesson

PRACTICE/APPLY

☐ **Leveled Text** Read the lesson vocabulary in the context of leveled text. **DAY 1** *LR19–LR27*

Leveled Readers

☐ **Words in Context** Read the lesson vocabulary and apply *context clues* in the context of *The Dinosaurs of Waterhouse Hawkins*. **DAY 2** *320–327*, **DAY 3** *328–338*,

☐ **Writing/Vocabulary Center** Write and illustrate the steps in making a dinosaur model on index cards. **ANY DAY** *316k*

Main Selection—Nonfiction

☐ **Homework** Practice Book pp. 124–125. **DAY 1** *318b*, **DAY 2** *319*

☐ **Word Play** Have students compile a list of scientific terms from *The Dinosaurs of Waterhouse Hawkins*, and define each word using context clues or a dictionary. **ANY DAY** *345c*

ASSESS

☐ **Selection Test** Use the Selection Test to determine students' understanding of the lesson vocabulary words. **DAY 3**

RETEACH/REVIEW

☐ **Reteach Lesson** If necessary, use this lesson to reteach and review *context clues*. **DAY 5** *345c*

① Use assessment data to determine your instructional focus.

② Preview this week's instruction by strand.

③ Choose instructional activities that meet the needs of your classroom.

COMPREHENSION

SKILL FACT AND OPINION You can prove a *statement of fact* true or false. You can do this by using your own knowledge, asking an expert, or checking a reference source such as an encyclopedia or a nonfiction text. A *statement of opinion* gives ideas or feelings, not facts. It cannot be proven true or false.

STRATEGY PREDICT The ability to think about what is going to happen next is predicting. Good readers look for clues and combine those clues with what they already know to tell what is going to happen next. Predicting can help you become a better reader and writer.

TEACH

☐ **Skill/Strategy Lesson** Use the skill/ strategy lesson in the Student Edition to introduce and model *fact and opinion* and *predict*. **DAY 1** *316–317*

Skill/Strategy Lesson

☐ **Extend Skills** Teach steps in a process. **ANY DAY** *345b*

PRACTICE/APPLY

☐ **Leveled Text** Apply *fact and opinion* and *predict* to read leveled text. **DAY 1** *LR19–LR27*

☐ **Skills and Strategies in Context** Read *The Dinosaurs of Waterhouse Hawkins*, using the Guiding Comprehension questions to apply *fact and opinion* and *predict*. **DAY 2** *320–327*, **DAY 3** *328–338*

Leveled Readers

☐ **Skills and Strategies in Context** Read "A Model Scientist," guiding students as they apply *fact and opinion* and *predict*. Then have students discuss and write across texts. **DAY 4** *340–345*

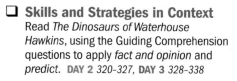

Main Selection—Nonfiction

☐ **Homework** Practice Book pp. 123, 127, 128 **DAY 1** *317*, **DAY 3** *337*, **DAY 5** *345b*

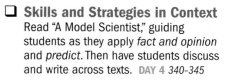

☐ **Fresh Reads for Differentiated Test Practice** Have students practice *fact and opinion* with a new passage. **DAY 3**

Paired Selection—Nonfiction

ASSESS

☐ **Selection Test** Determine students' understanding of the selection and their use of *fact and opinion*. **DAY 3**

☐ **Retell** Have students retell *The Dinosaurs of Waterhouse Hawkins*. **DAY 3** *338–339*

RETEACH/REVIEW

☐ **Reteach Lesson** If necessary, reteach and review *fact and opinion*. **DAY 5** *345b*

FLUENCY

SKILL PHRASING Phrasing is grouping related words, such as prepositional phrases, verbal phrases, and other clauses, to reinforce meaning. Phrasing allows the reader and listener to better understand the meaning of the text.

TEACH

☐ **Read Aloud** Model fluent reading by rereading "Graveyards of the Dinosaurs." Focus on this week's fluency skill, phrasing. **DAY 1** *316l–316m, 345a*

PRACTICE/APPLY

☐ **Echo Reading** Read aloud selected paragraphs from *The Dinosaurs of Waterhouse Hawkins*, placing emphasis on grouping related words together. Then practice as a class, doing three echo readings of the selected paragraphs. **DAY 2** *345a*, **DAY 3** *345a*

☐ **Partner Reading** Have partners practice reading aloud, reading with careful phrasing, and offering each other feedback. As students reread, monitor their progress toward their individual fluency goals. **DAY 4** *345a*

☐ **Listening Center** Have students follow along with the AudioText for this week's selections. **ANY DAY** *316j*

☐ **Reading/Library Center** Have students reread a selection of their choice. **ANY DAY** *316j*

☐ **Fluency Coach** Have students use Fluency Coach to listen to fluent readings or practice reading on their own. **ANY DAY**

ASSESS

☐ **Check Fluency** WCPM Do a one-minute timed reading, paying special attention to this week's skill—phrasing. Provide feedback for each student. **DAY 5** *345a*

☑ Customize Your Plan *by Strand*

SKILL PRINCIPAL PARTS OF IRREGULAR VERBS The principal parts of a verb are the present, present participle, past, and past participle. An irregular verb does not add *-ed* to form the past tense. Most irregular verbs have different spellings for the past and the past participle.

TEACH

☐ **Grammar Transparency 13** Use Grammar Transparency 13 to teach the principal parts of irregular verbs. **DAY 1** *345e*

Grammar Transparency 13

PRACTICE/APPLY

☐ **Develop the Concept** Review the concept of principal parts of irregular verbs and provide guided practice. **DAY 2** *345e*

☐ **Apply to Writing** Have students review something they have written and apply what they learned about principal parts of irregular verbs. **DAY 3** *345f*

☐ **Test Preparation** Examine common errors in principal parts of irregular verbs to prepare for standardized tests. **DAY 4** *345f*

☐ **Homework** Grammar and Writing Practice Book pp. 49–51. **DAY 2** *345e*, **DAY 3** *345f*, **DAY 4** *345f*

ASSESS

☐ **Cumulative Review** Use Grammar and Writing Practice Book p. 52. **DAY 5** *345f*

RETEACH/REVIEW

☐ **Daily Fix-It** Have students find and correct errors in grammar, spelling, and punctuation. **EVERY DAY** *345e–345f*

☐ **The Grammar and Writing Book** Use pp. 122–125 of The Grammar and Writing Book to extend instruction for principal parts of irregular verbs. **ANY DAY**

The Grammar and Writing Book

Trait of the Week

ORGANIZATION/PARAGRAPHS Good writers have organization to their writing. Their ideas are written in a logical order that helps readers with understanding and that shows connections among those ideas.

TEACH

☐ **Writing Transparency 13A** Use the model to introduce and discuss the Trait of the Week. **DAY 1** *345g*

☐ **Writing Transparency 13B** Use the transparency to show students how knowing what makes a paragraph can improve their writing. **DAY 2** *345g*

Writing Transparency 13A   **Writing Transparency 13B**

PRACTICE/APPLY

☐ **Write Now** Examine the model on Student Edition p. 339. Then have students write their own feature story. **DAY 3** *339, 345h,* **DAY 4** *345h*

> **Prompt** *The Dinosaurs of Waterhouse Hawkins* tells about the introduction of dinosaur models to the world. Think about the introduction of something new in your school or community. Now write a feature story about the event.

Write Now p. 339

☐ **Writing/Vocabulary Center** Write and illustrate the steps in making a dinosaur model on index cards. **ANY DAY** *316k*

ASSESS

☐ **Writing Trait Rubric** Use the rubric to evaluate students' writing. **DAY 4** *345h*

RETEACH/REVIEW

☐ **The Grammar and Writing Book** Use pp. 122–127 of The Grammar and Writing Book to extend instruction for principal parts of irregular verbs, what makes a paragraph, and feature stories. **ANY DAY**

The Grammar and Writing Book

❶ Use assessment data to determine your instructional focus.

❷ Preview this week's instruction by strand.

❸ Choose instructional activities that meet the needs of your classroom.

SPELLING

GENERALIZATION CONSONANT SOUNDS /J/, /KS/, /SK/, AND /S/
The sound /j/ can be spelled g, j, and dge: _ginger_, _journal_, _dodge_. The sound /ks/ can be spelled x: e_x_cuse. The sound /sk/ can be spelled sch: _sch_edule. The sound /s/ can be spelled sc: _sc_ene. Some consonant sounds can be spelled in different ways.

TEACH

❑ **Pretest** Give the pretest for words with consonant sounds /j/, /ks/, /sk/, and /s/. Guide students in self-correcting their pretests and correcting any misspellings. **DAY 1** _345i_

❑ **Think and Practice** Connect spelling to the phonics generalization for words with consonant sounds /j/, /ks/, /sk/, and /s/. **DAY 2** _345i_

PRACTICE/APPLY

❑ **Connect to Writing** Have students use spelling words to write opening sentences. Then review frequently misspelled words: _except, excited, school_. **DAY 3** _345j_

❑ **Homework** Word Study and Spelling Practice Book pp. 49–52. **EVERY DAY**

RETEACH/REVIEW

❑ **Review** Review spelling words to prepare for the posttest. Then provide students with a spelling strategy—memory tricks. **DAY 4** _345j_

ASSESS

❑ **Posttest** Use dictation sentences to give the posttest for words with consonant sounds /j/, /ks/, /sk/, and /s/. **DAY 5** _345j_

Spelling Words

1. excuse	8. schedule	15. ginger
2. scene	9. gigantic	16. scholar
3. muscle	10. scheme	17. scent
4. explore	11. Japan	18. dodge
5. pledge	12. excellent	19. smudge
6. journal	13. exclaim	20. schooner
7. science	14. fascinate	

Challenge Words

21. extraordinary	23. acknowledge	25. allergic
22. reminisce	24. prejudice	

*Word from the selection

RESEARCH AND INQUIRY

❑ **Internet Inquiry** Have students conduct an Internet inquiry on dinosaurs. **EVERY DAY** _345k_

❑ **Schedule** Review how information is organized in a schedule and discuss how students can use a schedule to locate information. **DAY 5** _345l_

❑ **Unit Inquiry** Allow time for students to analyze the information they have found about inventors and artists. **ANY DAY** _261_

SPEAKING AND LISTENING

❑ **Introduction** Have students imagine that they are going to introduce Dinosaur Hawkins's dinosaur at the Grand Opening. Have them create an introduction that will be informational as well as captivating. **DAY 5** _345d_

❑ **Listen to Audio CD** Have students listen to the AudioText of _The Dinosaurs of Waterhouse Hawkins_ and answer questions. **DAY 5** _345d_

Resources for Differentiated Instruction

LEVELED READERS

▶ **Comprehension**
- 🎯 **Skill** Fact and Opinion
- 🎯 **Strategy** Predict

▶ **Lesson Vocabulary**
- 🎯 **Context Clues**

erected foundations
mold occasion proportion
tidied workshop

▶ **Science Standards**
- **Fossils**
- **Dinosaurs**
- **Paleontology**
- **Extinction**

Leveled Reader Database ONLINE

PearsonSuccessNet.com

Use the Online Database of over 600 books to
- Download and print additional copies of this week's leveled readers.
- Listen to the readers being read online.
- Search for more titles focused on this week's skills, topic, and content.

On-Level

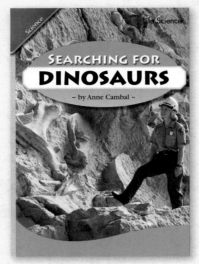

On-Level Reader

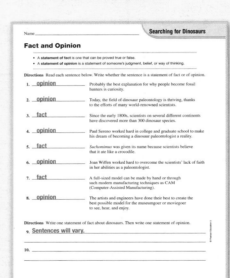

On-Level Practice TE p. LR23

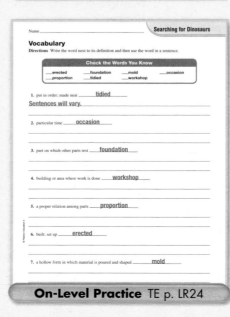

On-Level Practice TE p. LR24

Strategic Intervention

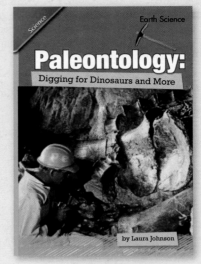

Below-Level Reader

Below-Level Practice TE p. LR20

Below-Level Practice TE p. LR21

Advanced

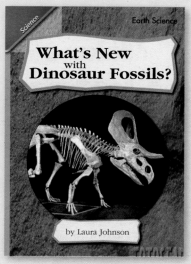

Advanced Reader

What's New with Dinosaur Fossils?
by Laura Johnson

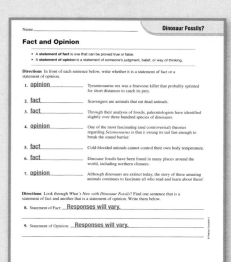

Name _____ Dinosaur Fossils?

Fact and Opinion

- A **statement of fact** is one that can be proved true or false.
- A **statement of opinion** is a statement of someone's judgment, belief, or way of thinking.

Directions In front of each sentence below, write whether it is a statement of fact or a statement of opinion.

1. **opinion** — Tyrannosaurus rex was a fearsome killer that probably sprinted for short distances to catch its prey.
2. **fact** — Scavengers are animals that eat dead animals.
3. **fact** — Through their analysis of fossils, paleontologists have identified slightly over three hundred species of dinosaurs.
4. **opinion** — One of the most fascinating (and controversial) theories regarding *Seismosaurus* is that it swung its tail fast enough to break the sound barrier.
5. **fact** — Cold-blooded animals cannot control their own body temperature.
6. **fact** — Dinosaur fossils have been found in many places around the world, including northern climates.
7. **opinion** — Although dinosaurs are extinct today, the story of these amazing animals continues to fascinate all who read and learn about them!

Directions Look through *What's New with Dinosaur Fossils?* Find one sentence that is a statement of fact and another that is a statement of opinion. Write them below.

8. Statement of Fact: **Responses will vary.**

9. Statement of Opinion: **Responses will vary.**

Advanced Practice TE p. LR26

Name _____ Dinosaur Fossils?

Vocabulary
Directions Use the vocabulary words to answer the questions below. Each word can only be used once.

Check the Words You Know

___avid	___carnivorous	___collaborator	___consensus
___contention	___descendants	___herbivorous	___olfactory bulbs
___theropods	___trackways	___vertebrae	

1. **herbivorous** — What kind of animal eats only plants?
2. **trackways** — Which word refers to certain kinds of footprints?
3. **collaborator** — What kind of person would you choose to work with you on a scientific project?
4. **vertebrae** — What is your backbone made up of?
5. **theropods** — Which word names certain meat-eating dinosaurs with sharp claws and sharp teeth that may be the ancestors of birds?
6. **olfactory bulbs** — Which word has to do with the sense of smell?
7. **avid** — Which word would you use for someone who is extremely enthusiastic?
8. **descendants** — What are grandchildren and great-grandchildren?
9. **carnivorous** — Which word describes lions, tigers, and other meat-eating animals?
10.–11. **consensus** / **contention** — Which two words mean opposite things?

Advanced Practice TE p. LR27

DINOSAUR TIME LINE
by Carl Escobedo
Illustrated by Gary Torrisi

ELL Reader

ELL Poster 13

Teacher's Edition Notes

ELL notes throughout this lesson support instruction and reference additional resources at point of use.

Teaching Guide pp. 85–91, 236–237

- Multilingual summaries of the main selection
- Comprehension lesson
- Vocabulary strategies and word cards
- ELL Reader 5.3.3 lesson

ELL and Transition Handbook

Ten Important Sentences

- Key ideas from every selection in the Student Edition
- Activities to build sentence power

More Reading

Readers' Theater Anthology

- Fluency practice
- Five scripts to build fluency
- Poetry for oral interpretation

Leveled Trade Books

Below-Level

Advanced

On-Level

- Extended reading tied to the unit concept
- Lessons in the Trade Book Library Teaching Guide

School + Home

Homework

- Family Times Newsletter
- ELL Multilingual Selection Summaries

Take-Home Books

- Leveled Readers

Family Times

Cross-Curricular Centers

 Listening

Listen to the *Selections*

MATERIALS `SINGLES`
CD player, headphones, AudioText CD, student book

LISTEN TO LITERATURE Listen to *The Dinosaurs of Waterhouse Hawkins* and "A Model Scientist" as you follow or read along in your book. Listen to identify both the facts and the opinions in each selection.

If there is anything you don't understand, you can listen again to any section.

 Reading/Library

Read It Again!

MATERIALS `SINGLES` `PAIRS` `GROUPS`
Collection of books for self-selected reading, reading logs, student book

Select a book you have already read. Record the title of the book in your reading log. You may want to read with a partner.

Choose from the following:

- **Leveled Readers**
- **ELL Readers**
- **Stories Written by Classmates**
- **Books from the Library**
- ***The Dinosaurs of Waterhouse Hawkins***

TEN IMPORTANT SENTENCES Read the Ten Important Sentences for *The Dinosaurs of Waterhouse Hawkins*. Then locate the sentences in the student book.

BOOK CLUB Discuss what makes Waterhouse Hawkins an interesting person to write about. Read other biographies and get together with a group to share your favorites.

Art

Make a Sketch

MATERIALS `SINGLES`
Drawing materials, paper, sculpting clay, reference materials, Internet access

Waterhouse Hawkins created life-size dinosaur models by first drawing them. Choose an animal that you would like to sketch.

1. **Research information on the animal's physical appearance and structure. Use a student-friendly search engine and follow classroom Internet rules.**
2. **Sketch a picture of the animal including all of the physical features of your animal.**
3. **Label the parts of your animal.**

EARLY FINISHERS Use sculpting clay to build a model of the animal.

Scott Foresman Reading Street Centers Survival Kit

Use the *Dinosaurs of Waterhouse Hawkins* materials from the Reading Street Centers Survival Kit to organize this week's centers.

Writing/Vocabulary

Science

Technology

List the Steps

MATERIALS `SINGLES`
Writing and drawing materials, index cards

Use the information in *The Dinosaurs of Waterhouse Hawkins* and "A Model Scientist" to explain how to make a dinosaur model.

1. List and number each step in the process on a separate index card.
2. Illustrate the index cards with a simple picture showing each step.

EARLY FINISHERS List the steps in the process for making another art project, like a paper collage.

1. Study the bones.

Compare Information

MATERIALS `SINGLES`
Books on dinosaurs, Internet access, writing materials

Make a T-chart to compare Hawkins's findings about dinosaurs to current research.

1. List three of Hawkins's findings about dinosaurs.
2. Locate current research about dinosaurs.
3. List three recent findings.

EARLY FINISHERS Using the information you find write a brief report.

Hawkins's Research	Current Research
Thought that dinosaurs probably looked like larger versions of present-day reptiles.	Paleontologists have discovered more fossils and now have a better idea of what dinosaurs really looked like.

Research Careers Online

MATERIALS `SINGLES`
Internet access, reference materials, e-mail programs

Learn more about another interesting job.

1. Follow classroom rules for using the Internet and using a student-friendly search engine.
2. Conduct a search about a career that interests you.
3. List 3–5 facts about this career.

EARLY FINISHERS Send an e-mail to a family member or friend telling about this career.

Search Engine

becoming a pilot

ALL CENTERS

OBJECTIVES

- Build vocabulary by finding words related to the lesson concept.
- Listen for statements of fact and opinion.

Concept Vocabulary

fossils the hardened remains or traces of something that lived in a former age

paleontologists scientists who study the forms of life in prehistoric time

sandstone a sedimentary rock made mostly of sand

Monitor Progress

Check Vocabulary

If...	then... review the
students are unable to place words on the web,	lesson concept. Place the words on the web and provide additional words for practice, such as *professor* and *field workers.*

SUCCESS PREDICTOR

DAY 1 — Grouping Options

Reading

Whole Group
Introduce and discuss the Question of the Week. Then use pp. 316l–318b.

Group Time
Differentiated Instruction
Read this week's Leveled Readers. See pp. 316h–316i for the small group lesson plan.

Whole Group
Use p. 345a.

Language Arts
Use pp. 345e–345k.

Build Concepts

FLUENCY

MODEL PHRASING As you read "Graveyards of the Dinosaurs," appropriately group together groups of words into phrases. Pay special attention to prepositional phrases such as, "of his career" and "in the Valley of the Moon."

LISTENING COMPREHENSION

After reading "Graveyards of the Dinosaurs," use the following questions to assess listening comprehension.

1. **Read the first introductory sentence. Is this a statement of fact or opinion? Why?** *(It is a statement of fact because it can be proved true by doing research.)* ***Fact and Opinion***

2. **The author compares paleontologists' work to grunt work. Is this a statement of fact or opinion? Why?** *(It is a statement of opinion because it cannot be proved true.)* ***Fact and Opinion***

BUILD CONCEPT VOCABULARY

Start a web to build concepts and vocabulary related to this week's lesson and the unit theme.

- Draw the Dinosaurs and Paleontology Concept Web.
- Read the sentence with the word *fossils* again. Ask students to pronounce *fossils* and discuss its meaning.
- Place *fossils* in an oval attached to *Evidence*. Explain that paleontologists search for *fossils*. Read the sentences in which *paleontologists* and *sandstone* appear. Have students pronounce the words, place them on the web, and provide reasons.
- Brainstorm additional words and categories for the web. Keep the web on display and add words throughout the week.

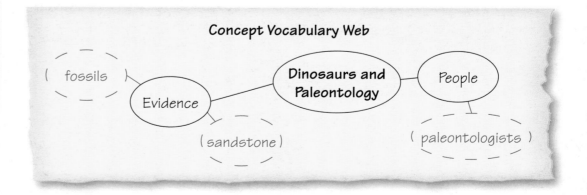

Concept Vocabulary Web

GRAVEYARDS OF THE DINOSAURS

BY SHELLEY TANAKA

Paul Sereno is a university professor who has discovered dinosaur fossils on five continents. He is one of the most respected dinosaur experts in the world.

One of Sereno's most dramatic discoveries came near the beginning of his career, when he set out to chart the entire evolution of dinosaurs. To do this, he had to start with the earliest dinosaur yet known—*Herrerasaurus*. Although a number of *Herrerasaurus* fossils had been found, there weren't enough bones to tell him exactly what the creature had looked like. Most important, no one had ever discovered a complete skull.

Sereno decided to look for a complete skeleton himself. That is how he ended up in the Valley of the Moon [in Argentina], the place where the other *Herrerasaurus* fossils had been found.

And just how was he going to find this rare skeleton? As [someone] has said, finding fossils is painfully simple. You walk, and you look.

It was like looking for a needle in a haystack.

Sereno and his team were combing the area piece by piece, gradually making their way along the valley. As they drove away from one spot, he realized there was a small ravine that they had missed. They moved on anyway, but that small triangle of land nagged at him. He couldn't sleep. So, a few weeks later, they drove back to it.

Most paleontologists will tell you that there are some field workers who have a special knack for finding fossils. Some call it accident or luck. Some say it's a sixth sense, an uncanny instinct.

Whatever it is, Sereno had it that day. He laid his backpack on a rock and headed down into the little valley. He walked a dozen paces, straight to where a fossil was poking out of a sandstone ledge.

He was too experienced to get excited right away. The fossil most likely belonged to a rhynchosaur. The bones of those ancient owl-faced lizards had been popping out of the rock so often that the team had stopped collecting them.

Then Sereno looked more closely. A few neck bones had started to roll down the slope. Sereno rolled them back into place. And he realized that the neck bones led to the back of a skull. A *Herrerasaurus* skull.

For a few seconds he was frozen. Then he let out a huge yell that bounced off the distant cliffs and brought his teammates running.

As the others crowded around the skeleton to examine it closely, Sereno walked away. He couldn't bear to look.

So much of what paleontologists do is pure grunt work. They spend their summers in dusty deserts, living on warm water, stale crackers, and tinned tuna, tripping over snakes and scorpions, going for weeks without a shower. Sereno was

(Continued on TR1.)

Activate Prior Knowledge

Before students listen to the Read Aloud, ask them what they know about dinosaurs and dinosaur fossils.

Set Purpose

Read aloud the title and have students predict what the selection will be about.

Read the introduction aloud. Encourage students to listen for both facts and opinions.

Creative Response

Have a group of students reenact the scene in which Sereno finds the *Herrerasaurus* skull. Encourage them to improvise dialogue that might have taken place between Sereno and his team. **Drama**

Access Content Before reading, share this summary: Paul Sereno went to Argentina to look for dinosaur fossils. He one day passed by a ravine, and went back to explore it a few weeks later. There he found the skeleton of a *Herrerasaurus*.

School + Home **Homework** Send home this week's Family Times newsletter.

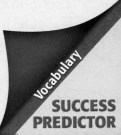

○ SKILLS ◆▶ STRATEGIES IN CONTEXT

Fact and Opinion Predict

○ Identify statements of fact and opinion.

○ Use statements of fact and opinion to make predictions.

Skills Trace	
○ **Fact and Opinion**	
Introduce/Teach	TE: 5.2 208–209; 5.3 316–317; 5.6 700–701
Practice	Practice Book: 83, 87, 88, 116, 123, 127, 128, 136, 283, 287, 288
Reteach/Review	TE: 5.2 229b, DI·55; 5.3 301, 345b, 355, DI·54; 5.6 725b, DI·55
Test	Selection Test: 33–36, 49–52, 113–116; Benchmark Test: Unit 3

INTRODUCE

Write the following sentences on the board: *Dinosaurs lived millions of years ago. (fact) They were a part of the reptile family. (fact) Dinosaurs are interesting to study. (opinion)* Have students read each sentence and tell whether it is a statement of fact or opinion.

Have students read the information on p. 316. Explain the following:

• Statements of fact can be proved true or false with one's own knowledge and reference sources. Statements of opinion can not be proved.

• Making predictions about whether a text will contain mostly statements of fact or statements of opinion can help you focus on the content of the selection.

Use Skill Transparency 13 to teach fact and opinion and predict.

Comprehension

Skill
Fact and Opinion

Strategy
Predict

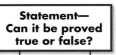

○ **Fact and Opinion**

• You can prove a statement of fact true or false. You can do this by using your own knowledge, asking an expert, or checking a reference source such as an encyclopedia, a nonfiction text, or a dictionary.

• A statement of opinion gives ideas or feelings, not facts. It cannot be proved true or false.

• A sentence may contain both a statement of fact and a statement of opinion.

```
        ┌─────────────────┐
        │   Statement—    │
        │  Can it be proved │
        │  true or false? │
        └─────────────────┘
   ┌──────────┐  ┌──────────┐  ┌──────────────┐
   │ Opinion—No │  │ Fact—Yes │  │ How to check? │
   └──────────┘  └──────────┘  └──────────────┘
```

○ **Strategy: Predict**

Active readers try to predict what they will learn when they read a nonfiction article. Preview the article. Predict whether you will read mostly statements of fact or statements of opinion. This will help focus your reading. After you read, see whether your prediction was correct.

Write to Read

1. Read "Dinosaurs." Use the graphic organizer above to find two opinions and three facts. For each fact you write, explain how you could check it.

2. Write two facts you know about dinosaurs and one opinion you have about them.

316

Strategic Intervention

○ **Fact and Opinion** Review the definitions for statements of fact and opinion. Create a two-column Fact and Opinion chart. Provide students with sentences and have them sort the sentences into the correct columns: *Many dinosaurs were green or brown. (fact) I would love to have seen a red dinosaur. (opinion) The argentinosaurus was the largest dinosaur of all. (fact) He was scary! (opinion)*

ELL

Access Content

Beginning/Intermediate For a Picture It! lesson on fact and opinion, see ELL Teaching Guide, pp. 85–86.

Advanced Ask a volunteer to read aloud the first sentence on p. 317. Help students determine that this sentence states an opinion. Identify the words that help you know this. Read with students the first sentence in the next two paragraphs to determine if they are statements of fact or opinion.

DINOSAURS

By far the most fascinating creatures ever to walk the earth were the dinosaurs. Dinosaurs lived from about 215 million years ago until about 65 million years ago. Their name comes from two Greek words that mean "terrible lizard." When you see drawings or models of certain dinosaurs, it is very easy to understand how they got their name.

Types of dinosaurs Some dinosaurs were herbivores, meaning that they ate only plants. Apatosaurus and Iguanodon were herbivores. Other dinosaurs were carnivores, or meat eaters. The most feared dinosaur of all, Tyrannosaurus, was a carnivore.

Dinosaur characteristics Dinosaurs were marked by special body features. Stegosaurus had armor that it used for protection. Pterosaur had wings like a bat's. Tyrannosaurus had strong back legs but short, weak front ones.

What happened to the dinosaurs? No one knows for sure, though there are several ideas about why they disappeared. Some of these ideas are as interesting as the dinosaurs themselves.

 1 **Strategy** Consider the title and the headings. Scan the article. Do you predict that the statements you will read will be mostly fact or opinion?

2 **Skill** Clue words can help you find two opinions in this first paragraph.

3 **Skill** Which statements were facts in the section you just read? What could you use to check whether they are true or false?

4 **Strategy** What about the prediction you made at the beginning of the article? Was it correct?

317

Available as **Skill Transparency** 13

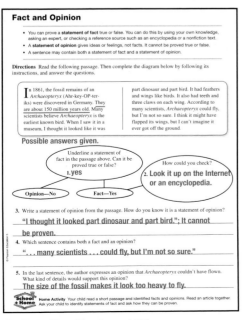

Fact and Opinion

- You can prove a **statement of fact** true or false. You can do this by using your own knowledge, asking an expert, or checking a reference source such as an encyclopedia or a nonfiction text.
- A **statement of opinion** gives ideas or feelings, not facts. It cannot be proved true or false.
- A sentence may contain both a statement of fact and a statement of opinion.

Directions Read the following passage. Then complete the diagram below by following its instructions, and answer the questions.

In 1861, the fossil remains of an *Archaeopteryx* (Ahr-key-OP-ter-iks) were discovered in Germany. They are about 150 million years old. Many scientists believe *Archaeopteryx* is the earliest known bird. When I saw it in a museum, I thought it looked like it was part dinosaur and part bird. It had feathers and wings like birds. It also had teeth and three claws on each wing. According to many scientists, *Archaeopteryx* could fly, but I'm not so sure. I think it might have flapped its wings, but I can't imagine it ever got off the ground.

Possible answers given.

Underline a statement of fact in the passage above. Can it be proved true or false? **1.yes**

How could you check? **2. Look it up on the Internet or an encyclopedia.**

Opinion—No   Fact—Yes

3. Write a statement of opinion from the passage. How do you know it is a statement of opinion? **"I thought it looked part dinosaur and part bird."; It cannot be proven.**

4. Which sentence contains both a fact and an opinion? **". . . many scientists . . . could fly, but I'm not so sure."**

5. In the last sentence, the author expresses an opinion that *Archaeopteryx* couldn't have flown. What kind of details would support this opinion? **The size of the fossil makes it look too heavy to fly.**

School + Home Home Activity Your child read a short passage and identified facts and opinions. Read an article together. Ask your child to identify statements of fact and ask how they can be proven.

▲ **Practice Book** p. 123

TEACH

1 **STRATEGY** Use the title and headings to model how to make predictions about the selection.

 Think Aloud **MODEL** I see that the title is very short and to-the-point. The headings remind me of headings I'd see in a science textbook. Based on what I see here, I predict that the article will be mostly statements of fact.

2 **SKILL** Use paragraph 1 to model how to find an author's opinion.

Think Aloud **MODEL** When I read, I look for things the author says that express feelings or ideas. In paragraph 1, I see the words *most fascinating* in the first sentence. This must be an opinion. I see the word *easy* in the last sentence. This must be another opinion.

PRACTICE AND ASSESS

3 **SKILL** All the statements in paragraph 2 are statements of fact. They can be proved in reference books or on the Internet.

4 **STRATEGY** Answers will vary. Have students explain whether or not their predictions were correct.

WRITE Have students complete steps 1 and 2 of the Write to Read activity. You might consider using this as a whole-class activity.

Monitor Progress

🔍 Fact and Opinion

If... students are unable to complete **Write to Read** on p. 316,	then... use Practice Book p. 123 to provide additional practice.

Tech Files
ONLINE

Students can find out more about dinosaurs by using a student-friendly search engine and the keyword *dinosaurs*. Be sure to follow classroom guidelines for Internet use.

E L L

Build Background Use ELL Poster 13 to build background and vocabulary for the lesson concept of dinosaurs and paleontology.

▲ **ELL Poster** 13

Build Background

ACTIVATE PRIOR KNOWLEDGE

BEGIN A KWL CHART about dinosaurs.

• Give students two to three minutes to write as many things as they can about dinosaurs. Record what students know on a KWL chart.

• Give students two minutes to write three questions they would like to find out about dinosaurs. Record questions on the KWL chart. Add a question of your own.

• Tell students that, as they read, they should look for the answers to their questions and note any new information to add to the chart.

Topic	Dinosaur Models	
K	**W**	**L**
You can find dinosaur models in museums.	How do they make dinosaur models today?	
They can be life-size.	What is the largest dinosaur model?	

▲ **Graphic Organizer** 4

BACKGROUND BUILDING AUDIO This week's audio is about the making of a dinosaur model. After students listen, discuss whether they would like to make a dinosaur model. Ask why or why not.

Background Building Audio

Introduce Vocabulary

WORD RATING CHART

Create word rating charts using the categories *Know*, *Have Seen*, and *Don't Know*.

Word Rating Chart

Word	Know	Have Seen	Don't Know
erected			✓
foundations		✓	
mold	✓		
occasion		✓	
proportion			✓
tidied	✓		
workshop	✓		

▲ **Graphic Organizer** 5

Read each word to students and have them place it in one of the three columns: *Know* (know and can use); *Have Seen* (have seen or heard the word; don't know meaning); *Don't Know* (don't know the word). ***Activate Prior Knowledge***

Have students share where they may have seen some of these words. Point out that some of this week's words have the ending *-ion (foundation, occasion, proportion)*. Ask students to think of other words with the *-ion* ending. ***Suffixes***

Check charts with students at the end of the week and have them make changes to their ratings.

Use the Multisyllabic Word Routine on p. DI·1 to help students read multisyllabic words.

Lesson Vocabulary

WORDS TO KNOW

T erected put up; built

T foundations parts on which the other parts rest for support; bases

T mold a hollow shape in which anything is formed, cast, or solidified

T occasion a special event

T proportion a proper relation among parts

T tidied put in order; made neat

T workshop space or building where work is done

MORE WORDS TO KNOW

anatomy structure of a living thing

dignitaries people who have positions of honor

monumental very great

T = Tested Word

▲ **Practice Book** p. 124

Vocabulary Strategy

OBJECTIVE

⊙ Use context clues to determine the meanings of homonyms.

INTRODUCE

Discuss the strategy for context clues using the steps on p. 318.

TEACH

• Have students read "The Artist of the Hour," paying attention to how vocabulary is used.

• Model using context clues to determine the meaning of the homonym *mold*.

Think Aloud **MODEL** I read the words around *mold* and see the clues "has the exact shape of the bird" and "pour cement into." *Mold* can mean "a hollow shape" or "a green fungus growth that can appear on food." I'll read the sentence again with each meaning to see which one fits best. The meaning, "a hollow shape" makes sense in the sentence.

Words to Know

- workshop
- proportion
- mold
- tidied
- foundations
- erected
- occasion

Remember

Try the strategy. Then, if you need more help, use your glossary or dictionary.

Vocabulary Strategy
for Homonyms

Context Clues Homonyms are words with the same spelling but different histories and meanings. Sometimes an unfamiliar word is a homonym. You can use context to help figure out its meaning. The words and sentences around the homonym offer clues.

1. Read the words and sentences around the homonym to find clues.

2. Think about the different meanings the homonym might have. For example, the word *bill* can mean "a statement of money owed" or "the beak of a bird."

3. Try each meaning in the sentence.

4. Decide which meaning makes sense in the sentence.

As you read "The Artist of the Hour," look for words that are homonyms. Decide which meaning the author is using.

318

DAY 2 Grouping Options

Reading
Whole Group Discuss the Question of the Day. Then use pp. 318–321.

Group Time Differentiated Instruction
Read *The Dinosaurs of Waterhouse Hawkins.* See pp. 316h–316i for the small group lesson plan.

Whole Group Use p. 345a.

Language Arts
Use pp. 345e–345k.

Strategic Intervention

⊙ **Context Clues** If students have trouble understanding how you determined the meaning of *mold*, walk them through each step listed on p. 318, having them follow each step as you go.

ELL

Access Content Use ELL Poster 13 to preteach vocabulary. Choose from the following to meet language proficiency levels.

Beginning Point out clues in the fourth sentence in the second paragraph on p. 319 that show the meaning of *mold*.

Intermediate Explain that the words *occasion* and *proportion* have Spanish cognates: *ocasión* and *proporción.*

Advanced Teach the lesson on pp. 312–313. Have students return to the word rating chart from 318b and make appropriate changes to their ratings.

Resources for home-language words may include parents, bilingual staff members, bilingual dictionaries, or online translation sources.

THE
ARTIST OF THE HOUR

Imagine that you are an artist at work in your workshop. You have been asked to make a sculpture for the new hospital. When people look at this sculpture, they are supposed to think about freedom and hope. You have decided to make a group of birds in flight.

First, you make a clay shape of each bird. You must measure carefully to be sure the proportion of the wings to the body is just right. Then you cover the shapes with melted plastic and let it get hard. Each mold has the exact shape of the bird you made. Next, you pour cement into each mold. After it hardens, any crumbs of cement and plastic must be tidied up. Then you have a whole bird shape.

Meanwhile, you have to build foundations for the birds. These are bases made of wood or cement, with iron pipes sticking up. When they are fastened to the rods, the birds will look as though they are sailing into the sky.

You hope your work of art will be erected in the flower garden at the hospital. When it is put in place, you will be honored for your work. There will be a party to celebrate the occasion.

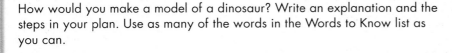

Words to Write

How would you make a model of a dinosaur? Write an explanation and the steps in your plan. Use as many of the words in the Words to Know list as you can.

319

PRACTICE AND ASSESS

- Have small groups work together to define any remaining lesson vocabulary words. Ask them to explain the context clues they used.

- Explain that if the meanings they do know of a homonym don't make sense in the sentence, they can check a dictionary to find other meanings of the word.

- If you began a word rating chart (p. 318b), have students update their charts.

- Have students complete Practice Book p. 125.

WRITE Students' explanations should include as many lesson vocabulary words as possible. When they finish, have them check to be sure they've used all vocabulary correctly.

Monitor Progress

↻ Context Clues

If... students need more practice with the lesson vocabulary,	then... use Tested Vocabulary Cards.

Vocabulary · Context Clues

- **Homonyms** are words with the same spelling but different meanings.
- Sometimes an unfamiliar word is a homonym. The words around the homonym can offer clues to its meaning.

Directions Read the following passage. Then answer the questions below.

Fossil collectors know that they are not allowed to remove fossils from most places. It is against the law to remove fossils from someone else's property and from public lands. In order to collect fossils, collectors meet at a "fossil fair" to buy fossils from other collectors. It's also possible they might add to their collection by keeping a file with photographs and drawings of fossils. Sometimes collectors make copies of fossils by pouring plaster into a mold. They can look very realistic.

1. *Fair* can mean "not favoring one more than others" or "a gathering of buyers or sellers." How is it used in the passage? How can you tell?
   "a gathering of buyers or sellers"; the word *buy*

2. *Might* can mean "possibly would" or "great power." How is it used in the passage? How can you tell?
   "possibly would"; the word *possible*

3. *File* can mean "a container, drawer, or folder for keeping papers in order" or "a steel tool used to smooth rough surfaces." How is it used in the passage? How can you tell?
   ***File* means "a container, drawer, or folder for keeping papers in order"; The sentence is about keeping photographs and drawings.**

4. *Mold* can mean "a furry, fungus growth" or "a shape in which anything is formed or cast." How is it used in the passage? How can you tell?
   Mold* means "a shape in which anything is formed or cast"; the words *pouring plaster

5. Write a sentence using the meaning of *mold* not used in the passage.
   Possible answer: The old bread had green mold growing on it.

Home Activity Your child read a short passage and used context clues to understand new homonyms in a passage. Read an article with your child. Identify homonyms in that article. Write sentences that use each meaning of the homonyms.

▲ **Practice Book** p. 125

Prereading Strategies

OBJECTIVES

- Identify statements of fact and opinion to improve comprehension.
- Use statements of fact and opinion to make predictions as you read.

GENRE STUDY

Biography

The Dinosaurs of Waterhouse Hawkins is a biography. Explain that a biography is the story of one person's life written by another person. It may cover a person's whole life or only part of it.

PREVIEW AND PREDICT

Have students preview the selection title and illustrations and discuss the topics or ideas they think this selection will cover. Have students use selection vocabulary words as they talk about what they expect to learn.

Strategy Response Log

Predict Have students write their predictions in their strategy response logs. Students will confirm their predictions in the Strategy Response Log activity on p. 327.

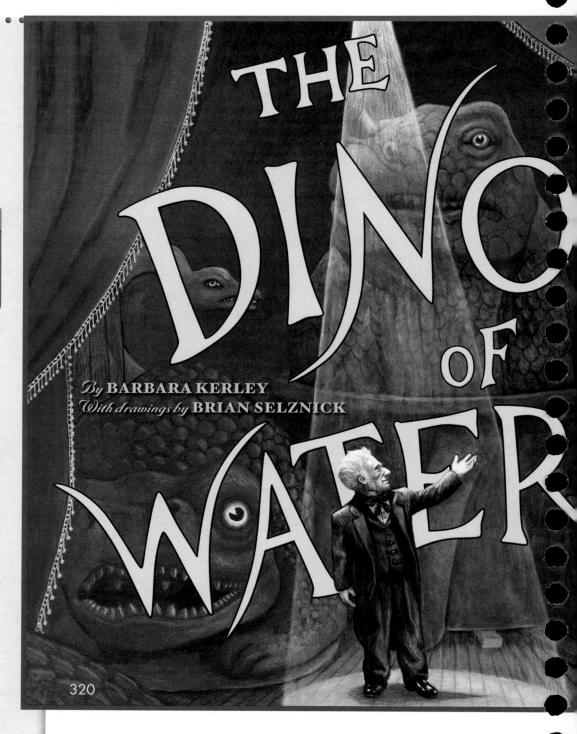

320

Activate Prior Knowledge Ask students if they have ever seen a full-size model of dinosaur bones. Use the pictures to introduce the *iguanodon* (p. 327) and the *megalosaurus* (p. 328).

Consider having students read the selection summary in English or in students' home languages. See the Multilingual Summaries in the ELL Teaching Guide, pp. 89–91.

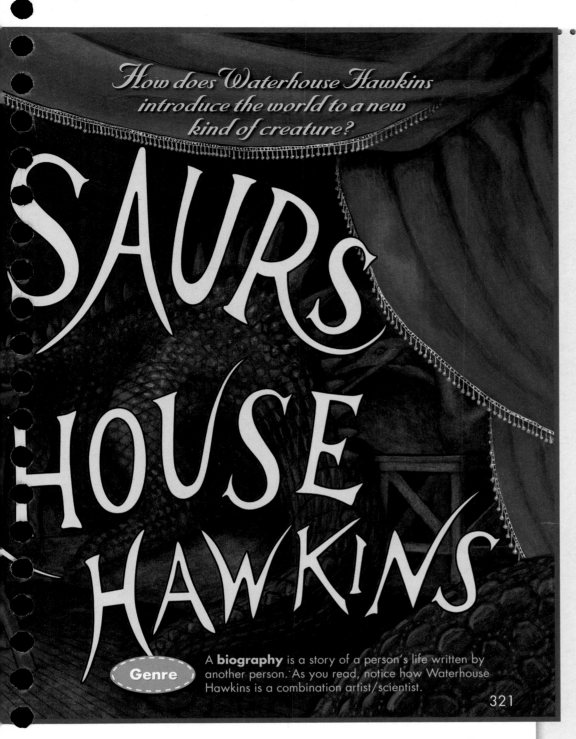

How does Waterhouse Hawkins introduce the world to a new kind of creature?

SAURS HOUSE HAWKINS

Genre

A **biography** is a story of a person's life written by another person. As you read, notice how Waterhouse Hawkins is a combination artist/scientist.

321

SET PURPOSE

Read the first page of the selection aloud to students. Have them consider their preview discussion and tell what they hope to understand as they read the selection.

Remind students to look for statements of fact and opinion as they read.

STRATEGY RECALL

Students have now used these before-reading strategies:

- preview the selection to be aware of its genre, features, and possible content;
- activate prior knowledge about that content and what to expect of that genre;
- make predictions;
- set a purpose for reading.

Remind students to be aware of and flexibly use the during-reading strategies they have learned:

- link prior knowledge to new information;
- summarize text they have read so far;
- ask clarifying questions;
- answer questions they or others pose;
- check their predictions and either refine them or make new predictions;
- recognize the text structure the author is using, and use that knowledge to make predictions and increase comprehension;
- visualize what the author is describing;
- monitor their comprehension and use fix-up strategies.

After reading, students will use these strategies:

- summarize or retell the text;
- answer questions they or others pose;
- reflect to make new information become part of their prior knowledge.

Audio CD **AudioText**

Guiding Comprehension

1  **Fact and Opinion • Inferential**

Is the first sentence on p. 322 a statement of fact or opinion?

The first sentence about horse-drawn carriages in London in 1853 is a fact. I can do research about London in 1853 to prove it.

Monitor Progress

Fact and Opinion

If... students are unable to determine a statement of fact,	then... use the skill and strategy instruction on p. 323.

2 **Characters • Inferential**

Based on what you have read on pp. 322–323, describe Benjamin Waterhouse Hawkins.

Possible responses: hard-working, committed, serious, creative, artistic.

Tech Files
ONLINE

Students can use a student-friendly search engine to learn more about the life of Benjamin Waterhouse Hawkins. Be sure to follow classroom rules for Internet use.

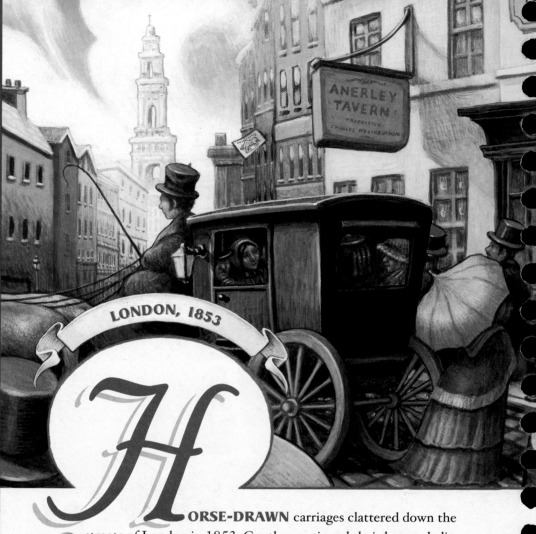

LONDON, 1853

1 **H**ORSE-DRAWN carriages clattered down the streets of London in 1853. Gentlemen tipped their hats to ladies passing by. Children ducked and dodged on their way to school.

But Benjamin Waterhouse Hawkins had no time to be out and about. Waterhouse, as he liked to call himself, hurried toward his workshop in a park south of town. He was expecting some very important visitors. He didn't want to be late.

322

ELL

Extend Language Point to the word *horse-drawn* on p. 322 and tell students that it is a compound word. Ask a volunteer to name the two words that make up the compound and to tell what each of the words means. Challenge students to find another compound word on p. 322. *(Waterhouse, workshop)*

As he neared his workshop, Waterhouse thought of the hours he'd spent outside as a boy. Like many artists, he had grown up sketching the world around him. By the time he was a young man, he'd found his true passion: animals. He loved to draw and paint them. But what he really loved was sculpting models of them. Through his care and hard work, they seemed to come to life.

 2

323

Fact and Opinion

TEACH

- A statement of fact can be proved true or false.

- A statement of opinion is someone's judgment, belief, or way of thinking about something.

Think Aloud **MODEL** The first sentence is about horse-drawn carriages in London in 1853. I can determine if this statement is true or false by doing research. So, I know it is a statement of fact.

PRACTICE AND ASSESS

Have students find a statement of opinion on pp. 322–323. Possible response: *He was expecting some very important visitors.*

EXTEND SKILLS

Illustrator's Craft

Point out that pictures in books do more than illustrate the story. They add information in a visual format. They can also mirror the mood, tone, main idea, setting, and more of a selection. Ask students to explain how the artwork on pp. 322–323 complements the text on the pages.

Guiding Comprehension

3 Main Idea/Details • Inferential

What is the main idea of p. 324? Name one detail.

Main idea: Waterhouse was creating models of dinosaurs although scientists weren't sure what dinosaurs looked like. Detail: Only bits and pieces of fossils had been found.

Monitor Progress

REVIEW Main Idea

If... students have difficulty identifying main idea,	then... use the skill and strategy instruction on p. 325.

4 Draw Conclusions • Inferential

How was Waterhouse helping people "see into the past"?

He used fossils to create models of dinosaurs at a time when no one knew what they looked like. In this way, he helped people see what life on earth may have been like millions of years ago.

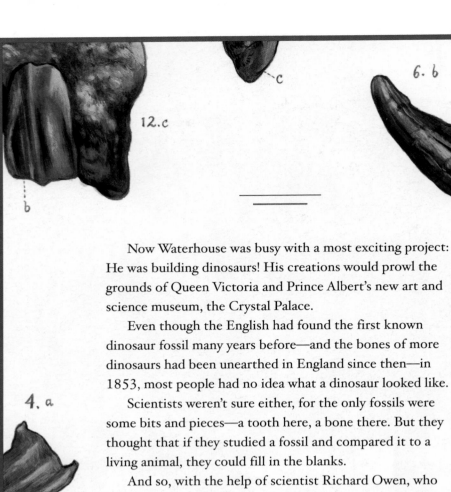

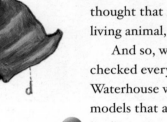

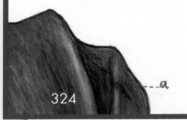

Now Waterhouse was busy with a most exciting project: He was building dinosaurs! His creations would prowl the grounds of Queen Victoria and Prince Albert's new art and science museum, the Crystal Palace.

Even though the English had found the first known dinosaur fossil many years before—and the bones of more dinosaurs had been unearthed in England since then—in 1853, most people had no idea what a dinosaur looked like.

Scientists weren't sure either, for the only fossils were some bits and pieces—a tooth here, a bone there. But they thought that if they studied a fossil and compared it to a living animal, they could fill in the blanks.

And so, with the help of scientist Richard Owen, who checked every muscle, bone, and spike, that's exactly what Waterhouse was doing. He wanted to create such perfect models that anyone—a crowd of curious children, England's leading scientists, even the Queen herself!—could gaze at his dinosaurs and see into the past.

324

ELL

Build Background Explain that fossils are the hardened remains of a plant or animal that lived long ago. Ask students to speculate why scientists didn't know what a dinosaur looked like even though they had found fossils.

325

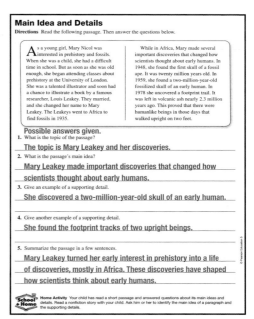

Iguanodon
Iguana

Main Idea REVIEW

TEACH

- A main idea is the most important point about the topic and has at least one supporting detail.

- Supporting details are smaller pieces of information that develop the main idea.

Think Aloud **MODEL** The first three paragraphs tell me that although scientists weren't sure what dinosaurs looked like, Waterhouse was creating models of them. This is the main idea. The third paragraph says scientists had to fill in the blanks from the bits of fossils. This is a detail.

PRACTICE AND ASSESS

- Have students reread p. 324, paragraph 4 to find the main idea. *(Hawkins wanted to create a perfect dinosaur model.)*

- To assess, use Practice Book p. 126.

Main Idea and Details

Directions Read the following passage. Then answer the questions below.

As a young girl, Mary Nicol was interested in prehistory and fossils. When she was a child, she had a difficult time in school. But as soon as she was old enough, she began attending classes about prehistory at the University of London. She was a talented illustrator and soon had a chance to illustrate a book by a famous researcher, Louis Leakey. They married, and she changed her name to Mary Leakey. The Leakeys went to Africa to find fossils in 1935.

While in Africa, Mary made several important discoveries that changed how scientists thought about early humans. In 1948, she found the first skull of a fossil ape. It was twenty million years old. In 1959, she found a two-million-year-old fossilized skull of an early human. In 1978 she uncovered a footprint trail. It was left in volcanic ash nearly 2.3 million years ago. This proved that there were humanlike beings in those days that walked upright on two feet.

Possible answers given.

1. What is the topic of the passage?
   The topic is Mary Leakey and her discoveries.

2. What is the passage's main idea?
   Mary Leakey made important discoveries that changed how scientists thought about early humans.

3. Give an example of a supporting detail.
   She discovered a two-million-year-old skull of an early human.

4. Give another example of a supporting detail.
   She found the footprint tracks of two upright beings.

5. Summarize the passage in a few sentences.
   Mary Leakey turned her early interest in prehistory into a life of discoveries, mostly in Africa. These discoveries have shaped how scientists think about early humans.

School + Home **Home Activity** Your child has read a short passage and answered questions about its main ideas and details. Read a nonfiction story with your child. Ask him or her to identify the main idea of a paragraph and the supporting details.

▲ **Practice Book** p. 126

Dinosaur Extinction

TIME FOR Science

Scientists have different theories to explain why dinosaurs died out over 60 million years ago. Some believe that dinosaurs disappeared slowly over time. Others believe an asteroid or comet crashed into Earth, making life impossible for dinosaurs. Still others believe that dinosaurs became extinct from widespread diseases.

Guiding Comprehension

5 🎯 **Predict • Inferential**

How do you think Queen Victoria and Prince Albert will react to the creatures?

Possible responses: shocked, impressed.

6 **Characters • Literal**

What was Richard Owen's job in creating the creatures?

Richard Owen imagined the shapes of the dinosaurs for Waterhouse.

7 **Prior Knowledge • Critical**

Text to Self **Describe a painting, statue, or museum exhibit you've seen that impressed or surprised you.**

Answers will vary but students should describe a specific experience they have had.

---

5 Waterhouse threw open the doors to his workshop. Nervously, he tidied up here and there. His assistants came, then Richard Owen.

At last, the visitors arrived: Queen Victoria and Prince Albert!

The Queen's eyes grew wide in surprise. Waterhouse's creatures were extraordinary! How on earth had he made them?

He was happy to explain: The iguanodon, for instance, had teeth that were quite similar to the teeth of an iguana. The iguanodon, then, must surely have looked like a giant iguana. Waterhouse pointed out that the few iguanodon bones helped determine the model's size and proportion. And another bone—almost a spike—most likely sat on the nose, like a rhino's horn.

Just so for the megalosaurus. Start with its jawbone. Compare it to the anatomy of a lizard. Fill in the blanks. And voilà! A dinosaur more than forty feet long.

Waterhouse was also making ancient reptiles and

6 amphibians. While Richard Owen could imagine their shapes, it took an artist to bring the animals to life.

7

326

Build Background Tell students that the words *reptiles* and *amphibians* have Spanish cognates (*reptil* and *anfibio*). Both reptiles and amphibians are cold-blooded animals with backbones.

327

STRATEGY SELF-CHECK

Predict

Tell students that predicting means guessing what may happen in a selection before reading it. Predicting also occurs during reading. Explain that predictions can be confirmed, checked, and refined as they read the text.

SELF-CHECK

Students can ask themselves these questions to assess their ability to use the skill and strategy.

- Did I recognize statements of fact and opinion as I read?
- Did this help me make predictions?

Monitor Progress
Fact and Opinion

If... students have difficulty recognizing statements of fact and opinion,	**then...** revisit the skill lesson on pp. 316–317. Reteach as necessary.

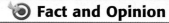

Strategy Response Log

Confirm Predictions Provide the following prompt: Was your prediction accurate? Revise your old prediction. (See p. 320.) Then make a new prediction about the rest of the selection.

Develop Vocabulary

PRACTICE LESSON VOCABULARY

Students orally respond *yes* or *no* to each question and provide a reason.

1. After Waterhouse *tidied* up his workshop, was it cluttered? *(No; it was clean and orderly.)*

...side his *workshop*? *(Yes; his ...work.)*

...*ted* the creatures? *(No; ...use built them.)*

...BULARY

... Ask if students have come ...ewhere that they would ... Concept Web, such as

If you want to teach this selection in two sessions, stop here.

The Dinosaurs of Waterhouse Hawkins   **327**

Guiding Comprehension

If you are teaching the selection in two days, discuss the statements of fact and opinion so far and review the vocabulary.

8 ⟳ **Predict • Inferential**

Before reading the text, look at the illustrations on pp. 328–329 and make a prediction about what this page will cover.

Possible answer: I predict that it will be about the six steps in the process of making a dinosaur.

9 ⟳ **Fact and Opinion • Inferential**

Is the last sentence on p. 328, paragraph 2, a statement of fact or of opinion?

It is a statement of fact because it can be proved by doing research.

Monitor Progress

⟳ Fact and Opinion

If... students have difficulty recognizing fact and opinion,	**then...** use the skill and strategy instruction on p. 329.

DAY 3 Grouping Options

Reading
Whole Group Discuss the Question of the Day.

Group Time Differentiated Instruction
Read *The Dinosaurs of Waterhouse Hawkins.* See pp. 316h–316i for the small group lesson plan.

Whole Group Discuss the Reader Response questions on p. 338. Then use p. 345a.

Language Arts
Use pp. 345e–345k.

Designing the creatures was only the first step. There was still the monumental task of building them.

Waterhouse showed his guests the small models he'd made, correct in every detail, from scales on the nose to nails on the toes. With the help of his assistants, he had formed the life-size clay figures and created the molds from them. Then he erected iron skeletons, built brick foundations, and covered the whole thing with cement casts from the dinosaur-shaped molds.

"It is no less," Waterhouse concluded, "than building a house upon four columns."

ELL

Extend Language Point out the word *scales* on p. 328, paragraph 2. Explain that the word has multiple meanings. Give students four possible definitions: a) a balance used to weigh things, b) a series of musical tones, c) relative size or extent as on a map, and d) thin flat plates that cover the body of fish, snakes, and lizards. Ask which definition fits in the selection. *(Choice d)*

4
Mold

5
Iron Skeleton
(must support tons
of dinosaur)

6
Finished Dinosaur
(bricks, tiles and broken
stones, all held together
with cement, covered with
casts and painted)

Tiles &
Broken
Stones

329

⊙ SKILLS ⟷ STRATEGIES IN CONTEXT

Fact and Opinion
Predict

TEACH

- Tell students that recognizing statements of fact and opinion can help them make predictions.

- Model recognizing a statement of fact in the last sentence of paragraph 2 on p. 328.

 MODEL The second paragraph on this page talks about how Waterhouse built his dinosaur models. The last sentence describes how he did it, step by step. I think this is a statement of fact because if I did research, I could prove that this is how he built his models.

PRACTICE AND ASSESS

- Have students reread p. 328 and predict whether or not Waterhouse will succeed in finishing the dinosaur.

- Ask them to explain their answers.

Guiding Comprehension

10 **Cause and Effect • Inferential**

Waterhouse showed his dinosaurs at a formal New Year's Eve party. What caused him to do that?

He wanted to be accepted by England's leading scientists.

11  **Vocabulary • Context Clues**

Use context clues to determine the meaning of *stage* on p. 330.

Clues: an event; Waterhouse would show them. Meaning: to organize; carry out.

Monitor Progress

 Context Clues

If... students have difficulty using context to determine the meaning of *stage*,	**then**... use the vocabulary strategy instruction on p. 331.

---

12  **Predict • Inferential**

Make a prediction about the party that Waterhouse is planning.

Possible answer: I think the party is going to be a special event and that the scientists are going to be amazed by his creatures. I think the party will be a success.

In the weeks to follow, Waterhouse basked in the glow of the Queen's approval. But he would soon face a much tougher set of critics: England's leading scientists. Waterhouse wanted to be accepted into this circle of eminent men. What would they think of his dinosaurs?

There was only one way to find out. Waterhouse **10** would show them. But why not do it with a little style?

A dinner party. On New Year's Eve, no less. And **11** not just any dinner party. Waterhouse would stage an event that no one would ever forget!

He sketched twenty-one invitations to the top scientists and supporters of the day, the words inscribed on a drawing of a pterodactyl wing. He pored over menus with the caterer.

The iguanodon mold was hauled outside. A platform was built. A tent erected.

As the hour drew near, the table was elegantly set, and names of famous scientists—the fathers of paleontology—were strung above the tent walls. All was ready.

With great anticipation, Waterhouse dressed for **12** the occasion in his finest attire. He was ready to reveal his masterpiece!

330

Access Content Point to the word *eminent*. Tell students that this word has a Spanish cognate *(eminente)*. Explain that *eminent* means famous or outstanding. Ask students why the men mentioned here were eminent.

 VOCABULARY STRATEGY

Context Clues

TEACH

Reread p. 330, paragraphs 1–3. Model using context clues to determine the meaning of *stage*.

Think Aloud **MODEL** In the third paragraph it says "Waterhouse would *stage* an event that no one would ever forget." The sentences that follow describe how Waterhouse plans and prepares for his dinner party. I think in this paragraph, *stage* means "to organize."

PRACTICE AND ASSESS

Have students use context clues to determine the meaning of *attire* in the last paragraph of p. 330. *(formal or fancy clothing)*

Tech Files
ONLINE

Encourage students to use a student-friendly search engine and the keyword *dinosaurs* to find information about different types of dinosaurs. Be sure to follow classroom rules for Internet use.

TIME FOR Science

Fossils

Fossils have provided scientists with a history of life on Earth by preserving organisms in rock. Fossils are the remains or traces of organisms or traces of activities set in stone. Paleontologists, or scientists who study prehistoric plant and animal life, use fossils to determine the period in which a dinosaur lived.

The Dinosaurs of Waterhouse Hawkins   **331**

Guiding Comprehension

13 **Mood • Inferential**

How would you describe the mood of the party? How do you know?

The mood of the party is festive. The words *delight*, *smiled*, and *feast* describe the atmosphere.

14 **Graphic Sources • Critical**

What does the illustration on pp. 326–327 show you that is not stated in the text?

Possible response: The illustration shows you that all of the scientists are sitting inside of the iguanodon.

15 **Fact and Opinion • Inferential**

Is the first sentence on p. 333 a statement of fact or opinion? Why?

It is a statement of fact because it can be proved.

Monitor Progress	
Fact and Opinion	
If... students have difficulty distinguishing a statement of fact from a statement of opinion,	**then...** use the skill and strategy instruction on p. 333.

When the guests arrived, they gasped with delight!
Waterhouse smiled as he signaled for dinner to begin.
With solemn formality, the footmen served course after course from silver platters. Up and down the steps of the platform they carried the lavish feast: rabbit soup, fish, ham, and even pigeon pie. For dessert, there were nuts, **13** pastries, pudding, and plums.

332

ELL

Fluency Help students read aloud the verse of the song, placing emphasis on rhyme and rhythm: The jolly old beast / is not deceased / there's life in him again! Point out that although *beast* and *deceased* are written differently, they rhyme.

For eight hours, the men rang in the New Year. They laughed and shouted. They made speech after speech, toasting Waterhouse Hawkins. All the guests agreed: The iguanodon was a marvelous success. By midnight they were belting out a song created especially for the occasion:

THE JOLLY OLD BEAST IS NOT DECEASED
THERE'S LIFE IN HIM AGAIN!

333

Fact and Opinion

TEACH

- A statement of fact can be true or false.
- An opinion is a statement of someone's belief or way of thinking about something. It cannot be proved true or false but can be supported or explained.
- A colon in a sentence is often used to tell a fact or list of facts. *(Paragraph 2, p. 332)*
- Model distinguishing a statement of fact from a statement of opinion with the first sentence on p. 333.

Think Aloud **MODEL** This statement about the New Year's celebration is a fact because it can be proved true or false by doing research.

PRACTICE AND ASSESS

Have students distinguish statements of fact from opinion with this example from p. 333: "The iguanodon was a marvelous success." *(It is an opinion because it states a belief and cannot be proved true or false.)*

Guiding Comprehension

16 **Main Idea • Inferential**

State the main idea of p. 334, paragraph 1.

Possible response: Waterhouse got his dinosaurs ready for the grand opening of the Crystal Palace.

17 **Cause and Effect • Literal**

What effect did the dinosaur models have on the crowd?

The people gasped, shrieked, laughed, and cried.

The next months passed by in concrete, stone, and iron, as Waterhouse put the finishing touches on his dinosaurs. Inside the iguanodon's lower jaw he signed the work: B. HAWKINS, BUILDER, 1854. The models were now ready for the grand opening of the Crystal Palace at Sydenham Park.

Forty thousand spectators attended the regal ceremony. In the sun-filled center court, Waterhouse mingled with scientists and foreign dignitaries. At last, the Queen arrived! The crowd cheered, "Hurrah!"

334

ELL

Extend Language Point to the words *spectators* and *dignitaries*. Explain that spectators are people who look on at an event, but do not participate and dignitaries are people with a position of honor.

Cannons boomed, music swelled, and a choir of one thousand voices sang. Waterhouse bowed before the Queen. Then she and Prince Albert invited the spectators to enjoy the amazing sights.

Waterhouse hurried to the lake and waited for the crowd to arrive.

First two, then ten, then a dozen more . . . Gasped! Shrieked! Laughed and cried: So this was a dinosaur!

335

Crystal Palace

TIME FOR **Science**

The Crystal Palace was built in 1851 for the Great Exhibition, which was meant to show off the great industrial achievements of Britain. After the Great Exhibition, the Crystal Palace was moved to Penge Place Estate, Sydenham, and rebuilt as a theme park. Part of the park included a dinosaur exhibit with a replication of the environment in which dinosaurs lived.

SKILLS ◆➤ STRATEGIES IN CONTEXT

Main Idea REVIEW

TEACH

- Remind students that the main idea may be implied.
- Tell students they can find an implied main idea by asking questions like: What or who is this about? What is the most important idea about this topic? What are some of the details that tell me more about the topic?

 MODEL In the first paragraph on p. 334, it says Waterhouse put finishing touches on his dinosaurs, signed his work, and the models were ready. I think the main idea is that Waterhouse completed his dinosaurs and got them ready for the Crystal Palace.

PRACTICE AND ASSESS

- Have students find the main idea of p. 335. *(Possible response: The Queen and Prince opened the Crystal Palace and the visitors were amazed by Waterhouse's creatures.)*
- To assess, use Practice Book p. 126.

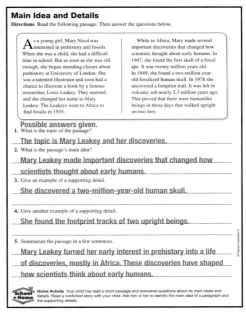

▲ **Practice Book** p. 126

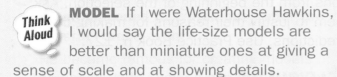

Reader Response

Open for Discussion Personal Response

Think Aloud **MODEL** If I were Waterhouse Hawkins, I would say the life-size models are better than miniature ones at giving a sense of scale and at showing details.

Comprehension Check Critical Response

1. Answers will vary, but be sure that students address both questions. **Author's Purpose**

2. People think the dinosaurs are fantastic. They express this with gasps, toasts, songs, and laughter. **Fact and Opinion**

3. Possible response: Waterhouse's desire to create scientifically accurate models leads readers to predict his success. **Predict**

4. Possible response: Waterhouse wanted to *erect* life-size dinosaur *models* in his *workshop* that would delight the Queen. **Vocabulary**

 Look Back and Write For test practice, assign a 10–15 minute time limit. For assessment, see the Scoring Rubric at the right.

Retell

Have students retell *The Dinosaurs of Waterhouse Hawkins.*

Monitor Progress

Check Retelling Rubric 4 3 2 1

If... students have difficulty retelling the selection,	then... use the Retelling Cards and the Scoring Rubric for Retelling on p. 339 to assist fluent retelling.

SUCCESS PREDICTOR

Check Retelling Suggest that students use the illustrations to guide their retellings of the selection. For more ideas on assessing students' retellings, see the ELL and Transition Handbook.

Reader Response

Open for Discussion Say you are Waterhouse Hawkins. You get a letter saying that miniature model dinosaurs are fine to play with but life-size dinosaur models are expensive and not useful. What would you reply?

1. This biography is about an artist and his art. It does not tell personal information, such as whether Waterhouse had children or liked to swim. Do you wish this information were in the book or are you happy with what's there? What needs to be told in a biography? Think Like an Author

2. Look back at pages 332–335. What are people's opinions of the dinosaurs? Discuss the different ways the people express their opinions. Fact and Opinion

3. Look back at page 324. What would lead readers to predict that Waterhouse Hawkins would one day amaze the people of Victorian England? Predict

4. Describe Waterhouse's plan for impressing England's leading scientists. Use words from the Words to Know list and other words from the selection. Vocabulary

 Look Back and Write Look back at pages 328–329 for Waterhouse's six steps for building a dinosaur model. List them. Then write two questions you would need to ask to get more information before building your own model.

Meet author **Barbara Kerley on page 762** and illustrator **Brian Selznick on page 775.**

Scoring Rubric **Look Back and Write**

Top-Score Response A top-score response will use details from pp. 328–329 of the selection to list the steps Waterhouse used to build his model and will use this information to formulate questions an actual builder would have to answer.

Example of a Top-Score Response
1. Make a drawing.
2. Make a small clay model.
3. Create a life-sized clay model.
4. Create a mold.
5. Build an iron skeleton for support.
6. Using the mold, cast a cement model on the skeleton.
How big was the actual dinosaur? How much cement will I need?

For additional rubrics, see p. WA10.

Write Now

Feature Story

Prompt

The Dinosaurs of Waterhouse Hawkins tells about the introduction of dinosaur models to the world.

Think about the introduction of something new in your school or community.

Now write a feature story about the event.

Writing Trait

Logical **organization** of details in **paragraphs** makes a feature story clear and engaging.

Student Model

Vivid description at beginning gets readers' attention.

Last Monday the Pleasanton Public Library was bursting with patrons choosing books and using computers. Twenty preschoolers attended a story time. This scene may seem ordinary, but it was an exciting event in Pleasanton.

Organization holds readers' interest: sets scene in first paragraph; gives facts in second paragraph.

Pleasanton long ago outgrew its old library. After years of fundraising, construction on a new library began last spring. Hundreds of people came to the grand opening last week. They admired the cheerful children's room and the cozy reading nooks.

Head librarian Ann Myer showed off the library's new artwork. "We're thrilled," she said.

Direct quotation in conclusion adds interest and sums up main idea.

"The people of Pleasanton finally have a public library to be proud of."

Use the model to help you write your own feature story.

339

Write Now

Look at the Prompt Have students identify and discuss key words and phrases in the prompt. *(introduction of something new, school or community, feature story)*

Strategies to Develop Organization/ Paragraphs

Have students

- read two feature stories and discuss their organization.
- organize details in different ways, such as spatial order or order of importance.
- begin the first paragraph with vivid images.

The rousing sounds of our school chorus echoed in a brand new auditorium today.

For additional suggestions and rubric, see pp. 345g–345h.

Hints for Better Writing

- Carefully read the prompt.
- Use a graphic organizer to plan your writing.
- Support your ideas with information and details.
- Use words that help readers understand.
- Proofread and edit your work.

Scoring Rubric — Expository Retelling

Rubric 4 3 2 1	4	3	2	1
Connections	Makes connections and generalizes beyond the text	Makes connections to other events, texts, or experiences	Makes a limited connection to another event, text, or experience	Makes no connection to another event, text, or experience
Author's Purpose	Elaborates on author's purpose	Tells author's purpose with some clarity	Makes some connection to author's purpose	Makes no connection to author's purpose
Topic	Describes the main topic	Identifies the main topic with some details early in retelling	Identifies the main topic	Retelling has no sense of topic
Important Ideas	Gives accurate information about events, steps, and ideas using details and key vocabulary	Gives accurate information about events, steps, and ideas with some detail and key vocabulary	Gives limited or inaccurate information about events, steps, and ideas	Gives no information about events, steps, and ideas
Conclusions	Draws conclusions and makes inferences to generalize beyond the text	Draws conclusions about the text	Is able to draw few conclusions about the text	Is unable to draw conclusions or make inferences about the text

Retelling Plan

- ☑ **Week 1** Assess Strategic Intervention students.
- ☑ **Week 2** Assess Advanced students.
- ☑ **This week assess Strategic Intervention students.**
- ☐ **Week 4** Assess On-Level students.
- ☐ **Week 5** Assess any students you have not yet checked during this unit.

Use the Retelling Chart on p. TR17 to record retelling.

Retelling

Selection Test To assess with *The Dinosaurs of Waterhouse Hawkins*, use Selection Tests, pp. 49–52.

Fresh Reads for Differentiated Test Practice For weekly leveled practice, use pp. 73–78.

SUCCESS PREDICTOR

Science in Reading

DAY 4 Grouping Options

OBJECTIVES

- Examine features of interviews.
- Practice a test-taking strategy.
- Compare and contrast across texts.

PREVIEW/USE TEXT FEATURES

As students preview "A Model Scientist," have them look at the introduction and questions. After they preview ask:

- **Why do you think an introduction was included?** *(Possible response: to provide some background information about the person being interviewed)*

- **Who is asking the questions?** *(someone from Owl Magazine)*

Link to Science

Students can do this activity with partners or in small groups, sharing their findings in a class discussion.

DAY 4 Grouping Options

Reading
Whole Group Discuss the Question of the Day.

Group Time Differentiated Instruction
Read "A Model Scientist." See pp. 316h–316i for the small group lesson plan.

Whole Group Use p. 345a.

Language Arts
Use pp. 345e–345k.

Science in Reading

Interview

Genre

- In an interview, the interviewer asks questions and the subject answers them.

- Interviews are often found in magazines and newspapers.

Text Features

- The interview first introduces the subject, or the person being interviewed.

- An interview gives the actual words spoken by the subject and interviewer.

- Preview the questions in bold type. What do they tell you about the interview?

Link to Science

Research how scientists use other kinds of models in their work, such as computer models. Explain to a classmate what you have learned.

340

A Model SCIENTIST

FROM OWL MAGAZINE

Meet Garfield Minott. He's been making dinosaur models since he was seven years old. Back then, he made dinosaurs just for fun. Today, his passion for the prehistoric has turned into a cool and unusual dinosaur job.

Content-Area Vocabulary — Science

paleo-artist	an artist who deals with ancient forms or conditions
prehistoric	belonging to times before histories were written
scales	thin, flat, hard plates forming the outer covering of some living things

ELL

Access Content Preview the text, reading the questions aloud and asking students to predict the answers to some of them.

- Point out the words *real-life models* and *rough drawing* (p. 341) and help students determine their meanings.

- After reading, ask students to check and correct their predictions.

Q: OWL: What exactly do you do?

A: Garfield: I'm a paleo-artist. I bring dinosaurs back to life!

Q: How do you do that?

A: I build real-life models of the dinosaurs scientists discover. My models help dinosaur scientists to gain a better understanding of these incredible creatures. I get bags of bones shipped to me from scientists, and I use these bones to plan my models. When it comes to learning about dino bones, nothing beats the real thing!

Q: What can you tell from a simple bone?

A: Lots of stuff! If you took all the muscles off of a bone, you'd be left with marks on the bone called "scarring." These marks tell me how the muscles were attached. Then, I can tell how the skin formed around the muscles. As I build up, layer after layer from the inside out, I can bring an animal back to life!

Q: How do you make your models?

A: Once I've researched in books and bones, I make a rough drawing. Then, I make a skeleton of the body out of welded steel. Next, I start layering on the muscles, which are made out of clay. When that's done, I start on the skin. If the dinosaur had scales, then I make the scales and layer them on one at a time. This could take three to five weeks. I want my dinosaur models to look as close as possible to the real thing.

Predict What will this be about? How quickly will you read it?

341

INTERVIEW

Use the sidebar on p. 340 to guide discussion.

- Explain to students that an interview is a written record of a conversation between two people.

- Tell students that an interview provides the actual words of the interviewer and the person being interviewed.

- Discuss with students why it is important to use the actual spoken words in a written interview.

 **AudioText**

Predict

Possible response: This will be about someone who builds dinosaur models. I will read it quickly because the question-and-answer format helps me understand the information.

Strategies for Nonfiction

USE QUESTIONS Explain to students that an interviewer's questions let a reader know what information he or she will be reading. Students can use the questions to help answer test questions. Provide the following strategy.

Use the Strategy

1. Read the test question and locate a key word or phrase.
2. Scan the questions in the interview, looking for matches to your key word or phrase.
3. When you find a match, read the information to find an answer to the test question.

GUIDED PRACTICE Have students discuss how they would use the strategy to answer the following question.

How is a dinosaur model created?

INDEPENDENT PRACTICE After students answer the following test question, discuss the process they used to find information.

What would happen to humans if dinosaurs still roamed the Earth today?

Q: When did you become interested in models?
A: I've been making models ever since I was a kid growing up in Jamaica. My mom used to bake a lot and whenever she did, she would teach me how to mold things out of flour. In those days, I was crazy about lizards so that's mostly the kind of models I made.

Q: When did you get hooked on dinosaurs?
A: When I was seven years old my family moved to Canada. Because I was in a new country, I became a pretty shy kid. One day my teacher asked me what kind of animals I liked. Of course I said, "Lizards." She said, "Well, if you like lizards you must like dinosaurs." I had no idea what a dinosaur was. She took me to the library, pulled a book off the shelf, and showed me my first dinosaur. I went totally bananas!

342

ELL

Test Practice Write the Independent Practice test question on the board. Have students suggest a word they might use as a key word. Work with students to follow the strategy steps with each suggested key word. For key words that fail to help answer the question, point out why the chosen word did not work.

30'   36'   42'   48'

Q: And you've been crazy about dinos ever since?

A: Yes! And I especially loved hearing all those long
and crazy dinosaur names. *Tyrannosaurus rex* is my
favorite. That name still makes me flip out!

Q: Did you ever imagine a career with dinosaurs?

A: When I was a kid, I had a kit that came with tiny
models of dinosaurs. I used these models to play
"dinosaurs" with friends. But, after a while I learned
about more kinds of dinosaurs than I had in my kit—so
I made the ones I didn't have out of Plasticine™. And, if
my *T. rex* got hungry and ate a whole herd of models, I
had to make new dinosaurs very quickly! I did this so
often that I became good at building models in no time
at all. That's how I became a model expert.

 Predict Did you predict accurately? Should you change your rate?

343

 **Predict**

Possible response: I did correctly predict what
the selection is about. However, the interview is
harder to follow than I predicted. I need to slow
down.

Extend Language Reread aloud the expressions "I
went totally bananas!" (p. 342) and ". . . makes me flip
out" (p. 343). Explain that the artist uses these expressions to show great enthusiasm. Encourage students
to name other expressions that they use to show their
enthusiasm.

The Dinosaurs of Waterhouse Hawkins **343**

USE TEXT FEATURES

Discuss with students how the interview questions shape the interview content. Use the following questions.

- **How does Minott know what to talk about in the interview?** *(Owl Magazine's questions tell Minott what subjects to address.)*
- **Why is it important to ask good questions in an interview?** *(Possible response: So that readers learn important information.)*

Q: How did model building become your job?

A: I found out about a paleo-artist who worked at the Royal Ontario Museum in Toronto. One day I went to meet him. He saw that I was interested in dinosaurs and a good model builder, so he suggested that I volunteer at the museum. I did, and I've been building models ever since.

Q: Do you wish dinosaurs still roamed Earth?

A: If they did, humans wouldn't be here. We'd be eaten! I'd like to see a live dinosaur on an island somewhere, and just observe it.

344

Q: What's the coolest fact you've learned about dinosaurs?

A: Dinosaurs never stopped growing the way humans do. Some were as long as a football field! That's unbelievable. To me, dinosaurs are amazing. Right now I'm working on a model of an Afro Titan. It's the biggest one I've ever made. I could lay down inside its head! If this dinosaur were alive, it could eat me whole in one bite.

Reading Across Texts

Both Waterhouse Hawkins and Garfield Minott enjoy what they do. Make notes on places in each selection that show this statement to be true.

Writing Across Texts Present your results in two paragraphs, one for each selection.

○ **Fact & Opinion**   On what facts does Garfield Minott base his opinions?

345

Paleontology

TIME FOR Science

The Royal Ontario Museum (ROM), where Minott volunteered, contains more than five million objects related to Earth's natural and cultural history. The museum has a number of research departments, including the Department of Paleobiology. This department researches, collects, and displays the remains of prehistoric animals and plants from all over the world. Members of the department share their research findings by giving public talks, creating museum exhibits, and publishing books about the history of life on Earth.

CONNECT TEXT TO TEXT
Reading Across Texts

Brainstorm with students a list of things a person might say or do that would lead them to believe the person enjoys his or her occupation or hobby. Then have students reread the selections, looking for details to support the statement that Hawkins and Minott enjoy what they do. Suggest they record the page numbers on which they find the details.

Writing Across Texts To give unity to their writing, students can write a similar topic sentence for each paragraph.

○ **Fact and Opinion**

Minott bases his opinions on dinosaur bones and scientific research.

Fluency Assessment Plan

- ☑ **Week 1** Assess Advanced students.
- ☑ **Week 2** Assess Strategic Intervention students.
- ☑ **This week assess On-Level students.**
- ☐ **Week 4** Assess Strategic Intervention students.
- ☐ **Week 5** Assess any students you have not yet checked during this unit.

Set individual goals for students to enable them to reach the year-end goal.

- Current Goal: 115–122 wcpm
- Year-End Goal: 140 wcpm

English language learners may be able to decode some English words but still not know the meanings. Help students recognize that they will understand sentences better and read more fluently as they learn more English words.

To develop fluent readers, use Fluency Coach.

DAY 5 Grouping Options

Reading
Whole Group
Revisit the Question of the Week.

Group Time
Differentiated Instruction
Reread this week's Leveled Readers. See pp. 316h–316i for the small group lesson plan.

Whole Group
Use pp. 345b–345c.

Language Arts
Use pp. 345d–345l.

PHRASING

Fluency

DAY 1

Model Reread "Graveyards of the Dinosaurs" on p. 316m. Explain that you will group words together to reflect the intended meaning of the text. Model for students as you read.

DAY 2

Echo Reading Read aloud the last three paragraphs on p. 326. Have students notice how you use punctuation—commas, colons, and dashes—as clues for appropriate phrasing. Have students practice as a class doing three echo readings of these paragraphs.

DAY 3

Model Read aloud pp. 332–333. Have students notice how reading with appropriate phrasing helps them better understand the meaning of the text. Practice as a class by doing three echo readings.

DAY 4

Partner Reading Partners practice reading pp. 332–333, three times. Students should read with appropriate phrasing, using punctuation as a guide, and offer each other feedback.

Monitor Progress | Check Fluency WCPM

As students reread, monitor their progress toward their individual fluency goals. Current Goal: 115–122 words correct per minute. End-of-Year Goal: 140 words correct per minute.

If... students cannot read fluently at a rate of 115–122 words correct per minute,
then... make sure students practice with text at their independent level. Provide additional fluency practice, pairing nonfluent readers with fluent readers.

If... students already read at 140 words correct per minute,
then... they do not need to reread three to four times.

SUCCESS PREDICTOR

DAY 5

Assessment
Individual Reading Rate Use the Fluency Assessment Plan and do a one-minute timed reading of either selection from this week to assess students in Week 3. Pay special attention to this week's skill, phrasing. Provide corrective feedback for each student.

Fact and Opinion

TEACH

Review the definitions of *fact* and *opinion* on p. 316. Students can complete Practice Book p. 128 on their own, or you can complete it as a class. Point out that they must answer questions 1–3 in order to complete the graphic organizer.

ASSESS

Have students reread the afterword on p. 337. Have them tell if it is a statement of fact or opinion and give reasons for their answer. *(Possible response: Fact because whether or not Waterhouse created the first model of a dinosaur can be proved true or false by checking a reference source.)*

For additional instruction on fact and opinion, see DI·54.

EXTEND SKILLS

Steps in a Process

TEACH

Steps in a Process means recognizing and being able to retell the order of steps required to accomplish something.

- Steps in a Process is a type of sequence in which something happens or something is made in a predictable way.
- Steps in a Process usually involves people doing or making something.

Review pp. 328–329 with students and discuss the number of steps involved in the process of building models of life-size dinosaur skeletons. *(six)* Then, have students retell the steps in their own words. (Drawing; small model; clay life-sized model; mold; iron skeleton; finished dinosaur display)

ASSESS

Have students work with partners to write the steps in the process of conducting an interview, like the one they read about in "A Model Scientist."

OBJECTIVES

- Recognize statements of fact and opinion.
- Identify and retell the order of steps taken to complete an action.

Skills Trace
Fact and Opinion

Introduce/Teach	TE: 5.2 208–209; 5.3 316–317; 5.6 700–701
Practice	Practice Book: 83, 87, 88, 116, 123, 127, 128, 136, 283, 287, 288
Reteach/Review	**TE: 5.2 229b, DI•55; 5.3 301, 345b, 355, DI•54; 5.6 725b, DI•55**
Test	Selection Test: 33–36, 49–52, 113–116; Benchmark Test: Unit 3

E L L

Access Content Reteach the skill by reviewing the Picture It! lesson on fact and opinion in the ELL Teaching Guide, pp. 85–86.

▲ **Practice Book** p. 128

Grammar Principal Parts of Irregular Verbs

OBJECTIVES

- Define and identify principal parts of irregular verbs.
- Use principal parts of irregular verbs in writing.
- Become familiar with principal parts of irregular verbs on high-stakes tests.

Monitor Progress

Grammar

If... students have difficulty identifying principal parts of irregular verbs,	then... provide additional instruction and practice in The Grammar and Writing Book pp. 122–125.

DAILY FIX-IT

This week use Daily Fix-It Transparency 13.

Spiral REVIEW

Support Grammar See the Grammar Transition lessons in the ELL and Transition Handbook.

▲ **The Grammar and Writing Book**
For more instruction and practice, use pp. 122–125.

DAY 1 Teach and Model

DAILY FIX-IT

1. Have you saw the dinosaur exhibit. *(seen; exhibit?)*

2. It's displays include every dinosaur I ever knowed about. *(Its; knew)*

READING-GRAMMAR CONNECTION

Write this sentence from *The Dinosaurs of Waterhouse Hawkins* on the board:

Waterhouse threw open the doors to his workshop.

Explain that the verb *throw* is irregular. It does not use *-ed* to form its past and past participle forms. It has a different spelling for each form: *throw, threw, (have) thrown.*

Display Grammar Transparency 13. Read aloud the definitions and sample sentences. Work through the items.

Principal Parts of Irregular Verbs

Usually you add *-ed* to a verb to show past tense. **Irregular verbs** do not follow this rule. Instead of having *-ed* forms to show past tense, irregular verbs usually change to other words.

Present Tense	We see a model dinosaur.
Present Participle	We are seeing a model dinosaur.
Past Tense	We saw a model dinosaur.
Past Participle	We have seen a model dinosaur.

Present Tense	Present Participle	Past Tense	Past Participle
become	(am, is, are) becoming	became	(has, have, had) become
begin	(am, is, are) beginning	began	(has, have, had) begun
buy	(am, is, are) buying	bought	(has, have, had) bought
do	(am, is, are) doing	did	(has, have, had) done
freeze	(am, is, are) freezing	froze	(has, have, had) frozen
go	(am, is, are) going	went	(has, have, had) gone
am/is/are	(am, is, are) being	was/were	(has, have, had) been
know	(am, is, are) knowing	knew	(has, have, had) known
make	(am, is, are) making	made	(has, have, had) made
see	(am, is, are) seeing	saw	(has, have, had) seen
think	(am, is, are) thinking	thought	(has, have, had) thought
write	(am, is, are) writing	wrote	(has, have, had) written

Directions Write *present, present participle, past,* or *past participle* to identify the principal part of the underlined verb.

1. We <u>are seeing</u> enormous models of *T. rex.* **present participle**
2. <u>Have</u> you <u>thought</u> much about these fierce animals? **past participle**
3. The models <u>freeze</u> them in time and space. **present**
4. Suddenly, the models <u>began</u> moving! **past**
5. My cousins <u>buy</u> a small model. **present**
6. They <u>have become</u> dinosaur fans. **past participle**

Directions Write the sentence using the principal part of the underlined verb indicated in ( ).

7. Dinosaurs <u>are</u> popular with children for years. (past participle)
   Dinosaurs have been popular with children for years.
8. Many children <u>make</u> dinosaur models. (past participle)
   Many children have made dinosaur models.

Unit 3 The Dinosaurs of Waterhouse Hawkins   Grammar **13**

▲ **Grammar Transparency** 13

DAY 2 Develop the Concept

DAILY FIX-IT

3. The sientist speaked about dinosaur bones and fossils. *(scientist spoke)*

4. Them bones are bigger than any I have seed. *(Those; seen)*

GUIDED PRACTICE

Review the concept of principal parts of irregular verbs.

- Some principal parts of a verb are the present, past, and past participle.

- An **irregular verb** does not add *-ed* to form the past tense.

- Most irregular verbs have different spellings for the past and the past participle.

HOMEWORK Grammar and Writing Practice Book p. 49. Work through the first two items with the class.

Principal Parts of Irregular Verbs

Usually you add *-ed* to a verb to show past tense. **Irregular verbs** do not follow this rule. Instead of having *-ed* forms to show past tense, irregular verbs usually change to other words.

Present Tense	The king sees the Crystal Palace.
Present Participle	The king is seeing the Crystal Palace.
Past Tense	The king saw the Crystal Palace.
Past Participle	The king has seen the Crystal Palace.

Present Tense	Present Participle	Past Tense	Past Participle
bring	(am, is, are) bringing	brought	(has, have, had) brought
build	(am, is, are) building	built	(has, have, had) built
choose	(am, is, are) choosing	chose	(has, have, had) chosen
come	(am, is, are) coming	came	(has, have, had) come
draw	(am, is, are) drawing	drew	(has, have, had) drawn
eat	(am, is, are) eating	ate	(has, have, had) eaten
find	(am, is, are) finding	found	(has, have, had) found
grow	(am, is, are) growing	grew	(has, have, had) grown
run	(am, is, are) running	ran	(has, have, had) run
set	(am, is, are) setting	set	(has, have, had) set
speak	(am, is, are) speaking	spoke	(has, have, had) spoken
tell	(am, is, are) telling	told	(has, have, had) told

Directions Underline the verb in each sentence. Write *present, present participle, past,* or *past participle* to identify the principal part of the verb.

1. He <u>built</u> a studio in Manhattan. ____ **past**
2. Hawkins <u>had chosen</u> Central Park for his display. ____ **past participle**

Directions Write the sentence using the principal part of the underlined verb indicated in ( ).

3. Archaeologists <u>find</u> many more dinosaur bones. (past participle) **Archaeologists have found many more dinosaur bones.**

4. Today dinosaur exhibits <u>draw</u> huge crowds. (present participle) **Today dinosaur exhibits are drawing huge crowds.**

 **Home Activity** Your child learned about principal parts of irregular verbs. Ask your child to write the principal parts of *tell* and *write* and then use each part in a sentence telling what he or she could communicate about dinosaurs.

▲ **Grammar and Writing Practice Book** p. 49

DAY 3 · Apply to Writing

DAILY FIX-IT

5. How does the sculptor make a muscel on a jigantic model? *(muscle; gigantic)*

6. The artist had drawn a sene of dinosaurs, and prehistoric plants. *(scene; dinosaurs and)*

PARTICIPLES AND PAST TIME

Point out to students that past forms of irregular verbs are not used with a helping verb, but past participle forms are.

No: He has went. It has broke.

Yes: He has gone. It has broken.

Yes: He went. It broke.

- Have students review something they have written to see if they can improve it by correcting errors in use of past and past participle forms.

HOMEWORK Grammar and Writing Practice Book p. 50.

Principal Parts of Irregular Verbs

Directions Write a complete sentence using the past participle form of the verb in ( ) with *has* or *have.*

1. Mr. Hancock (run) the museum for five years.
   Mr. Hancock has run the museum for five years.

2. He (choose) May as membership drive month .
   He has chosen May as membership drive month.

3. He (speak) to many organizations.
   He has spoken to many organizations.

4. The membership list (grow) quite large.
   The membership list has grown quite large.

5. Mr. Hancock (do) it!
   Mr. Hancock has done it!

6. The new dinosaur education wing (draw) new members. **The new dinosaur education wing has drawn new members.**

Directions Write a paragraph about dinosaurs. Include some past and past participle forms of such irregular verbs as *be, find, come, know,* and *think.*
Possible answer: I have been crazy about dinosaurs for a long time. I have always thought they were awesome. For example, I found out out *T. rex* had huge, sharp teeth. If it came after you, you would have known it!

Home Activity Your child learned how to write principal parts of irregular verbs correctly. Ask your child to write about a favorite prehistoric animal. Encourage him or her to use forms of *become, is, see, think, go,* and *eat* when writing.

▲ **Grammar and Writing Practice Book** p. 50

DAY 4 · Test Preparation

DAILY FIX-IT

7. Scientists have wrote many books on dinosaurs! *(have written; dinosaurs.)*

8. They have telled how new discoverys were made. *(told; discoveries)*

STANDARDIZED TEST PREP

Test Tip

Irregular verbs do not add *-ed* to form the past tense. Some irregular verbs have the same spelling in the past tense and the past participle tense.

No: He telled her the truth.

Yes: He told her the truth.

Yes: He has told her the truth.

HOMEWORK Grammar and Writing Practice Book p. 51.

Principal Parts of Irregular Verbs

Directions Mark the letter of the item that correctly identifies the form of the underlined word or words in each sentence.

1. A sculptor is building a clay figure.
   A past
   B present
   C past participle
   D present participle

2. She makes a mold of the clay shape.
   A past
   B present
   C past participle
   D present participle

3. She chooses a metal for the mold.
   A past
   B present
   C past participle
   D present participle

4. Many sculptures have begun this way.
   A past
   B present
   C past participle
   D present participle

5. The critics have spoken.
   A past
   B present
   C past participle
   D present participle

6. I saw a wonderful statue.
   A past
   B present
   C past participle
   D present participle

7. He has bought several works by that sculptor.
   A past
   B present
   C past participle
   D present participle

8. I have chosen the artwork I want to buy.
   A past
   B present
   C past participle
   D present participle

9. Set the painting here.
   A past
   B present
   C past participle
   D present participle

10. Who is bringing picture hangers?
    A past
    B present
    C past participle
    D present participle

Home Activity Your child prepared for taking tests on principal parts of irregular verbs. Ask your child to name the principal parts of the verbs choose and find and then use each part in a sentence.

▲ **Grammar and Writing Practice Book** p. 51

DAY 5 · Cumulative Review

DAILY FIX-IT

9. Hawkins became famus for his dinosaur modles. *(famous; models)*

10. He brought dinosaurs to the public and people was fascinated. *(public,; were)*

ADDITIONAL PRACTICE

Assign pp. 122–125 in The Grammar and Writing Book.

EXTRA PRACTICE Grammar and Writing Practice Book p. 134.

ASSESSMENT

CUMULATIVE REVIEW Grammar and Writing Practice Book p. 52.

Principal Parts of Irregular Verbs

Directions Write *present, present participle, past,* or *past participle* to identify the underlined verb form.

1. The diners eat for eight hours. — **present**
2. Each diner has told at least one story. — **past participle**
3. Hawkins chose the iguanodon model. — **past**
4. He had set a dining table inside it. — **past participle**
5. His guests become excited. — **present**
6. Hawkins thought they would be. — **past**
7. The guests told about this event for years. — **past**
8. The dinosaur fad had begun. — **past participle**
9. Today we find Hawkins's models odd. — **present**
10. We are making more discoveries about dinosaurs. — **present participle**

Directions Write the sentence using the principal part of the underlined verb indicated in ( ).

11. We know a great deal about the past. (present)
    We know a great deal about the past.

12. In 1850, scientists know much less. (past)
    In 1850, scientists knew much less.

13. They find some fossils of dinosaur bones. (past participle)
    They had found some fossils of dinosaur bones.

14. Sometimes animals freeze in glaciers. (present)
    Sometimes animals freeze in glaciers.

15. Explorers find the remains of these animals. (present participle) **Explorers are finding the remains of these animals.**

16. A little of Earth's history freeze with them. (past participle)
    A little of Earth's history has frozen with them.

Home Activity Your child reviewed principal parts of irregular verbs. Have your child identify examples of the use of present, present participle, past, and past participle forms in a cookbook or history book.

▲ **Grammar and Writing Practice Book** p. 52

Writing Workshop Feature Story

OBJECTIVES

- Identify characteristics of a well-written feature story.
- Show understanding of paragraph structure.
- Focus on organization/paragraphs.
- Use a rubric.

Genre Feature Story
Writer's Craft Paragraph Structure
Writing Trait Organization/Paragraphs

ELL

Organization/Paragraphs Explain that transition words make order clear in writing. Write *in conclusion, however, and, so, before, consequently,* and *last* on index cards, one to a card, and model their meaning and use. Help language learners use these transition words in their writing. Display cards for reference.

Writing Traits

FOCUS/IDEAS The story focuses on one event. All details support the author's view of that event.

ORGANIZATION/PARAGRAPHS The lead draws in readers. Ideas are logically organized in unified paragraphs.

VOICE The writing entertains as it informs. The writer is engaged with the subject.

WORD CHOICE Supporting details are concrete and specific (*30-foot-long iguanodon, life-size models*).

SENTENCES Sentences vary in length and structure.

CONVENTIONS There is excellent control and accuracy. Principal parts of irregular verbs are used correctly.

DAY 1 Model the Trait

READING-WRITING CONNECTION

- *The Dinosaurs of Waterhouse Hawkins* explains how a sculptor made the first dinosaur models.
- The story uses time order words and well-crafted paragraphs.
- Students will write a **feature story** with logical organization and unified paragraphs.

MODEL ORGANIZATION/PARAGRAPHS

Discuss Writing Transparency 13A. Then discuss the model and the writing trait of organization/paragraphs.

Think Aloud The writer organized each sentence in each paragraph in a logical order. Paragraph two begins with the main idea: Hawkins is famous for his dinosaur models. The next sentence tells how Hawkins made the models. The final sentence in the paragraph tells how realistic the models were. Details are arranged to make sense, and no irrelevant details are present.

Feature Story

A **feature story** in a newspaper tells about an interesting event or person. Its purpose is to inform and entertain. A feature story needs a catchy lead. Its paragraphs should be logically developed and include lively details.

Dinosaurs Disappear—Again

Lead grabs attention with a surprising detail.
> A sculptor's dream of a museum filled with dinosaurs was broken last night—literally! Life-size models of dinosaurs by British sculptor Waterhouse Hawkins were bashed to pieces just as they were about to be placed in the Paleozoic Museum in Manhattan's Central Park.

Paragraph tells about Hawkins's unusual work.
> Hawkins, who came to the United States in 1868, is famous for his giant models of "terrible lizards." Working from bones of the extinct beasts, Hawkins had constructed life-size statues of dinosaurs such as the 30-foot-long iguanodon. The models were said to be frighteningly realistic.

The public was eagerly awaiting the unveiling at the opening of a special museum in New York's new showplace, Central Park. That hope was destroyed when unknown vandals broke into Hawkins's studio last night.

Quote by sculptor adds interest and captures mood of outrage.
> The enraged sculptor said, "This is awful! These creations cannot be replaced. How could anyone destroy them?"

Final sentence concludes story and gives reader something to think about.
Even the pieces of the statues are missing.
> Like the dinosaurs they represented, the statues have disappeared from the face of the Earth.

Unit 3 The Dinosaurs of Waterhouse Hawkins   Writing Model **13A**

▲ **Writing Transparency** 13A

DAY 2 Improve Writing

WRITER'S CRAFT
What Makes a Paragraph?

Display Writing Transparency 13B. Work together to identify a topic sentence and order support logically.

Think Aloud **DECIDE ORDER OF DETAILS** Tomorrow we will write a **feature story.** I could write about the new historic mural downtown. How should I order details? I might first describe the mural's theme and purpose. Then I could describe what it looks like generally. Finally, I might describe each part from left to right in detail. This arrangement would help readers picture the mural.

GUIDED WRITING Some students may need more help with understanding what makes a paragraph. Have them reread the paragraphs on pp. 330 and 331, identify the topic sentences, and tell how other sentences support them.

What Makes a Paragraph

A **paragraph** is organized around one main idea. A topic sentence usually expresses that main idea. Other sentences give supporting details to develop the main idea. Sentences in a paragraph should be arranged in a logical order. Use connecting words, such as *for example, then,* and *however,* to show how the sentences are related to each other.

Directions Read the sentences. Label the topic sentence *TS.* Number the rest of the sentences *1, 2,* and so on, to show how they should be placed in a paragraph.

_1_ A small, exact model of the dinosaur is created in clay.
_3_ She creates a hard mold around the clay dinosaur shape.
_5_ The concrete dinosaur is held in place by a metal skeleton and stone foundation.
_2_ The sculptor uses the small model as a guide to make a life-size clay model.
_TS_ Building a life-size model of a dinosaur is a monumental task.
_4_ This hollow mold is used to create a concrete casting of the dinosaur.

Directions Write a paragraph using the sentences from the first exercise. Add connecting words, such as *first, then, next,* and so on, to the detail sentences to make them fit together smoothly. End the paragraph with a concluding sentence. **Possible answers:**

Building a life-size model of a dinosaur is a monumental task. First, a small, exact model of the dinosaur is created in clay. Then the sculptor uses the small model as a guide to make a life-size clay model. Next, she creates a hard mold around the clay dinosaur shape. Finally, this hollow mold is used to create a concrete casting of the dinosaur. Under it all, the concrete dinosaur is held in place by a metal skeleton and stone foundation. The finished model is huge yet correct in every detail.

Unit 3 The Dinosaurs of Waterhouse Hawkins   Writer's Craft **13B**

▲ **Writing Transparency** 13B

DAY 3 — Prewrite and Draft

READ THE WRITING PROMPT
on page 339 in the Student Edition.

The Dinosaurs of Waterhouse Hawkins *tells about the introduction of dinosaur models to the world.*

Think about the introduction of something new in your school or community.

Now write a feature story about the event.

Writing Test Tips
- Think about what readers would want to know about the new item and its introduction.
- List details of interest.
- Make an outline with one part for each paragraph in the article.

GETTING STARTED Students can do any of the following:

- Order details and actions on a graphic organizer such as a sequence chart.
- Use word webs to collect vivid verbs, nouns, and describing words about each feature.
- Think what image or statement would grab readers' attention; brainstorm several possible leads.

DAY 4 — Draft and Revise

EDITING/REVISING CHECKLIST
- ☑ Is each topic sentence supported with strong details?
- ☑ Have I used principal parts of irregular verbs correctly?
- ☑ Have I spelled words with consonant sounds /j/, /ks/, /sk/, and /s/ correctly?

See *The Grammar and Writing Book,* pp. 122–127.

Revising Tips

Organization/ Paragraphs

- Sharpen the focus of your topic sentences; make sure the subjects and verbs are specific and concrete.
- Check order of sentences for logic.
- See if additional transitions will make paragraphs flow more smoothly.

PUBLISHING Students can input their stories on a computer and format them as news articles, adding a headline. Some students may wish to revise their work later.

ASSESSMENT Use the scoring rubric to evaluate students' work.

DAY 5 — Connect to Unit Writing

Compare and Contrast Essay	
Week 1	Skit 285g–285h
Week 2	Question/Answer Essay 313g–313h
Week 3	Feature Story 343g–343h
Week 4	Description 361g–361h
Week 5	Expository Writing 381g–381h

PREVIEW THE UNIT PROMPT

Write an essay comparing and contrasting an invention of long ago with a modern invention. Explain how they are alike and different in the way they affected people. Use clue words such as like, also, but, *and* unlike *to signal likenesses and differences.*

APPLY

- Paragraphs in a compare and contrast essay are organized logically and stay on topic.

Writing Trait Rubric

	4	3	2	1
Organization/ Paragraphs	Ideas well developed from beginning to end; strong closure	Ideas that progress from beginning to end; good closure	Some sense of movement from beginning to end; weak closure	No sense of movement from beginning to end; no closure
	Feature story organized with exceptional logic	Feature story organized adequately	Feature story not clearly organized	Feature story not organized

Spelling & Phonics

Consonant Sounds /j/, /ks/, /sk/ and /s/

OBJECTIVE

● Spell words with consonant sounds /j/, /ks/, /sk/, and /s/.

Generalization

Connect to Phonics The sound /j/ can be spelled *g, j,* and *dge: ginger, journal, dodge.* The sound /ks/ can be spelled *x: excuse.* The sound /sk/ can be spelled *sch: schedule.* The sound /s/ can be spelled *sc: scene.* Some consonant sounds can be spelled in different ways.

Spelling Words

1. excuse	11. Japan
2. scene	12. excellent
3. muscle	13. exclaim
4. explore	14. fascinate
5. pledge	15. ginger
6. journal	16. scholar
7. science	17. scent
8. schedule	18. dodge
9. gigantic	19. smudge
10. scheme	20. schooner

Challenge Words

21. extraordinary	24. prejudice
22. reminisce	25. allergic
23. acknowledge	

E L L

Spelling/Phonics Support See the ELL and Transition Handbook for spelling support.

DAY 1 Pretest and Sort

PRETEST

Use the Dictation Sentences from Day 5 to administer the pretest. Read the word, read the sentence, and then read the word again. Guide students in self-correcting their pretests and correcting any misspellings.

Monitor Progress

Spelling

If... students misspell more than 5 pre-test words,	**then...** use words 1–10 for Strategic Intervention.
If... students misspell 1–5 pretest words,	**then...** use words 1–20 for On-Level practice.
If... students correctly spell all pretest words,	**then...** use words 1–25 for Advanced Learners.

HOMEWORK Spelling Practice Book, p. 49.

▲ **Spelling Practice Book** p. 49

DAY 2 Think and Practice

TEACH

Some consonant sounds can be spelled in different ways. Write *gigantic, Japan,* and *pledge* and underline the first *g* in *gigantic*, the *J* in *Japan*, and the *dge* in *pledge*. Say the words and point out that all the underlined letters stand for /j/. Write *explore*, *scheme*, and *scent*. Lead students in saying the sounds of the underlined letters.

gigantic
Japan
pledge

FLASH CARD SPELLING Divide the class into small groups and have students write *g, j, dge, x, sch,* and *sc* on note cards. Have one student read the list words. Have the others hold up the letters that the words contain.

HOMEWORK Spelling Practice Book, p. 50.

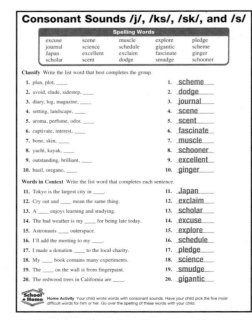

▲ **Spelling Practice Book** p. 50

DAY 3 — Connect to Writing

WRITE OPENING SENTENCES

Ask students to use at least five spelling words to write five attention-getting lead sentences they could use to begin newspaper human interest stories.

Frequently Misspelled Words

except   excited
school

These words may seem easy to spell, but they are often misspelled by fifth-graders. Alert students to these frequently misspelled words. Point out the *xc* in *except* and *excited.* Remind students that the first three letters of *school* are the same as the first three letters in *schedule.*

HOMEWORK Spelling Practice Book, p. 51.

Consonant Sounds /j/, /ks/, /sk/, and /s/

Proofread a Travel Poster There are seven spelling errors and one punctuation error. Circle the errors and write the corrections on the lines.

(Exsplore) Japan

This trip will (facinate) the (scolar) or the casual traveler.
(Exsellent) first-class hotels are available.
Experience the exotic taste of ginger and other spices.
Visit a typical school full of excited children.
Enjoy the (sent) of lotus flower in your own private spa.
Enjoy the peaceful (cene) of a
Japanese garden and teahouse.
The (skedule) is made to meet your needs.

Spelling Words
excuse
scene
muscle
explore
pledge
journal
science
schedule
gigantic
scheme

Japan
excellent
exclaim
fascinate
ginger
scholar
scent
dodge
smudge
schooner

1. Explore   2. fascinate
3. scholar   4. Excellent
5. scent   6. scene
7. schedule
8. The schedule is made to meet your needs.

Proofread Words Circle the correct spelling of the list words.

9. plege   pleje   (pledge)
10. sceme   (scheme)   skeme
11. (smudge) smuge   smuje
12. mussle   muscel   (muscle)
13. dodje   (dodge)   dogde
14. (journal) journle   jurnal
15. jigantic gidgantic   (gigantic)
16. skooner (schooner) scooner

Frequently Misspelled Words
except
excited
school

Home Activity Your child identified misspelled list words. Review the sch and sc words and their pronunciation with your child.

▲ **Spelling Practice Book** p. 51

DAY 4 — Review

REVIEW CONSONANT SOUNDS /j/, /ks/, /sk/, AND /s/

Have students use phonetic spellings, such as *skul* for *school,* to write ten list words. Tell them to exchange papers with a partner and have the partner spell the words correctly.

Spelling Strategy Memory Tricks

Some words seem so tricky to spell that we need to outsmart them with tricks of our own.

Step 1: Mark the letters that give you a problem.

Step 2: Find words you know with those same letters.

Step 3: Use your problem word and the word you know in a phrase or sentence.

Example:

jotting notes in my journal

HOMEWORK Spelling Practice Book, p. 52.

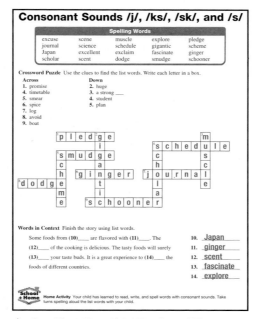

Consonant Sounds /j/, /ks/, /sk/, and /s/

Spelling Words

excuse	scene	muscle	explore	pledge
journal	science	schedule	gigantic	scheme
Japan	excellent	exclaim	fascinate	ginger
scholar	scent	dodge	smudge	schooner

Crossword Puzzle Use the clues to find the list words. Write each letter in a box.

Across
1. promise
4. timetable
5. smear
6. spice
7. log
8. avoid
9. boat

Down
2. huge
3. a strong ___
4. student
5. plan

Words in Context Finish the story using list words.

Some foods from (10)____ are flavored with (11)____. The
(12)____ of the cooking is delicious. The tasty foods will surely
(13)____ your taste buds. It is a great experience to (14)____ the
foods of different countries.

10. Japan
11. ginger
12. scent
13. fascinate
14. explore

Home Activity Your child has learned to read, write, and spell with consonant sounds. Take turns spelling aloud the list words with your child.

▲ **Spelling Practice Book** p. 52

DAY 5 — Posttest

DICTATION SENTENCES

1. Did you have an <u>excuse</u> for being late?

2. The picture shows a winter <u>scene</u>.

3. Exercise builds <u>muscle</u>.

4. It's fun to <u>explore</u> a new place.

5. I made a <u>pledge</u> never to smoke.

6. Do you ever write in a <u>journal</u>?

7. Jen's favorite class is <u>science</u>.

8. The <u>schedule</u> shows that the game is today.

9. The new swimming pool is <u>gigantic</u>.

10. The color <u>scheme</u> of the room was green and <u>white</u>.

11. <u>Japan</u> is an island.

12. You did an <u>excellent</u> job!

13. I heard him <u>exclaim</u>, "Hooray!"

14. Stamps <u>fascinate</u> me.

15. Would you like some <u>ginger</u> ale?

16. Ben is a history <u>scholar</u>.

17. The <u>scent</u> of flowers filled the air.

18. We had to <u>dodge</u> the ball.

19. The ink made a <u>smudge</u> on the paper.

20. An old sea <u>schooner</u> is docked in the harbor.

CHALLENGE

21. You have <u>extraordinary</u> talent.

22. Do you ever <u>reminisce</u> about the old days?

23. I <u>acknowledge</u> that you are the champ.

24. Some people have a <u>prejudice</u> against cats.

25. Are you <u>allergic</u> to milk?

- Formulate an inquiry question that is connected to this week's lesson focus.
- Effectively and efficiently find, evaluate, and communicate information related to an inquiry question using electronic sources.

New Literacies	
Day 1	Identify Questions
Day 2	Navigate/Search
Day 3	Analyze
Day 4	Synthesize
Day 5	Communicate

NEW LITERACIES
Internet Inquiry Activity
EXPLORE DINOSAURS

Use the following 5-day plan to help students conduct this week's Internet inquiry activity on dinosaurs. Remind students to follow classroom rules when using the Internet.

DAY 1

Identify Questions Discuss with students the lesson focus question: *How can paleontologists help us understand the past?* Recall the selection question on p. 321: *How does Waterhouse Hawkins introduce the world to a new kind of creature?* Brainstorm ideas for inquiry questions about the people who study dinosaurs. For example, students might want to find out about paleontology or why dinosaurs became extinct. Have students work individually, in pairs, or in small groups to write inquiry questions they want to answer.

DAY 2

Navigate/Search Continue your discussion of key Internet terms, including *World Wide Web* (a system of computers that are joined around the world) and *search engine* (a tool you can use to find specific Web sites on the Internet). Using keywords, have students locate Web sites they can use to gather and record information related to their inquiry questions from three or more sources.

DAY 3

Analyze Have students scan the Web sites they identified on Day 2. Ask them to pay particular attention to information that relates to their inquiry questions. When they finish, have students analyze the helpfulness of the sites they used. Which contained a lot of information? Which seemed the most reliable? If appropriate, have students print out and highlight relevant information or take notes about it.

DAY 4

Synthesize Have students synthesize information from Day 3. Ask them to create webs or charts that present key details about their topics. Then have them discuss their findings with partners.

DAY 5

Communicate Have students share their inquiry results. Direct them to use presentation software to create brief summaries of their research.

RESEARCH/STUDY SKILLS

Schedule

OBJECTIVES

- Review how information is organized in a schedule.
- Use a schedule to locate information.

TEACH

Ask students how they could find out when a bus leaves one station and arrives at another. Students may need prompting to identify the use of a bus schedule. Show a bus schedule to students and explain the following.

- A **schedule** is a kind of table that provides information about time and events.

- A schedule contains information arranged in **rows** and **columns**. Rows are horizontal. Columns are vertical. You match the information in the rows and columns to read the schedule.

- A **cell** is the box in the table where the row and column meet.

Give each student a schedule for the same bus route. (You can get schedules from your local transportation authority or print them online.) Point out any special features, such as arrows of direction, that will help students read the schedule. Then discuss questions such as the following:

1. **What bus route is shown on the schedule?** (The answer will be found in the schedule's title.)

2. **If you have an appointment at Broadway and Mercer St. at 12:30 P.M. When would you need to leave White Center Station to arrive at your appointment on time?** (11:02 A.M. on the schedule shown below. Adapt the question to your bus schedule.)

3. **How often does the bus run on weekdays?** (Every five hours from 6:02 A.M. to 9:02 P.M., on the schedule shown below. Adapt the question to your bus schedule.)

Route 60
Weekday to Broadway

White Center Station	Shoe Factory	VA Medical Center	12th Ave S & Jackson Street	Broadway & Mercer St.
6:02	6:17	6:33	6:45	6:57
11:02	11:17	11:33	11:45	11:57
4:02	4:17	4:33	4:45	4:57
9:02	9:17	9:33	9:45	9:57

AM - Lighter Type
PM - Darker Type

ASSESS

As students work with the schedule, check that they can navigate the rows and columns to find information.

For more practice or to assess students, use Practice Book pp. 129–130.

Schedule

A **schedule** is a kind of table with **rows** and **columns**. The rows and columns meet at boxes that are called **cells**. Schedules show times, dates, and locations for airplanes, trains, buses, activities, and sporting events.

Directions Use this train schedule to answer the questions.

Departure Schedule for Trains to Chicago

		A.M.	A.M.	A.M.	P.M.	P.M.	P.M.
Waukekee		5:01	7:30	11:30	1:00	3:30	5:00
Hampton		5:45	8:15	12:15	1:45	4:15	5:45
Rainville	*	6:15	8:45	12:45	2:15	4:45	6:15
Harbor Park	*	7:00	9:30	1:30	3:00	5:00	7:00
Arrive in Chicago		8:00	10:30	2:30	4:00	6:00	8:00

* Indicates food service.

1. How many trains go to Chicago every day? Which train leaves Waukekee in the morning, and arrives in Chicago in the afternoon?
   Six trains go to Chicago every day; 11:30 A.M.

2. Counting Waukekee, how many stops does the train make? What is the fourth stop?
   The train makes five stops; Harbor Park.

3. You live in Rainville. You want to meet your friends in Chicago at 10:30 A.M. What time do you have to catch the train in Rainville to be on time? How much extra time will you have when you arrive in Chicago?
   You need the 8:45 A.M. train; There will be no extra time.

4. You live in Harbor Park and have to take the train that leaves at 7:00 A.M. for Chicago. You don't have time to fix yourself breakfast. Will you be able to get something to eat on the train? How do you know?
   yes; The asterisk in the column indicates food service.

5. You live in Hampton. Every Monday at 5:00 P.M., you have violin lessons in Rainville. To be on time, which train do you have to catch? Will you have time to spare?
   You need the 4:15 P.M. train; You will have 15 minutes to spare.

▲ **Practice Book** p. 129

Directions Use this camp schedule to answer the questions.

Camp Want-To-Get-Away Schedule

	Monday	Tuesday	Wednesday	Thursday	Friday	Saturday	Sunday
8 A.M.	Breakfast in Olson Hall	Breakfast in Olson Hall	Breakfast in Olson Hall	Breakfast in Olson Hall	Breakfast in Olson Hall	Breakfast in Olson Hall	Breakfast in Olson Hall
10 A.M.	Swimming at Lake Beluga	Play Rehearsal	Archery	Swimming at Lake Beluga	Band Practice	You Choose	Play Rehearsal
1 P.M.	Crafts	Crafts	Horseback Riding	Letters Home	Horseback Riding	You Choose	Parents Visit
4 P.M.	Group Games	Archery	Water Sports	Group Games	Hiking	Group Games	Swimming at Lake Beluga
8 P.M.	Lights Out	Lights Out	Lights Out	Lights Out	MOVIE	Campfire Stories	Lights Out

6. How many time slots for each day are listed on this schedule? How many days are listed?
   There are five time slots listed each day; seven days.

7. You want to sharpen your swimming skills. What days and times can you go swimming?
   You can swim on Mondays and Thursdays at 10 A.M. and Sundays at 4 P.M.

8. You want your parents to come for a visit. What day and time is best?
   Sundays at 1 P.M. are the best time for parent visits.

9. What time can you eat breakfast everyday? Where is breakfast held?
   Breakfast is at 8 A.M.; Olson Hall

10. You love to act. What is a good activity to take part in? When is this activity available?
    Play Rehearsal; It is held on Tuesday and Sunday at 10 A.M.

School + Home Home Activity Your child learned about reading schedules. Look at the schedule of a sports team your child likes. Find out when the next game is and whether or not it takes place during school hours.

▲ **Practice Book** p. 130

Assessment Checkpoints *for the Week*

Selection Assessment

Use pp. 49–52 of Selection Tests **to check:**

 Selection Understanding

 Comprehension Skill *Fact and Opinion*

 Selection Vocabulary

erected	proportion
foundations	tidied
mold	workshop
occasion	

Leveled Assessment

 On-Level

Strategic Intervention

Advanced

Use pp. 73–78 of Fresh Reads for Differentiated Test Practice **to check:**

 Comprehension Skill *Fact and Opinion*

 REVIEW **Comprehension Skill** *Main Idea*

 Fluency *Words Correct Per Minute*

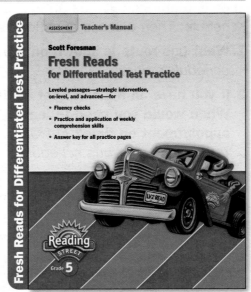

Managing Assessment

Use Assessment Handbook **for:**

 Observation Checklists

 Record-Keeping Forms

 Portfolio Assessment

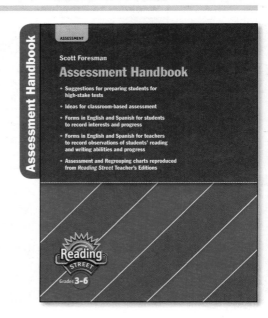

Illinois

Planning Guide for Performance Descriptors

Mahalia Jackson

Reading Street Teacher's Edition pages	Grade 5 English Language Arts Performance Descriptors
Oral Language **Speaking/Listening** Build Concept Vocabulary: 346l, 357, 363c Read Aloud: 346m	**1A.Stage E.1.** Use a combination of word analysis and vocabulary strategies within context to identify unknown words. **1B.Stage E.10.** Read age-appropriate material aloud with fluency and accuracy. **2A.Stage E.6.** Analyze the use of unfamiliar vocabulary.
Word Work One Consonant or Two: 363i–363j	**1A.Stage E.1.** Use a combination of word analysis and vocabulary strategies (e.g., word patterns, structural analyses) within context to identify unknown words.
Reading **Comprehension** Main Idea: 346–347, 350–357, 360–363, 363b Graphic Organizers: 346–347, 350–357, 360–363 **Vocabulary** Lesson Vocabulary: 348b, 357 Context Clues: 348–349, 363c **Fluency** Model Tempo and Rate: 346l–346m, 363a **Self-Selected Reading:** LR28–36, TR16–17 **Literature** Genre—Expository Nonfiction: 350 Reader Response: 358	**1B.Stage E.9.** Apply self-monitoring and self-correcting strategies continuously to clarify understanding during reading. **1C.Stage E.6.** Select reading strategies for text appropriate to the reader's purpose. **2A.Stage E.7.** Use comprehension strategies (e.g., association, categorization, graphic organizers) to enhance understanding. **2B.Stage E.6.** Read a wide range of nonfiction (e.g., books, newspapers, magazines, textbooks, visual media). **4B.Stage E.3.** Use details to elaborate and develop main ideas for purposes of informing, entertaining, and persuading. **4B.Stage E.6.** Use appropriate verbal and nonverbal communication elements (e.g., appropriate space, body language, pleasant tone, rate, volume).
Language Arts **Writing** Description: 363g–363h **Six-Trait Writing** Word Choice: 359, 363g–363h **Grammar, Usage, and Mechanics** Troublesome Verbs: 363e–363f **Research/Study** Technology—Card Catalog/Library Database: 363l **Technology** New Literacies: 363k	**3A.Stage E.4.** Use basic transition words to connect ideas. **3C.Stage E.3.** Write creatively for a specified purpose and audience. **3C.Stage E.4.** Use available technology to design, produce, and present compositions and multimedia works. **4B.Stage E.5.** Use appropriate grammar, word choice, and pacing. **5A.Stage E.1.** Generate questions of interest and narrow the focus of research.
Unit Skills **Writing** Compare and Contrast Essay: WA2–9 **Poetry:** 384–387 **Project/Wrap-Up:** 388–389	**3A.Stage E.2.** Develop multi-paragraph compositions that include an introduction, first and second level support, and a conclusion. **3C.Stage E.3.** Write creatively for a specified purpose and audience (e.g., short story, poetry, directions, song, friendly letter).

This Week's Leveled Readers

Below-Level

Nonfiction

2A.Stage E.1. Read a wide range of fiction.

4B.Stage E.3. Use details to elaborate and develop main ideas for purposes of informing, entertaining, and persuading.

On-Level

Nonfiction

2B.Stage E.1. Create an extension to a literary text (e.g., alternate ending, additional dialog for a character).

4B.Stage E.3. Use details to elaborate and develop main ideas for purposes of informing, entertaining, and persuading.

Advanced

Nonfiction

2A.Stage E.3. Predict how the story might be different if the author changed literary elements or techniques (e.g., dialect, setting, vocabulary).

4B.Stage E.3. Use details to elaborate and develop main ideas for purposes of informing, entertaining, and persuading.

Content-Area Illinois Performance Descriptors in This Lesson

Social Studies

14F.Stage E.1. Describe examples of the development of basic freedoms for the people of the United States.

14F.Stage E.2. Discuss consistencies and inconsistencies expressed in United States political traditions and actual practices (e.g., freedom of speech, the right to bear arms, slavery, voting rights).

16C.Stage E.3. Describe how slavery and indentured servitude were related to the wants of economic interest groups in the United States.

Science

11B.Stage E.1. Identify an innovative technological design from ordinary surroundings or circumstances.

13A.Stage E.2. Apply scientific habits of mind: explaining why similar investigations should but may not produce similar results.

Illinois!

A FAMOUS ILLINOISAN
Oprah Winfrey

Oprah Winfrey (1954–) was born in Kosciusko, Mississippi, and she lived in Milwaukee, Wisconsin, and Nashville, Tennessee. Winfrey worked as a television news reporter and anchor before co-hosting a morning show in Baltimore. She moved to Chicago in 1984 to host a morning TV show. The program was renamed the *Oprah Winfrey Show* the following year. In addition to hosting the show, Winfrey formed a television production company and a film production company, and she started a magazine.

Students can . . .
Think about a career they would like to have as an adult and write the steps they would need to take to achieve that goal.

A SPECIAL ILLINOIS PLACE
Cairo

Cairo is the county seat of Alexander County, at the southern tip of Illinois. Bridges over the Mississippi and Ohio Rivers connect Cairo with Kentucky and Missouri. The town was established in 1818. Because some people thought the low-lying area in which the town sits resembled the landscape around Cairo, Egypt, people started calling the area Little Egypt.

Students can . . .
Find pictures of Cairo, Egypt, and Cairo, Illinois, as they appear today and make a Venn diagram to show how the cities are alike and how they are different.

ILLINOIS FUN FACTS
Did You Know?

• The Potawatomi surrendered control of much of their land in what is now Illinois through the Treaty of Greenville. The treaty, signed in 1795, gave the land to the United States.

• The original Fort Dearborn was built in 1803 near the mouth of the Chicago River. It was rebuilt in 1816 after being burned down.

• Most Illinois counties are divided into government units called townships.

Students can . . .
Find out more about the township in which they live. Ask students to create a township information sheet to record the facts they gather.

Unit 3
Inventors and Artists

CONCEPT QUESTION
What do people gain from the work of inventors and artists?

Week 1
How do inventors inspire our imaginations?

Week 2
How do artists inspire future generations?

Week 3
How can paleontologists help us understand the past?

Week 4
How does an artist use music to inspire others?

Week 5
How do artists create special effects to entertain us?

EXPAND THE CONCEPT
How does an artist use music to inspire others?

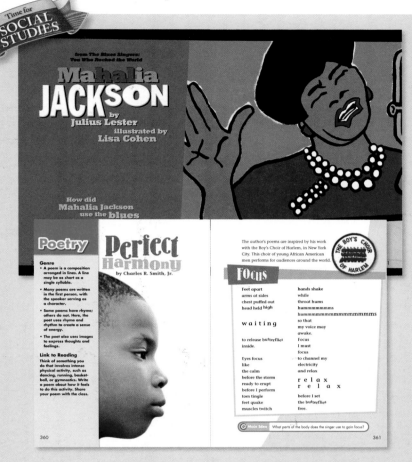

CONNECT THE CONCEPT

▶ **Build Background**
beat, blended, time

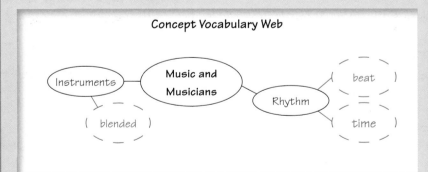

Concept Vocabulary Web

▶ **Social Studies Content**
Roots of Blues Music, Blues Artists, Boy's Choir of Harlem

▶ **Writing**
Description

▶ **Internet Inquiry**
Music and Musicians

Mahalia Jackson   **346a**

Preview Your Week

How does an artist use music to inspire others?

from *The Blues Singers: Ten Who Rocked the World*

Mahalia JACKSON

by **Julius Lester**

illustrated by **Lisa Cohen**

How did **Mahalia Jackson** use the **blues** in a **new** and **different** way?

Genre

Expository nonfiction explains what certain things are and how they came to be. As you read, notice how the author explains a musical form known as the blues and how it came to be.

Student Edition pages 350–357

Audio CD

Genre	Expository Nonfiction
⊙ **Vocabulary Strategy**	Context Clues
⊙ **Comprehension Skill**	Main Idea
⊙ **Comprehension Strategy**	Graphic Organizers

Paired Selection

Reading Across Texts
Compare Singing Techniques

Genre
Poetry

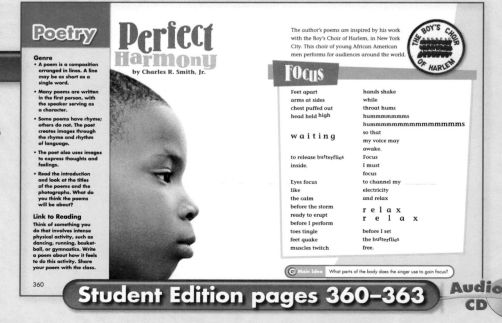

Poetry

Perfect Harmony
by Charles R. Smith, Jr.

Genre
- A poem is a composition arranged in lines. A line may be as short as a single word.
- Many poems are written in the first person, with the speaker serving as a character.
- Some poems have rhyme; others do not. The poet creates images through the rhyme and rhythm of language.
- The poet also uses images to express thoughts and feelings.
- Read the introduction and look at the titles of the poems and the photographs. What do you think the poems will be about?

Link to Reading
Think of something you do that involves intense physical activity, such as dancing, running, basketball, or gymnastics. Write a poem about how it feels to do this activity. Share your poem with the class.

The author's poems are inspired by his work with the Boy's Choir of Harlem, in New York City. This choir of young African American men performs for audiences around the world.

THE BOY'S CHOIR OF HARLEM

Focus

Feet apart	hands shake
arms at sides	while
chest puffed out	throat hums
head held high	hummmmmmms
	hummmmmmmmmmmmmmms
	so that
waiting	my voice may
	awake.
to release butterflies	Focus
inside.	I must
	focus
Eyes focus	to channel my
like	electricity
the calm	and relax
before the storm	
ready to erupt	r e l a x
before I perform	r e l a x
toes tingle	
feet quake	before I set
muscles twitch	the butterflies
	free.

⊙ **Main Idea** What parts of the body does the singer use to gain focus?

Student Edition pages 360–363

Audio CD

Read It
ONLINE
PearsonSuccessNet.com
• Student Edition
• Leveled Readers

Leveled Readers

🎯 **Skill** Main Idea
🎯 **Strategy** Graphic Organizers
Lesson Vocabulary

Below-Level

On-Level

Advanced

ELL Reader
· Concept Vocabulary
· Text Support
· Language Enrichment

Willie Dixon's Blues
A Talk with Marie Dixon
by Robert Jackson

Integrate Social Studies Standards
• U.S. History
• Contributions of African Americans
• 20th Century Culture

✓ **Read**

"Mahalia Jackson,"
pp. 350–357

Perfect Harmony,
pp. 360–363

Leveled Readers

Below-Level   **On-Level**   **Advanced**
• Support Concepts • Develop Concepts • Extend Concepts
• Social Studies Extension Activity

ELL Reader

✓ **Build Concept Vocabulary**
Music and Musicians,
pp. 346l–346m

✓ **Teach Social Studies Concepts**
Roots of Blues Music, p. 353
Blues Artists, p. 355
Boy's Choir of Harlem, p. 361

✓ **Explore Social Studies Center**
Explore the Blues, p. 346k

Weekly Plan

READING

45–90 minutes

TARGET SKILLS OF THE WEEK

- **Comprehension Skill**
  Main Idea

- **Comprehension Strategy**
  Graphic Organizers

- **Vocabulary Strategy**
  Context Clues

LANGUAGE ARTS

30–60 minutes

Trait of the Week

Word Choice

DAY 1
PAGES 346l–348b, 363a, 363e–363k

Oral Language

QUESTION OF THE WEEK *How does an artist use music to inspire others?*

Read Aloud: "Bud, not Buddy," 346m
Build Concepts, 346l

Comprehension/Vocabulary

Comprehension Skill/Strategy Lesson, 346–347
- Main Idea and Details **T**
- Graphic Organizers

Build Background, 348a

Introduce Lesson Vocabulary, 348b
appreciate, barber, choir, released, religious, slavery, teenager **T**

Read Leveled Readers

Grouping Options 346f–346g

Fluency

Model Tempo and Rate, 346l–346m, 363a

Grammar, 363e
Introduce Troublesome Verbs **T**

Writing Workshop, 363g
Introduce Description
Model the Trait of the Week: Word Choice

Spelling, 363i
Pretest for One Consonant or Two

Internet Inquiry, 363k
Identify Questions

DAY 2
PAGES 348–353, 363a, 363e–363k

Oral Language

QUESTION OF THE DAY *How did African Americans use music to fight against slavery?*

Comprehension/Vocabulary

Vocabulary Strategy Lesson, 348–349
- Context Clues **T**

Read "Mahalia Jackson," 350–353

Grouping Options 346f–346g

- Main Idea and Details **T**
Develop Vocabulary

Fluency

Echo Reading, 363a

Grammar, 363e
Develop Troublesome Verbs **T**

Writing Workshop, 363g
Improve Writing with Use Specific Words

Spelling, 363i
Teach the Generalization

Internet Inquiry, 363k
Navigate/Search

DAILY WRITING ACTIVITIES	**Day 1** Write to Read, 346	**Day 2** Words to Write, 349 Strategy Response Log, 350, 353
DAILY SOCIAL STUDIES CONNECTIONS	**Day 1** Music and Musicians Concept Web, 346l	**Day 2** Time for Social Studies: Roots of Blues Music, 353

DAILY SUCCESS PREDICTORS
for Adequate Yearly Progress

Monitor Progress and Corrective Feedback

Vocabulary — Check Vocabulary, *346l*

RESOURCES FOR THE WEEK

- Practice Book, *pp. 131–140*
- Word Study and Spelling Practice Book, *pp. 53–56*
- Grammar and Writing Practice Book, *pp. 53–56*
- Selection Test, *pp. 53–56*
- Fresh Reads for Differentiated Test Practice, *pp. 79–84*
- The Grammar and Writing Book, *pp. 128–133*

Grouping Options for Differentiated Instruction

Turn the page for the small group lesson plan.

DAY 3 — PAGES 354–359, 363a, 363e–363k

Oral Language

QUESTION OF THE DAY *How might young people today be inspired by Mahalia Jackson?*

Comprehension/Vocabulary

Read "Mahalia Jackson," 354–358

Grouping Options 346f–346g

- Graphic Organizers
- **REVIEW** Fact and Opinion **T**
- Develop Vocabulary

Reader Response

Selection Test

Fluency

Model Tempo and Rate, 363a

Grammar, 363f
Apply Troublesome Verbs in Writing **T**

Writing Workshop, 359, 363h
Write Now
Prewrite and Draft

Spelling, 363j
Connect Spelling to Writing

Internet Inquiry, 363k
Analyze Sources

Day 3 Strategy Response Log, 356
Look Back and Write, 358

Day 3 Time for Social Studies: Blues Artists, 355
Revisit the Music and Musicians Concept Web, 357

DAY 4 — PAGES 360–363a, 363e–363k

Oral Language

QUESTION OF THE DAY *What do you think inspires an artist to create a work of art, such as a piece of music or a poem?*

Comprehension/Vocabulary

Read *Perfect Harmony,* 360–363

Grouping Options 346f–346g

Poetry

Reading Across Texts

Fluency

Partner Reading, 363a

Grammar, 363f
Practice Troublesome Verbs for Standardized Tests **T**

Writing Workshop, 363h
Draft, Revise, and Publish

Spelling, 363j
Provide a Strategy

Internet Inquiry, 363k
Synthesize Information

Day 4 Writing Across Texts, 363

Day 4 Time for Social Studies: Boys Choir of Harlem, 361

DAY 5 — PAGES 363a–363l

Oral Language

QUESTION OF THE WEEK *To wrap up the week, revisit the Day 1 question.*
Build Concept Vocabulary, 363c

Fluency

Read Leveled Readers

Grouping Options 346f–346g

Assess Reading Rate, 363a

Comprehension/Vocabulary

- Reteach Main Idea, 363b **T**
- Persuasive Devices, 363b
- Review Context Clues, 363c **T**

Speaking and Listening, 363d
Oral Presentation
Listen to Music

Grammar, 363f
Cumulative Review

Writing Workshop, 363h
Connect to Unit Writing

Spelling, 363j
Posttest for One Consonant or Two

Internet Inquiry, 363k
Communicate Results

Research/Study Skills, 363l
Card Catalog/Library Database

Day 5 Persuasive Devices, 363b

Day 5 Revisit the Music and Musicians Concept Web, 363c

KEY ⊙ = Target Skill **T** = Tested Skill

Comprehension Check Retelling, *358*

Fluency Check Fluency WCPM, *363a*

Vocabulary Check Vocabulary, *363c*

SUCCESS PREDICTOR

Small Group Plan for Differentiated Instruction

Reading

Whole Group
- Oral Language
- Comprehension/Vocabulary

Group Time

Differentiated Instruction

Meet with small groups to provide:
- Skill Support
- Reading Support
- Fluency Practice

Read

This week's lessons for daily group time can be found behind the Differentiated Instruction (DI) tab on pp. DI·32–DI·41.

Whole Group
- Fluency

Language Arts
- Grammar
- Writing
- Spelling
- Research/Inquiry
- Speaking/Listening/Viewing

Use *My Sidewalks on Reading Street* for Tier III intensive reading intervention.

DAY 1

On-Level	Strategic Intervention	Advanced
Teacher-Led *Page DI·33*	**Teacher-Led** *Page DI·32*	**Teacher-Led** *Page DI·33*
• Develop Concept Vocabulary • **Read** On-Level Reader *Legends of the Blues*	• Reinforce Concepts • **Read** Below-Level Reader *Roots of the Blues*	• **Read** Advanced Reader *Music Gets the Blues* • Independent Extension Activity

(i) Independent Activities

While you meet with small groups, have the rest of the class...

- Visit the Reading/Library Center
- Listen to the Background Building Audio
- Finish Write to Read, p. 346
- Complete Practice Book pp. 133–134
- Visit Cross-Curricular Centers

DAY 2

On-Level	Strategic Intervention	Advanced
Teacher-Led *Pages 352-353*	**Teacher-Led** *Page DI·34*	**Teacher-Led** *Page DI·35*
• **Read** "Mahalia Jackson"	• Practice Lesson Vocabulary • Read Multisyllabic Words • **Read** or Listen to "Mahalia Jackson"	• Extend Vocabulary • **Read** "Mahalia Jackson"

(i) Independent Activities

While you meet with small groups, have the rest of the class...

- Visit the Reading/Library Center
- Listen to the AudioText for "Mahalia Jackson"
- Finish Words to Write, p. 349
- Complete Practice Book pp. 135–136
- Write in their Strategy Response Logs, pp. 350, 353
- Visit Cross-Curricular Centers
- Work on inquiry projects

DAY 3

On-Level	Strategic Intervention	Advanced
Teacher-Led *Pages 354–357*	**Teacher-Led** *Page DI·36*	**Teacher-Led** *Page DI·37*
• **Read** "Mahalia Jackson"	• Practice Main Idea and Graphic Organizers • **Read** or Listen to "Mahalia Jackson"	• Extend Main Idea and Graphic Organizers • **Read** "Mahalia Jackson"

(i) Independent Activities

While you meet with small groups, have the rest of the class...

- Visit the Reading/Library Center
- Listen to the AudioText for "Mahalia Jackson"
- Write in their Strategy Response Logs, p. 356
- Finish Look Back and Write, p. 358
- Complete Practice Book p. 137
- Visit Cross-Curricular Centers
- Work on inquiry projects

① Begin with whole class skill and strategy instruction.

② Meet with small groups to provide differentiated instruction.

③ Gather the whole class back together for fluency and language arts.

DAY 4

On-Level	Strategic Intervention	Advanced
Teacher-Led Pages 360–363	**Teacher-Led** Page DI · 38	**Teacher-Led** Page DI · 39
• **Read** *Perfect Harmony*	• Practice Retelling • **Read** or Listen to *Perfect Harmony*	• **Read** *Perfect Harmony* • Genre Study

ⓘ Independent Activities

While you meet with small groups, have the rest of the class...

- Visit the Reading/Library Center
- Listen to the AudioText for *Perfect Harmony*
- Visit the Writing/Vocabulary Center
- Finish Writing Across Texts, p. 363
- Visit Cross-Curricular Centers
- Work on inquiry projects

DAY 5

On-Level	Strategic Intervention	Advanced
Teacher-Led Page DI · 41	**Teacher-Led** Page DI · 40	**Teacher-Led** Page DI · 41
• **Reread** Leveled Reader *Legends of the Blues* • Retell *Legends of the Blues*	• **Reread** Leveled Reader *Roots of the Blues* • Retell *Roots of the Blues*	• **Reread** Leveled Reader *Music Gets the Blues* • Share Extension Activity

ⓘ Independent Activities

While you meet with small groups, have the rest of the class...

- Visit the Reading/Library Center
- Complete Practice Book pp. 138–140
- Visit Cross-Curricular Centers
- Work on inquiry projects

Grouping Place English language learners in the groups that correspond to their reading abilities in English.

Use the appropriate Leveled Reader or other text at students' instructional level.

TiP Send home the appropriate Multilingual Summary of the main selection on Day 1.

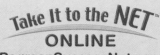

Take It to the **NET**
ONLINE
PearsonSuccessNet.com

P. David Pearson
For research on comprehension, see the article "Comprehension Instruction" by Scott Foresman author P. D. Pearson and L. Fielding.

TEACHER TALK

Keywords are words in a test question that tell who or what the question is about and what the question is asking for. *Alike, different, explain,* and *why* are examples of keywords.

Be sure to schedule time for students to work on the unit inquiry project "Inventors and Artists." This week students synthesize information they have gathered about the lives and contributions of inventors and artists.

Looking Ahead

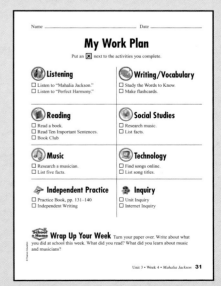

▲ **Group-Time Survival Guide** p. 31, Weekly Contract

Mahalia Jackson **346g**

☑ Customize Your Plan *by Strand*

ORAL LANGUAGE

Concept Development

 SOCIAL STUDIES

How does an artist use music to inspire others?

CONCEPT VOCABULARY
beat   time   blended

BUILD

- ☐ **Question of the Week** Introduce and discuss the question of the week. This week students will read a variety of texts and work on projects related to the concept *music and musicians*. Post the question for students to refer to throughout the week. **DAY 1** *346d*

- ☐ **Read Aloud** Read aloud "Bud, not Buddy." Then begin a web to build concepts and concept vocabulary related to this week's lesson and the unit theme, Inventors and Artists. Introduce the concept words *beat, time,* and *blended* and have students place them on the web. Display the web for use throughout the week. **DAY 1** *346l-346m*

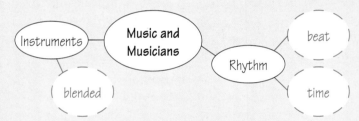

DEVELOP

- ☐ **Question of the Day** Use the prompts from the Weekly Plan to engage students in conversations related to this week's reading and the unit theme. **EVERY DAY** *346d-346e*

- ☐ **Concept Vocabulary Web** Revisit the Music and Musicians Concept Web and encourage students to add concept words from their reading and life experiences. **DAY 3** *357*

CONNECT

- ☐ **Looking Back/Moving Forward** Revisit the Music and Musicians Concept Web and discuss how it relates to this week's lesson and the unit theme. Then make connections to next week's lesson. **DAY 5** *363c*

CHECK

- ☐ **Concept Vocabulary Web** Use the Music and Musicians Concept Web to check students' understanding of the concept vocabulary words *beat, time,* and *blended*. **DAY 1** *346l*, **DAY 5** *363c*

VOCABULARY

⟳ STRATEGY CONTEXT CLUES
When you are reading, you may come to a word you do not know. An author may put an antonym near a difficult word to help you discover what it means. An antonym is a word that has the opposite meaning of another word.

LESSON VOCABULARY
appreciate   religious
barber   slavery
choir   teenager
released

TEACH

- ☐ **Words to Know** Give students the opportunity to tell what they already know about this week's lesson vocabulary words. Then discuss word meaning. **DAY 1** *348b*

- ☐ **Vocabulary Strategy Lesson** Use the vocabulary strategy lesson in the Student Edition to introduce and model this week's strategy, *context clues*. **DAY 2** *348-349*

Vocabulary Strategy Lesson

PRACTICE/APPLY

- ☐ **Leveled Text** Read the lesson vocabulary in the context of leveled text. **DAY 1** *LR28-LR36*

- ☐ **Words in Context** Read the lesson vocabulary and apply *context clues* in the context of "Mahalia Jackson." **DAY 2** *350-353*, **DAY 3** *354-358*

Leveled Readers

- ☐ **Writing/Vocabulary Center** Make flashcards for lesson vocabulary words. **ANY DAY** *346k*

Main Selection—Nonfiction

- ☐ **Homework** Practice Book pp. 134-135. **DAY 1** *348b*, **DAY 2** *349*

- ☐ **Word Play** Have partners list examples of sensory language in "Mahalia Jackson" and identify which sense is being stimulated. **ANY DAY** *363c*

ASSESS

- ☐ **Selection Test** Use the Selection Test to determine students' understanding of the lesson vocabulary words. **DAY 3**

RETEACH/REVIEW

- ☐ **Reteach Lesson** If necessary, use this lesson to reteach and review *context clues*. **DAY 5** *363c*

❶ Use assessment data to determine your instructional focus.

❷ Preview this week's instruction by strand.

❸ Choose instructional activities that meet the needs of your classroom.

COMPREHENSION

⊙ SKILL MAIN IDEA AND DETAILS The *main idea* is the most important idea about a paragraph, passage, or article. *Details* are small pieces of information that tell more about the main idea.

⊙ STRATEGY GRAPHIC ORGANIZERS Creating charts, making lists, or setting up time lines can help you organize your thoughts as you read and remember what you read. Using graphic organizers can help you figure out the main idea and the details that support it.

TEACH

☐ **Skill/Strategy Lesson** Use the skill/strategy lesson in the Student Edition to introduce and model *main idea and details* and *graphic organizers*. **DAY 1** 346-347

Skill/Strategy Lesson

☐ **Extend Skills** Teach persuasive devices. **ANY DAY** 363b

PRACTICE/APPLY

☐ **Leveled Text** Apply *main idea and details* and *graphic organizers* to read leveled text. **DAY 1** LR28-LR36

Leveled Readers

☐ **Skills and Strategies in Context** Read "Mahalia Jackson," using the Guiding Comprehension questions to apply *main idea and details* and *graphic organizers*. **DAY 2** 350-353, **DAY 3** 354-357

Main Selection—Nonfiction

☐ **Skills and Strategies in Context** Read *Perfect Harmony*, guiding students as they apply *main idea and details* and *graphic organizers*. Then have students discuss and write across texts. **DAY 4** 360-363

Paired Selection—Poetry

☐ **Homework** Practice Book pp. 133, 137, 138. **DAY 1** 347, **DAY 3** 357, **DAY 5** 363b

☐ **Fresh Reads for Differentiated Test Practice** Have students practice *main idea and details* with a new passage. **DAY 3**

ASSESS

☐ **Selection Test** Determine students' understanding of the selection and their use of *main idea and details*. **DAY 3**

☐ **Retell** Have students retell "Mahalia Jackson." **DAY 3** 358-359

RETEACH/REVIEW

☐ **Reteach Lesson** If necessary, reteach and review *main idea and details*. **DAY 5** 363b

FLUENCY

SKILL TEMPO AND RATE Reading with appropriate tempo means that you take breaths at appropriate times and pause at punctuation. Reading with appropriate rate means that you do not read too fast or too slow.

TEACH

☐ **Read Aloud** Model fluent reading by rereading "Bud, not Buddy." Focus on this week's fluency skill, tempo and rate. **DAY 1** 346l-346m, 363a

PRACTICE/APPLY

☐ **Echo Reading** Read aloud selected paragraphs from "Mahalia Jackson," modeling appropriate reading tempo and rate. Have students practice by doing three echo readings of the selected paragraphs. **DAY 2** 363a, **DAY 3** 363a

☐ **Partner Reading** Have partners practice reading aloud, using appropriate tempo and rate, and offering each other feedback. As students reread, monitor their progress toward their individual fluency goals. **DAY 4** 363a

☐ **Listening Center** Have students follow along with the AudioText for this week's selections. **ANY DAY** 346j

☐ **Reading/Library Center** Have students reread a selection of their choice. **ANY DAY** 346j

☐ **Fluency Coach** Have students use Fluency Coach to listen to fluent readings or practice reading on their own. **ANY DAY**

ASSESS

☐ **Check Fluency** WCPM Do a one-minute timed reading, paying special attention to this week's skill—tempo and rate. Provide feedback for each student. **DAY 5** 363a

☑ Customize Your Plan *by Strand*

GRAMMAR

SKILL TROUBLESOME VERBS Verbs that have similar meanings or look alike can be confusing and troublesome. Examples of verbs that are often confusing are *sit/set, lie/lay,* and *leave/let.*

TEACH

- ☐ **Grammar Transparency 14** Use Grammar Transparency 14 to teach troublesome verbs. DAY 1 *363e*

Grammar Transparency 14

PRACTICE/APPLY

- ☐ **Develop the Concept** Review the concept of troublesome verbs and provide guided practice. **DAY 2** *363e*

- ☐ **Apply to Writing** Have students review something they have written and apply knowledge of troublesome verbs. **DAY 3** *363f*

- ☐ **Test Preparation** Examine common errors in troublesome verbs to prepare for standardized tests. **DAY 4** *363f*

- ☐ **Homework** Grammar and Writing Practice Book pp. 53–55. **DAY 2** *363e,* **DAY 3** *363f,* **DAY 4** *363f*

ASSESS

- ☐ **Cumulative Review** Use Grammar and Writing Practice Book p. 56. **DAY 5** *363f*

RETEACH/REVIEW

- ☐ **Daily Fix-It** Have students find and correct errors in grammar, spelling, and punctuation. **EVERY DAY** *363e–363f*

- ☐ **The Grammar and Writing Book** Use pp. 128–131 of The Grammar and Writing Book to extend instruction for troublesome verbs. **ANY DAY**

The Grammar and Writing Book

WRITING

Trait of the Week

WORD CHOICE Good writers choose their words carefully. Strong verbs, specific nouns, and vivid adjectives help writers elaborate on their ideas. Well-chosen words make writing clear and lively and can create images that appeal to readers' senses.

TEACH

- ☐ **Writing Transparency 14A** Use the model to introduce and discuss the Trait of the Week. DAY 1 *363g*

- ☐ **Writing Transparency 14B** Use the transparency to show students how using specific words can improve their writing. DAY 2 *363g*

Writing Transparency 14A **Writing Transparency 14B**

PRACTICE/APPLY

- ☐ **Write Now** Examine the model on Student Edition p. 359. Then have students write their own description. **DAY 3** *359, 363h,* **DAY 4** *363h*

  Prompt "Mahalia Jackson" describes the voice of a talented singer. Think about a unique sound. Now write a description of that sound, using vivid sensory words.

Write Now p. 359

- ☐ **Writing/Vocabulary Center** Make flashcards for lesson vocabulary words. **ANY DAY** *346k*

ASSESS

- ☐ **Writing Trait Rubric** Use the rubric to evaluate students' writing. DAY 4 *363h*

RETEACH/REVIEW

- ☐ **The Grammar and Writing Book** Use pp. 128–133 of The Grammar and Writing Book to extend instruction for troublesome verbs, using specific words, and descriptions. **ANY DAY**

The Grammar and Writing Book

❶ Use assessment data to determine your instructional focus.

❷ Preview this week's instruction by strand.

❸ Choose instructional activities that meet the needs of your classroom.

SPELLING

GENERALIZATION ONE CONSONANT OR TWO Many words have two consonants that stand for the same sound: _address, committee_. When the same consonant appears twice in a row in a word, it stands for a single sound.

TEACH

❑ **Pretest** Give the pretest for words with one consonant or two. Guide students in self-correcting their pretests and correcting any misspellings. DAY 1 _363i_

❑ **Think and Practice** Connect spelling to the phonics generalization about one consonant or two. DAY 2 _363i_

PRACTICE/APPLY

❑ **Connect to Writing** Have students use spelling words to write song titles. Then review frequently misspelled words: _different, happened_. DAY 3 _363j_

❑ **Homework** Word Study and Spelling Practice Book pp. 53–56. EVERY DAY

RETEACH/REVIEW

❑ **Review** Review spelling words to prepare for the posttest. Then provide students with a spelling strategy—memory tricks. DAY 4 _363j_

ASSESS

❑ **Posttest** Use dictation sentences to give the posttest for words with one consonant or two. DAY 5 _363j_

Spelling Words

1. address
2. college
3. mirror
4. recess
5. committee
6. collect
7. Mississippi
8. immediate
9. command
10. appreciate*
11. announce
12. possess
13. Tennessee
14. gallop
15. opponent
16. barricade
17. broccoli
18. accomplish
19. allowance
20. zucchini

Challenge Words

21. silhouette
22. millionaire
23. dilemma
24. embarrassment
25. compassionate

*Word from the selection

RESEARCH AND INQUIRY

❑ **Internet Inquiry** Have students conduct an Internet inquiry on how musicians appeal to their audiences. EVERY DAY _363k_

❑ **Card Catalog/Library Database** Review the features and terms associated with library card catalogs and databases and discuss how students can use a card catalog or database to locate books. DAY 5 _363l_

❑ **Unit Inquiry** Allow time for students to synthesize information they have gathered about the lives and contributions of inventors and artists. ANY DAY _261_

SPEAKING AND LISTENING

❑ **Oral Presentation** Have students give an oral presentation describing a unique sound using vivid sensory details. DAY 5 _363d_

❑ **Listen to Music** Have students listen to a variety of blues music and answer questions. DAY 5 _363d_

Resources for Differentiated Instruction

▶ **Comprehension**

🎯 **Skill** Main Idea

🎯 **Strategy** Graphic Organizers

▶ **Lesson Vocabulary**

🎯 **Context Clues**

teenager
barber
choir
released
slavery
religious
appreciate

▶ **Social Studies Standards**

• U.S. History

• Contributions of African Americans

• 20th Century Culture

Leveled Reader Database ONLINE

PearsonSuccessNet.com

Use the Online Database of over 600 books to

• Download and print additional copies of this week's leveled readers.

• Listen to the readers being read online.

• Search for more titles focused on this week's skills, topic, and content.

On-Level

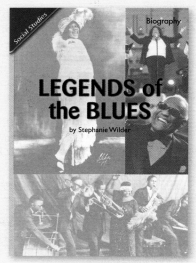

On-Level Reader

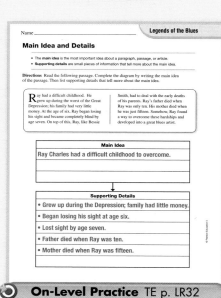

On-Level Practice TE p. LR32

On-Level Practice TE p. LR33

Strategic Intervention

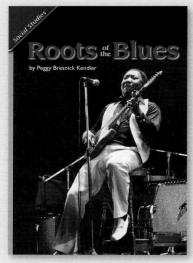

Below-Level Reader

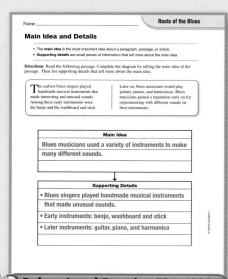

Below-Level Practice TE p. LR29

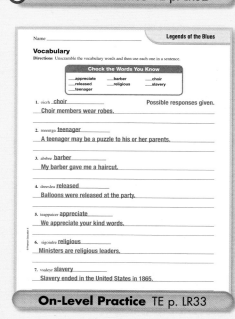

Below-Level Practice TE p. LR30

Advanced

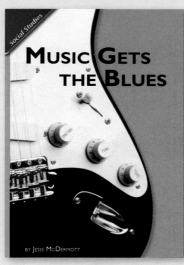

Advanced Reader

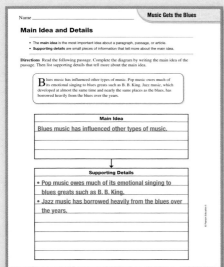

Advanced Practice TE p. LR35

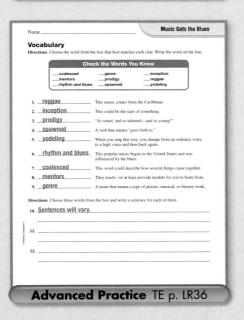

Advanced Practice TE p. LR36

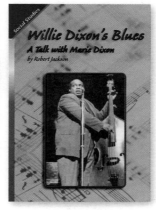

ELL Reader

ELL Poster 14

Teacher's Edition Notes

ELL notes throughout this lesson support instruction and reference additional resources at point of use.

Teaching Guide
pp. 92–98, 238–239

- Multilingual summaries of the main selection
- Comprehension lesson
- Vocabulary strategies and word cards
- ELL Reader 5.3.4 lesson

ELL and Transition Handbook

Ten Important Sentences

- Key ideas from every selection in the Student Edition
- Activities to build sentence power

More Reading

Readers' Theater Anthology

- Fluency practice
- Five scripts to build fluency
- Poetry for oral interpretation

Leveled Trade Books

- Extended reading tied to the unit concept
- Lessons in the Trade Book Library Teaching Guide

School + Home

Homework

- Family Times Newsletter
- ELL Multilingual Selection Summaries

Take-Home Books

- Leveled Readers

Cross-Curricular Centers

Listening

Listen to the Selections

MATERIALS — SINGLES
CD player, headphones,
AudioText CD, student book

LISTEN TO LITERATURE Listen to
"Mahalia Jackson" and *Perfect
Harmony* as you follow or read
along in your book. Listen for the
main idea about Mahalia Jackson's
life.

If there is anything you don't
understand, you can listen again
to any section.

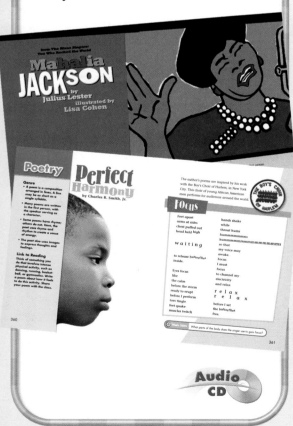

Reading/Library

Read It *Again!*

MATERIALS — SINGLES, PAIRS, GROUPS
Collection of books for self-
selected reading, reading logs,
student book

Select a book you have already
read. Record the title of the book
in your reading log. You may want
to read with a partner.

Choose from the following:

- Leveled Readers
- ELL Readers
- Stories Written by Classmates
- Books from the Library
- "Mahalia Jackson"

TEN IMPORTANT SENTENCES Read
the Ten Important Sentences for
"Mahalia Jackson." Then locate
the sentences in the student book.

BOOK CLUB Look at "Meet
Authors" on p. 767 of the student
book to help you set up an author
study of Julius Lester. Read
other books by Lester and get
together with a group to share your
favorites.

Music

Research a Musician

MATERIALS — GROUPS
Writing materials, books about
musicians, Internet access

Find out more about another
musician or singer like Mahalia
Jackson.

1. Use reference books or the Internet
   to research another musician or
   singer.
2. List five interesting facts about that
   person.

EARLY FINISHERS Try to locate a
piece of the musician's music and
read the lyrics.

Scott Foresman Reading Street Centers Survival Kit

Use the "Mahalia Jackson" materials from the Reading Street Centers Survival Kit to organize this week's centers.

Writing/ Vocabulary

Make
Flashcards

MATERIALS `GROUPS`
Writing materials, index cards

Make flashcards for vocabulary words.

1. **Write lesson vocabulary words on the front of individual index cards.**
2. **Write the definition of the words on the back of the cards.**
3. **Quietly quiz your classmates using the flashcards.**

EARLY FINISHERS Name an antonym for each word after you say its meaning.

Choir

Group of singers who sing together, often in a church service

Social Studies

Explore
THE BLUES

MATERIALS `SINGLES`
Books on the history of the blues, Internet access, writing materials

Find out more about the history of blues music.

1. **Use reference books or the Internet to research the history of blues music.**
2. **Make a list of 3–5 interesting facts about the history of blues music.**

EARLY FINISHERS Draw a time line of key events in the history of the blues movement.

History of Music
The Blues
Blues Greats

Blues History
The history of blues music can be traced back to the 1860s.

Technology

Make a
Play List

MATERIALS `SINGLES` `PAIRS`
Internet access, word processing program

Use a student-friendly search engine to find out about Mahalia Jackson's music.

1. **Conduct a search for a list of Mahalia Jackson's songs.**
2. **Using your word processing program, make a list of 3–5 song titles that you like and would like to hear.**

EARLY FINISHERS Complete your list by writing the year each song was recorded.

Search Engine
Mahalia Jackson

Mahalia Jackson's Songs
1. "Move On Up A Little Higher"
2. "Down By the Riverside"
3. "Didn't It Rain"
4. "When the Saints Go Marching In"
5. "How I Got Over"

ALL CENTERS

Build Concepts

OBJECTIVES

- Build vocabulary by finding words related to the lesson concept.
- Listen for main idea.

Concept Vocabulary

beat a sound made by striking something again and again

time rate of movement in music

blended mixed together

Monitor Progress

Check Vocabulary

If...	then...
students are unable to place words on the web,	... review the lesson concept. Place the words on the web and provide additional words for practice, such as *note* and *fiddle*.

SUCCESS PREDICTOR

DAY 1   Grouping Options

Reading

Whole Group
Introduce and discuss the Question of the Week. Then use pp. 346l–348b.

Group Time

Differentiated Instruction
 Read this week's Leveled Readers. See pp. 346h–346i for the small group lesson plan.

Whole Group
Use p. 363a.

Language Arts
Use pp. 363e–363k.

FLUENCY

MODEL TEMPO AND RATE As you read "Bud, Not Buddy," use tempo and rate to model reading with expression. You can use a slow or fast tempo, like in jazz music as you read words and phrases like "the soft rain commencing to fall on someone's tin roof" or "one deep, sad moan."

LISTENING COMPREHENSION

After reading "Bud, Not Buddy," use the following questions to assess listening comprehension.

1. **What is the main idea of the last paragraph?** *(Miss Thomas's voice was the most beautiful instrument of all.)* **Main Idea**

2. **How many different musical instruments are mentioned in this selection?** *(six)* **Details**

BUILD CONCEPT VOCABULARY

Start a web to build concepts and vocabulary related to this week's lesson and the unit theme.

- Draw the Music and Musicians Concept Web.
- Read the sentence with the word *beat* again. Ask students to pronounce *beat* and discuss its meaning.
- Place *beat* in an oval attached to *Rhythm*. Explain that *beat* is related to this concept. Read the sentences in which *time* and *blended* appear. Have students pronounce the words, place them on the web, and provide reasons.
- Brainstorm additional words and categories for the web. Keep the web on display and add words throughout the week.

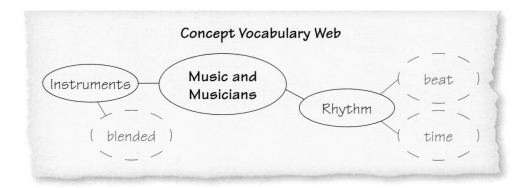

Concept Vocabulary Web

by Christopher Paul Curtis

Listen in on a group of jazz musicians having a jam session.

"One, two, one two three!"....

The Thug was brushing his sticks across the round gold metal thing next to his drums and making it sound like a soft rain was commencing to fall on someone's tin roof. Only instead of sounding like rain splashing any time it wanted to, the Thug had it sounding like it was coming down in a steady, bouncing way.

Then Dirty Deed started making the piano sound like it was a kind of drum, for a second it fell right in with the rain pats that the Thug was making, then it took off and made you think of what Niagara Falls must sound like, it sounded like big, bright drops of water splashing up and over, over and up. The drops would fall loud and clear as anything, then before you knew it they were right back into the Thug's steady, bouncy beat.

Steady Eddie started snapping his fingers real soft, in time with the piano and the drum, his toothpick jumping right along with his fingers. He put his sax in his mouth and blew, but instead of the horn making music it seemed like Steady made it talk. He blew one long, low, rumbly sound and I knew right then, with that one deep, sad moan, what the most beautiful sound in the world was. Steady held the note for a long time, then made the sax drift away from the rest of the storm of music. It swirled and floated back and joined the rain sound that the Thug and Dirty Deed kept going....

Mr. Jimmy picked up his horn and joined in the storm. Miss Thomas sat on a stool, closed her eyes and ducked her head up and down, up and down. Herman E. Calloway stood next to his giant fiddle and started bobbing his head too. He put one of his hands near the top of the fiddle and began pulling at the strings with his other hand.

Every time he patted the strings it seemed like something wide and heavy was walking by slow and easy. Or it seemed like he was the thunder, soft and far away but getting closer all the time.

All of the instruments blended up together and....you'd have a real hard time trying to figure out which instrument was your favorite. Until Miss Thomas opened her mouth. While the rest of the band was being a storm, she was the sun busting through thick, gray clouds....

Prereading Strategies

- Identify main ideas and supporting details to improve comprehension.
- Use graphic organizers to help determine main ideas.

GENRE STUDY

Expository Nonfiction

"Mahalia Jackson" is expository nonfiction. Explain that expository nonfiction is organized by topic and provides information about real-life people, events, ideas, or themes.

PREVIEW AND PREDICT

Have students preview the selection title and illustrations and discuss the topics or ideas they think this selection will cover. Have students use lesson vocabulary words as they talk about what they expect to learn.

Strategy Response Log

Predict Have students write their predictions in their strategy response logs. Students will check their predictions in the Strategy Response Log activity on p. 355.

---

from *The Blues Singers: Ten Who Rocked the World*

Mahalia JACKSON

by **Julius Lester**

illustrated by **Lisa Cohen**

How did **Mahalia Jackson** use the **blues** in a **new** and **different** way?

350

ELL

Access Content Point to the picture of Mahalia Jackson on the opening spread and talk with students about her expression. Help them use the other pictures to talk about the blues, blues singers, and any experience they have had with the music. Have students take turns reading aloud the captions.

Consider having students read the selection summary in English or in students' home languages. See the Multilingual Summaries in the ELL Teaching Guide, pp. 96–98.

Genre

Expository nonfiction explains what certain things are and how they came to be. As you read, notice how the author explains a musical form known as the blues and how it came to be.

351

SET PURPOSE

Read the first page of the selection aloud to students. Have them consider their preview discussion and tell what they hope to find out as they read.

Remind students to look for main ideas and supporting details as they read.

STRATEGY RECALL

Students have now used these before-reading strategies:

- preview the selection to be aware of its genre, features, and possible content;
- activate prior knowledge about that content and what to expect of that genre;
- make predictions;
- set a purpose for reading.

Remind students that, as they read, they should monitor their own comprehension. If they realize something does not make sense, they can regain their comprehension by using fix-up strategies they have learned, such as:

- use phonics and word structure to decode new words;
- use context clues or a dictionary to figure out meanings of new words;
- adjust their reading rate—slow down for difficult text, speed up for easy or familiar text, or skim and scan just for specific information;
- reread parts of the text;
- read on (continue to read for clarification);
- use text features such as headings, subheadings, charts, illustrations, and so on as visual aids to comprehension;
- make a graphic organizer or a semantic organizer to aid comprehension;
- use reference sources, such as an encyclopedia, dictionary, thesaurus, or synonym finder;
- use another person, such as a teacher, a peer, a librarian, or an outside expert, as a resource.

After reading, students will use these strategies:

- summarize or retell the text;
- answer questions they or others pose;
- reflect to make new information become part of their prior knowledge.

Audio CD AudioText

Strategies for Fiction

USE IMAGERY Explain to students that they will be asked to read fiction pieces, including poems, and will be asked to answer questions about them on tests. Poems, like "Focus" and "Deep Breaths," include many images that express feelings and thoughts. Provide the following strategy.

Use the Strategy

1. Read the test question and be sure you understand what the question is asking.
2. Use your own experiences to help you understand the images and the feelings being expressed.
3. Reread the poems, if necessary, to find the answer to the question.

GUIDED PRACTICE Have students discuss how they would use the strategy to answer the following question.

How does the speaker feel just before he performs? Use details from "Focus" to support your answer.

INDEPENDENT PRACTICE After students answer the following test question, discuss the process they used to find information.

According to the speaker, what is the process of singing? Support your answer with images from the poem, "Deep Breaths."

Deep Breaths

Ex-
hale
s l o w.
In-
hale
d e e p.
Thoughts focus.
Ready.
Release.

Breath
breathes life
into words
on a page
gives them
a stage
to showcase
sound

and express
rage
drown sorrows
and engage
ears
with musical
notes
that jump
leap
and
shout
from throats
voicing words
floating
on air
built up
in lungs
singing

singing
a song
that began
with a breath
transformed
from air
to notes
to words
in voice
waiting
to be
sung.

Energy spent.
Ex-
hale
and
done.

362

Test Practice Write the Guided Practice question on the board. Work with students to identify the details in the poem "Focus" that express how the speaker feels before he performs. Students may need help understanding some of the images and the language. Identify and explain some of the images such as "like the calm before the storm," "toes tingle," and "feet quake."

Reading Across Texts

Compare how Mahalia Jackson and the speaker of the poems use their bodies when they sing.

Writing Across Texts Make a list of tips that Mahalia and the speaker might give to people who want to sing with great energy and power. Share your tips with the class.

 **Main Idea** What does it mean to "breathe life into words"?

363

CONNECT TEXT TO TEXT

Reading Across Texts

Suggest that students create a T-chart with the heading *Mahalia* on one side and *Speaker* on the other. As they reread "Mahalia Jackson" and *Perfect Harmony*, they can use the chart to record information.

Writing Across Texts Have students use the information in their T-charts to develop a list of tips.

Main Idea

Possible response: When you "breathe life" into words, you make the words come alive. They have meaning. Without breath, words could not be heard.

Fluency Assessment Plan

- ☑ **Week 1** Assess Advanced students.
- ☑ **Week 2** Assess Strategic Intervention students.
- ☑ **Week 3** Assess On-Level students.
- ☑ **This week assess Strategic Intervention students.**
- ☐ **Week 5** Assess any students you have not yet checked during this unit.

Set individual goals for students to enable them to reach the year-end goal.
- Current Goal: 115–122 wcpm
- Year-End Goal: 140 wcpm

Build students' fluency by encouraging them to repeatedly read aloud passages from familiar and favorite selections, including books that reflect their cultures.

To develop fluent readers, use Fluency Coach.

DAY 5 Grouping Options

Reading
Whole Group
Revisit the Question of the Week.

Group Time
Differentiated Instruction
ReRead this week's Leveled Readers. See pp. 346h–346i for the small group lesson plan.

Whole Group
Use pp. 363b–363c.

Language Arts
Use pp. 363d–363l.

TEMPO AND RATE

Fluency

DAY 1

Model Reread "Bud, Not Buddy" on p. 346m. Explain using different tempos, or rates of speed, mimics the flow of everyday language. Model expressing and emphasizing different words for effect as you read.

DAY 2

Echo Reading Read aloud the last three paragraphs on p. 352. Have students notice how you pause at questions and slow the tempo down for emphasis. Have them practice as a class doing three echo readings of these paragraphs.

DAY 3

Model Read aloud the last two paragraphs on p. 355. Have students notice how you slow down for reflection and emphasis, and increase your speed to express the energy in the text. Practice expression as a class by doing three echo readings of these paragraphs.

DAY 4

Partner Reading Partners practice reading the last two paragraphs on p. 355, three times. Students should read with appropriate tempo, rate, and expression. Have them offer each other feedback.

Monitor Progress | **Check Fluency wcpm**

As students reread, monitor their progress toward their individual fluency goals. Current Goal: 115–122 words correct per minute. End-of-Year Goal: 140 words correct per minute.

If... students cannot read fluently at a rate of 115–122 words correct per minute,
then... make sure students practice with text at their independent level. Provide additional fluency practice, pairing nonfluent readers with fluent readers.

If... students already read at 140 words correct per minute,
then... they do not need to reread three to four times.

SUCCESS PREDICTOR

DAY 5

Assessment
Individual Reading Rate Use the Fluency Assessment Plan and do a one-minute timed reading of either selection from this week to assess students in Week 4. Pay special attention to this week's skill, tempo and rate. Provide corrective feedback for each student.

RETEACH

Main Idea

TEACH

Review the definitions of *main idea* and *supporting details* on p. 346. Students can complete Practice Book p. 138 on their own, or you can complete it as a class. Point out that students need to carefully read the passage and write the main idea and supporting details in each circle to complete the graphic organizer.

ASSESS

Have students work with partners to reread p. 353, paragraph 1, to determine the main idea *(slaves fought against slavery with song)*, and supporting details *(singing spirituals, only bodies were in slavery)*.

For additional instruction on main idea, see DI・55.

EXTEND SKILLS

Persuasive Devices

TEACH

Authors use persuasive devices, also known as propaganda, to persuade people to be for or against someone or something. It is an extreme form of biased writing.

- Some types of persuasive devices are bandwagon, testimonial, and loaded words.
- It is up to the reader to decide whether or not he or she agrees or disagrees with an author's ideas.

Point out the author's use of persuasive devices on p. 352 when he describes the blues.

ASSESS

Have students write a persuasive paragraph about the type of music they like best and why.

OBJECTIVES

- Determine main idea and identify details.
- Identify persuasive devices in a story.

Skills Trace
Main Idea

Introduce/Teach	TE: 5.3 288–289, 346–347; 5.6 654–655
Practice	Practice Book: 113, 117, 118, 126, 133, 137, 138, 156, 216, 263, 267, 268, 286
Reteach/Review	**TE: 5.3 315b, 325, 335, 363b, DI•53, DI•55; 5.4 401; 5.5 545; 5.6 673b, 711, 717, DI•53**
Test	Selection Test: 45–48, 53–56, 105–108; Benchmark Test: Unit 3

Access Content Reteach the skill by reviewing the Picture It! lesson on main idea in the ELL Teaching Guide, pp. 92–93.

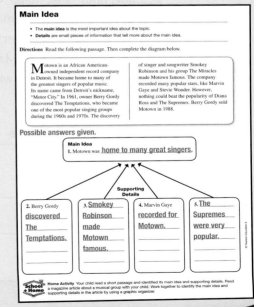

▲ **Practice Book** p. 138

Spelling & Phonics One Consonant or Two

Spelling Words

1. address	11. announce
2. college	12. possess
3. mirror	13. Tennessee
4. recess	14. gallop
5. committee	15. opponent
6. collect	16. barricade
7. Mississippi	17. broccoli
8. immediate	18. accomplish
9. command	19. allowance
10. appreciate*	20. zucchini

Challenge Words

21. silhouette	24. embarrassment
22. millionaire	25. compassionate
23. dilemma	

* Word from the selection

Spelling/Phonics Support See the ELL and Transition Handbook for spelling support.

DAY 1 Pretest and Sort

PRETEST

Use the Dictation Sentences from Day 5 to administer the pretest. Read the word, read the sentence, and then read the word again. Guide students in self-correcting their pretests and correcting any misspellings.

Monitor Progress

Spelling

If... students misspell more than 5 pretest words,	**then**... use words 1–10 for Strategic Intervention.
If... students misspell 1–5 pretest words,	**then**... use words 1–20 for On-Level practice.
If... students correctly spell all pretest words,	**then**... use words 1–25 for Advanced Learners.

HOMEWORK Spelling Practice Book, p. 53.

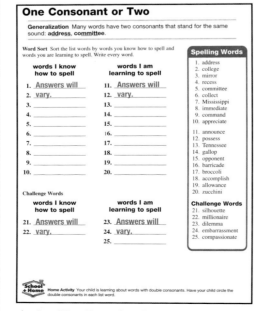

▲ **Spelling Practice Book** p. 53

DAY 2 Think and Practice

TEACH

A single consonant sound is often spelled with a double consonant. Write and say *Mississippi.* Point out that the letter *s* appears four times, but /s/ is only heard twice. Underline each double *s.* Ask what other letters stand for one sound, and underline the double *p.* Have students point out double consonants that stand for a single sound in *command* and *possess.*

M<u>i</u>ss<u>issi</u>ppi

CRACK THE CODE Have students write the list words, replacing each single consonant with a triangle and each pair of double consonants with a star. Tell students to exchange papers and write each spelling word correctly.

HOMEWORK Spelling Practice Book, p. 54.

▲ **Spelling Practice Book** p. 54

DAY 3 — Connect to Writing

WRITE SONG TITLES

Ask students to use at least four spelling words to make up silly song titles.

Frequently Misspelled Words

different   happened

These words may seem easy to spell, but they are often misspelled by fifth-graders. Alert students to these frequently misspelled words. Point out the double consonants that stand for one sound in each word.

HOMEWORK Spelling Practice Book, p. 55.

One Consonant or Two

Proofread a Newspaper Article Circle six misspelled words. Write the words correctly. Find one capitalization error. Write the sentence correctly.

Something odd (hapenned) in the (colledge) dining room. Some students wanted (brocoli) at every meal. Their opponents wanted (zuchinni). A (commitee) was formed. They decided to take a vote. No one expected an (immediat) result. The committee had something surprising to announce. (mst) of the students preferred carrots!

1. happened
2. college
3. broccoli
4. zucchini
5. committee
6. immediate
7. Most of the students preferred carrots!

Proofread Words Circle the correct spelling of the list words.

8. Memphis and Nashville are cities in ____.
   Tennese   Tennesse   (Tennessee)
9. Most students love ____ after being inside.
   (recess)   reccess   recces
10. I ____ a collection of old comic books.
    possess   (possess)   posses
11. The settlers used a wooden plank to ____ the door.
    (barricade)   barricad   barricade
12. I am hoping to ____ a lot this school year.
    acomplish   (accomplish)   accommplish
13. The bathroom ____ was foggy because of the steam from the shower.
    mirrer   mirror   (mirror)
14. I will ____ the winner at the end of the game.
    (announce)   anounce   announc

Spelling Words
address
college
mirror
recess
committee
collect
Mississippi
immediate
command
appreciate
announce
possess
Tennessee
gallop
opponent
barricade
broccoli
accomplish
allowance
zucchini

Frequently Misspelled Words
different
happened

School + Home **Home Activity** Your child identified misspelled list words. Have your child tell you the three most difficult list words and then spell them to you.

▲ **Spelling Practice Book** p. 55

DAY 4 — Review

REVIEW WORDS WITH ONE CONSONANT OR TWO

Have pairs of students take turns writing list words, using a blank line for each single consonant or pair of consonants and writing the vowels in the correct place. Have the partners guess and spell the word.

Spelling Strategy
Memory Tricks

We can use memory tricks to remember when to write two consonants.

Step 1: Mark the double consonants.

Step 2: Find two related words that begin with those consonants.

Step 3: Use the related words and the problem word in a phrase or sentence.

Example: What is my <u>dear</u> <u>dad</u>dy's ad<u>d</u>ress?

HOMEWORK Spelling Practice Book, p. 56.

One Consonant or Two

Spelling Words

address	college	mirror	recess	committee
collect	Mississippi	immediate	command	appreciate
announce	possess	Tennessee	gallop	opponent
barricade	broccoli	accomplish	allowance	zucchini

Double Puzzle Unscramble the words. Write the numbered letters in the boxes below to find the answer to the riddle.

Riddle: What is the name of a dark, rich chocolate dessert?

1. CINUCZIH   z u c c h i n i
2. GPLALO   g a l l o p
3. MIRORR   m i r r o r
4. SADDRSE   a d d r e s s
5. DETIAMME   i m m e d i a t e
6. UNOCEANN   a n n o u n c e
7. SSNEEEENT   T e n n e s s e e
8. POICSHCLAM   a c c o m p l i s h
9. BDCIERARA   b a r r i c a d e
10. TAIARPECEP   a p p r e c i a t e
11. PSESSSO   p o s s e s s
12. EIOETTCMM   c o m m i t t e e

M i s s i s s i p p i   m u d   p i e

Synonyms Write the list word that has the same or nearly the same meaning.

13. foe   opponent   14. higher education   college
15. green vegetable broccoli   16. order   command
17. payment   allowance   18. gather   collect
19. speak to   address   20. time off   recess

School + Home **Home Activity** Your child has learned to read, write, and spell words with double consonants. Look at magazines and newspapers with your child and find three other words that have double consonants.

▲ **Spelling Practice Book** p. 56

DAY 5 — Posttest

DICTATION SENTENCES

1. What is your home <u>address</u>?
2. What will you study in <u>college</u>?
3. I see my face in the <u>mirror</u>.
4. We go out for <u>recess</u> after lunch.
5. The <u>committee</u> planned the party.
6. Both boys <u>collect</u> baseball cards.
7. The steamboat sails on the <u>Mississippi</u> River.
8. I need an <u>immediate</u> answer.
9. I <u>command</u> you to sit down.
10. We <u>appreciate</u> the gift.
11. Who will <u>announce</u> the winner?
12. Jay hopes to <u>possess</u> the new video game soon.
13. The mountains in <u>Tennessee</u> are beautiful.
14. The horses <u>gallop</u> on the trail.
15. His <u>opponent</u> won the game.
16. A <u>barricade</u> blocked the sidewalk.
17. We had steamed <u>broccoli</u> for dinner.
18. We can <u>accomplish</u> this task.
19. Dan spent his <u>allowance</u> quickly.
20. It is easy to grow <u>zucchini</u>.

CHALLENGE

21. The artist cut a <u>silhouette</u> from black paper.
22. A <u>millionaire</u> donated the money.
23. The two choices present a <u>dilemma</u>.
24. Sue blushed in <u>embarrassment</u>.
25. Some <u>compassionate</u> people rescued the kitten.

OBJECTIVES

- Formulate an inquiry question that is connected to this week's lesson focus.
- Effectively and efficiently find, evaluate, and communicate information related to an inquiry question using electronic sources.

New Literacies

Day 1	Identify Questions
Day 2	Navigate/Search
Day 3	Analyze
Day 4	Synthesize
Day 5	Communicate

NEW LITERACIES

Internet Inquiry Activity

EXPLORE MUSIC AND MUSICIANS

Use the following 5-day plan to help students conduct this week's Internet inquiry activity on how musicians appeal to their audiences. Remind students to follow classroom rules when using the Internet.

DAY 1

Identify Questions Discuss the lesson focus question: *How does an artist use music to inspire others?* Brainstorm ideas for specific inquiry questions about today's most popular musicians. For example, students might want to learn what certain musical artists do to appeal to their audiences. Have students work individually, in pairs, or in small groups to write inquiry questions they want to answer.

DAY 2

Navigate/Search Explain how to begin a simple Internet search using a student-friendly search engine. Discuss how to use search engine results to identify a few helpful Web sites. Students can scan the URLs to determine if a site contains relevant information.

DAY 3

Analyze Have students explore the Web sites they identified on Day 2. Tell them to skim each site for information that helps answer their inquiry questions. Explain how to use links and how they are helpful in researching a topic further. Students should analyze information for credibility, reliability, and usefulness. They can take notes from the site, or if appropriate, print out and highlight relevant information.

DAY 4

Synthesize Have students synthesize information from Day 3. Remind them that when they synthesize, they combine relevant ideas and information from different sources to develop answers to their inquiry questions.

DAY 5

Communicate Have students share their inquiry results. They can use a word processing program to create fact sheets about the musicians they chose to research.

RESEARCH/STUDY SKILLS
Card Catalog/Library Database

OBJECTIVES

- Understand terms associated with library card catalogs and databases.
- Use a card catalog or database to locate books.

TEACH

Ask students to imagine that they are researching a report on the American Revolution or that they'd like to read a book by their favorite author. Ask them how they would begin looking for the books they want in the library. Guide them to suggest a card catalog or library database. Use a library computer with the class, if possible, to discuss these features of a database.

- A **library database** is a computerized or online version of a **card catalog.** It can be searched on a computer at a library or sometimes at home.

- A database search can be by subject, author, or title to locate books in the library. For authors, use the last name first.

- A **call number** is an identification number assigned to books, DVDs, and CDs in the library. Numbers are based on the Dewey Decimal System, which divides materials into ten major subject areas.

- A subject search is best for specific topics, such as a place or a person. A **keyword** search is more flexible, so it's more useful when searching for broader topics, such as *African American singers.*

If available, allow students to search an online database using a classroom or library computer. Or, if possible, bring them to the library to use the traditional card catalog to locate books. Have pairs discuss these questions:

1. **What kind of search would you do to find information about Ray Charles?** *(subject)*

2. **If you are looking for more books to read by the author, Andrew Clements, would a keyword search be best? Explain.** *(No, I would search by author to find more books by Andrew Clements.)*

ASSESS

As students work with a library database, check that they understand the variety of search options and when it is appropriate to use each.

For more practice or to assess students, use Practice Book pp. 139–140.

▲ **Practice Book** p. 139

▲ **Practice Book** p. 140

Assessment Checkpoints *for the Week*

Selection Assessment

Use pp. 53–56 of Selection Tests **to check:**

 Selection Understanding

 Comprehension Skill *Main Idea*

 Selection Vocabulary

appreciate	religious
barber	slavery
choir	teenager
released	

Leveled Assessment

- On-Level
- Strategic Intervention
- Advanced

Use pp. 79–84 of Fresh Reads for Differentiated Test Practice **to check:**

 Comprehension Skill *Main Idea*

 REVIEW Comprehension Skill
Fact and Opinion

 Fluency *Words Correct Per Minute*

Managing Assessment

Use Assessment Handbook **for:**

 Observation Checklists

 Record-Keeping Forms

 Portfolio Assessment

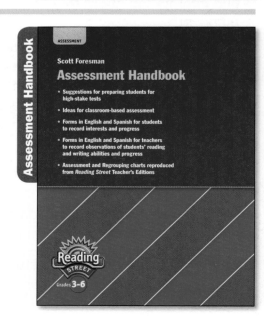

Illinois

Planning Guide for Performance Descriptors

Special Effects in Film and Television

Reading Street Teacher's Edition pages	Grade 5 English Language Arts Performance Descriptors
Oral Language **Speaking/Listening** Build Concept Vocabulary: 364l, 373, 377, 383c Read Aloud: 364m **Viewing** Analyze Film Media: 383d	**1B.Stage E.10.** Read age-appropriate material aloud with fluency and accuracy. **4A.Stage E.5.** Paraphrase and summarize the content of a formal/informal spoken presentation or message. **4B.Stage E.10.** Contribute meaningfully to small and large group discussions by following accepted guidelines for verbal interaction.
Word Work Prefixes *un-, de-, dis-*: 383i–383j	**1A.Stage E.1.** Use a combination of word analysis and vocabulary strategies (e.g., word patterns, structural analyses) within context to identify unknown words.
Reading **Comprehension** Graphic Sources: 364–365, 368–377, 380–383, 383b Prior Knowledge: 364–365, 368–377, 380–383 **Vocabulary** Lesson Vocabulary: 366b, 373, 377 Word Structure: 366–367, 373, 383c **Fluency** Model Tempo and Rate: 364l–364m, 383a **Self-Selected Reading:** LR37–45, TR16–17 **Literature** Genre—Expository Nonfiction: 368 Reader Response: 378	**1A.Stage E.1.** Use a combination of word analysis and vocabulary strategies (e.g., word patterns, structural analyses) within context to identify unknown words. **1B.Stage E.4.** Make judgments based on prior knowledge during reading. **1B.Stage E.7.** Identify structure (e.g., description, compare, cause/effect, sequence) of nonfiction text to improve comprehension. **1C.Stage E.6.** Select reading strategies for text appropriate to the reader's purpose. **2A.Stage E.7.** Use comprehension strategies (e.g., association, categorization, graphic organizers) to enhance understanding. **4B.Stage E.6.** Use appropriate verbal and nonverbal communication elements (e.g., appropriate space, body language, pleasant tone, rate, volume).
Language Arts **Writing** Expository Writing: 383g–383h **Six-Trait Writing** Sentences: 379, 383g–383h **Grammar, Usage, and Mechanics** Prepositions and Prepositional Phrases: 383e, 383f **Research/Study** Graphics/Symbols: 383l **Technology** New Literacies: 383k	**3B.Stage E.1.** Use prewriting strategies to choose a topic and generate ideas (e.g., webbing, brainstorming, listing, note taking, outlining, drafting, graphic organizers). **3B.Stage E.7.** Use adjectives, adverbs, and prepositional phrases to enrich written language. **3C.Stage E.2.** Use the characteristics of a well-developed narrative, expository, and persuasive piece. **3C.Stage E.4.** Use available technology to design, produce, and present compositions and multimedia works.
Unit Skills **Writing** Compare and Contrast Essay: WA2–9 **Poetry:** 384–387 **Project/Wrap-Up:** 388–389	**3A.Stage E.2.** Develop multi-paragraph compositions that include an introduction, first and second level support, and a conclusion. **3C.Stage E.3.** Write creatively for a specified purpose and audience (e.g., short story, poetry, directions, song, friendly letter).

This Week's Leveled Readers

Below-Level

Nonfiction

1C.Stage E.11. Interpret information from tables, maps, visual aids, and charts to enhance understanding of text.

2A.Stage E.7. Use comprehension strategies (e.g., association, categorization, graphic organizers) to enhance understanding.

On-Level

Nonfiction

1C.Stage E.8. Interpret imagery and figurative language (e.g., alliteration, metaphor, simile, personification).

2A.Stage E.7. Use comprehension strategies (e.g., association, categorization, graphic organizers) to enhance understanding.

Advanced

Nonfiction

2A.Stage E.7. Use comprehension strategies (e.g., association, categorization, graphic organizers) to enhance understanding.

2B.Stage E.5. Make inferences and draw conclusions about contexts, events, character, and settings.

Content-Area Illinois Performance Descriptors in This Lesson

Science

11A.Stage E.2. Conduct scientific inquiry investigation: observing safety precautions and following procedural steps accurately over multiple trials.

11A.Stage E.4. Organize and display data: determining most appropriate visualization strategies for collected data; using graphs and technologies.

12C.Stage E.2. Apply scientific inquiries or technological designs to distinguish the properties of matter.

13B.Stage E.3. Investigate the interactions of societal decisions in science and technology innovations and discoveries.

Social Studies

14F.Stage E.5. Identify significant changes in communication or technology that have had an affect on the spread of political information and influence (e.g., telegraph, television, Internet).

15B.Stage E.2. Identify factors that affect consumer choices (e.g., prices of goods and services; quality; income; preferences/tastes).

Math

7C.Stage E.1. Select appropriate tools to measure, draw, or construct figures.

Illinois!

NATIVE AMERICANS OF ILLINOIS
The Sauk

During the 1800s the Sauk people moved from the area that is now Wisconsin and settled along the Mississippi River near Rock Island. They lived in bark houses in villages during the summer, staying near fields where the women grew crops. In the winter, family groups lived together in houses covered with reed mats. The men hunted bison and other animals in the spring.

Students can . . .
Research the Sauk, Fox, and Kickapoo Native American groups. Have students make a chart to compare and contrast how each group lived.

A SPECIAL ILLINOIS PLACE
Du Quoin

The original settlement of Du Quoin grew out of a Kaskaskia winter camp, but the community was never formally established. When a railroad was built in the area, many settlers moved to be closer to the railroad, and they called their new community Du Quoin. The original settlement became known as Old Du Quoin. Du Quoin is named for Jean Baptiste Du Quoin, the son of a Frenchman and a Tamaroa woman. He later became a leader of the Tamaroa.

Students can . . .
Find out about the Du Quoin State Fair held every year in August and September. Have them draw a picture of one of the featured attractions or events at the fair.

ILLINOIS FUN FACTS
Did You Know?

• Coal is mined in twelve counties in Illinois.

• Well-known science-fiction writer Ray Bradbury was born in Waukegan.

• Everett Dirksen, a U.S. senator from Illinois, helped pass the Voting Rights Act of 1965, which is generally considered to be the most successful piece of civil rights legislation ever adopted by the United States Congress. The act enforces the Fifteenth Amendment's permanent guarantee that, throughout the nation, no person can be denied the right to vote because of race or color.

Students can . . .
Find out more about Everett Dirksen and use their findings to write a brief biography of the senator.

Unit 3
Inventors and Artists

CONCEPT QUESTION
What do people gain from the work of inventors and artists?

Week 1

How do inventors inspire our imaginations?

Week 2

How do artists inspire future generations?

Week 3

How can paleontologists help us understand the past?

Week 4

How does an artist use music to inspire others?

Week 5

How do artists create special effects to entertain us?

EXPAND THE CONCEPT
How do artists create special effects to entertain us?

CONNECT THE CONCEPT

▶ **Build Background**
digital effects, illusion, props

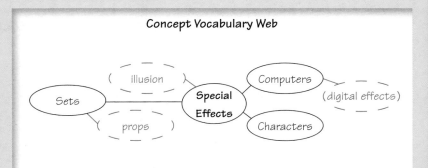

Concept Vocabulary Web

▶ **Science Content**
Careers, Blue Screen Technology

▶ **Writing**
Expository Writing

▶ **Internet Inquiry**
Special Effects

Preview Your Week

How do artists create special effects to entertain us?

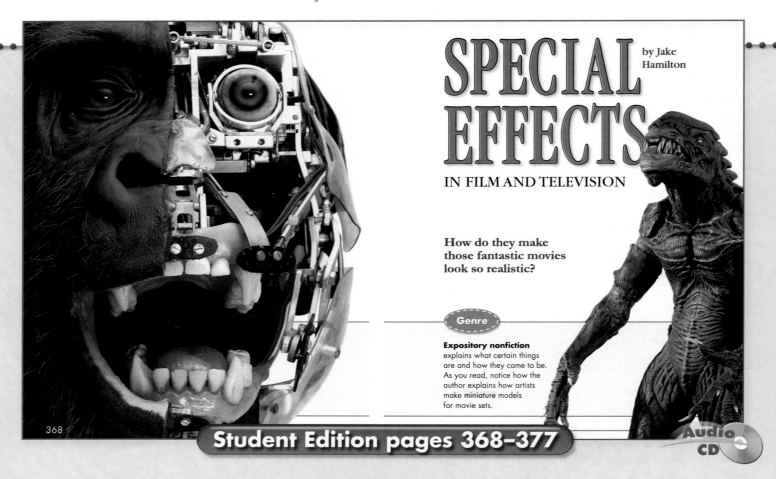

by Jake Hamilton

SPECIAL EFFECTS
IN FILM AND TELEVISION

How do they make those fantastic movies look so realistic?

Genre

Expository nonfiction explains what certain things are and how they came to be. As you read, notice how the author explains how artists make miniature models for movie sets.

368

Student Edition pages 368–377

Audio CD

Genre	Expository Nonfiction
Vocabulary Strategy	Word Structure
Comprehension Skill	Graphic Sources
Comprehension Strategy	Prior Knowledge

Paired Selection

SOCIAL STUDIES

Reading Across Texts
Make a List of Special Effects and Animation Tricks

Genre
Search Engines

Text Features
Search Window
Keywords
Search Results
Web Site

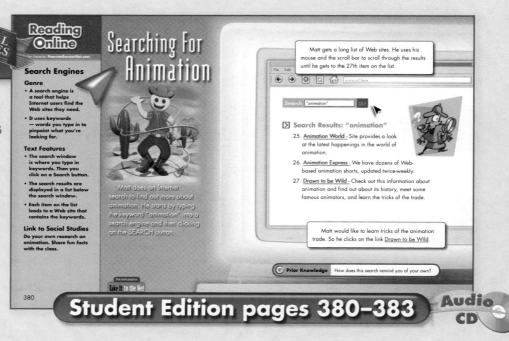

Reading Online
For literacy: PearsonSuccessNet.com

Search Engines

Genre
- A search engine is a tool that helps Internet users find the Web sites they need.
- It uses keywords — words you type in to pinpoint what you're looking for.

Text Features
- The search window is where you type in keywords. Then you click on a Search button.
- The search results are displayed in a list below the search window.
- Each item on the list leads to a Web site that contains the keywords.

Link to Social Studies
Do your own research on animation. Share fun facts with the class.

Searching For Animation

Matt does an Internet search to find out more about animation. He starts by typing the keyword "animation" into a search engine and then clicking on the SEARCH button.

Matt gets a long list of Web sites. He uses his mouse and the scroll bar to scroll through the results until he gets to the 27th item on the list.

Search: "animation" GO

Search Results: "animation"

25. Animation World - Site provides a look at the latest happenings in the world of animation.

26. Animation Express - We have dozens of Web-based animation shorts, updated twice-weekly.

27. Drawn to be Wild - Check out this information about animation and find out about its history, meet some famous animators, and learn the tricks of the trade.

Matt would like to learn tricks of the animation trade. So he clicks on the link Drawn to be Wild.

Prior Knowledge How does this search remind you of your own?

For more practice
Take It to the Net

380

Student Edition pages 380–383

Audio CD

Read It
ONLINE
PearsonSuccessNet.com
• Student Edition
• Leveled Readers

Leveled Readers

⊙ **Skill** Graphic Sources
⊙ **Strategy** Prior Knowledge
Lesson Vocabulary

Below-Level

On-Level

Advanced

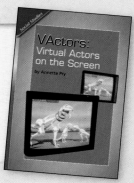

ELL Reader
· Concept Vocabulary
· Text Support
· Language Enrichment

VActors:
Virtual Actors
on the Screen
by Annette Fry

Time for
SOCIAL
STUDIES

Integrate Social Studies Standards
• Careers
• Technology
• Entertainment Industry

✓ **Read**

Special Effects in Film and Television,
pp. 368–377

"Searching for Animation,"
pp. 380–383

Leveled Readers

Below-Level   On-Level   Advanced
• Support Concepts • Develop Concepts • Extend Concepts
                                        • Extension Activity

ELL Reader

✓ **Build Concept Vocabulary**
Special Effects, pp. 364l–364m

✓ **Teach Social Studies Concepts**
Careers, p. 371
Blue Screen Technology, p. 375

✓ **Explore Social Studies Center**
Research Reptiles, p. 364k

Weekly Plan

READING

45–90 minutes

TARGET SKILLS OF THE WEEK

Comprehension Skill
Graphic Sources

Comprehension Strategy
Prior Knowledge

Vocabulary Strategy
Word Structure

LANGUAGE ARTS

30–60 minutes

Trait of the Week

Sentences

DAY 1 — PAGES 364l–366b, 383a, 383e–383k

Oral Language

QUESTION OF THE WEEK *How do artists create special effects to entertain us?*

Read Aloud: "The Making of The Lord of the Rings," 364m
Build Concepts, 364l

Comprehension/Vocabulary

Comprehension Skill/Strategy Lesson, 364–365
Graphic Sources **T**
Prior Knowledge
Build Background, 366a
Introduce Lesson Vocabulary, 366b
background, landscape, miniature, prehistoric, reassembled **T**

Read Leveled Readers

Grouping Options 364f–364g

Fluency

Model Tempo and Rate, 364l–364m, 383a

Grammar, 383e
Introduce Prepositions and Prepositional Phrases **T**

Writing Workshop, 383g
Introduce Expository Writing
Model the Trait of the Week: Sentences

Spelling, 383i
Pretest for Prefixes *un-, de-, dis-*

Internet Inquiry, 383k
Identify Questions

DAY 2 — PAGES 366–373, 383a, 383e–383k

Oral Language

QUESTION OF THE DAY *Why do special effects artists create miniature models of movie scenes?*

Comprehension/Vocabulary

Vocabulary Strategy Lesson, 366–367
Word Structure **T**

Read *Special Effects in Film and Television,* 368–373

Grouping Options 364f–364g

Graphic Sources **T**
Word Structure **T**
Develop Vocabulary

Fluency

Choral Reading, 383a

Grammar, 383e
Develop Prepositions and Prepositional Phrases **T**

Writing Workshop, 383g
Improve Writing with Parallelism

Spelling, 383i
Teach the Generalization

Internet Inquiry, 383k
Navigate/Search

DAILY WRITING ACTIVITIES

Day 1 Write to Read, 364

Day 2 Words to Write, 367
Strategy Response Log, 368, 373

DAILY SOCIAL STUDIES CONNECTIONS

Day 1 Special Effects Concept Web, 364l

Day 2 Time for Social Studies: Careers, 371
Revisit the Special Effects Concept Web, 373

DAILY SUCCESS PREDICTORS
for Adequate Yearly Progress

Monitor Progress and Corrective Feedback

Vocabulary | Check Vocabulary, *364l*

RESOURCES FOR THE WEEK

- Practice Book, *pp. 141–150*
- Word Study and Spelling Practice Book, *pp. 57–60*
- Grammar and Writing Practice Book, *pp. 57–60*
- Selection Test, *pp. 57–60*
- Fresh Reads for Differentiated Test Practice, *pp. 85–90*
- The Grammar and Writing Book, *pp. 134–139*

Grouping Options for Differentiated Instruction

Turn the page for the small group lesson plan.

DAY 3 — PAGES 374–379, 383a, 383e–383k

Oral Language

QUESTION OF THE DAY *How can an artist make a prehistoric setting look realistic?*

Comprehension/Vocabulary

Read *Special Effects in Film and Television,* 374–378

Grouping Options 364f–364g

🔵 Prior Knowledge
REVIEW Author's Purpose **T**
Develop Vocabulary

Reader Response

Selection Test

Fluency

Model Tempo and Rate, 383a

Grammar, 383f
Apply Prepositions and Prepositional Phrases in Writing **T**

Writing Workshop, 379, 383h
Write Now
Prewrite and Draft

Spelling, 383j
Connect Spelling to Writing

Internet Inquiry, 383k
Analyze Sources

Day 3 Strategy Response Log, 376
Look Back and Write, 378

Day 3 Time for Social Studies: Blue Screen Technology, 375; Revisit the Special Effects Concept Web, 377

DAY 4 — PAGES 380–383a, 383e–383k

Oral Language

QUESTION OF THE DAY *Why do you think many films and television programs with spectacular special effects are so popular?*

Comprehension/Vocabulary

Read "Searching for Animation," 380–383

Grouping Options 364f–364g

Search Engines/Text Features

Reading Across Texts

Fluency

Partner Reading, 383a

Grammar, 383f
Practice Prepositions and Prepositional Phrases for Standardized Tests **T**

Writing Workshop, 383h
Draft, Revise, and Publish

Spelling, 383j
Provide a Strategy

Internet Inquiry, 383k
Synthesize Information

Day 4 Writing Across Texts, 383

Day 4 Social Studies Center: Research Reptiles, 364k

DAY 5 — PAGES 383a–383l

Oral Language

QUESTION OF THE WEEK *To wrap up the week, revisit the Day 1 question.*
Build Concept Vocabulary, 383c

Fluency

Read Leveled Readers

Grouping Options 364f–364g

Assess Reading Rate, 383a

Comprehension/Vocabulary

🔵 Reteach Graphic Sources, 383b **T**
Steps in a Process, 383b
🔵 Review Word Structure, 383c **T**

Speaking and Viewing, 383d
Advertisement
Analyze Film Media

Grammar, 383f
Cumulative Review

Writing Workshop, 383h
Connect to Unit Writing

Spelling, 383j
Posttest for Prefixes *un-, de-, dis-*

Internet Inquiry, 383k
Communicate Results

Research/Study Skills, 383l
Graphics/Symbols

Day 5 Steps in a Process, 383b

Day 5 Revisit the Special Effects Concept Web, 383c

KEY 🔵 = Target Skill **T** = Tested Skill

Comprehension — Check Retelling, *378*

Fluency — Check Fluency WCPM, *383a*

Vocabulary — Check Vocabulary, *383c*

SUCCESS PREDICTOR

Small Group Plan *for Differentiated Instruction*

Daily Plan
AT A GLANCE

Reading

Whole Group
- Oral Language
- Comprehension/Vocabulary

Group Time

Differentiated Instruction

Meet with small groups to provide:
- Skill Support
- Reading Support
- Fluency Practice

Read

This week's lessons for daily group time can be found behind the Differentiated Instruction (DI) tab on pp. DI·42–DI·51.

Whole Group
- Fluency

Language Arts
- Grammar
- Writing
- Spelling
- Research/Inquiry
- Speaking/Listening/Viewing

Use *My Sidewalks on Reading Street* for Tier III intensive reading intervention.

DAY 1

On-Level	Strategic Intervention	Advanced
Teacher-Led *Page DI·43*	**Teacher-Led** *Page DI·42*	**Teacher-Led** *Page DI·43*
• Develop Concept Vocabulary • **Read** On-Level Reader *Very Special Effects: Computers in Filmmaking*	• Reinforce Concepts • **Read** Below-Level Reader *The Art of Makeup: Going Behind the Mask*	• **Read** Advanced Reader *Hollywood Special Effects* • Independent Extension Activity

(i) Independent Activities

While you meet with small groups, have the rest of the class...

- Visit the Reading/Library Center
- Listen to the Background Building Audio
- Finish Write to Read, p. 364
- Complete Practice Book pp. 143–144
- Visit Cross-Curricular Centers

DAY 2

On-Level	Strategic Intervention	Advanced
Teacher-Led *Pages 370–373*	**Teacher-Led** *Page DI·44*	**Teacher-Led** *Page DI·45*
• **Read** *Special Effects in Film and Television*	• Practice Lesson Vocabulary • Read Multisyllabic Words • **Read** or Listen to *Special Effects in Film and Television*	• Extend Vocabulary • **Read** *Special Effects in Film and Television*

(i) Independent Activities

While you meet with small groups, have the rest of the class...

- Visit the Reading/Library Center
- Listen to the AudioText for *Special Effects in Film and Television*
- Finish Words to Write, p. 367
- Complete Practice Book pp. 145–146
- Write in their Strategy Response Logs, pp. 368, 373
- Visit Cross-Curricular Centers
- Work on inquiry projects

DAY 3

On-Level	Strategic Intervention	Advanced
Teacher-Led *Pages 374–377*	**Teacher-Led** *Page DI·46*	**Teacher-Led** *Page DI·47*
• **Read** *Special Effects in Film and Television*	• Practice Prior Knowledge and Graphic Sources • **Read** or Listen to *Special Effects in Film and Television*	• Extend Prior Knowledge and Graphic Sources • **Read** *Special Effects in Film and Television*

(i) Independent Activities

While you meet with small groups, have the rest of the class...

- Visit the Reading/Library Center
- Listen to the AudioText for *Special Effects in Film and Television*
- Write in their Strategy Response Logs, p. 376
- Finish Look Back and Write, p. 378
- Complete Practice Book p. 147
- Visit Cross-Curricular Centers
- Work on inquiry projects

① Begin with whole class skill and strategy instruction.

② Meet with small groups to provide differentiated instruction.

③ Gather the whole class back together for fluency and language arts.

On-Level

Teacher-Led
Pages 380–383

- **Read** "Searching for Animation"

Strategic Intervention

Teacher-Led
Page DI · 48

- Practice Retelling
- **Read** or Listen to "Searching for Animation"

Advanced

Teacher-Led
Page DI · 49

- **Read** "Searching for Animation"
- Genre Study

DAY 4

(i) Independent Activities

While you meet with small groups, have the rest of the class...

- Visit the Reading/Library Center
- Listen to the AudioText for "Searching for Animation"
- Visit the Writing/Vocabulary Center

- Finish Writing Across Texts, p. 383
- Visit Cross-Curricular Centers
- Work on inquiry projects

On-Level

Teacher-Led
Page DI · 51

- **Reread** Leveled Reader *Very Special Effects: Computers in Filmmaking*
- Retell *Very Special Effects: Computers in Filmmaking*

Strategic Intervention

Teacher-Led
Page DI · 50

- **Reread** Leveled Reader *The Art of Makeup: Going Behind the Mask*
- Retell *The Art of Makeup: Going Behind the Mask*

Advanced

Teacher-Led
Page DI · 51

- **Reread** Leveled Reader *Hollywood Special Effects*
- Share Extension Activity

DAY 5

(i) Independent Activities

While you meet with small groups, have the rest of the class...

- Visit the Reading/Library Center
- Complete Practice Book pp. 148–150

- Visit Cross-Curricular Centers
- Work on inquiry projects

Grouping Place English language learners in the groups that correspond to their reading abilities in English.

Use the appropriate Leveled Reader or other text at students' instructional level.

TiP Send home the appropriate Multilingual Summary of the main selection on Day 1.

ELL

Take It to the NET ONLINE
PearsonSuccessNet.com

Edward Kame'enui
For effective activities to develop vocabulary, see the article "Research on Vocabulary Instruction" by J. F. Baumann and Scott Foresman author Edward Kame'enui.

TEACHER TALK

A **base word** is a word that can stand alone or take endings and affixes, such as *walk* or *happy*.

Be sure to schedule time for students to work on the unit inquiry project "Inventors and Artists." This week students create a class display on the inventors and artists they researched. They may also write biographies and compile a class book.

Looking Ahead

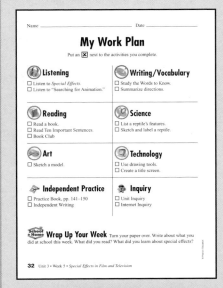

Name _____ Date _____

My Work Plan
Put an ☒ next to the activities you complete.

Listening
☐ Listen to *Special Effects*.
☐ Listen to "Searching for Animation."

Writing/Vocabulary
☐ Study the Words to Know.
☐ Summarize directions.

Reading
☐ Read a book.
☐ Read Ten Important Sentences.
☐ Book Club

Science
☐ List a reptile's features.
☐ Sketch and label a reptile.

Art
☐ Sketch a model.

Technology
☐ Use drawing tools.
☐ Create a title screen.

Independent Practice
☐ Practice Book, pp. 141–150
☐ Independent Writing

Inquiry
☐ Unit Inquiry
☐ Internet Inquiry

Wrap Up Your Week Turn your paper over. Write about what you did at school this week. What did you read? What did you learn about special effects?

32 Unit 3 • Week 5 • *Special Effects in Film and Television*

▲ **Group-Time Survival Guide**
p. 32, Weekly Contract

☑ Customize Your Plan *by Strand*

 SOCIAL STUDIES

Concept Development

How do artists create special effects to entertain us?

CONCEPT VOCABULARY
digital effects   illusion   props

BUILD

❑ **Question of the Week** Introduce and discuss the question of the week. This week students will read a variety of texts and work on projects related to the concept *special effects.* Post the question for students to refer to throughout the week. DAY 1 *364d*

❑ **Read Aloud** Read aloud "The Making of the Lord of the Rings." Then begin a web to build concepts and concept vocabulary related to this week's lesson and the unit theme, Inventors and Artists. Introduce the concept words *digital effects, illusion,* and *props* and have students place them on the web. Display the web for use throughout the week. DAY 1 *364l–364m*

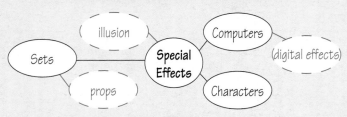

Sets — Special Effects
illusion
props
Computers
(digital effects)
Characters

DEVELOP

❑ **Question of the Day** Use the prompts from the Weekly Plan to engage students in conversations related to this week's reading and the unit theme. **EVERY DAY** *364d–364e*

❑ **Concept Vocabulary Web** Revisit the Special Effects Concept Web and encourage students to add concept words from their reading and life experiences. DAY 2 *373*, DAY 3 *377*

CONNECT

❑ **Looking Back** Revisit the Special Effects Concept Web and discuss how it relates to this week's lesson and the unit theme. DAY 5 *383c*

CHECK

❑ **Concept Vocabulary Web** Use the Special Effects Concept Web to check students' understanding of the concept vocabulary words *digital effects, illusion,* and *props.* DAY 1 *364l* DAY 5 *383c*

⟳ **STRATEGY WORD STRUCTURE**
Recognizing a prefix can help you figure out the meaning of an unfamiliar word. A prefix is a syllable added at the beginning of a base word that has a meaning of its own.

LESSON VOCABULARY
background   prehistoric
landscape   reassembled
miniature

TEACH

❑ **Words to Know** Give students the opportunity to tell what they already know about this week's lesson vocabulary words. Then discuss word meaning. DAY 1 *366b*

❑ **Vocabulary Strategy Lesson** Use the vocabulary strategy lesson in the Student Edition to introduce and model this week's strategy, *word structure.* DAY 2 *366-367*

Vocabulary Strategy Lesson

PRACTICE/APPLY

❑ **Leveled Text** Read the lesson vocabulary in the context of leveled text. DAY 1 *LR37–LR45*

Leveled Readers

❑ **Words in Context** Read the lesson vocabulary and apply *word structure* in the context of *Special Effects in Film and Television.* DAY 2 *368-373*, DAY 3 *374-378*

❑ **Writing/Vocabulary Center** Summarize the steps in the miniature model-making process. **ANY DAY** *364k*

Main Selection—Nonfiction

❑ **Homework** Practice Book pp. 144–145. DAY 1 *366b*, DAY 2 *367*

❑ **Word Play** Have small groups brainstorm lists of abbreviations and acronyms that use initials for phrases, such as ASAP and FYI. Then have students make up their own abbreviations and acronyms for common phrases, like SYL for "see you later." **ANY DAY** *383c*

ASSESS

❑ **Selection Test** Use the Selection Test to determine students' understanding of the lesson vocabulary words. DAY 3

RETEACH/REVIEW

❑ **Reteach Lesson** If necessary, use this lesson to reteach and review *word structure.* DAY 5 *383c*

❶ Use assessment data to determine your instructional focus.

❷ Preview this week's instruction by strand.

❸ Choose instructional activities that meet the needs of your classroom.

COMPREHENSION

⊙ SKILL GRAPHIC SOURCES Graphic sources are maps, timelines, charts, diagrams, and pictures with captions. A graphic source makes information easy to see and understand.

⊙ STRATEGY PRIOR KNOWLEDGE Prior knowledge is what the reader already knows. Good readers use their prior knowledge to help them understand what they read and then take the new information and connect it to something they already know to create new meaning.

TEACH

❑ **Skill/Strategy Lesson** Use the skill/ strategy lesson in the Student Edition to introduce and model *graphic sources* and *prior knowledge*. DAY 1 *364-365*

Skill/Strategy Lesson

❑ **Extend Skills** Teach steps in a process. **ANY DAY** *383b*

PRACTICE/APPLY

❑ **Leveled Text** Apply *graphic sources* and *prior knowledge* to read leveled text. DAY 1 *LR37-LR45*

Leveled Readers

❑ **Skills and Strategies in Context** Read *Special Effects in Film and Television,* using the Guiding Comprehension questions to apply *graphic sources* and *prior knowledge*. DAY 2 *368-373*, DAY 3 *374-378*

Main Selection—Nonfiction

❑ **Skills and Strategies in Context** Read "Searching for Animation," guiding students as they apply *graphic sources* and *prior knowledge*. Then have students discuss and write across texts. DAY 4 *380-383*

Paired Selection—Nonfiction

❑ **Homework** Practice Book pp. 143, 147, 148. DAY 1 *365*, DAY 3 *377*, DAY 5 *383b*

❑ **Fresh Reads for Differentiated Test Practice** Have students practice *graphic sources* with a new passage. DAY 3

ASSESS

❑ **Selection Test** Determine students' understanding of the selection and their use of *graphic sources*. DAY 3

❑ **Retell** Have students retell *Special Effects in Film and Television*. DAY 3 *378-379*

RETEACH/REVIEW

❑ **Reteach Lesson** If necessary, reteach and review *graphic sources*. DAY 5 *383b*

FLUENCY

SKILL TEMPO AND RATE Reading with an even tempo means that you take breaths at appropriate times and pause at punctuation. Reading with appropriate rate means that you do not read too fast or too slow.

TEACH

❑ **Read Aloud** Model fluent reading by rereading "The Making of the Lord of the Rings." Focus on this week's fluency skill, tempo and rate. DAY 1 *364l-364m, 383a*

PRACTICE/APPLY

❑ **Choral Reading** Read aloud selected paragraphs from *Special Effects in Film and Television,* modeling appropriate reading rate and tempo. Have students practice, doing three choral readings of the selected paragraphs. DAY 2 *383a*, DAY 3 *383a*

❑ **Partner Reading** Have partners practice reading aloud, using appropriate tempo and rate, and offering each other feedback. As students reread, monitor their progress toward their individual fluency goals. DAY 4 *383a*

❑ **Listening Center** Have students follow along with the AudioText for this week's selections. **ANY DAY** *364j*

❑ **Reading/Library Center** Have students reread a selection of their choice. **ANY DAY** *364j*

❑ **Fluency Coach** Have students use Fluency Coach to listen to fluent readings or practice reading on their own. **ANY DAY**

ASSESS

❑ **Check Fluency** WCPM Do a one-minute timed reading, paying special attention to this week's skill—tempo and rate. Provide feedback for each student. DAY 5 *383a*

☑ Customize Your Plan *by Strand*

SKILL PREPOSITIONS AND PREPOSITIONAL PHRASES A *preposition* begins a group of words called a *prepositional phrase.* The noun or pronoun that follows the preposition is called the *object of the preposition.* Prepositional phrases can be used to tell more about the words they accompany.

TEACH

❑ **Grammar Transparency 15** Use Grammar Transparency 15 to teach prepositions and prepositional phrases. DAY 1 *383e*

Grammar Transparency 15

PRACTICE/APPLY

❑ **Develop the Concept** Review the concept of prepositions and prepositional phrases and provide guided practice. DAY 2 *383e*

❑ **Apply to Writing** Have students review something they have written and apply prepositions and prepositional phrases. DAY 3 *383f*

❑ **Test Preparation** Examine common errors in prepositions and prepositional phrases to prepare for standardized tests. DAY 4 *383f*

❑ **Homework** Grammar and Writing Practice Book pp. 57–59. DAY 2 *383e*, DAY 3 *383f*, DAY 4 *383f*

ASSESS

❑ **Cumulative Review** Use Grammar and Writing Practice Book p. 60. DAY 5 *383f*

RETEACH/REVIEW

❑ **Daily Fix-It** Have students find and correct errors in grammar, spelling, and punctuation. EVERY DAY *383e-383f*

❑ **The Grammar and Writing Book** Use pp. 134–137 of The Grammar and Writing Book to extend instruction for prepositions and prepositional phrases. ANY DAY

The Grammar and Writing Book

Trait of the Week

SENTENCES Good writers express their thoughts in lively, varied sentences. Sentences that have a natural flow as well as vary in structure and length create a rhythm and style.

TEACH

❑ **Writing Transparency 15A** Use the model to introduce and discuss the Trait of the Week. DAY 1 *383g*

❑ **Writing Transparency 15B** Use the transparency to show students how parallelism can improve their writing. DAY 2 *383g*

Writing Transparency 15A   **Writing Transparency 15B**

PRACTICE/APPLY

❑ **Write Now** Examine the model on Student Edition p. 379. Then have students write their own expository writing. DAY 3 *379, 383h*, DAY 4 *383h*

> **Prompt** *Special Effects in Film and Television* explains how filmmakers create effects. Think about a movie and a television show in the same genre. Now use expository writing to tell how they are alike and different.

Write Now p. 379

❑ **Writing/Vocabulary Center** Summarize the steps in the miniature model-making process. ANY DAY *364k*

ASSESS

❑ **Writing Trait Rubric** Use the rubric to evaluate students' writing. DAY 4 *383h*

RETEACH/REVIEW

❑ **The Grammar and Writing Book** Use pp. 134–139 of The Grammar and Writing Book to extend instruction for prepositions and prepositional phrases, parallelism, and expository writing. ANY DAY

The Grammar and Writing Book

SPELLING

GENERALIZATION PREFIXES *UN-*, *DE-*, *DIS-* When prefixes *un-*, *de-*, and *dis-* are added to words, the base word does not change: <u>un</u>cover, <u>de</u>frost, <u>dis</u>courage. The prefixes *un-*, *de-*, and *dis-* mean "not" or "the opposite of."

TEACH

❑ **Pretest** Give the pretest for words with prefixes *un-*, *de-*, *dis-*. Guide students in self-correcting their pretests and correcting any misspellings. **DAY 1** *383i*

❑ **Think and Practice** Connect spelling to the phonics generalization for words with prefixes *un-*, *de-*, *dis-*. **DAY 2** *383i*

PRACTICE/APPLY

❑ **Connect to Writing** Have students use spelling words to write about a change. Then review frequently misspelled words: *until, before.* **DAY 3** *383j*

❑ **Homework** Word Study and Spelling Practice Book pp. 57–60. **EVERY DAY**

RETEACH/REVIEW

❑ **Review** Review spelling words to prepare for the posttest. Then provide students with a spelling strategy—words with prefixes. **DAY 4** *383j*

ASSESS

❑ **Posttest** Use dictation sentences to give the posttest for words with prefixes *un-*, *de-*, *dis-*. **DAY 5** *383j*

Spelling Words

1. uncover	8. disability	15. disapprove
2. defrost	9. discomfort	16. disappoint
3. uncomfortable	10. deodorant	17. unpleasant
4. discourage	11. unemployed	18. dehydrated
5. disadvantage	12. deflate	19. disqualify
6. unfortunate	13. disbelief	20. undecided
7. unfamiliar	14. unpredictable	

Challenge Words

21. unnecessary	23. dehumidifier	25. disenchanted
22. disobedient	24. disinfectant	

*Word from the selection

RESEARCH AND INQUIRY

❑ **Internet Inquiry** Have students conduct an Internet inquiry on special effects. **EVERY DAY** *383k*

❑ **Graphics/Symbols** Review how to recognize and understand graphics and symbols within a text and discuss how students can interpret graphics and symbols to understand information. **DAY 5** *383l*

❑ **Unit Inquiry** Allow time for students to create a class display on the inventors and artists they researched. They may also write biographies and compile a class book. **ANY DAY** *261*

SPEAKING AND VIEWING

❑ **Advertisement** Have students work with partners to create an advertisement for the movie in *Special Effects in Film and Television.* **DAY 5** *383d*

❑ **Analyze Film Media** Have students discuss TV shows or movies they have seen which use special effects, and then answer questions. **DAY 5** *383d*

Resources for
Differentiated Instruction

LEVELED READERS

▶ **Comprehension**
- ◎ **Skill** Graphic Sources
- ◎ **Strategy** Prior Knowledge

▶ **Lesson Vocabulary**
- ◎ **Word Structure**

background   landscape

prehistoric

miniature   reassembled

▶ **Social Studies Standards**
- **Careers**
- **Technology**
- **Entertainment Industry**

Leveled Reader Database
ONLINE
PearsonSuccessNet.com

Use the Online Database of over 600 books to
- Download and print additional copies of this week's leveled readers.
- Listen to the readers being read online.
- Search for more titles focused on this week's skills, topic, and content.

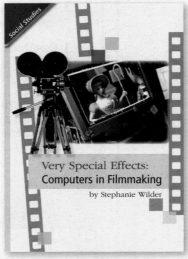

Social Studies

Very Special Effects:
Computers in Filmmaking
by Stephanie Wilder

On-Level Reader

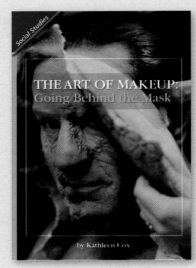

Social Studies

THE ART OF MAKEUP:
Going Behind the Mask

by Kathleen Cox

Below-Level Reader

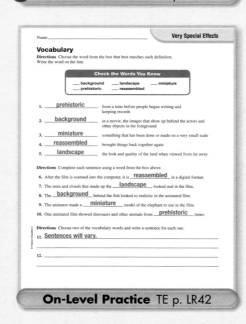

Name _____ Very Special Effects

Graphic Sources

- **Graphic sources** include items such as advertisements, charts, diagrams, graphs, maps, menus, photographs, recipes, and timetables.
- Use graphic sources to help you understand text and to draw conclusions as you read.

Directions Use the graphic source on pages 20–21 of *Very Special Effects: Computers in Filmmaking* to answer the questions below.

1. What type of graphic source is shown on these pages? Possible responses given.
   a chart
2. Give one *pro* of computer-based movies that is related to their cost.
   Computer-based movies cost less to make and distribute than regular movies.
3. What is one *con* of computer-based movies that relates to computer memory?
   They take up a lot of space as computer files.
4. Why might movie-theater owners resist converting to computer-based films?
   It would be expensive, so they might have to raise ticket prices.
5. Why might moviemakers prefer computer-based movies?
   They can see a result immediately.
6. What are some words that mean the same as *con* as it is used in this graphic source?
   drawback, disadvantage
7. What are some words that mean the same as *pro* as it is used in this graphic source?
   benefit, advantage, strength
8. If you were a moviegoer, would you be in favor of or opposed to computer-based movies? Explain your reasoning.
   Possible responses: In favor, because the special effects are really great. Opposed, because ticket prices may go up and because they look grainy on a big screen.

On-Level Practice TE p. LR41

Name _____ The Art of Makeup

Graphic Sources

- **Graphic sources** include items such as advertisements, charts, diagrams, graphs, maps, menus, photographs, recipes, and timetables.
- Use graphic sources to help you understand text and to draw conclusions as you read.

Directions Look at the graphic sources throughout *The Art of Makeup: Going Behind the Mask.* Then answer the questions below.

1. What type of graphic source is shown on page 17? Possible responses given.
   photographs that show steps in a process
2. Review the steps for making a foam latex mask discussed in the text on pages 8–11. What step or steps are shown in the photos on page 10?
   attaching the mask to the actor's face and applying makeup to the mask
3. Look at pages 12–15. How do the photos shown here work with the text? How do the arrows help?
   They show many of the steps in making false teeth. The arrows show the order of the steps.
4. What is the black-and-white graphic source on page 17?
   It is a drawing of wig-making in the seventeenth century.
5. What does the "inset" photograph on page 17 show?
   the creation of a wig for a modern film
6. Did the graphic sources in this book help you understand the text better? Explain.
   Possible response: Yes; they helped me understand that there are many steps to making masks.
7. List two techniques makeup artists use to create characters.
   applying makeup; creating wigs

Below-Level Practice TE p. LR38

Name _____ Very Special Effects

Vocabulary
Directions Choose the word from the box that best matches each definition. Write the word on the line.

Check the Words You Know
| ___ background | ___ landscape | ___ miniature |
| ___ prehistoric | ___ reassembled | |

1. prehistoric — from a time before people began writing and keeping records
2. background — in a movie, the images that show up behind the actors and other objects in the foreground
3. miniature — something that has been done or made on a very small scale
4. reassembled — brought things back together again
5. landscape — the look and quality of the land when viewed from far away

Directions Complete each sentence using a word from the box above.

6. After the film is scanned into the computer, it is reassembled in a digital format.
7. The trees and clouds that made up the landscape looked real in the film.
8. The background behind the fish looked so realistic in the animated film.
9. The animator made a miniature model of the elephant to use in the film.
10. One animated film showed dinosaurs and other animals from prehistoric times.

Directions Choose two of the vocabulary words and write a sentence for each one.

11. Sentences will vary.
   _____
12. _____

On-Level Practice TE p. LR42

Name _____ The Art of Makeup

Vocabulary
Directions Choose the word from the box that best matches each definition. Write the word on the line.

Check the Words You Know
| ___ background | ___ landscape | ___ miniature |
| ___ prehistoric | ___ reassembled | |

1. prehistoric — of or belonging to times before histories were written
2. background — the part of a picture or scene behind the subject
3. miniature — done or made on a very small scale; tiny
4. reassembled — brought together again
5. landscape — view of scenery on land

Directions Choose the word from the box that best completes each sentence. Write the word on the line.

6. The makeup artist reassembled his tray of makeup after it fell on the floor.
7. The makeup artist created a miniature model of the ape before creating a larger mask for the actor.
8. The landscape of distant flowers and trees looked very realistic.
9. The character's makeup looked especially scary set against the background of moldy old dungeon walls.
10. Artists need to rely on fossil remains and their imaginations when they try to create makeup for prehistoric cave-dwelling characters.

Below-Level Practice TE p. LR39

Advanced

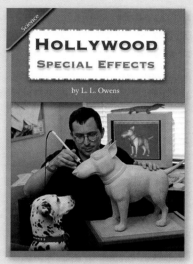

HOLLYWOOD SPECIAL EFFECTS
by L. L. Owens

Advanced Reader

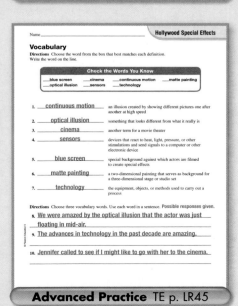

Advanced Practice TE p. LR44

Advanced Practice TE p. LR45

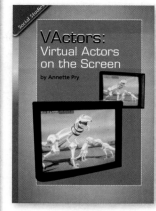

VActors: Virtual Actors on the Screen
by Annette Pry

ELL Reader

ELL Poster 15

Teacher's Edition Notes
ELL notes throughout this lesson support instruction and reference additional resources at point of use.

Teaching Guide pp. 99–105, 240–241
- Multilingual summaries of the main selection
- Comprehension lesson
- Vocabulary strategies and word cards
- ELL Reader 5.3.5 lesson

ELL and Transition Handbook

Ten Important Sentences
- Key ideas from every selection in the Student Edition
- Activities to build sentence power

More Reading

Readers' Theater Anthology
- Fluency practice
- Five scripts to build fluency
- Poetry for oral interpretation

Leveled Trade Books

Below-Level

Advanced

On-Level

- Extended reading tied to the unit concept
- Lessons in the Trade Book Library Teaching Guide

School + Home

Homework
- Family Times Newsletter
- ELL Multilingual Selection Summaries

Take-Home Books
- Leveled Readers

Family Times

Cross-Curricular Centers

Listening

Listen to the SELECTIONS

MATERIALS `SINGLES`
CD player, headphones, AudioText CD, student book

LISTEN TO LITERATURE Listen to *Special Effects in Film and Television* and "Searching for Animation" as you follow or read along in your book.

If there is anything you don't understand, you can listen again to any section.

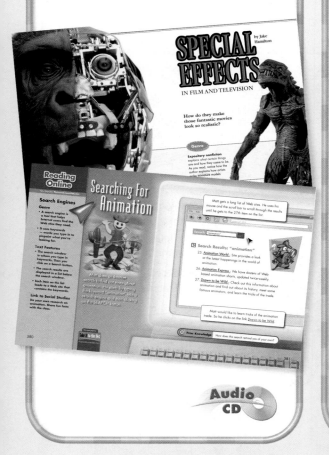

Audio CD

Reading/Library

Read it AGAIN!

MATERIALS `SINGLES` `PAIRS` `GROUPS`
Collection of books for self-selected reading, reading logs, student book

Select a book you have already read. Record the title of the book in your reading log. You may want to read with a partner.

Choose from the following:

- **Leveled Readers**
- **ELL Readers**
- **Stories Written by Classmates**
- **Books from the Library**
- ***Special Effects in Film and Television***

TEN IMPORTANT SENTENCES
Read the Ten Important Sentences for *Special Effects in Film and Television*, then locate the sentences in the student book.

BOOK CLUB Discuss the way that the author has organized the text in *Special Effects in Film and Television*. How is it different from other examples of expository nonfiction you may have read? Read other examples of expository nonfiction and get together with a group to share your favorites.

Art

Design a Model

MATERIALS `SINGLES`
Writing and art materials

Design a concept model to explore the process of creating special effects.

1. Review the first step for building a concept model for a miniature landscape in *Special Effects in Film and Television*.
2. Sketch a model you would build if you were designing a miniature landscape for a movie. Include details such as plants, water, mountains, or any other landscape features.

EARLY FINISHERS Color and label your sketch.

Scott Foresman Reading Street Centers Survival Kit

Use the *Special Effects* materials from the Reading Street
Centers Survival Kit to organize this week's centers.

Writing/Vocabulary

Summarize *Directions*

MATERIALS   SINGLES
Writing and drawing materials

Summarize the steps in the miniature model-making process.

1. Review the steps for making a miniature landscape model in *Special Effects in Film and Television*.
2. Summarize each step in the process.

EARLY FINISHERS Draw an illustration for each of the steps.

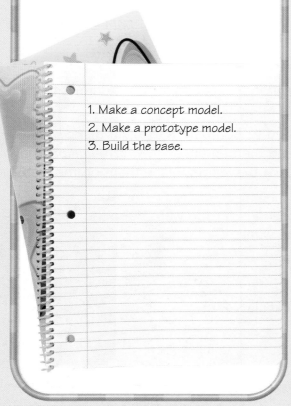

1. Make a concept model.
2. Make a prototype model.
3. Build the base.

Science

Research Reptiles

MATERIALS   SINGLES
Books on reptiles, Internet   PAIRS
access, writing and art
materials

Sketch a reptile to be used for building a realistic model.

1. Gather information on the physical features of one type of reptile, such as an iguana. List details like the color and texture of its skin.
2. Make a sketch of the reptile based on the details in your list. Label each physical feature.

EARLY FINISHERS With a partner, draw another picture that shows the reptile in a landscape that might appear in a movie.

Spiny crest

Yellowish
colored
with bro
blotche

Desert Iguana

1. About 1.2 meters in length.
2. Yellowish colored with brown blotches on its sides and legs.
3. Spiny crest running down along its back from its head.

Technology

Use Graphics

MATERIALS   SINGLES
Word processing program with   PAIRS
drawing tools

Use computer drawing tools to create a title screen for a movie.

1. Follow classroom rules for using computer software.
2. Use graphics and drawing tools to create a title screen for the prehistoric film described in *Special Effects in Film and Television*.

EARLY FINISHERS Expand the title screen into a movie poster advertising the movie.

Prehistoric Passages

ALL CENTERS

OBJECTIVES

- Build vocabulary by finding words related to the lesson concept.
- Listen for details and facts.

Concept Vocabulary

digital effects pictures and sounds created by a computer

illusion something that appears to be different from what it actually is

props any piece of furniture or small item used in performing or making a movie or TV show

Monitor Progress

Check Vocabulary

If...	then... review the
students are unable to place words on the web,	lesson concept. Place the words on the web and provide additional words for practice, such as *landscapes* and *air brushing*.

SUCCESS PREDICTOR

DAY 1 Grouping Options

Reading

Whole Group
Introduce and discuss the Question of the Week. Then use pp. 364I–364b.

Group Time

Differentiated Instruction
Read this week's Leveled Readers. See pp. 364h–364i for the small group lesson plan.

Whole Group
Use p. 383a.

Language Arts
Use pp. 383e–383k.

Build Concepts

FLUENCY

MODEL TEMPO AND RATE As you read "The Making of *The Lord of the Rings*," model reading with the appropriate tempo and rate. Pause for a moment at the end of each sentence, and for several moments at the end of each paragraph. Read more slowly when the content is technical in nature such as in this sentence: "Then the two were merged using the magic of digital technology."

LISTENING COMPREHENSION

After reading "The Making of *The Lord of the Rings*," use the following questions to assess listening comprehension.

1. **Name two tricks that were used to make the Middle-earth set look realistic.** (*Possible response: adding digital effects from the computer; making identical props in small and large sizes; making feet out of rubber molds.*) ***Details and Facts***

2. **Make a generalization about making movies.** (*Movie making is not all glamorous; there is a lot of hard work involved.*) ***Generalize***

BUILD CONCEPT VOCABULARY

Start a web to build concepts and vocabulary related to this week's lesson and the unit theme.

- Draw the Special Effects Concept Web.
- Read the sentence with the words *digital effects* again. Ask students to pronounce *digital effects* and discuss its meaning.
- Place *digital effects* in an oval attached to *Computers*. Explain that *digital effects* is related to this concept. Read the sentences in which *illusion* and *props* appear. Have students pronounce the words, place them on the web, and provide reasons.
- Brainstorm additional words and categories for the web. Keep the web on display and add words throughout the week.

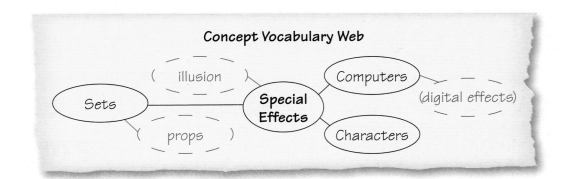

Concept Vocabulary Web

The Making of
THE LORD OF THE RINGS

from *Owl Magazine*

Middle-earth is home to the hobbits, wizards, orcs, and elves in *The Lord of the Rings* movies. Because Middle-earth doesn't exist anywhere in real life, the land, its characters, and all of their gear had to be created for the films.

Director Peter Jackson needed to find a location that was as much like Middle-earth as possible. Peter and his team chose New Zealand to film the three *The Lord of the Rings* movies because it has so many different landscapes—mountains, deserts, lakes, fields, and volcanoes—just like Middle-earth. If the natural scenery wasn't quite right, digital effects were used to enhance the sets. "With digital wizardry, we were able to add craggy little mountains, put buildings where they have never been," says Peter. "With a little help from the computer, we turned [the landscape] into a magical Middle-earth."

Middle-earth is a world filled with creatures of all shapes and sizes, from towering wizards to tiny hobbits. Since the actors weren't as short as hobbits or as tall as wizards, designers had to create the illusion of size difference, making them look bigger or smaller than they actually were. Special lighting and camera angles wouldn't do the trick. But props would. If a prop, like a table, was small, it would make the actor look big. If it was built in an extra-large size, an average-sized actor would look small beside it. So, one of New Zealand's top special effects companies, went on double duty, creating every prop in two different sizes. When characters of different sizes were in the same scene, they were filmed separately with their props. Then, the two were merged using the magic of digital technology.

Local New Zealand artists built sets, made props, and designed costumes for the film. The special effects team made wrinkly, elephant-like skin suits and black armor for the hideous-looking orcs. They gave creatures a gruesome finishing touch by hand-weaving unique hairstyles into the top of each orc mask, using yak hair. And for orc blood, they came up with an oozy, black, tar-like substance that could be applied to wounds during battle scenes.

Since hobbits never wear shoes, the special effects team had to create hobbit feet that would stand up to Middle-earth's mountains, rivers, and deserts—and an occasional game of hackey sack between takes. So designers used foam latex, a type of rubber, to make their feet. They whipped it up with an egg beater, poured it into hobbit-feet molds, and baked them in an oven. Each pair lasted no more than three days, so the team had to keep baking fresh feet. By the end of filming, they'd baked about 4,000 pairs! To get the hobbit feet on in time for shooting, the actors had to be up between 4:30 and 5:30 a.m. Artists used make-up and air brushing to add scratches, burns, and mud to the feet. They topped it all off with strands of hobbit hair.

Activate Prior Knowledge

Before students listen to the Read Aloud, ask them what they know about the book or the movie, *The Lord of the Rings*.

Set Purpose

Read aloud the title and have students predict what the selection will be about.

Read the introduction aloud. Have students listen for details about creating Middle-earth for the big screen.

Creative Response

Have pairs of students improvise interviews between Peter Jackson and the magazine writer. The interviewer should ask questions about the Middle-earth Jackson created for his movies. ***Drama***

Access Content Before reading, share this summary: Peter Jackson, the director of *The Lord of the Rings,* shot the movie in New Zealand because it had many different landscapes. He used special effects to make characters look big and small. The special effects team made wrinkly skin suits and hobbit feet. Digital technology helped bring all the special effects together.

'School'+Home **Homework** Send home this week's Family Times newsletter.

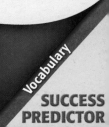

SKILLS ⟷ STRATEGIES IN CONTEXT

Graphic Sources
Prior Knowledge

OBJECTIVES

- Interpret graphic sources.

- Use prior knowledge to understand graphic sources and increase comprehension.

Skills Trace	
Graphic Sources	
Introduce/Teach	TE: 5.3 364–365; 5.4 436–437; 5.5 536–537
Practice	Practice Book: 143, 147, 148, 166, 173, 177, 178, 213, 217, 218, 226, 246
Reteach/Review	TE: 5.3 383b, DI·56; 5.4 421, 457b, DI·54; 5.5 559b, 569, 613, DI·53
Test	Selection Test: 57-60, 69-72, 85-88; Benchmark Test: Unit 5

INTRODUCE

Draw a bar graph on the board to show the following lunch count: *pizza 15, turkey sandwich 5, soup and salad 3, peanut butter and jelly sandwich 2.* Ask which lunch choice was most popular and which one was least popular. *(pizza; peanut butter and jelly sandwich)*

Have students read the information on p. 364. Explain the following:

- Graphic sources may add new information or explain difficult information in text.

- Personal experience can be helpful in understanding what you see and what you read in a text.

Use Skill Transparency 15 to teach graphic sources and using prior knowledge.

Comprehension

Skill
Graphic Sources

Strategy
Prior Knowledge

Graphic Sources

- Some graphic sources are maps, time lines, charts, diagrams, and pictures with captions.

- A graphic source makes information easy to see and understand.

- Preview graphic sources to help predict what an article or story may be about.

- As you read, compare the information in graphic sources with the information in the text.

Strategy: Prior Knowledge

Good readers use what they already know to help them understand what they read. Connect what you are reading with what you have read before and what you know from personal experience. Use what you already know to understand the information in graphic sources.

Write to Read

1. Read "Computer Art and What It Takes." As you read, make a list of computer graphics tools that are new to you.

2. Write down three things you learned as you read the article and studied the picture.

364

Strategic Intervention

Graphic Sources Bring in kid-friendly magazines. Have partners choose an article and work together to explain how the visuals support the article.

ELL

Access Content

Beginning/Intermediate For a Picture It! lesson on graphic sources, see the ELL Teaching Guide, pp. 99–100.

Advanced Before students read "Computer Art and What It Takes," have them study the picture carefully. Ask students to point to each component of the computer system and name it. Provide vocabulary as needed.

Computer Art
and What It Takes

What do all these things share: the characters you play with in video games, the weather maps you see on TV, and the cartoons you laugh at in modern movies? They have all been created on computers. They are all examples of computer graphics.

It does not take much to put together a computer graphics system. Graphics software allows you to create the pictures. A computer hard drive stores the graphics, or pictures, and lets you work with them. A monitor shows you the pictures.

Also necessary are a mouse and a keyboard to input commands. Some equipment to input pictures is needed as well. This could be a digital pad or camera, a scanner, or a light pen. If you want to make a copy of the pictures on paper, you'll need a printer too.

 Skill Preview the picture below. What does it suggest this article will be about?

 Strategy Which of the tools pictured below have you already used or seen someone else use?

 Skill Which items that you are reading about are pictured here?

 Strategy Did the text match what you already know about some of these items? Did you learn anything new about any of them? If so, you have just added to your prior knowledge.

365

Available as **Skill Transparency** 15

TEACH

1 **SKILL** Model how to preview the graphic sources to determine the article's content.

Think Aloud **MODEL** I see a girl working at a computer. It looks like the girl is working on a picture. I think this article will be about art created with a computer.

2 **STRATEGY** Use the tools in the picture to think about your personal experience.

Think Aloud **MODEL** I recognize most of the tools shown in the photograph. I've used a computer, keyboard, graphic pen, and graphics program. My experience with this equipment makes me confident that I will understand the information in the article.

PRACTICE AND ASSESS

3 **SKILL** The text mentions a computer and a monitor, which are pictured. There is a picture on the computer screen that was created with graphics software.

4 **STRATEGY** A response should show that students have reflected upon personal experience and prior knowledge.

WRITE Have to Read students complete steps 1 and 2 of the Write to Read activity. You might consider using this as a whole-class activity.

Monitor Progress
Graphic Sources

If... students are unable to complete **Write to Read** on p. 364,	then... use Practice Book p. 143 to provide additional practice.

Graphic Sources

- Some graphic sources are maps, time lines, charts, diagrams, and pictures with captions.
- A graphic source makes information easy to see and understand.

Directions Study the circle graph below. Then answer the following questions.

Small Films Company Annual Budget for Special Effects

21% Sound
17% Props
10% Make-up
30% Lighting
22% Costumes

1. What do the percentages show?
   They show how much of the budget was spent in each area.
2. On what special effect did the company spend the most money?
   The company spent the most money on lighting.
3. How much more of the budget went toward costumes than make-up?
   twelve percent
4. In what kind of article might you see a circle graph?
   Possible answers: An article about the costs of special effects, making a movie, or budgets in general.
5. What prior knowledge did you use to help you understand the graphic source?
   Possible answer: I saw a play once and noticed all the different elements that go into putting it together.

School + Home Home Activity Your child learned how to interpret a graphic source. Together, imagine you are both writing an article about a favorite subject. Draw a graphic source that could be included in the article.

ELL

Build Background Use ELL Poster 15 to build background and vocabulary for the lesson concept of special effects.

▲ **ELL Poster** 15

Build Background

ACTIVATE PRIOR KNOWLEDGE

BEGIN A SEMANTIC WEB about making movies.

Have students use a semantic web to brainstorm the things that are needed to make a movie.

Write "Making Movies" in the center oval. Write ideas from students in the outer ovals. Add more ovals if needed.

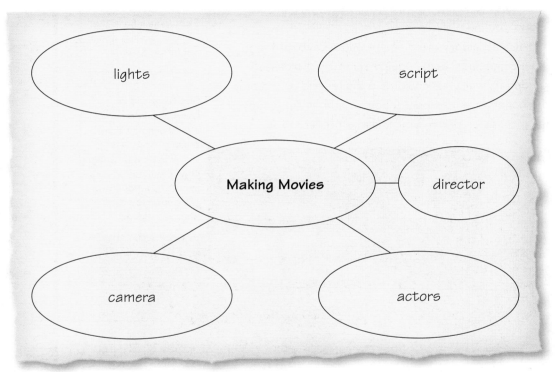

▲ **Graphic Organizer** 15

Encourage students to add to the web throughout the week as they learn more about the subject.

BACKGROUND BUILDING AUDIO This week's audio explores special effects and how they are created. After students listen, discuss with them what they found most interesting.

Background Building Audio

Introduce Vocabulary

USE CONTEXT CLUES

Present the following scene to students with words in context:

Two days ago David bumped his desk spilling his collection of *miniature* dinosaurs onto the floor. He threw the little critters into a box. Yesterday, he'd *reassembled* them on his desk. He would set them up again the same way today. David turned out his lights and went to bed. Suddenly, he heard loud explosions that sounded like giant cannon blasts. He opened his eyes and found himself outdoors, looking at a strange *landscape*, a field of grass and shrubs. In the distance, a volcano was puffing smoke. Also in the *background*, a herd of dinosaurs was grazing. How could that be? They looked so real, but dinosaurs lived in *prehistoric* times. "I must be dreaming!" David told himself. And then he woke up.

Read the scene to students and ask them to listen for the five lesson vocabulary words. ***Activate Prior Knowledge***

Have students number a sheet 1–5. Then reread one or two sentences at a time. Encourage students to notice how each vocabulary word is used. Ask them to write down a synonym or meaning for each vocabulary word. Invite volunteers to explain what context clue helped them identify each word meaning. ***Context Clues***

Have students write analogies for this week's vocabulary words. Provide this example on the board:

> **Landscape is to scenery as miniature is to small in scale.**

Encourage students to use electronic and print dictionaries, glossaries, or thesauruses to find analogous words. **Analogies**

Have students keep their word lists. At the end of the week, ask them to revise word meanings as needed.

Also, have students use these steps for reading multisyllabic words. (See the Multisyllabic Word Routine on p. DI·1.)

1 **Look for Meaningful Word Parts** (base words, endings, prefixes, suffixes, roots) Think about the meaning of each part. Use the parts to read the word. Model: I see the prefix *re-* in front of *reassembled* and the ending *-ed* after it. *Assemble* means "to gather or bring together," and *re-* means "again" and *-ed* means it happened in the past. Therefore, *reassembled* means "came together again."

2 **Chunk Words with No Recognizable Parts** Say each chunk slowly. Then say the chunks fast to make a word. Model: *spec, tac, u, lar—spectacular.*

Lesson Vocabulary

WORDS TO KNOW

T background the part of a picture or scene toward the back

T landscape a view of scenery on land

T miniature reduced image or likeness; done on a small scale.

T prehistoric belonging to periods before recorded history

T reassembled came, brought, or put together again

MORE WORDS TO KNOW

boundaries limits

prototype the first or original type or model of anything that is designed or constructed

spectacular making a great display

T = Tested Word

Vocabulary

Directions Choose the word from the box that best matches each definition. Write the word on the line.

prehistoric _____ 1. of or belonging to periods before recorded history

reassembled _____ 2. put back together again

landscape _____ 3. view of scenery on land

miniature _____ 4. done or made on an extremely small scale

background _____ 5. the part of a picture or scene toward the back

Check the Words You Know
___background
___landscape
___miniature
___prehistoric
___reassembled

Directions Choose the word from the box that best completes the sentence. Write the word on the line shown to the left.

reassembled _____ 6. Three hours after the storm, the set for the movie had already been _____.

miniature _____ 7. In preparing for the movie, the crew created a _____ village.

background _____ 8. The film crew built a ruined temple to appear in the _____ of the scene.

prehistoric _____ 9. The dinosaur film used models of huge, _____ creatures.

landscape _____ 10. The park provided a perfect _____ for the film.

Write a Movie Review
On a separate sheet of paper write a review of a movie that had lots of special effects. Describe the special effects and how they worked. Use as many vocabulary words as you can.

Movie reviews should include words from the vocabulary list and details about special effects used in the movies.

Home Activity Your child identified and used vocabulary words from *Special Effects in Film and Television*. Read the review of a movie with your child. Have him or her point out unfamiliar words. Work together to try to figure out the meaning of each word.

▲ **Practice Book** p. 144

Vocabulary Strategy

OBJECTIVE

Use word structure to determine the meaning of words with prefixes.

INTRODUCE

Discuss the strategy for word structure using the steps on p. 366.

TEACH

- Have students read "Visiting the Past," paying attention to how vocabulary is used.

- Model how to use word structure to determine the meaning of *prehistoric*.

Think Aloud **MODEL** The word *prehistoric* has the base word *historic,* which refers to written history. The prefix *pre-* means "before." *Prehistoric* must mean "before the time of written history."

Words to Know

prehistoric

landscape

background

miniature

reassembled

Remember
Try the strategy. Then, if you need more help, use your glossary or dictionary.

Vocabulary Strategy
for Prefixes

Word Structure A prefix is a syllable added at the beginning of a base word that has a meaning of its own. Recognizing a prefix can help you figure out the word's meaning. For example, *pre-* means "before." If you *prearrange* something, you arrange it ahead of time. The prefix *re-* means "again." If you *reheat* soup, you warm it up again.

1. Look at an unfamiliar word to see if it has a base word you know.

2. Check to see if a prefix has been added to the base word.

3. Ask yourself how the prefix changes the meaning of the base word.

4. Try the meaning in the sentence. Does it make sense?

As you read "Visiting the Past," find words with prefixes. Use the prefixes to help you figure out the meanings of the words.

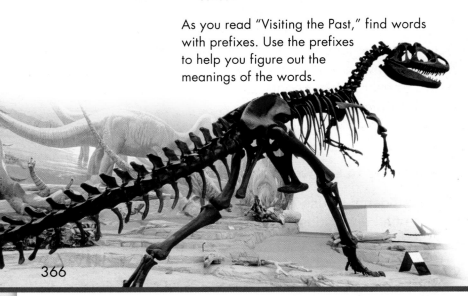

366

DAY 2 **Grouping Options**

Reading
Whole Group Discuss the Question of the Day. Then use pp. 366–369.

Group Time Differentiated Instruction
Read *Special Effects in Film and Television.* See pp. 364h–364i for the small group lesson plan.

Whole Group Use p. 383a.

Language Arts
Use pp. 383e–383k.

Strategic Intervention

Word Structure Have students work in pairs to follow the steps on p. 366 to figure out the meaning of *reassembled.*

ELL

Access Content Use ELL Poster 15 to preteach vocabulary. Choose from the following to meet language proficiency levels.

Beginning Point to the word *reproduce* on p. 367, paragraph 1. Ask students what the base word *produce* means. Remind them that the prefix *re-* means "again." Have them use this information to tell the meaning of *reproduce.*

Intermediate Point out that the words *prehistoric* and *miniature* have Spanish cognates, or related words: *prehistórico* and *miniatura.*

Advanced Teach the lesson on pp. 366–367. Have students find home-language terms for some of the tested words.

Resources for home-language words may include parents, bilingual staff members, bilingual dictionaries, or online translation sources.

Visiting the Past

While we were on vacation, our family visited an incredible theme park. It had models that reproduce scenes from the past. Once we entered the park, we split up and went our own ways.

I went straight to the exhibit of prehistoric times. Paintings of huge, strange plants created the feeling of an ancient landscape. The model dinosaurs were life-sized, looked real, and even moved! A tape of background noises, such as animal cries and splashes, added to the realism. In one large room, artists had shaped a past world in miniature.

When we reassembled as a family for lunch, my brother described the Old West community he had visited. It had a whole street from a mining town—complete with general store, hotel, and jail. He rode a cart into a deep tunnel. Down there, the exhibit showed how miners worked. Occasionally, he said, you felt a tremor and heard a boom. Somehow they reproduced the explosions when ore was blasted from a mountain! We agreed that this was the best theme park we have ever visited.

Words to Write

What place have you visited that uses special effects? Write an article about the place for the school newspaper. Use words from the Words to Know list.

Connect to Phonics

Word Study/Decoding Explain that students can break words into syllables, or sound chunks, and read each part separately before putting them together to form the word. Model identifying syllabication by using *prehistoric* from p. 367, paragraph 2. Have students suggest other multisyllabic words they know. Have them break each word into sound chunks, read each separately, and then put them back together. Check dictionaries or glossaries for correct syllabication.

PRACTICE AND ASSESS

- Have students use word structure to determine the meanings of other words with prefixes they find in the story.

- Point out that dictionaries often include definitions of prefixes.

- If you began practicing with context clues on p. 366b, ask students to revise the meanings they wrote for vocabulary words, if necessary, and see if they can think of more synonyms.

- Have students complete Practice Book p. 145.

WRITE Students' articles should include several lesson vocabulary words to describe their observations of a place with special effects.

Monitor Progress

Prefixes

If... students need more practice with the lesson vocabulary,	then... use Tested Vocabulary Cards.

Vocabulary · Word Structure

- A **prefix** is added at the beginning of a base word to change its meaning. Recognizing a prefix will help you figure out the word's meaning.
- The prefix *re–* means "to do over again."
- The prefix *pre–* means "before."

Directions Read the following passage. Then answer the questions below.

On our first trip to L.A., we toured a special-effects studio. In one room the workers had just reassembled a landscape scene with prehistoric animals. Huge reptile-like birds with feathers flew in the background. In another room we saw a miniature village. Tiny houses were placed among even tinier bushes and trees. Next, we visited the basement. We heard explosions going off. We were told that technicians were testing small explosive devices and that we should be careful. Down the hall we saw a room full of what looked like snow and ice. It was going to be used as an Arctic landscape with below-zero temperatures. By the end of the afternoon, we were weary but eager to redo the tour soon. We felt like we had been treated to our own sneak preview of several of the coolest movies coming out in the future.

1. What does *reassembled* mean? What prefix helped you to determine the meaning?
   It means put back together again; the prefix *re–*

2. What does *prehistoric* mean? What does its prefix mean?
   It means before history; The prefix *pre–* means "before".

3. If you replaced the prefix in *preview* with the prefix *re–*, how would the meaning change?
   Instead of seeing something before, you would be seeing something again.

4. Can you use a prefix to determine the meaning of *real*? Why or why not?
   No, because *–al* is not a base word.

5. Write at least three examples of words that either begin with the prefix *re–* or *pre–*.
   Possible answer: retest; redo; prepaid

Home Activity Your child identified the meanings of words with prefixes. Make a list of all the words you can think of that begin with the prefixes *re–* or *pre–*. Then, have a silly conversation in which you try to use as many words on the list as possible.

▲ **Practice Book** p. 145

Prereading Strategies

- Use graphic sources to improve comprehension.
- Use prior knowledge to understand graphic sources.

GENRE STUDY

Expository Nonfiction

Special Effects in Film and Television is expository nonfiction. Explain that expository nonfiction is organized around topics and gives information about real-life things, ideas, or happenings.

PREVIEW AND PREDICT

Have students read the title, note the photographs, and read the numbered steps. Ask them to predict what information may be covered in the article. Have students use the lesson vocabulary in their discussion.

Strategy Response Log

Activate Prior Knowledge Encourage students to record what they know about special effects in films or television in their Strategy Response Logs. They will review their notes in the Strategy Response Logs activity on p. 373.

368

Access Content Lead a picture walk to reinforce vocabulary, such as *landscape* (p. 371); *backdrop*, *overhead* (p. 373); *foreground*; and *camera's eye-view* (p. 376).

Consider having students read the selection summary in English or in students' home languages. See the Multilingual Summaries in the ELL Teaching Guide, pp. 103–105.

SPECIAL EFFECTS

by Jake Hamilton

IN FILM AND TELEVISION

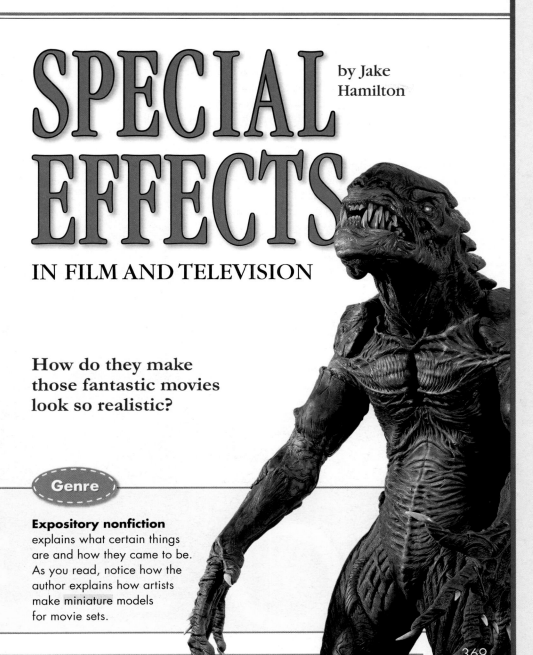

How do they make those fantastic movies look so realistic?

Genre

Expository nonfiction explains what certain things are and how they came to be. As you read, notice how the author explains how artists make miniature models for movie sets.

SET PURPOSE

Read the first paragraph of the selection aloud to students. Have them consider their preview discussion and identify what they would like to find out as they read.

Tell students to study each photograph and relate it to their own experience of watching movies with special effects. Explain that they should also use the photographs to help them understand what they are reading.

STRATEGY RECALL

Students have now used these before-reading strategies:

- preview the selection to be aware of its genre, features, and possible content;
- activate prior knowledge about that content and what to expect of that genre;
- make predictions;
- set a purpose for reading.

Remind students to be aware of and flexibly use the during-reading strategies they have learned:

- link prior knowledge to new information;
- summarize text they have read so far;
- ask clarifying questions;
- answer questions they or others pose;
- check their predictions and either refine them or make new predictions;
- recognize the text structure the author is using, and use that knowledge to make predictions and increase comprehension;
- visualize what the author is describing;
- monitor their comprehension and use fix-up strategies.

After reading, students will use these strategies:

- summarize or retell the text;
- answer questions they or others pose;
- reflect to make new information become part of their prior knowledge.

AudioText

Guiding Comprehension

1 **Main Idea • Inferential**

What is the main idea of p. 370?

Possible response: Movie makers use special effects, including miniatures, to create realistic-looking scenes that would otherwise be too expensive or impossible to film.

2 ⚙ **Graphic Sources • Inferential**

The photo next to Step 1 on p. 371 doesn't look very realistic. Why is it included?

Possible Response: It is a concept model, meant to give an idea of what the finished model will look like.

Monitor Progress
⚙ **Graphic Sources**
If... students are unable to use the photo to understand the text,	**then...** use the skill and strategy instruction on p. 371.

3 **Compare and Contrast • Inferential**

How are concept models different from prototype models?

Prototype models have more detail, are larger, and give a clearer picture of what the finished product will look like than the concept models, which are more general.

Tech Files
ONLINE

Students can find out more about special effects by using a student-friendly search engine and the keywords *movie special effects*. Be sure to follow classroom guidelines for Internet use.

IN MINIATURE

Special effects (SFX) is the art of making the impossible into a fantastic reality. Special effects has always pushed the boundaries of human imagination. It keeps today's movie and television audiences glued to their seats in starry-eyed wonder.

The art of miniature model-making has always been an important part of special effects in movies. Some movie stories have big, spectacular, action-filled scenes. They may call for fights between dinosaurs, explosions on the Golden Gate Bridge, or an armed force charging through the desert. Movie-makers can save time and money by making models for these scenes. This article tells the story of the building of a miniature landscape for **1** a television show.

400-foot (120m) film magazine with running time of $4\frac{1}{4}$ minutes at normal speed

Prime lens interchangeable with the zoom lens

Matte box reduces lens flares.

ARRIFLEX

370

ELL

Understanding Idioms Explain that "glued to their seats" on p. 370, paragraph 1 means "too excited to move."

Concept model is 1 ft x 1 ft
(0.3 meter x 0.3 meter)

1 A General Idea

A special effects team must build a **prehistoric** world in a workshop. The team's first step is to make a "concept" model of this mini-world. The model will give a general view of what the finished product will look like. This model shows that the landscape will include a fallen tree and a circular lake.

2 Getting Larger

The movie-makers study this concept model to decide on the size and shape of the finished product. Then they make a larger and more detailed "prototype" model. This gives them a clearer picture of how the finished product will look. The prototype comes in sections that are fitted together like puzzle pieces. This 2 ft x 2 ft (0.6 m x 0.6 m) prototype is fully painted and fitted with bushes and trees. Now the team can work on the final product.

Final model landscape will be in three main sections— white areas show where the divides are between the main sections.

Cameraman's eyepiece

Camera door is opened to thread the film past the gate.

Cardboard representation of early reptile

371

Graphic Sources

TEACH

- Remind students that graphics, such as photographs, are meant to give information and help the reader understand the text.
- Model using a photograph to understand text.

Think Aloud **MODEL** The text for Step 1 on p. 371 says that the concept model gives a general view of what the scene will look like. The photo shows only a few details. This helps me understand that a concept model only includes the main features the scene will have when it is done.

PRACTICE AND ASSESS

Ask students to explain how the photograph next to Step 2 helps them understand the text. *(The photo shows the additional details that a prototype model includes and how it's put together.)*

Careers

There are many different jobs in the special effects field—from computer programming images on screen to building strange creatures that move. Special effects also include "atmospherics"—producing fake snow, wind, and rain—and "physical effects"— objects that do something, like a car that falls apart bit by bit. And that's not all. Special costumes and amazing props are also part of special effects.

Time for
SOCIAL STUDIES

EXTEND SKILLS

Photo Essay

Explain that a photo essay is a collection of photographs on one topic that goes along with a written explanation. In a photo essay, the photographs allow the reader to visualize the information in the text. As they read *Special Effects in Film and Television*, have students discuss how the photos help them understand the text.

Guiding Comprehension

If you are teaching the selection in two days, discuss graphic sources so far and review the vocabulary.

7 Author's Purpose • Inferential

Why do you think the author wrote this article?

To inform readers about how miniature landscape models are used to create special effects.

Monitor Progress

REVIEW Author's Purpose

If... students have difficulty determining author's purpose,	**then...** use the skill and strategy instruction on p. 375.

8 Text Structure • Inferential

Why is some material set off in the sidebar on p. 375?

The sidebar is titled "Reptile Modeling," and it presents information on how the dinosaur models that appear in the landscape were made.

DAY 3 Grouping Options

Reading
Whole Group Discuss the Question of the Day.

Group Time Differentiated Instruction
Read *Special Effects in Film and Television.*
See pp. 364h–364i for the small group lesson plan.

Whole Group Discuss the Reader Response questions on p. 378. Then use p. 383a.

Language Arts
Use pp. 383e–383k.

Appropriate large potted plants are used for the foreground.

8 Fixing in Place
Model-makers use a special glue to make sure the sections will not come apart. The glue is carefully dried by hand. Technicians use the same kind of blow-dryer people use on their hair. That way they can aim the hot wind just right so it will not disturb any delicate details on the landscape's surface.

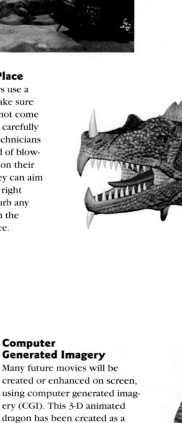

Computer Generated Imagery
Many future movies will be created or enhanced on screen, using computer generated imagery (CGI). This 3-D animated dragon has been created as a wire frame image before being fleshed out, enhanced, and lit carefully—all on a computer.

7

374

Access Content Explain to students that *fleshed out* means "filled out in structure or framework." Have students draw a sketch of an animal. Then ask them to "flesh it out" by adding detail and coloring it in.

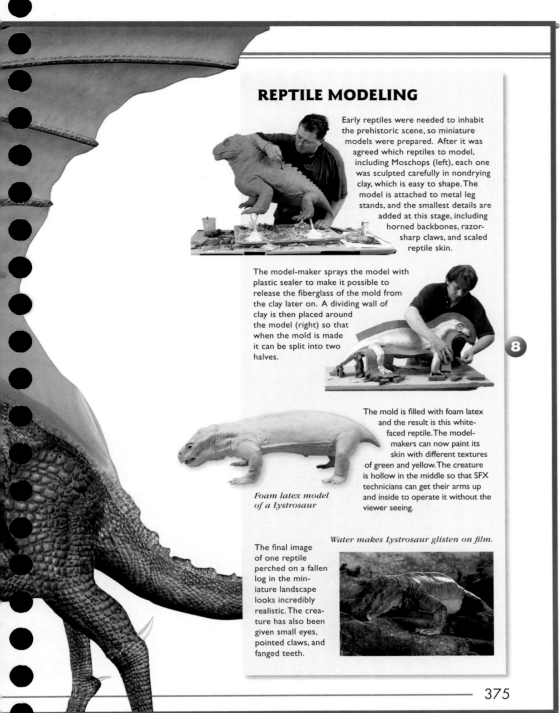

REPTILE MODELING

Early reptiles were needed to inhabit the prehistoric scene, so miniature models were prepared. After it was agreed which reptiles to model, including Moschops (left), each one was sculpted carefully in nondrying clay, which is easy to shape. The model is attached to metal leg stands, and the smallest details are added at this stage, including horned backbones, razor-sharp claws, and scaled reptile skin.

The model-maker sprays the model with plastic sealer to make it possible to release the fiberglass of the mold from the clay later on. A dividing wall of clay is then placed around the model (right) so that when the mold is made it can be split into two halves.

Foam latex model of a Lystrosaur

The mold is filled with foam latex and the result is this white-faced reptile. The model-makers can now paint its skin with different textures of green and yellow. The creature is hollow in the middle so that SFX technicians can get their arms up and inside to operate it without the viewer seeing.

Water makes Lystrosaur glisten on film.

The final image of one reptile perched on a fallen log in the miniature landscape looks incredibly realistic. The creature has also been given small eyes, pointed claws, and fanged teeth.

375

Blue Screen Technology

Time for SOCIAL STUDIES

Blue screen photography is a form of technology used in many movies. It is a technique in which an actor performs in front of a blue (or green) screen. An optical printer with a projector and camera is used to remove the blue background from around the actor. Two pieces of film, one with the actor and one with the background, are put in the projector to create one piece of film showing the actor against the background.

SKILLS ⬌ STRATEGIES IN CONTEXT

Author's Purpose REVIEW

TEACH

- Review with students the four common reasons that authors write: to persuade, to inform, to entertain, and to express an idea or opinion.

- Model how to determine an author's purpose.

Think Aloud **MODEL** As I read the article, I notice there are a lot of details used to describe the process of creating special effects. The information explains this process so I think the author's purpose is to inform.

PRACTICE AND ASSESS

- The introduction on p. 370 states this model landscape was created for a television show. What kind of show do you think it was? For what purpose would a program like that be produced? (Possible response: *The television show might be written to entertain if it is fictional, or to inform if it is informational.*)

- To assess, use Practice Book p. 146.

Author's Purpose
Directions Read the passage. Then answer the questions below.

Jack had studied dinosaurs for twenty years, and he'd lived in Dinosaur Park for all twenty of them. Nothing about dinosaurs could surprise him. This thought calmed his nerves as he walked toward the lodge at the other end of the park.

After an hour, he pulled out his GPS-DL (dinosaur locator) to check the position of the dinosaurs. The path was still clear for miles. So why did he feel so uneasy? Sweat was running down his cheeks. He felt dizzy.

Then a thundering blast filled the air. The earth shook. A foul smell hit him like a punch. A roar split the sky. It was like nothing he'd heard before. And it was coming straight toward him.

1. What is the author's purpose?
   The author's purpose is to entertain.
2. How do you know?
   The author created suspense with the plot.
3. Do you think the author met his or her purpose for writing? Why or why not?
   yes; The story made me want to read on to see what would happen.
4. Notice the sentences get shorter in the second half of the passage. Why do you think the author did this?
   The shorter sentences create suspense, which makes the reader want to keep reading.
5. How did the author's purpose affect your reading pace?
   Possible answer: The author's purpose was to entertain and to build action, so I wanted to read faster.

Home Activity Your child has read a fictional passage and identified the author's purpose for writing it. Choose a story to read. Have your child preview the story first, looking at the cover, title, and pictures, to predict the author's purpose. Read the story to find out if the prediction was correct.

▲ **Practice Book** p. 146

Guiding Comprehension

9 🔊 **Prior Knowledge • Critical**

From your experience watching television and movies, why is it important for special effects to look realistic?

Possible response: If the special effects look real, it's easier to believe the story.

10 🔊 **Graphic Sources • Critical**

Study the photograph of Steven Spielberg on p. 377. What special understanding do you get from this photograph about the landscape model?

Possible response: You get a sense of scale, of how relatively small the model is. Spielberg looks like a giant compared to the miniature soldiers, tents, and vehicles in the model.

11 **Compare and Contrast • Critical**

Text to World **What impact have special effects and new technology had on movies and television today?**

Answers will vary but should include something about how they have made them more thrilling or realistic.

Strategy Response Log

Summarize When students finish reading the selection, provide this prompt: Imagine that you and a friend just finished watching a movie with cool special effects. In a few sentences, explain what you learned about special effects in *Special Effects in Film and Television*.

Tricks of the Trade
The model-makers go to great lengths to make a miniature look as realistic as possible. Here, they are working on a slight depression in the surface that was carved out for a lake. It is filled with water to a depth of just 1.5 in. (4 cm.). The model-makers are layering the shallow water with fabric to make it look more like a deep lake.

Model-makers refer to television monitor for camera's eye-view.

Large, potted trees are used for foreground section.

9

Real log is used in foreground of landscape.

376

ELL

Extend Language Tell students that the phrase *tricks of the trade* is used to talk about the methods or techniques that are helpful to a person doing a specific job. Model-makers use all sorts of tricks to make a miniature look as real as possible.

Toy Soldiers

Director Steven Spielberg used a miniature model to plan shots for the film *Raiders of the Lost Ark*. Directors often use miniature models to plan the way a scene should look, including actors' movements, the scenery, and any special lighting or camera angles.

Spielberg decides where to position the camera for the desert shot.

Sand dunes are constructed from polystyrene and beach sand.

10

Miniature models of tents, tanks and other vehicles are used.

Miniature trees are planted in the section behind muslin-coated pond.

Landscape is supported on timber platform.

Sand used on ground of miniature and to cover cracks in model surface.

Finally Ready

It has taken most of the day to reassemble the entire miniature landscape. Now the scene is ready for filming. During filming, SFX team members beneath the platform can reach up and move the reptile models around from below. Notice how the trees in the background section of the landscape are much smaller than the trees in the foreground section. This makes the scene seem to roll back away rapidly into the distance. The large painted backdrop and studio lighting add to the effect of a vast prehistoric landscape roamed by early reptiles.

11

377

Develop Vocabulary

PRACTICE LESSON VOCABULARY

As a class, have students answer the following questions orally.

1. Which would most likely appear in the *background* of a scene, an actor or mountain scenery? *(mountain scenery)*

2. What objects might you see in a *landscape* model for a movie about the moon? *(craters and rocks)*

BUILD CONCEPT VOCABULARY

Review previous concept words with students. Ask if they have come across any words today in their reading or elsewhere that they would like to add to the Special Effects Concept Web, such as *layering* and *enhanced*.

STRATEGY SELF-CHECK

Prior Knowledge

Discuss with students how their prior knowledge of movies and television helped them understand the text and the photos in the article.

SELF-CHECK

Students can ask themselves these questions to assess their ability to use the skill and strategy.

- Did I use my prior knowledge about movies and television to help me understand the article?
- Did the photographs help me better understand the meaning of the text?

Monitor Progress

Graphic Sources

If... students are unable to use photographs and prior knowledge to understand the text,	then... use the Reteach lesson on p. 383b.

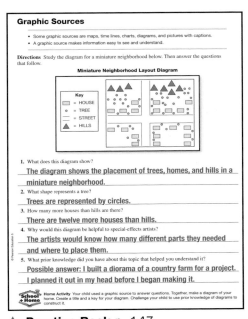

▲ **Practice Book** p. 147

Reader Response

Open for Discussion Personal Response

MODEL I'd think about things I'm likely to see in a prehistoric scene, like dinosaurs, exotic plants, rumbling earthquakes, and smoking volcanoes.

Comprehension Check Critical Response

1. Responses should include intermediary steps or tools. Students should support their opinions. **Author's Purpose**

2. Captions should reflect an understanding of each photograph. **Graphic Sources**

3. Responses should describe a personal experience with an art project that is similar in some way to the selection. **Prior Knowledge**

4. Possible response: The *miniature* models and *background* items like the trees, rocks, and sky make the *landscape* look realistic. **Vocabulary**

Look Back and Write For test practice, assign a 10–15 minute time limit. For assessment, see the Scoring Rubric at the right.

Retell

Have students retell *Special Effects in Film and Television*.

Monitor Progress

Check Retelling [4] [3] [2] [1] Rubric

| If... students have difficulty retelling the selection, | then... use the Retelling Cards and the Scoring Rubric for Retelling on p. 379 to assist fluent retelling. |

SUCCESS PREDICTOR

Check Retelling Have students use the numbered headings along with the photographs to guide their retellings. For more ideas on assessing students' retellings, see the ELL and Transition Handbook.

Reader Response

Open for Discussion The miniature landscape is being made for a TV show. What might that show be like? Use what you know from the selection to imagine different scenes and the sounds that would go with them.

1. The selection includes photographs to help you visualize the process that the author describes in words. What are some steps and tools that are not shown? Would showing them make the selection better? Explain. **Think Like an Author**

2. Think up additional captions for the photographs. **Graphic Sources**

3. Look back at the selection as you recall art projects you have done in school or at home. Which project does the selection most remind you of? Describe it. **Prior Knowledge**

4. What makes this prehistoric landscape look realistic? Use words from the Words to Know list in your answer. **Vocabulary**

Look Back and Write Imagine that you have the entire team of technicians from the selection in front of you. You are the boss, explaining in general what they must do. Write what you would say to them.

Meet author Jake Hamilton on page 766.

378

Scoring Rubric Look Back and Write

Top-Score Response A top-score response will summarize the most important steps and processes technicians must follow to create a prehistoric world onscreen and will address the technicians directly.

Example of a Top-Score Response First, you will make a small model of the set and decide how big to make the real set. Next, you will make a bigger prototype out of plastic, section by section. After you assemble the sections in the studio, spray them with foam. Finally, add details, such as rocks, bushes, and trees. Get materials, such as paint and glue, before you start.

For additional rubrics, see p. WA10.

Write Now

Expository Writing

Prompt

Special Effects in Film and Television explains how filmmakers create effects. Think about a movie and a television show in the same genre. Now use expository writing to tell how they are alike and different.

Writing Trait

Different kinds, lengths, and structures of **sentences** give expository writing a smooth flow.

Student Model

Subjects to be compared are identified at beginning.

Writer uses sentences of different lengths.

Signal words alert readers to comparisons and contrasts.

The Shaggy Dog is a movie remake. _The Bill Cosby Show_ is an old TV show. Both are comedies about happy families with funny dads, but they are also different.

    In _The Shaggy Dog_, Tim Allen plays a dad who sometimes turns into a dog. Allen uses silly expressions and movements when he is a dog.

    Bill Cosby is also funny. Sometimes he uses slapstick, but usually his humor is verbal. Unlike _The Shaggy Dog_, the show is realistic.

    In both shows, dads learn to communicate better with their kids. Both are good family comedies with funny father characters.

Use the model to help you with your own expository writing.

Write Now

Look at the Prompt Have students identify and discuss key words and phrases in the prompt. *(movie, television show, same genre, expository writing, alike and different)*

Strategies to Develop Sentences

Have students

- use words that signal similarities *(both, also, too, in addition)* and differences *(but, however, unlike, on the other hand)*.
- combine similarities and differences if possible. Both are scary science fiction stories. They also use close-up shots to reveal panic and fear.

For additional suggestions and rubric, see pp. 383g–383h.

Hints for Better Writing

- Carefully read the prompt.
- Use a graphic organizer to plan your writing.
- Support your ideas with information and details.
- Use words that help readers understand.
- Proofread and edit your work.

379

Scoring Rubric — Expository Retelling

Rubric 4 3 2 1	4	3	2	1
Connections	Makes connections and generalizes beyond the text	Makes connections to other events, texts, or experiences	Makes a limited connection to another event, text, or experience	Makes no connection to another event, text, or experience
Author's Purpose	Elaborates on author's purpose	Tells author's purpose with some clarity	Makes some connection to author's purpose	Makes no connection to author's purpose
Topic	Describes the main topic	Identifies the main topic with some details early in retelling	Identifies the main topic	Retelling has no sense of topic
Important Ideas	Gives accurate information about events, steps, and ideas using details and key vocabulary	Gives accurate information about events, steps, and ideas with some detail and key vocabulary	Gives limited or inaccurate information about events, steps, and ideas	Gives no information about events, steps, and ideas
Conclusions	Draws conclusions and makes inferences to generalize beyond the text	Draws conclusions about the text	Is able to draw few conclusions about the text	Is unable to draw conclusions or make inferences about the text

Retelling Plan

☑ **Week 1** Assess Strategic Intervention students.

☑ **Week 2** Assess Advanced students.

☑ **Week 3** Assess Strategic Intervention students.

☑ **Week 4** Assess On-Level students.

☑ **This week assess any students you have not yet checked during this unit.**

Use the Retelling Chart on p. TR17 to record retelling.

Selection Test To assess students on *Special Effects*, use Selection Tests, pp. 57–60.

Fresh Reads for Differentiated Test Practice For weekly leveled practice, use pp. 85–90.

SUCCESS PREDICTOR

Reading Online

PREVIEW/USE TEXT FEATURES

Have students preview "Searching for Animation." Ask:

- **Why does Matt type the word *animation* in the search window?** *(He wants to find information about animation.)*

- **What does the numbered list on the screen on p. 381 show? Why does the list begin with number 25?** *(The list shows three of the Web sites that resulted from Matt's search. The list is too long to fit on one screen, so Matt scrolled down to read all of the results.)*

If students need help understanding how to use a search engine, use the Technology Tools.

Link to Social Studies

Have students brainstorm a list of questions that relate to animation. Have them identify keywords that will help them search for the answers to their questions.

DAY 4 Grouping Options

Reading
Whole Group Discuss the Question of the Day.

Group Time Differentiated Instruction
Read "Searching for Animation." See pp. 364h–364i for the small group lesson plan.

Whole Group Use p. 383a.

Language Arts
Use pp. 383e–383k.

Reading Online

New Literacies: **PearsonSuccessNet.com**

Searching For Animation

Search Engines

Genre
- A search engine is a tool that helps Internet users find the Web sites they need.

- It uses keywords — words you type in to pinpoint what you're looking for.

Text Features
- The search window is where you type in keywords. Then you click on a Search button.

- The search results are displayed in a list below the search window.

- Each item on the list leads to a Web site that contains the keywords.

Link to Social Studies
Do your own research on animation. Share fun facts with the class.

Matt does an Internet search to find out more about animation. He starts by typing the keyword "animation" into a search engine and then clicking on the SEARCH button.

For more practice
Take It to the Net
PearsonSuccessNet.com

380

TECHNOLOGY TOOLS

Search Engine

Search Window The search window is where you type the keyword or phrase you want to find information about. In some search engines, you may need to click on the box before typing. To start the search, click on a word like *Search* or *Go,* or press *Enter.*

Search Results The results of a search are displayed in a list below the search window. This list includes links to Web sites that contain the keywords you typed into the search window.

Scroll Bar The scroll bar is located on the right side of the screen. Many search result lists are long and take up more than one screen. Clicking on the scroll bar with your mouse allows you to move up and down a list.

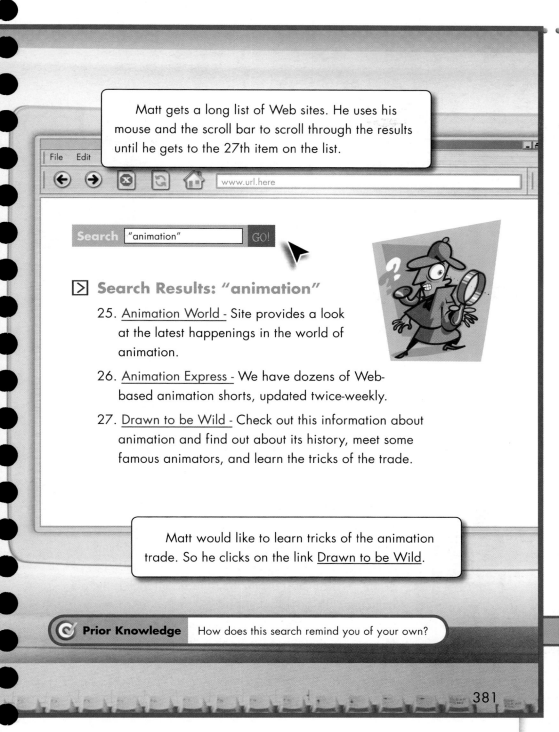

Matt gets a long list of Web sites. He uses his mouse and the scroll bar to scroll through the results until he gets to the 27th item on the list.

File   Edit

www.url.here

Search "animation" GO!

⊳ **Search Results: "animation"**

25. Animation World - Site provides a look at the latest happenings in the world of animation.

26. Animation Express - We have dozens of Web-based animation shorts, updated twice-weekly.

27. Drawn to be Wild - Check out this information about animation and find out about its history, meet some famous animators, and learn the tricks of the trade.

Matt would like to learn tricks of the animation trade. So he clicks on the link Drawn to be Wild.

Ⓒ Prior Knowledge   How does this search remind you of your own?

WEB-IQUETTE

Search Engine

Tell students that, while search engines are a quick and efficient way to find information, there are rules of etiquette they should follow:

- Research using a search engine that locates age-appropriate sites approved for use in your classroom. Avoid clicking on links that appear with pop-up advertisements, and close all pop-up windows immediately.
- Read the descriptions of the different Web sites in the search results list first in order to judge which sites are best suited to your topic.
- Plan ahead in order to use your time more efficiently when conducting Internet searches. If you're sharing computer time, brainstorm keywords related to your topic ahead of time so that you don't keep others waiting.

NEW LITERACIES: SEARCH ENGINE

Use the sidebar on p. 380 to guide discussion.

- A search engine helps Internet users find Web sites that contain the information they need. By typing a keyword into a search engine, the user tells the search engine to find sites on the Internet that relate to that word.

- Search results may include brief descriptions of the sites. Here, Matt chooses to click on link 27 because he is interested in learning tricks of the animation trade.

- Discuss with students how they would review search results and decide which sites to explore if their searches yielded long lists of Web sites.

 **AudioText**

Ⓒ Prior Knowledge

Possible response: My search produced a long list of results, and I had to scroll down through several screens to find what I was looking for. I read the descriptions of the different Web sites in order to choose the one that best related to my topic.

ⒺⓁⓁ

Access Content Lead a picture walk to reinforce technology vocabulary, such as *keyword* and *search engine* (p. 380), and *Web sites* (p. 381).

Special Effects in Film and Television   **381**

Strategies for Navigation

USE TITLES Point out that some search engines may yield many results, more than a student has time to explore. To be efficient, researchers may sometimes make decisions about which Web sites to visit based on the sites' titles.

Use the Strategy

1. The next time you use a search engine and get many results, read the Web site titles carefully before you click on any links. The name of a Web site can often tell you something about the content of the site.

2. When you review your search results, ask yourself two questions about each link: *Based on the title of the Web site, is it likely to have the kind of information I'm looking for? Is the site affiliated with a reliable organization that is likely to provide me with facts rather than opinions?*

3. Choose a few of the sites that look the most promising, and explore those links first.

PRACTICE Think about the ways you use titles at home and at school.

The next time you use print resources to find information for a report, note how helpful the titles are in deciding which sources to use and which ones to eliminate.

The next time you use a search engine, print a copy of the search results. Next to each Web site title, write how helpful you think the site will be and why. Then check out a few of the sites to confirm your predictions.

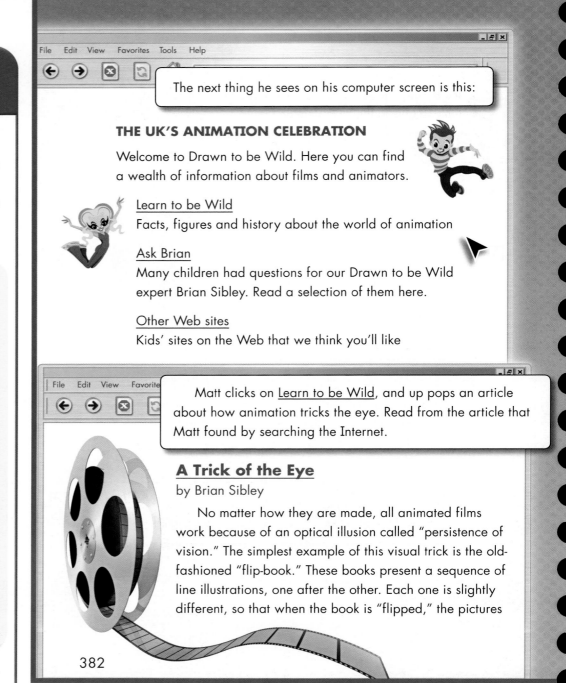

The next thing he sees on his computer screen is this:

THE UK'S ANIMATION CELEBRATION

Welcome to Drawn to be Wild. Here you can find a wealth of information about films and animators.

Learn to be Wild
Facts, figures and history about the world of animation

Ask Brian
Many children had questions for our Drawn to be Wild expert Brian Sibley. Read a selection of them here.

Other Web sites
Kids' sites on the Web that we think you'll like

Matt clicks on Learn to be Wild, and up pops an article about how animation tricks the eye. Read from the article that Matt found by searching the Internet.

A Trick of the Eye
by Brian Sibley

No matter how they are made, all animated films work because of an optical illusion called "persistence of vision." The simplest example of this visual trick is the old-fashioned "flip-book." These books present a sequence of line illustrations, one after the other. Each one is slightly different, so that when the book is "flipped," the pictures

382

Guided Practice If there is time, have students log onto the Internet. Show them how to use a title to evaluate whether a site will provide the information that is needed. Help students make connections between the steps they are doing and related vocabulary terms.

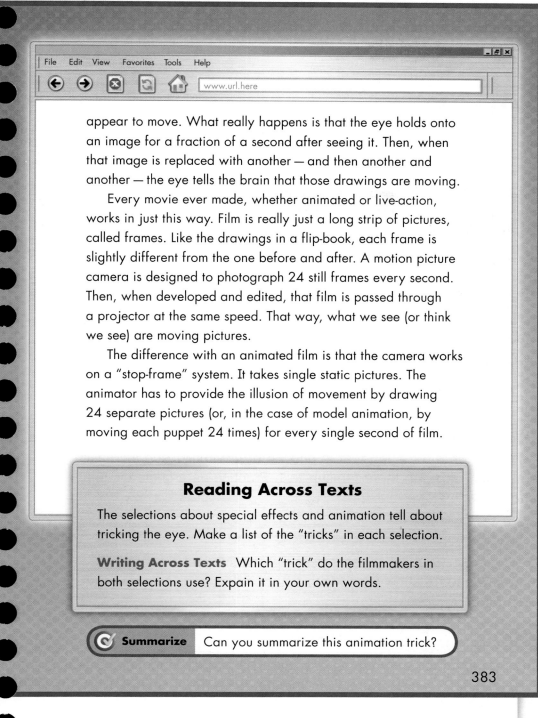

appear to move. What really happens is that the eye holds onto an image for a fraction of a second after seeing it. Then, when that image is replaced with another — and then another and another — the eye tells the brain that those drawings are moving.

Every movie ever made, whether animated or live-action, works in just this way. Film is really just a long strip of pictures, called frames. Like the drawings in a flip-book, each frame is slightly different from the one before and after. A motion picture camera is designed to photograph 24 still frames every second. Then, when developed and edited, that film is passed through a projector at the same speed. That way, what we see (or think we see) are moving pictures.

The difference with an animated film is that the camera works on a "stop-frame" system. It takes single static pictures. The animator has to provide the illusion of movement by drawing 24 separate pictures (or, in the case of model animation, by moving each puppet 24 times) for every single second of film.

Reading Across Texts

The selections about special effects and animation tell about tricking the eye. Make a list of the "tricks" in each selection.

Writing Across Texts Which "trick" do the filmmakers in both selections use? Expain it in your own words.

Summarize Can you summarize this animation trick?

383

CONNECT TEXT TO TEXT

Reading Across Texts

Discuss the different ways that animators and special effects artists "trick" viewers. Focus on the methods that animators and artists use, as well as the illusion that results.

Writing Across Texts Before writing, students may want to practice explaining "the trick" to a partner, using their own words. If their partner feels the explanation is unclear, they may review the selection again.

Summarize

Possible response: The eye holds onto an image for a fraction of a second after seeing it. Therefore, when a series of images is projected, each one slightly different from the one before, the brain interprets the images as moving.

Fluency Assessment Plan

- ☑ **Week 1** Assess Advanced students.
- ☑ **Week 2** Assess Strategic Intervention students.
- ☑ **Week 3** Assess On-Level students.
- ☑ **Week 4** Assess Strategic Intervention students.
- ☑ **This week assess any students you have not yet checked during this unit.**

Set individual goals for students to enable them to reach the year-end goal.

- Current Goal: 115–122 wcpm
- Year-End Goal: 140 wcpm

Fluency, particularly for English learners reading texts in English, develops gradually and through much practice. Focus on each student's improvement rather than solely monitoring the number of words correct per minute.

 To develop fluent readers, use Fluency Coach.

DAY 5 Grouping Options

Reading
Whole Group
Revisit the Question of the Week.

Group Time
Differentiated Instruction
Reread this week's Leveled Readers. See pp. 364h–364i for the small group lesson plan.

Whole Group
Use pp. 383b–383c.

Language Arts
Use pp. 383d–383l.

TEMPO AND RATE

Fluency

DAY 1

Model Reread "The Making of the Lord of the Rings" on p. 364m. Explain you will use different tempos and rates of reading depending on the importance of the information and the possible need for reflection. Model for students as you read.

DAY 2

Choral Reading Read aloud item number 2 on p. 371. Have students notice the adjustments you make to your tempo and rate when you come to challenging vocabulary (*concept, prototype*), and numbers or measurements. Have students practice as a class by doing three choral readings.

DAY 3

Model Read aloud items 3 and 4 on p. 372. Have students notice how you slow down for information that is difficult or unfamiliar and increase your tempo and rate with more familiar text. Practice as a class by doing three choral readings.

DAY 4

Partner Reading Partners practice reading items 3 and 4 on p. 372, three times. Students should read with appropriate tempo and rate and offer each other feedback.

Monitor Progress | Check Fluency WCPM

As students reread, monitor their progress toward their individual fluency goals. Current Goal: 115–122 words correct per minute. End-of-Year Goal: 140 words correct per minute.

If... students cannot read fluently at a rate of 115–122 words correct per minute,
then... make sure students practice with text at their independent level. Provide additional fluency practice, pairing nonfluent readers with fluent readers.

If... students already read at 140 words correct per minute,
then... they do not need to reread three to four times.

SUCCESS PREDICTOR

DAY 5

Assessment
Individual Reading Rate Use the Fluency Assessment Plan and do a one-minute timed reading of either selection from this week to assess students in Week 5. Pay special attention to this week's skill, tempo and rate. Provide corrective feedback for each student.

RETEACH

⌖ Graphic Sources

TEACH

Review the examples and purposes of *graphic sources* on p. 364. Students can complete Practice Book p. 148 on their own, or you can complete it as a class. Explain they must interpret the information in the graph to answer the questions.

ASSESS

Have students work in small groups to reread the "Reptile Modeling" sidebar on p. 375 and compare the information in the text with the illustrations. Ask students how the illustrations help them better understand the text.

For additional instruction on graphic sources, see DI·56.

EXTEND SKILLS

Steps in a Process

TEACH

The steps in a process usually involve people doing or making something in a particular sequence or order. When you come across steps in a process in your reading:

- Read each step carefully.
- Try to visualize each step.
- Use clue words and common sense to keep track of order.

Point out the seven steps in the process of rebuilding a miniature model on pp. 371–373.

ASSESS

Have students write out the steps in the process for writing and mailing a letter. Ask:

1. Have you numbered the steps?

2. Did you try to picture each step to make sure the order makes sense?

3. Did you double-check to be sure you didn't leave anything out?

OBJECTIVES

- ⌖ Use graphic sources to understand text.
- Identify steps in a process.

Skills Trace
⌖ **Graphic Sources**

Introduce/Teach	TE: 5.3 364–365; 5.4 436–437; 5.5 536–537
Practice	Practice Book: 143, 147, 148, 166, 173, 177, 178, 213, 217, 218, 226, 246
Reteach/Review	**TE: 5.3 383b, DI•56; 5.4 421, 457b, DI•54; 5.5 559b, 569, 613, DI•53**
Test	Selection Test: 57–60, 69–72, 85–88; Benchmark Test: Unit 5

ELL

Access Content Reteach the skill by reviewing the *Picture It!* lesson on graphic sources in the ELL Teaching Guide, pp. 99–100.

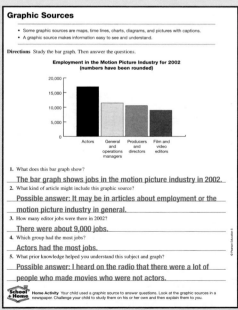

Graphic Sources

- Some graphic sources are maps, time lines, charts, diagrams, and pictures with captions.
- A graphic source makes information easy to see and understand.

Directions Study the bar graph. Then answer the questions.

Employment in the Motion Picture Industry for 2002
(numbers have been rounded)

1. What does this bar graph show?
   The bar graph shows jobs in the motion picture industry in 2002.
2. What kind of article might include this graphic source?
   Possible answer: It may be in articles about employment or the motion picture industry in general.
3. How many editor jobs were there in 2002?
   There were about 9,000 jobs.
4. Which group had the most jobs?
   Actors had the most jobs.
5. What prior knowledge helped you understand this subject and graph?
   Possible answer: I heard on the radio that there were a lot of people who made movies who were not actors.

Home Activity Your child used a graphic source to answer questions. Look at the graphic sources in a newspaper. Challenge your child to study them on his or her own and then explain them to you.

▲ **Practice Book** p. 148

Vocabulary and Word Study

VOCABULARY STRATEGY

Word Structure

PREFIXES Remind students that a prefix is a syllable added at the beginning of a base word that has a meaning of its own. Prefixes can help you figure out the meaning of an unknown word. Have students brainstorm words with the prefixes *pre-* and *re-* and the prefixes *im-* and *in-* like those below from *Special Effects in Film and Television*. For each word, students should give the prefix and its meaning, the base word, and the meaning of the whole word.

Prefix (Meaning)		Base		New Word (Meaning)
im- (not)	+	possible	=	impossible (not possible)
	+		=	
	+		=	
in- (into; toward; within)		habit		inhabit: live in
	+		=	

BUILD CONCEPT VOCABULARY

Special Effects

LOOKING BACK Remind students of the unit theme: Inventors and Artists. Discuss the unit focus question, *What do people gain from the work of inventors and artists?* Ask students how the Concept Vocabulary from each week of this unit relates to the unit theme and unit focus question. Ask students if they have any words or categories to add. If time permits, create a Unit Concept Web.

Monitor Progress

Check Vocabulary

If... students suggest words or categories that are not related to the concept,	**then...** review the words and categories on the Concept Web and discuss how they relate to the lesson concept.

SUCCESS PREDICTOR

Abbreviations and Acronyms

Abbreviations are shortened forms of words or phrases. Although word abbreviations like *St.* for *street* and *Mon.* for *Monday* are common, abbreviations using initials for phrases like *SFX* (special effects) are less common. Have small groups brainstorm other abbreviations using initials for phrases such as *ASAP* and *FYI*. Explain that words formed from the first letters or syllables of other words are known as acronyms, for example, *scuba* for "self-contained underwater breathing apparatus." Then have students make up their own abbreviations or acronyms for common phrases, like *SYL* for "see you later." Note that a period is used after most abbreviations.

Speaking and Viewing

SPEAKING

Advertisement

SET-UP Have students work with partners to create an advertisement for the movie in *Special Effects in Film and Television.* Students should give the movie an appropriate title. They can cast the movie with their favorite actors, or they can make up names for fictitious actors.

AUDIENCE Remind students that their audience will be people who like movies with action and adventure, and that their purpose is to convince people to come to see the movie. Explain that their advertisement should appeal to these people by focusing on the special effects that are featured in the movie.

MULTI-MEDIA PRESENTATION Explain that students can use sound, computer art, or visual models or aids to help advertise the movie. Offer these suggestions:

- Use persuasive language and images.
- Vary your tone and volume for emphasis.
- Use visual displays that can easily be seen by all audience members.
- Present images that support your words.

Remind students, that even with visual displays or music, this project should still emphasize the spoken word.

VIEWING

Analyze Film Media

Discuss with students TV shows or movies they have seen which use special effects. With partners, they can answer these questions orally or in writing.

1. **Give examples of special effects in the movie.**
2. **How do you think the special effects were created?** *(Responses will vary but should show some reflection upon the selection.)*
3. **What special effect from a movie do you think is most impressive? Why?**

ELL

Support Vocabulary Use the following to review and extend vocabulary and to explore lesson concepts further:
- ELL Poster 15, Days 3–5 instruction
- Vocabulary Activities and Word Cards in ELL Teaching Guide, pp. 101–102

Assessment For information on assessing students' speaking, listening, and viewing, see the ELL and Transition Handbook.

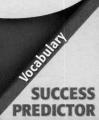
Vocabulary

SUCCESS PREDICTOR

Grammar
Prepositions and Prepositional Phrases

Monitor Progress

Grammar

If... students have difficulty identifying prepositions and prepositional phrases,	then... provide additional instruction and practice in The Grammar and Writing Book pp. 134–137.

DAILY FIX-IT

This week use Daily Fix-It Transparency 15.

Spiral REVIEW

ELL

Support Grammar See the Grammar Transition lessons in the ELL and Transition Handbook.

▲ **The Grammar and Writing Book**
For more instruction and practice, use pp. 134–137.

DAY 1 Teach and Model

DAILY FIX-IT

1. Grandma is infamiliar about the new cartoon shows. *(unfamiliar; with)*

2. Her would disaprove of the violence in some cartoons. *(She; disapprove)*

READING-GRAMMAR CONNECTION

Write this sentence on the board:

People in film and television use computers.

Explain that *in film and television* is a prepositional phrase that tells about the subject *people.* The preposition is *in,* and both *film* and *television* are objects of the preposition.

Display Grammar Transparency 15. Read aloud the definitions and sample sentences. Work through the items.

Prepositions and Prepositional Phrases

A **preposition** begins a group of words called a **prepositional phrase.** The noun or pronoun that follows the preposition is called the **object of the preposition.** Prepositional phrases provide details about the rest of the sentence.

Animation is created from careful drawings. (preposition)
Animation is created from careful drawings. (prepositional phrase)
Animation is created from careful drawings. (object of the preposition)

Common Prepositions

about	around	by	into	over	until
above	at	down	near	through	up
across	before	for	of	to	with
after	below	from	on	toward	
against	between	in	onto	under	

Directions Underline the prepositional phrase in each sentence. Circle the preposition.

1. The first animated cartoons were made by Walt Disney.
2. Disney created Mickey Mouse in 1928.
3. This film used sound for the first time.
4. Viewers loved the little mouse with the silly grin.
5. Mickey's looks changed over time.
6. Today he is beloved around the world.
7. Many millions of people visit Disney World and Disneyland.
8. There you can see Mickey strolling across the grounds.

Directions Write *P* if the underlined word is a preposition. Write *O* if it is the object of the preposition.

9. Animated movies have been around for a long time. P
10. Disney produced *Snow White and the Seven Dwarfs* in 1937. P
11. Each image in that movie was hand drawn. O
12. Every movement of a character requires hundreds of drawings. O
13. Compare this movie with a newer cartoon film such as *Mulan.* P
14. Computers make life easier for the cartoon artist. P
15. Animated movies draw huge crowds into the theaters. O
16. People of all ages love these entertaining films. O

Unit 3 Special Effects in Film and Television   Grammar **15**

▲ **Grammar Transparency** 15

DAY 2 Develop the Concept

DAILY FIX-IT

3. Have you ever maked a flip book. *(made; book?)*

4. It werks like a simpel animated cartoon. *(works; simple)*

GUIDED PRACTICE

Review the concept of prepositions and prepositional phrases.

- A **preposition** begins a group of words called a **prepositional phrase.**
- The noun or pronoun that follows the preposition is called the **object of the preposition.**
- Prepositional phrases can be used to tell more about the words they accompany.

HOMEWORK Grammar and Writing Practice Book p. 57. Work through the first two items with the class.

Prepositions and Prepositional Phrases

A **preposition** begins a group of words called a **prepositional phrase.** The noun or pronoun that follows the preposition is called the **object of the preposition.** Prepositional phrases provide details about the rest of the sentence.

People have watched animated movies for a long time. (preposition)
People have watched animated movies for a long time. (prepositional phrase)
People have watched animated movies for a long time. (object of the preposition)

Common Prepositions

about	around	by	into	over	until
above	at	down	near	through	up
across	before	for	of	to	with
after	below	from	on	toward	
against	between	in	onto	under	

Directions Underline the prepositional phrase in each sentence. Write *P* above the preposition. Write *O* above the object of the preposition.

1. The characters in animated films often seem quite real. P O
2. Young viewers may identify with the superheroes. P O
3. Ariel was a mermaid who lived under the sea. P O
4. She wanted a life on dry land. P O
5. Her father was Neptune, king of the sea. P O

Directions Underline the prepositional phrases. The number in ( ) tells how many prepositional phrases are in that sentence.

6. Many fairy tales have been made into animated movies for children. (2)
7. Their stories take youngsters from childhood into adulthood. (2)
8. The hero of the tale must pass through trials and adventures. (2)
9. At the end, he or she has shown great strength of character. (2)

School-Home CONNECTION **Home Activity** Your child learned about prepositions and prepositional phrases. Read a favorite story with your child. Ask him or her to point out prepositional phrases and identify the preposition and object of the preposition in each.

▲ **Grammar and Writing Practice Book** p. 57

DAY 3 — Apply to Writing

DAILY FIX-IT

5. The chilren watch cartoons in Saturday morning. *(children; on)*

6. Can your draw cartoons good? *(you; well)*

ADD PREPOSITIONAL PHRASES

Prepositional phrases can add important details that make your writing clearer and more informative.

Without Prepositional Phrases: Animators make drawings and photograph them.

With Prepositional Phrases: Animators make drawings <u>in a series</u> and photograph them <u>in order</u>.

- Have students review something they have written and improve it by adding prepositional phrases to modify nouns and verbs.

HOMEWORK Grammar and Writing Practice Book p. 58.

Prepositions and Prepositional Phrases

Directions Add a preposition to complete each sentence. Write the sentence on the line.
Possible answers:
1. I usually lie _____ the floor when I watch TV.
   I usually lie on the floor when I watch TV.

2. When I get hungry, I get a snack _____ the refrigerator. **When I get hungry, I get a snack from the refrigerator.**

3. We have several movies stored _____ the television. **We have several movies stored under the television.**

4. I would rather see a movie _____ the theater.
   I would rather see a movie at the theater.

5. The big screen and the smell _____ popcorn create a memorable experience.
   The big screen and the smell of popcorn create a memorable experience.

Directions Add a prepositional phrase of your own to complete each sentence. Write the sentence.
Possible answers:
6. Let's make Dad a cartoon _____
   Let's make Dad a cartoon about a superhero.

7. I'll get the paper and markers _____
   I'll get the paper and markers from my room.

8. You draw the scenes in pencil, and I'll color them _____ **You draw the scenes in pencil, and I'll color them with these markers.**

9. What colors shall we use _____?
   What colors shall we use for the costumes?

10. Dad will hang this cartoon _____
    Dad will hang this cartoon on his office bulletin board.

School-Home Connection **Home Activity** Your child learned how to use prepositions and prepositional phrases in writing. Ask your child to write about his or her favorite animated film using at least one prepositional phrase in each sentence.

▲ **Grammar and Writing Practice Book** p. 58

DAY 4 — Test Preparation

DAILY FIX-IT

7. Jiminy Cricket is Pinocchios conscience to the movie. *(Pinocchio's; in)*

8. However, jiminy cannot keep the pupet from temptation. *(Jiminy; puppet)*

STANDARDIZED TEST PREP

> **Test Tip**
>
> Some words can serve as either conjunctions or prepositions. A conjunction introduces a clause. A preposition introduces a phrase and links a noun or pronoun to the rest of the sentence.
>
> *Conjunction:* I'll watch a movie <u>after</u> I do my homework.
>
> *Preposition:* What shall we do <u>after</u> the movie?

HOMEWORK Grammar and Writing Practice Book p. 59.

Prepositions and Prepositional Phrases

Directions Mark the letter of the preposition that correctly completes each sentence in the paragraph.

(1) *Pinocchio* was released ___ 1940. (2) It is a tale ___ a puppet who wants to be a real boy. (3) He was carved ___ a woodcarver named Gepetto. (4) A fairy princess turns Pinocchio ___ a wooden boy. (5) ___ his way to school, Pinocchio is lured away by a con artist named Honest John. (6) The con artist sells Pinocchio ___ the puppeteer Stromboli. (7) Next, Pinocchio winds up ___ Pleasure Island. (8) Boys run wild there until they turn ___ donkeys. (9) Then the puppet is swallowed ___ Monstro the whale. (10) Finally, father and son are reunited, and Pinocchio becomes a real boy ___ the end.

1. A between
   B with
   C in
   D at

2. **A** about
   B from
   C for
   D into

3. A behind
   B before
   C by
   D over

4. A from
   B into
   C to
   D down

5. A Against
   B Through
   C Across
   D On

6. **A** until
   B to
   C about
   D under

7. **A** on
   B above
   C under
   D after

8. A for
   B by
   C around
   D into

9. A down
   B by
   C behind
   D toward

10. A under
    B around
    C at
    D to

School-Home Connection **Home Activity** Your child prepared for taking tests on prepositions and prepositional phrases. Ask your child to make flash cards for prepositions he or she has learned. Show each card and have him or her use the preposition in a sentence.

▲ **Grammar and Writing Practice Book** p. 59

DAY 5 — Cumulative Review

DAILY FIX-IT

9. Paula kin use an computer skillfully. *(can; a)*

10. She has brung we more information. *(brought; us)*

ADDITIONAL PRACTICE

Assign pp. 134–137 in The Grammar and Writing Book.

EXTRA PRACTICE Grammar and Writing Practice Book p. 136.

ASSESSMENT

CUMULATIVE REVIEW Grammar and Writing Practice Book p. 60.

Prepositions and Prepositional Phrases

Directions Underline each prepositional phrase. The number in ( ) tells how many prepositional phrases are in that sentence.

1. *Bambi* is an animated movie about a deer. (1)

2. It begins with Bambi's birth in the forest. (2)

3. All the forest creatures are filled with joy at the birth. (2)

4. They welcome the new prince of the forest. (1)

5. Bambi makes two friends of the closest kind. (1)

6. Thumper is a bunny with attitude, who has a sense of fun. (2)

7. Bambi discovers a shy skunk in the flowers and names him Flower. (1)

Directions Write *P* if the underlined word is a preposition. Write *O* if it is the object of the preposition.

8. Today we learned about computer animation. — **P**

9. We enjoy cartoons thanks to this technique. — **P**

10. Artists create drawings on the computer. — **O**

11. With software, they manipulate these drawings. — **O**

12. Before computers, animation artists drew every frame. — **P**

13. Now computers move the cartoon for the artist. — **P**

14. Software also applies colors in the shapes. — **O**

Directions Underline the prepositional phrase in each sentence. Write *P* above the preposition. Write *O* above the object of the preposition.

15. *Toy Story* is an animated film about a boy's toys. — P O

16. The toys remain loyal to their owner. — P O

17. There is jealousy and competition between the toys. — P O

18. They finally become friends and work together for their own good. — P O

School-Home Connection **Home Activity** Your child reviewed prepositions and prepositional phrases. Have your child see how many prepositional phrases he or she can find on the label of a box or can of food. Have your child identify the prepositions.

▲ **Grammar and Writing Practice Book** p. 60

Writing for Tests Expository Writing

Sentences Read imperative, exclamatory, and interrogative sentences aloud to English learners, using tone to show how these sentences add excitement to writing. Add think-aloud comments to explain how punctuation helps readers understand sentences.

Writing Traits

FOCUS/IDEAS All details are focused on explaining how the films are alike and different.

ORGANIZATION/PARAGRAPHS Similarities are discussed first, then differences are described.

VOICE The writer speaks directly and clearly to the reader and is interested in the subject.

WORD CHOICE Details inform with facts (*created in different centuries*) and exact descriptions (*every image . . . drawn and colored by hand*).

SENTENCES Prepositional phrases (*made before computers, colored by hand*) create variety in sentences.

CONVENTIONS There is excellent control and accuracy.

DAY 1 Model the Trait

READING-WRITING CONNECTION

- When you write a response for tests, remember that sentences with parallel structure strengthen your answer.

- Think about how the writer uses parallel structure in *Computer Animation* to express ideas clearly.

MODEL SENTENCES Discuss Writing Transparency 15A. Point out underlined words in the prompt. Then discuss the model and the writing trait of sentences.

 The writer of this essay has made it strong and easy to follow by using parallel sentences. I see "Both films present" and "both films were animated." Then I see "However" to signal differences, and sentences about *Pinocchio* followed by sentences about *Finding Nemo.*

Writing for Tests

Think about an older animated film and a recent animated film you can compare. For example, *Snow White and the Seven Dwarfs* is older, and *The Lion King* is newer. Use expository writing to explain to your class ways they are alike and different. Use parallel structure to present your ideas.

Pinocchio and Finding Nemo

Topic sentence sets up the essay.

Although they were created in different centuries, *Pinocchio* and *Finding Nemo* are animated films with much in common. Both films present an exciting story of adventure. In each movie, a father searches for a lost son who is in danger. In addition, both films were animated so skillfully that you forget that you are looking at drawings. The artistry of the animation results in characters, action, and images that captivate viewers.

Parallel structure is used to present three nouns naming similar characteristics.

Transitions show likenesses and differences.

However, these films are from different eras, and the technology used to produce each movie is quite different. Because it was made before computers, *Pinocchio* required detailed illustrations by artists. Every image that was photographed was drawn and colored by hand. On the other hand, *Finding Nemo* is a film of the computer age. Computer animation saved its creators thousands of drawings because software could create "in-between" drawings after the originals were done. Computers were used to add color, texture, and light to drawings. Despite the difference in technology, both films are entertaining and artistic.

Unit 3 Special Effects in Film and Television Writing Model **15A**

▲ **Writing Transparency** 15A

DAY 2 Improve Writing

WRITER'S CRAFT
Parallelism

Display Writing Transparency 15B. Read the directions and work together to identify parallel structure.

 BUILD SENTENCES WITH A LOGICAL PATTERN Tomorrow we will write an **expository explanation.** How could I use parallel structure to compare *Pinocchio* and *Finding Nemo*? I could write, "Both movies give human traits to nonhuman things, involve lost sons, and teach a life lesson." The verbs *give, involve,* and *teach* begin three phrases that are alike in structure.

GUIDED WRITING Some students may need more help with parallel structure. Write simple sentences with similar elements and help students combine them using parallel structures.

Parallelism

If a sentence has two or more parts that are alike, those parts should have the same form or pattern. **Parallel structure** refers to the pattern, or organization, of similar sentence parts, such as verbs, nouns, and prepositional phrases. Note how the second sentence below, which lists three nouns as steps in a process, sounds smoother than the first.

Not Parallel The steps in filmmaking are preproduction, production, and what happens after production.

Parallel The steps in filmmaking are preproduction, production, and postproduction.

Directions Mark the letter of the parallel sentence in each pair.

1. A I love drawing, painting, and to sculpt.
   Ⓑ I love drawing, painting, and sculpting.
2. Ⓐ I hope to become an artist, a cartoonist, or an animator.
   B I hope to become an artist, a cartoonist, or a person who makes animated films.
3. A Computer animation is used to create special effects, short cartoons, and movies that are animated.
   Ⓑ Computer animation is used to create special effects, short cartoons, and animated movies.
4. Ⓐ Rendering involves computer software that colors objects, adds texture, and introduces light.
   B Rendering involves computer software that colors objects, adds texture, and can even introduce light.
5. A Computers create animated cartoons quickly, efficiently, and with precision.
   Ⓑ Computers create animated cartoons quickly, efficiently, and precisely.

Directions Rewrite the sentences in this paragraph to make them parallel.

Walt put down his pen, looked at the drawing, and sighing with satisfaction. The little mouse looked perky, friendly, and like a character you could love. Soon the animator and his little mouse would gain fame, a bundle of money, and affection around the world.

Possible answer: Walt put down his pen, looked at the drawing, and sighed with satisfaction. The little mouse looked perky, friendly, and lovable. Soon the animator and his little mouse would gain fame, fortune, and affection around the world.

Unit 3 Special Effects in Film and Television Writer's Craft **15B**

▲ **Writing Transparency** 15B

DAY 3 Prewrite and Draft

READ THE WRITING PROMPT

on page 379 in the Student Edition.

Special Effects in Film and Television *explains how filmmakers create effects.*

Think about a movie and a television show in the same genre.

Now use expository writing to tell how they are alike and different.

Writing Test Tips

1. **Read the prompt carefully.**
   - Find key words.
   - Consider the purpose and audience. How will they affect your writing?

2. **Develop a plan.** Think of what you want to say before writing. Fill out a simple graphic organizer.

3. **Support your ideas.** Use facts, examples, and details to strengthen your response. Avoid making general statements that are unsupported.

4. **Use a variety of sentence structures.** Include complex and compound sentences, varied sentence beginnings, and different sentence lengths and types.

5. **Choose clear, precise words.** Use words that create pictures and help readers understand what you mean.

6. **Check your writing.** If this is a timed test, you may not have time to recopy your work. However, you can neatly add, delete, or change words and make corrections in spelling, punctuation, or grammar. Make sure your handwriting is legible. It pays to reread your work before handing it in.

DAY 4 Draft and Revise

EDITING/REVISING CHECKLIST

☑ **Focus** Are explanations supported by enough details? Are all details relevant?

☑ **Organization** Have I used parallel structure in sentence parts that are alike?

☑ **Support** Have I used prepositional phrases to clarify meaning and add interest?

☑ **Conventions** Are words with prefixes *un-, de-,* and *dis-* spelled correctly?

See *The Grammar and Writing Book,* pp. 134–139.

Revising Tips

Sentences

- Combine like ideas in a sentence if possible to show similarities or differences.
- Make each element in a list the same in its form: all nouns, all prepositional phrases, and so on.
- Use exact words to express ideas in a list of like parts.

ASSESSMENT Use the scoring rubric to evaluate students' work.

DAY 5 Connect to Unit Writing

Compare and Contrast Essay

Week 1	Skit 285g–285h
Week 2	Question/Answer Essay 313g–313h
Week 3	Feature Story 343g–343h
Week 4	Description 361g–361h
Week 5	Expository Writing 381g–381h

PREVIEW THE UNIT PROMPT

Write an essay comparing and contrasting an invention of long ago with a modern invention. Explain how they are alike and different in the way they affected people. Use clue words such as like, also, but, *and* unlike *to signal likenesses and differences.*

APPLY

- Use parallel structures to help present likenesses and differences in a clear manner.

Writing Trait Rubric

	4	3	2	1
Sentences	Clear, interesting, unique sentences; excellent variety of sentence structure	Clear sentences; variety of sentence structure	Some sentences clear; limited variety of sentence structure	Most sentences unclear; no variety of sentence structure
	Exceptional sentence variety in expository writing	Some sentence variety in expository writing	Needs more sentence variety in expository writing	Little or no sentence variety in expository writing

OBJECTIVES

- Formulate an inquiry question that is connected to this week's lesson focus.
- Effectively and efficiently find, evaluate, and communicate information related to an inquiry question using electronic sources.

New Literacies

Day 1	Identify Questions
Day 2	Navigate/Search
Day 3	Analyze
Day 4	Synthesize
Day 5	Communicate

Internet Inquiry Activity

EXPLORE SPECIAL EFFECTS

Use the following 5-day plan to help students conduct this week's Internet inquiry activity on special effects. Remind students to follow classroom rules when using the Internet.

DAY 1

Identify Questions Discuss the lesson focus question: *How do artists create special effects to entertain us?* Brainstorm ideas for specific inquiry questions about special effects. For example, students might want to find out about the special effects used for one of their favorite movies. Have students work individually, in pairs, or in small groups to write inquiry questions.

DAY 2

Navigate/Search Remind students about the importance of scanning through Web site descriptions before they search sites. Checking the contents in advance can help them avoid sites that are strictly commercial; for example, sites that sell special effects props or costumes.

DAY 3

Analyze Have students skim Web sites they identified on Day 2. Explain how to identify a reliable, credible site by identifying the background of the author or publisher of the site, and by noting how recently it was updated. If appropriate, students can print out and highlight relevant information or take notes directly from the sites.

DAY 4

Synthesize Encourage students to synthesize information from Day 3. Remind them to use their own words to restate information or to use quotation marks when citing actual text from a site.

DAY 5

Communicate Invite students to share their inquiry results. They can use a word processor to write short summaries or create charts or diagrams summarizing the information they find.

RESEARCH/STUDY SKILLS
Graphics/Symbols

OBJECTIVES

- Understand and recognize *graphics* and *symbols*.
- Interpret graphics and symbols to understand information.

TEACH

Ask students if they can think of examples of graphics or visual information. Students may need prompting to identify maps, time lines, diagrams, etc. Show examples of graphics you have in the classroom, such as maps or graphics from textbooks. Then, define these terms for students.

- **Graphics** are visual representations of information.
- Graphics can include graphs, diagrams, tables, charts, maps, time lines, and storyboards.
- Graphics support and aid in the comprehension of text.
- **Symbols** are icons or small drawings that stand for ideas and information.

Working in groups, have students locate examples of graphics in their science or social studies textbooks. Have them examine the graphics and symbols. Then students can identify the information presented, the symbols used, and their meanings. As a class, discuss these questions:

1. **What types of graphics did you look at? What information was being presented?** (Possible response: diagram of the water cycle)

2. **What symbols were used to represent information? What did the symbols stand for?** (Possible response: Arrows represent movement of water through the process, and clouds and rain represent precipitation)

3. **Why are symbols used with graphics?** (Possible response: Symbols give detailed information in a concise way and can further help you understand the graphic.)

MAP KEY

- Sunny
- Rain
- Snow
- Partly Cloudy
- Thunderstorms

ASSESS

As students examine graphics and symbols, check for student understanding of the information being presented, how symbols are used, and their meanings. Be sure students understand the purpose of different types of graphics and where they are usually found.

For more practice or to assess students, use Practice Book pp. 149–150.

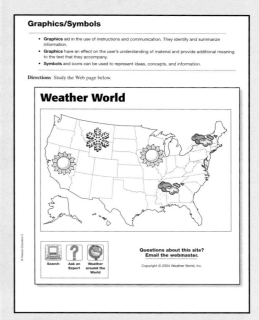

▲ **Practice Book** p. 149

▲ **Practice Book** p. 150

Unit 3
Reading Poetry

OBJECTIVES

- Listen and respond to poems.
- Identify how meaning is conveyed through word choice.
- Read poetry fluently.
- Connect ideas and themes across texts.

Model Fluent Reading

When reading "Chemistry 101" aloud, vary your rate to show the teacher's excitement and the students' initial boredom. Point out that the rate of your voice adds meaning to the poem.

Discuss the Poem

1 Metaphor • Critical

To what are the students compared and why?

Possible responses: The students are compared to "a claque of ducklings hatched by hens," possibly because they all think alike and follow one another.

2 Compare and Contrast • Inferential

Why does the speaker describe items first as the teacher sees them and then as the students see them?

Possible response: The speaker is showing two different perspectives.

EXTEND SKILLS

Tone

Explain that tone is the author's attitude toward the subject or audience. By recognizing the tone of a poem, the reader can better understand its intended emotional meaning. Tone should not be confused with mood, which is the atmosphere or feeling of a written work.

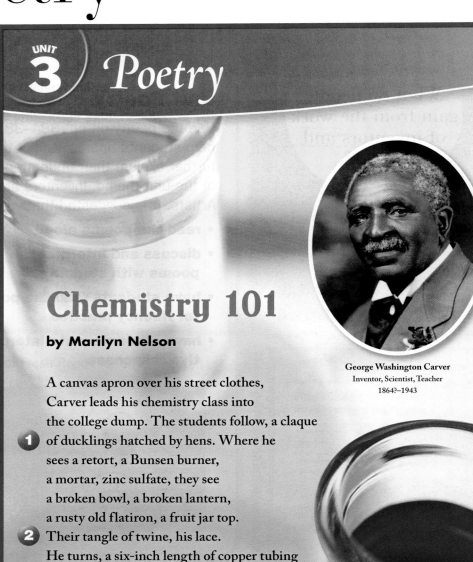

UNIT 3 Poetry

Chemistry 101

by Marilyn Nelson

George Washington Carver
Inventor, Scientist, Teacher
1864?–1943

A canvas apron over his street clothes,
Carver leads his chemistry class into
the college dump. The students follow, a claque
1 of ducklings hatched by hens. Where he
sees a retort, a Bunsen burner,
a mortar, zinc sulfate, they see
a broken bowl, a broken lantern,
a rusty old flatiron, a fruit jar top.
2 Their tangle of twine, his lace.
He turns, a six-inch length of copper tubing
in one hand. "Now, what can we do with this?"
Two by two, little lights go on.
One by hesitant one, dark hands are raised.
The waters of imagining, their element.

384

Practice Fluent Reading

Have partners take turns reading "Chemistry 101" aloud. Tell them to read the poem at least three times—once quickly, once slowly, and once at a varying rate. Then have students listen to the AudioText of the poem and compare and contrast their readings with the CD recording.

Audio CD AudioText

The Bronze Horse

by Beverly McLoughland

The museum guard is fast asleep
Chin on his chest in his fold-up chair,
The bronze horse paws at the marble floor
His muscles quiver, his nostrils flare

His bronze mane flows as though a breeze
Has blown through the door, while the breath of sun
In the empty room holds summer fields
Of tender green, where the horses run. **1**

And feeling his bronze soul come to life,
He lifts one foot from the marble floor,
Nuzzles the silence which stirs to hear
Hoofbeats echo through the open door. **2**

385

Model Fluent Reading

Read "The Bronze Horse" aloud. Tell students to listen for how your pitch and rate change as the poem progresses. The poem begins with a sleeping guard and ends with a horse running across the room.

Discuss the Poem

1 Compare and Contrast • Inferential
What contrast is set up between the guard and the horse?

Possible responses: The poem creates an ironic contrast between the guard and the horse. The guard is alive—but is calm and quiet, asleep. The horse is a statue—but becomes powerful and energetic, very much alive.

2 Tone • Inferential
How does the speaker feel about the horse?

Possible response: The speaker sees the horse as frozen in marble with a soul that wishes to run free. The speaker seems thrilled by the horse's power and energy.

WRITING POETRY

Have students write poems about a piece of art in a museum that comes to life. Encourage students to imagine and describe what their piece of art would think, feel, or do.

Unit 3
Reading Poetry

Model Fluent Reading

Read "The Termites" aloud. Point out that the poem will lose meaning if you pause at the end of every line. Instead, readers should let the punctuation tell them when to pause.

Discuss the Poem

1 **Rhyme • Inferential**

What are some examples of rhyme from the poem? How are some of them "hidden"?

Possible responses: Examples of rhyme include *mound, ground, underground; immense, defense, fence; enemies, degrees, guarantees;* and *assign, design, fine.* Since the lines of the poem are broken to create the shape of a termite mound, rhymes sometimes fall in the middle of lines and may be harder to see.

2 **Draw Conclusions • Inferential**

The speaker in the poem is a termite. What does the speaker admire about the architectural design of its mound?

Possible responses: The termite mound is huge. It protects termites from enemies and the elements of nature. It may not be pretty, but it serves the termites' needs perfectly.

The Termites
by Douglas Floriatt

Our
high and
mighty
termite
mound
arises
far above
the ground,
and just as
deep, grows
underground.
Our nest is
blessed to be
immense. It gives
us all a firm
defense, superior
to any fence. It
shields us from our
enemies. It keeps us
cooler, by degrees.
From floods and droughts
it guarantees. A prize
nobody will assign in
architectural design, but
still our hill suits us just fine.

386

EXTEND SKILLS

Symbolism

Explain that a symbol is a person, place, event, or object that has meaning in itself but suggests other meanings as well. Point out that a termite mound might symbolize the power of teamwork. Ask students to discuss what else a termite mound might symbolize.

Practice Fluent Reading

Have partners take turns reading "The Termites" aloud. Tell students to ignore the line breaks and let the punctuation tell them when to pause. Point out how reading the poem this way makes the rhymes easier to hear.

Audio CD AudioText

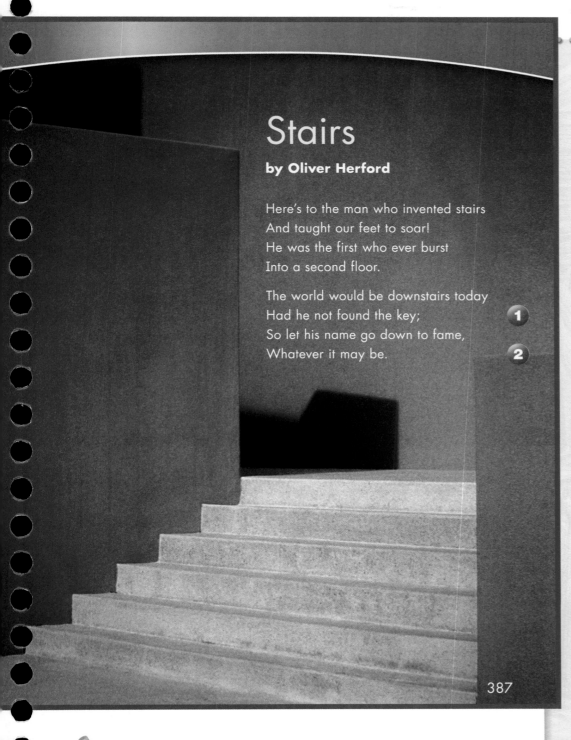

Stairs

by Oliver Herford

Here's to the man who invented stairs
And taught our feet to soar!
He was the first who ever burst
Into a second floor.

The world would be downstairs today
Had he not found the key;
So let his name go down to fame,
Whatever it may be.

1

2

387

WRITING POETRY

Have students write a concrete poem about an invention. For example, students might write about the Internet, placing the words in the shape of a computer.

Model Fluent Reading

Read "Stairs" aloud using a celebratory tone of voice. When you get to the last line, change your tone to flat and disappointed. Point out that the reader's tone of voice can show his or her attitude toward the subject.

Discuss the Poem

1 **Draw Conclusions • Critical**

Why do you think the speaker is celebrating the person who invented stairs?

Possible responses: With the invention of stairs, people were able to build taller buildings. Stairs may also represent inventions that have allowed people to *soar.*

2 **Irony • Inferential**

What is ironic about the last two lines of the poem?

Possible response: The speaker wants the person who invented stairs to be remembered, but we don't know his or her name.

Connect Ideas and Themes

This unit deals with what people gain from the work of inventors and artists. Ask if students were surprised by the inventors or artists presented in the poems. For example, did they expect to read a poem about termites? Then have students discuss other unrecognized inventors or artists and what they have contributed to society.

Unit 3
Wrap-Up

OBJECTIVES

- Critically analyze unit theme.
- Connect content across selections.
- Combine content and skills in meaningful activities that build literacy.
- Respond to unit selections through a variety of modalities.

INVENTORS AND ARTISTS

Discuss the Big Idea

What do people gain from the work of inventors and artists?

Write the unit theme and Big Idea question on the board. Ask students to think about the selections they have read in the unit. Discuss how each selection and lesson concept can help them answer the Big Idea question from this unit.

Model this for students by choosing a selection and explaining how the selection and lesson concept address the Big Idea.

Invent It Yourself

connect to **SCIENCE**

Think of the inventions in this unit. Each one was an attempt to make people's lives better. Make a chart like the one below and put each one on it. Then plan and describe your own invention using the chart. Make a drawing of your invention.

What It Is Made Of	What It Is For	How It Works

388

What do people gain from the work of inventors and artists?

Inventors in the News

connect to
WRITING

Leonardo da Vinci looked ahead to a time when people would fly. Waterhouse Hawkins helped people visualize the dinosaurs of the distant past. Become a newspaper reporter at the time of one of these men. Write a news article on the man and his work. Include details on how people of the time feel about your subject.

Today's Times

Leonardo Tackles High and Mighty Problems

Creative Influences

connect to
SOCIAL STUDIES

Apart from the inventors and artists you met in this unit, whose creative work has been important in your life? Research and make notes on this person and his or her work. Then present an oral report from your notes. Describe this person's work, telling why it is important to you.

Sandra's Report on Monet

Claude Monet was a famous artist who painted pictures of beautiful flowers. He used a style called Impressionism. I like his flowers because they remind me of my mom's garden. She works in the garden all weekend. Sometimes she lets me help plant bulbs.

389

ACTIVITIES

Invent It Yourself

Plan an Invention Discuss one invention from the unit as a class and help students complete the first row of their charts. After students complete their charts, have them brainstorm invention ideas in pairs or small groups and then draw their own inventions. Students' drawings should include the name of the invention, labels for key parts, and a short description of its purpose and how it works.

Inventors in the News

Write a News Article Suggest students review the selection about the man they will write about, taking notes about his life and work. They can also use print or online resources to find out more about the man and the time he lived. Remind them to write as if they were living at that time. Their articles should answer the questions *Who? What? Where? When? Why?* and *How?*

Creative Influences

Give an Oral Report Brainstorm possible inventors and artists students could research. Then have each student choose a person and find out more about the person's life and work using online or print resources. Remind students to take clear notes and organize them into a logical sequence for their oral reports. Students could show examples of the person's work as part of their reports.

Glossary

im·mi·grant (im′ə grənt), *N.* someone who comes into a country or region to live there: *Canada has many immigrants from Europe.* ❑ *N. PL.* **im·mi·grants.**

in·con·ceiv·a·ble (in′kən sē′və bəl), *ADJ.* hard to imagine or believe; incredible: *It is inconceivable that two nations so friendly for centuries should now be at odds.*

in·con·ven·ience (in′kən vē′nyəns), *N.* something inconvenient; cause of trouble, difficulty, or bother.

in·de·pend·ence (in′di pen′dəns), *N.* freedom from the control, influence, support, or help of others: *The American colonies won independence from England.*

in·no·va·tion (in′ə vā′shən), *N.* change made in the established way of doing things: *The principal made many innovations.* ❑ *N. PL.* **in·no·va·tions.**

in·spire (in spīr′), *V.* to fill with a thought or feeling; influence: *A chance to try again inspired her with hope.* ❑ *V.* **in·spired, in·spir·ing.**

in·tact (in takt′), *ADJ.* with nothing missing or broken; whole; untouched; uninjured: *The missing money was found and returned to the bank intact.*

in·te·ri·or (in tir′ē ər), *N.* inner surface or part; inside: *The interior of the house was beautifully decorated.*

theater interior

in·ter·sec·tion (in′tər sek′shən), *N.* point, line, or place where one thing crosses another: *a dangerous intersection.*

in·ves·ti·ga·tion (in ves′tə gā′shən), *N.* a careful search; detailed or careful examination: *An investigation of the accident by the police put the blame on the drivers of both cars.*

i·ras·ci·ble (i ras′ə bəl), *ADJ.* easily made angry.

is·sue (ish′ü), *V.* to send out; put forth: *The government issues money and stamps.* ❑ *V.* **is·sued, is·su·ing.**

Jj

jam (jam), **1.** *V.* to press or squeeze tightly between two surfaces: *The ship was jammed between two rocks.* **2.** *V.* to make music with other musicians without having practiced (*SLANG*). ❑ *V.* **jammed, jamm·ing. 3.** *N.* preserve made by boiling fruit with sugar until thick: *strawberry jam.*

Kk

kelp (kelp), *N.* any of various large, tough, brown seaweeds.

Ll

lair (lãr), *N.* den or resting place of a wild animal.

la·ment (lə ment′), **1.** *V.* to feel or show grief for; mourn aloud for: *We lament the dead.* **2.** *V.* to say sadly, with grief: *She lamented his absence.* ❑ *V.* **la·ment·ed, la·ment·ing.**

land·scape (land′ skāp), *N.* 1 view of scenery on land. 2 picture showing a land scene.

life·less (līf′lis), *ADJ.* without life: *a lifeless statue.*

lime·light (līm′līt′), *N.* center of public attention and interest: *Some people are never happy unless they are in the limelight.*

lin·ger (ling′gər), *V.* to stay on; go slowly, as if unwilling to leave: *He lingers after the others leave.* ❑ *V.* **ling·ered, ling·er·ing.**

784

log·ger (lô′gər), *N.* a person whose work is cutting down and removing trees. ❑ *N. PL.* **log·gers.**

lul·la·by (lul′ə bī), *N.* song for singing to a child in a cradle; soft song to lull a baby to sleep.

lux·ur·y (luk′shər ē), **1.** *N.* use of the best and most costly food, clothes, houses, furniture, and amusements: *The movie star was accustomed to luxury.* **2.** *N.* something pleasant but not necessary: *Candy is a luxury.*

Mm

mag·ni·fy (mag′nə fī), *V.* to cause something to look larger than it actually is; increase the apparent size of an object: *A microscope magnifies bacteria so that they can be seen and studied.* ❑ *V.* **mag·ni·fied, mag·ni·fy·ing.**

match·mak·er (mach′mā′kər), *N.* person who arranges, or tries to arrange, marriages for others.

mer·can·tile (mèr′kən til), *ADJ.* of merchants or trade; commercial: *a mercantile company.*

midst (midst), *N.* in the middle of.

mi·grant (mī′ grənt), *ADJ.* migrating; roving: *a migrant worker.*

min·i·a·ture (min′ē ə chùr, min′ə chər), *ADJ.* a reduced image or likeness: *miniature furniture for a dollhouse.*

mock (mok), *V.* to laugh at; make fun of: *The student was punished for mocking the kindergartner.* ❑ *V.* **mocked, mock·ing.**

mold¹ (mōld), *N.* a hollow shape in which anything is formed, cast, or solidified, such as the mold into which melted metal is poured to harden into shape, or the mold in which gelatin is left to stiffen.

mold² (mōld), *N.* loose or broken earth.

mon·i·tor (mon′ə tər), **1.** *N.* a television set connected to a computer. ❑ *N. PL.* **mon·i·tors. 2.** *V.* to listen to and check radio or television transmissions, telephone messages, etc., by using a receiver. ❑ *V.* **mon·i·tored, mon·i·tor·ing.**

mon·u·men·tal (mon′yə men′tl), *ADJ.* very great: *monumental ignorance.*

mu·cus (myü′kəs), *N.* a slimy substance produced in the nose and throat to moisten and protect them.

Nn

nau·se·at·ing (nô′shē āt ing), *ADJ.* sickening; causing nausea.

Na·zi (nä′tsē or nat′sē), *N.* member of the National Socialist Party, a fascist political party in Germany, led by Adolf Hitler. ❑ *N. PL.* **Nazis.**

new·com·er (nü′kum′ər), *N.* person who has just come or who came not long ago.

news·reel (nüz rēl′), *N.* a short news story for a movie audience. ❑ *N. PL.* **news·reels.**

night·time (nīt′tim′), *N.* time between evening and morning.

nu·tri·tious (nü trish′əs), *ADJ.* valuable as food; nourishing.

a	in hat	o	in open	sh	in she
ā	in age	ō	in all	th	in thin
ä	in care	ô	in order	ᴛʜ	in then
ä	in far	oi	in oil	zh	in measure
e	in let	ou	in out	ə	= a in about
ē	in equal	u	in cup	ə	= e in taken
ėr	in term	ù	in put	ə	= i in pencil
i	in it	ü	in rule	ə	= o in lemon
ī	in ice	ch	in child	ə	= u in circus
o	in hot	ng	in long		

785

Oo

oc·ca·sion (ə kā′zhən), *N.* a special event: *The jewels were worn only on great occasions.*

on·stage (on′stāj′), *ADV.* on the part of a stage that the audience can see: *walk onstage.*

ooze (üz), *N.* a soft mud or slime, especially at the bottom of a pond or river or on the ocean bottom.

out·field (out′fēld′), **1.** *N.* the part of a baseball field beyond the diamond or infield. **2.** *N.* the three players in the outfield.

o·ver·run (ō′vər run′), *V.* to spread over: *Vines overran the wall.* ❑ *V.* **o·ver·ran, o·ver·run·ning.**

Pp

par·a·pet (par′ə pet), *N.* a low wall at the edge of a balcony, roof, or bridge.

parapet

par·a·site (par′ə sīt), *N.* any living thing that lives on or in another, from which it gets its food, often harming the other in the process. Lice and tapeworms are parasites. ❑ *N. PL.* **par·a·sites.**

pa·vil·ion (pə vil′yən), *N.* a light building, usually somewhat open, used for shelter, pleasure, etc.: *The swimmers took shelter from the sudden storm in the beach pavilion.*

ped·dler (ped′lər), *N.* person who travels about selling things carried in a pack or in a truck, wagon, or cart.

per·mit (pər mit′), **1.** *V.* to let; allow: *My parents will not permit me to stay up late.* ❑ *V.* **per·mit·ted, per·mit·ting. 2.** *N.* license or written order giving permission to do something: *Do you have a permit to fish in this lake?*

phi·los·o·pher (fə los′ə fər), *N.* a person who attempts to discover and understand the basic nature of knowledge and reality. (*Philosopher* comes from a Greek word *philosophia* meaning "love of wisdom.")

pitch (pich), **1.** *V.* to throw or fling; hurl; toss: *They were pitching horseshoes.* ❑ *V.* **pitched, pitch·ing. 2.** *N.* thick, black, sticky substance made from tar or turpentine, used to fill the seams of wooden ships, to cover roofs, to make pavements, etc.

ple·si·o·saur·us (plē′sē ə sôr′əs), *N.* any of several large sea reptiles that lived about 200 million years ago. They had long necks and flippers instead of legs.

plesiosaurus

plunge (plunj), *V.* to fall or move suddenly downward or forward: *The sea turtle plunged into the water.* ❑ *V.* **plunged, plung·ing.**

pon·der (pon′dər), *V.* to consider carefully; think over: *ponder a problem.* ❑ *V.* **pon·dered, pon·der·ing.** (*Ponder* comes from a Latin word *pondus* meaning "weight.")

786

post·hu·mous·ly (pos′chə məs lē), *ADV.* happening after death: *The author was honored posthumously.*

pot·hole (pot′hōl′), *N.* a deep hole in the surface of a street or road. ❑ *N. PL.* **pot·holes.**

pre·cious (presh′əs), *ADJ.* having great value; worth much; valuable. Gold, platinum, and silver are often called the precious metals. Diamonds, rubies, and sapphires are precious stones.

pred·a·tor (pred′ə tər), *N.* animal or person that lives by killing and eating other animals.

pre·his·tor·ic (prē′hi stôr′ik), *ADJ.* Of or belonging to periods before recorded history: *Some prehistoric people lived in caves.*

pro·ce·dure (prə sē′jər), *N.* way of proceeding; method of doing things: *What is your procedure in making bread?* ❑ *N. PL.* **pro·ce·dures.**

pro·ces·sion (prə sesh′ən), *N.* something that moves forward; persons marching or riding: *The opening procession started at noon.*

pro·file (prō′fīl), **1.** *N.* a side view, especially of the human face. **2.** *N.* low profile; moderate attitude or position, deliberately chosen in order to avoid notice (*IDIOMATIC*).

pro·por·tion (prə pôr′shən), *N.* a proper relation among parts: *The dog's short legs were not in proportion to its long body.*

pros·per·i·ty (pro sper′ə tē), *N.* prosperous condition; good fortune; success: *a time of peace and prosperity.*

pro·to·type (prō′tə tīp), *N.* the first or primary type of anything: *A modern ship has its prototype in the hollowed log used by primitive peoples.*

push·cart (pùsh′kärt′), *N.* a light cart pushed by hand. ❑ *N. PL.* **push·carts.**

Rr

ra·vine (rə vēn′), *N.* a long, deep, narrow valley eroded by running water.

realm (relm), *N.* kingdom.

re·as·sem·ble (rē′ə sem′ bəl), *V.* come or bring together again. ❑ *V.* **re·as·sem·bled, re·as·sem·bling.**

rec·om·mend (rek′ə mend′), *V.* to speak in favor of; suggest favorably: *The teacher recommended him for the job.* ❑ *V.* **rec·om·men·ded, rec·om·men·ding.**

ref·u·gee (ref′yə jē′ or ref′yə jē′), *N.* person who flees for refuge or safety, especially to a foreign country, in time of persecution, war, or disaster: *Refugees from the war were cared for in neighboring countries.* ❑ *N. PL.* **refugees.**

re·lease (ri lēs′), *V.* to permit to be published, shown, sold, etc. ❑ *V.* **re·leased, re·leas·ing.**

re·li·gious (ri lij′əs), *ADJ.* much interested in the belief, study, and worship of God or gods; devoted to religion: *He is very religious and prays often.*

a	in hat	o	in open	sh	in she
ā	in age	ō	in all	th	in thin
ä	in care	ô	in order	ᴛʜ	in then
ä	in far	oi	in oil	zh	in measure
e	in let	ou	in out	ə	= a in about
ē	in equal	u	in cup	ə	= e in taken
ėr	in term	ù	in put	ə	= i in pencil
i	in it	ü	in rule	ə	= o in lemon
ī	in ice	ch	in child	ə	= u in circus
o	in hot	ng	in long		

787

Ren·ais·sance (ren′ə säns′ *or* ren′ə säns), *N.* the great revival of art and learning in Europe during the 1300s, 1400s, and 1500s; the period of time when this revival occurred.

rep·re·sent·a·tive (rep′ri zen′tə tiv), *N.* person appointed or elected to act or speak for others: *She is the club's representative at the convention.* ❑ *N. PL.* **rep·re·sent·a·tives.**

re·proach·ful·ly (ri prōch′fəl lē), *ADV.* with disapproval.

rep·u·ta·tion (rep′yə tā′shən), *N.* what people think and say the character of someone or something is; character in the opinion of others; name; repute: *This store has an excellent reputation for fair dealing.*

re·source·ful (ri sôrs′fəl), *ADJ.* good at thinking of ways to do things; quick-witted: *The resourceful children mowed lawns to earn enough money to buy new bicycles.*

ri·val (rī′vəl), *N.* person who wants and tries to get the same thing as another or who tries to equal or do better than another; competitor: *The two girls were rivals for the same class office.*

ro·bot·ic (rō bot′ik), *ADJ.* of or for a machine with moving parts and sensing devices controlled by a computer: *robotic design.*

role (rōl), **1.** *N.* an actor's part in a play, movie, etc.: *She played the leading role in the school play.* **2.** *N.* role model, a person whose patterns of behavior influence someone else's actions and beliefs: *Parents are important role models for children.*

rus·tle (rus′əl), *V.* to make or cause to make a light, soft sound of things gently rubbing together: *The leaves were rustling in the breeze.* ❑ *V.* **rus·tled, rus·tling.**

Ss

sa·cred (sā′krid), **1.** *ADJ.* worthy of reverence: *the sacred memory of a dead hero.* **2.** *ADJ.* not to be violated or disregarded: *a sacred promise.* (*Sacred* comes from a Latin word *sacrare* meaning "holy.")

scarce (skârs), *ADJ.* hard to get; rare: *Water is becoming scarce.*

scin·til·late (sin′tl āt), *V.* to sparkle; flash: *Her brilliant wit scintillates.* ❑ *V.* **scin·til·lat·ed, scin·til·lat·ing.**

scoun·drel (skoun′drəl), *N.* an evil, dishonorable person; villain; rascal: *The scoundrels who set fire to the barn have been caught.*

scrawl (skrôl), *V.* to write or draw poorly or carelessly. ❑ *V.* **scrawled, scrawl·ing.**

scraw·ny (skrô′nē), *ADJ.* having little flesh; lean; thin; skinny: *Turkeys have scrawny necks.*

sea ur·chins (sē′ ėr′chəns), *N.* any of numerous small, round sea animals with spiny shells.

sec·ond·hand (sek′ənd hand′), **1.** *ADJ.* not new; used already by someone else: *secondhand clothes.* **2.** *ADV.* from other than the original source; not firsthand: *The information came to us secondhand.*

sed·i·ment (sed′ə mənt), *N.* material that settles to the bottom of a liquid: *A film of sediment covered the underwater wreck.*

seed·ling (sēd′ling), *N.* a young plant grown from a seed. ❑ *N. PL.* **seed·lings.**

sem·i·pro (sem′i prō′), *N.* a part-time professional athlete.

ser·pent (sėr′pənt), *N.* snake, especially a big snake.

se·vere (sə vir′), *ADJ.* serious; grave: *a severe illness.*

shell·fish (shel′fish′), *N.* a water animal with a shell. Oysters, clams, crabs, and lobsters are shellfish.

shut·down (shut′doun′), **1.** *N.* act of closing of a factory, or the like, for a time: *The factory had a partial shutdown last week to fix some faulty equipment.* **2.** *N.* a stopping; a checking of (*INFORMAL*): *His reply was a real shutdown to her negative comment.*

side·track (sīd′trak′), *V.* to draw someone's attention away from something: *Don't sidetrack me with pointless questions.* ❑ *V.* **side·tracked, side·track·ing.**

sin·ew (sin′yü), *N.* tendon.

sketch (skech), *V.* to draw roughly and quickly. ❑ *V.* **sketched, sketch·ing.**

skid (skid), *V.* to slip or slide sideways while moving: *The car skidded on the slippery road.* ❑ *V.* **skid·ded, skid·ding.**

slav·er·y (slā′vər ē), *N.* the condition of being owned by another person and being made to work without wages.

sol·i·tar·y (sol′ə ter′ē), *ADJ.* without companions; away from people; lonely.

som·ber (som′bər), **1.** *ADJ.* having deep shadows; dark; gloomy: *A cloudy winter day is somber.* **2.** *ADJ.* sad; gloomy; dismal: *His losses made him somber.*

a **somber** picture (def. 2)

som·er·sault (sum′ər sôlt), *V.* to run or jump, turning the heels over the head. ❑ *V.* **som·er·saul·ted, som·er·saul·ting.**

so·nar (sō′när), *N.* device for finding the depth of water or for detecting and locating underwater objects. Sonar sends sound waves into water, and they are reflected back when they strike the bottom or any object.

So·vi·et (sō′vē et), *N.* a person belonging to or fighting for the former Soviet Union. ❑ *N. PL.* **So·vi·ets.**

spe·cial·ize (spesh′ə līz), *V.* to develop in a special way: *Animals and plants are specialized to fit their surroundings.* ❑ *V.* **spe·cial·ized, spe·cial·iz·ing.**

spe·cif·ic (spi sif′ik), *ADJ.* definite; precise; particular: *There was no specific reason for the party.*

spec·ta·cles (spek′tə kəlz), *N. PL.* eyeglasses. (*Spectacles* comes from a Latin word *spectare* meaning "to watch.")

spec·tac·u·lar (spek tak′ yə lər), *ADJ.* making a great display or show; very striking or imposing to the eye: *a spectacular storm.*

spin·dly (spind′lē), *ADJ.* very long and slender; too tall and thin: *a spindly plant.*

spir·i·tu·al (spir′ə chü əl), *N.* a religious song which originated among African Americans of the southern United States. ❑ *N. PL.* **spir·i·tu·als.**

a	in hat	ō	in open	sh	in she
ā	in age	ò	in all	th	in thin
â	in care	ô	in order	ᴛʜ	in then
ä	in far	oi	in oil	zh	in measure
e	in let	ou	in out	ə	= a in about
ē	in equal	u	in cup	ə	= e in taken
ėr	in term	ů	in put	ə	= i in pencil
i	in it	ü	in rule	ə	= o in lemon
ī	in ice	ch	in child	ə	= u in circus
o	in hot	ng	in long		

spoon·ful (spün′fůl), *N.* as much as a spoon can hold.

star·va·tion (stär vā′shən), *N.* suffering from extreme hunger; being starved: *Starvation caused his death.*

stealth·y (stel′thē), *ADJ.* done in a secret manner; secret; sly: *The cat crept in a stealthy way toward the bird.*

steed (stēd), *N.* horse, especially a riding horse.

ster·ile (ster′əl), *ADJ.* free from germs: *Bandages should always be kept sterile.*

stern·ly (stėrn′ lē), *ADV.* strictly; firmly: *The teacher frowned sternly.*

strat·e·gy (strat′ə jē), *N.* the skillful planning and management of anything.

strict (strikt), *ADJ.* very careful in following a rule or in making others follow it: *The teacher was strict but fair.*

stroke (strōk), *N.* a sudden attack of illness, especially one caused by a blood clot or bleeding in the brain; apoplexy.

sub·ject (sub′jikt), **1.** *N.* something that is thought about, discussed, investigated, etc.; topic: *The subject for our composition was "An Exciting Moment."* **2.** *N.* person under the power, control, or influence of another: *subjects of the king.*

su·per·i·or (sə pir′ē ər), *N.* person who is higher in rank, position, or ability: *A captain is a lieutenant's superior.* ❑ *N. PL.* **su·per·i·ors.**

sus·pend·ers (sə spen′dərz), *N. PL.* straps worn over the shoulders to hold up the trousers.

sus·pi·cion (sə spish′ən), *N.* belief; feeling; thought: *I have a suspicion that the weather will be very hot today.* ❑ *N. PL.* **sus·pi·cions.**

Tt

tape·worm (tāp′wėrm′), *N.* any of the numerous long, flat worms that live during their adult stage as parasites in the intestines of human beings and other animals. ❑ *N. PL.* **tape·worms.**

teen·ag·er (tēn′ā′jər), *N.* person in his or her teens.

ther·a·pist (ther′ə pist), *N.* person who specializes in the treatment of diseases, injuries, or disorders.

thieve (thēv), *V.* to steal. ❑ *V.* **thieved, thiev·ing.**

throb (throb), *V.* to beat rapidly or strongly: *My injured foot throbbed.* ❑ *V.* **throb·bed, throb·bing.**

ti·dy (tī′dē), *V.* to put in order; make neat: *I tidied the room.* ❑ *V.* **ti·died, ti·dy·ing.**

to·ga (tō′gə), *N.* a loose, outer garment worn in public. ❑ *N. PL.* **to·gas.**

tra·di·tion (trə dish′ən), *N.* custom or belief handed down from generation to generation: *According to tradition, Betsy Ross made the first American flag.* ❑ *N. PL.* **tra·di·tions.**

trans·at·lan·tic (tran′sət lan′tik), *ADJ.* crossing the Atlantic: *a transatlantic liner.*

tum·ble·down (tum′bəl doun′), *ADJ.* ready to fall down; not in good condition; dilapidated: *a tumbledown shack in the mountains.*

tun·dra (tun′drə), *N.* a vast, level, treeless plain in the arctic regions. The ground beneath its surface is frozen even in summer.

tweez·ers (twē′zərz), *N.* small pincers for pulling out hairs, picking up small objects, etc.

Uu

u·nique (yü nēk′), *ADJ.* having no like or equal; being the only one of its kind: *a unique specimen of rock, a unique experience.*

un·screw (un skrü′), *V.* to loosen or take off by turning: *Can you help me unscrew this tight lid?* ❑ *V.* **un·screwed, un·screw·ing.**

Vv

va·cant (vā′kənt), *ADJ.* not occupied: *a vacant chair, a vacant house.*

var·mint (vär′mənt), *N.* an objectionable animal or person (*DIALECT*).

vein (vān), *N.* **1.** membranous tubes forming part of the system of vessels that carry blood to the heart. **2.** a small natural channel within the earth through which water trickles or flows. ❑ *N. PL.* **veins.**

vi·bra·phone (vī′brə fōn), *N.* musical instrument similar to the xylophone, with metal bars and artificially increased vibration; vibraharp.

view·port (vyü′pôrt), *N.* small window in a small vessel, such as a space capsule or mini-submarine.

vi·sa (vē′zə), *N.* an official signature or endorsement upon a passport, showing that it has been examined and approved. A visa is granted by the consul or other representative of the country to which a person wishes to travel.

Ww

wai·tress (wā′tris), *N.* woman who serves or brings food to people in a restaurant.

weak·ness (wēk′nis), *N.* a weak point; slight fault: *Putting things off is her weakness.*

weight·less·ness (wāt′lis nis), *N.* the condition of being free from the pull of gravity: *weightless travelers in space.*

wheel·chair (wēl′châr′), *N.* chair on wheels, used especially by people who are sick or unable to walk. It can be moved by the person who is sitting in the chair.

wince (wins), *V.* to draw back suddenly; flinch slightly: *I winced when the dentist's drill touched my tooth.* ❑ *V.* **winced, winc·ing.**

wind·up (wind′up′), *N.* (in baseball), a swinging movement of the arms while twisting the body just before pitching the ball.

with·er (wiᴛʜ′ər), *V.* to lose or cause to lose freshness; make or become dry and lifeless; dry up; fade; shrivel: *Age had withered the old woman's face.* ❑ *V.* **with·ered, with·er·ing.**

work·shop (wėrk′shop′), *N.* space or building where work is done.

wor·ship (wėr′ship), *V.* to pay great honor and reverence to: *to worship God.* ❑ *V.* **wor·shipped, wor·ship·ping.**

worth·less (wėrth′lis), *ADJ.* without value; good-for-nothing; useless: *Throw those worthless, broken toys away.*

a	in hat	ō	in open	sh	in she
ā	in age	ò	in all	th	in thin
â	in care	ô	in order	ᴛʜ	in then
ä	in far	oi	in oil	zh	in measure
e	in let	ou	in out	ə	= a in about
ē	in equal	u	in cup	ə	= e in taken
ėr	in term	ů	in put	ə	= i in pencil
i	in it	ü	in rule	ə	= o in lemon
ī	in ice	ch	in child	ə	= u in circus
o	in hot	ng	in long		

English/Spanish Selection Vocabulary List

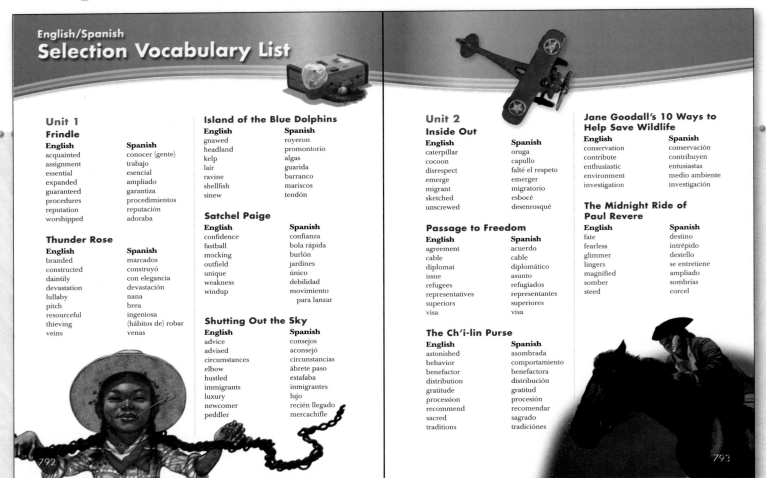

English/Spanish
Selection Vocabulary List

Unit 1
Frindle

English	Spanish
acquainted	conocer (gente)
assignment	trabajo
essential	esencial
expanded	ampliado
guaranteed	garantiza
procedures	procedimientos
reputation	reputación
worshipped	adoraba

Thunder Rose

English	Spanish
branded	marcados
constructed	construyó
daintily	con elegancia
devastation	devastación
lullaby	nana
pitch	brea
resourceful	ingeniosa
thieving	(hábitos de) robar
veins	venas

Island of the Blue Dolphins

English	Spanish
gnawed	royeron
headland	promontorio
kelp	algas
lair	guarida
ravine	barranco
shellfish	mariscos
sinew	tendón

Satchel Paige

English	Spanish
confidence	confianza
fastball	bola rápida
mocking	burlón
outfield	jardines
unique	único
weakness	debilidad
windup	movimiento para lanzar

Shutting Out the Sky

English	Spanish
advice	consejos
advised	aconsejó
circumstances	circunstancias
elbow	ábrete paso
hustled	estafaba
immigrants	inmigrantes
luxury	lujo
newcomer	recién llegado
peddler	mercachifle

Unit 2
Inside Out

English	Spanish
caterpillar	oruga
cocoon	capullo
disrespect	falté el respeto
emerge	emerger
migrant	migratorio
sketched	esbocé
unscrewed	desenrosqué

Passage to Freedom

English	Spanish
agreement	acuerdo
cable	cable
diplomat	diplomático
issue	asunto
refugees	refugiados
representatives	representantes
superiors	superiores
visa	visa

The Ch'i-lin Purse

English	Spanish
astonished	asombrada
behavior	comportamiento
benefactor	benefactora
distribution	distribución
gratitude	gratitud
procession	procesión
recommend	recomendar
sacred	sagrado
traditions	tradiciónes

Jane Goodall's 10 Ways to Help Save Wildlife

English	Spanish
conservation	conservación
contribute	contribuyen
enthusiastic	entusiastas
environment	medio ambiente
investigation	investigación

The Midnight Ride of Paul Revere

English	Spanish
fate	destino
fearless	intrépido
glimmer	destello
lingers	se entretiene
magnified	ampliado
somber	sombrías
steed	corcel

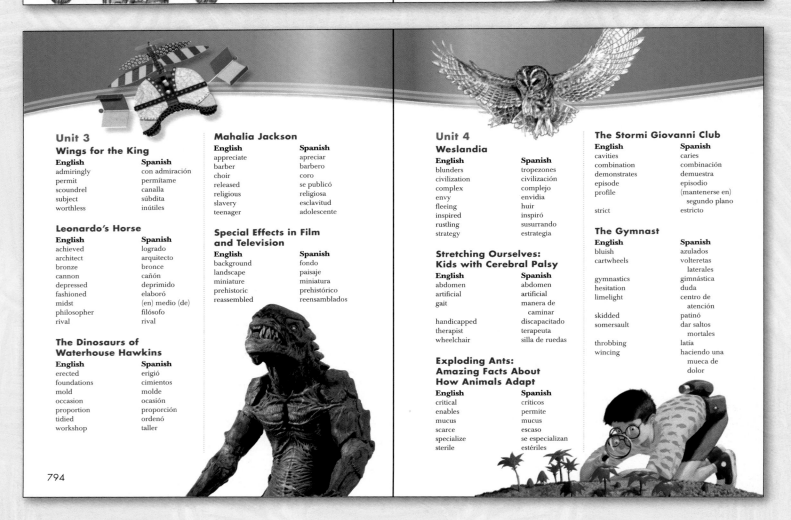

Unit 3
Wings for the King

English	Spanish
admiringly	con admiración
permit	permítame
scoundrel	canalla
subject	súbdita
worthless	inútiles

Leonardo's Horse

English	Spanish
achieved	logrado
architect	arquitecto
bronze	bronce
cannon	cañón
depressed	deprimido
fashioned	elaboró
midst	(en) medio (de)
philosopher	filósofo
rival	rival

The Dinosaurs of Waterhouse Hawkins

English	Spanish
erected	erigió
foundations	cimientos
mold	molde
occasion	ocasión
proportion	proporción
tidied	ordenó
workshop	taller

Mahalia Jackson

English	Spanish
appreciate	apreciar
barber	barbero
choir	coro
released	se publicó
religious	religiosa
slavery	esclavitud
teenager	adolescente

Special Effects in Film and Television

English	Spanish
background	fondo
landscape	paisaje
miniature	miniatura
prehistoric	prehistórico
reassembled	reensamblados

Unit 4
Weslandia

English	Spanish
blunders	tropezones
civilization	civilización
complex	complejo
envy	envidia
fleeing	huir
inspired	inspiró
rustling	susurrando
strategy	estrategia

Stretching Ourselves: Kids with Cerebral Palsy

English	Spanish
abdomen	abdomen
artificial	artificial
gait	manera de caminar
handicapped	discapacitado
therapist	terapeuta
wheelchair	silla de ruedas

Exploding Ants: Amazing Facts About How Animals Adapt

English	Spanish
critical	críticos
enables	permite
mucus	mucus
scarce	escaso
specialize	se especializan
sterile	estériles

The Stormi Giovanni Club

English	Spanish
cavities	caries
combination	combinación
demonstrates	demuestra
episode	episodio
profile	(mantenerse en) segundo plano
strict	estricto

The Gymnast

English	Spanish
bluish	azulados
cartwheels	volteretas laterales
gymnastics	gimnástica
hesitation	duda
limelight	centro de atención
skidded	patinó
somersault	dar saltos mortales
throbbing	latía
wincing	haciendo una mueca de dolor

English/Spanish Selection Vocabulary List

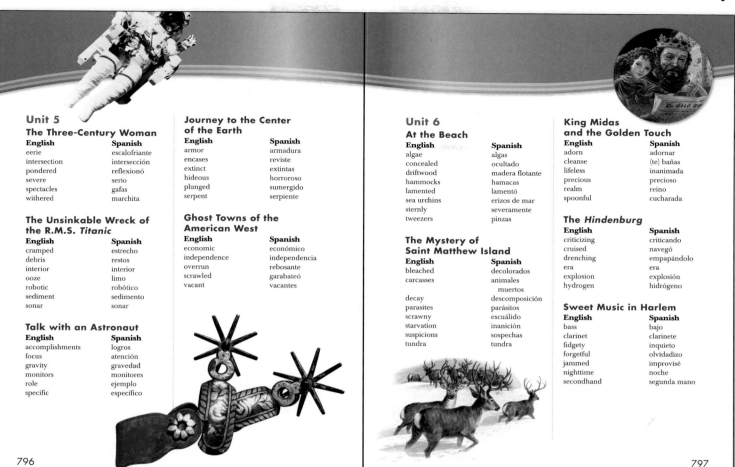

Unit 5

The Three-Century Woman

English	Spanish
eerie	escalofriante
intersection	intersección
pondered	reflexionó
severe	serio
spectacles	gafas
withered	marchita

The Unsinkable Wreck of the R.M.S. *Titanic*

English	Spanish
cramped	estrecho
debris	restos
interior	interior
ooze	limo
robotic	robótico
sediment	sedimento
sonar	sonar

Talk with an Astronaut

English	Spanish
accomplishments	logros
focus	atención
gravity	gravedad
monitors	monitores
role	ejemplo
specific	específico

Journey to the Center of the Earth

English	Spanish
armor	armadura
encases	reviste
extinct	extintas
hideous	horroroso
plunged	sumergido
serpent	serpiente

Ghost Towns of the American West

English	Spanish
economic	económico
independence	independencia
overrun	rebosante
scrawled	garabateó
vacant	vacantes

Unit 6

At the Beach

English	Spanish
algae	algas
concealed	ocultado
driftwood	madera flotante
hammocks	hamacas
lamented	lamentó
sea urchins	erizos de mar
sternly	severamente
tweezers	pinzas

The Mystery of Saint Matthew Island

English	Spanish
bleached	decolorados
carcasses	animales muertos
decay	descomposición
parasites	parásitos
scrawny	escuálido
starvation	inanición
suspicions	sospechas
tundra	tundra

King Midas and the Golden Touch

English	Spanish
adorn	adornar
cleanse	(te) bañas
lifeless	inanimada
precious	precioso
realm	reino
spoonful	cucharada

The *Hindenburg*

English	Spanish
criticizing	criticando
cruised	navegó
drenching	empapándolo
era	era
explosion	explosión
hydrogen	hidrógeno

Sweet Music in Harlem

English	Spanish
bass	bajo
clarinet	clarinete
fidgety	inquieto
forgetful	olvidadizo
jammed	improvisé
nighttime	noche
secondhand	segunda mano

796

797

Acknowledgments

Writing

Writing Trait of the Week

Writing Traits.. WA1

Writing Workshop

Unit 1   Personal Narrative
Unit 2   How-to Report
Unit 3   Compare and Contrast Essay WA2
Unit 4   Story
Unit 5   Persuasive Essay
Unit 6   Research Report

Writer's Craft:
   Stick to the Topic.. WA4
   Elaboration: Parallelism WA5
Differentiated Instruction with Leveled Prompts and Support WA8

Rubrics

Look Back and Write Rubrics WA10

Writing Rubrics WA11

Assessment

Assessment

Monitoring Fluency WA15

Assess and Regroup WA17

Student Tips for Making Top Scores in Writing Tests

1 **Use transitions such as those below to relate ideas, sentences, or paragraphs.**

in addition	nevertheless	finally	however
then	instead	therefore	as a result
for example	in particular	first	such as

2 **Write a good beginning. Make readers want to continue.**
- I shouldn't have opened that green box.
- Imagine being locked in a crate at the bottom of the sea.
- When I was four, I saw a purple dog.
- Have you ever heard of a talking tree?

3 **Focus on the topic.**
If a word or detail is off-topic, get rid of it. If a sentence is unrelated or loosely related to the topic, drop it or connect it more closely.

4 **Organize your ideas.**
Have a plan in mind before you start writing. Your plan can be a list, bulleted items, or a graphic organizer. Five minutes spent planning your work will make the actual writing go much faster and smoother.

5 **Support your ideas.**
- Develop your ideas with fully elaborated examples and details.
- Make ideas clear to readers by choosing vivid words that create pictures.
- Avoid dull *(get, go, say)*, vague *(thing, stuff, lots of)*, or overused *(really, very)* words.
- Use a voice that is appropriate to your audience.

6 **Make writing conventions as error-free as possible.**
Proofread your work line by line, sentence by sentence. Read for correct punctuation, then again for correct capitalization, and finally for correct spelling.

7 **Write a conclusion that wraps things up but is more than a repeating of ideas or "The end."**
- After all, he was my brother, weird or not.
- The Internet has changed our lives for better and for worse.
- It's not the largest planet but the one I'd choose to live on.
- Now tell me you don't believe in a sixth sense.

Rubric

| 4 | 3 | 2 | 1 |

Focus/Ideas

Organization/
Paragraphs

Voice

Word Choice

Sentences

Conventions

Writing Traits

- **Focus/Ideas** refers to the main purpose for writing and the details that make the subject clear and interesting. It includes development of ideas through support and elaboration.

- **Organization/Paragraphs** refers to the overall structure of a piece of writing that guides readers. Within that structure, transitions show how ideas, sentences, and paragraphs are connected.

- **Voice** shows the writer's unique personality and establishes a connection between writer and reader. Voice, which contributes to style, should be suited to the audience and the purpose for writing.

- **Word Choice** is the use of precise, vivid words to communicate effectively and naturally. It helps create style through the use of specific nouns, lively verbs and adjectives, and accurate, well-placed modifiers.

- **Sentences** covers strong, well-built sentences that vary in length and type. Skillfully written sentences have pleasing rhythms and flow fluently.

- **Conventions** refers to mechanical correctness and includes grammar, usage, spelling, punctuation, capitalization, and paragraphing.

Compare and Contrast Essay

OBJECTIVES

- Develop an understanding of a compare and contrast essay.
- Stick to the topic of the essay.
- Use parallel structure to compare and contrast.
- Establish criteria for evaluating a compare and contrast essay.

Key Features

Compare and Contrast Essay

In a compare and contrast essay, a writer explains similarities and differences between two things.

- Compares and contrasts two things
- Uses transition words and details to show likenesses and differences
- Follows a pattern of organization
- Has a clear topic sentence

Connect to Weekly Writing

Week 1	Skit (Scene) 287g–287h
Week 2	Question/Answer Essay 315g–315h
Week 3	Feature Story 345g–345h
Week 4	Description 363g–363h
Week 5	Expository Writing 383g–383h

Strategic Intervention

See Differentiated Instruction p. WA8.

Advanced

See Differentiated Instruction p. WA9.

ELL

See Differentiated Instruction p. WA9.

Additional Resource for Writing
Writing Rubrics and Anchor Papers, pp. 54–61

Writing Prompt: Inventors and Artists

Write an essay comparing and contrasting an invention of long ago with a modern invention. Explain how they are alike and different in the way they affected people. Use clue words such as *like*, *also*, *but*, and *unlike* to signal likenesses and differences.

Purpose: Compare and contrast two inventions

Audience: Your teacher or another adult

READ LIKE A WRITER

Look back at *Wings for the King.* Remind students that Isaac Summerville taught the king and queen how books are like wings. They came to understand that books transport a person to "the land of knowledge" and "the land of fun." They also learned that, unlike actual travel, reading can take you to imaginary places and introduce you to many characters and ideas. Tell students that they will write an essay in which they **compare and contrast** two things.

EXAMINE THE MODEL AND RUBRIC

GUIDED WRITING Read the model aloud. Point out transition words such as *but, too, both,* and *however* that the writer uses to signal similarities and differences. Discuss how the model reflects traits of good writing.

From Portable Tape Players to MP3 Players

Many kids listen to music on headphones. You may have a modern invention called the MP3 player. Kids used to listen to tapes and CDs on a portable player, such as a Walkman, but not many people carry them anymore.

The MP3 player is a terrific invention because you can carry all of your favorite tunes with you. Music is recorded digitally and stored on a hard drive inside the player. Some of these players can store as many as 10,000 songs! It's hard to believe all that music fits into a tiny MP3 player. If you had the same number of songs on cassettes or CDs, you would have to carry a couple of suitcases around with you. And a Walkman is bigger than a digital recorder too.

Both a Walkman and an MP3 player are portable. You can carry them anywhere you go. But the way music is recorded is another major difference. A Walkman can't be hooked up to your computer. However, an MP3 player can be hooked up to the computer, and music can be downloaded from the Internet. With a Walkman, only one tape can play at a time. With an MP3 player, all the digitally recorded music is available, and you can skip from track to track and artist to artist.

The main advantage of MP3 players is the large number of songs you can listen to anytime, anywhere. The Walkman was a good invention because it started the idea of portable music, but I'm glad my headphones are connected to an MP3 player!

Unit 3 Compare and Contrast Essay • PREWRITE Writing Process **15**

Traits of a Good Compare and Contrast Essay

Focus/Ideas	The essay explains the similarities and differences between two kinds of portable music players.
Organization/ Paragraphs	The writer has organized the report into paragraphs, using transition words such as *too, but, both,* and *however* to signal a comparison or a contrast.
Voice	The voice is lively and informative. The writer provides supporting details about the two things being compared and contrasted.
Word Choice	The writer uses specific words to explain similarities and differences.
Sentences	The sentence structure is correct. The writer uses some parallel sentences.
Conventions	Correct spelling, punctuation, and grammar are used throughout the report.

Unit 3 Compare and Contrast Essay • PREWRITE Writing Process **16**

▲ **Writing Transparency** WP15   ▲ **Writing Transparency** WP16

FINDING A TOPIC

- Discuss the modern inventions students use every day, such as cars, computers, and refrigerators. Ask what devices people used before each item was invented.
- Suggest conducting firsthand interviews with older people about inventions once new but are now obsolete. Help students craft formal letters requesting information about old inventions from local historians or inventors.

NARROW A TOPIC Have students evaluate their ideas to refine their topic.

Typewriters and word processors These inventions are too similar.
Typewriters and adding machines These inventions are too different.
Typewriters and computers These would be good to compare and contrast.

PREWRITING STRATEGY

GUIDED WRITING Display Writing Transparency WP17. Model how to complete a Venn diagram.

Think Aloud **MODEL** This student is going to write about computers and typewriters. He filled in this Venn diagram. In the center section, he wrote ways that typewriters and computers are alike. In the outer parts of the circles, he wrote ways that typewriters and computers are different. Now he can use these details to write his essay.

PREWRITING ACTIVITIES

- Have students use Grammar and Writing Practice Book p. 168 to list similarities and differences between their two inventions.
- Students can make a list of modern inventions and pair it with a list of their past counterparts.

Inventions

Now	Then
computer	typewriter
microwave oven	stove
refrigerator	icebox
MP3 player	portable CD player

Venn Diagram
Directions Fill in the Venn Diagram with similarities and differences about the two animals you are comparing.

Typewriter | Both | Computer

Typewriter:
can write only one thing at a time
had to use carbon paper to make a copy
difficult to make corrections
can make only two copies at a time
heavy and not easily moved

Both:
keyboards are the same
used to write essays, letters, reports
create nice-looking, formal documents
inventions created to save time

Computer:
can save material and make many documents
easy to go back and make corrections
can easily print out many copies
some lightweight and portable

Unit 3 Compare and Contrast Essay • PREWRITE   Writing Process **17**

▲ **Writing Transparency** WP17

Monitor Progress

Differentiated Instruction

If... students have trouble thinking of a suitable pair of inventions,	**then...** have them discuss modern life in the past with a partner.

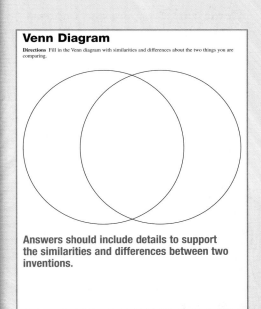

Venn Diagram
Directions Fill in the Venn diagram with similarities and differences about the two things you are comparing.

Answers should include details to support the similarities and differences between two inventions.

▲ **Grammar and Writing Practice Book** p. 168

Inventors and Artists **WA3**

Writing Workshop

1 PREWRITE 2 DRAFT 3 REVISE 4 EDIT 5 PUBLISH

Think Like a Writer

Explain Your Purpose Write an opening sentence that both grabs your reader's attention and explains your purpose, to compare and contrast two inventions. Also, make sure that your reader finds out right at the beginning what two inventions you are comparing and contrasting.

ELL

Support Writing Invite students to talk with you about what they plan to write. Record key words and ideas that they mention and help them generate language for other key words and ideas. See the ELL and Transition Handbook for additional strategies to support the writing process.

Words That Compare and Contrast

Directions The words in the box signal that two things are alike or different. Write two sentences that explain how your two inventions are alike, using words from the box. Then write two sentences that explain how your two inventions are different, using words from the box.

Words That Signal Similarity	Words That Signal Difference
and	but
also	however
too	unlike
as well	on the other hand
like	

How the two things are alike

1. Answers should include specific details about the similarities and differences of the two inventions being compared.

2. _____

How the two things are different

1. _____

2. _____

▲ **Grammar and Writing Practice Book** p. 169

WRITING THE FIRST DRAFT

GUIDED WRITING Use Writing Transparency WP18 to practice using words that compare and contrast.

- Remind students that when we compare and contrast, we tell how two things are alike and how they are different.
- Have students list words that signal likenesses *(both, like, also, too),* and words that signal differences *(but, however, on the other hand).*

Think Aloud **MODEL** When I read the first pair of sentences, I notice that they tell one way a stove and a microwave oven are different—a stove cooks slowly; a microwave oven cooks quickly. I can combine these two sentences using a comma and the word *but* to signal a difference.

Words That Compare and Contrast

A compare and contrast essay uses transition words such as *like, unlike, but, however, also,* and *too* that signal similarities or differences.

Directions Add an appropriate compare or contrast transition word to each pair of sentences. You might combine some of the sentence pairs into a compound sentence. **Possible answers:**

1. A stove cooks food slowly. A microwave oven is fast.
   A stove cooks food slowly, but a microwave oven is fast.

2. Stoves can make foods very hot. Microwave ovens heat foods to high temperatures.
   Stoves can make foods very hot. Microwave ovens heat foods to high temperatures too.

3. Microwaves are perfect for cooks on the go. Ovens suit leisurely cooks.
   Microwaves are perfect for cooks on the go, unlike ovens, which suit leisurely cooks.

4. Stoves are easy to operate. Microwaves are even easier.
   Stoves are easy to operate, but microwaves are even easier.

5. You can burn yourself on a stove. A microwave can't burn you.
   You can burn yourself on a stove. However, a microwave can't burn you.

Unit 3 Compare and Contrast Essay • DRAFT   Writing Process **18**

▲ **Writing Transparency** WP18

WRITER'S CRAFT Stick to the Topic

Here are some ways writers can keep their essay focused:

- Include only details that tell about either a likeness or a difference.
- Make sure every sentence tells about a likeness or a difference.
- Organize likenesses in one paragraph and differences in another paragraph.

DRAFTING STRATEGIES

- Have students review their Venn diagram before they write.
- Students can think about where compare and contrast words might be used.
- Remind students to keep their audience and purpose in mind.
- Students should review their essay to make sure all details tell about the topic.
- Have students use Grammar and Writing Practice Book p. 169 to choose words that compare and contrast.

WRITER'S CRAFT Elaboration

PARALLELISM Explain that one way to elaborate is to use parallelism. Parallelism, or parallel structure, refers to the organization of similar sentence parts, such as verbs and adjectives.

Note how parallelism can make a sentence sound smoother.

Not Parallel E-mail is useful for sending, receiving, and to read mail.

Parallel E-mail is useful for sending, receiving, and reading mail.

Use Grammar and Writing Practice Book p. 170 to practice using parallel structure.

REVISING STRATEGIES

GUIDED WRITING Use Writing Transparency WP19 to model revising. Point out the Revising Marks, which students should use when they revise their work.

 MODEL This is part of the essay that compares and contrasts the typewriter and the computer. The first sentence in the first paragraph has been deleted. It tells an interesting fact but is off topic because it does not tell about a likeness or a difference. The word *more* has also been deleted because it is unnecessary. A topic sentence has been added at the beginning of the second paragraph to provide a smooth transition. The vague word *papers* has been changed to the more specific word *reports*. The word *Also* has been added to the beginning of the last sentence to signal that that sentence further supports the similarities between the typewriter and the computer.

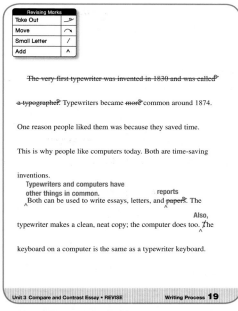

▲ **Writing Transparency** WP19

PEER REVISION Write the Revising Checklist on the board or make copies to distribute. Students can use this checklist to revise their compare and contrast essays. Have partners read each other's first drafts. Remind them to be courteous and specific with suggestions.

Trait Checklist

REVISING

Focus/Ideas

✔ Is the compare and contrast essay focused and informative?

✔ Do all the details tell about similarities and differences?

Organization/Paragraphs

✔ Are words that compare and contrast used to signal similarities and differences?

Voice

✔ Is the writer engaged with the topic?

Word Choice

✔ Are specific words used to tell about similarities and differences?

Sentences

✔ Are sentences written using parallel structure?

Elaboration
Parallelism

If a sentence has parts that are alike, those parts should have the same form or pattern. **Parallelism, or parallel structure,** refers to the pattern, or organization, of similar sentence parts, such as verbs or adjectives.

Not Parallel Riders were expected to ride a horse, facing dangers, and go for hours without sleep.

Parallel Riders were expected to ride a horse, face dangers, and go for hours without sleep.

Directions Rewrite the sentences to make them parallel. **Possible answers:**

1. The Pony Express carried mail, rode long distances, and they travel at 10 miles per hour.
   The Pony Express carried mail, rode long distances, and traveled at 10 miles per hour.

2. Today, e-mail makes modern communication much quicker, cheaper, and easy to use.
   Today, e-mail makes modern communication much quicker, cheaper, and easier to use.

3. Riders for the Pony Express rode 75–100 miles at a time, changed horses every 10–15 miles, and are earning $100 a month. **Riders for the Pony Express rode 75–100 miles at a time, changed horses every 10–15 miles, and earned $100 a month.**

4. Unlike the Pony Express, you can send an e-mail, are receiving a reply, and respond in just minutes! **Unlike the Pony Express, you can send an e-mail, receive a reply, and respond in just minutes!**

5. Do you communicate by e-mail, letters, or talking on the telephone? **Do you communicate by e-mail, letters, or telephone?**

▲ **Grammar and Writing Practice Book** p. 170

UNIT 3

EDITING STRATEGY

SENTENCE BY SENTENCE Suggest that students use an editing strategy. Have them read through their essay sentence by sentence, looking for correct punctuation, verb tense, and spelling, one sentence at a time.

GUIDED WRITING Use Writing Transparency WP20 to model the process of editing sentence by sentence. Indicate the Proofreading Marks, which students should use when they edit their work. Write the Editing Checklist on the board or make copies to distribute. Students can use this checklist to edit their work.

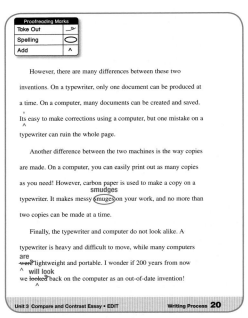

▲ **Writing Transparency** WP20

 **MODEL** As I go through the writing sentence by sentence, I see that first the writer corrected his deletion of an apostrophe in *It's,* which is a contraction. Then he corrected his spelling of the word *smudges.* Next, he realized that the two verbs in a sentence weren't parallel, so he changed *were* to *are.* He also recognized that a verb in the last sentence wasn't in the correct tense, so he changed *looked* to *will look.* Those were good catches.

 USING TECHNOLOGY Students who have written or revised their compare and contrast essays on computers should keep these points in mind as they edit.

- Do not rely on search engines for getting consistent, accurate information. Access information from encyclopedias, dictionaries, and other reference sources online.

- When you have questions about using a menu item or function, check with a friend or use the Help menu.

- You can determine margins, line lengths, borders, shading, paragraph indents, and other features using the Format menu.

Monitor Progress

Differentiated Instruction

If... students are using incorrect verb tenses,	then... review the grammar lesson on pp. 285e–285f.

Editing Checklist

✔ Did I spell words with the consonant sounds /j/, /ks/, /sk/, and /s/ correctly?

✔ Did I use the correct tense for all verbs?

✔ Did I check contractions for missing apostrophes?

✔ Did I indent the first sentence of each paragraph?

ELL

Support Writing When reviewing a student's draft, focus on ideas more than errors. Keep in mind that a consistent grammatical error may reflect the writing conventions of the home language. Choose one or two skills, and use the appropriate Grammar Transition Lessons in the ELL and Transition Handbook to explicitly teach the English conventions.

SELF-EVALUATION

Prepare students to fill out a Self-Evaluation Guide. Display Writing Transparency WP21 to model the self-evaluation process.

Think Aloud **MODEL** I would give the compare and contrast essay a *4.*

Focus/Ideas This essay focuses on how a typewriter and a computer are alike and different.

Organization/Paragraphs Compare and contrast words signal similarities and differences.

Voice The voice is thoughtful, lively, and informative.

Word Choice The writer uses specific words in the supporting details.

Sentences Sentences are of different lengths and structures.

Conventions Grammar, capitalization, and spelling are excellent.

EVALUATION Assign Grammar and Writing Practice Book p. 171. Tell students that when they evaluate their own compare and contrast essays, assigning a score of 3, 2, or even 1 does not necessarily indicate a bad paper. The ability to identify areas for improvement in future writing is a valuable skill.

Typewriters vs. Computers

Over half the homes in the United States have a computer. However, most of those homes do not have a typewriter. Typewriters have been replaced by computers.

Typewriters became common around 1874. One reason people liked them was because they saved time. This is why people like computers today. Both are time-saving inventions.

Typewriters and computers have other things in common. Both can be used to write essays, letters, and reports. The typewriter makes a clean, neat copy; the computer does too. Also, the keyboard on a computer is the same as a typewriter keyboard.

However, there are many differences between these two inventions. On a typewriter, only one document can be produced at a time. On a computer, many documents can be created and saved. It's easy to make corrections using a computer, but one mistake on a typewriter can ruin the whole page.

Another difference between the two machines is the way copies are made. On a computer, you can easily print out as many copies as you need! However, carbon paper is used to make a copy on a typewriter. It makes messy smudges on your work, and no more than two copies can be made at a time.

Finally, the typewriter and computer do not look alike. A typewriter is heavy and difficult to move, while many computers are lightweight and portable. I wonder if 200 years from now we will look back on the computer as an out-of-date invention!

Unit 3 Compare and Contrast Essay • PUBLISH   Writing Process **21**

▲ **Writing Transparency** WP21

Ideas for Publishing

E-Mail an Expert Have students send their essays to a grandparent or another adult, sharing the information they gathered about two inventions.

Idea Exchange Students can share their essays in small groups, reading one another's work to learn more about inventions.

Self-Evaluation Guide
Compare and Contrast Essay

Directions Think about the final draft of your compare and contrast essay. Then rate yourself on a scale of from 4 to 1 (4 is the highest) on each writing trait. After you fill out the chart, answer the questions.

Writing Traits	4	3	2	1
Focus/Ideas				
Organization/Paragraphs				
Voice				
Word Choice				
Sentences				
Conventions				

1. What is the best part of your compare and contrast essay? Students' responses should show that they have given thought to the essays they have written.

2. Write one thing you would change about this compare and contrast essay if you had the chance to write it again.

▲ **Grammar and Writing Practice Book** p. 171

Scoring Rubric — Compare and Contrast Essay

Rubric 4 3 2 1	4	3	2	1
Focus/Ideas	Compare and contrast essay well focused and clearly developed	Compare and contrast essay generally focused and developed	Compare and contrast essay that strays from topic or lacks details	Compare and contrast essay with no focus or few details
Organization/ Paragraphs	Well organized; uses words that compare and contrast	Organized; uses some words that compare and contrast	Unclear organization; few words that compare and contrast	No organization; no words that compare or contrast
Voice	Informative voice; shows writer's knowledge	Fairly informative voice	Weak voice; lacks knowledge of subject	No clear voice
Word Choice	Uses specific words to tell about similarities and differences	Uses some specific words in details	Uses few specific words in details	No attempt to use specific words
Sentences	Variety of sentences; use of parallel structure	Some variety in sentences; use of parallel structure attempted	Little variety in sentences; incorrect use of parallel structure	Lacks sentence variety; no parallel structure attempted
Conventions	Few, if any, errors	Some minor errors	Many errors that detract from writing	Errors that prevent understanding of writing

For 6-, 5-, and 3-point Scoring Rubrics, see pp. WA11–WA14.

WRITING Workshop

Compare and Contrast Essay
Differentiated Instruction

WRITING PROMPT: Inventors and Artists

Write an essay comparing and contrasting an invention of long ago with a modern invention. Explain how they are alike and different, focusing on how they affect people's everyday lives. Use clue words such as *like*, *also*, *but*, and *unlike* to signal likenesses and differences.

Purpose: Compare and contrast two inventions

Audience: Your teacher or another adult

Pick One

MODIFY INSTRUCTION →

ALTERNATIVE PROMPTS ▼

ALTERNATIVE PROMPTS: Expository Writing

Strategic Intervention Compare and contrast a ballpoint pen to a pencil or a zipper to buttons. Write a paragraph that tells two ways the two things are alike and two ways they are different.

On-Level Think of a specific subject area that you are interested in, such as space exploration, medicine, or the environment. Focus on two inventions in that subject area. Write about the similarities and differences between the two inventions.

Advanced Go beyond inventions to the inventors themselves. Compare and contrast two inventors, their work, their backgrounds, and their inspirations. Tell how these inventors are alike and different.

Strategic Intervention

MODIFY THE PROMPT

Help emerging writers choose two simple inventions to compare and contrast in their essay. Encourage them to choose familiar everyday items that require little or no research to compare and contrast.

1 PREWRITE **2 DRAFT** **3 REVISE** **4 EDIT** **5 PUBLISH**

PREWRITING SUPPORT

- Allow linear thinkers to make a chart or list for their compare and contrast ideas if the Venn diagram doesn't suit their needs.

- Encourage students to brainstorm details about several pairs of inventions and then use the pair for which they have the most supporting material.

- Interview students to check their facts. Ask them to explain the similarities and differences to you, and have them think about how they will use compare and contrast words in each paragraph.

OPTIONS

- Give students the option of writing a group compare and contrast essay under your supervision.

CHECK PROGRESS Segment the assignment into manageable pieces. Check work at intervals, such as graphic organizers and first drafts, to make sure writing is on track.

MODIFY THE PROMPT

Expect advanced writers to produce writing with a clear focus on the chosen topics and strong supporting details that tell only about similarities and differences between the topics. Their essays should be organized in one of two ways: all similarities followed by all differences, or feature by feature, whether similar or different.

APPLY SKILLS

- As students revise their work, have them consider some ways to improve it.

  Check each paragraph to make sure it has a topic sentence.

  Use specific words to support the ideas.

  Use more sophisticated words to compare and contrast, such as *similarly* and *on the other hand.*

OPTIONS

- Students can follow these steps to create their own class rubrics.

  1. Read examples of class compare and contrast essays and rank them 1–4, with 4 the highest.

  2. Discuss how they arrived at each rank.

  3. Isolate the six traits and make a rubric based on them.

CHECK PROGRESS Discuss the students' Self-Evaluation Guides. Work with students to monitor their growth and identify their strengths and weaknesses as writers.

MODIFY THE PROMPT

Provide a framework of partial sentences that compare and contrast familiar objects. Let beginning speakers fill in the blanks in the sentences.

BUILD BACKGROUND

- Write the words *same* and *different* on the board. Explain to students that when we see things that are the *same* in two inventions, we *compare.* Write *compare* under the word *same.* When we see things about two inventions that are different, we *contrast.* Write *contrast* under the word *different.* Discuss the list of Key Features of a compare and contrast essay that appears in the left column of p. WA2.

OPTIONS

- As students write their compare and contrast essays, guide them toward books, magazines, or Web sites that provide comprehension support through features such as the following:

  strong picture/text correspondence

  detailed photographs

  text in the home-language

- For more suggestions on scaffolding the Writing Workshop, see the ELL and Transition Handbook.

CHECK PROGRESS You may need to explain certain traits and help students fill out their Self-Evaluation Guides. Downplay conventions and focus more on ideas. Recognize examples of vocabulary growth and efforts to use language in more complex ways.

Scoring Rubric Look Back and Write

2 points The response indicates that the student has a complete understanding of the reading concept embodied in the task. The response is accurate, complete, and fulfills all the requirements of the task. Necessary support and/or examples are included, and the information given is clearly text-based.

1 point The response indicates that the student has a partial understanding of the reading concept embodied in the task. The response includes information that is essentially correct and text-based, but the information is too general or too simplistic. Some of the support and/or examples may be incomplete or omitted.

0 points The response indicates that the student does not demonstrate an understanding of the reading concept embodied in the task. The student has either failed to respond or has provided a response that is inaccurate or has insufficient information.

Scoring Rubric Look Back and Write

4 points The response indicates that the student has a thorough understanding of the reading concept embodied in the task. The response is accurate, complete, and fulfills all the requirements of the task. Necessary support and/or examples are included, and the information is clearly text-based.

3 points The response indicates that the student has an understanding of the reading concept embodied in the task. The response is accurate and fulfills all the requirements of the task, but the required support and/or details are not complete or clearly text-based.

2 points The response indicates that the student has a partial understanding of the reading concept embodied in the task. The response that includes information is essentially correct and text-based, but the information is too general or too simplistic. Some of the support and/or examples and requirements of the task may be incomplete or omitted.

1 point The response indicates that the student has a very limited understanding of the reading concept embodied in the task. The response is incomplete, may exhibit many flaws, and may not address all requirements of the task.

0 points The response indicates that the student does not demonstrate an understanding of the reading concept embodied in the task. The student has either failed to respond or has provided a response that is inaccurate or has insufficient information.

Scoring Rubric — Narrative Writing

Rubric 4 3 2 1	6	5	4	3	2	1
Focus/Ideas	Excellent, focused narrative; well elaborated with quality details	Good, focused narrative; elaborated with telling details	Narrative focused; adequate elaboration	Generally focused narrative; some supporting details	Sometimes unfocused narrative; needs more supporting details	Rambling narrative; lacks development and detail
Organization/ Paragraphs	Strong beginning, middle, and end; appropriate order words	Coherent beginning, middle, and end; some order words	Beginning, middle, and end easily identifiable	Recognizable beginning, middle, and end; some order words	Little direction from beginning to end; few order words	Lacks beginning, middle, end; incorrect or no order words
Voice	Writer closely involved; engaging personality	Reveals personality	Pleasant but not compelling voice	Sincere voice but not fully engaged	Little writer involvement, personality	Careless writing with no feeling
Word Choice	Vivid, precise words that bring story to life	Clear words to bring story to life	Some specific word pictures	Language adequate but lacks color	Generally limited or redundant language	Vague, dull, or misused words
Sentences	Excellent variety of sentences; natural rhythm	Varied lengths, styles; generally smooth	Correct sentences with some variations in style	Correctly constructed sentences; some variety	May have simple, awkward, or wordy sentences; little variety	Choppy; many incomplete or run-on sentences
Conventions	Excellent control; few or no errors	No serious errors to affect understanding	General mastery of conventions but some errors	Reasonable control; few distracting errors	Weak control; enough errors to affect understanding	Many errors that prevent understanding

Scoring Rubric — Narrative Writing

Rubric 4 3 2 1	5	4	3	2	1
Focus/Ideas	Excellent, focused narrative; well elaborated with quality details	Good, focused narrative; elaborated with telling details	Generally focused narrative; some supporting details	Sometimes unfocused narrative; needs more supporting details	Rambling narrative; lacks development and detail
Organization/ Paragraphs	Strong beginning, middle, and end; appropriate order words	Coherent beginning, middle, and end; some order words	Recognizable beginning, middle, and end; some order words	Little direction from beginning to end; few order words	Lacks beginning, middle, end; incorrect or no order words
Voice	Writer closely involved; engaging personality	Reveals personality	Sincere voice but not fully engaged	Little writer involvement, personality	Careless writing with no feeling
Word Choice	Vivid, precise words that bring story to life	Clear words to bring story to life	Language adequate but lacks color	Generally limited or redundant language	Vague, dull, or misused words
Sentences	Excellent variety of sentences; natural rhythm	Varied lengths, styles; generally smooth	Correctly constructed sentences; some variety	May have simple, awkward, or wordy sentences; little variety	Choppy; many incomplete or run-on sentences
Conventions	Excellent control; few or no errors	No serious errors to affect understanding	Reasonable control; few distracting errors	Weak control; enough errors to affect understanding	Many errors that prevent understanding

Scoring Rubric — Narrative Writing

Rubric 4 3 2 1	3	2	1
Focus/Ideas	Excellent, focused narrative; well elaborated with quality details	Generally focused narrative; some supporting details	Rambling narrative; lacks development and detail
Organization/ Paragraphs	Strong beginning, middle, and end; appropriate order words	Recognizable beginning, middle, and end; some order words	Lacks beginning, middle, end; incorrect or no order words
Voice	Writer closely involved; engaging personality	Sincere voice but not fully engaged	Careless writing with no feeling
Word Choice	Vivid, precise words that bring story to life	Language adequate but lacks color	Vague, dull, or misused words
Sentences	Excellent variety of sentences; natural rhythm	Correctly constructed sentences; some variety	Choppy; many incomplete or run-on sentences
Conventions	Excellent control; few or no errors	Reasonable control; few distracting errors	Many errors that prevent understanding

Scoring Rubric — Descriptive Writing

Rubric 4 3 2 1	6	5	4	3	2	1
Focus/Ideas	Excellent, focused description; well elaborated with quality details	Good, focused description; elaborated with telling details	Description focused; good elaboration	Generally focused description; some supporting details	Sometimes unfocused description; needs more supporting details	Rambling description; lacks development and detail
Organization/ Paragraphs	Compelling ideas enhanced by order, structure, and transitions	Appealing order, structure, and transitions	Structure identifiable and suitable; transitions used	Adequate order, structure, and some transitions to guide reader	Little direction from beginning to end; few transitions	Lacks direction and identifiable structure; no transitions
Voice	Writer closely involved; engaging personality	Reveals personality	Pleasant but not compelling voice	Sincere voice but not fully engaged	Little writer involvement, personality	Careless writing with no feeling
Word Choice	Vivid, precise words that create memorable pictures	Clear, interesting words to bring description to life	Some specific word pictures	Language adequate; appeals to senses	Generally limited or redundant language	Vague, dull, or misused words
Sentences	Excellent variety of sentences; natural rhythm	Varied lengths, styles; generally smooth	Correct sentences with variations in style	Correctly constructed sentences; some variety	May have simple, awkward, or wordy sentences; little variety	Choppy; many incomplete or run-on sentences
Conventions	Excellent control; few or no errors	No serious errors to affect understanding	General mastery of conventions but some errors	Reasonable control; few distracting errors	Weak control; enough errors to affect understanding	Many errors that prevent understanding

Scoring Rubric — Descriptive Writing

Rubric 4 3 2 1	5	4	3	2	1
Focus/Ideas	Excellent, focused description; well elaborated with quality details	Good, focused description; elaborated with telling details	Generally focused description; some supporting details	Sometimes unfocused description; needs more supporting details	Rambling description; lacks development and detail
Organization/ Paragraphs	Compelling ideas enhanced by order, structure, and transitions	Appealing order, structure, and transitions	Adequate order, structure, and some transitions to guide reader	Little direction from beginning to end; few transitions	Lacks direction and identifiable structure; no transitions
Voice	Writer closely involved; engaging personality	Reveals personality	Sincere voice but not fully engaged	Little writer involvement, personality	Careless writing with no feeling
Word Choice	Vivid, precise words that create memorable pictures	Clear, interesting words to bring description to life	Language adequate; appeals to senses	Generally limited or redundant language	Vague, dull, or misused words
Sentences	Excellent variety of sentences; natural rhythm	Varied lengths, styles; generally smooth	Correctly constructed sentences; some variety	May have simple, awkward, or wordy sentences; little variety	Choppy; many incomplete or run-on sentences
Conventions	Excellent control; few or no errors	No serious errors to affect understanding	Reasonable control; few distracting errors	Weak control; enough errors to affect understanding	Many errors that prevent understanding

Scoring Rubric — Descriptive Writing

Rubric 4 3 2 1	3	2	1
Focus/Ideas	Excellent, focused description; well elaborated with quality details	Generally focused description; some supporting details	Rambling description; lacks development and detail
Organization/ Paragraphs	Compelling ideas enhanced by order, structure, and transitions	Adequate order, structure, and some transitions to guide reader	Lacks direction and identifiable structure; no transitions
Voice	Writer closely involved; engaging personality	Sincere voice but not fully engaged	Careless writing with no feeling
Word Choice	Vivid, precise words that create memorable pictures	Language adequate; appeals to senses	Vague, dull, or misused words
Sentences	Excellent variety of sentences; natural rhythm	Correctly constructed sentences; some variety	Choppy; many incomplete or run-on sentences
Conventions	Excellent control; few or no errors	Reasonable control; few distracting errors	Many errors that prevent understanding

Scoring Rubric — Persuasive Writing

Rubric 4 3 2 1

	6	5	4	3	2	1
Focus/Ideas	Persuasive argument carefully built with quality details	Persuasive argument well supported with details	Persuasive argument focused; good elaboration	Persuasive argument with one or two convincing details	Persuasive piece sometimes unfocused; needs more support	Rambling persuasive argument; lacks development and detail
Organization/ Paragraphs	Information chosen and arranged for maximum effect	Evident progression of persuasive ideas	Progression and structure evident	Information arranged in a logical way with some lapses	Little structure or direction	No identifiable structure
Voice	Writer closely involved; persuasive but not overbearing	Maintains persuasive tone	Persuasive but not compelling voice	Sometimes uses persuasive voice	Little writer involvement, personality	Shows little conviction
Word Choice	Persuasive words carefully chosen for impact	Argument supported by persuasive language	Uses some persuasive words	Occasional persuasive language	Generally limited or redundant language	Vague, dull, or misused words; no persuasive words
Sentences	Excellent variety of sentences; natural rhythm	Varied lengths, styles; generally smooth	Correct sentences with variations in style	Carefully constructed sentences; some variety	Simple, awkward, or wordy sentences; little variety	Choppy; many incomplete or run-on sentences
Conventions	Excellent control; few or no errors	No serious errors to affect understanding	General mastery of conventions but some errors	Reasonable control; few distracting errors	Weak control; enough errors to affect understanding	Many errors that prevent understanding

Scoring Rubric — Persuasive Writing

Rubric 4 3 2 1

	5	4	3	2	1
Focus/Ideas	Persuasive argument carefully built with quality details	Persuasive argument well supported with details	Persuasive argument with one or two convincing details	Persuasive piece sometimes unfocused; needs more support	Rambling persuasive argument; lacks development and detail
Organization/ Paragraphs	Information chosen and arranged for maximum effect	Evident progression of persuasive ideas	Information arranged in a logical way with some lapses	Little structure or direction	No identifiable structure
Voice	Writer closely involved; persuasive but not overbearing	Maintains persuasive tone	Sometimes uses persuasive voice	Little writer involvement, personality	Shows little conviction
Word Choice	Persuasive words carefully chosen for impact	Argument supported by persuasive language	Occasional persuasive language	Generally limited or redundant language	Vague, dull, or misused words; no persuasive words
Sentences	Excellent variety of sentences; natural rhythm	Varied lengths, styles; generally smooth	Carefully constructed sentences; some variety	Simple, awkward, or wordy sentences; little variety	Choppy; many incomplete or run-on sentences
Conventions	Excellent control; few or no errors	No serious errors to affect understanding	Reasonable control; few distracting errors	Weak control; enough errors to affect understanding	Many errors that prevent understanding

Scoring Rubric — Persuasive Writing

Rubric 4 3 2 1

	3	2	1
Focus/Ideas	Persuasive argument carefully built with quality details	Persuasive argument with one or two convincing details	Rambling persuasive argument; lacks development and detail
Organization/ Paragraphs	Information chosen and arranged for maximum effect	Information arranged in a logical way with some lapses	No identifiable structure
Voice	Writer closely involved; persuasive but not overbearing	Sometimes uses persuasive voice	Shows little conviction
Word Choice	Persuasive words carefully chosen for impact	Occasional persuasive language	Vague, dull, or misused words; no persuasive words
Sentences	Excellent variety of sentences; natural rhythm	Carefully constructed sentences; some variety	Choppy; many incomplete or run-on sentences
Conventions	Excellent control; few or no errors	Reasonable control; few distracting errors	Many errors that prevent understanding

Unit 3
Assess and Regroup

FYI In Grade 5 there are opportunities for regrouping every five weeks—at the end of Units 2, 3, 4, and 5. These options offer sensitivity to each student's progress, although some teachers may prefer to regroup less frequently.

Regroup for Unit 4
To make regrouping decisions at the end of Unit 3, consider students' end-of-unit scores for
- Unit 3 Retelling
- Fluency (WCPM)
- Unit 3 Benchmark Test

Group Time

On-Level	Strategic Intervention	Advanced
To continue On-Level or to move into the On-Level group, students should	**Students would benefit from Strategic Intervention if they**	**To move to the Advanced group, students should**
• score 3 or better on their cumulative unit rubric scores for Retelling	• score 2 or lower on their cumulative unit rubric scores for Retelling	• score 4 on their cumulative unit rubric scores for Retelling and demonstrate expansive vocabulary and ease of language in their retellings
• meet the current benchmark for fluency (115–122 WCPM), reading On-Level text such as Student Edition selections	• do not meet the current benchmark for fluency (115–122 WCPM)	• score 95% on the Unit 3 Benchmark Test
• score 80% or better on the Unit 3 Benchmark Tests	• score below 60% on the Unit 3 Benchmark Tests	• read above-grade-level material fluently (115–122 WCPM)
• be capable of working in the On-Level group based on teacher judgment	• are struggling to keep up with the On-Level group based on teacher judgment	• be capable of handling the problem solving and investigative work of the Advanced group based on teacher judgment

QUESTIONS TO CONSIDER

- What types of test questions did the student miss? Are they specific to a particular skill or strategy?
- Does the student have adequate background knowledge to understand the test passages or selections for retelling?

- Has the student's performance met expectations for daily lessons and assessments with little or no reteaching?
- Is the student performing more like students in another group?
- Does the student read for enjoyment, different purposes, and varied interests?

Benchmark Fluency Scores

Current Goal: **115–122 WCPM**

End-of-Year Goal: **140 WCPM**

Leveled Readers

Table of Contents

Student Edition Selections

Wings for the King

Leonardo's Horse

The Dinosaurs of Waterhouse Hawkins

Mahalia Jackson

Special Effects in Film and Television

Lesson Plans and Practice for Leveled Readers .... Page

5.3.1 BELOW-LEVEL *What a Great Idea!* **LR1**

ON-LEVEL *The Story of Flight* **LR4**

ADVANCED *The Patent Process* **LR7**

5.3.2 BELOW-LEVEL *Da Vinci's Designs* **LR10**

ON-LEVEL *Michelangelo and The Italian Renaissance* **LR13**

ADVANCED *The Inspiration of Art* **LR16**

5.3.3 BELOW-LEVEL *Paleontology: Digging for Dinosaurs and More* **LR19**

ON-LEVEL *Searching for Dinosaurs* **LR22**

ADVANCED *What's New with Dinosaur Fossils?* **LR25**

5.3.4 BELOW-LEVEL *Roots of the Blues* **LR28**

ON-LEVEL *Legends of the Blues* **LR31**

ADVANCED *Music Gets the Blues* **LR34**

5.3.5 BELOW-LEVEL *The Art of Makeup: Going Behind the Mask* **LR37**

ON-LEVEL *Very Special Effects: Computers in Filmmaking* **LR40**

ADVANCED *Hollywood Special Effects* **LR43**

Answer Key for Leveled Readers **LR46**

What a Great Idea!

⊙ **AUTHOR'S PURPOSE**

⊙ **TEXT STRUCTURE**

LESSON VOCABULARY admiringly, permit, scoundrels, subject, worthless

SUMMARY Kids have created inventions dating from 5,000 years ago. This book describes five such inventions, explains the process for getting a patent, and encourages students to invent too.

INTRODUCE THE BOOK

BUILD BACKGROUND Invite students to name inventions with which they are familiar and to discuss how those inventions have helped them in their daily lives. Encourage students to think about why inventions are created.

PREVIEW/USE TEXT FEATURES Look through the book with students and note text features that help with the book's organization: Table of Contents, charts, diagrams, and flow charts. Ask students what they expect to learn.

ELL Point out words such as *inventor* (page 4), *empress* (page 5), *earmuffs* (page 6), and others with which students may not be familiar.

TEACH/REVIEW VOCABULARY Write the vocabulary words on the board. Invite students to define familiar words and then explain words that students don't know. Next, create an add-on story. Start the story with a single sentence using one vocabulary word. Have each student add to the story using another vocabulary word. Continue until all students have had a turn. Repeating vocabulary words is fine.

TARGET SKILL AND STRATEGY

⊙ **AUTHOR'S PURPOSE** Remind students that there are four main reasons for writing: *to persuade, to inform, to entertain,* and *to express.* Explain that authors often have more than one purpose for writing.

⊙ **TEXT STRUCTURE** Review the external, or obvious, features of text structure (titles, headings, subheadings, lists, flow charts, etc.). Then introduce the idea of internal structure—the pattern of ideas and logical connections in the text. Explain that a description/definition structure, such as that in *What a Great Idea!,* provides information about a topic.

READ THE BOOK

Use the following questions to support comprehension.

PAGE 5 How did Hsi Ling Shi invent silk? *(A cocoon fell into her tea and threads appeared.)*

PAGE 11 Why do inventors need patent lawyers? *(Lawyers make sure the invention is new, and they fill out paperwork.)*

PAGE 17 What is the author's purpose in including a flow chart? *(to inspire kids to become inventors and to inform them of a sensible process)*

TALK ABOUT THE BOOK

READER RESPONSE
1. Possible response: The author wanted readers to know kids have been inventing for thousands of years.
2. Charts could show each invention and why it was invented.
3. Descriptions should reflect students' understanding on the word *scoundrel.*
4. The illustrations and sketches make the patent process clearer and show how earmuffs work.

RESPONSE OPTIONS

SPEAKING Have students prepare a drawing of an invention they would like to create and a paragraph explaining how the invention works. Students may present their ideas to the class.

CONTENT CONNECTIONS

SOCIAL STUDIES Except for Hsi Ling Shi, the book does not detail when or where the inventions were made. Invite students to research and to write short biographies of the inventors in this text or other young inventors.

Time for SOCIAL STUDIES

Author's Purpose

- The **author's purpose** is his or her reason for writing.
- Four common reasons are *to persuade, to inform, to entertain,* and *to express.*

Directions Read the paragraph below. Then answer the questions.

> In the late 1800s, Chester Greenwood invented earmuffs. Chester lived in Maine, which has cold winters. Chester's ears got so cold during winter that he could only play outside for brief periods of time. Chester wanted to keep playing outside without his ears getting cold. Then he hit upon an idea! He bent a piece of wire to the shape of his head. Then he had his grandmother sew two padded circles. Chester attached the circles to the ends of the wires. Then he put his creation onto his head! At first people thought Chester looked funny with his earmuffs. But when they saw how long he could stay out in the cold, they looked at him admiringly. Soon, people were buying earmuffs from Chester!

1. What is one of the author's purposes in writing this paragraph? How do you know?

_____

_____

2. What is another purpose that the author has for writing? How do you know?

_____

_____

3. Might the author have a third purpose for writing? Give some examples to justify your answer.

_____

_____

4. Does it seem the author wants to persuade the reader? How do you know?

_____

_____

5. If you wanted to write about an invention, what invention would you select, and what would be your purpose?

_____

_____

© Pearson Education 5

54

Vocabulary

Directions Choose the word from the box that best matches each definition.
Write the word on the line.

Check the Words You Know

___admiringly ___permit ___scoundrels
___subject ___worthless

1. _____ evil, dishonorable people; villains or rascals

2. _____ a person who is bound by loyalty to a king or queen

3. _____ to let or allow

4. _____ with wonder, pleasure, and approval

5. _____ without value; good-for-nothing; useless

Directions Choose the word from the box that best completes each sentence.
Write the word on the line.

6. People who saw Chester Greenwood's invention looked at him _____.

7. When Jeannie Low invented her step stool, she realized that a magnet would

_____ her to keep the step in place.

8. People in Florida may have thought Chester's invention was _____,
but for people from cold climates, earmuffs became essential.

9. After the young empress Hsi Ling Shi invented silk, all of her _____
began weaving silk.

10. Over the years, some _____ have tried to steal the ideas of creative
inventors, but few have succeeded.

© Pearson Education 5

Vocabulary

Directions Write a sentence using each of the vocabulary words. Try to make them relate to airplanes and flight.

Check the Words You Know

___admiringly   ___permit   ___scoundrels   ___subject   ___worthless

1. _____

_____

2. _____

_____

3. _____

_____

4. _____

_____

5. _____

_____

Directions Draw a line from the vocabulary word to its definition.

6. admiringly   to make possible or allow

7. permit   having no value

8. scoundrels   a person who lives under a king's or queen's rule

9. subject   with respect and awe

10. worthless   dishonest people

55

The Patent Process
by Donna Latham

Unit 3 Week 1

The Patent Process

🔘 **AUTHOR'S PURPOSE**

🔘 **TEXT STRUCTURE**

LESSON VOCABULARY clients, eligible, exclusive rights, intellectual property, notary, patent, patent attorney, patentee, provisional patent

SUMMARY The author describes a variety of aspects of the patent process and refers to inventions that have been patented.

INTRODUCE THE BOOK

BUILD BACKGROUND Discuss with students what they know about patents. Ask: Do you have ideas for inventions?

PREVIEW/USE TEXT FEATURES Have students examine the chart on page 5. Discuss the difference between one type of patent and another.

ELL Explain that a *patent* is a way of protecting an inventor. Inventors seek patents to get recognition and to make sure they get paid for their work.

TEACH/REVIEW VOCABULARY Discuss with students the vocabulary words and their meanings.

TARGET SKILL AND STRATEGY

🔘 **AUTHOR'S PURPOSE** Remind students that authors write for their audience with a particular purpose in mind: *to inform, to entertain, to persuade,* or *to express* ideas.

🔘 **TEXT STRUCTURE** Remind students that text is written with a particular structure, or organization, both *internal* and *external.* Suggest that they look over the headings in the book to assess how this material is structured for the reader.

READ THE BOOK

Use the following questions to support comprehension.

PAGE 5 What reasons might people have for wanting exclusive rights to their inventions? *(They might not want someone else to make or sell their inventions.)*

PAGE 10 What seems to be the author's purpose? *(to inform of how to apply for a provisional patent)*

PAGE 19 Examine the chart. What does the structure of the chart allow the reader to do? *(The reader can compare the number of patents that people in each state received during a particular year.)*

TALK ABOUT THE BOOK

READER RESPONSE

1. Possible response: The information is complicated; easier to read and understand in the form of a chart

2. Possible response: *18th century:* Samuel Hopkins, soap; Ben Franklin, bifocals; George Washington Carver, peanut butter, chili sauce, wood stain; *19th century:* Levi Strauss, jeans; Alexander Graham Bell, telephone; John Dunlop, bicycle tires; Thomas Edison, development of light bulb; George Ferris, Ferris wheel; *20th century:* Wright Brothers, working airplane; Martin Cooper, cell phone; Arthur Fry, Post-it Notes; Ellen Ochoa, robotic systems; Marc Andreesen, Mosaic® ; Parkinson and Getting, GPS

3. Possible response: because they come from someone's intellect, or mind

4. Possible response: page 11, because it shows a four-year-old's invention

RESPONSE OPTIONS

WRITING Invite students to write about a modern invention no one can live without. They should support their reasoning with examples.

CONTENT CONNECTIONS

TIME FOR Science

SCIENCE Encourage students to go to the library or on the Internet to research patent disputes. (They can use keywords *patent dispute.*) Have them share their findings with their classmates. Invite them to discuss the disputes and tell, if the information is available, who won the patent.

Name_____

Author's Purpose

- **Author's purpose** refers to what the author is trying to accomplish.
- The author may want to *inform, entertain, persuade,* or *express* himself or herself.

Directions Reread the following excerpt from *The Patent Process*. Then answer the questions.

> On July 31, 1790, President George Washington signed the first United States patent. It went to Samuel Hopkins of Philadelphia, Pennsylvania, who had developed a method for mixing potash and pearl ash to be used for making soap.
>
> George Washington isn't the only United States president linked to the first patents. Thomas Jefferson, who became President in 1801, examined the very first patent applications while serving on the original three-person patent board . . . According to the United States Patent and Trademark Office, it now takes about 6,500 people to do the job that three people once did!

1. Based on these paragraphs, what seems to be the author's purpose?

_____

_____

2. Which sentence tells you information about the person who earned the first United States patent?

_____

_____

3. Which sentence tells about the president who was involved in granting the first United States patent?

_____

_____

4. What kind of comparison is made between how patents were processed during Jefferson's time and how they are processed today?

_____

_____

5. What conclusion might you draw about why the author wants to give readers the information in this paragraph?

_____

_____

© Pearson Education 5

54

Name_____

Vocabulary

Directions Write a paragraph about an inventor and his or her invention. It can be imaginary. Use all of the vocabulary words.

Check the Words You Know

___clients   ___eligible   ___exclusive rights

___intellectual property   ___notary   ___patent

___patent attorney   ___patentee   ___provisional patent

_____

_____

_____

_____

_____

_____

_____

_____

_____

_____

_____

_____

_____

_____

© Pearson Education 5

55

Main Idea and Details

- The **main idea** is the most important idea about a paragraph, passage, or article.
- **Supporting details** are small pieces of information that tell more about the main idea.

Directions Read the paragraph below. Then complete the graphic organizer by writing the main idea of that passage. List details that tell more about the main idea.

Artists shifted art away from its original focus on religion. Their paintings focused less on religious teachings and more on human emotions and the drama of everyday life. Historians now use the term *humanism* to describe this style of art.

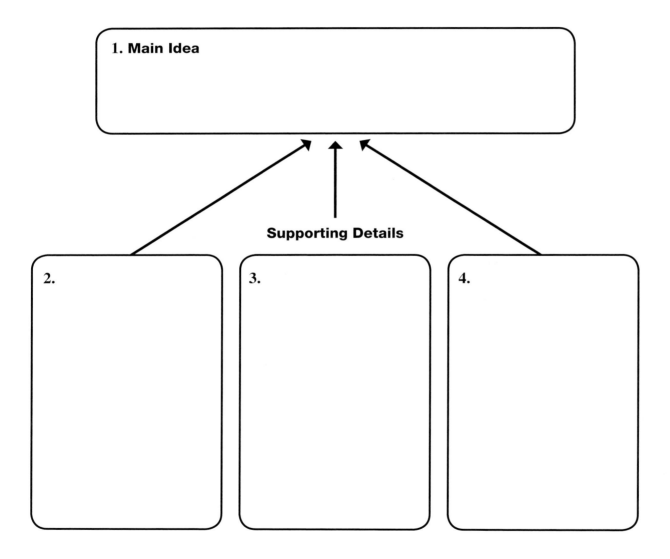

1. Main Idea

Supporting Details

2.

3.

4.

© Pearson Education 5

58

Vocabulary

Directions Draw a line from each word to its definition.

Check the Words You Know		
___achieved	___architect	___bronze
___cannon	___depressed	___fashioned
___midst	___philosopher	___rival

1. achieved   gloomy

2. architect   person who tries to understand the nature of reality

3. bronze   formed

4. cannon   accomplished

5. depressed   the middle of

6. fashioned   competitor

7. midst   person who designs buildings

8. philosopher   alloy of copper and tin

9. rival   big gun

Directions Write a sentence for each of the following words: *architect, fashioned, midst, philosopher, rival.*

10. _____

11. _____

12. _____

13. _____

14. _____

© Pearson Education 5

Fact and Opinion

- A **statement of fact** is one that can be proved true or false.
- A **statement of opinion** is a statement of someone's judgment, belief, or way of thinking.

Directions Read the following passage. Some of the sentences are statements of fact, and some are statements of opinion. On the lines below, write the sentence or sentences that are statements of facts. Then write the sentence or sentences that are statements of opinion.

> Many scientists believe that Tyrannosaurus rex was mainly a hunter. However, new information about its sense of smell suggests that it might also have been a scavenger. Scavengers are animals that eat dead and decaying things.

1. **Statements of Fact** _____

_____

_____

2. **Statements of Opinion** _____

_____

_____

Directions Answer the following question.

3. How did you figure out which sentences showed facts and which showed opinions?

_____

_____

_____

© Pearson Education 5

62

Vocabulary

Directions Choose the word that best completes each sentence.

> ### Check the Words You Know
>
> ___erected   ___foundations   ___mold   ___occasion
> ___proportion   ___tidied   ___workshop

1. I _____ my messy room.

2. The scientists made a _____ of the fossil.

3. Good buildings have strong _____.

4. A good ice-cream sundae has the right _____ of ice cream to syrup.

5. We made the kitchen table in our _____.

6. After we _____ the frame, we were able to attach the dinosaur bones.

7. The day I won the pie-eating contest was a very special _____.

Directions Write a sentence of your own for each vocabulary word.

8. _____

9. _____

10. _____

11. _____

12. _____

13. _____

14. _____

63

Fact and Opinion

- A **statement of fact** is one that can be proved true or false.
- A **statement of opinion** is a statement of someone's judgment, belief, or way of thinking.

Directions In front of each sentence below, write whether it is a statement of fact or a statement of opinion.

1. _____ Tyrannosaurus rex was a fearsome killer that probably sprinted for short distances to catch its prey.

2. _____ Scavengers are animals that eat dead animals.

3. _____ Through their analysis of fossils, paleontologists have identified slightly over three hundred species of dinosaurs.

4. _____ One of the most fascinating (and controversial) theories regarding *Seismosaurus* is that it swung its tail fast enough to break the sound barrier.

5. _____ Cold-blooded animals cannot control their own body temperature.

6. _____ Dinosaur fossils have been found in many places around the world, including northern climates.

7. _____ Although dinosaurs are extinct today, the story of these amazing animals continues to fascinate all who read and learn about them!

Directions Look through *What's New with Dinosaur Fossils?* Find one sentence that is a statement of fact and another that is a statement of opinion. Write them below.

8. Statement of Fact: _____

_____

9. Statement of Opinion: _____

_____

© Pearson Education 5

62

Vocabulary

Directions Use the vocabulary words to answer the questions below. Each word can only be used once.

Check the Words You Know

___avid   ___carnivorous   ___collaborator   ___consensus
___contention   ___descendants   ___herbivorous   ___olfactory bulbs
___theropods   ___trackways   ___vertebrae

1. _____ What kind of animal eats only plants?

2. _____ Which word refers to certain kinds of footprints?

3. _____ What kind of person would you choose to work with you on a scientific project?

4. _____ What is your backbone made up of?

5. _____ Which word names certain meat-eating dinosaurs with sharp claws and sharp teeth that may be the ancestors of birds?

6. _____ Which word has to do with the sense of smell?

7. _____ Which word would you use for someone who is extremely enthusiastic?

8. _____ What are grandchildren and great-grandchildren?

9. _____ Which word describes lions, tigers, and other meat-eating animals?

10–11. _____ Which two words mean opposite things?

_____

Name _____

Main Idea and Details

- The **main idea** is the most important idea about a paragraph, passage, or article.
- **Supporting details** are small pieces of information that tell more about the main idea.

Directions Read the following passage. Complete the diagram by writing the main idea of the passage. Then list supporting details that tell more about the main idea.

Ray had a difficult childhood. He grew up during the worst of the Great Depression; his family had very little money. At the age of six, Ray began losing his sight and became completely blind by age seven. On top of this, Ray, like Bessie Smith, had to deal with the early deaths of his parents. Ray's father died when Ray was only ten. His mother died when he was just fifteen. Somehow, Ray found a way to overcome these hardships and developed into a great blues artist.

Main Idea

Supporting Details

© Pearson Education 5

66

Vocabulary

Directions Unscramble the vocabulary words and then use each one in a sentence.

Check the Words You Know
___appreciate ___barber ___choir
___released ___religious ___slavery
___teenager

1. oicrh _____

_____

_____

2. reeentga _____

_____

_____

3. abrbre _____

_____

_____

4. dreeslea _____

_____

_____

5. teappaicer _____

_____

_____

6. sigoiulre _____

_____

_____

7. vsaleyr _____

_____

_____

© Pearson Education 5

67

Vocabulary

Directions Choose the word from the box that best matches each clue. Write the word on the line.

Check the Words You Know

___coalesced	___genre	___inception
___mentors	___prodigy	___reggae
___rhythm and blues	___spawned	___yodeling

1. _____ This music comes from the Caribbean.

2. _____ This could be the start of something.

3. _____ "So smart, and so talented—and so young!"

4. _____ A verb that means "gave birth to."

5. _____ When you sing this way, you change from an ordinary voice to a high voice and then back again.

6. _____ This popular music began in the United States and was influenced by the blues.

7. _____ This word could describe how several things came together.

8. _____ They teach—or at least provide models for you to learn from.

9. _____ A noun that means a type of artistic, musical, or literary work.

Directions Choose three words from the box and write a sentence for each of them.

10. _____

_____

11. _____

_____

12. _____

_____

67

The Art of Makeup

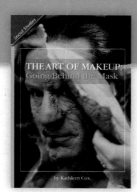

⊙ **GRAPHIC SOURCES**

⊙ **PRIOR KNOWLEDGE**

LESSON VOCABULARY background, landscape, miniature, prehistoric, reassembled

SUMMARY Today's makeup artists can easily transform a human actor into a fantastic creature with masks, false teeth, or wigs. This book describes the detailed processes for making these special effects.

INTRODUCE THE BOOK

BUILD BACKGROUND Invite students to discuss films they've seen with actors wearing heavy makeup (for example, *Harry Potter* or *The Lord of the Rings* series). Ask students what tricks or techniques they imagine makeup artists use to create these characters.

PREVIEW/USE TEXT FEATURES Have students preview the text by looking at chapter titles and subheads. Remind students that such text features help organize reading.

TEACH/REVIEW VOCABULARY Have students define vocabulary words they know and discuss words they don't. Note the two vocabulary words that have prefixes *(prehistoric and reassembled)*. Define these prefixes for students. (*pre-* means "before"; *re-* means "again") Invite students to suggest other words with these prefixes.

TARGET SKILL AND STRATEGY

⊙ **GRAPHIC SOURCES** Remind students that a *graphic source* is a way of showing information visually and may help resolve confusing text. Graphics used in this text include photos with captions. Explain that the two- or three-step photo diagrams (pages 10, 12–13, and 14) are meant to help readers see the steps of a process in order.

⊙ **PRIOR KNOWLEDGE** Tell students that *prior knowledge* obtained from reading or from life experiences can help them understand this book. Any student who has had braces will know about *dental impressions*. Many students will have seen films featuring actors with heavy makeup. Students can connect this prior knowledge with text features and photos.

READ THE BOOK

Use the following questions to support comprehension.

PAGE 4 Tell why makeup takes long to apply. *(Artists must get every detail right; substances must set or dry properly; actor safety—makeup can be dangerous.)*

PAGES 10–11 How does the pair of photos help explain how a mask connects to an actor's skin? *(It shows the makeup artist blending in the edges of the mask.)*

PAGE 15 What is the last step in the creation of false teeth? *(Adjustments are made if the teeth hurt.)*

ELL Have students make a graphic organizer outlining the steps for each type of makeup discussed.

TALK ABOUT THE BOOK

READER RESPONSE
1. Possible response: They helped explain each step in the process.
2. Responses will vary.
3. Possible response: It provides the setting for the action.
4. Possible response: The process is long and complicated, and it involves potentially dangerous materials.

RESPONSE OPTIONS

WRITING Have students work in groups to create a character and describe the special mask, teeth, and wig it will need. Have a student from each group draw the character. Then have students explain their group characters to the class.

CONTENT CONNECTIONS

SOCIAL STUDIES Have students research famous makeup artists from the film industry. Those with an interest in history may also enjoy researching the process of *ventilating,* invented during the reign of Louis XVI.

Time for SOCIAL STUDIES

Name_____

Graphic Sources

- **Graphic sources** include items such as advertisements, charts, diagrams, graphs, maps, menus, photographs, recipes, and timetables.
- Use graphic sources to help you understand text and to draw conclusions as you read.

Directions Look at the graphic sources throughout *The Art of Makeup: Going Behind the Mask.* Then answer the questions below.

1. What type of graphic source is shown on page 17?

_____

2. Review the steps for making a foam latex mask discussed in the text on pages 8–11. What step or steps are shown in the photos on page 10?

_____

_____

3. Look at pages 12–15. How do the photos shown here work with the text? How do the arrows help?

_____

_____

4. What is the black-and-white graphic source on page 17?

_____

5. What does the "inset" photograph on page 17 show?

_____

6. Did the graphic sources in this book help you understand the text better? Explain.

_____

_____

7. List two techniques makeup artists use to create characters.

_____

_____

70

© Pearson Education 5

Name_____

Vocabulary

Directions Choose the word from the box that best matches each definition.
Write the word on the line.

Check the Words You Know

____ background   ____ landscape   ____ miniature
____ prehistoric   ____ reassembled

1. _____ of or belonging to times before histories were written

2. _____ the part of a picture or scene behind the subject

3. _____ done or made on a very small scale; tiny

4. _____ brought together again

5. _____ view of scenery on land

Directions Choose the word from the box that best completes each sentence.
Write the word on the line.

6. The makeup artist _____ his tray of makeup after it fell on the floor.

7. The makeup artist created a _____ model of the ape before creating a larger mask for the actor.

8. The _____ of distant flowers and trees looked very realistic.

9. The character's makeup looked especially scary set against the _____ of moldy old dungeon walls.

10. Artists need to rely on both fossil remains and their imaginations when they try to create makeup

for _____ cave-dwelling characters.

© Pearson Education 5

Graphic Sources

- **Graphic sources** include items such as advertisements, charts, diagrams, graphs, maps, menus, photographs, recipes, and timetables.
- Use graphic sources to help you understand text and to draw conclusions as you read.

Directions Look at the graphic sources throughout *Hollywood Special Effects*. Then answer the questions below.

1. What type of graphic source is shown on page 8?

_____

2–3. What is the purpose of the graphic source on page 8? What does it show?

_____

_____

4. How does the graphic source on page 8 compare with the one on page 11?

_____

_____

5. Why might the author have included the photograph on pages 12–13?

_____

_____

6–7. What does the photograph on page 15 show? How does it help your understanding of the text?

_____

_____

8–9. What is the graphic source shown on page 19? What conclusion can you draw from that graphic source?

_____

_____

10. What conclusion can you draw from studying the graphic sources used in this book?

_____

_____

© Pearson Education 5

70

Vocabulary

Directions Choose the word from the box that best matches each definition.
Write the word on the line.

Check the Words You Know
___blue screen ___cinema ___continuous motion ___matte painting ___optical illusion ___sensors ___technology

1. _____ an illusion created by showing different pictures one after another at high speed

2. _____ something that looks different from what it really is

3. _____ another term for a movie theater

4. _____ devices that react to heat, light, pressure, or other stimulations and send signals to a computer or other electronic device

5. _____ special background against which actors are filmed to create special effects

6. _____ a two-dimensional painting that serves as background for a three-dimensional stage or studio set

7. _____ the equipment, objects, or methods used to carry out a process

Directions Choose three vocabulary words. Use each word in a sentence.

8. _____

9. _____

10. _____

© Pearson Education 5

71

Answer Key for Below-Level Reader Practice

What a Great Idea!   LR1

🎯 Author's Purpose, LR2
1. To inform. The author provides details and information to teach us about Chester Greenwood's invention. **2.** To entertain. The author presents her information in the form of a story. She uses exclamation points to get the reader excited. **3.** To express. The author wants us to be able to visualize the cold Maine winters. **4.** No. The author is not giving us her opinion of the earmuffs or of Chester Greenwood. **5.** Answers will vary. Example: I would write about the invention of the calculator and teach people the steps the inventor used.

Vocabulary, LR3
1. scoundrels **2.** subject **3.** permit **4.** admiringly **5.** worthless **6.** admiringly **7.** permit **8.** worthless **9.** subjects **10.** scoundrels

Da Vinci's Designs   LR10

🎯 Main Idea and Details, LR11
Possible responses given. **1.** Da Vinci tried to learn the secret of flying. **2.** studied wings of bats and birds **3.** studied wind currents **4.** studied flight patterns

Vocabulary, LR12
1. midst **2.** rival **3.** achieved **4.** architect **5.** cannon **6.** philosopher **7.** fashioned **8.** bronze **9.** depressed **10–12.** Sentences will vary.

Paleontology: Digging for Dinosaurs and More   LR19

🎯 Fact and Opinion, LR20
1. Scavengers are animals that eat dead and decaying things. **2.** Many scientists believe that Tyrannosaurus rex was mainly a hunter. However, new information about its sense of smell suggests that it might also have been a scavenger. **3.** Possible response: Opinion sentences included words like *believe* and *suggest.*

Vocabulary, LR21
1. tidied **2.** mold **3.** foundations **4.** proportion **5.** workshop **6.** erected **7.** occasion **8–14.** Sentences will vary.

Roots of the Blues   LR28

🎯 Main Idea and Details, LR29
Main idea: Blues musicians used a variety of instruments to make many different sounds. **Supporting details:** Blues singers played handmade musical instruments that made unusual sounds. **Early instruments:** banjo, washboard and stick **Later instruments:** guitar, piano, and harmonica.

Vocabulary, LR30
1. release **2.** slave **3.** X **4.** No X **5.** No X **6.** X **7.** X **8.** Possible responses are given. A *teenager* sang in a *religious choir* made up of many adults. *I appreciate* that the *barber* gave the *teenager* a great haircut.

The Art of Makeup   LR37

🎯 Graphic Sources, LR38
Possible responses given. **1.** photographs that show steps in a process **2.** attaching the mask to the actor's face and applying makeup to the mask **3.** They show many of the steps in making false teeth. The arrows show the order of the steps. **4.** It is a drawing of wig-making in the seventeenth century. **5.** the creation of a wig for a modern film **6.** Possible response: Yes; they helped me understand that there are many steps to making masks. **7.** applying makeup, creating wigs

Vocabulary, LR39
1. prehistoric **2.** background **3.** miniature **4.** reassembled **5.** landscape **6.** reassembled **7.** miniature **8.** landscape **9.** background **10.** prehistoric

Answer Key for On-Level Reader Practice

The Story of Flight — LR4

Author's Purpose, LR5

Possible responses given. **1.** to inform the reader about how jet engines changed air travel **2.** It had room for up to 181 passengers. **3.** It could travel 600 miles per hour. **4.** "That year, more than one million people flew between the Unites States and Europe. For the first time in history, more people crossed the Atlantic by plane than by ship." **5.** The author wants the reader to have an idea of how much air travel changed during the year 1958.

Vocabulary, LR6

Possible responses given. **1.** The passengers looked *admiringly* at the shiny jumbo jet. **2.** The pilot did not *permit* passengers to unfasten their seat belts. **3.** Only *scoundrels* would try to sit in your airplane seat. **4.** The King's loyal *subject* tried to design a way for people to fly. **5.** Early designs for airplanes were sometimes found to be *worthless*. **6.** admiringly—with respect and awe **7.** permit—to make possible or allow **8.** scoundrels—dishonest people **9.** subject—a person who lives under a king's or queen's rule **10.** worthless—having no value

Michelangelo and The Italian Renaissance — LR13

Main Idea and Details, LR14

Possible responses given. **1.** Artists shifted to a style of art called *humanism*. **2.** Their paintings focused less on religious teachings. **3.** They focused more on human emotions. **4.** They focused more on the drama of everyday life.

Vocabulary, LR15

1. achieved—accomplished **2.** architect—person who designs buildings **3.** bronze—alloy of copper and tin **4.** cannon—big gun **5.** depressed—gloomy **6.** fashioned—formed **7.** midst—the middle of **8.** philosopher—a person who tries to understand the nature of reality **9.** rival—competitor **10–14.** Sentences will vary.

Searching for Dinosaurs — LR22

Fact and Opinion, LR23

1. opinion **2.** opinion **3.** fact **4.** opinion **5.** fact **6.** opinion **7.** fact **8.** opinion **9–10.** Sentences will vary.

Vocabulary, LR24

1. tidied **2.** occasion **3.** foundation **4.** workshop **5.** proportion **6.** erected **7.** mold
Sentences will vary.

Legends of the Blues — LR31

Main Idea and Details, LR32

Main Idea—Ray Charles had a difficult childhood to overcome. Supporting Details: Grew up during the Depression; family had little money. Began losing his sight at age six. Lost sight by age seven. Father died when Ray was ten. Mother died when Ray was fifteen.

Vocabulary, LR33

Possible responses given. **1.** choir: Choir members wear robes. **2.** teenager: A teenager may be a puzzle to his or her parents. **3.** barber: My barber gave me a haircut. **4.** released: Balloons were released at the party. **5.** appreciate: We appreciate your kind words. **6.** religious: Ministers are religious leaders. **7.** slavery: Slavery ended in the United States in 1865.

Very Special Effects: Computers in Filmmaking — LR40

Graphic Sources, LR41

Possible responses given. **1.** a chart **2.** Computer-based movies cost less to make and distribute than regular movies. **3.** They take up a lot of space as computer files. **4.** It would be expensive, so they might have to raise ticket prices. **5.** They can see a result immediately. **6.** drawback, disadvantage **7.** benefit, advantage, strength **8.** Possible responses: In favor, because the special effects are really great. Opposed, because ticket prices may go up and because they look grainy on a big screen.

Vocabulary, LR42

1. prehistoric **2.** background **3.** miniature **4.** reassembled **5.** landscape **6.** reassembled **7.** landscape **8.** background **9.** miniature **10.** prehistoric **11–12.** Sentences will vary.

Answer Key for Advanced-Level Reader Practice

The Patent Process   LR7

Author's Purpose, LR8

Possible responses given. **1.** to inform the reader about the relationship of early presidents to the development of the patent process **2.** It went to Samuel Hopkins of Philadelphia, who had developed a method for making soap. **3.** On July 31, 1790, George Washington signed the first U.S. patent. **4.** Jefferson and his board used only three people. Today it takes about 6,500 people. **5.** The author wants the reader to have an appreciation for the early development of the patent process.

Vocabulary, LR9

Possible response given. Jackie Morante hoped she would be able to find a lot of *clients* who would buy her new invention. She had managed to get *exclusive rights* to a new pancake flipper. She thought she'd attract customers by saying that the first one hundred buyers were *eligible* to get two for the price of one. But first she had to apply for a *patent.* She sketched her design on a piece of paper and went to a *notary* to make it official. Then she found a *patent attorney* to guide her through the process. A few months later, she was given a *provisional patent,* so she started making infomercials to sell it on television. By the end of the year she was an official *patentee,* and the flipper was her *intellectual property.* Her pancake flippers were selling like crazy.

The Inspiration of Art   LR16

Main Idea and Details, LR17

Possible responses given. **1.** Borrowing designs from other artists was common and considered a compliment at that time. **2.** Artists have always studied the art of earlier times. **3.** Copying showed respect and admiration for older artists. **4.** Copying contributed to the preservation of past artistic styles.

Vocabulary, LR18

1. incorporated **2–3.** baroque; sinuous **4.** cast **5–6.** intricate; facade **7.** cubism **8–9.** innovative; razing.
Paragraphs will vary.

What's New with Dinosaur Fossils?   LR25

Fact and Opinion, LR26

1. opinion **2.** fact **3.** fact **4.** opinion **5.** fact **6.** fact **7.** opinion **8.** Responses will vary. **9.** Responses will vary.

Vocabulary, LR27

1. herbivorous **2.** trackways **3.** collaborator **4.** vertebrae **5.** theropods **6.** olfactory bulbs **7.** avid **8.** descendants **9.** carnivorous **10–11.** consensus, contention

Music Gets the Blues   LR34

Main Idea and Details, LR35

Main Idea: Blues music has influenced other types of music. Supporting Details: Pop music owes much of its emotional singing to blues greats such as B. B. King. Jazz music has borrowed heavily from the blues over the years.

Vocabulary, LR36

1. reggae **2.** inception **3.** prodigy **4.** spawned **5.** yodeling **6.** rhythm and blues **7.** coalesced **8.** mentors **9.** genre **10–12.** Sentences will vary.

Hollywood Special Effects   LR43

Graphic Sources, LR44

Possible responses given. **1.** a poster **2–3.** The poster is designed to interest moviegoers in seeing the movie *It,* that starred the actress Clara Bow. **4.** Both are movie posters, but the one on page 11 shows the special effects makeup that is part of the movie *Frankenstein.* **5.** The author may have wanted to show that special effects could create seemingly everyday events. **6–7.** It shows how a moviemaker used a split screen to create the illusion of twins. It shows what the author is describing in the text. **8–9.** a cover from *Time* magazine; that special effects, and especially those of George Lucas, were getting national attention **10.** Possible answer: Special effects are very important in making movies.

Vocabulary, LR45

1. continuous motion **2.** optical illusion **3.** cinema **4.** sensors **5.** blue screen **6.** matte painting **7.** technology **8–10.** Sentences will vary.

Differentiated Instruction

Table of Contents

Routine Cards ....DI•1

Daily Group Time Lessons

Week 1 **Wings for the King**
- (Strategic Intervention) Days 1–5 .... DI•2, 4, 6, 8, 10
- (On-Level) Days 1 and 5 ....DI•3, 11
- (Advanced) Days 1–5 .... DI•3, 5, 7, 9, 11

Week 2 **Leonardo's Horse**
- (Strategic Intervention) Days 1–5 .... DI•12, 14, 16, 18, 20
- (On-Level) Days 1 and 5 ....DI•13, 21
- (Advanced) Days 1–5 .... DI•13, 15, 17, 19, 21

Week 3 **The Dinosaurs of Waterhouse Hawkins**
- (Strategic Intervention) Days 1–5 .... DI•22, 24, 26, 28, 30
- (On-Level) Days 1 and 5 ....DI•23, 31
- (Advanced) Days 1–5 .... DI•23, 25, 27, 29, 31

Week 4 **Mahalia Jackson**
- (Strategic Intervention) Days 1–5 .... DI•32, 34, 36, 38, 40
- (On-Level) Days 1 and 5 ....DI•33, 41
- (Advanced) Days 1–5 .... DI•33, 35, 37, 39, 41

Week 5 **Special Effects in Film and Television**
- (Strategic Intervention) Days 1–5 .... DI•42, 44, 46, 48, 50
- (On-Level) Days 1 and 5 ....DI•43, 51
- (Advanced) Days 1–5 .... DI•43, 45, 47, 49, 51

Reteach Lessons ....DI•52

Matching Students to Text

Reading Levels ....DI•57

Independent Reading Chart..DI•58

Running Record...DI•59

Routine Cards

Oral Rereading Routine

Use this Routine when students read orally.

1 Read Have students read the entire book orally.

2 Reread For optimal fluency, students should reread the text three or four times.

3 Provide Feedback Listen as students read and provide corrective feedback regarding their oral reading and their use of decoding strategies.

Choral Reading Routine

Use this Routine when students read chorally.

1 Select a Passage Choose an appropriate passage from the selection.

2 Divide into Groups Assign each group a part to read.

3 Model Have students track the print as you read.

4 Read Together Have students read along with you.

5 Independent Reading Have the groups read aloud without you. Monitor progress and provide feedback. For optimal fluency, students should reread three to four times.

Fluent Word Reading Routine

Teach students to read words fluently using this Routine.

1 Connect Write an example word. Isolate the sound-spelling or word structure element you will focus on and ask students to demonstrate their understanding.

2 Model When you come to a new word, look at all the letters in the word and think about its vowel sound. Say the sounds in the word to yourself and then read the word. Model reading the example words in this way. When you come to a new word, what are you going to do?

3 Group Practice Write other similar words. Let's read these words. Look at the letters, think about the vowel sounds, and say the sounds to yourself. When I point to the word, let's read it together. Allow 2-3 seconds previewing time for each word.

Paired Reading Routine

Use this Routine when students read in pairs.

1 Reader 1 Begins Students read the entire book, switching readers at the end of each page.

2 Reader 2 Begins Have partners reread; now the other partner begins.

3 Reread For optimal fluency, students should reread three or four times.

4 Provide Feedback Listen as students read. Provide corrective feedback regarding their oral reading and their use of decoding strategies.

Routine Cards

Multisyllabic Word Routine

Teach students this Routine to read long words with meaningful parts.

1 Teach Tell students to look for meaningful parts and to think about the meaning of each part. They should use the parts to read the word and determine meaning.

2 Model Think aloud to analyze a long word for the base word, ending, prefix, and/or suffix and to identify the word and determine its meaning.

3 Guide Practice Provide examples of long words with endings (*-ing, -ed, -s*), prefixes (*un-, re-, dis-, mis-, non-*), and/or suffixes (*-ly, -ness, -less, -ful,* and so on). Help students analyze base words and parts.

4 Provide Feedback Encourage students to circle parts of the words to help identify parts and determine meaning.

Picture Walk Routine

To build concepts and vocabulary, conduct a structured picture walk before reading.

1 Prepare Preview the selection and list key concepts and vocabulary you wish to develop.

2 Discuss As students look at the pages, discuss illustrations, have students point to pictured items, and/or ask questions that target key concepts and vocabulary.

3 Elaborate Elaborate on students' responses to reinforce correct use of the vocabulary and to provide additional exposure to key concepts.

4 Practice For more practice with key concepts, have each student turn to a partner and do the picture walk using the key concept vocabulary.

Multisyllabic Word Routine

Teach students this Routine to chunk words with no recognizable parts.

1 Teach Tell students to look for chunks in words with no meaningful parts. They should say each chunk slowly and then say the chunks fast to make a whole word.

2 Model Think aloud to demonstrate breaking a word into chunks, saying each chunk slowly, and then saying the chunks fast to make a word.

3 Guide Practice Provide examples of long words with no meaningful parts. Help students chunk the words.

4 Provide Feedback If necessary, reteach by modeling how to break words into chunks.

Concept Vocabulary

Use this Routine to teach concept vocabulary.

1 Introduce the Word Relate the word to the week's concept. Supply a student-friendly definition.

2 Demonstrate Provide several familiar examples to demonstrate meaning.

3 Apply Have students demonstrate understanding with a simple activity.

4 Display the Word Relate the word to the concept by displaying it on a concept web. Have students identify word parts and practice reading the word.

5 Use the Word Often Encourage students to use the word often in their writing and speaking. Ask questions that require students to use the word.

© Pearson Education, Inc.

Group Time

DAY 2

Audio CD AudioText

1 Word Study/Phonics

LESSON VOCABULARY Use p. 264b to review the meanings of *admiringly, permit, scoundrels, subject,* and *worthless.* Students can practice saying all of the words. Have individuals read the words from word cards.

DECODING MULTISYLLABIC WORDS Write *parapet* and say the word as you write it. Then model how to decode when there are no meaningful word parts. I see a chunk at the beginning: *par.* I see an *a* in the middle. A single vowel in the middle of a word usually has the schwa sound, *uh.* I see a chunk at the end: *pet.* I say each chunk slowly: *par a pet.* I say the chunks fast to make a whole word: *parapet.* Is it a real word? Yes, a parapet is a high castle tower.

Use the Multisyllabic Word routine on p. DI·1 to help students read these other words from *Wings for the King: rotors, dungeon, propeller, hobbyhorse,* and *fanfare.* Be sure students understand the meanings of words such as *rotors* and *fanfare.*

Use *Strategies for Word Analysis,* Lesson 11, with students who have difficulty mastering word analysis and need practice with decodable text.

2 Read *Wings for the King,* pp. 266–273

BEFORE READING Yesterday we read about many different inventors. Today we will read a play about a king who wants an invention that will make it possible for him to fly.

Using the Picture Walk routine on p. DI·1, guide students through the text, asking questions such as those listed below. Then read the question on p. 266. Together, set a purpose for reading.

pp. 268–269 Why do you think the king is pointing at a bird? (*He likes birds. He wants to be like a bird.*)

pp. 270–271 What do you think the picture on these pages shows? (*perhaps unusual wings for the king*) In this play we'll read why the king wants wings.

DURING READING Follow the Guiding Comprehension routine on pp. 268–273. Have students read along with you while tracking the print or do a choral reading of the selection. Stop every two pages to ask what students have learned so far. Prompt as necessary.

- Describe what you think a page is. What is a page's job?
- What do you think Geraldine is going to warn the king about?

AFTER READING What has happened in the play so far? What do you think will happen next? Reread sections of the play with students for comprehension as needed.

Monitor Progress

Word and Story Reading

If... students have difficulty reading multisyllabic words in the selection,	then... have them look for and read meaningful parts in the words or have them chunk words with no recognizable parts.
If... students need practice reading words fluently,	then... use the Fluent Word Reading Routine on the DI tab.
If... students have difficulty reading along with the group,	then... have them follow along as they listen to the AudioText.

Advanced

DAY 2

1 Extend Vocabulary

CONTEXT CLUES Choose and read a sentence or passage containing a homonym or a word with multiple meanings, such as this sentence from p. 4 of *The Patent Process*: "During the California gold rush, Levi Strauss realized that miners needed rugged pants that would not wear out as they dug for gold." Does the word *pants* in this sentence mean short, quick breaths of air or an article of clothing? How did you know? *(from the context "wear out")* Remind students to use the strategy as they read *Wings for the King*.

2 Read *Wings for the King*, pp. 266–273

BEFORE READING In *The Patent Process,* you read about the steps people take to get their inventions recognized and protected. Today you will read a play about a king who wants a particular invention. As you read, think about how the two pieces are alike, and how they are different.

Have students write the sequence of events in the play in their Strategy Response Logs (p. 266).

CRITICAL/CREATIVE THINKING Have students read pp. 266–273 independently. Encourage them to think critically and creatively. For example, ask:

- Why would Tina think that the kite would hold the king's weight?
- What kind of wings would you design for the king?

AFTER READING Have partners discuss the selection and share their Strategy Response Log entries. Have them record the sequence of events so far in their Strategy Response Logs (p. 273). Then have students discuss the events and what they think might happen next. Give students an opportunity to share their thoughts with you.

WINGS for the KING

Audio CD **AudioText**

Group Time

DAY **4**

Audio CD AudioText

ROUTINE

① Practice Retelling

REVIEW STORY ELEMENTS Help students identify the main characters and the setting of *Wings for the King*. Then guide them in using the Retelling Cards to list story events in sequence. Prompt students to include important details.

RETELL Using the Retelling Cards, have students work in pairs to retell *Wings for the King*. Monitor retelling and prompt students as needed. For example, ask:

Retelling Cards
Grade 5
PEARSON
Scott Foresman

- Where and when does the play take place?
- Tell me what happened in this part of the play in a few sentences.
- What is the main character like?

If students struggle, model a fluent retelling.

② Read "Becky Schroeder: Enlightened Thinker"

BEFORE READING Read the genre information on p. 282. Point out that narrative nonfiction tells a true story but in a way that sounds more like fiction. As we read "Becky Schroeder: Enlightened Thinker," pay attention to the process Becky went through to create her invention.

Read the rest of the panel on p. 282. Have students read the title and identify the topic of this selection. *(how a girl invented a way to write in the dark)* Ask: How is the selection about Becky similar to "What's the Big Idea, Ben Franklin?" *(Both selections are about inventors who solved problems.)* How are the writing styles different?

DURING READING Have students read along with you while tracking the print or do a choral reading of the selection. Stop to discuss difficult vocabulary, such as *glimmered, inspiration,* and *commandeered*.

AFTER READING Have students share their reactions to the selection. Then guide them through the Reading Across Texts and Writing Across Texts activities, prompting if necessary.

- What character in *Wings for the King* is Becky Schroeder most like? Why do you think so?
- What personal traits helped Becky to come up with a solution to her problem?

Monitor Progress

Word and Selection Reading

If... students have difficulty reading multisyllabic words in the selection,	**then...** have them look for and read meaningful parts in the words or have them chunk words with no recognizable parts.
If... students have difficulty reading along with the group,	**then...** have them follow along as they listen to the AudioText.

Advanced

1 **Read** "Becky Schroeder: Enlightened Thinker"

CREATIVE THINKING Have students read pp. 282–287 independently. Encourage them to think creatively. For example, ask:

• What other uses could there be for Becky's invention?
• What are some potential problems that might arise by using the Glo-Sheet?

AFTER READING Have students meet with you to discuss the selection and Reading Across Texts. Have students do Writing Across Texts independently.

2 **Extend Genre Study**

RESEARCH Have students use the library and online sources to find more inventions that were created by young inventors.

WRITE Have students write a description of another successful invention from a child inventor.

AudioText

Wings for the King

Group Time

Leveled Reader Database ONLINE

PearsonSuccessNet.com

Strategic Intervention

ROUTINE

1 Reread for Fluency

MODEL Tell students that good readers read with different tones to show emotion. Listeners should be able to detect excitement, frustration, happiness, sadness, and other emotions from the reader's tone. Then model, reading aloud p. 6 of the Leveled Reader *What a Great Idea!* Use a tone of voice that shows discomfort while reading about how cold Chester's ears would get. Use a different tone of voice while reading about the excitement that the development of earmuffs caused. Discuss how tone of voice makes reading more interesting and makes what we read easier to understand.

PRACTICE Have individuals silently reread passages from *What a Great Idea!* Encourage students to self-correct. Then have partners reread passages aloud. For optimal fluency, they should reread three or four times. As students read, monitor fluency and provide corrective feedback. Students in this group are assessed in Weeks 2 and 4.

2 Retell Leveled Reader *What a Great Idea!*

Model how to use skimming to retell the events on pp. 3–6. Then ask students to retell *What a Great Idea!*, skimming the book. Prompt them as needed.

- Tell me what this passage is about in a few sentences.
- What did you learn from reading this selection?

Monitor Progress

Fluency

If... students have difficulty reading fluently,	**then...** provide additional fluency practice by pairing nonfluent readers with fluent ones.

For alternate Leveled Reader lesson plans that teach
🎯 **Author's Purpose,** 🎯 **Story Structure,** and
Lesson Vocabulary, see pp. LR1–LR9.

On-Level

1 Reread for Fluency ROUTINE

MODEL Tell students that good readers use tone of voice to communicate the emotion in the passage. Point out that the genre of *Wings for the King* is a play, and each character shows many emotions, which can be illustrated with tone of voice. In *The Story of Flight*, the reader's tone of voice can help listeners understand the struggles and excitement felt by the inventors of airplanes. Then model pacing, reading p. 4 of the Leveled Reader *The Story of Flight*. Discuss how tone of voice makes reading more interesting and meaningful to listeners.

PRACTICE Have students reread passages from *The Story of Flight* with a partner or individually. For optimal fluency, students should reread three or four times. As students read, monitor fluency and provide corrective feedback. Students in this group are assessed in Week 3.

2 Retell Leveled Reader *The Story of Flight*

Have students use chapter titles as a guide to summarize important facts they learned from each section of the book. Prompt as needed.

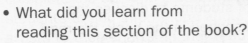

- What did you learn from reading this section of the book?
- What was the author trying to tell us?

Advanced

1 Reread for Fluency ROUTINE

PRACTICE Have students silently reread passages from the Leveled Reader *The Patent Process*. Then have them reread aloud with a partner or individually. As students read, monitor fluency and provide corrective feedback. If students read fluently on the first reading, they do not need to reread three to four times. Assess the fluency of students in this group using p. 287a.

2 Revisit Leveled Reader *The Patent Process*

RETELL Have students retell the Leveled Reader *The Patent Process*.

NOW TRY THIS Have students complete their plans for an invention. You may wish to review the plans with students and suggest ideas, if needed. Have them share their inventions with classmates.

Leonardo's Horse

Group Time

Audio CD — AudioText

DAY 2

Strategic Intervention

ROUTINE

1 Word Study/Phonics

LESSON VOCABULARY Use p. 290b to review the meanings of *achieved, architect, bronze, cannon, depressed, fashioned, midst, philosopher,* and *rival*. Students can practice saying all of the words. Have individuals read the words from word cards.

DECODING MULTISYLLABIC WORDS Write *landscape* and model how to decode a word with recognizable word parts. First I ask myself if I see any parts that I know. I see *land* at the beginning of the word, and *scape* at the end. I know that *land* is the ground or the earth. I also know that this passage is about art. So I think *landscape* has something to do with art and land.

Use the Multisyllabic Word routine on p. DI·1 to help students read these other words from *Leonardo's Horse: lightweight, chariots, recommend, fluid, deathbed,* and *archers*. Be sure students understand the meanings of words such as *fluid* and *archers*.

Use *Strategies for Word Analysis*, Lesson 12, with students who have difficulty mastering word analysis and need practice with decodable text.

2 Read *Leonardo's Horse*, pp. 292–303

BEFORE READING Yesterday we read about Leonardo da Vinci's many designs. Today we will read a biography about da Vinci that focuses on one of his very special projects.

Using the Picture Walk routine on p. DI·1, guide students through the text, asking questions such as those listed below. Then read the question on p. 292. Together, set a purpose for reading.

pp. 294–295 What can you learn about Leonardo da Vinci by looking at the picture? *(Leonardo liked to draw. He probably liked horses.)* In *Leonardo's Horse,* you will read about a dream Leonardo had and whether it came true.

p. 296 What do see in the picture? *(bicycles, boats, wings, human body)* Leonardo had ideas for many kinds of inventions and art.

DURING READING Follow the Guiding Comprehension routine on pp. 294–303. Have students read along with you while tracking the print or do a choral reading of the selection. Stop every two pages to ask what students have learned so far. Prompt as necessary.

• Why did the duke want da Vinci to create a statue of a horse?
• What was the hardest part about making such a large sculpture?

AFTER READING What have you learned so far? What do you think you will read about tomorrow? Reread sections as needed.

Monitor Progress

Word and Story Reading

If... students have difficulty reading multisyllabic words in the selection,	**then...** have them look for and read meaningful parts in the words or have them chunk words with no recognizable parts.
If... students need practice reading words fluently,	**then...** use the Fluent Word Reading Routine on the DI tab.
If... students have difficulty reading along with the group,	**then...** have them follow along as they listen to the AudioText.

Advanced

1 Extend Vocabulary

🔊 **WORD STRUCTURE** Choose and read a sentence or passage containing a difficult word with identifiable word parts, such as this sentence from p. 303 of *Leonardo's Horse:* "It was shown at one of the duke's special occasions, and it was a sensation." What does the word *sensation* mean? *(a sense of great excitement)* How did you figure out the word's meaning? *(Sensation reminds me of* sense, *which means "to feel." The feeling I have when I see amazing things is excitement.)* Remind students to use the strategy as they read *Leonardo's Horse.*

2 Read *Leonardo's Horse,* pp. 292–303

BEFORE READING In "The Inspiration of Art," you read about how artists get their ideas. Today you will read a biography of Leonardo da Vinci. As you read, think about how artists like da Vinci get their ideas.

Have students write questions about da Vinci's dream in their Strategy Response Logs (p. 292).

CREATIVE THINKING Have students read pp. 292–303 independently. Encourage them to think creatively. For example, ask:

• If you were inspired to create a giant sculpture, what would you create?

AFTER READING Have partners discuss the selection and share their Strategy Response Log entries. Have them record the answers they found to their questions about da Vinci's dream in their Strategy Response Logs (p. 303). Then have students discuss the questions and what they think might happen next. Give students an opportunity to share their thoughts with you.

DAY 2

AudioText

Group Time

ROUTINE

DAY 4

1 Practice Retelling

REVIEW MAIN IDEAS Help students identify the main ideas of *Leonardo's Horse.* List the ideas students mention. Then ask questions to help students differentiate between important and not so important information.

RETELL Using the Retelling Cards, have students work in pairs to retell the important ideas in *Leonardo's Horse.* Show partners how to summarize in as few words as possible. Monitor retelling and prompt students as needed. For example, ask:

- What is this selection mostly about?
- Tell me about the major events in order.
- What did you learn from reading this selection?

If students struggle, model a fluent retelling.

2 Read "Humans with Wings"

BEFORE READING Read the genre information on p. 312. Point out that narrative nonfiction relates facts but sounds like a story. As we read "Humans with Wings," pay attention to the inventors and their unique attempts to fly.

Read the rest of the panel on p. 312. Have students read the title and identify the topic of the selection. *(different inventions to help humans fly)* Ask: How are art and inventing related? *(Inventors can use art to represent their ideas before they build them.)* Was da Vinci more an inventor or an artist?

DURING READING Have students read along with you while tracking the print or do a choral reading of the selection. Stop to discuss difficult vocabulary, such as *gravity, humanpowered,* and *cautious.*

AFTER READING Have students share their reactions to the selection. Then guide them through the Reading Across Texts and Writing Across Texts activities, prompting if necessary.

- What events could be placed in both the *Triumph* and *Tragedy* lists?
- What are some traits that you would expect an inventor to have?

Social Studies in Reading

HUMANS with WINGS
BY ROGER YEPSEN

Narrative Nonfiction

Genre

Text Features

Link to Social Studies

Audio CD **AudioText**

Monitor Progress

Word and Selection Reading

If... students have difficulty reading multisyllabic words in the selection,	**then...** have them look for and read meaningful parts in the words or have them chunk words with no recognizable parts.
If... students have difficulty reading along with the group,	**then...** have them follow along as they listen to the AudioText.

Advanced

ROUTINE

1 Read "Humans with Wings"

CREATIVE THINKING Have students read pp. 312–315 independently. Encourage them to think creatively. For example, ask:

- What are some safety rules or devices the inventors could have used?
- What objects could be used today to build a new flying machine?

AFTER READING Have students meet with you to discuss the selection and Reading Across Texts. Have students do Writing Across Texts independently.

2 Extend Genre Study

RESEARCH Have students use the library and online sources to compare da Vinci's flying machine ideas to existing inventions.

WRITE Have students write a one-page description of how close da Vinci was to creating a successful design.

AudioText

Group Time

ROUTINE

1 Build Background

REINFORCE CONCEPTS Display the Dinosaurs and Paleontology Concept Web. This week's concept is *dinosaurs and paleontology*. Paleontologists are scientists who study animal and plant fossils for information about the past. Discuss the meaning of each word on the web, using the definitions on p. 316l and the Concept Vocabulary routine on p. DI·1.

CONNECT TO READING This week you will read about paleontologists and how they learn about prehistoric life. In "Graveyards of the Dinosaurs," why didn't Paul Sereno get excited when he first found the fossil in the Valley of the Moon in Argentina? *(He thought it was the fossil of a much more common lizard.)*

2 Read Leveled Reader *Paleontology: Digging for Dinosaurs and More*

BEFORE READING Using the Picture Walk routine on p. DI·1, guide students through the text focusing on key concepts and vocabulary. Ask questions such as:

p. 3 These are photographs of two things that paleontologists commonly look for: body fossils and trace fossils. What is the difference between the two kinds of fossils?

pp. 14–15 The drawings on pp. 14–15 show a *Seismosaurus*. Why are the buses part of the illustration? *(to show how long the dinosaur was)* Artists, photographers, and writers often use a known object as a point of reference to compare the size or shape of a different object.

DURING READING Read pp. 3–5 aloud while students track the print. Do a choral reading of pp. 6–9. If students are capable, have them read and discuss the remainder of the book with a partner. Ask: What did you find most interesting about a paleontologist's job?

AFTER READING Encourage pairs of students to discuss the process of finding and rebuilding dinosaur remains as described in the book. We read *Paleontology: Digging for Dinosaurs and More* to understand how scientists learn about the past through fossils. Understanding how paleontologists work will help you understand *The Dinosaurs of Waterhouse Hawkins.*

Leveled Reader
Database
ONLINE
PearsonSuccessNet.com

Monitor Progress

Selection Reading and Comprehension

If... students have difficulty reading the selection with a partner,	**then**... have them follow along as they listen to the Online Leveled Reader Audio.
If... students are unsure of what paleontologists do,	**then**... reread pp. 6–7 and talk about what paleontologists specifically look for and do.

DAY 1

For alternate Leveled Reader lesson plans that teach
🕐 **Fact and Opinion,** 🕐 **Predict,** and **Lesson Vocabulary,** see pp. LR19–LR27.

On-Level

DAY 1 · ROUTINE

1 Build Background

DEVELOP VOCABULARY Write the word *sandstone* and ask students to define it in their own words. *(stone made mostly of compressed sand)* Many dinosaur fossils are found in sandstone because of how they died and got buried. Repeat this activity with the word *expedition* and other words from the Leveled Reader *Searching for Dinosaurs.* Use the Concept Vocabulary routine on p. DI·1 as needed.

2 Read Leveled Reader *Searching for Dinosaurs*

BEFORE READING Have students create two webs to complete as they read, one labeled Field Work: Finding Fossils and the other labeled Animatronics: Bringing Fossils to "Life." This book gives information about paleontologists who search for fossils that will give them information about dinosaurs and about people who work with computers and models of dinosaurs. Add to the webs as you learn about the people and work in each area of discovery.

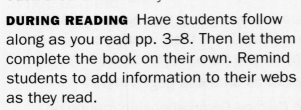

DURING READING Have students follow along as you read pp. 3–8. Then let them complete the book on their own. Remind students to add information to their webs as they read.

AFTER READING Have students share the entries in their webs. Point out that understanding how scientists work with dinosaur fossils will help them as they read tomorrow's selection *The Dinosaurs of Waterhouse Hawkins.*

Advanced

DAY 1 · ROUTINE

1 Read Leveled Reader *What's New with Dinosaur Fossils?*

BEFORE READING Recall the Read Aloud "Graveyards of the Dinosaurs." Why was it important for Paul Sereno to find the fossils of a *Herrerasaurus? (Sereno wanted to chart the entire evolution of dinosaurs, and* Herrerasaurus *was the earliest dinosaur known.)* Today you will read about past and modern paleontologists and their discoveries.

CRITICAL THINKING Have students read the Leveled Reader independently. Encourage them to think about how paleontologists' ideas about dinosaurs have changed over the years. For example, ask:

• Where have dinosaur fossils been found? Why were scientists so surprised that dinosaur fossils were found in Alaska?
• Why do scientists think dinosaurs became extinct? What did scientists in the past think?
• How might birds and dinosaurs be connected?

AFTER READING Have students review the selection to find five or more unfamiliar words and find their meanings. Then have partners write a paragraph about dinosaurs using the words they chose. Have students meet with you to discuss the selection and share the paragraphs they developed.

2 Independent Extension Activity

NOW TRY THIS Assign "Now Try This" on pp. 22–23 of *What's New with Dinosaur Fossils?* for students to work on throughout the week.

Group Time

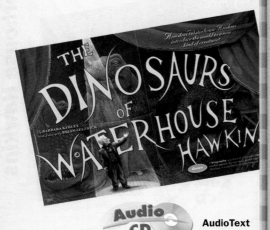

Audio CD AudioText

DAY 3

ROUTINE

1 Reinforce Comprehension

◎ SKILL FACT AND OPINION Have students explain the difference between a statement of fact and a statement of opinion. *(Statements of fact can be proved true or false; statements of opinion can't be proved true or false but can be supported by facts and logic.)* Explain that writers use facts to communicate things like history, and include opinions to make reading more interesting. As you look for statements of fact and opinion as you read, remember that facts can be researched and proved true or false, and opinions are a viewpoint and are often added to make the story more interesting.

Write the following sentences on the board. Have students tell whether the statements are fact or opinion, and tell how they know.

The Crystal Palace Exhibition was wonderful. *(opinion; The word* wonderful *tells how someone might feel about the exhibition. It cannot be proved.)*

The Crystal Palace Exhibition was the first World's Fair. *(fact; This can be proved true.)*

2 Read *The Dinosaurs of Waterhouse Hawkins,* pp. 328–337

BEFORE READING Have students retell what happened in the selection so far. Reread p. 326. Model how to predict as you read. On this page, I see that Waterhouse is presenting his sculptures to the Queen. I think she will be happy to have them in the Crystal Palace. Remind students to predict as they read the rest of *The Dinosaurs of Waterhouse Hawkins.* **◎ STRATEGY Predict**

DURING READING Follow the Guiding Comprehension routine on pp. 328–337. Have students read along with you while tracking the print or do a choral reading. Stop every two pages to ask students what has happened so far. Prompt as necessary.

• Why did Waterhouse need to take so many steps to recreate the life-size dinosaur?
• Why did Waterhouse want to impress the scientists?
• What do you think it would have been like to eat inside the dinosaur's head?

AFTER READING How did people react to the dinosaurs when the Crystal Palace opened? Why do you think they reacted this way? Reread with students for comprehension as needed. Tell them that tomorrow they will read "A Model Scientist," an interview with a modern artist who builds dinosaur models.

Monitor Progress

Word and Selection Reading

If...	then...
If... students have difficulty reading multisyllabic words in the selection,	**then...** have them look for and read meaningful parts in the words or have them chunk words with no recognizable parts.
If... students have difficulty reading along with the group,	**then...** have them follow along as they listen to the AudioText.

Advanced

1 Extend Comprehension

SKILL FACT AND OPINION Ask students to look at the story to find statements of fact and opinion. Ask students to explain how they can identify statements as fact or opinion.

STRATEGY PREDICT Have students think about the events so far in *The Dinosaurs of Waterhouse Hawkins.* Have students predict what they think might happen next and explain why they think so.

• How do you think other scientists will react to the dinosaur sculptures?

2 Read *The Dinosaurs of Waterhouse Hawkins,* pp. 328–337

BEFORE READING Have students recall what has happened in the selection so far. Remind them to identify which parts are fact and which are opinion and to make predictions about the passage as they read the remainder of *The Dinosaurs of Waterhouse Hawkins.*

PROBLEM SOLVING Have students read pp. 328–337 independently. Encourage them to problem solve. For example, ask students:

• How would you go about locating and digging up the pieces of Waterhouse's dinosaurs buried in New York City's Central Park?

AFTER READING Have students complete the Strategy Response Log activity (p. 336). Then have them write a summary of the passage. Give students an opportunity to meet with you as they write the summary to discuss the selection.

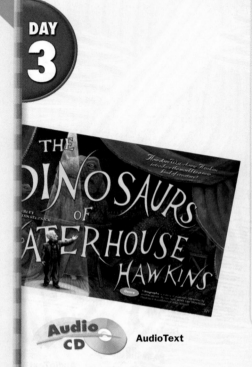

AudioText

The Dinosaurs of Waterhouse Hawkins

Group Time

DAY 5

Paleontology: Digging for Dinosaurs and More

Leveled Reader Database ONLINE

PearsonSuccessNet.com

Strategic Intervention

ROUTINE

1 Reread for Fluency

MODEL Tell students that good readers read with different phrasing so words and groups of words make sense. Punctuation clues the reader where to pause. Then model, reading aloud pp. 6–7 of the Leveled Reader *Paleontology: Digging for Dinosaurs and More.* Pause at the ends of phrases and at signals such as commas and end punctuation to demonstrate phrasing. Then reread the same pages in an expressionless monotone. Discuss how proper phrasing made the first reading easier to understand.

PRACTICE Have students reread passages from *Paleontology: Digging for Dinosaurs and More* with a partner or individually. Encourage students to self-correct. For optimal fluency, they should reread three or four times. As students read, monitor fluency and provide corrective feedback. Students in this group are assessed in Weeks 2 and 4.

2 Retell Leveled Reader *Paleontology: Digging for Dinosaurs and More*

Model how to use skimming to retell the events on pp. 3–7. Then ask students to retell *Paleontology: Digging for Dinosaurs and More*, skimming the book. Prompt them as needed.

- What is this section mostly about?
- What did you learn from reading this selection?

Monitor Progress

Fluency

If... students have difficulty reading fluently,	then... provide additional fluency practice by pairing nonfluent readers with fluent ones.

For alternate Leveled Reader lesson plans that teach
🔄 **Fact and Opinion,** 🔄 **Predict,** and **Lesson Vocabulary,** see pp. LR19–LR27.

On-Level

DAY 5

ROUTINE

① Reread for Fluency

MODEL Tell students that good readers use phrasing to make words and groups of words clear. In *Searching for Dinosaurs,* there are many complex sentences that need proper phrasing. Then model phrasing, reading p. 4 of the Leveled Reader *Searching for Dinosaurs.* Discuss how the punctuation gave you clues about when to pause.

PRACTICE Have students reread passages from *Searching for Dinosaurs* with a partner or individually. Remind them to self-correct if they misread or skip a word. For optimal fluency, students should reread three or four times. As students read, monitor fluency and provide corrective feedback. Assess the fluency of students in this group using p. 345a.

② Retell Leveled Reader *Searching for Dinosaurs*

Have students use heads as a guide to summarize important facts they learned from each section of the book. Prompt as needed.

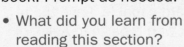

• What did you learn from reading this section?
• What was the author trying to teach us?

Advanced

DAY 5

ROUTINE

① Reread for Fluency

PRACTICE Have students reread passages from the Leveled Reader *What's New with Dinosaur Fossils?* with a partner or individually. As students read, monitor fluency and provide corrective feedback. If students read fluently on the first reading, they do not need to reread three to four times. Students in this group were assessed in Week 1.

② Revisit Leveled Reader *What's New with Dinosaur Fossils?*

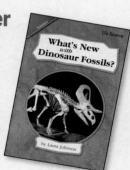

RETELL Have students retell the Leveled Reader *What's New with Dinosaur Fossils?* Remind them to use the heads as prompts for retelling.

NOW TRY THIS Have students complete their new fossil design and the related news article. You may wish to review the articles with students. Have them share their fossils with classmates.

Group Time

Leveled Reader
Database
ONLINE
PearsonSuccessNet.com

DAY 1

① Build Background

REINFORCE CONCEPTS Display the Music and Musicians Concept Web. This week's concept is *music and musicians*. Blues is a style of music that has its roots in the music that enslaved people from Africa brought to America. Discuss the meaning of each word on the web, using the definitions on p. 346l and the Concept Vocabulary routine on p. DI·1.

CONNECT TO READING This week you will read about the history of the musical style known as the blues. In "Bud, Not Buddy," how did the author describe the music? *(The music sounded like a dark storm.)*

② Read Leveled Reader *Roots of the Blues*

BEFORE READING Using the Picture Walk routine on p. DI·1, guide students through the text focusing on key concepts and vocabulary. Ask questions such as:

p. 4 What do you notice about the West African banjo compared to the North American banjo? *(It is much smaller.)* Yes, musical entertainers called *griots* traveled from village to village in Africa playing music on these kinds of banjos. The small banjo was easy to carry as they traveled.

p. 8 Why do you think one of these pictures is a photograph and one is a drawing? *(The photograph is of present times and the drawing was done before there were cameras.)* Yes, the pictures show two different times, but some of the songs these two groups sang are the same. These songs played an important role in blues music.

DURING READING Read pp. 3–5 aloud while students track the print. Do a choral reading of pp. 6–9. If students are capable, have them read and discuss the remainder of the book with a partner. Ask: For how long have people been playing and listening to blues music?

AFTER READING Encourage pairs of students to discuss the instruments used by blues musicians and how these instruments are used in other styles of music. We read *Roots of the Blues* to understand the origins of this style of music. Understanding the music and its history will help you as you read "Mahalia Jackson."

Monitor Progress

Selection Reading and Comprehension

If... students have difficulty reading the selection with a partner,	**then**... have them follow along as they listen to the Online Leveled Reader Audio.
If... students have difficulty relating music to geography,	**then**... reread pp. 14–15 and point out the locations on the map as you read the passage.

For alternate Leveled Reader lesson plans that teach
🔵 **Main Idea,** 🔵 **Graphic Organizers,** and **Lesson Vocabulary,** see pp. LR28–LR36.

On-Level

DAY 1

1 Build Background

DEVELOP VOCABULARY Write the word *blended* and ask students to define it and give examples of some things that are blended. *(mixed together)* Repeat this activity with the word *released* and other words from the Leveled Reader *Legends of the Blues.* Use the Concept Vocabulary routine on p. DI·1 as needed.

2 Read Leveled Reader *Legends of the Blues*

BEFORE READING Have students create a three-column chart to complete as they read. This book gives information about famous blues musicians. Complete the chart with the first column having the names of the musicians discussed; the second column having what instrument, if any, that they played; and the third having the time period they were most active in blues music. As you find information during your reading, add important facts to your chart.

DURING READING Have students follow along as you read pp. 3–9. Then let them complete the book on their own. Remind students to add information to their three-column chart as they read.

AFTER READING Have students share the entries in their charts. Point out that knowing about some famous blues musicians will help as they read tomorrow's selection "Mahalia Jackson."

Advanced

DAY 1

1 Read Leveled Reader *Music Gets the Blue*

BEFORE READING Recall the Read Aloud "Bud, Not Buddy." What types of instruments did the musicians have? *(piano, horn, drum, bass)* Today you will read about how the blues has influenced popular music.

PROBLEM SOLVING Have students read the Leveled Reader independently. Encourage them to think of the problems that early blues musicians would have faced. For example, ask:

- What sorts of challenges do you think early African American blues musicians would have experienced when trying to perform?
- What problems do you think early blues music might have told about?
- How might blues music be different today if the early blues musicians had not been able to overcome these problems?

AFTER READING Have students review the selection to list five or more unfamiliar words and then find their meanings. Then have students, working with partners, write lyrics to a short song using these words. Have students meet with you to discuss the selection and share the songs that they wrote.

2 Independent Extension Activity

NOW TRY THIS Assign "Now Try This" on pp. 22–23 of *Music Gets the Blues* for students to work on throughout the week.

Mahalia Jackson

Group Time

ROUTINE

DAY 2

Audio CD AudioText

1 Word Study/Phonics

LESSON VOCABULARY Use p. 348b to review the meanings of *appreciate, barber, choir, released, religious, slavery,* and *teenager.* Students can practice saying all of the words. Have individuals read the words from word cards.

DECODING MULTISYLLABIC WORDS Write *directed* and model how to decode when there are meaningful word parts. First I ask myself if I see any parts that I know. I see *direct* at the beginning of the word, and the suffix *-ed* at the end. I know that in music *direct* means "to lead." The suffix *-ed* tells me that the word is past tense. So I think *directed* means "led."

Use the Multisyllabic Word routine on p. DI·1 to help students read these other words from "Mahalia Jackson": *reputation, posthumously,* and *expressive.* Be sure students understand the meanings of words such as *reputation* and *expressive.*

Use *Strategies for Word Analysis*, Lesson 14, with students who have difficulty mastering word analysis and need practice with decodable text.

2 Read "Mahalia Jackson," pp. 350–353

BEFORE READING Yesterday we read about how blues musicians work together to make great music. Today we will read a true story about a singer who was influenced by the blues.

Using the Picture Walk routine on p. DI·1, guide students through the text, asking questions such as those listed below. Then read the question on p. 350. Together, set a purpose for reading.

pp. 350–351 Mahalia Jackson is singing in this picture. What does her expression tell you? *(She probably sings with a lot of emotion.)*

pp. 352–353 What does the style of the artwork in "Mahalia Jackson" tell you about blues music? *(Blues music is colorful and has a message.)*

DURING READING Follow the Guiding Comprehension routine on pp. 352–353. Have students read along with you while tracking the print or do a choral reading of the selection. Then ask what students have learned so far. Prompt as necessary.

- How is blues a feeling?
- What does "The blues is life" mean?

AFTER READING What have you learned in the passage so far? What do you think you will read about tomorrow? Reread sections of the passage with students for comprehension as needed.

Monitor Progress

Word and Story Reading

If... students have difficulty reading multisyllabic words in the selection,	**then...** have them look for and read meaningful parts in the words or have them chunk words with no recognizable parts.
If... students need practice reading words fluently,	**then...** use the Fluent Word Reading Routine on the DI tab.
If... students have difficulty reading along with the group,	**then...** have them follow along as they listen to the AudioText.

Advanced

ROUTINE

1 Extend Vocabulary

CONTEXT CLUES Choose and read a sentence or passage containing a synonym or an antonym for a word in the sentence or a word defined in a sentence, such as this sentence from p. 6 of *Music Gets the Blues:* "The enslaved plantation workers sang not only call-and-response work songs, but also religious songs, called *spirituals.*" What does the word *spirituals* mean? *(Spirituals are religious songs.)* How did you figure out the word's meaning? *(The word* spirituals *is defined in the sentence, set off by a comma and the word* called.) Remind students to use this strategy as they read "Mahalia Jackson."

2 Read "Mahalia Jackson," pp. 350–353

BEFORE READING In "Bud, Not Buddy," you read about a group of blues musicians playing together. Today you will read a biography of a singer named Mahalia Jackson. As you read, think about how blues music might make you feel.

Have students write a prediction about what they will read in the passage in their Strategy Response Logs (p. 350). Tell them to look for answers during reading and to record other questions as they arise.

CRITICAL/CREATIVE THINKING Have students read pp. 350–353 independently. Encourage them to think critically while reading. Then ask them to answer questions such as the following:

- How might spirituals have been passed on to people in Mahalia Jackson's time?
- How has what you've read helped you understanding why blues music was important to slaves?

AFTER READING Have partners discuss the selection and share their Strategy Response Log entries. Then have students discuss their predictions and what they think blues music has to do with Mahalia Jackson. Give students an opportunity to share their thoughts with you and with the group.

DAY 2

AudioText

Mahalia Jackson
Group Time

ROUTINE

DAY
3

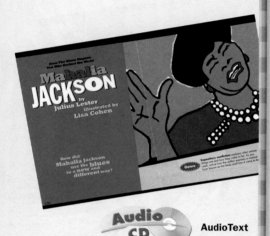

Audio CD   AudioText

1 Reinforce Comprehension

SKILL MAIN IDEA Have students define *main idea*. *(The main idea is the most important idea or concept.)* Explain that readers who look for main ideas remember more about what they read. When you look for the main idea as you read, you will understand what the writer is trying to tell you.

Write the following paragraph on the board. Have students identify the main idea and explain how they decided what the main idea was.

Mahalia Jackson was a famous gospel singer, but she influenced many different types of music. She was even inducted into the Rock and Roll Hall of Fame in 1977. Early rock musician Little Richard claims that she is one of his biggest influences. Jackson herself said that rock and roll was stolen right out of church music. *(Students should identify the first sentence as the main idea.)*

2 Read "Mahalia Jackson," pp. 354–357

BEFORE READING Have students retell the main ideas in the selection so far. Ask: What questions do you have about what you think will happen in the passage? Reread p. 353. Model how to predict as you read. On this page, I see that the author wants us to understand why people sing the blues. I think that Mahalia Jackson may have had reason to sing the blues too. I will find out if I am right as I keep reading. Remind students to predict as they read the rest of "Mahalia Jackson." **STRATEGY Predict**

DURING READING Follow the Guiding Comprehension routine on pp. 354–357. Have students read along with you while tracking the print or do a choral reading. Stop every two pages to ask students what has happened so far. Prompt as necessary.

- What happened first?
- What did you learn about Mahalia Jackson?

AFTER READING What does the author think of Mahalia Jackson's ability to sing? Reread with students for comprehension as needed. Tell them that tomorrow they will read two poems about making music.

Monitor Progress

Word and Selection Reading

If... students have difficulty reading multisyllabic words in the selection,	**then...** have them look for and read meaningful parts in the words or have them chunk words with no recognizable parts.
If... students have difficulty reading along with the group,	**then...** have them follow along as they listen to the AudioText.

Advanced

ROUTINE

1 Extend Comprehension

SKILL MAIN IDEA Ask students to look at the passage to find the main idea of different paragraphs. Ask students to give important details that support the main ideas.

STRATEGY PREDICT Have students think about the events so far in "Mahalia Jackson." Have students predict what they think the author will talk about next and explain why they think so.

• How do you think blues music will influence Mahalia Jackson?

2 Read "Mahalia Jackson," pp. 354–357

BEFORE READING Have students recall the main ideas in the passage so far. Remind them to look for the main ideas in the paragraphs they read and to make predictions about the passage as they read the remainder of "Mahalia Jackson."

PROBLEM SOLVING Have students read pp. 354–357 independently. Encourage them to think critically. For example, ask students:

• Why do you think so many blues musicians also sang gospel music?

AFTER READING Have students complete the Strategy Response Log activity (p. 356). Then have them write a sentence to either confirm or refute each of their predictions. Give students an opportunity to meet with you to discuss the selection and their sentences about their predictions.

Audio CD   AudioText

Mahalia Jackson
Group Time

Audio CD AudioText

ROUTINE

1 Practice Retelling

REVIEW MAIN IDEAS Help students identify the main ideas in "Mahalia Jackson." List the ideas students mention. Then ask questions to help students differentiate between essential and nonessential information.

RETELL Using the Retelling Cards, have students work in pairs to retell the important ideas. Show partners how to summarize in as few words as possible. Monitor retelling and prompt students as needed. For example, ask:

Grade 5
Retelling Cards
PEARSON
Scott Foresman

• What was this selection mostly about?
• What did you learn from reading this selection?
• Why do you think the author wrote this selection?

If students struggle, model a fluent retelling.

2 Read *Perfect Harmony*

BEFORE READING Read the genre information on p. 360. Point out that the two poems that are part of *Perfect Harmony* are not organized in rhyming stanzas but use words to create interesting sounds and rhythm. As we read *Perfect Harmony*, think about why the poet might have arranged the words the way he did.

Read the rest of the panel on p. 360. Have students read the titles and identify the topics of the poems. *(getting ready to sing and then singing)* Ask: How does the way the poet has arranged the words add to your feelings about the poem? *(Accept reasonable answers.)*

DURING READING Have students read along with you while tracking the print or do a choral reading of the selection. Stop to discuss difficult vocabulary, such as *focus, erupt,* and *channel.*

AFTER READING Have students share their reactions to the poems. Then guide them through the Reading Across Texts and Writing Across Texts activities, prompting if necessary.

• How do singers use other parts of their bodies while singing?
• What words would you use to describe Mahalia Jackson and the Harlem Boys Choir?

Monitor Progress

Word and Poetry Reading

If... students have difficulty reading multisyllabic words in the poems,	then... have them look for and read meaningful parts in the words or have them chunk words with no recognizable parts.
If... students have difficulty reading along with the group,	then... have them follow along as they listen to the AudioText.

Advanced

1 Read *Perfect Harmony*

CREATIVE THINKING Have students read pp. 360–363 independently. Encourage them to think creatively. For example, ask:

- What words could you use to describe yourself when you are doing something you love to do?
- What kinds of music give you feelings similar to those described in these poems?

AFTER READING Have students meet with you to discuss the poems and Reading Across Texts. Have students do Writing Across Texts independently.

2 Extend Genre Study

RESEARCH Have students use the library and online sources to research their favorite musical group or singer.

WRITE Have students write a poem, either free verse or having rhyme and rhythm, that describes how their favorite song by their favorite musical group or singer makes them feel.

AudioText

Group Time

ROUTINE

DAY 1

ONLINE

PearsonSuccessNet.com

① Build Background

REINFORCE CONCEPTS Display the Special Effects Concept Web. This week's concept is *special effects*. Special effects are visual or sound devices that filmmakers use to make things that aren't real appear to look real or sound real. Discuss the meaning of each word on the web, using the definitions on p. 364l and the Concept Vocabulary routine on p. DI · 1.

CONNECT TO READING This week you will read about how filmmakers use special effects in movies. In "The Making of the Lord of the Rings," how did the director make the set look like Middle Earth? *(The director used digital effects and props.)*

② Read Leveled Reader *The Art of Makeup: Going Behind the Mask*

BEFORE READING Using the Picture Walk routine on p. DI · 1, guide students through the text focusing on key concepts and vocabulary. Ask questions such as:

p. 7 These photographs show changes in the appearance of an actor. What changes were made in his appearance? *(The actor's hair and face were changed.)*

pp. 13–15 False teeth can change the way an actor looks. What does it seem to take to make false teeth? *(making a mold, then forming the teeth, and then making sure they fit)* Yes. People who have gone to the dentist for a bridge or a crown on broken teeth or teeth that can't receive any more fillings know that this is also the procedure a dentist uses to make an impression of the patient's teeth.

DURING READING Read pp. 4–6 aloud while students track the print. Do a choral reading of pp. 7–11. If students are capable, have them read and discuss the remainder of the book with a partner. Ask: Which kind of special effects makeup did you find most interesting?

AFTER READING Encourage pairs of students to discuss why special effects makeup is so important. We read The *Art of Makeup: Going Behind the Mask* to understand how makeup can be used for creating special effects in films. Understanding one type of special effects will help you understand *Special Effects in Film and Television*.

Monitor Progress

Selection Reading and Comprehension

If... students have difficulty reading the selection with a partner,	then... have them follow along as they listen to the Online Leveled Reader Audio.
If... students have difficulty understanding the concept of three-dimensional makeup,	then... reread pp. 7–8 and talk about the pictures as they correspond to the text.

For alternate Leveled Reader lesson plans that teach
🔊 **Graphic Sources,** 🔊 **Prior Knowledge,** and
Lesson Vocabulary, see pp. LR37–LR45.

On-Level

ROUTINE

DAY 1

❶ Build Background

DEVELOP VOCABULARY Write the word *illusion* and ask students to define it in their own words. *(something that appears different from what it actually is)* What are some illusions you have seen or know about? Repeat this activity with the word *time-consuming* and other words from the Leveled Reader *Very Special Effects: Computers in Filmmaking.* Use the Concept Vocabulary routine on p. DI·1 as needed.

❷ Read Leveled Reader *Very Special Effects: Computers in Filmmaking*

BEFORE READING Have students create a web to complete as they read. This book gives information about how computers are used to make films. Complete the web with words and ideas related to making movies with computers. As you find ideas during your reading, add them to your web.

DURING READING Have students follow along as you read pp. 3–7. Then let them complete the book on their own. Remind students to add words and ideas to their webs as they read.

AFTER READING Have students share the entries in their webs. Point out that knowing the different ways that filmmakers use computers to make movies will help as they read tomorrow's selection *Special Effects in Film and Television.*

Advanced

ROUTINE

DAY 1

❶ Read Leveled Reader *Hollywood Special Effects*

BEFORE READING Recall the Read Aloud "The Making of *The Lord of the Rings.*" What interesting special effects did the filmmakers use? *(skin suits, hobbit feet, miniature props)* Today you will read about other special effects that filmmakers use.

PROBLEM SOLVING Have students read the Leveled Reader independently. Encourage them to think of the problems that filmmakers have faced in the past. For example, ask:

- What challenges would actors have faced when changing from acting in silent films to acting in "talkies," or movies with sound?
- What problems could occur in filming when the film uses matte paintings and models?
- What older types of special effects can be replaced today by special effects created with computers?

AFTER READING Have students review the selection to find five or more unfamiliar words and then find their meanings. Then have students, working with a partner, create a poster for a new film using the words they selected. Have students meet with you to discuss the selection and share the poster they created.

❷ Independent Extension Activity

NOW TRY THIS Assign "Now Try This" on pp. 22–23 of *Hollywood Special Effects* for students to work on throughout the week.

Group Time

Strategic Intervention

ROUTINE

1 Word Study/Phonics

LESSON VOCABULARY Use p. 366b to review the meanings of *background, landscape, miniature, prehistoric,* and *reassembled.* Students can practice saying all of the words. Have individuals read the words from word cards.

DECODING MULTISYLLABIC WORDS Write *respirator,* saying the word as you write it. Then model how to chunk the word parts. I see a chunk at the beginning: *res.* I see a part in the middle: *pir,* and another part: *a.* I see a chunk at the end: *tor.* I say each chunk slowly: *res pir a tor.* I say the chunks smoothly to make a whole word: *respirator.* A *respirator* is "a device that helps a person breathe."

Use the Multisyllabic Word routine on p. DI·1 to help students read these other words from *Special Effects in Film and Television: inhabit, foreground, reality, prototype,* and *lighting.* Be sure students understand the meanings of words such as *reality* and *prototype.*

Use *Strategies for Word Analysis,* Lesson 15, with students who have difficulty mastering word analysis and need practice with decodable text.

2 Read *Special Effects in Film and Television,* pp. 368–373

BEFORE READING Yesterday we read about how filmmakers use makeup to change an actor's appearance. Today we will read about some other types of special effects.

Using the Picture Walk routine on p. DI·1, guide students through the text, asking questions such as those listed below. Then read the question on p. 369. Together, set a purpose for reading.

p. 368–369 What do the two halves of the picture on p. 368 reveal? Using what the picture on p. 368 shows, what do you think might be under the "skin" of the creature in the picture on p. 369?

pp. 371–373 Why are the pictures on pp. 371–373 numbered? Yes, they are steps a special effects team follows to build a setting.

DURING READING Follow the Guiding Comprehension routine on pp. 370–373. Have students read along with you while tracking the print or do a choral reading of the selection. Stop every two pages to ask what students have learned so far. Prompt as necessary.

• What did you learn about the cameras needed to film miniatures?
• What did you learn that you didn't know about special effects?

AFTER READING What have you learned so far? What do you think you will learn about tomorrow? **Reread passages as needed.**

DAY 2

AudioText

Monitor Progress

Word and Story Reading

If...	then...
If... students have difficulty reading multisyllabic words in the selection,	**then...** have them look for and read meaningful parts in the words or have them chunk words with no recognizable parts.
If... students need practice reading words fluently,	**then...** use the Fluent Word Reading Routine on the DI tab.
If... students have difficulty reading along with the group,	**then...** have them follow along as they listen to the AudioText.

Advanced

DAY 2

1 Extend Vocabulary

WORD STRUCTURE Choose and read a sentence or passage containing a difficult word with identifiable word parts, such as this sentence from p. 9 of *Hollywood Special Effects:* "Talkies allowed actors to act in a far more natural manner, as they no longer needed to overcompensate for the lack of sound." Write *overcompensate* on the board. What is this word? How can you figure out its meaning? *(To* compensate *means "to make up for something that is missing." Over means "more than necessary." To overcompensate is to do more than is necessary to make up for something missing or lacking.)* Remind students to use the strategy as they read *Special Effects in Film and Television.*

2 Read *Special Effects in Film and Television,* pp. 368–373

BEFORE READING In "The Making of *The Lord of the Rings,*" you read about a movie that needed many kinds of special effects. Today you will read a more detailed explanation of how some special effects are made. As you read, think about movies that you may have seen that used special effects.

Have students write notes about different special effects techniques they know about in their Strategy Response Logs (p. 368). They will use their notes to summarize the passage to this point on p. 373.

CRITICAL THINKING Have students read pp. 368–373 independently. Encourage them to think critically. For example, ask:

• How might computers be used in making concept models?

AFTER READING Have partners discuss the selection and share their Strategy Response Log entries. Have them record their notes about the passage in their Strategy Response Logs (p. 373). Then have students discuss their notes with classmates. Give students an opportunity to share their notes with you.

Audio CD AudioText

Group Time

DAY 3

Audio CD   AudioText

Strategic Intervention

ROUTINE

1 Reinforce Comprehension

SKILL GRAPHIC SOURCES Have students define a *graphic source*. *(an illustration or design that explains)* Explain that readers can look at graphic sources in a passage to better understand what they are reading about. When you take time to look at graphics, you see what the writer is saying in a visual way.

Write the following sentences on the board. Have students describe a graphic source that would help make the meaning clearer.

In movies that combine live actors with animated characters, filmmakers use a "green screen." *(Possible answer: A photograph depicting an actor in front of a green screen.)* A computer places the animation in the place of the green screen later. *(Possible answer: A photograph of a programmer placing the animation on the green screen.)*

2 Read *Special Effects in Film and Television,* pp. 374–377

BEFORE READING Have students retell what they have learned from the selection so far. Ask: What questions do you have about the information in the selection? Reread p. 373. Model how to use prior knowledge as you read. In Step 7, the author mentions that there are lights to make the scene look more realistic. I know that when I take pictures with my camera, the flash can make a big difference in how a picture comes out. Using these lights while making a film may be like using the flash on my camera. Remind students to use prior knowledge as they read the rest of *Special Effects in Film and Television.* **STRATEGY Prior Knowledge**

DURING READING Follow the Guiding Comprehension routine on pp. 374–377. Have students read along with you while tracking the print or do a choral reading. Stop every two pages to ask students the main ideas so far. Prompt as necessary.

- What did you learn about the dinosaur model?
- What was foam used for?
- What did you learn that you didn't already know about directors using models while making a film?

AFTER READING What kind of special effects most interested you? Reread passages with students for comprehension as needed. Tell them that tomorrow they will read "Searching for Animation," an explanation of how to use Internet search engines.

Monitor Progress

Word and Selection Reading

If... students have difficulty reading multisyllabic words in the selection,	**then...** have them look for and read meaningful parts in the words or have them chunk words with no recognizable parts.
If... students have difficulty reading along with the group,	**then...** have them follow along as they listen to the AudioText.

Advanced

ROUTINE

1 Extend Comprehension

SKILL GRAPHIC SOURCES Ask students to look at the passage to find the different graphic sources that were included. Ask students to explain how the graphics helped their understanding of the reading.

STRATEGY PRIOR KNOWLEDGE Have students think about what they already knew about filmmaking and special effects before reading the selection.

• What did you already know about filmmaking and special effects that helped your understanding of the passage so far?

2 Read *Special Effects in Film and Television,* pp. 374–377

BEFORE READING Have students recall the main ideas in the selection so far. Remind them to look at the graphic sources included in the selection and to use their prior knowledge about special effects and films as they read the remainder of *Special Effects in Film and Television.*

CREATIVE THINKING Have students read pp. 374–377 independently. Encourage them to think creatively. For example, ask students:

• What other common objects could be used to make the landscape?

AFTER READING Have students complete the Strategy Response Log activity (p. 376). Then have them write a summary of the passage. Have students meet with you to discuss the selection and their summaries.

DAY 3

Audio CD AudioText

Group Time

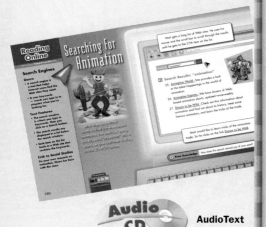

Audio CD AudioText

Strategic Intervention

ROUTINE

1 Practice Retelling

REVIEW MAIN IDEAS Help students identify the main ideas in *Special Effects in Film and Television.* List the ideas students mention. Then ask questions to help students differentiate between essential and nonessential information.

RETELL Using the Retelling Cards, have students work with partners to retell the important ideas. Show partners how to summarize in as few words as possible. Monitor retelling and prompt students as needed. For example, ask:

Grade 5
Retelling Cards
PEARSON
Scott Foresman

• What was this selection mostly about?
• Tell me the steps the filmmakers follow.
• What did you learn from reading this selection?

If students struggle, model a fluent retelling.

2 Read "Searching for Animation"

BEFORE READING Read the genre information on p. 380. Point out that there are different types of search engines that help people locate information on the Internet. As we read "Searching for Animation," think about how you can use search engines to find information about other topics that you might need to research or that might interest you.

Read the rest of the panel on p. 380. Have students read the title and identify the topic of this selection. *(using search engines to find information)* Ask: How do search engines help you use the Internet? *(They help me look for the information I need.)* What can you use a search engine for? *(accept reasonable answers)*

DURING READING Have students read along with you while tracking the print or do a choral reading of the selection. Stop to discuss difficult vocabulary, such as *scroll, wealth,* and *optical.*

AFTER READING Have students share their reactions to the passage. Then guide them through the Reading Across Texts and Writing Across Texts activities, prompting if necessary.

• What is a flip book?
• What trick is common both in filmmaking and in reading your responses from an Internet search?

Monitor Progress

Word and Selection Reading

If... students have difficulty reading multisyllabic words in the selection,	then... have them look for and read meaningful parts in the words or have them chunk words with no recognizable parts.
If... students have difficulty reading along with the group,	then... have them follow along as they listen to the AudioText.

Advanced

ROUTINE

1 Read "Searching for Animation"

CRITICAL THINKING Have students read pp. 380–383 independently. Encourage them to think critically. For example, ask:

- What would happen if Matt searched for "animation world" instead of just "animation"?
- What ways could Matt use to find more information about animation and optical illusions?

AFTER READING Have students meet with you to discuss the selection and Reading Across Texts. Have students do Writing Across Texts independently.

2 Extend Genre Study

RESEARCH Have students use an online search engine to find more articles about animation and film.

WRITE Have students write a paragraph describing a new technique in film animation.

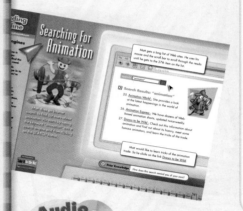

 AudioText

Group Time

ONLINE
PearsonSuccessNet.com

DAY 5

ROUTINE

1 Reread for Fluency

MODEL Tell students that good readers read with different tempo and rate when the passage has important information or when the listener needs time to reflect on the words. New and complicated concepts may require a slower tempo. Then model, reading aloud p. 11 of the Leveled Reader *The Art of Makeup: Going Behind the Mask*. Pause after each step to be sure students have time to understand what is described. Then reread the same page in an even monotone voice. Point out how important concepts are lost in that kind of reading.

PRACTICE Have students reread passages from *The Art of Makeup: Going Behind the Mask* with a partner or individually. Encourage students to self-correct. For optimal fluency, they should reread three or four times. As students read, monitor fluency and provide corrective feedback. Assess any students you have not yet checked during this unit.

2 Retell Leveled Reader *The Art of Makeup: Going Behind the Mask*

Model how to use skimming to retell the ideas on pp. 4–6. Then ask students to retell *The Art of Makeup: Going Behind the Mask*, skimming the selection. Prompt them as needed.

- What is this section about?
- What was the author trying to teach us?
- What did you learn from reading this selection?

Monitor Progress

Fluency

If... students have difficulty reading fluently,	**then...** provide additional fluency practice by pairing nonfluent readers with fluent ones.

Main Idea

Determining the main idea in a text helps readers distinguish between important and less important information. When students can correctly identify the main idea, they understand the gist of what they read. Use this routine to teach main idea.

1 EXPLAIN ITS USE

Explain that finding the main idea is an important tool in helping students understand and remember what they read.

2 DEFINE THE TERMS

Explain that the topic is the subject, what the selection is all about. The main idea is the most important idea about the topic. The main idea can be stated in a sentence.

3 MODEL FINDING THE MAIN IDEA

Read a nonfiction paragraph with a stated main idea. Have students identify the topic by asking: *What is this paragraph about?* Then model how you determine the main idea.

4 FINDING SUPPORTING DETAILS

Explain that supporting details are small pieces of information that tell more about the main idea. Model how to identify supporting details.

5 USE A GRAPHIC ORGANIZER

Have students find the main idea and supporting details in a nonfiction selection. Use a main idea chart to help students organize their thoughts.

Choose passages carefully to practice this succession of skills:

- Paragraphs: stated main idea (Grades 2–6); implied main idea (Grades 3–6)

- Articles: stated main idea (Grades 4–6); implied main idea (Grades 4–6)

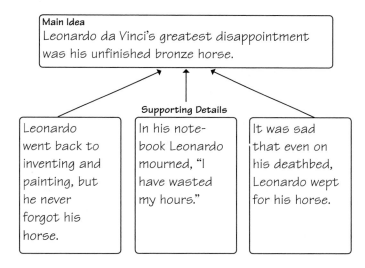

▲ **Graphic Organizer** 17

Research on Main Idea

"When great readers are reading this stuff that has so many ideas in it, they have to listen to that mental voice tell them which words, which sentences or paragraphs, and which ideas are most important. Otherwise they won't get it."

Ellin Oliver Keene and Susan Zimmermann,
Mosaic of Thought

Keene, Ellin Oliver, and Susan Zimmermann. *Mosaic of Thought: Teaching Comprehension in a Reader's Workshop.* Heinemann, 1997, p. 86.

Fact and Opinion

When students can identify statements of fact and opinion, they are able to make critical judgments concerning what they hear, read, and write. Use this routine to help students recognize statements of fact and statements of opinion and distinguish between them.

1 DEFINE FACT AND OPINION

Explain that a statement of fact can be proved true or false. A statement of opinion is someone's judgment, belief, or way of thinking about something. It cannot be proved true or false, but it can be supported or explained.

2 GIVE EXAMPLES

Write three statements on the board:

Charlotte's Web *was published in 1952. E. B. White wrote* Charlotte's Web. *You should read* Charlotte's Web.

Ask: *Which sentences are statements of fact? (the first two) How can you tell?* Elicit ways the facts could be verified, such as looking at the book or asking the school librarian. Talk about other ways to check statements of fact (observing, weighing, measuring, asking an expert).

Ask: *Which sentence is a statement of opinion? (the third one)* Point out the judgment word *should.* Explain opinions often contain judgment words such as *should, I think, cute,* and *best.*

3 PROVIDE PRACTICE

- Partners can read nonfiction selections and use a T-chart to list statements of fact and opinion.

- Have small groups read newspaper editorials. Students can list opinions and their supporting arguments.

Facts	Opinions
1. Waterhouse Hawkins sculpted models of animals.	1. The animals that Waterhouse sculpted seemed to come to life through his care and hard work.
2. Waterhouse built models of the dinosaurs he created.	2. Building a model of a dinosaur is like building a house.
3. The dinosaurs were unveiled at the grand opening for the Crystal Palace in 1854.	3. The sights at the Crystal Palace were amazing.

▲ **Graphic Organizer** 25

Research on Fact and Opinion

"Students will—and should—argue about the difference between fact and opinion . . .; they will often dispute one another about inferences . . . . The point of such discussions is to help students sensitize themselves to the kinds of statements they encounter and make them aware of the inferences of others."

Thomas G. Devine,
Teaching Reading Comprehension

Devine, Thomas G. *Teaching Reading Comprehension.* Allyn and Bacon, Inc., 1986.1992, p. 238.

Main Idea

Determining the main idea in a text helps readers distinguish between important and less important information. When students can correctly identify the main idea, they understand the gist of what they read. Use this routine to teach main idea.

1 EXPLAIN ITS USE

Explain that finding the main idea is an important tool in helping students understand and remember what they read.

2 DEFINE THE TERMS

Explain that the topic is the subject, what the selection is all about. The main idea is the most important idea about the topic. The main idea can be stated in a sentence.

3 MODEL FINDING THE MAIN IDEA

Read a nonfiction paragraph with a stated main idea. Have students identify the topic by asking: *What is this paragraph about?* Then model how you determine the main idea.

4 FINDING SUPPORTING DETAILS

Explain that supporting details are small pieces of information that tell more about the main idea. Model how to identify supporting details.

5 USE A GRAPHIC ORGANIZER

Have students find the main idea and supporting details in a nonfiction selection. Use a main idea chart to help students organize their thoughts.

Choose passages carefully to practice this succession of skills:

- Paragraphs: stated main idea (Grades 2–6); implied main idea (Grades 3–6)

- Articles: stated main idea (Grades 4–6); implied main idea (Grades 4–6)

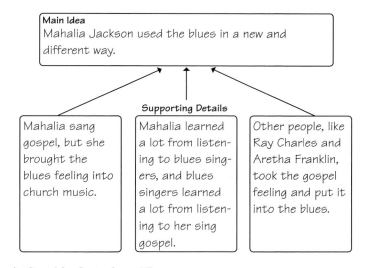

▲ **Graphic Organizer** 17

Research on Main Idea

"When great readers are reading this stuff that has so many ideas in it, they have to listen to that mental voice tell them which words, which sentences or paragraphs, and which ideas are most important. Otherwise they won't get it."

Ellin Oliver Keene and Susan Zimmermann,
Mosaic of Thought

Keene, Ellin Oliver, and Susan Zimmermann. *Mosaic of Thought: Teaching Comprehension in a Reader's Workshop.* Heinemann, 1997, p. 86.

Graphic Sources

Graphic sources can be a valuable aid to readers in previewing and comprehending text. When students interpret and create graphics as they read, they often strengthen their understanding of the text. Use this routine to teach graphic sources.

1 DISCUSS GRAPHIC SOURCES

Explain that a graphic is a way of showing information visually. Graphics can include pictures, charts, graphs, maps, diagrams, schedules, and so on. Graphics often show information from the text in a visual way. They can organize many facts or ideas.

2 USE GRAPHICS TO PREVIEW

Remind students to look for graphics when they preview. Graphics are often a good way to discover what the story or article is about.

3 COMPARE GRAPHICS TO TEXT

Have students compare the text with graphics in a selection and discuss the author's purpose for including graphics. Captions, charts, diagrams, and maps may present information that is nowhere else in the article, or they may help the reader better understand text information.

4 CREATE GRAPHICS

Give students opportunities to create their own pictures, charts, and other graphics to help them organize and understand text information.

5 USE A GRAPHIC ORGANIZER

Have students create a chart from information in a selection. Depending on the content, they may use a two-, three-, four-, or five-column chart.

Details About Landscape Modeling	Details About Reptile Modeling
1. Make a "concept" model.	1. Sculpt each miniature reptile model in clay.
2. Make a larger, more detailed prototype model.	2. Attach each model to a metal stand.
3. Make a base for the full-size model.	3. Add specific details, such as skin and claws.
4. Add landscape details, such as miniature trees and bushes.	4. Spray model with sealer

▲ **Graphic Organizer** 25

Research on Graphic Sources

"Teaching students to organize the ideas that they are reading about in a systematic, visual graph benefits the ability of the students to remember what they read and may transfer, in general, to better comprehension and achievement in Social Studies and Science content areas."

National Reading Panel,
Teaching Children to Read

National Reading Panel. *Teaching Children to Read: Reports of the Subgroups.* National Institute of Child Health & Human Development, National Institutes of Health, 2000, p. 4-45.

Providing students with reading materials they can and want to read is an important step toward developing fluent readers. A running record allows you to determine each student's instructional and independent reading level. Information on how to take a running record is provided on pp. DI·59–DI·60.

Instructional Reading Level

Only approximately 1 in 10 words will be difficult when reading a selection from the Student Edition for students who are at grade level. (A typical fifth-grader reads approximately 120–140 words correct per minute.)

- Students reading at grade level should read regularly from the Student Edition and On-Level Leveled Readers, with teacher support as suggested in the Teacher's Editions.
- Students reading below grade level can read the Strategic Intervention Leveled Readers. Instructional plans can be found in the Teacher's Edition and the Leveled Reader Teaching Guide.
- Students who are reading above grade level can read the Advanced Leveled Readers. Instructional plans can be found in the Teacher's Edition and the Leveled Reader Teaching Guide.

Independent Reading Level

Students should read regularly in independent-level texts in which no more than approximately 1 in 20 words is difficult for the reader. Other factors that make a book easy to read include the student's interest in the topic, the amount of text on a page, how well illustrations support meaning, and the complexity and familiarity of the concepts. Suggested books for self-selected reading are provided for each lesson on p. TR14 in this Teacher's Edition.

Guide students in learning how to self-select books at their independent reading level. As you talk about a book with students, discuss the challenging concepts in it, list new words students find in sampling the book, and ask students about their familiarity with the topic. A blackline master to help students evaluate books for independent reading is provided on p. DI·58.

Self-Selected/Independent Reading

While oral reading allows you to assess students' reading level and fluency, independent reading is of crucial importance to students' futures as readers and learners. Students need to develop their ability to read independently for increasing amounts of time.

- Schedule a regular time for sustained independent reading in your classroom. During the year, gradually increase the amount of time devoted to independent reading.
- Encourage students to track the amount of time they read independently and the number of pages they read in a given amount of time. Tracking will help motivate them to gradually increase their duration and speed. Blackline masters for tracking independent reading are provided on pp. DI·58 and TR15.

Choosing a Book for Independent Reading

When choosing a book, story, or article for independent reading, consider these questions:

_____ 1. Do I know something about this topic?

_____ 2. Am I interested in this topic?

_____ 3. Do I like reading this kind of book (fiction, fantasy, biography, or whatever)?

_____ 4. Have I read other things by this author? Do I like this author?

If you say "yes" to at least one of the questions above, continue:

_____ 5. In reading the first page, was only about 1 of every 20 words hard?

If you say "yes," continue:

_____ 6. Does the number of words on a page look about right to me?

If you say "yes," the book or article is probably at the right level for you.

Silent Reading

Record the date, the title of the book or article you read, the amount of time you spent reading, and the number of pages you read during that time.

Date	Title	Minutes	Pages

Taking a Running Record

A running record is an assessment of a student's oral reading accuracy and oral reading fluency. Reading accuracy is based on the number of words read correctly. Reading fluency is based on the reading rate (the number of words correct per minute) and the degree to which a student reads with a "natural flow."

How to Measure Reading Accuracy

1. Choose a grade-level text of about 80 to 120 words that is unfamiliar to the student.
2. Make a copy of the text for yourself. Make a copy for the student or have the student read aloud from a book.
3. Give the student the text and have the student read aloud. (You may wish to record the student's reading for later evaluation.)
4. On your copy of the text, mark any miscues or errors the student makes while reading. See the running record sample on page DI·60, which shows how to identify and mark miscues.
5. Count the total number of words in the text and the total number of errors made by the student. Note: If a student makes the same error more than once, such as mispronouncing the same word multiple times, count it as one error. Self-corrections do not count as actual errors. Use the following formula to calculate the percentage score, or accuracy rate:

$$\frac{\text{Total Number of Words} - \text{Total Number of Errors}}{\text{Total Number of Words}} \times 100 = \text{percentage score}$$

Interpreting the Results

- A student who reads **95–100%** of the words correctly is reading at an **independent level** and may need more challenging text.
- A student who reads **90–94%** of the words correctly is reading at an **instructional level** and will likely benefit from guided instruction.
- A student who reads **89%** or fewer of the words correctly is reading at a **frustrational level** and may benefit most from targeted instruction with lower-level texts and intervention.

How to Measure Reading Rate (wcpm)

1. Follow Steps 1–3 above.
2. Note the exact times when the student begins and finishes reading.
3. Use the following formula to calculate the number of words correct per minute (wcpm):

$$\frac{\text{Total Number of Words Read Correctly}}{\text{Total Number of Seconds}} \times 60 = \text{words correct per minute}$$

Interpreting the Results

An appropriate reading rate for a fifth-grader is 120–140 (wcpm).

Running Record Sample

Running Record Sample

Did you know that every day in cities
across the United States, students like you
are helping others?

Each year in Louisiana, a young [.H.]
student and her younger brother have
gone around collecting stuffed animals
for children who live in a homeless shelter. [the]

In New York City, seventy-six
students from Harlem teamed up with
four Olympic athletes to transform a
run-down park into a playground featuring
a daffodil garden.

And each year in Indiana, a young [every]
student has gone around collecting
hundreds of bundles of baby clothes and [sc]
other baby items. In the fall she delivers
them to a home for mothers who are having
tough times. [/tof/]

—From *Using Special Talents*
On-Level Reader 5.2.1

Symbols

Accurate Reading
The student reads a word correctly.

Hesitation
The student hesitates over a word, and the teacher provides the word. Wait several seconds before telling the student what the word is.

Insertion
The student inserts words or parts of words that are not in the text.

Omission
The student omits words or word parts.

Substitution
The student substitutes words or parts of words for the words in the text.

Self-Correction
The student reads a word incorrectly but then corrects the error. Do not count self-corrections as actual errors. However, noting self-corrections will help you identify words the student finds difficult.

Mispronunciation/Misreading
The student pronounces or reads a word incorrectly.

Running Record Results ▶ **Reading Accuracy** ▶ **Reading Rate—WCPM**

Total Number of Words: **107**

Number of Errors: **5**

$$\frac{107 - 5}{107} \times 100 = 95.327 = 95\%$$

$$\frac{102}{51} \times 60 = 120 = 120 \text{ words correct per minute}$$

Reading Time: **51 seconds**

Accuracy Percentage Score: **95%**

Reading Rate: **120 WCPM**

Teacher Resources

Table of Contents

Read Aloud Overflow **TR1**

Word Lists **TR2**

Handwriting **TR10**

Bibliography for Self-Selected Reading **TR14**

Retelling Assessment **TR16**

Scope and Sequence **TR18**

Index **TR26**

Acknowledgments **TR42**

Graveyards of the Dinosaurs from p. 316m

a talented but very young professor who was leading the first expedition of his life. People thought he was crazy, that his chances of finding such a rare fossil in the middle of the desert were one in a million.

But, he had set out to do it anyway.

Sereno walked back to the group and took another look. It was indeed a *Herrerasaurus*—the most complete skeleton that had ever been found.

Unit 1   Vocabulary Words   Spelling Words

Frindle

Vocabulary Words

acquainted	guaranteed
assignment	procedures
essential	reputation
expanded	worshipped

Short vowel VCCV, VCV

distance	enjoy	husband	regular
method	perhaps	tissue	denim
anger	figure	mustard	
problem	channel	shuttle	
butter	admire	advance	
petals	comedy	drummer	

Thunder Rose

Vocabulary Words

branded	pitch
constructed	resourceful
daintily	thieving
devastation	veins
lullaby	

Long vowel VCV

fever	native	agent	legal
broken	silent	motive	solo
climate	labor	vital	
hotel	spider	acorn	
basic	label	item	
vocal	icon	aroma	

Island of the Blue Dolphins

Vocabulary Words

gnawed	ravine
headland	shellfish
kelp	sinew
lair	

Long vowel digraphs

coast	arrow	crease	complain
feast	needle	groan	sneeze
speech	charcoal	breeze	
wheat	praise	willow	
Spain	faint	appeal	
paint	maintain	bowling	

Satchel Paige

Vocabulary Words

confidence	unique
fastball	weakness
mocking	windup
outfield	

Adding -ed, -ing

supplied	included	qualified	satisfied
supplying	including	qualifying	satisfying
denied	admitted	identified	
denying	admitting	identifying	
decided	occurred	delayed	
deciding	occurring	delaying	

Shutting Out the Sky

Vocabulary Words

advice	immigrants
advised	luxury
circumstanc-es	newcomer
elbow	peddler
hustled	

Contractions

they're	what'll	wouldn't
you've	doesn't	who've
weren't	hadn't	shouldn't
needn't	could've	who'd
there'd	would've	this'll
they've	should've	couldn't
mustn't	might've	

Unit 2   Vocabulary Words   Spelling Words

Inside Out

Vocabulary Words: caterpillar, cocoon, disrespect, emerge, migrant, sketched, unscrewed

Digraphs th, sh, ch, ph

shovel	establish	shatter	attach
southern	although	ethnic	ostrich
northern	challenge	shiver	
chapter	approach	pharmacy	
hyphen	astonish	charity	
chosen	python	china	

Passage to Freedom

Vocabulary Words: agreement, cable, diplomat, issue, refugees, representatives, superiors, visa

Irregular plurals

staffs	chiefs	quizzes	chefs
ourselves	buffaloes	sheriffs	pianos
pants	flamingos	dominoes	
scissors	beliefs	thieves	
loaves	echoes	measles	
volcanoes	shelves	avocados	

The Ch'i-lin Purse

Vocabulary Words: astonished, behavior, benefactor, distribution, gratitude, procession, recommend, sacred, traditions

Vowel sounds with r

snore	report	repair	volunteer
tornado	prepare	sword	declare
spare	pioneer	ignore	
appear	chair	order	
career	beware	engineer	
square	smear	resort	

Jane Goodall's 10 Ways to Help Save Wildlife

Vocabulary Words: conservation, contribute, enthusiastic, environment, investigation

Final Syllables -en, -an, -el, -le, -il

example	oxygen	fossil	sudden
level	wooden	toboggan	beagle
human	double	veteran	
quarrel	travel	chisel	
scramble	cancel	suburban	
evil	chuckle	single	

The Midnight Ride of Paul Revere

Vocabulary Words: fate, fearless, glimmer, lingers, magnified, somber, steed

Final Syllables -er, -ar, -or

danger	surrender	caterpillar
wander	solar	rumor
tractor	sticker	glimmer
dollar	locker	linger
harbor	helicopter	sensor
eager	pillar	alligator
eraser	refrigerator	

Unit 3	Vocabulary Words		Spelling Words			
Wings for the King	admiringly permit scoundrel	subject worthless	**Schwas**			
			jewel kingdom gasoline factory garage tropical	pajamas estimate tomorrow humidity Chicago bulletin	carnival illustrate elegant census terrific celebrate	operate celery
Leonardo's Horse	achieved architect bronze cannon depressed	fashioned midst philosopher rival	**Compound words**			
			waterproof teaspoon grasshopper homesick barefoot courthouse	earthquake rowboat scrapbook countryside lightweight fishhook	spotlight blindfold whirlpool tablespoon greenhouse	postcard humming- bird thumbtack
The Dinosaurs of Waterhouse Hawkins	erected foundations mold occasion	proportion tidied workshop	**Consonant sounds /j/, /ks/, /sk/, and /s/**			
			excuse scene muscle explore pledge journal	science schedule gigantic scheme Japan excellent	exclaim fascinate ginger scholar scent dodge	smudge schooner
Mahalia Jackson	appreciate barber choir released	religious slavery teenager	**One consonant or two**			
			address college mirror recess committee collect	Mississippi immediate command appreciate announce possess	Tennessee gallop opponent barricade broccoli accomplish	allowance zucchini
Special Effects in Film and Television	background landscape miniature prehistoric reassembled		**Prefixes** *un-, de-, dis*			
			uncover defrost uncomfortable discourage disadvantage unfortunate unfamiliar	disability discomfort deodorant unemployed deflate disbelief	unpredict- able disapprove disappoint unpleasant dehydrated	disqualify undecided

Unit 4 | Vocabulary Words | Spelling Words

Weslandia

Vocabulary Words: blunders, civilization, complex, envy, fleeing, inspired, rustling, strategy

Words from many cultures

khaki	vanilla	cobra	karate
hula	canyon	koala	kiosk
banana	yogurt	barbecue	
ballet	banquet	safari	
waltz	macaroni	buffet	
tomato	polka	stampede	

Stretching Ourselves: Kids With Cerebral Palsy

Vocabulary Words: abdomen, artificial, gait, handicapped, therapist, wheelchair

Prefixes over-, under-, sub-, super-, out-

overlook	underground	submarine	subdivision
underline	overboard	undercover	subhead
subway	undercurrent	overcast	
subset	superstar	outfield	
supermarket	overtime	output	
outlet	supersonic	supernatural	

Exploding Ants: Amazing Facts About How Animals Adapt

Vocabulary Words: critical, enables, mucus, scarce, specialize, sterile

Homophones

cent	whether	tide	course
sent	their	tied	coarse
scent	there	pale	
threw	they're	pail	
through	chili	aloud	
weather	chilly	allowed	

The Stormi Giovanni Club

Vocabulary Words: cavities, combination, demonstrates, episode, profile, strict

Suffixes -ible, -able

sensible	flexible	laughable	responsible
washable	reasonable	sociable	tolerable
available	favorable	allowable	
agreeable	breakable	divisible	
fashionable	convertible	hospitable	
valuable	forgettable	reversible	

The Gymnast

Vocabulary Words: bluish, cartwheels, gymnastics, hesitation, limelight, skidded, somersault, throbbing, wincing

Negative prefixes

invisible	impatient	illogical
illiterate	independent	indefinite
irregular	incorrect	imperfect
irresistible	inactive	immobile
impossible	imperfect	irresponsible
informal	impolite	
illegal	immature	inexpensive

WORD LIST

Unit 5	Vocabulary Words		Spelling Words

The Three-Century Woman

Vocabulary Words: eerie, intersection, pondered, severe, spectacles, withered

Multisyllabic words

elementary	variety	mosaic	centennial
vehicle	literature	tuxedo	curiosity
miniature	elevator	meteorite	
probability	Pennsylvania	fascination	
definition	ravioli	cylinder	
substitute	cafeteria	intermediate	

The Unsinkable Wreck of the R.M.S. *Titanic*

Vocabulary Words: cramped, debris, interior, ooze, robotic, sediment, sonar

Unusual spellings

league	blood	intrigue	subtle
sergeant	vague	villain	disguise
yacht	anxious	cantaloupe	
doubt	foreign	flood	
fatigue	bargain	depot	
debt	condemn	cordial	

Talk with an Astronaut

Vocabulary Words: accomplishments, focus, gravity, monitors, role, specific

Greek word parts

geology	disaster	biosphere	ecology
thermometer	meteorology	thermos	mythology
astronaut	technology	asterisk	
atmosphere	hemisphere	thermostat	
biology	zoology	astronomy	
thermal	sociology	spherical	

Journey to the Center of the Earth

Vocabulary Words: armor, encases, extinct, hideous, plunged, serpent

Latin roots

project	decimal	audit	dejected
audience	injection	decimeter	terrain
decade	December	audition	
territory	reject	audible	
auditorium	eject	decathlon	
terrier	terrace	terrarium	

Ghost Towns of the American West

Vocabulary Words: economic, independence, overrun, scrawled, vacant

Related words

politics	signature	clean
political	arrive	cleanse
major	arrival	resign
majority	inspire	resignation
equal	inspiration	unite
equation	human	unity
sign	humanity	

Unit 6   Vocabulary Words   Spelling Words

At the Beach

algae	lamented
concealed	sea urchins
driftwood	sternly
hammocks	tweezers

Suffixes -ous, -sion, -ion, -ation

famous	nervous	tension	occupation
invention	explanation	humorous	destination
election	various	exhibition	
furious	decision	attraction	
imagination	relaxation	invasion	
education	conversation	creation	

The Mystery of Saint Matthew Island

bleached	scrawny
carcasses	starvation
decay	suspicions
parasites	tundra

Final Syllable -ant, -ent, -ance, -ence

important	absence	confidence	excellence
experience	appearance	conference	persistent
ignorant	intelligent	insurance	
entrance	evidence	ambulance	
difference	pollutant	hesitant	
instance	clearance	consistent	

King Midas and the Golden Touch

adorn	precious
cleanse	realm
lifeless	spoonful

Words with ei and ie

brief	seize	yield	shield
believe	ceiling	deceive	conceited
receive	field	achieve	
leisure	neither	grief	
piece	apiece	niece	
relief	receipt	protein	

The Hindenburg

criticizing	era
cruised	explosion
drenching	hydrogen

Compound words

ice cream	textbook	dead end	cartwheel
a lot	guidelines	password	root beer
keyboard	newspaper	teenager	fingerprint
fairy tale	space shut-tle	skateboard	
horseshoe		everything	
piggy bank	hay fever	barbed wire	

Sweet Music in Harlem

bass
clarinet
fidgety
forgetful
jammed
nighttime
secondhand

Easily confused words

quiet	than	from	medal
quite	then	form	metal
finely	since	later	
finally	sense	latter	
except	affect	adapt	
accept	effect	adopt	

Grade 4 Vocabulary

Use this list of fourth grade tested vocabulary words for review and leveled activities.

A

aboard
affords
amazed
amphibians
ancestors
ancient
anticipation
appeared
aquarium
astronauts
atlas
aviator
avoided
awkward

B

bargain
bawling
bewildered
biologist
bluff
boarding school
bow
brilliant
brisk
bustling

C

canopy
capable
capsule
cargo
celestial
chant
chorus
cockpit
colonel
conducted
Constitution
continent
convergence
cord

coward
coyote
cradle
crime
crumbled
curiosity

D

dangle
dappled
daring
depart
destruction
dignified
dismay
docks
dolphins
dormitory
draft
drag
dudes
duke
dungeon

E

elegant
enchanted
endurance
escape
etched
exhibit
expected

F

fascinated
favor
flex
flexible
forbidding
forecasts
fouled
fragrant

frost
furiously

G

generations
genius
glacier
gleamed
glider
glimpses
glint
glorious
grand
granite
grizzly

H

hangars
hatch
heaves
homeland
hoop
horizon
howling
humble

I

icebergs
immense
impressive
inland

J

jersey

L

lagoon
lassoed
link
lizard
longed
loomed

lunar
lurking

M

magician
majesty
manual
marveled
massive
mechanical
memorial
migrating
minister
miracle
module
monument

N

naturalist
navigation
noble
numerous

O

offended
outspoken

P

palettes
parlor
payroll
peasant
peculiar
politics
pollen
pollinate
porridge
positive
prairie
preserve
prideful
pulpit
pulses

Q

quaint
quarantine
quivered

R

recalls
reference
reptiles
reseats
resemblance
reservation
responsibility
rille
rim
riverbed
roundup
rudder
ruins
rumbling
runt

S

salamander
scan
scent
scholars
sculptures
seeker
selecting
shatter
shielding
shimmering
shrieked
slithered
slopes
society
solemnly
solo
species
speechless
spurs

staggered
stalled
stern
still
stumped
summoning
surface
surge
swatted

T

taunted
temple
terraced
terror
thickets
timid
torrent
towering
trench
triumph
tropical
trudged

U

unbelievable
uncover

V

vain
vanished
vehicle

W

wharf
wilderness
wondrous

Y

yearned

Grade 6 Vocabulary

Use this list of sixth grade tested vocabulary words for leveled activities.

A

absurd
abundant
access
accustomed
aggressive
aliens
apparently
application
architecture
artifacts
astronomers
authority

B

barge
basin
beacon
behalf
benefits
bondage
burden

C

campaigns
candidate
captive
caravans
characteristic
charities
collapse
collide
combustion
commissioned
compact
companionship
comrades
confidently
conformed
conquer
converts
corridors
corrode

counselor
customary

D

dean
decline
decrees
delirious
democracy
densest
destination
destiny
detect
devise
dingy
diploma
disgraced
dismounted
distressed
dramatic
dubiously

E

earthen
eaves
efficiency
emphasized
empire
encounter
engulfed
enraged
enrich
equator
erosion
eternity
evaporates
existence
expanse
expedition
exploit
exported
extract

F

fixtures
flimsy
flourish
foreigners
formal
former
fragile
frantic
frustration
fulfill

G

galaxy
generated
groping

H

hatchet
hoard
homesteaders
hospitable
hovers

I

ideal
identity
ignite
immortal
imprinted
incident
industrial
insulated
invaders
isolation

L

lance
legacy
leisure
lunging
lush

M

maintenance
manuscripts
materialize
medieval
menacing
migration
misfortune
moisture
molten
momentous
mongrel
mythology

N

navigator
negotiate
nub

O

obedient
observatory
obstacle
opera
ordeal
ore

P

painstaking
particles
patron
percentage
permission
persisted
physical
pleas
poisonous
prejudice
presence
prey
primitive
privileged
proclaimed

progress
promoted
provisions

Q

quests
quill

R

receded
recital
recycled
refrain
registered
reigned
reject
relish
renewed
renowned
repay
reproduce
resound
retreat
revolting
romping
rowdy
rural

S

sanctuaries
secretive
settlement
sluggish
slung
smoldered
specimens
speckled
squire
stiffened
stimulating
stunned
subscribe
sufficient

surplus
survive

T

technology
tolerated
toll
torment
transmitted
traversed
treacherous
treaded
tropics

U

unaccompanied
unison
universal
urban

V

ventured
verify
version
vigorously
volcanic

W

waft
waning
wilt

Legibility

When handwriting is legible, letters, words and numbers can be read easily. Handwriting that is not legible can cause problems for the reader and make communication difficult. Legibility can be improved if students are able to identify what is causing legibility problems in their handwriting. Focus instruction on the following five elements of legible handwriting.

Size

Letters need to be a consistent size. Students should focus on three things related to size: letters that reach to the top line, letters that reach halfway between the top and bottom line, and letters that extend below the bottom line. Writing letters the correct size can improve legibility. Often the letters that sit halfway between the top and bottom line cause the most problems. When students are writing on notebook paper, there is no middle line to help them size letters such as *m, a, i,* and *r* correctly. If students are having trouble, have them draw middle lines on their notebook paper.

Shape

Some of the most common handwriting problems are caused by forming letters incorrectly. These are the most common types of handwriting problems:

- round letters such as *a, o,* and *g* are not closed
- looped letters such as *i, e,* and *b* have no loops
- letters such as *i, t,* and *d* have loops that shouldn't be there

Have students examine one another's writing to indicate which words are hard to read, and then discuss which letters aren't formed correctly. They can then practice those particular letters.

Spacing

Letters within words should be evenly spaced. Too much or too little space can make writing difficult to read. A consistent amount of space should also be used between words in a sentence and between sentences. Suggest that students use the tip of their pencil to check the spacing between words and the width of their pencil to check the spacing between sentences.

Slant

Correct writing slant can be to the right or to the left, or there may be no slant at all. Slant becomes a legibility problem when letters are slanted in different directions. Suggest that students use a ruler to draw lines to determine if their slant is consistent.

Smoothness

Written letters should be produced with a line weight that is not too dark and not too light. The line should be smooth without any shaky or jagged edges. If students' writing is too dark, they are pressing too hard. If the writing is too light, they are not pressing hard enough. Usually shaky or jagged lines occur if students are unsure of how to form letters or if they are trying to draw letters rather than using a flowing motion.

D'Nealian™ Cursive Alphabet

a b c d e f g

h i j k l m n

o p q r s t u

v w x y z

A B C D E F G

H I J K L M N

O P Q R S T U

V W X Y Z . , ' ?

1 2 3 4 5 6

7 8 9 10

D'Nealian™ Alphabet

a b c d e f g h i
j k l m n o p q r s t
u v w x y z

A B C D E F G
H I J K L M N O
P Q R S T U V
W X Y Z . , ' ?

1 2 3 4 5 6
7 8 9 10

© Pearson Education

Manuscript Alphabet

Unit 3 *Inventors and Artists*

	Below-Level	On-Level	Advanced

Wings for the King

To Read Aloud!
One Fine Day: A Radio Play
by Elizabeth Van Steenwyk (Wm. B. Eerdmans Publishing, 2003) Written as a radio play, this is the history of the Wright brothers' first successful flight from their point of view.

More Than Anything Else
by Marie Bradby (Orchard Books, 1995) Nine-year-old Booker T. Washington worked with his father at the salt works but dreamed of the day when he'd be able to read.

The Skit Book: 101 Skits from Kids
by Margaret MacDonald and Marie-Louise Scull (Linnet Books, 1990) This book contains 101 skits of authentic folklore by, and for, children.

The Neverending Story
by Michael Ende (Doubleday, 1983) Through the pages of a book, an unlikely hero is literally taken to another world where he experiences incredible adventures and finds strength he did not know he had.

Leonardo's Horse

To Read Aloud!
Leonardo da Vinci
by Diane Stanley (HarperCollins, 1996) This biography gives a fascinating portrait of the brilliant Italian artist and inventor using quotes from his own writings and images from his notebooks.

Snowflake Bentley
by Jacqueline Martin (Houghton Mifflin, 1998) A man's perseverance and love of nature led him to make scientific and artistic advances, despite the ridicule of others.

Frank O. Gehry: Outside In
by Jan Greenberg and Sandra Jordan (DK Publishing, 2000) This book describes the life of the architect and designer of the Guggenheim Museum and looks at how he used his vision to mix art and science.

The Second Mrs. Giaconda
By E. L. Konigsberg (Aladdin, 1998) Told from the point of view of Leonardo da Vinci's servant, this mystery novel tells how the great artist came to paint the *Mona Lisa* and reconstructs the middle years of his life.

The Dinosaurs of Waterhouse Hawkins

To Read Aloud!
Dinosaur Named Sue: The World's Most Complete T. Rex
by Patricia Relf (Cartwheel, 2000) This book recounts the finding and reconstruction of, and controversy over, the most complete T. Rex skeleton ever found.

Dinosaurs, Strange and Wonderful
by Carol Heyer and Laurence Pringle (Puffin, 1996) This introduction to the world of dinosaurs describes different kinds of dinosaurs and how paleontologists study them.

Finding Out About Dinosaurs (Science Explorers)
By Elin Kelsey (Maple Tree Press, 2000) This fact-filled book contains lots of information about dinosaurs and the exciting new approaches scientists use to learn about them.

The Art of Science: A Pop-Up Adventure in Art
by Jay Young (Candlewick, 1999) This book explores the many and often surprising ways in which science influences and inspires well-known artists.

Mahalia Jackson

To Read Aloud!
Call Down the Moon: Poems of Music
edited by Myra Cohn Livingston (McElderry, 1995) This anthology of contemporary poems celebrates the many forms of music and the effect of music on us.

Satchmo's Blues
by Alan Shroeder (Dragonfly, 1999) This moving biography of Louis Armstrong follows the events in his life that led him to become one of the world's greatest jazz musicians.

Free at Last: Stories and Songs of Emancipation
by Doreen Rappaport (Candlewick, 2003) This colorful journey through African-American heritage includes famous and everyday heroes.

Walking to the Bus-Rider Blues
by Harriette Gillem Robinet (Aladdin, 2002) Alfa Merryfield and his family have the "blues" as they struggle for rent money, food, and dignity while participating in the 1956 Montgomery, Alabama, bus boycott.

Special Effects in Film and Television

To Read Aloud!
Backstage at a Movie Set
by Katherine Wessling (Children's Press, 2003) This book explains the historical background, technological advances, and process of creating a movie.

How a House is Built
by Gail Gibbons (Holiday House, 1996) This book introduces readers to the work of architects, surveyors, carpenters, and others who build houses.

Side by Side: Five Favorite Picture-Book Teams Go to Work
by Leonard Marcus (Walker, 2001) This fascinating book explains how authors and illustrators work together to create picture books.

Movie Science: 40 Mind-Expanding, Reality-Bending Starstruck Activities for Kids
by Jim Wiese (John Wiley, 2001) This entertaining science book explains how movies bring fantasy to life using science and special effects.

See also *Assessment Handbook*, p 119

Unit 3 Reading Log

Name _____

Dates Read	Title and Author	What is it about?	How would you rate it?	Explain your rating.
From _____ to _____			Great Awful 5 4 3 2 1	
From _____ to _____			Great Awful 5 4 3 2 1	
From _____ to _____			Great Awful 5 4 3 2 1	
From _____ to _____			Great Awful 5 4 3 2 1	
From _____ to _____			Great Awful 5 4 3 2 1	

Unit 3 Narrative Retelling Chart

Selection Title _____   **Name** _____   **Date** _____

Retelling Criteria/Teacher Prompt	Teacher-Aided Response	Student-Generated Response	Rubric Score (Circle one.)
Connections Has anything like this happened to you? How does this story remind you of other stories?			4 3 2 1
Author's Purpose Why do you think the author wrote this story? What was the author trying to tell us?			4 3 2 1
Characters Describe _____ (character's name) at the beginning and end of the story.			4 3 2 1
Setting Where and when did the story happen?			4 3 2 1
Plot Tell me what the story was about in a few sentences.			4 3 2 1

Summative Retelling Score   4   3   2   1

Comments _____
_____
_____

Unit 3 Expository Retelling Chart

Selection Title _____

Name _____

Date _____

Retelling Criteria/Teacher Prompt	Teacher-Aided Response	Student-Generated Response	Rubric Score (Circle one.)
Connections Did this selection make you think about something else you have read? What did you learn about as you read this selection?			4 3 2 1
Author's Purpose Why do you think the author wrote this selection?			4 3 2 1
Topic What was the selection mostly about?			4 3 2 1
Important Ideas What is important for me to know about _____ (topic)?			4 3 2 1
Conclusions What did you learn from reading this selection?			4 3 2 1

Summative Retelling Score 4 3 2 1

Comments _____
_____
_____

Reading

Concepts of Print and Print Awareness	Pre-K	K	1	2	3	4	5	6
Develop awareness that print represents spoken language and conveys and preserves meaning	•	•	•					
Recognize familiar books by their covers; hold book right side up	•	•						
Identify parts of a book and their functions (front cover, title page/title, back cover, page numbers)	•	•	•					
Understand the concepts of letter, word, sentence, paragraph, and story	•	•	•					
Track print (front to back of book, top to bottom of page, left to right on line, sweep back left for next line)	•	•	•					
Match spoken to printed words	•	•	•					
Know capital and lowercase letter names and match them	•	• T	•					
Know the order of the alphabet		•	•					
Recognize first name in print	•	•	•					
Recognize the uses of capitalization and punctuation			•	•				
Value print as a means of gaining information	•	•	•					

Phonological and Phonemic Awareness	Pre-K	K	1	2	3	4	5	6
Phonological Awareness								
Recognize and produce rhyming words	•	•	•					
Track and count each word in a spoken sentence and each syllable in a spoken word	•	•	•					
Segment and blend syllables in spoken words			•					
Segment and blend onset and rime in one-syllable words		•	•					
Recognize and produce words beginning with the same sound	•	•	•					
Identify beginning, middle, and/or ending sounds that are the same or different	•	•	•					
Understand that spoken words are made of sequences of sounds	•	•	•					
Phonemic Awareness								
Identify the position of sounds in words		•	•					
Identify and isolate initial, final, and medial sounds in spoken words	•	•	•					
Blend sounds orally to make words or syllables		•	•					
Segment a word or syllable into sounds; count phonemes in spoken words or syllables		•	•					
Manipulate sounds in words (add, delete, and/or substitute phonemes)	•	•	•					

Phonics and Decoding	Pre-K	K	1	2	3	4	5	6
Phonics								
Understand and apply the **alphabetic principle** that spoken words are composed of sounds that are represented by letters	•	•	•					
Know letter-sound relationships	•	• T	• T	• T				
Blend sounds of letters to decode		•	• T	• T	• T			
Consonants, consonant blends, and consonant digraphs		•	• T	• T	• T			
Short, long, and r-controlled vowels; vowel digraphs; diphthongs; common vowel patterns			• T	• T	• T			
Phonograms/word families		•	•	•	•			
Word Structure								
Decode words with common word parts		•	• T	• T	• T	•	•	•
Base words and inflected endings			• T	• T	•	•	•	•
Contractions and compound words			• T	• T	• T	•	•	•
Suffixes and prefixes			• T	• T	• T	•	•	•
Greek and Latin roots						•	•	•
Blend syllables to decode words			• T	• T	• T	•	•	•
Decoding Strategies								
Blending strategy: Apply knowledge of letter-sound relationships to decode unfamiliar words		•	•	•	•			
Apply knowledge of word structure to decode unfamiliar words		•	•	•	•	•	•	•
Use context and syntax along with letter-sound relationships and word structure to decode		•	•	•	•	•	•	•
Self-correct			•	•	•	•	•	•

Fluency	Pre-K	K	1	2	3	4	5	6
Read aloud fluently with accuracy, comprehension, appropriate pace/rate; with expression/intonation (prosody); with attention to punctuation and appropriate phrasing			• T	• T	• T	• T	• T	• T
Practice fluency in a variety of ways, including choral reading, partner/paired reading, Readers' Theater, repeated oral reading, and tape-assisted reading		•	•	•	•	•	•	•

• instructional opportunity　　　　**T** tested in standardized test format

	Pre-K	K	1	2	3	4	5	6
Work toward appropriate fluency goals by the end of each grade			•T	•T	•T	•T	•T	•T
Read regularly in independent-level material			•	•	•	•	•	•
Read silently for increasing periods of time			•	•	•	•	•	•

Vocabulary (Oral and Written)

Word Recognition

	Pre-K	K	1	2	3	4	5	6
Recognize regular and irregular high-frequency words	•	•	•T	•T				
Recognize and understand selection vocabulary		•	•	•T	•	•	•	•
Understand content-area vocabulary and specialized, technical, or topical words			•	•	•	•	•	•

Word Learning Strategies

	Pre-K	K	1	2	3	4	5	6
Develop vocabulary through direct instruction, concrete experiences, reading, listening to text read aloud	•	•	•	•	•	•	•	•
Use knowledge of word structure to figure out meanings of words			•	•T	•T	•T	•T	•T
Use context clues for meanings of unfamiliar words, multiple-meaning words, homonyms, homographs			•	•T	•T	•T	•T	•T
Use grade-appropriate reference sources to learn word meanings	•	•	•	•	•T	•T	•T	•T
Use picture clues to help determine word meanings	•	•	•	•	•			
Use new words in a variety of contexts	•	•	•	•	•	•	•	•
Examine word usage and effectiveness		•	•	•	•	•	•	•
Create and use graphic organizers to group, study, and retain vocabulary			•	•	•	•	•	•

Extend Concepts and Word Knowledge

	Pre-K	K	1	2	3	4	5	6
Academic language	•	•	•	•	•	•	•	•
Classify and categorize	•	•	•	•	•	•	•	•
Antonyms and synonyms			•	•T	•T	•T	•T	•T
Homographs, homonyms, and homophones				•	•T	•T	•T	•T
Multiple-meaning words			•	•	•T	•T	•T	•T
Related words and derivations					•	•	•	•
Analogies						•		
Connotation/denotation						•	•	•
Figurative language and idioms			•	•	•	•	•	•
Descriptive words (location, size, color, shape, number, ideas, feelings)	•	•	•	•	•	•	•	•
High-utility words (shapes, colors, question words, position/directional words, and so on)	•	•	•	•	•			
Time and order words	•	•	•	•	•	•	•	•
Transition words						•	•	•
Word origins: Etymologies/word histories; words from other languages, regions, or cultures						•	•	•
Shortened forms: abbreviations, acronyms, clipped words			•	•	•	•	•T	

Text Comprehension

Comprehension Strategies

	Pre-K	K	1	2	3	4	5	6
Preview the text and formulate questions	•	•	•	•	•	•	•	•
Set and monitor purpose for reading and listening	•	•	•	•	•	•	•	•
Activate and use prior knowledge	•	•	•	•	•	•	•	•
Make predictions	•	•	•	•	•	•	•	•
Monitor comprehension and use fix-up strategies to resolve difficulties in meaning: adjust reading rate, reread and read on, seek help from reference sources and/or other people, skim and scan, summarize, use text features				•	•	•	•	•
Create and use graphic and semantic organizers		•	•	•	•	•	•	•
Answer questions (text explicit, text implicit, scriptal), including *who, what, when, where, why, what if, how*	•	•	•	•	•	•	•	•
Look back in text for answers			•	•	•	•	•	•
Answer test-like questions			•	•	•	•	•	•
Generate clarifying questions, including *who, what, where, when, how, why,* and *what if*	•	•	•	•	•	•	•	•
Recognize text structure: story and informational (cause/effect, chronological, compare/contrast, description, problem/solution, propostion/support)	•	•	•	•	•	•	•	•
Summarize text		•	•	•	•	•	•	•
Recall and retell stories	•	•	•	•	•	•	•	•
Identify and retell important/main ideas (nonfiction)	•	•	•	•	•	•	•	•
Identify and retell new information			•	•	•	•	•	•
Visualize; use mental imagery		•	•	•	•	•	•	•
Use strategies flexibly and in combination			•	•	•	•	•	•

Comprehension Skills

	Pre-K	K	1	2	3	4	5	6
Author's purpose		•T	•T	•T	•T	•T	•T	•T
Author's viewpoint/bias/perspective					•	•	•	•T
Categorize and classify	•	•	•	•				
Cause and effect		•	•T	•T	•T	•T	•T	•T
Compare and contrast		•	•T	•T	•T	•T	•T	•T
Details and facts		•	•	•	•	•	•	•
Draw conclusions		•	•T	•T	•T	•T	•T	•T
Fact and opinion			•T	•T	•T	•T	•T	•T
Follow directions/steps in a process	•	•	•	•	•	•	•	•
Generalize					•T	•T	•T	•T
Graphic sources		•	•	•		•T	•T	•T
Main idea and supporting details		•T	•T	•T	•T	•T	•T	•T
Paraphrase				•	•	•	•	•
Persuasive devices and propaganda				•	•	•	•	•
Realism/fantasy		•	•T	•T	•T	•	•	•
Sequence of events		•T	•T	•T	•T	•T	•T	•T

Higher Order Thinking Skills

	Pre-K	K	1	2	3	4	5	6
Analyze				•	•	•	•	•
Describe and connect the essential ideas, arguments, and perspectives of a text				•	•	•	•	•
Draw inferences, conclusions, or generalizations, support them with textual evidence and prior knowledge		•	•	•	•	•	•	•
Evaluate and critique ideas and text				•	•	•	•	•
Hypothesize						•	•	•
Make judgments about ideas and text				•	•	•	•	•
Organize and synthesize ideas and information				•		•	•	•

Literary Analysis, Response, & Appreciation

	Pre-K	K	1	2	3	4	5	6
Genre and Its Characteristics								
Recognize characteristics of a variety of genre	•	•	•	•	•	•	•	•
Distinguish fiction from nonfiction		•	•	•	•	•	•	•
Identify characteristics of literary texts, including drama, fantasy, traditional tales		•	•	•	•	•	•	•
Identify characteristics of nonfiction texts, including biography, interviews, newspaper articles		•	•	•	•	•	•	•
Identify characteristics of poetry and song, including nursery rhymes, limericks, blank verse	•	•	•	•	•	•	•	•
Literary Elements and Story Structure								
Character	•	•T	•T	•T	•T	•T	•T	
Recognize and describe traits, actions, feelings, and motives of characters		•	•	•	•	•	•	•
Analyze characters' relationships, changes, and points of view		•	•	•	•	•	•	•
Analyze characters' conflicts				•	•	•	•	•
Plot and plot structure	•	•T	•T	•T	•T	•T	•T	
Beginning, middle, end	•	•	•	•	•			
Goal and outcome or problem and solution/resolution		•	•	•	•	•	•	•
Rising action, climax, and falling action/denouement; setbacks						•	•	•
Setting	•	•T	•T	•T	•T	•T		
Relate setting to problem/solution						•	•	•
Explain ways setting contributes to mood						•	•	•
Theme		•	•T	•T	•	•	•	•
Use Literary Elements and Story Structure	•	•	•	•	•	•	•	•
Analyze and evaluate author's use of setting, plot, character					•	•	•	•
Identify similarities and differences of characters, events, and settings within or across selections/cultures		•	•	•	•	•	•	•
Literary Devices								
Allusion								•
Dialect						•	•	•
Dialogue and narration	•			•	•	•	•	•
Exaggeration/hyperbole						•	•	•
Figurative language: idiom, jargon, metaphor, simile, slang			•	•	•	•	•	•

• instructional opportunity   **T** tested in standardized test format

	Pre-K	K	1	2	3	4	5	6
Flashback						•	•	•
Foreshadowing								•
Formal and informal language				•	•	•	•	•
Humor					•	•	•	•
Imagery and sensory words			•	•	•	•		•
Mood				•	•		•	•
Personification				•		•		
Point of view (first person, third person, omniscient)					•	•	•	•
Puns and word play					•	•	•	•
Sound devices and poetic elements	•	•	•	•	•	•	•	•
Alliteration, assonance, onomatopoeia	•	•	•	•	•	•	•	•
Rhyme, rhythm, repetition, and cadence	•	•	•		•	•	•	•
Word choice					•	•	•	•
Symbolism					•	•	•	•
Tone						•	•	

Author's and Illustrator's Craft

	Pre-K	K	1	2	3	4	5	6
Distinguish the roles of author and illustrator		•	•	•				
Recognize/analyze author's and illustrator's craft or style		•	•	•	•	•	•	•

Literary Response

	Pre-K	K	1	2	3	4	5	6
Recollect, talk, and write about books	•	•	•	•	•	•	•	•
Reflect on reading and respond (through talk, movement, art, and so on)	•	•	•	•	•	•	•	•
Ask and answer questions about text	•	•	•	•	•	•	•	•
Write about what is read	•	•	•	•	•	•	•	•
Use evidence from the text to support opinions, interpretations, or conclusions			•	•	•	•	•	•
Support ideas through reference to other texts and personal knowledge				•	•	•	•	•
Locate materials on related topic, theme, or idea				•	•	•	•	•
Generate alternative endings to plots and identify the reason for, and the impact of, the alternatives	•	•	•	•	•	•	•	•
Synthesize and extend the literary experience through creative responses	•	•	•	•	•	•	•	•
Make connections: text to self, text to text, text to world	•	•	•	•	•	•	•	•
Evaluate and critique the quality of the literary experience				•	•	•	•	•
Offer observations, react, speculate in response to text				•	•	•	•	•

Literary Appreciation/Motivation

	Pre-K	K	1	2	3	4	5	6
Show an interest in books and reading; engage voluntarily in social interaction about books	•	•	•	•	•	•	•	•
Choose text by drawing on personal interests, relying on knowledge of authors and genres, estimating text difficulty, and using recommendations of others	•	•	•	•	•	•	•	•
Read a variety of grade-level appropriate narrative and expository texts		•	•	•	•	•	•	•
Read from a wide variety of genres for a variety of purposes	•	•	•	•	•	•	•	•
Read independently		•	•	•	•	•	•	•
Establish familiarity with a topic		•	•	•	•	•	•	•

Cultural Awareness

	Pre-K	K	1	2	3	4	5	6
Develop attitudes and abilities to interact with diverse groups and cultures	•	•	•	•	•	•	•	•
Connect experiences and ideas with those from a variety of languages, cultures, customs, perspectives	•	•	•	•	•	•	•	•
Understand how attitudes and values in a culture or during a period in time affect the writing from that culture or time period						•	•	
Compare language and oral traditions (family stories) that reflect customs, regions, and cultures		•	•	•	•	•		•
Recognize themes that cross cultures and bind them together in their common humanness						•	•	•

Language Arts

Writing

Concepts of Print for Writing	Pre-K	K	1	2	3	4	5	6
Develop gross and fine motor skills and hand/eye coordination	•	•	•					
Print own name and other important words	•	•	•					
Write using pictures, some letters, and transitional spelling to convey meaning	•	•	•					
Dictate messages or stories for others to write	•	•	•					

	Pre-K	K	1	2	3	4	5	6
Create own written texts for others to read; write left to right on a line and top to bottom on a page	•	•	•					
Participate in shared and interactive writing	•	•	•					

Traits of Writing

Focus/Ideas

	Pre-K	K	1	2	3	4	5	6
Maintain focus and sharpen ideas		•	•	•	•	•	•	•
Use sensory details and concrete examples; elaborate		•	•	•	•	•	•	•
Delete extraneous information			•	•	•	•	•	•
Rearrange words and sentences to improve meaning and focus				•	•	•	•	•
Use strategies, such as tone, style, consistent point of view, to achieve a sense of completeness						•	•	•

Organization/Paragraphs

	Pre-K	K	1	2	3	4	5	6
Use graphic organizers to group ideas		•	•	•	•	•	•	•
Write coherent paragraphs that develop a central idea			•	•	•	•	•	•
Use transitions to connect sentences and paragraphs			•	•	•	•	•	•
Select an organizational structure based on purpose, audience, length						•	•	•
Organize ideas in a logical progression, such as chronological order or by order of importance		•			•	•	•	•
Write introductory, supporting, and concluding paragraphs						•	•	•
Write a multi-paragraph paper				•	•	•	•	•

Voice

	Pre-K	K	1	2	3	4	5	6
Develop personal, identifiable voice and an individual tone/style			•	•	•	•	•	•
Maintain consistent voice and point of view						•	•	•
Use voice appropriate to audience, message, and purpose						•	•	•

Word Choice

	Pre-K	K	1	2	3	4	5	6
Use clear, precise, appropriate language		•	•	•	•	•	•	•
Use figurative language and vivid words			•	•	•	•	•	•
Select effective vocabulary using word walls, dictionary, or thesaurus		•	•	•	•	•	•	•

Sentences

	Pre-K	K	1	2	3	4	5	6
Combine, elaborate, and vary sentences		•	•	•	•	•	•	•
Write topic sentence, supporting sentences with facts and details, and concluding sentence			•	•	•	•	•	•
Use correct word order			•	•	•	•	•	•
Use parallel structure in a sentence							•	•

Conventions

	Pre-K	K	1	2	3	4	5	6
Use correct spelling and grammar; capitalize and punctuate correctly		•	•	•	•	•	•	•
Correct sentence fragments and run-ons					•	•	•	•
Use correct paragraph indention				•	•	•	•	•

The Writing Process

	Pre-K	K	1	2	3	4	5	6
Prewrite using various strategies	•	•	•	•	•	•	•	•
Develop first drafts of single- and multiple-paragraph compositions		•	•	•	•	•	•	•
Revise drafts for varied purposes, including to clarify and to achieve purpose, sense of audience, precise word choice, vivid images, and elaboration		•	•	•	•	•	•	•
Edit and proofread for correct spelling, grammar, usage, and mechanics		•	•	•	•	•	•	•
Publish own work	•	c	•	•	•	•	•	•

Types of Writing

	Pre-K	K	1	2	3	4	5	6
Narrative writing (such as personal narratives, stories, biographies, autobiographies)	•	•	• T	• T	• T	• T	• T	• T
Expository writing (such as essays, directions, explanations, news stories, research reports, summaries)		•	• T	• T	• T	• T	• T	• T
Descriptive writing (such as labels, captions, lists, plays, poems, response logs, songs)	•	•	• T	• T	• T	• T	• T	• T
Persuasive writing (such as ads, editorials, essays, letters to the editor, opinions, posters)		•	• T	• T	• T	• T	• T	• T

Writing Habits and Practices

	Pre-K	K	1	2	3	4	5	6
Write on a daily basis	•	•	•	•	•	•	•	•
Use writing as a tool for learning and self-discovery			•	•	•	•	•	•
Write independently for extended periods of time			•	•	•	•	•	•

ENGLISH LANGUAGE CONVENTIONS in WRITING and SPEAKING

	Pre-K	K	1	2	3	4	5	6

Grammar and Usage in Speaking and Writing

Sentences

	Pre-K	K	1	2	3	4	5	6
Types (declarative, interrogative, exclamatory, imperative)	•	•	• T	• T	• T	• T	• T	• T
Structure (simple, compound, complex, compound-complex)	•	•	•	•	•	• T	• T	• T

• instructional opportunity   T tested in standardized test format

Skill	Pre-K	K	1	2	3	4	5	6
Parts (subjects/predicates: complete, simple, compound; phrases; clauses)				•T	•	•T	•T	•T
Fragments and run-on sentences		•	•	•	•	•	•	•
Combine sentences, elaborate			•	•	•	•	•	•
Parts of speech: nouns, verbs and verb tenses, adjectives, adverbs, pronouns and antecedents, conjunctions, prepositions, interjections		•	•T	•T	•T	•T	•T	•T
Usage								
Subject-verb agreement		•	•T	•	•	•T	•T	•T
Pronoun agreement/referents			•T	•	•	•T	•T	•T
Misplaced modifiers						•	•T	•T
Misused words					•	•	•	•T
Negatives; avoid double negatives					•	•	•	•

Mechanics in Writing

Skill	Pre-K	K	1	2	3	4	5	6
Capitalization (first word in sentence, proper nouns and adjectives, pronoun *I*, titles, and so on)	•	•	•T	•T	•T	•T	•T	•T
Punctuation (apostrophe, comma, period, question mark, exclamation mark, quotation marks, and so on)		•	•T	•T	•T	•T	•T	•T

Spelling	Pre-K	K	1	2	3	4	5	6
Spell independently by using pre-phonetic knowledge, knowledge of letter names, sound-letter knowledge	•	•	•	•	•	•	•	•
Use sound-letter knowledge to spell	•	•	•	•	•	•	•	•
Consonants: single, double, blends, digraphs, silent letters, and unusual consonant spellings		•	•	•	•	•	•	•
Vowels: short, long, *r*-controlled, digraphs, diphthongs, less common vowel patterns, schwa			•	•	•	•	•	•
Use knowledge of word structure to spell			•	•	•	•	•	•
Base words and affixes (inflections, prefixes, suffixes), possessives, contractions and compound words			•	•	•	•	•	•
Greek and Latin roots, syllable patterns, multisyllabic words			•	•	•	•	•	•
Spell high-frequency, irregular words		•	•	•	•	•	•	•
Spell frequently misspelled words correctly, including homophones or homonyms			•	•	•	•	•	•
Use meaning relationships to spell					•	•	•	•

Handwriting	Pre-K	K	1	2	3	4	5	6
Gain increasing control of penmanship, including pencil grip, paper position, posture, stroke	•	•	•	•				
Write legibly, with control over letter size and form; letter slant; and letter, word, and sentence spacing		•	•	•	•	•	•	•
Write lowercase and capital letters	•	•	•	•				
Manuscript	•	•	•	•	•	•	•	•
Cursive				•	•	•	•	•
Write numerals	•	•	•					

Listening and Speaking	Pre-K	K	1	2	3	4	5	6

Listening Skills and Strategies

Skill	Pre-K	K	1	2	3	4	5	6
Listen to a variety of presentations attentively and politely	•	•	•	•	•	•	•	•
Self-monitor comprehension while listening, using a variety of skills and strategies	•	•	•	•	•	•	•	•
Listen for a purpose								
For enjoyment and appreciation	•	•	•	•	•	•	•	•
To expand vocabulary and concepts	•	•	•	•	•	•	•	•
To obtain information and ideas	•	•	•	•	•	•	•	•
To follow oral directions	•	•	•	•	•	•	•	•
To answer questions and solve problems	•	•	•	•	•	•	•	•
To participate in group discussions	•	•	•	•	•	•	•	•
To identify and analyze the musical elements of literary language	•	•	•	•	•	•	•	•
To gain knowledge of one's own culture, the culture of others, and the common elements of cultures	•	•	•	•	•	•	•	•
Recognize formal and informal language				•	•	•	•	•
Listen critically to distinguish fact from opinion and to analyze and evaluate ideas, information, experiences		•		•	•	•	•	•
Evaluate a speaker's delivery				•	•	•	•	•
Interpret a speaker's purpose, perspective, persuasive techniques, verbal and nonverbal messages, and use of rhetorical devices					•	•	•	•

Speaking Skills and Strategies

Skill	Pre-K	K	1	2	3	4	5	6
Speak clearly, accurately, and fluently, using appropriate delivery for a variety of audiences, and purposes	•	•	•	•	•	•	•	•
Use proper intonation, volume, pitch, modulation, and phrasing		•	•	•	•	•	•	•
Speak with a command of standard English conventions	•	•	•	•	•	•	•	•
Use appropriate language for formal and informal settings	•	•	•	•	•	•	•	•

	Pre-K	K	1	2	3	4	5	6
Speak for a purpose								
To ask and answer questions	•	•	•	•	•	•	•	•
To give directions and instructions	•	•	•	•	•	•	•	•
To retell, paraphrase, or explain information			•	•	•	•	•	•
To communicate needs and share ideas and experiences	•	•	•	•	•	•	•	•
To participate in conversations and discussions	•	•	•	•	•	•	•	•
To express an opinion	•	•	•	•	•	•	•	•
To deliver dramatic recitations, interpretations, or performances	•	•	•	•	•	•	•	•
To deliver presentations or oral reports (narrative, descriptive, persuasive, and informational)	•	•	•	•	•	•	•	•
Stay on topic	•	•	•	•	•	•	•	•
Use appropriate verbal and nonverbal elements (such as facial expression, gestures, eye contact, posture)	•	•	•	•	•	•	•	•
Identify and/or demonstrate methods to manage or overcome communication anxiety						•	•	•
Viewing/Media	Pre-K	K	1	2	3	4	5	6
Interact with and respond to a variety of print and non-print media for a range of purposes	•	•	•	•	•	•	•	•
Compare and contrast print, visual, and electronic media					•	•	•	•
Analyze and evaluate media			•	•	•	•	•	•
Recognize purpose, bias, propaganda, and persuasive techniques in media messages			•	•	•	•	•	•

Research and Study Skills

Understand and Use Graphic Sources	Pre-K	K	1	2	3	4	5	6
Advertisement			•	•	•	•	•	•
Chart/table	•	•	•	•	•	•	•	•
Diagram/scale drawing			•	•	•	•	•	•
Graph (bar, circle, line, picture)			•	•	•	•	•	•
Illustration, photograph, caption, label	•	•	•	•	•	•	•	•
Map/globe	•	•	•	•	•	•	•	•
Order form/application						•	•	•
Poster/announcement	•	•	•	•	•	•	•	
Schedule						•	•	•
Sign	•	•	•	•	•			
Time line				•	•	•	•	•
Understand and Use Reference Sources	Pre-K	K	1	2	3	4	5	6
Know and use parts of a book to locate information	•	•	•	•	•	•	•	•
Use alphabetical order			•	•	•			
Understand purpose, structure, and organization of reference sources (print, electronic, media, Internet)	•	•	•	•	•	•	•	•
Almanac						•	•	•
Atlas		•		•	•	•	•	•
Card catalog/library database				•	•	•	•	•
Dictionary/glossary		•	•	•	•T	•T	•T	•T
Encyclopedia				•	•	•	•	•
Magazine/periodical				•	•	•	•	•
Newspaper and Newsletter			•	•	•	•	•	•
Readers' Guide to Periodical Literature						•	•	•
Technology (computer and non-computer electronic media)		•	•	•	•	•	•	•
Thesaurus					•	•	•	•
Study Skills and Strategies	Pre-K	K	1	2	3	4	5	6
Adjust reading rate			•	•	•	•	•	•
Clarify directions	•	•	•	•	•	•	•	•
Outline				•	•	•	•	•
Skim and scan			•	•	•	•	•	•
SQP3R						•	•	•
Summarize		•	•	•	•	•	•	•
Take notes, paraphrase, and synthesize			•	•	•	•	•	•
Use graphic and semantic organizers to organize information		•	•	•	•	•	•	•

• instructional opportunity   T tested in standardized test format

Test-Taking Skills and Strategies	Pre-K	K	1	2	3	4	5	6
Understand the question, the vocabulary of tests, and key words				•	•	•	•	•
Answer the question; use information from the text (stated or inferred)		•	•	•	•	•	•	•
Write across texts				•	•	•	•	•
Complete the sentence				•	•	•	•	•

Technology/New Literacies	Pre-K	K	1	2	3	4	5	6
Non-Computer Electronic Media								
Audio tapes/CDs, video tapes/DVDs	•	•	•	•	•	•	•	
Film, television, and radio		•	•	•	•	•	•	•
Computer Programs and Services: Basic Operations and Concepts								
Use accurate computer terminology	•	•	•	•	•	•	•	•
Create, name, locate, open, save, delete, and organize files			•	•	•	•	•	•
Use input and output devices (such as mouse, keyboard, monitor, printer, touch screen)	•	•	•	•	•	•	•	•
Use basic keyboarding skills			•	•	•	•	•	•
Responsible Use of Technology Systems and Software								
Work cooperatively and collaboratively with others; follow acceptable use policies	•	•	•	•	•	•	•	•
Recognize hazards of Internet searches			•	•	•	•	•	•
Respect intellectual property					•	•	•	•
Information and Communication Technologies: Information Acquisition								
Use electronic web (non-linear) navigation, online resources, databases, keyword searches			•	•	•	•	•	•
Use visual and non-textual features of online resources	•	•	•	•	•	•	•	•
Internet inquiry			•	•	•	•	•	•
Identify questions			•	•	•	•	•	•
Locate, select, and collect information			•	•	•	•	•	•
Analyze information			•	•	•	•	•	•
Evaluate electronic information sources for accuracy, relevance, bias				•	•	•	•	•
Understand bias/subjectivity of electronic content (about this site, author search, date created)					•	•	•	•
Synthesize information					•	•	•	•
Communicate findings				•	•	•	•	•
Use fix-up strategies (such as clicking *Back, Forward,* or *Undo;* redoing a search; trimming the URL)			•	•	•	•	•	•
Communication								
Collaborate, publish, present, and interact with others		•	•	•	•	•	•	•
Use online resources (e-mail, bulletin boards, newsgroups)			•	•	•	•	•	•
Use a variety of multimedia formats			•	•	•	•	•	•
Problem Solving								
Select the appropriate software for the task	•	•	•	•	•	•	•	•
Use technology resources for solving problems and making informed decisions			•	•	•	•	•	•
Determine when technology is useful				•	•	•	•	•

The Research Process	Pre-K	K	1	2	3	4	5	6
Choose and narrow the topic; frame and revise questions for inquiry		•	•	•	•	•	•	•
Choose and evaluate appropriate reference sources			•	•	•	•	•	•
Locate and collect information	•	•	•	•	•	•	•	•
Take notes/record findings				•	•	•	•	•
Combine and compare information				•	•	•	•	•
Evaluate, interpret, and draw conclusions about key information		•	•	•	•	•	•	•
Summarize information		•	•	•	•	•	•	•
Make an outline				•	•	•	•	•
Organize content systematically		•	•	•	•	•	•	•
Communicate information		•	•	•	•	•	•	•
Write and present a report			•	•	•	•	•	•
Include citations						•	•	•
Respect intellectual property/plagiarism						•	•	•
Select and organize visual aids		•	•	•	•	•	•	•

INDEX

A

Abbreviations. *See* **Vocabulary strategies.**

Accountability. *See* **Adequate yearly progress.**

Achieving English proficiency. *See* **ELL (English Language Learners) suggestions.**

Acronyms. *See* **Vocabulary strategies.**

Activate prior knowledge. *See* **Prereading strategies.**

Adequate yearly progress (AYP), 5.1 16g–16h, 5.2 140g–140h, 5.3 260g–260h, 5.4 390g–390h, 5.5 510g–540h, 5.6 632g–632h

Adjectives, 5.5 559e–559f, 581e–581f, 5.6 653e–653f
  articles, 5.5 559e–559f
  comparative and superlative, 5.5 603e–603f

Advanced learners
  group time, 5.1 18f–18g, 42f–42g, 68f–68g, 90f–90g, 112f–112g, DI·3, DI·5, DI·7, DI·9, DI·11, DI·13, DI·15, DI·17, DI·19, DI·21, DI·23, DI·25, DI·27, DI·29, DI·31, DI·33, DI·35, DI·37, DI·39, DI·41, DI·43, DI·45, DI·47, DI·49, DI·51, 5.2 142f–142g, 162f–162g, 186f–186g, 208f–208g, 230f–230g, DI·3, DI·5, DI·7, DI·9, DI·11, DI·13, DI·15, DI·17, DI·19, DI·21, DI·23, DI·25, DI·27, DI·29, DI·31, DI·33, DI·35, DI·37, DI·39, DI·41, DI·43, DI·45, DI·47, DI·49, DI·51, 5.3 262f–262g, 288f–288g, 316f–316g, 346f–346g, 364f–364g, DI·3, DI·5, DI·7, DI·9, DI·11, DI·13, DI·15, DI·17, DI·19, DI·21, DI·23, DI·25, DI·27, DI·29, DI·31, DI·33, DI·35, DI·37, DI·39, DI·41, DI·43, DI·45, DI·47, DI·49, DI·51, 5.4 392f–392g, 412f–412g, 436f–436g, 458f–458g, 484f–484g, DI·3, DI·5, DI·7, DI·9, DI·11, DI·13, DI·15, DI·17, DI·19, DI·21, DI·23, DI·25, DI·27, DI·29, DI·31, DI·33, DI·35, DI·37, DI·39, DI·41, DI·43, DI·45, DI·47, DI·49, DI·51, 5.5 512f–512g, 536f–536g, 560f–560g, 582f–582g, 604f–604g, DI·3, DI·5, DI·7, DI·9, DI·11, DI·13, DI·15, DI·17, DI·19, DI·21, DI·23, DI·25, DI·27, DI·29, DI·31, DI·33, DI·35, DI·37, DI·39, DI·41, DI·43, DI·45, DI·47, DI·49, DI·51, 5.6 634f–634g, 654f–654g, 674f–674g, 700f–700g, 726f–726g, DI·3, DI·5, DI·7, DI·9, DI·11, DI·13, DI·15, DI·17, DI·19, DI·21, DI·23, DI·25, DI·27, DI·29, DI·31, DI·33, DI·35, DI·37, DI·39, DI·41, DI·43, DI·45, DI·47, DI·49, DI·51. *See also* **Grouping students for instruction.**
  leveled readers, 5.1 LR7–LR9, LR16–LR18, LR25–LR27, LR34–LR36, LR43–LR45, 5.2 LR7–LR9, LR16–LR18, LR25–LR27, LR34–LR36, LR43–LR45, 5.3 LR7–LR9, LR16–LR18, LR25–LR27, LR34–LR36, LR43–LR45, 5.4 LR7–LR9, LR16–LR18, LR25–LR27, LR34–LR36, LR43–LR45, 5.5 LR7–LR9, LR16–LR18, LR25–LR27, LR34–LR36, LR43–LR45, 5.6 LR7–LR9, LR16–LR18, LR25–LR27, LR34–LR36, LR43–LR45
  resources, 5.1 18g, 42g, 68g, 90g, 112g, 5.2 142g, 162g, 186g, 208g, 230g, 5.3 262g, 288g, 316g, 346g, 364g, 5.4 392g, 412g, 436g, 458g, 484g, 5.5 512g, 536g, 560g, 582g, 604g, 5.6 634g, 654g, 674g, 700g, 726g
  writing, 5.1 WA9, 5.2 WA9, 5.3 WA9, 5.4 WA9, 5.5 WA9, 5.6 WA9

Adventure fiction. *See* **Genres.**

Adverbs, 5.5 625e–625f, 5.6 653e–653f

Advertisement. *See* **Graphic sources.**

Affective domain. *See* **Habits and attitudes, Literary response and appreciation.**

Affixes. *See* **Spelling,** word structure; **Word structure,** prefixes, suffixes.

Almanac. *See* **Reference sources.**

Alphabetical order, 5.1 70, 5.2 162–163, 5.5 536–537, 549, 5.6 634–635, 645

Analyzing. *See* **Reading across texts.** In addition, analytical thinking questions are raised throughout Guiding Comprehension and Reader Response.

Analogy. *See* **Vocabulary strategies.**

Answering questions. *See* **Questions, answering.**

Antonyms, 5.1 20b, 92–93, 5.3 348b, 348–349, 363c, 5.4 394b, 5.5 514b, 584b. *See also* **Vocabulary strategies.**

Apostrophe, 5.2 185e–185f, 5.5 535e–535f

Appreciating literature. *See* **Literary response and appreciation.**

Appropriate word meaning, 5.1 114–115, 133c, 5.2 164b, 5.3 264–265, 275, 287, 348b, 5.4 414b, 460b, 5.5 514b, 562–563, 581c

Art activities. *See* **Cross-curricular activities.**

Art, interpreting. *See* **Literary craft,** illustrator's craft/style.

Asking questions. *See* **Questions, asking.**

Assessment
  classroom-based. "If/then" assessment occurs throughout lessons and Guiding Comprehension.
  formal, 5.1 35, 41h, 41j, 65, 67h, 67j, 85, 89h, 89j, 109, 111h, 111j, 129, 133h, 133j, 134a, WA7, WA10–WA14, 5.2 159, 161h, 161j, 179, 185h, 185j, 205, 207h, 207j, 225, 229h, 229j, 249, 253h, 253j, 254a, WA7, WA10–WA14, 5.3 281, 287h, 287j, 311, 315h, 315j, 339, 345h, 345j, 359, 363h, 363j, 379, 383h, 383j, 384a, WA7, WA10–WA14, 5.4 409, 411h, 411j, 433, 435h, 435j, 453, 457h, 457j, 479, 483h, 483j, 499, 503h, 503j, 504a, WA7, WA10–WA14, 5.5 531, 535h, 535j, 553, 559h, 559j, 577, 581h, 581j, 599, 603h, 603j, 621, 625h, 625j, 626a, WA7, WA10–WA14, 5.6 651, 653h, 653j, 669, 673h, 673j, 697, 699h, 699j, 721, 725h, 725j, 749, 753h, 753j, 754a, WA7, WA10–WA14,
  fluency, 5.1 41a, 67a, 89a, 111a, 133a, WA15–WA16, DI·59–DI·60, 5.2 161a, 185a, 207a, 229a, 253a, WA15–WA16, DI·59–DI·60, 5.3 287a, 315a, 345a, 363a, 383a, WA15–WA16, DI·59–DI·60, 5.4 411a, 435a, 457a, 483a, 503a, WA15–WA16, DI·59–DI·60, 5.5 535a, 559a, 581a, 603a, 625a, WA15–WA16, DI·59–DI·60, 5.6 653a, 673a, 699a, 725a, 753a, WA15–WA16, DI·59–DI·60
  scoring guide (rubric), 5.1 34, 35, 41h, 64, 65, 67h, 84, 85, 89h, 108, 109, 111h, 128, 129, 133h, 134a, WA7, WA10–WA14, 5.2 158, 159, 161h, 178, 179, 185h, 204, 205, 207h,

224, 225, 229h, 248, 249, 253h, 254a, WA7, WA10–WA14, 5.3 280, 281, 287h, 310, 311, 315h, 338, 339, 345h, 358, 359, 363h, 378, 379, 383h, 384a, WA7, WA10–WA14, 5.4 408, 409, 411h, 432, 433, 435h, 452, 453, 457h, 478, 479, 483h, 498, 499, 503h, 504a, WA7, WA10–WA14, 5.5 530, 531, 535h, 552, 553, 559h, 576, 577, 581h, 598, 599, 603h, 620, 621, 625h, 626a, WA7, WA10–WA14, 5.6 650, 651, 653h, 668, 669, 673h, 696, 697, 699h, 720, 721, 725h, 748, 749, 753h, 754a, WA7, WA10–WA14
  self-assessment, 5.1 41h, 67h, 89h, 111h, 133h, WA7, 5.2 161h, 185h, 207h, 229h, 253h, WA7, 5.3 287h, 315h, 345h, 363h, 383h, WA7, 5.4 411h, 435h, 457h, 483h, 503h, WA7, 5.5 535h, 559h, 581h, 603h, 625h, WA7, 5.6 653h, 673h, 699h, 725h, 753h, WA7
  spelling, 5.1 41j, 67j, 89j, 111j, 133j, 5.2 161j, 185j, 207j, 229j, 253j, 5.3 287j, 315j, 345j, 363j, 383j, 5.4 411j, 435j, 457j, 483j, 503j, 5.5 535j, 559j, 581j, 603j, 625j, 5.6 653j, 673j, 699j, 725j, 753j
  test-taking strategies, 5.1 34, 64, 84, 108, 128, 133h, 5.2 158, 178, 204, 224, 248, 253h, 5.3 280, 310, 338, 358, 378, 383h, 5.4 408, 432, 452, 478, 498, 503h, 5.5 530, 552, 576, 598, 620, 5.6 650, 668, 696, 720, 748
  writing, 5.1 WA7, WA10–WA14, 5.2 WA7, WA10–WA14, 5.3 WA7, WA10–WA14, 5.4 WA7, WA10–WA14, 5.5 WA7, WA10–WA14, 5.6 WA7, WA10–WA14

Atlas. *See* **Reference sources.**

Attitudes, personal. *See* **Habits and attitudes.**

Authors (of reading selections)
  Aesop, 5.2 206–207
  Alexander, Sally Hobart, 5.4 434–435
  Archbold, Rich, 5.5 540–551
  Asch, Frank, 5.6 755
  Ballard, Robert D., 5.1 139f, 5.5 540–551
  Baylor, Byrd, 5.4 506
  Bial, Raymond, 5.5 608–619
  Biron, Debora, 5.2 180–185
  Brooks, Gwendolyn, 5.4 411
  Buckley, Susan, 5.5 622–625
  Carter, Alden, 5.4 416–431
  Clements, Andrew, 5.1 22–33
  Cline-Ransome, Lena, 5.1 94–107
  Craft, Charlotte, 5.6 678–695
  Delacre, Lulu, 5.6 638–649
  Diamond, Lydia R., 5.4 462–477
  Dickenson, Emily, 5.2 257
  Fang, Linda, 5.1 139f, 5.2 190–203
  Fisher, Lillian M., 5.4 507
  Fleischman, Paul, 5.4 396–407
  Floriatt, Douglas, 5.3 386
  Fritz, Jean, 5.1 139d, 5.3 292–309
  George, Kristine O'Connell, 5.4 504
  Giovanni, Nikki, 5.4 505
  Goodall, Jane, 5.2 212–223
  Hamilton, Jake, 5.3 368–377
  Hamilton, Virginia, 5.4 410
  Herford, Oliver, 5.3 387
  Hill, Donna, 5.5 554–559
  Hopkinson, Deborah, 5.1 116–127, 139h
  Jiménez, Francisco, 5.1 139j, 5.2 146–157
  Johnson, Georgia Douglas, 5.5 626
  Kerley, Barbara, 5.1 139d, 5.3 320–337
  Klages, Ellen, 5.1 110–111

Kumin, Maxine W., 5.1 134–135
Lame Deer, 5.6 652–653
Leacock, Elspeth, 5.5 622–625
Lear, Edward, 5.6 754
Lester, Julius, 5.1 139h, 5.3 350–357
Longfellow, Henry Wadsworth, 5.1 139l, 5.2 234–247
McClester, Cedric, 5.2 254–255
McKissack, Fredrick, 5.5 627
McKissack, Patricia, 5.5 627
McLoughland, Beverly, 5.3 385
Merriam, Eve, 5.2 256
Mochizuki, Ken, 5.2 166–177
Moon, Pat, 5.6 756
Nichols, bp, 5.5 628–629
Nelson, Marilyn, 5.3 384
Nolen, Jerdine, 5.1 46–63
Nye, Naomi Shihab, 5.1 136–137
O'Brien, Patrick, 5.6 704–719
Ochoa, Ellen, 5.5 564–575
O'Dell, Scott, 5.1 72–83, 139j
Ostrander, Emilie, 5.4 480–483
Peck, Richard, 5.5 516–529
Pulver, Robin, 5.1 36–41
Quinlan, Susan, 5.6 658–667
Roethke, Theodore, 5.6 757
Settel, Joanne, 5.1 139h, 5.4 440–451
Sibley, Brian, 5.3 382–383
Silverstein, Shel, 5.6 698–699
Smith, Charles R., 5.3 360–363
Soto, Gary, 5.4 488–497
Sroda, Anne, 5.3 266–279
Stewart, Jeanie, 5.5 532–535
Taylor, Debbie A., 5.6 730–747, 750–753
Thimmesh, Catherine, 5.6 670–673
Tilton, Buck, 5.1 86–89
Trueit, Trudi Strain, 5.1 66–67
Tucker, Tom, 5.3 282–287
Verne, Jules, 5.1 139l, 5.5 586–597
Wong, Janet S., 5.2 254, 257
Yepsen, Roger, 5.3 312–315

Author's craft/style/language. See **Literary craft.**

Author's note. See **Genres.**

Author's perspective/viewpoint/bias, 5.1 105, 111b, 136, 229b, 5.2 221, 256, 5.6 717. See also **Literary craft.**

Author's possible meanings. See **Author's perspective/viewpoint/bias; Literary craft,** author's perspective/viewpoint/bias; **Theme (as a story element).**

Authors, program, 5.1 xx, 5.2 iv, 5.3 iv, 5.4 iv, 5.5 iv, 5.6 iv
  Afflerbach, Peter
  Blachowicz, Camille
  Boyd, Candy Dawson
  Cheyney, Wendy
  Juel, Connie
  Kame'enui, Edward
  Leu, Donald
  Paratore, Jeanne
  Pearson, P. David
  Sebesta, Sam

  Simmons, Deborah
  Vaughn, Sharon
  Watts-Taffe, Susan
  Wixson, Karen Kring

Author's purpose, 5.2 151, 162l–162m, 162–163, 169, 175, 185b, DI·16, DI·17, DI·53, 5.3 262l–262m, 262–263, 269, 277, 283, 287b, 375, DI·6, DI·7, DI·52, 5.4 436l–436m, 445, 481, 5.5 521, 560l–560m, 560–561, 567, 573, 579, 581b, 591, DI·26, DI·27, DI·54

Author study, 5.1 139b–139n

Autobiography. See **Genres.**

B

Background, build. See **Concept development; Prereading strategies,** activate prior knowledge.

Base words with and without spelling changes. See **Spelling,** word structure; **Word structure.**

Bias, 5.1 105, 111b, 5.2 221, 5.6 717

Bibliography
  self-selected reading, 5.1 DI·57–DI·58, TR14–TR17, 5.2 DI·57–DI·58, TR14–TR17, 5.3 DI·57–DI·58, TR14–TR17, 5.4 DI·57–DI·58, TR14–TR17, 5.5 DI·57–DI·58, TR14–TR17, 5.6 DI·57–DI·58, TR14–TR17
  trade book library, 5.1 18i, 42i, 68i, 90i, 112i, 5.2 142i, 162i, 186i, 208i, 230i, 5.3 262i, 288i, 316i, 346i, 364i, 5.4 392i, 412i, 436i, 458i, 484i, 5.5 512i, 536i, 560i, 582i, 604i, 5.6 634i, 654i, 674i, 700i, 726i

Bilingual students. See **ELL (English Language Learners) suggestions.**

Biography. See **Genres.**

Build background. See **Concept development; Prereading strategies,** activate prior knowledge.

C

Capitalization
  nouns, proper, 5.1 133e–133f
  See also **Writing process,** edit.

Card catalog. See **Reference sources.**

Career awareness, 5.3 340–345, 5.5 578–581

Cartoons. See **Genres.**

Case study. See **Genres.**

Categorizing. See **Classifying.**

Cause and effect, 5.1 27, 42l–42m, 42–43, 51, 57, 59, 112l–112m, 112–113, 119, 125, 131, 133b, DI·16, DI·17, DI·46, DI·47, DI·53, DI·56, 5.3 271, 5.5 582l–582m, 582–583, 589, 593, 603, 603b, DI·36, DI·37, DI·55

Central message of text. See **Main idea, Theme (as a story element).**

Character, 5.1 18l–18m, 18–19, 25, 29, 37, 41b, 49, 77, DI·6, DI·7, DI·52, 5.5 512l–512m, 512–513, 519, 525, 533, 535, 535b, DI·6, DI·7, DI·52

Character Counts! See **Character education.**

Character education (as demonstrated in

literature selections)
  attentiveness, 5.1 86–89, 5.2 212–223, 5.4 416–431, 5.6 730–747
  caring, 5.2 146–157, 160–161, 190–203, 212–223, 5.4 462–477, 5.5 532–535
  citizenship, 5.2 234–247, 5.5 564–575
  fairness, 5.1 94–107, 110–111
  initiative, 5.1 46–63, 116–127, 5.3 282–287, 5.4 396–407, 5.5 622–625
  patience, 5.1 72–83, 5.3 292–309, 320–337
  respect, 5.1 94–107, 5.2 146–157, 166–177
  responsibility, 5.2 166–177, 212–223, 5.6 670–673
  trustworthiness, 5.2 212–223, 5.5 516–529, 5.6 638–649, 652–653

Choral reading. See **Fluency, reading.**

Chronology. See **Sequence.**

Chunking. See **Word structure,** chunking.

Classifying
  statements of evidence. See **Fact and opinion, statements of.**
  words into groups, 5.1 70b, 5.4 394b, 5.6 702b

Classroom-based assessment. "If/then" assessment occurs throughout lessons and Guiding Comprehension.

Classroom management, 5.1 18d–18e, 18f–18g, 18g-1–18g-4, 42d–42e, 42f–42g, 42g-1–42g-1, 68d–68e, 68f–68g, 68g-1–68g-4, 90d–90e, 90f–90g, 90g-1–90g-4, 112d–112e, 112f–112g, 112g-1–112g-4, 5.2 142d–142e, 142f–142g, 142g-1–142-4, 162d–162e, 162f–162g, 162g-1–162g-4, 186d–186e, 186f–186g, 186g-1–186g-4, 208d–208e, 208f–208g, 208g-1–208g-4, 230d–230e, 230f–230g, 230g-1–230g-4, DI·52, 5.3 262d–262e, 262f–262g, 262g-1–262g-4, 288d–288e, 288f–288g, 288g-1–288g-4, 316d–316e, 316f–316g, 316g-1–316g-4, 346d–346e, 346f–346g, 346g-1–346g-4, 364d–364e, 364f–364g, 364g-1–364g-4, 5.4 392d–392e, 329f–329g, 329g-1–329g-4, 412d–412e, 412f–412g, 412g-1–412g-4, 436d–436e, 436f–436g, 436g-1–436g-4, 458d–458e, 458f–458g, 458g-1–458g-4, 484d–484e, 484f–484g, 484g-1–484g-4, 5.5 512d–512e, 512f–512g, 512g-1–512g-4, 536d–536e, 536f–536g, 536g-1–536g-4, 560d–560e, 560f–560g, 560g-1–560g-4, 582d–582e, 582f–582g, 582g-1–582g-4, 604d–604e, 604f–604g, 604g-1–604g-4, 5.6 634d–634e, 634f–634g, 634g-1–634g-4, 654d–654e, 654f–654g, 654g-1–654g-4, 674d–674e, 674f–674g, 674g-1–674g-4, 700d–700e, 700f–700g, 700g-1–700g-4, 726d–726e, 726f–726g, 726g-1–726g-4

Clauses
  dependent, 5.1 89e–89f
  independent, 5.1 89e–89f

Colon, 5.1 40, 5.3 333, 5.6 753e–753f

Comma, 5.1 40, 89f, 111e–111f, 5.6 699e–699f

Common word parts. See **Word structure.**

Communication, effective. See **Listening,** tips; **Speaking,** tips.

Community, involvement of. See **School-home connection.**

Comparing and contrasting, 5.1 101, 5.2 142l–142m, 142–143, 149, 153, 161b, 186l–186m, 186–187, 193, 201, 207b, 217, DI·26, DI·27, DI·54, 5.2 DI·6, DI·7, 5.6 674l–674m, 674–675, 681, 689, 693, 699, 699b, DI·26, DI·27, DI·54

Composition. See **Six-trait writing, Writing forms/products, Writing modes, Writing process, Writing purpose.**

Compound words, 5.3 DI·14, 5.4 486b, 5.5 535c. See also **Spelling,** word structure; **Word structure.**

Comprehension skills, explicit/implicit instruction. See **Author's purpose; Cause and effect; Character; Classifying; Comparing and contrasting; Conclusions, drawing; Fact and opinion, statements of; Graphic sources; Main idea; Plot; Predicting; Sequence; Setting; Steps in a process; Summarizing; Theme (as a story element).**

Comprehension strategies. See **Graphic and semantic organizers; Monitor and fix up; Prereading strategies; Questions, answering; Questions, asking; Self-check; Story structure; Text structure; Visualizing.**

Computers, using. See **New literacies (for student reading); Reference sources; Technology; Writing, with technology.**

Concept development, 5.1 17a, 18a, 18l, 20a, 42a, 42l, 44a, 68a, 68l, 70a, 90a, 90l, 92a, 112a, 112l, 114a, 134a, 5.2 141a, 142a, 142l, 144a, 162a, 162l, 164a, 186a, 186l, 188a, 208a, 208l, 210a, 230a, 230l, 232a, 254a, 5.3 261a, 262a, 262l, 264a, 288a, 288l, 290a, 316a, 316l, 318a, 346a, 346l, 348a, 364a, 364l, 366a, 384a, 5.4 391a, 392a, 392l, 394a, 412l, 414a, 436l, 438a, 458l, 460a, 484a, 484l, 486a, 504a, 5.5 511a, 512a, 512l, 514a, 536a, 536l, 538a, 560a, 560l, 562a, 582a, 582l, 584a, 604a, 604l, 606a, 626a, 5.6 633a, 634a, 634l, 636a, 654a, 654l, 656a, 674a, 674l, 676a, 700a, 700l, 702a, 762a, 726l, 728a, 754a. See also **Prereading strategies,** activate prior knowledge.

Conclusions, drawing, 5.1 90l–90m, 5.4 392l–392m, 392–393, 399, 405, 411, 411b, 466, 467, 484l–484m, 484–485, 491, 503, 503b, DI·6, DI·7, DI·46, DI·47, DI·52, DI·56, 5.6 634l–634m, 634–635, 643, 647, 653b, 682, 683, 687, 735, 745, DI·6, DI·7, DI·52

Conjunctions, 5.1 111e–111f, 5.6 673e–673f

Connections, making
  text to self, 5.1 32, 76, 126, 5.2 172, 194, 202, 222, 240, 5.3 278, 308, 326, 356, 5.4 400, 420, 476, 492, 5.5 522, 566, 590, 5.6 644, 648, 694, 738
  text to text, 5.1 41, 62, 67, 82, 89, 111, 133, 5.2 161, 185, 207, 218, 229, 246, 253, 5.3 270, 287, 315, 345, 363, 372, 383, 5.4 411, 435, 457, 468, 483, 496, 503, 5.5 535, 542, 559, 581, 603, 618, 625, 5.6 653, 662, 673, 684, 699, 718, 725, 746, 753
  text to world, 5.1 100, 106, 118, 5.2 156, 176, 5.3 302, 336, 352, 376, 5.4 406, 430, 446, 450, 5.5 528, 550, 574, 596, 612, 5.6 666, 708

Connotation/denotation, 5.1 114b, 5.3 315c

Content-area texts
  science, 5.1 66–67, 86–89, 226–229, 5.3 340–345, 5.4 434–435, 454–457, 5.5 600–603, 5.6 670–673
  social studies, 5.1 110–111, 5.2 160–161, 180–185, 5.3 282–287, 312–315, 5.4 480–483, 5.5 554–559, 622–625, 750–753

Content-area vocabulary, 5.1 66, 70b, 86, 110, 5.2 160, 180, 226, 5.3 282, 290b, 312, 340, 5.4 434, 454, 480, 5.5 554, 600, 622, 5.6 636b, 670, 728b, 750

Context clues for meaning
  antonyms, 5.1 92–93, 5.3 348–349, 363c, DI·35, 5.5 581c
  homographs, 5.6 728–729, 753c, DI·45
  homonyms, 5.1 44–45, 53, 67c, 5.3 318–319, 345c, DI·5, DI·25, DI·35
  multiple-meaning words, 5.1 114–115, 123c, 133, 5.3 264–265, 275, 287c, 331, DI·5, 5.5 562–563, 581c
  synonyms, 5.2 232b, 5.3 366b, DI·35, 5.4 438–439, 447, 5.5 581c
  unfamiliar words, 5.1 99, 111c, DI·15, DI·35, DI·45, 5.2 210–211, 219, 229c, 5.3 331, DI·5, 5.4 414–415, 425, 435c, 457c, 460–461, 473, 483c, DI·15, DI·25, DI·35, 5.5 571, 584–585, 595, 603c, DI·25, DI·35, 5.6 702–703, 709, 725c, 737, 741, DI·35

Contractions. See **Spelling,** word structure; **Word structure, contractions.**

Contrasting. See **Comparing and contrasting.**

Conventions of standard language. See **Capitalization; Grammar and usage; Punctuation; Writing purpose,** edit.

Creative/dramatic activities, 5.1 18j, 41d, 5.2 162j, 207d, 230j, 5.6 634j, 653d, 753d. See also **Speaking,** activities.

Critical thinking
  analyzing, 5.1 34, 64, 84, 105, 108, 125, 128, 5.2 158, 178, 204, 221, 224, 248, 5.3 280, 297, 310, 338, 358, 378, 5.4 405, 408, 432, 452, 478, 498, 5.5 530, 552, 576, 598, 620, 5.6 650, 668, 696, 709, 717, 720, 748. In addition, analytical thinking questions are raised throughout Guiding Comprehension and Reader Response.
  comparing and contrasting across selections (intertextuality), 5.1 41, 62, 67, 82, 89, 111, 133, 5.2 161, 185, 207, 218, 229, 246, 253, 5.3 270, 287, 315, 345, 363, 372, 383, 5.4 411, 435, 457, 468, 483, 496, 503, 5.5 535, 542, 559, 581, 603, 618, 625, 5.6 653, 662, 673, 684, 699, 718, 725, 746, 753
  comparing and contrasting within a text, 5.1 101, 5.2 142l–142m, 142–143, 149, 153, 161b, 186l–186m, 186–187, 193, 201, 207b, 217, 5.6 674l–674m, 674–675, 681, 689, 693, 699, 699b
  deductive reasoning, 5.6 662
  evaluating and critiquing ideas and text, 5.1 34, 64, 84, 105, 108, 125, 128, 5.2 158, 178, 204, 221, 224, 248, 5.3 280, 297, 310, 338, 358, 378, 5.4 405, 408, 432, 452, 478, 498, 5.5 530, 552, 576, 598, 620, 5.6 650, 668, 696, 709, 717, 720, 748

hypothesize, 5.4 457k, 5.6 673k
inductive reasoning, 5.6 662
inferring, 5.1 34, 64, 84, 108, 128, 5.2 158, 178, 204, 224, 248, 5.3 280, 310, 338, 358, 378, 5.4 408, 432, 452, 478, 498, 5.5 530, 552, 576, 598, 620, 5.6 650, 668, 696, 720, 748
organizing ideas, 5.1 20a, 44a, 70a, 92a, 5.2 164a, 188a, 210a, 232a, 5.3 264a, 290a, 318a, 348a, 366a, 5.4 394a, 414a, 438a, 460a, 486a, 5.5 514a, 538a, 562a, 606a, 5.6 636a, 656a, 676a, 702a, 728a
organizing information, 5.1 20a, 44a, 70a, 92a, 5.2 164a, 188a, 210a, 232a, 5.3 264a, 290a, 318a, 348a, 366a, 5.4 394a, 414a, 438a, 460a, 486a, 5.5 514a, 538a, 562a, 606a, 5.6 636a, 656a, 676a, 702a, 728a
synthesizing ideas from different texts and media, 5.1 41k, 67k, 89k, 111k, 133k, 5.2 161k, 185k, 207k, 229k, 253k, 5.3 287k, 315k, 345k, 363k, 383k, 5.4 411k, 435k, 457k, 483k, 503k, 5.5 535k, 559k, 581k, 603k, 625k, 5.6 653k, 673k, 699k, 725k, 753k

See also **Conclusions, drawing; Generalizations, making; Problems, solving.** In addition, critical thinking questions appear throughout Guiding Comprehension in each lesson.

Cross-curricular activities
  art, 5.1 90j, 5.2 186j, 5.3 288j, 316j, 364j, 5.4 458j, 484j, 5.5 536j, 5.6 674j
  careers, 5.5 578–581
  drama, 5.1 18j, 41d, 5.2 162j, 207d, 230j, 5.6 634j, 653d, 753d
  health, 5.1 68j, 5.4 412j, 436j, 5.5 512j
  listening, 5.1 18j, 42j, 68j, 90j, 112j, 5.2 142j, 162j, 186j, 208j, 230j, 5.3 262j, 288j, 316j, 346j, 364j, 5.4 392j, 412j, 436j, 458j, 484j, 5.5 512j, 536j, 560j, 582j, 604j, 5.6 634j, 654j, 674j, 700j, 726j
  math, 5.1 42j, 112j, 5.2 208j, 5.4 392j, 5.5 560j, 582j, 5.6 654j, 700j
  music, 5.2 142j, 5.3 262j, 346j, 5.5 604j, 5.6 726j
  science, 5.1 42k, 49, 53, 59, 66–67, 5.2 208k, 215, 221, 226–227, 5.3 262k, 269, 275, 283, 288k, 312, 316k, 325, 331, 335, 340, 345, 364j, 5.4 412k, 421, 425, 434–435, 436k, 445, 449, 455, 5.5 536k, 543, 549, 560k, 567, 573, 582k, 589, 591, 595, 600–601, 5.6 634k, 641, 647, 653, 654k, 661, 665
  social studies, 5.1 18k, 27, 31, 37, 68k, 75, 77, 81, 87, 90k, 97, 101, 111, 112k, 5.2 142k, 149, 155, 161, 162k, 181, 186k, 207, 230k, 5.3 283, 297, 299, 307, 346k, 353, 361, 371, 375, 5.4 392k, 399, 405, 419, 458k, 467, 471, 473, 480, 484k, 491, 495, 5.5 512k, 554, 604k, 613, 617, 623, 5.6 674k, 681, 683, 689, 700k, 707, 715, 717, 726k, 733, 737, 743, 745
  technology, 5.1 18k, 42k, 68k, 90k, 112k, 5.2 142k, 162k, 186k, 208k, 230k, 5.3 262k, 288k, 316k, 346k, 364k, 5.4 392k, 412k, 436k, 458k, 484k, 5.5 512k, 536k, 560k, 582k, 604k, 5.6 634k, 654k, 674k, 700k, 726k
  writing/vocabulary, 5.1 18k, 42k, 68k, 90k, 112k, 5.2 142k, 162k, 186k, 208k, 230k, 5.3 262k, 288k, 316k, 346k, 364k, 5.4 392k, 412k, 436k, 458k, 484k, 5.5 512k, 536k, 560k, 582k, 604k, 5.6 634k, 654k, 674k, 700k, 726k

Cross-curricular Centers, 5.1 18j–18k, 42j–42k, 68j–68k, 90j–90k, 112j–112k, 5.2 142j–142k, 162j–162k, 186j–186k, 208j–208k, 230j–230k, 5.3 262j–262k, 288j–288k, 316j–316k, 346j–346k, 364j–364k, 5.4 392j–392k, 412j–412k, 436j–436k, 458j–458k, 484j–484k, 5.5 512j–512k, 536j–536k, 560j–560k, 582j–582k, 604j–604k, 5.6 634j–634k, 654j–654k, 674j–674k, 700j–700k, 726j–726k

Cross-textual comparisons. See **Connections, making; Reading across texts.**

Cultures, appreciating, See **Habits and attitudes,** toward other groups and people; **Multicultural connections.**

Cursive. See **Handwriting.**

D

Dash, 5.6 753e–753f

Decoding. See **Phonics, Word Structure.**

Deductive reasoning, 5.6 662. See also **Critical thinking.**

Details and facts, 5.3 295, 299, 335

Diagram. See **Graphic sources.**

Dialogue. See **Literary devices.**

Diary. See **Genres.**

Dictionary/glossary
  definition, 5.1 41l, 70–71
  multiple-meaning words, 5.1 41l, 5.2 164–165, 5.5 538–539, 549, 5.6 636–637, 645
  pronunciation, 5.1 41l, 70, 5.2 164, 5.5 538
  unfamiliar words, 5.1 70–71, DI·24, 5.2 DI·15, 5.5 538–539, 549, DI·15, 5.6 636–637, 645, DI·5
  See also **Reference sources.**

Differentiated instruction, 5.1 DI·2–DI·51, 5.2 DI·2–DI·51, 5.3 DI·2–DI·51, 5.4 DI·2–DI·51, 5.5 DI·2–DI·51, 5.6 DI·2–DI·51. See also **Advanced learners, Intervention.**

Directions, following
  oral, 5.4 411d
  written, 5.2 161l, 5.4 411l, 454–458, 5.6 653l

Discussion. See **Speaking, activities.**

Drama. See **Cross-curricular activities, Genres.**

Dramatic activities, 5.1 18j, 41d, 5.2 162j, 207d, 230j, 5.6 634j, 653d, 753d. See also **Speaking,** activities.

Drawing conclusions. See **Conclusions, drawing.**

E

Echo reading. See **Fluency, reading.**

Electronic information. See **Technology.**

ELL (English Language Learners) suggestions
  access content, 5.1 18m, 18–19, 20, 24, 30, 36, 39, 41b, 42, 42m, 44, 48, 52, 54, 67b, 68l, 68m, 68, 70, 72, 76, 78, 82, 87, 89b, 90, 92, 96, 100, 104, 111b, 112m, 112, 114, 116, 122, 124, 131, 133b, 5.2 142, 144, 146, 150, 154, 161b, 162m, 162, 164, 166, 168, 180, 183, 185b, 186m, 186, 188, 190, 194, 198, 202, 207b, 208m, 208, 210, 212, 214, 216, 229b, 230m, 230, 232, 234, 5.3 262m, 262, 264, 266, 274, 278, 283, 285, 287b, 288m, 288, 290, 292, 302, 304, 306, 308, 313, 315b, 316m, 316, 318, 330, 340, 345b, 346m, 346, 348, 350, 354, 363b, 364m, 364, 366, 368, 374, 381, 383b, 5.4 392m, 392, 394, 398, 404, 411b, 412m, 412, 414, 416, 422, 428, 430, 435b, 436m, 436, 438, 440, 444, 446, 455, 457b, 458m, 458, 460, 464, 468, 472, 480, 483b, 484m, 484, 486, 488, 492, 496, 501, 503b, 5.5 512m, 512, 514, 522, 526, 535b, 536m, 536, 538, 540, 542, 546, 550, 554, 558, 559b, 560m, 560, 562, 568, 572, 581b, 582m, 582, 584, 592, 594, 603b, 604m, 604, 606, 608, 612, 614, 623, 625b, 5.6 634m, 634, 636, 638, 640, 646, 648, 653b, 654m, 654, 656, 658, 662, 664, 671, 673b, 674m, 674, 676, 678, 680, 682, 690, 694, 699b, 700m, 700, 702, 704, 708, 712, 716, 723, 725b, 726m, 726, 728, 730, 732, 738, 744, 746, 751, 753b
  access language, 5.5 544
  activate prior knowledge, 5.1 22, 5.2 227, 5.3 296, 320, 360, 5.4 396, 474, 5.5 516, 532, 564, 579
  assessment, 5.1 35, 41d, 65, 67d, 85, 89d, 109, 111d, 129, 133d, 5.2 159, 161d, 179, 185d, 205, 207d, 225, 229d, 249, 253d, 5.3 281, 287d, 311, 315d, 339, 345d, 359, 363d, 379, 383d, 5.4 409, 411d, 433, 435d, 453, 457d, 479, 483d, 499, 503d, 5.5 503d, 530, 535d, 552, 559d, 576, 581d, 599, 603d, 620, 625d, 5.6 636a, 650, 653d, 668, 673d, 696, 699d, 720, 725d, 748, 753d
  build background, 5.1 20a, 32, 44a, 46, 70a, 92a, 94, 114a, 118, 5.2 142m, 144a, 148, 164a, 188a, 210a, 232a, 238, 251, 5.3 264a, 272, 290a, 298, 318a, 324, 326, 348a, 366a, 372, 5.4 394a, 414a, 424, 438a, 460a, 486a, 494, 5.5 514a, 538a, 552a, 557, 582m, 584a, 586, 606a, 5.6 636a, 642, 656a, 660, 676a, 702a, 728a, 742
  check retelling, 5.1 34, 64, 84, 108, 128, 5.2 158, 178, 204, 224, 248, 5.3 280, 310, 338, 358, 378, 5.4 408, 432, 452, 478, 498, 5.5 598
  comprehension. See **ELL (English Language Learners),** access content.
  context clues, 5.1 58, 126, 5.2 172, 192, 5.4 442
  extend language, 5.1 50, 56, 60, 74, 98, 106, 120, 5.2 152, 156, 170, 174, 184, 220, 242, 5.3 268, 270, 276, 286, 294, 300, 322, 328, 334, 336, 343, 352, 356, 376, 5.4 400, 402, 420, 426, 448, 476, 490, 5.5 518, 520, 524, 528, 548, 570, 574, 588, 590, 610, 616, 618, 5.6 644, 686, 688, 692, 710, 714, 734, 736, 740
  fluency, 5.1 80, 5.2 176, 236, 244, 5.3 332, 5.6 706
  grammar support, 5.1 41e, 67e, 89e, 111e, 133e, 5.2 161e, 185e, 207e, 229e, 253e, 5.3 287e, 315e, 345e, 363e, 383e, 5.4 411e, 435e, 457e, 483e, 503e, 5.5 535e, 559e, 581e, 603e, 625e, 5.6 653e, 673e, 699e, 725e, 753e
  guided practice, 5.1 132, 252, 5.3 382, 5.4 502, 5.5 556, 580, 6.2 724, 752
  idioms, 5.1 26, 40, 102, 5.3 370, 5.4 450, 466, 470, 5.5 556, 596, 5.6 666, 684
  independent practice, 5.4 482, 5.5 624

  resources, 5.1 18g, 42g, 68g, 90g, 112g, 5.2 142g, 162g, 186g, 208g, 230g, 5.3 262g, 288g, 316g, 346g, 364g, 5.4 392g, 412g, 436g, 458g, 484g, 5.5 512g, 536g, 560g, 582g, 604g, 5.6 634g, 654g, 674g, 700g, 726g
  spelling/phonics support, 5.1 41i, 67i, 89i, 111i, 133i, 5.2 161i, 185i, 207i, 229i, 253i, 5.3 287i, 315i, 345i, 363i, 383i, 5.4 411i, 435i, 457i, 483i, 503i, 5.5 535i, 559i, 581i, 603i, 625i, 5.6 653i, 673i, 699i, 725i, 753i
  test practice, 5.1 38, 88, 5.2 182, 228, 5.3 284, 314, 342, 362, 5.4 456, 5.5 534, 602, 624, 5.6 672
  vocabulary support, 5.1 41d, 67d, 89d, 111d, 133d, 5.2 161d, 185d, 207d, 229d, 253d, 5.3 287d, 315d, 345d, 363d, 383d, 5.4 411d, 435d, 457d, 483d, 503d, 5.5 535d, 559d, 581d, 603d, 625d, 5.6 653d, 673d, 699d, 725d, 753d
  writing support, 5.1 41g, 67g, 89g, 111g, 133g, WA4, WA6, WA9, 5.2 161g, 185g, 207g, 229g, 253g, WA4, WA6, WA9, 5.3 287g, 315g, 345g, 363g, 383g, WA4, WA6, WA9, 5.4 411g, 435g, 457g, 483g, 503g, WA4, WA6, WA9, 5.5 535g, 559g, 581g, 603g, 625g, WA4, WA6, WA9, 5.6 653g, 673g, 699g, 725g, 753g, WA4, WA6, WA9

E-mail. See **Genres, Technology.**

Endings. See **Spelling,** word structure; **Word structure.**

End punctuation. See **Exclamation mark, Period, Question mark.**

English, conventions of. See **Capitalization, Grammar and usage; Punctuation; Writing process,** edit.

ESL (English as a Second Language). See **ELL (English Language Learners) suggestions.**

Etymologies. See **Word structure,** etymology.

Essential message. See **Main idea, Theme (as a story element).**

Evaluating sources. See **Research,** process and strategies.

Evaluation. See **Assessment.**

Exaggeration. See **Literary devices.**

Exclamation mark, 5.1 41e–41f

Experiment. See **Genres.**

Expository nonfiction. See **Genres.**

Expression/intonation (prosody). See **Fluency, reading.**

F

Fact and fiction. See **Fact and opinion, statements of.**

Fact and nonfact. See **Fact and opinion, statements of.**

Fact and opinion, statements of, 5.2 208l–208m, 208–209, 215, 221d, 229, 229b, DI·36, DI·37, DI·55, 5.3 301, 316l–316m, 316–317, 323, 329, 333, 345, 345b, 355, DI·26, DI·27, DI·54, 5.6 700l–700m, 700–701, 707, 715, 725, 725b, DI·36, DI·37, DI·55

Family involvement. *See* **School-home connection.**

Fantasy. *See* **Genres.**

Fiction. *See* **Genres.**

Figurative language
  hyperbole, 5.1 58
  idiom, 5.4 411b
  metaphor, 5.3 287b, 5.4 457b
  simile, 5.4 435b, 503b, 5.5 595

Fix-up strategies. *See* **Monitor and fix up.**

Flashback. *See* **Literary devices.**

Flexible grouping. *See* **Grouping students for instruction.**

Fluency, reading
  assessment (taking a running record), 5.1 41a, 67a, 89a, 111a, 133a, WA15–WA16, 5.2 161a, 185a, 207a, 229a, 253a, WA15–WA16, 5.3 287a, 315a, 345a, 363a, 383a, WA15–WA16, 5.4 411a, 435a, 457a, 483a, 503a, WA15–WA16, 5.5 535a, 559a, 581a, 603a, 625a, WA15–WA16, 5.6 653a, 673a, 699a, 725a, 753a, WA15–WA16
  characterization/dialogue, 5.2 142l, 161a, 5.6 634l, 653a
  choral reading, 5.1 41a, 89a, 5.2 185a, 207a, 229a, 5.3 287a, 383a, 5.4 411a, 435a, 483a, 5.5 535a, 559a, 603a, 625a, 5.6 653a, 725a
  echo reading, 5.1 67a, 111a, 133a, 5.2 161a, 253a, 5.3 315a, 345a, 363a, 5.4 457a, 503a, 5.5 581a, 5.6 673a, 699a, 753a
  emotion, 5.4 412l, 435a, 5.5 536l, 559a
  expression/intonation (prosody), 5.2 185a, 5.3 363a
  modeling by teacher, 5.1 18l, 19a, 42l, 43a, 68l, 69a, 90l, 91a, 112l, 113a, 5.2 142l, 143a, 162l, 163a, 186l, 187a, 208l, 209a, 230l, 231a, 5.3 262l, 263a, 288l, 289a, 316l, 317a, 346l, 347a, 364l, 365a, 5.4 392l, 393a, 412l, 413a, 436l, 437a, 458l, 459a, 484l, 485a, 5.5 512l, 513a, 536l, 537a, 560l, 561a, 582l, 583a, 604l, 605a, 5.6 634l, 635a, 654l, 655a, 674l, 675a, 700l, 701a, 726l, 727a
  paired reading, 5.1 41a, 67a, 89a, 111a, 133a, 5.2 161a, 185a, 207a, 229a, 253a, 5.3 287a, 315a, 345a, 363a, 383a, 5.4 411a, 435a, 457a, 483a, 503a, 5.5 535a, 559a, 581a, 603a, 625a, 5.6 653a, 673a, 699a, 725a, 753a
  pauses, 5.1 112l, 133a, 5.5 582l, 603a
  phrasing, 5.1 90l, 111a, 5.2 208l, 229a, 5.3 316l, 345a, 5.6 700l, 725a, 726l, 753a
  pitch, 5.1 68l, 89a, 5.2 186l, 207a
  punctuation, attention to, 5.4 392l, 411a, 484l, 503a, 5.6 654l, 673a
  rate/pace, 5.3 288l, 315a, 346l, 363a, 364l, 383a, 5.4 436l, 457a
  rhythmic patterns of language, 5.6 674l, 699a
  tone of voice, 5.1 18l, 41a, 42l, 67a, 5.2 162l, 185a, 230l, 253a, 5.3 262l, 287a, 5.4 458l, 483a, 560l, 581a, 5.5 604l, 625a
  volume, 5.5 512l, 535a

Folk literature. *See* **Genres.**

Following directions. *See* **Directions, following.**

Foreshadowing. *See* **Literary devices.**

Functional reading, 5.1 86–89, 5.2 212–223, 5.4 434–435

G

Generalizations, making, 5.4 412l–412m, 412–413, 419, 427, 429, 435, 435b, 458l–458m, 458–459, 465, 471, 475, 483, 483b, 493, DI·16, DI·17, DI·36, DI·37, DI·53, DI·55, 5.5 604l–604m, 604–605, 611, 617, 623, 625, 625b, DI·46, DI·47, DI·56

Generate questions. *See* **Questions, asking; Prereading strategies,** ask questions.

Genres
  adventure fiction, 5.5 554–559
  author's note, 5.6 750–753
  autobiography, 5.2 180–185, 5.4 488–497
  biography, 5.1 94–107, 5.2 166–177, 5.3 292–309, 320–337
  cartoons, 5.6 698
  case study, 5.6 658–667
  diary/journal, 5.3 307
  drama, 5.3 266–279, 5.4 462–477
  e-mail, 5.1 130–133, 5.2 160–161
  experiment, 5.4 454–457
  expository nonfiction, 5.1 66–67, 110–111, 116–127, 5.2 212–223, 226–229, 5.3 350–357, 368–377, 5.4 416–431, 434–435, 440–451, 5.6 608–619, 704–719
  fantasy, 5.1 36–41
  fiction, 5.4 396–407
  folk literature, 5.2 190–203, 206–207, 5.6 652–653
  historical fiction, 5.1 72–83
  humorous fiction, 5.1 22–33, 5.5 516–529
  informational article, 5.5 600–603
  Internet article, 5.2 250–253, 5.3 380–383, 5.4 500–503, 5.5 578–581, 5.6 722–725
  interview, 5.1 86–89, 5.3 340–345, 5.5 564–575
  journal, 5.3 306–309
  legend, 5.6 652–653
  magazine article, 5.2 215
  mystery, 5.6 661
  myth, 5.6 678–695
  narrative nonfiction, 5.3 282–287, 312–315, 5.5 540–551, 622–625, 5.6 670–673
  new literacies, 5.1 130–133, 5.2 250–253, 5.3 380–383, 5.4 500–503, 5.5 573, 578–581, 5.6 722–725
  newspaper article, 5.4 480–483
  online reference sources and directories, 5.4 500–503, 5.5 578–581
  personal essay, 5.4 495
  photo essay, 5.3 368–377, 5.4 416–431, 5.5 608–619
  play, 5.3 266–279, 5.4 462–477
  poetry, 5.1 134–137, 5.2 234–247, 254–257, 5.3 360–363, 384–387, 5.4 410–411, 504–507, 5.5 626–629, 5.6 698–699, 754–757
  realistic fiction, 5.2 146–157, 5.6 638–649, 730–747
  science fiction, 5.5 586–597
  search engines, 5.3 380–383
  short story, 5.5 532–535
  song, 5.3 353
  tall tale, 5.1 46–63
  textbook article, 5.5 600–603
  Web site, 5.2 250–253, 5.3 380–383, 5.4 500–503, 5.5 573, 578–581, 5.6 722–725

Genre study, 5.1 139a–139k, DI·9, DI·19, DI·29, DI·39, DI·49, 5.2 DI·9, DI·19, DI·29, DI·39,

DI·49, 5.3 DI·9, DI·19, DI·29, DI·39, DI·49, 5.4 DI·9, DI·19, DI·29, DI·39, DI·49, 5.5 DI·9, DI·19, DI·29, DI·39, DI·49, 5.6 DI·9, DI·19, DI·29, DI·39, DI·49

Gifted students. *See* **Advanced learners.**

Glossary. *See* **Dictionary/glossary.**

Goal and outcome. *See* **Plot, Story structure.**

Grammar and usage. *See* **Adjectives, Adverbs, Clauses, Conjunctions, Interjections, Negatives, Nouns, Prepositions and prepositional phrases, Pronouns, Sentences, Subject/verb agreement, Verbs.**

Grammar reference book. *See* **Reference sources.**

Graph. *See* **Graphic sources.**

Graphic and semantic organizers, 5.2 230–231, 241, 243, 247, 253, DI·46, DI·47, 5.3 346–347, 357, 5.5 604–605, 617, 619, DI·47
  as comprehension tool, 5.1 18, 42, 68, 90, 112, 5.2 162, 186, 208, 230–231, 241, 243, 247, 253, DI·46, DI·47, 5.3 262, 288, 316, 346–347, 5.4 412, 458, 484, 5.5 512, 560, 582, 604–605, 5.6 634, 654, 674, 700, 726
  as concept development tool, 5.1 18l, 41c, 42l, 67c, 68l, 89c, 90l, 111c, 112l, 133c, 5.2 142l, 161c, 162l, 185c, 186l, 207c, 208l, 229c, 230l, 253c, 5.3 262l, 287c, 288l, 315c, 316l, 345c, 346l, 363c, 364l, 5.4 392l, 411c, 412l, 435c, 457c, 458l, 483c, 484l, 503c, 5.5 512l, 535c, 536l, 559c, 560l, 581c, 582l, 603c, 604l, 5.6 634l, 653c, 654l, 673c, 674l, 699c, 700l, 725c, 726l, 753c
  as prereading tool, 5.1 20a, 44a, 70a, 92a, 114a, 5.2 164a, 188a, 210a, 232a, 5.3 264a, 290a, 318a, 348a, 366a, 5.4 394a, 414a, 438a, 460a, 486a, 5.5 514b, 538a, 562a, 606a, 5.6 636a, 656a, 676a, 702a, 728a
  as prewriting tool, 5.1 41h, 67h, 89h, 111h, 133h, WA3, 5.2 161h, 185h, 207h, 229h, 253h, WA3, 5.3 287h, 315h, 345h, 363h, 383h, WA3, 5.4 411h, 435h, 457h, 503h, WA3, 5.5 535h, 559h, 581h, 603h, WA3, 5.6 653h, 699h, WA3
  as vocabulary/word structure tool, 5.1 41c, 44b, 67c, 70b, 89c, 111c, 133c, 5.2 161c, 164b, 185c, 207c, 229c, 253c, 5.3 264b, 287c, 290b, 315c, 318b, 345c, 348b, 363c, 383c, 5.4 394b, 411c, 435b, 457c, 460b, 483c, 486b, 5.5 514b, 535c, 559c, 581c, 584b, 603c, 625c, 5.6 636b, 653c, 673c, 699c, 702b, 725c, 753c
  types
    author's purpose chart, 5.2 162, 5.3 262, 5.5 560
    cause and effect chart, 5.1 42, 112, 5.5 582
    character and plot chart, 5.5 512
    column chart, 5.1 41c, 44b, 70b, 89c, 111c, 133c, 5.2 161c, 164b, 185h, 207c, 229c, 253c, 5.3 264b, 287c, 290b, 315c, 318b, 348b, 5.4 394b, 411c, 435c, 483c, 5.5 535c, 559c, 603c, 625c, 5.6 653c, 673c, 702h, 725c, 753c
    compare and contrast chart, 5.2 186, 5.6 674
    conclusions, draw chart, 5.4 484, 5.6 634
    fact and opinion chart, 5.2 208, 5.3 316, 5.6 700

generalization chart, 5.4 412, 458, 5.5 604–605, DI·46

how-to chart, 5.2 WA3

KWL chart, 5.1 92a, 5.2 164a, 210a, 5.3 264a, 290a, 316a, 348a, 5.4 414a, 486a, 5.5 538a, 562a, 5.6 656a, 728a, WA3

list, 5.5 603h

main idea and details chart, 5.3 288, 346–347, 5.6 654

notes for personal narrative, 5.1 WA3

persuasive argument chart, 5.5 WA3

plot chart, 5.1 18

sequence chart, 5.1 67h, 89h, 90, 111h, 5.2 161h, 241, 247, 5.3 345h, 5.5 559h, 581h, 5.6 726

story chart, 5.4 WA3

story plan, 5.3 287h, 5.4 457h

synonym and antonym chart, 5.6 584b

T-chart, 5.1 20a, 67c, 133h, 5.2 185c, 188a, 253h, 5.3 363c, 383h, 5.4 503h, 5.5 535h, 581c, 606a, 5.6 699c

theme and setting chart, 5.1 68

time line, 5.2 230–231, 243, 253, DI·46

Venn diagram, 5.1 133h, 5.2 253h, 5.3 383h, WA3, 5.4 503h, 5.6 DI·54

vocabulary, 5.2 144b, 232b, 5.3 366b, 5.4 414b, 5.5 538b, 584b, 5.6 676b

web, 5.1 18l, 41c, 41h, 42l, 44a, 67c, 68l, 70a, 89c, 90l, 111c, 111h, 112l, 133c, WA3, 5.2 142l, 161c, 162l, 185c, 185h, 186l, 207c, 208l, 229c, 229h, 230l, 232a, 253c, 5.3 262l, 287c, 288l, 315c, 315h, 316l, 345c, 346l, 363c, 363h, 364l, 366a, 383c, 5.4 392l, 394a, 411c, 411h, 412l, 435c, 435h, 436l, 438a, 457c, 458l, 460h, 483c, 484l, 503c, 5.5 512l, 514b, 535c, 536l, 559c, 560l, 581c, 582l, 603c, 604l, 5.6 634l, 636a, 653c, 653h, 654l, 673c, 674l, 676a, 699c, 699h, 700l, 702a, 725c, 726l, 753c

word frame, 5.4 457c

word meaning chart, 5.4 394b

word rating chart, 5.1 44b, 5.2 164b, 5.3 290b, 318b, 348b, 5.4 460b, 486b, 5.5 514b, 5.6 636b

Graphic sources, 5.1 67, 5.3 364–365, 371, DI·46, DI·47, DI·56, 5.4 421, 436–437, 443, 449, 455, 457b, DI·26, DI·27, DI·54, 5.5 536–537, 543, 547, 559b, 569, 613, DI·16, DI·53

advertisement, 5.3 287l

application, 5.6 699l

chart/table, 5.1 67, 5.3 383l

diagram/scale drawing, 5.3 383l, 5.5 603l

graph, 5.3 364, 383l, 5.4 503l

graphics, 5.3 383l

illustration (photograph or art) and/or caption, 5.2 253l

map/globe, 5.3 383l, 5.5 536–537, 5.6 725l

order form, 5.6 699l

poster/announcement, 5.6 753l

schedule, 5.3 345l

symbols, 5.3 383l

time line, 5.3 383l, 5.6 673l

Greek and Latin roots. See Word structure.

Grouping students for instruction

advanced learners, 5.1 18f–18g, 42f–42g, 68f–68g, 90f–90g, 112f–112g, DI·3, DI·5, DI·7, DI·9, DI·11, DI·13, DI·15, DI·17, DI·19, DI·21, DI·23, DI·25, DI·27, DI·29, DI·31, DI·33, DI·35, DI·37, DI·39, DI·41, DI·43, DI·45, DI·47, DI·49, DI·51, 5.2 142f–142g, 162f–162g, 186f–186g, 208f–208g, 230f–230g, DI·3, DI·5, DI·7, DI·9, DI·11, DI·13, DI·15, DI·17, DI·19, DI·21, DI·23, DI·25, DI·27, DI·29, DI·31, DI·33, DI·35, DI·37, DI·39, DI·41, DI·43, DI·45, DI·47, DI·49, DI·51, 5.3 262f–262g, 288f–288g, 316f–316g, 346f–346g, 364f–364g, DI·3, DI·5, DI·7, DI·9, DI·11, DI·13, DI·15, DI·17, DI·19, DI·21, DI·25, DI·27, DI·29, DI·31, DI·33, DI·35, DI·37, DI·39, DI·41, DI·43, DI·45, DI·47, DI·49, DI·51, 5.4 392f–392g, 412f–412g, 436f–436g, 458f–458g, 484f–484g, DI·3, DI·5, DI·7, DI·9, DI·11, DI·13, DI·15, DI·17, DI·19, DI·21, DI·23, DI·25, DI·27, DI·29, DI·31, DI·33, DI·35, DI·37, DI·39, DI·41, DI·43, DI·45, DI·47, DI·49, DI·51, 5.5 512f–512g, 536f–536g, 560f–560g, 582f–582g, 604f–604g, DI·3, DI·5, DI·7, DI·9, DI·11, DI·13, DI·15, DI·17, DI·19, DI·21, DI·23, DI·25, DI·27, DI·29, DI·31, DI·33, DI·35, DI·37, DI·39, DI·41, DI·43, DI·45, DI·47, DI·49, DI·51, 5.6 634f–634g, 654f–654g, 674f–674g, 700f–700g, 726f–726g, DI·3, DI·5, DI·7, DI·9, DI·11, DI·13, DI·15, DI·17, DI·19, DI·21, DI·23, DI·25, DI·27, DI·29, DI·31, DI·33, DI·35, DI·37, DI·39, DI·41, DI·43, DI·45, DI·47, DI·49, DI·51

intervention, 5.1 18f–18g, 42f–42g, 68f–68g, 90f–90g, 112f–112g, DI·2, DI·4, DI·6, DI·8, DI·10, DI·12, DI·14, DI·16, DI·18, DI·20, DI·22, DI·24, DI·26, DI·28, DI·30, DI·32, DI·34, DI·36, DI·38, DI·40, DI·42, DI·44, DI·46, DI·48, DI·50, 5.2 142f–142g, 162f–162g, 186f–186g, 208f–208g, 230f–230g, DI·2, DI·4, DI·6, DI·8, DI·10, DI·12, DI·14, DI·16, DI·18, DI·20, DI·22, DI·24, DI·26, DI·28, DI·30, DI·32, DI·34, DI·36, DI·38, DI·40, DI·42, DI·44, DI·46, DI·48, DI·50, 5.3 262f–262g, 288f–288g, 316f–316g, 346f–346g, 364f–364g, DI·2, DI·4, DI·6, DI·8, DI·10, DI·12, DI·14, DI·16, DI·18, DI·20, DI·22, DI·24, DI·26, DI·28, DI·30, DI·32, DI·34, DI·36, DI·38, DI·40, DI·42, DI·44, DI·46, DI·48, DI·50, 5.4 392f–392g, 412f–412g, 436f–436g, 458f–458g, 484f–484g, DI·2, DI·4, DI·6, DI·8, DI·10, DI·12, DI·14, DI·16, DI·18, DI·20, DI·22, DI·24, DI·26, DI·28, DI·30, DI·32, DI·34, DI·36, DI·38, DI·40, DI·42, DI·44, DI·46, DI·48, DI·50, 5.5 512f–512g, 536f–536g, 560f–560g, 582f–582g, 604f–604g, DI·2, DI·4, DI·6, DI·8, DI·10, DI·12, DI·14, DI·16, DI·18, DI·20, DI·22, DI·24, DI·26, DI·28, DI·30, DI·32, DI·34, DI·36, DI·38, DI·40, DI·42, DI·44, DI·46, DI·48, DI·50, 5.6 634f–634g, 654f–654g, 674f–674g, 700f–700g, 726f–726g, DI·2, DI·4, DI·6, DI·8, DI·10, DI·12, DI·14, DI·16, DI·18, DI·20, DI·22, DI·24, DI·26, DI·28, DI·30, DI·32, DI·34, DI·36, DI·38, DI·40, DI·42, DI·44, DI·46, DI·48, DI·50

Guiding Reading. See Grouping students for instruction. Guiding Comprehension and leveled readers are a part of every lesson plan.

H

Habits and attitudes

consequences of actions/behaviors/choices (as demonstrated in literature selections). See Character education.

humanity and compassion (as demonstrated in literature selections). See Character education.

toward other groups and people (multicultural values), 5.1 72–83, 94–107, 130–133, 5.2 166–177, 190–203, 5.6 652–653, 730–747. See also Multicultural connections.

toward reading, writing, listening, speaking, viewing, 5.1 18l, 20a, 42l, 44a, 68l, 70a, 90l, 92a, 112l, 114a, 5.2 142l, 144a, 162l, 164a, 186l, 188a, 208l, 210a, 230l, 232a, 5.3 262l, 264a, 288l, 290a, 316l, 318a, 346l, 348a, 364l, 366a, 5.4 392l, 394a, 412l, 414a, 436l, 438a, 458l, 460a, 484l, 486a, 5.5 512l, 514a, 536l, 538a, 560l, 562a, 582l, 584a, 604l, 606a, 5.6 634l, 636a, 654l, 656a, 674l, 676a, 700l, 702a, 726l, 728a

Handwriting, 5.1 TR10–TR13, 5.2 TR10–TR13, 5.3 TR10–TR13, 5.4 TR10–TR13, 5.5 TR10–TR13, 5.6 TR10–TR13

Health activities. See Cross-curricular activities.

Higher-order thinking skills. See Critical thinking.

Historical fiction. See Genres.

Home-school connection. See School-home connection.

Homework. See School-home connection.

Homographs, 5.4 394b, 5.6 728–729, 753c. See also Vocabulary strategies.

Homonyms, 5.1 44b, 44–45, 53, 67c, 5.3 318, 345c. See also Vocabulary strategies.

Homophones, 5.4 414b, 435c

Humorous fiction. See Genres.

Hyperbole. See Literary devices, exaggeration/hyperbole.

Hyphen, 5.6 753e–753f

Hypothesize, 5.4 457k, 5.6 673k

I

Idioms. See Figurative language, Literary devices.

Illustrations. See Graphic sources, diagram/scale drawing, illustration and/or caption; Prereading strategies, use illustrations.

Illustrator's craft/style. See Literary craft.

Illustrator study, 5.1 139m–139p

Imagery. See Literary devices.

Manual. *See* **Reference sources.**

Map/globe. *See* **Graphic sources.**

Mapping selections. *See* **Graphic and semantic organizers,** types.

Mass media. *See* **Viewing.**

Mathematics activities. *See* **Cross-curricular activities.**

Mechanics (of English grammar and writing). *See* **Capitalization, Punctuation.**

Media. *See* **Viewing.**

Metacognition. *See* **Monitor and fix up, Self-check.**

Metaphor, 5.3 287b, 5.4 457b. *See also* **Figurative language.**

Modeling. Teacher modeling and think-alouds are presented throughout Skills in Context lessons and After Reading lessons.

Modern realistic fiction. *See* **Genres,** realistic fiction.

Monitor and fix up, 5.1 42–43, 55, 57, 63, DI·17, 5.2 162–163, 175, 177, 183, 185, 5.4 436–437, 449, 451, 457, DI·27, 5.5 560–561, 572, 573, 575, 581, DI·27
  adjust reading rate, 5.2 162–163, 5.4 455, 5.5 560, 573, 579, 5.6 661, 723
  ask questions, 5.1 42–43, 57
  read on, 5.1 42–43
  reread, 5.1 55, 5.2 183, DI·17, 5.4 457, DI·26, 5.5 581
  summarize, 5.1 63
  take notes, 5.5 560–561
  use a graphic organizer, 5.1 63, 5.4 457
  use graphic sources, 5.4 436–437
  use reference sources, 5.4 436, 449, 451

Monitor comprehension. *See* **Monitor and fix up, Self-check.**

Mood. *See* **Literary devices.**

Motivation, 5.1 18l, 20a, 42l, 44a, 68l, 70a, 90l, 92a, 112l, 114a, 5.2 142l, 144a, 162l, 164a, 186l, 188a, 208l, 210a, 230l, 232a, 5.3 262l, 264a, 288l, 290a, 316l, 318a, 346l, 348a, 364l, 366a, 5.4 392l, 394a, 412l, 414a, 436l, 438a, 458l, 460a, 484l, 486a, 5.5 512l, 514a, 536l, 538a, 560l, 562a, 582l, 584a, 604l, 606a, 5.6 634l, 636a, 654l, 656a, 674l, 676a, 700l, 702a, 726l, 728a

Multicultural connections, 5.1 72–83, 94–107, 130–133, 5.2 166–177, 190–203, 5.6 652–653, 730–747. *See also* **Habits and attitudes.**

Multiple-meaning words, 5.1 114–115, 133c, 5.2 164b, 5.3 264–265, 275, 287, 348b, 5.4 414b, 460b, 5.5 514b, 562–563, 581c

Multisyllabic words. *See* **Spelling,** word structure; **word structure,** chunking; endings, inflected and uninflected; syllabication; word parts.

Music activities. *See* **Cross-curricular activities.**

Mystery. *See* **Genres.**

Myth. *See* **Genres.**

Narrative nonfiction. *See* **Genres.**

Negatives, 5.5 535e–535f

New literacies (for student reading), 5.1 130–133, 5.2 250–253, 5.3 380–383, 5.4 500–503, 5.5 573, 578–581, 5.6 722–725. *See also* **Technology.**

Newsletter. *See* **Reference sources.**

Newspaper (as reference sources). *See* **Reference sources.**

Newspaper article. *See* **Genres, Reference sources.**

Nonverbal communication. *See* **Listening,** tips; **Speaking,** tips.

Note-taking, 5.5 559l, 5.6 673g–673h

Nouns
  common/proper, 5.1 133e–133f
  possessive, 5.2 185e–185f
  singular/plural, 5.2 161e–161f
    See also **Capitalization.**

Online reference sources and directories. *See* **Genres; Reference sources,** Internet and World Wide Web.

Opinion and fact. *See* **Fact and opinion, statements of.**

Oral reading ability
  choral reading, 5.1 41a, 89a, 5.2 185a, 207a, 229a, 5.3 287a, 383a, 5.4 411a, 435a, 483a, 5.5 535a, 559a, 603a, 625a, 5.6 653a, 725a
  expression/intonation (prosody), 5.2 185a, 5.3 363a
  fluency, 5.1 41a, 67a, 89a, 111a, 111d, 133a, 5.2 161a, 185a, 207a, 229a, 253a, 253d, 5.3 287a, 315a, 345a, 363a, 383a, 5.4 411a, 435a, 457a, 483a, 503a, 5.5 535a, 559a, 581a, 603a, 625a, 5.6 653a, 673a, 699a, 725a, 753a
  paired reading, 5.1 41a, 67a, 89a, 111a, 133a, 5.2 161a, 185a, 207a, 229a, 253a, 5.3 287a, 315a, 345a, 363a, 383a, 5.4 411a, 435a, 457a, 483a, 503a, 5.5 535a, 559a, 581a, 603a, 625a, 5.6 653a, 673a, 699a, 725a, 753a

Order form. *See* **Graphic sources.**

Organizing information
  classifying, 5.1 70b, 5.4 394b, 5.6 702b
  outlining, 5.5 625l, 5.6 725g–725h
  summarizing, 5.1 112–113, 125, 127, 133, 5.3 288–289, 303, 307, 309, 315, 383, 5.5 582–583, 593, 597, 601, 625
  taking notes, 5.5 559l, 5.6 673g–673h
  See also **Graphic and semantic organizers; Logs, strategy response.**

Outlining, 5.5 625l, 5.6 725g–725h

Own life, text's relation to. *See* **Character education; Connections, making; Habits and attitudes.**

Paired reading. *See* **Fluency, reading.**

Paraphrasing, 5.1 133b, 5.5 559l, 581b. *See also* **Summarizing.**

Parentheses, 5.1 123

Parents. *See* **School-home connection.**

Parts of a book, 5.1 75, 5.2 185l

Penmanship. *See* **Handwriting.**

Period, 5.1 41e–41f

Personal essay. *See* **Genres.**

Personal reading programs. *See* **Bibliography, self-selected reading.**

Persuasion, 5.5 625b. *See also* **Author's perspective/viewpoint/bias.**

Phonics
  chunking. *See* **Word structure,** chunking.
  common word (vowel) patterns
    VCCV, 5.1 41i–41j
    VCV, 5.1 41i–41j, 67i–67j
  consonant digraphs, 5.2 161i–161j
  consonant sounds and patterns, 5.3 345i–345j
  consonants, double, 5.3 363i–363j
  graphophonic cues, 5.1 21, 5.2 233, 5.3 367, 5.4 395, 5.5 607, 5.6 677
  strategies. *See* **Spelling,** phonics, connection to.
  vowels
    digraphs, 5.1 89i–89j
    long, 5.1 67i–67j
    r-controlled, 5.2 207i–207j, 253i–253j
    schwa sound, 5.2 287i–287j
    short, 5.1 41i–41j
    sounds and patterns, 5.1 41i–41j, 67i–67j

Photo essay. *See* **Genres.**

Phrasing. *See* **Fluency, reading.**

Pictures. *See* **Graphic sources,** illustration and/or caption; **Prereading strategies,** use illustrations.

Pitch. *See* **Fluency, reading.**

Play. *See* **Genres.**

Plot, 5.1 18l–18m, 18–19, 25, 29, 39, 41b, 49, 61, 77, DI·6, DI·7, 5.5 512l–512m, 512–513, 519, 525, 535, 535b, DI·6, DI·7

Poetic devices. *See* **Sound devices and poetic elements.**

Poetry. *See* **Genres.**

Poetry selections
  "Almost Human," Pat Moon, 5.6 756
  "Bat, The," Theodore Roethke, 5.6 757
  "Bronze Horse, The," Beverly McLoughland, 5.3 385
  "Camel," Lillian M. Fisher, 5.4 507
  "Chemistry 101," Marilyn Nelson, 5.3 384
  "Desert Tortoise," Byrd Baylor, 5.4 506
  "Drum, The," Nikki Giovanni, 5.4 505
  "For Peace Sake," Cedric McClester, 5.2 254–255
  "Full Day," Naomi Shihab Nye, 5.1 136–137
  "Jimmy Jet and His TV Set," Shel Silverstein, 5.6 698–699
  "Keziah," Gwendolyn Brooks, 5.4 411

"Limericks," Edward Lear, 5.6 754

"Microscope, The," Maxine W. Kumin, 5.1 134–135

"Midnight Ride of Paul Revere, The," Henry Wadsworth Longfellow, 5.2 234–247

"Not in Vain," Emily Dickenson, 5.2 257

"Path to the Moon, A," bp Nichol, 5.5 628–629

"Perfect Harmony," Charles R. Smith, 5.3 360–363

"Share the Adventure," Patricia and Fredrick McKissack, 5.5 627

"Stairs," Oliver Herford, 5.3 387

"Strangers," Janet S. Wong, 5.2 257

"Sunflakes," Frank Asch, 5.6 755

"Termites, The," Douglas Floriatt, 5.3 386

"Two People I Want to Be Like," Eve Merriam, 5.2 256

"Under the Back Porch," Virginia Hamilton, 5.4 410

"Which Lunch Table?," Kristine O'Connell George, 5.4 504

"Your World," Georgia Douglas Johnson, 5.5 626
See also **Genres.**

Point of view. See **Literary devices.**

Poster. See **Graphic sources,** poster/announcement.

Predicting
    confirming predictions, 5.3 337
    outcomes, 5.2 186–187, 197, 201, 203, 207, DI·26, DI·27, 5.3 316–317, 327, 329, 337, 341, 343, DI·36, DI·37, DI·26, DI·27, 5.4 412–413, 423, 427, 431, DI·17
    previewing and predicting, 5.1 22, 36, 46, 66, 72, 86, 94, 110, 116, 130, 5.2 146, 160, 166, 180, 190, 206, 212, 226, 234, 250, 5.3 266, 282, 292, 312, 320, 340, 350, 360, 368, 380, 5.4 396, 410, 416, 434, 440, 454, 462, 480, 488, 500, 5.5 516, 532, 540, 554, 564, 578, 586, 600, 608, 622, 5.6 638, 652, 658, 670, 678, 698, 704, 722, 730, 750

Prefixes, 5.2 144–145, 155, 161c, 5.3 366–367, 373, 383c, 5.5 606–607, 625c. See also **Spelling,** word structure; **Word structure.**

Prepositions and prepositional phrases, 5.3 383e–383f

Prereading strategies
    activate prior knowledge, 5.1 18–19, 20a, 29, 33, 41, 44a, 70a, 92a, 114a, DI·6, DI·7, 5.2 144a, 164a, 188a, 210a, 232a, 5.3 264a, 290a, 318a, 348a, 364–365, 366a, 377, 381, DI·46, DI·47, 5.4 394a, 414a, 438a, 460a, 486a, 5.5 512–513, 514a, 535, 538a, 562a, 584a, 606a, DI·6, DI·7, 5.6 636a, 656a, 676a, 702a, 726–727, 728a, 739, 743, 747, DI·46, DI·47
    ask questions, 5.1 92a, 5.2 164a, 210a, 5.3 264a, 290a, 318a, 348a, 5.4 414a, 486a, 5.5 538a, 562a, 5.6 656a, 728a
    graphic organizers
        KWL, 5.1 92a, 5.2 164a, 210a, 5.3 264a, 290a, 318a, 348a, 5.4 414a, 486a, 5.5 538a, 562a, 5.6 656a, 728a
        T-chart, 5.1 20a, 5.2 188a, 5.5 606a, 5.6 702a
        web, 5.1 44a, 70a, 5.2 232a, 5.3 366a, 5.4 394a, 438a, 460a, 5.5 514a, 5.6 636a, 676a
    See also **Graphic and semantic organizers.**

preview and predict, 5.1 22, 36, 46, 66, 72, 86, 94, 110, 116, 130, 5.2 146, 160, 166, 180, 190, 206, 212, 226, 234, 250, 5.3 266, 282, 292, 312, 320, 340, 350, 360, 368, 380, 5.4 396, 410, 416, 434, 440, 454, 462, 480, 488, 500, 5.5 516, 532, 540, 554, 564, 578, 586, 600, 608, 622, 5.6 638, 652, 658, 670, 678, 698, 704, 722, 730, 750
set purposes for reading, 5.1 23, 47, 73, 95, 117, 5.2 147, 167, 191, 213, 235, 5.3 267, 293, 321, 351, 369, 5.4 397, 417, 441, 463, 489, 5.5 517, 541, 565, 587, 609, 5.6 639, 659, 679, 705, 731
skim and scan, 5.2 180
use illustrations, 5.1 22, 36, 46, 72, 94, 110, 116, 5.2 146, 166, 190, 206, 226, 234, 5.3 266, 282, 292, 312, 320, 350, 360, 368, 5.4 396, 410, 416, 434, 454, 462, 480, 488, 5.5 516, 532, 540, 554, 564, 586, 600, 608, 5.6 638, 652, 658, 678, 698, 704, 750
use reading strategy, 5.1 92a, 5.2 164a, 210a, 5.3 264a, 290a, 318a, 348a, 5.4 414a, 486a, 5.5 538a, 562a, 5.6 656a, 728a
use text features, 5.1 66, 86, 130, 5.2 160, 180, 212, 226, 250, 5.3 282, 312, 340, 360, 380, 5.4 434, 454, 480, 500, 5.5 578, 600, 622, 5.6 670, 722

Previewing. See **Prereading strategies.**

Prior knowledge. See **Prereading strategies,** activate prior knowledge.

Problems, solving, 5.2 DI·3, DI·13, DI·33, 5.3 DI·13, DI·27, DI·33, DI·43, 5.4 DI·5, DI·23, 5.5 559g–559h, DI·9, DI·37, 5.6 DI·3, DI·5, DI·13, DI·17, DI·27, DI·43

Projects, 5.1 16–17, 134a, 138–139, 5.2 140–141, 254a, 258–259, 5.3 260–261, 384a, 388–389, 5.4 390–391, 504a, 508–509, 5.5 510–511, 626a, 630–631, 5.6 632–633, 754a, 758–759

Pronouns
    case, 5.4 457e–457f
    demonstrative, 5.5 581e–581f
    indefinite, 5.4 483e–483f
    object, 5.4 411e–411f, 503e–503f
    pronoun/antecedent agreement, 5.4 435e–435f
    reflexive, 5.4 483e–483f
    subject, 5.4 411e–411f, 503e–503f

Proofreading. See **Writing process,** edit.

Propaganda, 5.3 297, 5.6 709

Prosody. See **Fluency, reading,** expression/intonation (prosody).

Punctuation. See **Apostrophe; Colon; Comma; Dash; Exclamation mark; Hyphen; Italics; Parentheses; Period; Question mark; Quotation marks; Semicolon; Underlining; Writing process,** edit.

Punctuation, attention to. See **Fluency, reading.**

Purposes for reading. See **Monitor and fix up; Prereading strategies,** set purposes for reading.

Put Reading First text comprehension strategies. See **Graphic and semantic organizers; Questions, answering; Questions, asking; Summarizing.**

Q

Question-answer relationship (QAR). See **Questions, answering.**

Question mark, 5.1 41e–41f

Questions, answering (QAR), 5.2 142–143, 153, 157, 161, 5.4 392–393, 405, 407, DI·6, DI·7, 5.6 674–675, 685, 689, 695, DI·26, DI·27

Questions, asking, 5.1 90–91, 103, 105, 107, DI·36, DI·37, 5.2 208–209, 227, DI·6, DI·7, DI·36, DI·37, 5.5 536–537, 547, 551, 557, 559, DI·16, DI·17, 5.6 700–701, 713, 715, 719, 722, DI·36, DI·37. See also **Prereading strategies,** set purposes for reading; **Speaking, activities.**

Quotation marks, 5.1 40, 5.4 411k, 5.6 725e–725f

R

Rate. See **Fluency, reading; Monitor and fix up.**

Read-aloud, 5.1 18m, 42m, 68m, 90m, 112m, TR14, 5.2 142m, 162m, 186m, 208m, 230m, TR14, 5.3 262m, 288m, 316m, 346m, 364m, TR14, 5.4 392m, 412m, 436m, 458m, 484m, TR14, 5.5 512m, 536m, 560m, 582m, 604m, TR14, 5.6 634m, 654m, 674m, 700m, 726m, TR14

Reader response. See **Connections, making; Response to literature.**

Reader's Guide to Periodical Literature. See **Reference sources.**

Reading across texts, 5.1 41, 62, 67, 82, 89, 111, 133, 5.2 161, 185, 207, 218, 229, 246, 253, 5.3 270, 287, 315, 345, 363, 372, 383, 5.4 411, 435, 457, 468, 483, 496, 503, 5.5 535, 542, 559, 581, 603, 618, 625, 5.6 653, 662, 673, 684, 699, 718, 725, 746, 753

Reading fluency. See **Fluency, reading; Oral reading ability.**

Reading rate. See **Fluency, reading; Monitor and fix up.**

Reading strategies. See **Strategies.**

Reading to students. See **Read-aloud.**

Realistic fiction. See **Genres.**

Recreational reading. See **Bibliography,** self-selected reading.

Reference sources
    almanac, 5.1 67l
    atlas, 5.6 725l
    card catalog/library database, 5.3 363l
    dictionary/glossary, 5.1 41l
    encyclopedia, 5.1 133l
    grammar/reference book, 5.2 161l
    Internet and World Wide Web, 5.1 41k, 67k, 89k, 111k, 133k, 5.2 161k, 185k, 207k, 229k, 253k, 5.3 287k, 315k, 345k, 363k, 383k, 5.4 411k, 435k, 457k, 483k, 503k, 5.5 535k, 559k, 581k, 603k, 625k, 5.6 653k, 673k, 699k, 725k, 753k
    magazine/periodical, 5.4 457l
    manual, 5.2 161l, 5.4 411l

newsletter, 5.1 111l
newspaper, 5.1 111l
Reader's Guide to Periodical Literature, 5.5 581l
  technology. See **Technology,** new literacies.
telephone directory, 5.4 435l
textbook, 5.2 185l, 207l
thesaurus, 5.4 483l
trade book, 5.2 207l

Repetition. See **Sound devices and poetic elements.**

Rereading. See **Monitor and fix up.**

Research
  activities, 5.1 41l, 67l, 89l, 111l, 133l, 5.2 161l, 185l, 207l, 229l, 253l, 5.3 287l, 315l, 345l, 363l, 383l, 5.4 411l, 435l, 457l, 483l, 503l, 5.5 535l, 559l, 581l, 603l, 625l, 5.6 653l, 673l, 699l, 725l, 753l
  process and strategies
    evaluating sources, 5.6 722–725
    locating and collecting information, 5.1 41k, 67k, 89k, 111k, 133k, 5.2 161k, 185k, 207k, 229k, 229l, 253k, 5.3 287k, 315k, 345k, 363k, 383k, 5.4 411k, 435k, 435l, 457k, 483k, 503k, 5.5 535k, 559k, 581k, 603k, 625k, 5.6 653k, 673k, 699k, 725d, 725k, 753k
    notecards, using, 5.6 725d
    outlining, 5.5 625l, 5.6 725g–725h
    paraphrase and synthesize, 5.1 41k, 67k, 89k, 111k, 133k, 5.2 161k, 185k, 207k, 229k, 253k, 5.3 287k, 315k, 345k, 363k, 383k, 5.4 411k, 435k, 457k, 483k, 503k, 5.5 535k, 559k, 559l, 581k, 603k, 625k, 5.6 653k, 673k, 699k, 725k, 753k
    procedures and instructions, 5.2 161l, 5.4 411l, 5.6 653l
    questions for inquiry, 5.1 41k, 67k, 89k, 111k, 133k, 5.2 161k, 185k, 207k, 229k, 253k, 5.3 287k, 315k, 345k, 363k, 383k, 5.4 411k, 435k, 457k, 483k, 503k, 5.5 535k, 559k, 581k, 603k, 625k, 5.6 653k, 673k, 699k, 725k, 753k
    record, 5.5 559l
    skimming/scanning, 5.3 315l, 383k
    SPQ3R, 5.1 89l
    study strategy to find or learn information, 5.1 89l
    taking notes/recording findings, 5.5 559l, 5.6 725d
    using graphic sources. See **Graphic sources.**
    using reference sources. See **References sources.**

Response to literature
  oral, 5.1 34, 64, 84, 108, 128, 133h, 5.2 158, 178, 204, 224, 248, 253h, 5.3 280, 310, 338, 358, 378, 383h, 5.4 408, 432, 452, 478, 498, 503h, 5.5 530, 552, 576, 598, 620, 5.6 650, 668, 696, 720, 748
  written, 5.1 34, 41, 64, 67, 84, 89, 108, 111, 128, 133, 5.2 158, 159, 161, 161g–161h, 178, 179, 185, 185g–185h, 204, 207, 224, 229, 248, 253, 5.3 280, 287, 310, 315, 338, 345, 358, 363, 378, 383, 5.4 408, 411, 432, 435, 452, 457, 478, 483, 498, 503, 5.5 530, 535, 552, 559, 576, 581, 598, 603, 5.6 650, 653, 668, 673, 696, 699, 720, 725, 748, 753
  See also **Connections, making; Literary response and appreciation.**

Retelling. See **Speaking,** activities.

Rhyme. See **Sound devices and poetic elements.**

Rhythm. See **Sound devices and poetic elements.**

Root words. See **Spelling,** word structure; **Word structure,** Greek and Latin roots.

Rubric. See **Assessment,** scoring guide (rubric).

Running record, taking a, 5.1 41a, 67a, 89a, 111a, 133a, DI·59–DI·60, 5.2 161a, 185a, 207a, 229a, 253a, DI·59–DI·60, 5.3 287a, 315a, 345a, 363a, 383a, DI·59–DI·60, 5.4 411a, 435a, 457a, 483a, 503a, DI·59–DI·60, 5.5 535a, 559a, 581a, 603a, 625a, DI·59–DI·60, 5.6 653a, 673a, 699a, 725a, 753a, DI·59–DI·60. See also **Fluency, reading; Oral reading ability.**

S

Safety information. See **Character education.**

Scaffolded instruction, 5.1 19, 25, 43, 41f, 51, 53, 67f, 69, 75, 89f, 91, 97, 99, 111f, 113, 119, 123, 133f, DI·1, 5.2 143, 149, 161f, 163, 185f, 187, 193, 207f, 209, 218, 229f, 231, 239, 253f, DI·1, 5.3 263, 269, 275, 287f, 289, 295, 315f, 317, 331, 345f, 347, 349, 353, 363f, 365, 371, 383f, DI·1, 5.4 393, 399, 411f, 413, 425, 435f, 437, 443, 447, 457f, 459, 473, 483f, 485, 491, 503f, DI·1, 5.5 513, 519, 535f, 537, 543, 559f, 561, 567, 571, 581f, 583, 595, 603f, 605, 625f, DI·1, 5.6 635, 643, 653f, 655, 661, 673f, 675, 699f, 675, 681, 701, 709, 725f, 727, 733, 737, 753f, DI·1

Scale drawing. See **Graphic sources,** diagram/scale drawing.

Schedule. See **Graphic sources.**

School-home connection, 5.1 18i, 18m, 42i, 42m, 68i, 68m, 90i, 90m, 112i, 112m, 5.2 142i, 142m, 162i, 162m, 186i, 186m, 208i, 208m, 230i, 230m, 5.3 262i, 262m, 288i, 288m, 316i, 316m, 346i, 346m, 364i, 364m, 5.4 392i, 392m, 412i, 412m, 436i, 436m, 458i, 458m, 484i, 484m, 5.5 512i, 512m, 536i, 536m, 560i, 560m, 582i, 582m, 604i, 604m, 5.6 634i, 634m, 654i, 654m, 674i, 674m, 700i, 700m, 726i, 726m

Science activities. See **Cross-curricular activities.**

Science fiction. See **Genres.**

Science in reading, 5.1 66–67, 86–89, 5.2 226–229, 5.3 340–345, 5.4 434–435, 454–457, 5.5 600–603, 5.6 670–673

Search engines. See **Genres; Technology,** new literacies.

Self-appraisal and self-correction. See **Monitor and fix up.**

Self-check, 5.1 33, 55, 63, 83, 103, 107, 127, 5.2 157, 177, 197, 203, 223, 247, 5.3 273, 279, 303, 309, 327, 337, 357, 377, 5.4 407, 423, 431, 451, 469, 477, 497, 5.5 523, 529, 551, 575, 597, 619, 5.6 649, 667, 685, 695, 713, 719, 739, 747

Self-monitor and use fix-up strategies. See **Monitor and fix up.**

Self-questioning to assess understanding. See **Self-check.**

Self-selected reading, 5.1 DI·57–DI·58, TR14–TR17, 5.2 DI·57–DI·58, TR14–TR17, 5.3 DI·57–DI·58, TR14–TR17, 5.4 DI·57–DI·58, TR14–TR17, 5.5 DI·57–DI·58, TR14–TR17, 5.6 DI·57–DI·58, TR14–TR17

Semicolon, 5.1 111e, 5.6 753e–753f

Sensory words. See **Literary devices.**

Sentences
  fragment, 5.1 111f
  parts of
    predicate, 5.1 67e–67f
    subject, 5.1 67e–67f
    run-ons, 5.1 111f
  structure
    complex, 5.1 111e–111f
    compound, 5.1 67f, 111e–111f, 5.3 DI·14, 5.4 486b, 5.5 535c
  types of
    declarative, 5.1 41e–41f
    exclamatory, 5.1 41e–41f
    imperative, 5.1 41e–41f
    interrogative, 5.1 41e–41f

Sequence
  directions, following, 5.2 161l, 5.4 411l, 5.6 653l
  sequence of events (time sequence/chronology), 5.1 90–91, 96, 97, 105, 121, DI·36, DI·37, DI·55, 5.2 173, 199, 230l–230m, 230–231, 239, 243, 253b, DI·46, DI·47, DI·56, 5.6 641, 665, 726l–726m, 726–727, 733, 743, 751, 753b, DI·46, DI·47, DI·56
  steps in a process, 5.3 345b

Setting, 5.1 68l–68m, 68–69, 75, 81, 89b, DI·25, DI·26, DI·54, 5.5 237

Setting purposes for reading. See **Monitor and fix up, Prereading strategies.**

Short story. See **Genres.**

Simile, 5.4 435b, 503b, 5.5 595. See also **Figurative language.**

Six-trait writing
  conventions, 5.1 41g–41h, 67g–67h, 89g–89h, 111g–111h, 133g–133h, WA1, WA6, WA7, 5.2 161g–161h, 185g–185h, 207g–207h, 229g–229h, 253g–253h, WA1, WA6, WA7, 5.3 281, 287g–287h, 315g–351h, 345g–345h, 363g–363h, 383g–383h, WA1, WA6, WA7, 5.4 409, 411g–411h, 435g–435h, 457g–457h, 483g–483h, 503g–503h, WA1, WA6, WA7, 5.5 535g–535h, 559g–559h, 581g–581h, 603g–603h, 625g–625h, WA1, WA6, WA7, 5.6 651, 653g–653h, 673g–673h, 699g–699h, 725g–725h, 753g–753h, WA1, WA6, WA7
  focus/ideas, 5.1 41g, 67g, 89g, 111g, 133g, WA1, WA5, WA7, 5.2 159, 161g–161h, 179, 185g–185h, 207g, 229g, 253g, WA1, WA7, 5.3 287g, 311, 315g–315h, 345g, 363g, 383g,

WA1, WA5, WA7, 5.4 411g, 433, 435g, 457g, 483g, 503g, WA1, WA5, WA7, 5.5 531, 535g–535h, 559g, 581g, 603g, 625g, WA1, WA5, WA7, 5.6 653g, 669, 673g–673h, 699g, 725g, 753g, WA1, WA5, WA7

organization/paragraphs, 5.1 41g–41h, 67g–67h, 85, 89g–89h, 111g–111h, 133g–133h, WA1, WA3, WA5, WA7, 5.2 161g–161h, 185g–185h, 205, 207g–207h, 229g–229h, 249, 253g–253h, WA1, WA3, WA5, WA7, 5.3 287g–287h, 315g–315h, 339, 345g–345h, 363g–363h, 383g–383h, WA1, WA3, WA5, WA7, 5.4 411g–411h, 435g–435h, 457g–457h, 483g–483h, 503g–503h, WA1, WA3, WA5, WA7, 5.5 535g–535h, 559g–559h, 581g–581h, 603g–603h, 625g–625h, WA1, WA3, WA5, WA7, 5.6 653g–653h, 673g–673h, 699g–699h, 721, 725g–725h, 753g–753h, WA1, WA3, WA5, WA7

sentences, 5.1 41g, 67g, 89g, 111g, 133g, WA1, WA5, WA7, 5.2 161g, 185g, 207g, 229g, 253g, WA1, WA5, WA7, 5.3 287g, 315g, 345g, 363g, 379, 383g–383h, WA1, WA5, WA7, 5.4 411g, 435g, 457g, 483g, 503g, WA1, WA5, WA7, 5.5 535g, 559g, 577, 581g–581h, 603g, 621, 625g–625h, WA1, WA5, WA7, 5.6 653g, 673g, 699g, 725g, 749, 753g–753h, WA1, WA5, WA7

voice, 5.1 35, 41g–41h, 67g, 89g, 111g, 133g, WA1, WA5, WA7, 5.2 161g, 185g, 207g, 229g, 253g, WA1, WA5, WA7, 5.3 287g, 315g, 345g, 363g, 383g, WA1, WA5, WA7, 5.4 411g, 435g, 457g, 479, 483g–483h, 503g, WA1, WA5, WA7, 5.5 535g, 559g, 581g, 599, 603g–603h, 625g, WA1, WA5, WA7, 5.6 653g, 673g, 697, 699g–699h, 725g, 753g, WA1, WA5, WA7

word choice, 5.1 41g, 65, 67g–67h, 89g, 109, 111g–111h, 129, 133g–133g, WA1, WA5, WA7, 5.2 161g, 185g, 207g, 225, 229g–229h, 253g, WA1, WA5, WA7, 5.3 287g, 315g, 345g, 359, 363g–363h, 383g, WA1, WA5, WA7, 5.4 411g, 435g, 453, 457g–457h, 483g, 499, 503g–503h, WA1, WA5, WA7, 5.5 535g, 553, 559g–559h, 581g, 603g, 625g, WA1, WA5, WA7, 5.6 653g, 673g, 699g, 725g, 753g, WA1, WA5, WA7

Skimming and scanning, 5.3 315l, 383k

Slang. See Literary devices.

Social studies activities. See Cross-curricular activities.

Social studies in reading, 5.1 110–111, 5.2 160–161, 180–185, 5.3 282–285, 312–315, 5.4 480–483, 5.5 554–559, 622–625, 5.6 750–753

Solving problems. See Problems, solving.

Song. See Genres.

Sound devices and poetic elements
    alliteration, 5.6 757
    repetition, 5.4 399
    rhyme, 5.3 361, 5.4 410, 5.6 698, 699
    rhythm, 5.2 239, 5.3 361, 5.4 410

Speaking
    activities
        advertisement, 5.3 383d
        advice, 5.4 483d
        ask questions, 5.1 103, 105, 107, 5.2 208–209, 227, 5.5 547, 551, 557, 559, 5.6 700–701, 713, 715, 719, 722

debate, 5.2 229d, 5.5 625d
demonstration, 5.4 411d
description, 5.4 457d
dramatization, 5.1 41d
informational speech, 5.4 503d, 5.5 581d
interview, 5.1 133d, 5.6 673d
introductions, 5.3 345d, 5.5 535d
literature, 5.5 603d
interpret fiction, 5.5 603d
multimedia presentation, 5.3 383d, 5.4 503d
newscast, 5.3 315d, 5.6 725d
oral book report, 5.2 185d
oral presentation/report, 5.2 185d, 5.3 363d, 5.4 435d, 5.5 559d
oral reading, 5.1 41a, 67a, 89a, 111a, 133a, 5.2 161a, 185a, 207a, 229a, 253a, 5.3 287a, 315a, 345a, 363a, 383a, 5.4 411a, 435a, 457a, 483a, 503a, 5.5 535a, 559a, 581a, 603a, 625a, 5.6 653a, 673a, 699a, 725a, 753a
panel discussion, 5.2 229d
persuasive speech, 5.2 161d
radio feature story, 5.2 253d
Readers' Theater, 5.2 207d, 5.6 653d, 753d
retelling, 5.1 35, 65, 85, 109, 129, 5.2 159, 179, 205, 225, 249, 5.3 281, 311, 339, 359, 379, 5.4 409, 433, 453, 499, 5.5 531, 553, 577, 599, 621, 5.6 651, 669, 697, 721, 749
review, 5.1 89d, 5.3 287d
sportscast, 5.1 111d
storytelling, 5.6 699d
tall tale, 5.1 67d
purpose/reasons for speaking
    expository, 5.1 89d, 111d, 133d, 5.2 185d, 5.3 315d, 345d, 363d, 5.4 435d, 5.5 535d, 559d, 581d, 603d, 5.6 673d, 725d
    expressive, 5.1 41d, 67d, 5.2 207d, 253d, 5.4 457d, 5.6 653d, 699d, 725d
    narrative, 5.1 41d, 67d, 5.2 207d, 253d, 5.6 653d, 699d, 725d
    persuasive, 5.2 161d, 229d, 5.3 287d, 383d, 5.4 411d, 5.5 625d
    problem solving, 5.4 483d
tips, 5.1 67d, 111d, 5.2 161d, 185d, 207d, 253d, 5.3 345d, 5.4 435d, 457d, 503d, 5.5 535d, 603d, 625d, 5.6 653d, 673d, 699d, 725d, 753d

Spelling
    common word (vowel) patterns
        VCCV, 5.1 41i–41j
        VCV, 5.1 41i–41j, 67i–67j
    five-step plan for learning words, 5.1 41i–41j, 67i–67j, 89i–89j, 111i–111j, 133i–133j, 5.2 161i–161j, 185i–185j, 207i–207j, 229i–229j, 253i–253j, 5.3 287i–287j, 315i–315j, 345i–345j, 363i–363j, 383i–383j, 5.4 411i–411j, 435i–435j, 457i–457j, 483i–483j, 503i–503j, 5.5 535i–535j, 559i–559j, 581i–581j, 603i–603j, 625i–625j, 5.6 653i–653j, 673i–673j, 699i–699j, 725i–725j, 753i–753j
    meaning relationships
        easily confused words, 5.6 753i–753j
        homophones, 5.4 457i–457j
        related words, 5.5 625i–625j
        words with multiple spellings, 5.3 275, 287c
    phonics, connection to
        consonant digraphs, 5.2 161i–161j
        consonant sounds and patterns, 5.3 345i–345j
        consonants, double, 5.3 363i–363j

vowel digraphs, 5.1 89i–89j
vowel sounds and patterns, 5.1 41i–41j, 67i–67j
vowels in final syllable, 5.1 67i–67j
vowels, long, 5.1 67i–67j
vowels, r-controlled, 5.2 207i–207j, 253i–253j
vowels, schwa, 5.2 287i–287j
vowels, short, 5.1 41i–41j
words with ei and ie, 5.6 699i–699j
word structure
    adding -en, -an, -el, -le, -il, 5.2 229i–229j
    affixes, 5.3 383i–383j, 5.4, 435i–435j, 483i–483j, 503i–503j, 5.6 653i–653j
    compound words, 5.3 315i–315j, 5.6 725i–725j
    contractions, 5.1 133i–133j
    Greek word parts, 5.5 581i–581j
    inflected endings, 5.1 111i–111j
    Latin roots, 5.5 603i–603j
    plurals, irregular, 5.2 185i–185j
    multisyllabic words, 5.5 535i–535j
    syllables, final, -ant, -ent, -ance, -ence, 5.6 673i–673j
    unusual spellings, 5.5 559i–559j

Standard book features. See Parts of a book.

Steps in a process, 5.3 345b

Stereotypes, 5.1 125, 5.4 405

Story elements. See Character, Plot, Setting, Theme (as a story element).

Story structure, 5.3 262–263, 273, 279, DI·6, DI·7, 5.4 458–459, 469, 471, DI·36, DI·37

Strategic intervention. See Intervention.

Strategies
    comprehension, 5.1 18–19, 42–43, 68–69, 90–91, 112–113, 5.2 142–143, 162–163, 186–187, 208–209, 230–231, 5.3 262–263, 288–289, 316–317, 346–347, 364–365, 5.4 392–393, 412–413, 436–437, 458–459, 484–485, 5.5 512–513, 536–537, 560–561, 582–583, 604–605, 5.6 634–635, 654–655, 674–675, 700–701, 726–727
    concept development, 5.1 17a, 18a, 18l, 42a, 42l, 68a, 68l, 90a, 90l, 112a, 112l, 5.2 141a, 142a, 142l, 162a, 162l, 186a, 186l, 208a, 208l, 230a, 230l, 5.3 261a, 262a, 262l, 288a, 288l, 316a, 316l, 346a, 346l, 364a, 364l, 5.4 391a, 392a, 392l, 412a, 412l, 436a, 436l, 458a, 458l, 484a, 484l, 5.5 511a, 512a, 512l, 536a, 536l, 560a, 560l, 582a, 582l, 604a, 604l, 5.6 633a, 634a, 634l, 654a, 654l, 674a, 674l, 700a, 700l, 762a, 726l
    context, 5.1 44–45, 53, 67c, 92–93, 99, 111c, 114–115, 123c, 133, 5.2 210–211, 219, 229c, 232b, 5.3 264–265, 275, 287c, 318–319, 331, 345c, 348–349, 363c, 366b, 5.4 414–415, 425, 435c, 438–439, 447, 457c, 460–461, 473, 483c, 5.5 562–563, 571, 581c, 584–585, 595, 603c, 5.6 702–703, 709, 725c, 728–729, 737, 741, 753c
    decoding, 5.1 41i–41j, 67i–67j, 89i–89j, 111i–111j, 133i–133j, 5.2 161i–161j, 185i–185j, 207i–207j, 229i–229j, 253i–253j, 5.3 287i–287j, 315i–315j, 345i–345j, 363i–363j, 383i–383j, 5.4 411i–411j, 435i–435j, 457i–457j, 483i–483j, 503i–503j, 5.5 535i–535j, 559i–559j, 581i–581j, 603i–603j, 625i–625j, 5.6 653i–653j, 673i–673j, 699i–699j, 725i–725j, 753i–753j

fluent reading, 5.1 41a, 67a, 89a, 111a, 133a, 5.2 161a, 185a, 207a, 229a, 253a, 5.3 287a, 315a, 345a, 363a, 383a, 5.4 411a, 435a, 457a, 483a, 503a, 5.5 535a, 559a, 581a, 603a, 625a, 5.6 653a, 673a, 699a, 725a, 753a

graphophonic cues, using, 5.1 21, 5.2 233, 5.3 367, 5.4 395, 5.5 607, 5.6 677

monitor and fix up, 5.1 42–43, 55, 57, 63, DI·17, 5.2 162–163, 175, 177, 183, 185, 5.4 436–437, 449, 451, 456, 457, 5.5 560–561, 572, 573, 575, 581

prereading, 5.1 22, 46, 72, 94, 116, 5.2 146, 166, 190, 212, 234, 5.3 266, 292, 320, 350, 368, 5.4 396, 416, 440, 462, 488, 5.5 516, 540, 564, 586, 608, 5.6 638, 658, 678, 704, 730

research, 5.1 41l, 67l, 89l, 111l, 133l, 5.2 161l, 185l, 207l, 229l, 253l, 5.3 287l, 315l, 345l, 363l, 383l, 5.4 411l, 435l, 457l, 483l, 503l, 5.5 535l, 559l, 581l, 603l, 625l, 5.6 653l, 673l, 699l, 725l, 753l

spelling, 5.1 41i–41j, 67i–67j, 89i–89j, 111i–111j, 133i–133j, 5.2 161i–161j, 185i–185j, 207i–207j, 229i–229j, 253i–253j, 5.3 287i–287j, 315i–315j, 345i–345j, 363i–363j, 383i–383j, 5.4 411i–411j, 435i–435j, 457i–457j, 483i–483j, 503i–503j, 5.5 535i–535j, 559i–559j, 581i–581j, 603i–603j, 625i–625j, 5.6 653i–653j, 673i–673j, 699i–699j, 725i–725j, 753i–753j

viewing, 5.1 67d, 5.2 207d, 5.3 315d, 5.4 503d, 5.5 559d

vocabulary. See **Vocabulary strategies.**

Structural analysis. See **Word structure.**

Study strategies, 5.1 41l, 67l, 89l, 111l, 133l, 5.2 161l, 185l, 207l, 229l, 253l, 5.3 287l, 315l, 345l, 363l, 383l, 5.4 411l, 435l, 457l, 483l, 503l, 5.5 535l, 559l, 581l, 603l, 625l, 5.6 653l, 673l, 699l, 725l, 753l. See also **Assessment,** test-taking strategies; **Content-area texts; Graphic sources; Organizing information; Parts of a book; Reference sources; Textbook-reading techniques.**

Style, author's. See **Literary craft.**

Style, illustrator's. See **Literary craft.**

Subject-verb agreement, 5.2 253e–253f

Suffixes. See **Vocabulary strategies, Word structure.**

Summarizing, 5.1 112–113, 125, 127, 133, DI·46, DI·47, 5.3 288–289, 303, 307, 309, 315, 383, DI·16, DI·17, 5.5 582–583, 593, 597, 601, 625, DI·36, DI·37

Sustained silent reading. See **Self-selected reading.**

Syllables. See **Spelling,** word structure; **Word structure,** chunking, syllabication.

Synonyms, 5.1 20b, 92–93, 5.2 188b, 5.4 394b, 438–439, 447, 5.5 584b. See also **Vocabulary strategies.**

Synthesizing. See **Connections, making; Reading across texts.**

T

Tables. See **Graphic sources,** chart/table.

Taking notes. See **Note-taking.**

Tall tale. See **Genres.**

Target comprehension skills. See **Comprehension skills, explicit/implicit instruction** for a total listing of these skills.

Target comprehension strategies. See **Comprehension strategies, explicit/implicit instruction** for a total listing of these strategies.

Teaching strategies
informal assessment. See **Running record, taking a.**
modeling. This strategy is part of every lesson.
think-aloud. This strategy is part of every lesson. See also **Graphic and semantic organizers,** types.

Technology
e-mail, 5.1 130–133, 5.4 483k
information and communication technologies. See **Technology,** new literacies.
Internet article, 5.2 250–253, 5.3 380–383, 5.4 500–503, 5.5 578–581, 5.6 722–725
Internet/World Wide Web. See **Technology,** new literacies.
new literacies
bias, 5.1 111k
bookmarks, 5.1 67k, 5.2 207k, 253k, 5.4 501, 5.5 579, 625k, 5.6 653k
documentation of Web sites, 5.1 67, 5.2 161k, 253k, 5.3 287k, 315k, 5.4 411k, 457k, 5.5 535k, 603k, 5.6 673k
electronic media, 5.1 20a, 41k, 44a, 48, 58, 67k, 70a, 74, 81, 84, 89k, 92a, 96, 111k, 114a, 118, 133k, 5.2 144a, 156, 161k, 164a, 168, 185k, 188a, 192, 207k, 210a, 222, 229k, 232a, 236, 253k, 5.3 264a, 268, 287k, 290a, 294, 315k, 318a, 322, 331, 345k, 348b, 352, 363k, 366a, 370, 383k, 5.4 394a, 402, 411k, 414a, 418, 435k, 438a, 444, 457k, 460a, 466, 483k, 486a, 490, 503k, 5.5 514a, 518, 531, 535k, 538a, 542, 559k, 562a, 566, 581k, 584a, 588, 603k, 606a, 610, 625k, 5.6 636a, 644, 653k, 656a, 664, 673k, 676a, 680, 699k, 702a, 708, 725k, 728a, 732, 753k
e-mail, 5.1 130–133, 5.2 160, 161, 5.4 483k
etiquette, 5.1 131, 5.2 251, 5.3 381, 5.4 483k, 501, 5.5 579, 5.6 723
evaluating Internet information and sources, 5.1 41k, 67k, 89k, 111k, 5.2 161k, 207k, 229k, 251, 253k, 5.3 287k, 315k, 345k, 363k, 381, 382, 383k, 5.4 411k, 435k, 457k, 483k, 500–503, 503k, 5.5 535k, 559k, 579, 581k, 603k, 625k, 5.6 653k, 673k, 699k, 722–725, 725k, 753k
folder, 5.1 132
homepage, 5.1 5.4 500, 5.6 722
Internet article, 5.2 250–253, 5.3 380–383, 5.4 500–503, 5.5 578–581, 5.6 722–725
Internet inquiry, 5.1 20a, 41k, 44a, 48, 58, 67k, 70a, 74, 81, 84, 89k, 92a, 96, 111k, 114a, 118, 133k, 5.2 144a, 156, 161k, 164a, 168, 185k, 188a, 192, 207k, 210a, 222, 229k, 232a, 236, 253k, 5.3 264a, 268, 287k, 290a, 294, 315k, 318a, 322, 331, 345k, 348b, 352, 363k, 366a, 370, 383k, 5.4 394a, 402, 411k, 414a, 418, 435k, 438a, 444, 457k, 460a, 466, 483k, 486a, 490, 503k, 5.5 514a, 518, 535k, 538a, 542, 559k, 562a, 566, 581k, 584a, 588, 603k, 606a, 610, 625k, 5.6 636a, 644, 653k, 656a, 664, 673k, 676a, 680, 699k, 702a, 708, 725k, 728a, 732, 753k
keyword, 5.1 20a, 44a, 48, 58, 67k, 70a, 74, 81, 84, 89k, 92a, 96, 114a, 118, 5.2 144a, 156, 161k, 168, 185k, 188a, 192, 210a, 222, 229k, 232a, 236, 250, 252, 253k, 5.3 264a, 268, 290a, 294, 315k, 318a, 331, 348a, 352, 366a, 370, 380, 381, 5.4 394a, 402, 411k, 414a, 418, 432, 435k, 438a, 444, 457k, 460a, 483k, 486a, 490, 501, 503k, 5.5 514a, 535k, 538a, 542, 559k, 562a, 566, 578, 584a, 588, 606a, 610, 625k, 5.6 636a, 644, 653a, 656a, 664, 676a, 680, 699k, 702a, 708, 725k, 728a, 732, 753k
library catalog, 5.6 749
links, 5.1 111k, 5.2 250, 5.3 380, 381, 382, 5.4 435k, 500, 501, 502, 5.5 559k, 578–580, 5.6 724, 725k, 753k
online reference sources and directories, 5.1 5.2 250, 5.3 5.4 500–503, 503k, 5.5 562a, 578–581, 5.6 721
presentation software, 5.1 41k, 111k, 133k, 5.2 161k, 185k, 207k, 229k, 253k, 5.3 287k, 315k, 363k, 383k, 5.4 411k, 435k, 457k, 483k, 5.5 559k, 581k, 603k, 625k, 5.6 673k, 699k, 725k, 753k
reference source. See **Reference sources.**
search engines, 5.1 20a, 41k, 44a, 48, 58, 67k, 74, 81, 84, 89k, 92a, 114a, 118, 5.2 156, 161k, 164a, 168, 185k, 188a, 192, 207k, 210a, 222, 229k, 232a, 236, 250, 253k, 5.3 264a, 268, 287k, 290a, 294, 315k, 318a, 322, 331, 345k, 348a, 352, 363k, 366a, 370, 380–383, 5.4 394a, 402, 411k, 414a, 418, 435k, 438a, 444, 457k, 460a, 466, 486a, 490, 501, 502, 503k, 5.5 514a, 518, 538a, 542, 562a, 566, 580, 581k, 584a, 588, 606a, 610, 5.6 636a, 644, 656a, 664, 673k, 676a, 699k, 702a, 708, 725k, 728a, 732
searching and navigating the Internet, 5.1 20a, 41k, 44a, 48, 58, 67k, 70a, 74, 81, 84, 89k, 92a, 96, 111k, 114a, 118, 133k, 5.2 144a, 456, 459, 161k, 164a, 168, 185k, 188a, 192, 207k, 210a, 222, 229k, 232a, 236, 253k, 5.3 264a, 268, 287k, 290a, 294, 315k, 318a, 322, 331, 345k, 348b, 352, 363k, 366a, 370, 383k, 5.4 394a, 402, 411k, 414a, 418, 435k, 438a, 444, 457k, 460a, 466, 483k, 486a, 490, 503k, 5.5 514a, 518, 535k, 538a, 542, 559k, 562a, 566, 581k, 584a, 588, 603k, 606a, 610, 625k, 5.6 636a, 644, 653k, 656a, 664, 673k, 676a, 680, 699k, 702a, 708, 725k, 728a, 753k
technology tools, 5.1 130, 5.2 250, 5.3 380, 5.4 500, 5.5 578, 5.6 722
URLs, 5.1 67k, 111k, 133k, 5.2 253k, 5.3 287k, 363k, 5.4 435k, 5.5 603k, 625k, 5.6 699k, 722
use graphic sources, 5.4 502
use web site features, 5.1 130–131, 5.2 160, 250, 251, 252, 5.3 380, 382, 5.4 500, 5.5 578, 5.6 722, 724, 753k

website, 5.1 41k, 67k, 111k, 130–133,
5.2 144a, 156, 160–161, 161k, 185k, 207k,
250–253, 253k, 5.3 287k, 315k, 345k,
363k, 380, 381, 382, 383k, 5.4 435k,
457k, 483k, 500–503, 503k, 5.5 535k,
559k, 578–581, 603k, 625k, 5.6 653k,
673k, 680, 699k, 722, 723, 724, 725k, 753k

Scott Foresman Reading Street technology
Background Building CD, 5.1 20a, 44a,
70a, 92a, 114a, 5.2 144a, 164a, 188a,
210a, 232a, 5.3 264a, 290a, 318a, 348a,
366a, 5.4 394a, 414a, 438a, 460a, 486a,
5.5 514a, 538a, 562a, 584a, 606a,
5.6 636a, 656a, 676a, 702a, 728a

Leveled Reader Database, 5.1 18h, 42h,
68h, 90h, 112h, 5.2 142h, 162h, 186h,
208h, 230h, 5.3 262h, 288h, 316h, 346h,
364h, 5.4 392h, 412h, 436h, 458h, 484h,
5.5 512h, 536h, 560h, 582h, 604h,
5.6 634h, 654h, 674h, 700h, 726h

**professional development (PearsonSuccessNet.
com),** 5.1 18i, 42i, 68i, 90i, 112i, 5.2 142i,
162i, 186i, 208i, 230i, 5.3 262i, 288i, 316i,
346i, 364i, 5.4 392i, 412i, 436i, 458i, 484i,
5.5 512i, 536i, 560i, 582i, 604i, 5.6 634i,
654i, 674i, 700i, 726i

Selection AudioText CD (Student Edition),
5.1 23, 47, 73, 95, 117, 5.2 147, 167, 191,
213, 235, 5.3 267, 293, 321, 351, 369,
5.4 397, 417, 441, 463, 489, 5.5 517, 541,
565, 587, 609, 5.6 639, 659, 679, 705, 731

skill for using technology, 5.1 20a, 41k, 44a,
48, 58, 67k, 70a, 74, 81, 84, 89k, 92a,
96, 111k, 114a, 118, 133k, 5.2 144a,
156, 161k, 164a, 168, 185k, 188a, 192,
207k, 210a, 222, 229k, 232a, 236, 253k,
5.3 264a, 268, 287k, 290a, 294, 315k,
318a, 322, 331, 345k, 348b, 352, 363k,
366a, 370, 383k, 5.4 394a, 402, 411k,
414a, 418, 435k, 438a, 444, 457k, 460a,
466, 483k, 486a, 490, 503k, 5.5 514a,
518, 535k, 538a, 542, 559k, 562a, 566,
581k, 584a, 588, 603k, 606a, 610, 625k,
5.6 636a, 644, 653k, 656a, 664, 673k,
676a, 680, 699k, 702a, 708, 725k, 728a,
732, 753k

basic knowledge and skills, 5.1 41k, 67k, 89k,
111k, 130–133, 133k, 5.2 161k, 185k,
207k, 229k, 250–253, 253k, 5.3 287k,
315k, 345k, 363k, 380–383, 383k,
5.4 411k, 435k, 457k, 483k, 500–503,
503k, 5.5 535k, 559k, 578–581, 581k,
603k, 625k, 5.6 653k, 673k, 699k, 722–
725k, 728k, 753k

communication, 5.1 41k, 67k, 89k, 111k,
130–133, 133k, 5.2 161k, 185k, 207k,
229k, 253k, 5.3 287k, 315k, 345k, 363k,
383k, 5.4 411k, 435k, 457k, 483k,
503k, 5.5 535k, 559k, 581k, 603k, 625k,
5.6 653k, 673k, 699k, 728k, 753k

information acquisition, 5.1 41k, 67k, 89k,
111k, 133k, 5.2 161k, 185k, 207k, 229k,
250–253, 253k, 5.3 287k, 315k, 345k,
363k, 380–383, 383k, 5.4 411k, 435k,
457k, 483k, 500–503, 503k, 5.5 535k,
559k, 578–581, 581k, 603k, 625k,
5.6 653k, 673k, 699k, 722–725, 725k, 753k

operations and concepts, 5.1 41k, 67k, 89k,
111k, 133k, 5.2 161k, 185k, 207k, 229k,
253k, 5.3 287k, 315k, 345k, 363k,

383k, 5.4 411k, 435k, 457k, 483k,
503k, 5.5 535k, 559k, 581k, 603k, 625k,
5.6 653k, 673k, 699k, 728k, 753k

responsible use, 5.1 41k, 67k, 89k, 111k,
133k, 5.2 161k, 185k, 207k, 229k, 253k,
5.3 287k, 315k, 345k, 363k, 383k,
5.4 411k, 435k, 457k, 483k, 503k,
5.5 535k, 559k, 581k, 603k, 625k,
5.6 653k, 673k, 699k, 728k, 753k

See also **Cross-curricular activities,
Reference sources.**

Testing, formal and informal. *See* **Assessment.**

Test-taking practice
look back and write, 5.1 34, 64, 84, 108, 128,
5.2 158, 178, 204, 224, 248, 5.3 280, 310,
338, 358, 378, 5.4 408, 432, 452, 478, 498,
5.5 530, 552, 576, 598, 620, 5.6 650, 668,
696, 720, 748
strategies in fiction
use dialogue, 5.1 38
use location phrases, 5.5 534
use questions, 5.3 342
use story details, 5.5 556, 5.6 653
use theme, 5.2 207
strategies in nonfiction
use charts, 5.1 67
use graphic sources, 5.3 314, 5.5 624
use headings, 5.2 161, 5.4 435
use introduction/conclusions, 5.1 88, 5.2 228
use leads, 5.4 482
use quotation marks, 5.3 284
use subheads, 5.4 456
use time phrases, 5.2 182
writing for tests, 5.1 133g-133h, 5.2 253g-253h,
5.3 383g-383h, 5.4 503g-503h

Textbook (as reference source). *See* **Reference
sources.**

Textbook article. *See* **Genres.**

Textbook-reading techniques, 5.2 185l, 207l

Text features, 5.1 66, 86, 110, 130, 5.2 160,
180, 206, 226, 250, 5.3 282, 312, 340, 380,
5.4 434, 454, 480, 500, 5.5 532, 554, 578,
600, 622, 5.6 670, 722, 750

**Text structure (method of presenting
information),** 5.2 180, 182, 5.3 282, 283, 285,
287, 5.6 654–655, 667, 671, DI·16, DI·17

Theme (as a story element), 5.1 68l–68m, 68–
69, 75, 81, 89b, DI·25, DI·26, 5.2 237

Themes for teaching and learning, 5.1 16–17,
17a, 18a, 42a, 68a, 90a, 112a, 138–139,
5.2 140–141, 141a, 142a, 162a, 186a, 208a,
230a, 258–259, 5.3 260–261, 261a, 262a,
288a, 316a, 346a, 364a, 388–389, 5.4 390–
391, 391a, 392a, 412a, 436a, 458a, 484a, 508–
509, 5.5 510–511, 511a, 512a, 536a, 560a,
582a, 604a, 630–631, 5.6 632–633, 633a,
634a, 654a, 674a, 700a, 762a, 758–759

Thesaurus. *See* **Reference sources.**

Think-aloud statements. Think-alouds and teacher
modeling are demonstrated throughout weekly
lessons as a basic teaching strategy.

Thinking strategies. *See* **Critical thinking.**

Time line. *See* **Graphic organizers, Graphic
sources.**

Time sequence. *See* **Sequence.**

Tone. *See* **Literary devices.**

Topic, recognizing. *See* **Main idea.**

Trade books
as reference source, 5.2 207l
trade book library, 5.1 18g, 42g, 68g, 90g, 112g,
5.2 142g, 162g, 186g, 208g, 230g, 5.3 262g,
288g, 316g, 346g, 364g, 5.4 392g, 412g,
436g, 458g, 484g, 5.5 512g, 536g, 560g,
582g, 604g, 5.6 634g, 654g, 674g, 700g,
726g

Types of literature. *See* **Genres.**

U

Underlining, 5.6 753e–753f

Unfamiliar word meaning, 5.1 70–71, 99, 111c,
5.2 210–211, 219, 229c, 5.3 331, 5.4 414–415,
425, 435c, 457c, 460–461, 473, 483c, 5.5 571,
584–585, 595, 603c, 5.6 702–703, 709, 725c,
737, 741. *See also* **Vocabulary strategies.**

Unit Inquiry Projects. *See* **Projects.**

Usage. *See* **Adjectives, Adverbs, Clauses,
Conjunctions, Interjections, Negatives,
Nouns, Prepositions and prepositional
phrases, Pronouns, Sentences, Subject/verb
agreement, Verbs.**

V

Venn diagram. *See* **Graphic and semantic
organizers,** types.

Verbs
action, 5.2 207e–207f
helping, 5.2 229e–229f
linking, 5.2 207e–207f
main, 5.2 229e–229f
principle parts of, 5.3 315e–315f, 345e–345f,
363e–363f
tense, 5.3 287e–287f

Viewing
kinds of media
art, 5.3 315d
illustration, 5.1 67d, 5.2 207d, 5.4 411d,
5.5 603d, 5.6 725d
movies/video, 5.1 89d, 5.2 229d, 5.3 383d,
5.4 503d, 5.5 625d
multimedia, 5.3 383d, 5.4 503d, 5.5 535k
photography, 5.1 133d, 5.5 559d, 5.6 653d,
699d
television, 5.1 89d, 5.2 229d, 5.3 383d,
5.5 625d
responding to media
oral, 5.1 89d, 5.2 207d, 229d, 5.3 315d,
383d, 5.4 411d, 503d, 5.5 559d, 5.6 653d,
699d, 725d
written, 5.1 67d, 89d, 133d, 5.2 207d, 229d,
5.3 315d, 383d, 5.4 411d, 5.5 559d, 603d,
625d, 5.6 653d, 699d, 725d
uses of media
analysis, 5.1 67d, 89d, 133d, 5.2 207d, 229d,
5.3 315d, 383d, 5.4 411d, 5.5 559d, 603d,
625d, 5.6 653d, 699d, 725d

enjoyment, 5.1 89d, 5.2 229d, 5.3 383d,
5.4 503d, 5.5 625d, 5.6 653d, 699d, 725d
research, 5.5 559d, 5.6 653d

Visualizing, 5.1 68–69, 81, 83, 87, 89, DI·25,
DI·26, 5.4 484–485, 497, 501, DI·16, DI·46,
DI·47, 5.6 634–635, 647, 649, 653, DI·6, DI·7

Vocabulary development
classifying words, 5.1 70b, 5.4 394b, 5.6 702b
content-area vocabulary, 5.1 66, 70b, 86, 110,
5.2 160, 180, 226, 5.3 282, 290b, 312,
340, 5.4 434, 454, 480, 5.5 554, 600, 622,
5.6 636b, 670, 728b, 750
etymology for meaning, 5.2 188–189, 195, 207c,
5.3 290–291, 297, 305, 315c, 5.5 514–515,
527
graphic organizers for grouping, studying, and
retaining, 5.1 41c, 44b, 67c, 70b, 89c, 111c,
133c, 5.2 161c, 164b, 185c, 207c, 229c,
253c, 5.3 264b, 287c, 290b, 315c, 318b,
345c, 348b, 363c, 383c, 5.4 394b, 411c,
435b, 457c, 460b, 483c, 486b, 5.5 514b,
535c, 559c, 581c, 584b, 603c, 625c,
5.6 636b, 653c, 673c, 699c, 702b, 725c, 753c
introducing selection vocabulary, 5.1 20b, 44b,
70b, 92b, 114b, 5.2 144b, 164b, 188b, 210b,
232b, 5.3 264b, 290b, 318b, 348b, 366b,
5.4 394b, 414b, 438b, 460b, 486b, 5.5 514b,
538b, 562b, 584b, 606b, 5.6 636b, 656b,
676b, 702b, 728b
listening for vocabulary development, 5.1 18l–
18m, 42l–42m, 68l–68m, 90l–90m, 112l–
112m, 5.2 142l–142m, 162l–162m, 186l–
186m, 208l–208m, 230l–230m, 5.3 262l–
262m, 288l–288m, 316l–316m, 346l–346m,
364l–364m, 5.4 392l–392m, 412l–412m,
436l–436m, 458l–458m, 484l–484m,
5.5 512l–512m, 536l–536m, 560l–560m,
582l–582m, 604l–604m, 5.6 634l–634m,
654l–654m, 674l–674m, 700l–700m, 726l–
726m
practice lesson vocabulary, 5.1 29, 33, 55,
63, 79, 83, 103, 107, 123, 127, 5.2 153,
157, 173, 177, 197, 203, 219, 223, 241, 247,
5.3 273, 279, 303, 309, 327, 337, 357, 373,
377, 5.4 403, 407, 423, 431, 447, 451, 469,
477, 493, 497, 5.5 523, 529, 547, 551, 571,
575,593, 597, 615, 619, 5.6 645, 649, 663,
667, 685, 695, 713, 719, 739, 747
predict definitions, 5.1 20b, 5.4 438b,
5.5 606b, 5.6 656b
reading for vocabulary development, 5.1 20b,
44b, 70b, 92b, 114b, 5.2 144b, 164b, 188b,
210b, 232b, 5.3 264b, 290b, 318b, 348b,
366b, 5.4 394b, 414b, 438b, 460b, 486b,
5.5 514b, 538b, 562b, 584b, 606b, 5.6 636b,
656b, 676b, 702b, 728b
related words, 5.4 457c
roots, Greek and Latin, 5.2 188–189, 195, 207c,
5.3 290–291, 297, 305, 315c, 5.5 514–515,
527
speaking for vocabulary development, 5.1 18l,
42l, 68l, 90l, 112l, 114b, 5.2 142l, 162l, 186l,
208l, 230l, 5.3 262l, 288l, 316l, 346l, 364l,
5.4 392l, 412l, 436l, 458l, 484l, 5.5 512l,
536l, 560l, 562b, 582l, 604l, 5.6 634l, 654l,
674l, 700l, 726l, 728b
writing vocabulary, 5.1 41g, 67g–67h, 89g,
111g–111h, 133g–133h, 5.2 161g, 185g,
207g, 229g–229h, 253g, 5.3 287g, 315g,
345g, 363g–363h, 383g, 5.4 411g, 435g,
457g–457h, 483g, 503g, 5.5 535g, 559g–

559h, 581g, 603g, 625g, 5.6 653g, 673g,
699g, 725g, 753g. See also **Vocabulary
strategies.**

Vocabulary strategies
abbreviations, 5.3 383c
acronyms, 5.3 383c
analogies, 5.2 188b, 5.3 366b
antonyms, 5.1 20b, 92–93, 5.3 348b, 348–349,
363c, 5.4 394b, 5.5 514b, 584b
base words, 5.5 538b
compound words, 5.4 486b, 5.5 535c
connotation/denotation, 5.1 114b, 5.3 315c
context clues, 5.1 44–45, 53, 67c, 92–93, 99,
111c, 114–115, 123, 133c, 5.2 210–211, 219,
232b, 5.3 264–265, 275, 287, 318–319, 331,
345c, 348–349, 363c, 366b, 5.4 414–415,
425, 435c, 438–439, 447, 457c, 460–461,
473, 483c, 5.5 562–563, 571, 581c, 584–
585, 595, 603c, 5.6 702–703, 709, 725c,
728–729, 737, 741, 753c
dictionary/glossary, 5.1 70–71, 79, 89c,
5.2 164–165, 171, 185c, 5.5 538–539, 549,
559c, 5.6 636–637, 645, 653c, 656b
endings, 5.1 20b, 5.2 144b, 232–233, 245,
253c, 5.4 394–395, 403, 411c, 5.5 603e–
603f, 5.6 656b, 663, 673c
environmental words, 5.1 70b
graphophonic cues, using, 5.1 21, 5.2 233,
5.3 367, 5.4 395, 5.5 607, 5.6 677
Greek and Latin roots, 5.2 188–189, 195, 207c,
5.3 290–291, 297, 305, 315c, 5.5 514–515,
527
homographs, 5.4 394b, 5.6 728–729, 753c
homonyms, 5.1 44b, 44–45, 53, 67c, 5.3 318–
319, 345c
homophones, 5.4 414b, 435c
meaning, 5.1 92b, 99, 123, 5.3 331, 373,
5.4 425, 473, 5.5 571, 615, 702b, 709, 737,
741
multiple meaning words, 5.1 114–115, 133c,
5.2 164b, 5.3 264–265, 275, 287, 348b,
5.4 414b, 460b, 5.5 514b, 562–563, 581c
predict definitions, 5.4 438b
prefixes, 5.2 144–145, 155, 161c, DI·14,
5.3 366–367, 373, 383c, 5.5 606b, 606–607,
625c, DI·45, 5.6 DI·4
reading for vocabulary building, 5.1 20b, 44b,
70b, 92b, 114b, 5.2 144b, 164b, 188b, 210b,
232b, 5.3 264b, 290b, 318b, 348b, 366b,
5.4 394b, 414b, 438b, 460b, 486b, 5.5 514b,
538b, 562b, 584b, 606b, 5.6 636b, 656b,
676b, 702b, 728b
reference materials, 5.1 70–71, 79, 89c,
5.2 164–165, 171, 185c, 5.5 538–539, 549,
559c, 5.6 636–637, 645, 653c, 656b
suffixes, 5.1 20–21, 31, 41c, DI·4, DI·5, DI·44,
5.2 DI·4, DI·5, DI·34, 5.3 264b, 318b, DI·34,
5.4 486–487, 503c, DI·24, DI·45, 5.5 DI·14,
5.6 676–677, 691, 699c, DI·25, DI·44
synonyms, 5.1 20b, 92–93, 5.2 188b, 5.4 394b,
438–439, 447, 5.5 584b
unfamiliar words, 5.1 44b, 70–71, 89c, 111c,
5.2 164b, 164–165, 171, 185c, 210–211, 219,
5.4 414–415, 435c, 457c, 460–461, 483c,
5.5 538–539, 559c, 584–585, 595, 603c,
5.6 636–637, 653c, 702–703, 725c
word/definition match, 5.2 210b, 5.5 538b,
5.6 676b
word parts, 5.4 495
word structure, 5.1 79, 99, 112–113, 5.2 208–
209, 219, 5.3 262–263, 275, 316–317, 331,
346–347, 5.4 412–413, 425, 436–437, 447,

458–459, 473, 5.5 560–561, 571, 582–583,
595, 5.6 700–701, 709, 726–727, 737, 741
See also **Context clues for meaning,
Vocabulary development.**

Volume. See **Fluency, reading.**

W

Web site. See **Genres, Technology.**

Webbing. See **Graphic and semantic
organizers,** types.

Word attack skills. See **Context clues for
meaning, Dictionary/glossary, Phonics,
Vocabulary strategies, Word structure.**

Word histories. See **Word structure,** etymology.

Word identification. See **Context clues for
meaning, Dictionary/glossary, Vocabulary
strategies, Word structure.**

Word structure
base words
with spelling changes, 5.1 DI·14, 5.2 233,
5.4 495, DI·5, DI·45, 5.6 663
without spelling changes, 5.1 31, DI·4, DI·5,
DI·44, 5.2 DI·4, DI·14, DI·34, 5.4 DI·24,
DI·34, 5.5 DI·24, 5.6 DI·14, DI·24, DI·44
chunking, 5.1 20b, 92b, DI·23, 5.2 144b, DI·24,
DI·44, 5.3 366b, DI·4, DI·44, 5.4 414b, DI·14,
DI·34, DI·44, 5.5 538b, DI·34, 5.6 656b
compound words, 5.3 DI·14, 5.4 486b, 5.5 535c
contractions, 5.5 535e–535f
endings, inflected and uninflected, 5.1 20b, 31,
DI·14, DI·23, DI·34, 5.2 144b, 232–233, 245,
253c, DI·14, 5.4 394–395, 403, 411c, DI·5,
5.5 603e–603f, 5.6 663, DI·15
etymology, 5.2 188–189, 195, 207c, 5.3 290–
291, 297, 305, 315c, 5.5 514–515, 527
Greek and Latin roots, 5.2 188–189, 195, 207c,
5.3 290–291, 297, 305, 315c, 5.5 514–515,
527
plurals
irregular, 5.2 161e–161f
regular, 5.2 161e–161f, 5.6 656–657
possessives
irregular, 5.2 185e–185f
regular, 5.2 185e–185f
prefixes, 5.2 144–145, 155, 161c, DI·14,
5.3 366–367, 373, 383c, 5.5 606b, 606–607,
625c, DI·45, 5.6 DI·4
suffixes, 5.1 20–21, 31, 41c, DI·4, DI·5, DI·44,
5.2 DI·4, DI·5, DI·34, 5.3 264b, 318b, DI·34,
5.4 486–487, 503c, DI·24, DI·45, 5.5 DI·14,
5.6 676–677, 691, 699c, DI·25, DI·44
syllabication, 5.3 367
word parts, 5.3 DI·14, DI·15, DI·24, DI·34,
DI·45, 5.4 495, DI·4, DI·34, 5.5 DI·4, DI·24,
DI·44, 5.6 DI·4, DI·14, DI·24, DI·34
See also **Spelling.**

Word study. See **Context clues for meaning,
Dictionary/glossary, Vocabulary strategies,
Word structure.**

Working with words. See **Context clues for
meaning, Dictionary/glossary, Vocabulary
development, Vocabulary strategies.**

Work stations. *See* **Cross-Curricular Centers.**

Writer's craft. *See* **Literary craft,** author's craft/style/language.

Writing assessment. *See* **Assessment,** scoring guide (rubric).

Writing forms/products
  advertisement, 5.5 621, 625g–625h
  advice, 5.4 479, 483g–483h
  article, 5.1 109, 111g–111h, 5.6 749, 753g–753h
  biography, 5.5 577, 581g–581h
  character sketch, 5.1 35, 41g–41h
  comparison/contrast, 5.3 379, 383g–383h, WA2–WA9
  description, 5.3 359, 363g–363h, 5.4 499, 503g–503h
  editorial, 5.5 531, 535g–535h
  email, 5.4 409, 411g–411h
  essay, 5.3 311, 315g–315h, 5.5 553, 559g–559h
  explanatory paragraph/essay, 5.6 651, 653g–653h, 749, 753g–753h
  feature story, 5.3 339, 345g–345h
  how-to report, 5.2 WA2–WA9
  interview, 5.2 249, 253g–253h
  journal, 5.4 433, 435g–435h
  letter, friendly, 5.1 85, 89g–89h, 5.4 479, 483g–489h
  letter, thank you, 5.1 85, 89g–89h
  narrative, 5.1 129, 133g–133h, WA2–WA9
  news article/report/story, 5.2 205, 207g–207h
  notes, 5.6 669, 673g–673h
  outline, 5.6 721, 725g–725h
  personal narrative, 5.1 WA2–WA9
  persuasive argument/essay/paragraph, 5.5 WA2–WA9
  persuasive letter, 5.5 531, 535g–535h, 599, 603g–603h
  poem, 5.6 697, 699g–699h
  problem/solution, 5.5 553, 559g–559h
  research report, 5.6 WA2–WA9
  response log. *See* **Logs, strategy response.**
  review, 5.2 179, 185g–185h
  rules, 5.2 225, 229g–229h
  skit, 5.3 281, 287g–287h
  story, 5.4 453, 457g–457h, WA2–WA9
  summary, 5.2 159, 161g–161h
  tall tale, 5.1 65, 67g–67h

Writing modes
  descriptive, 5.1 35, 41g–41h, 5.3 359, 363g–363h, 5.4 433, 435g–435h, 499, 503g–503h
  expository, 5.1 109, 111g–111h, 5.2 178, 185g–185h, 225, 229g–229h, WA2–WA9, 5.3 311, 315g–315h, 379, 383g–383h, WA2–WA9, 5.5 553, 559g–559h, 5.6 651, 653g–653h, 669, 673g–673h, 721, 725g–725h, 749, 753g–753h, WA2–WA9
  expressive, 5.1 85, 89g–89h, 5.2 249, 253g–253h, 5.3 281, 287g–287h, 5.4 409, 411g–411h, 479, 483g–483h, 5.6 697, 699g–699h, 721, 725g–725

  narrative, 5.1 65, 67g–67h, 129, 133g–133h, WA2–WA9, 5.2 159, 161g–161h, 205, 207g–207h, 5.3 339, 345g–345h, 5.4 453, 457g–457h, WA2–WA9, 5.5 577, 581g–581h
  persuasive, 5.5 531, 535g–535h, 599, 603g–603h, 621, 625g–625h, WA2–WA9

Writing process
  assessing/scoring guide (rubric), 5.1 41h, 67h, 89h, 111h, 133h, WA7, 5.2 161h, 185h, 207h, 229h, 253h, WA7, 5.3 287h, 315h, 345h, 363h, 383h, WA7, 5.4 411h, 435h, 457h, 483h, 503h, WA7, 5.5 535h, 559h, 581h, 603h, 625h, WA7, 5.6 653h, 673h, 699h, 725h, 753h, WA7
  draft, 5.1 41h, 67h, 89h, 111h, 133h, WA4–WA5, 5.2 161h, 185h, 207h, 229h, 253h, WA4–WA5, 5.3 287h, 315h, 345h, 363h, 383h, WA4–WA5, 5.4 411h, 435h, 457h, 483h, 503h, WA4–WA5, 5.5 535h, 559h, 581h, 603h, 625h, WA4–WA5, 5.6 653h, 673h, 699h, 725h, 753h, WA4–WA5
  edit, 5.1 41h, 67h, 89h, 111h, 133h, WA6, 5.2 161h, 185h, 207h, 229h, 253h, WA6, 5.3 287h, 315h, 345h, 363h, 383h, WA6, 5.4 411h, 435h, 457h, 483h, 503h, WA6, 5.5 535h, 559h, 581h, 603h, 625h, WA6, 5.6 653h, 673h, 699h, 725h, 753h, WA6
  prewrite, 5.1 41h, 67h, 89h, 111h, 133h, WA3, WA8, 5.2 161h, 185h, 207h, 229h, 253h, WA3, WA8, 5.3 287h, 315h, 345h, 363h, 383h, WA3, WA8, 5.4 411h, 435h, 457h, 483h, 503h, WA3, WA8, 5.5 535h, 559h, 581h, 603h, 625h, WA3, WA8, 5.6 653h, 673h, 699h, 725h, 753h, WA3, WA8
  publish, 5.1 41h, 67h, 89h, 111h, WA7, 5.2 161h, 185h, 207h, 229h, WA7, 5.3 287h, 315h, 345h, 363h, WA7, 5.4 411h, 435h, 457h, 483h, WA7, 5.5 535h, 559h, 581h, 603h, WA7, 5.6 653h, 673h, 699h, 725h, 753h, WA7
  revise, 5.1 41h, 67h, 89h, 111h, 133h, WA5, WA9, 5.2 161h, 185h, 207h, 229h, 253h, WA5, WA9, 5.3 287h, 315h, 345h, 363h, 383h, WA5, WA9, 5.4 411h, 435h, 457h, 483h, 503h, WA5, WA9, 5.5 535h, 559h, 581h, 603h, 625h, WA5, WA9, 5.6 653h, 673h, 699h, 725h, 753h, 759g, WA5

Writing purpose
  clarify information, 5.2 159, 161g–161h, 203, 205, 207g–207h, 5.4 409, 411g–411h, 479, 483g–483h
  express ideas, 5.1 109, 111g–111h, 5.2 179, 185g–185h, 225, 229g–229h, WA2–WA9, 5.3 359, 363g–363h, 383g–383h, 379, WA2–WA9, 5.4 433, 435g–435h, 5.5 531, 535g–535h, 599, 603g–603h, WA2–WA9, 5.6 653g–653h, 725g–725h, 753g–753h, WA2–WA9
  respond to literature, 5.1 34, 41, 64, 67, 84, 89, 108, 111, 128, 133, 5.2 158, 159, 161, 161g–161h, 178, 185, 185g–185h, 204, 207, 224, 229, 248, 253, 5.3 280, 287, 310, 315, 338, 345, 358, 363, 378, 383, 5.4 408, 411, 432,

435, 452, 457, 478, 483, 498, 503g, 5.5 530, 535, 552, 559, 576, 581, 598, 603g, 5.6 650, 653, 668, 673, 696, 699, 720, 725, 748, 753
  share experiences, 5.1 129, 133g–133h, WA2–WA9, 5.4 408, 411g–411h, 5.5 621, 631g–631h
  share ideas/information, 5.1 35, 41g–41h, 109, 111g–111h, 5.2 159, 161g–161h, 179, 185g–185h, 225, 229g–229h, 249, 253g–253h, WA2–WA9, 5.3 311, 315g–315h, 379, 383g–383h, WA2–WA9, 5.5 553, 559g–559h, 577, 581g–581h, 5.6 651, 653g–653h, 669, 673g–673h, 721, 725g–725h, 749, 753g–753h, WA2–WA9
  share stories/poems, 5.1 65, 67g–67h, 129, 133g–133h, WA2–WA9, 5.2 205, 207g–207h, 5.3 281, 287g–287h, 339, 345g–345h, 5.4 453, 457g–457h, 499, 503g–503h, WA2–WA9, 5.6 697, 699g-699h
  specific audience, 5.1 85, 89g–89h, 5.2 WA2–WA9, 5.4 408, 411g–411h, 478, 483g–483h, 5.5 599, 603g–603h

Writing, six-trait. *See* **Six-trait writing.**

Writing strategies. *See* **Writing process.**

Writing with technology, 5.1 WA6, WA9, 5.2 WA6, WA9, 5.3 287k, 315k, 363k, WA6, WA9, 5.4 411k, WA6, WA9, 5.5 535k, 559k, 581k, 603k, 625k, WA6, WA9, 5.6 673k, 725k, 753k, WA6, WA9

ACKNOWLEDGMENTS

Teacher's Edition

Text

KWL Strategy: The KWL Interactive Reading Strategy was developed and is used by permission of Donna Ogle, National-Louis University, Evanston, Illinois, co-author of *Reading Today and Tomorrow*, Holt, Rinehart & Winston Publishers, 1988. (See also *The Reading Teacher*, February 1986, pp. 564–570.)

Page 262m: From *What's the Big Idea, Ben Franklin?* by Jean Fritz. Copyright © 1976 by Jean Fritz, text. Reprinted by permission of Coward-McCann, a Division of Penguin Young Readers Group, a Member of Penguin Group (USA) Inc., 345 Hudson Street, New York, NY 10014. All rights reserved.

Page 288m: From "Kid with the Camera Eye," *Norman Rockwell: Storyteller with a Brush* by Beverly Gherman. Text copyright © 2000 by Beverly Gherman. Reprinted by permission of Atheneum Books for Young Readers, an imprint of Simon & Schuster Children's Publishing Division.

Page 316m: From *Graveyards of the Dinosaurs* by Shelley Tanaka. Copyright © 1998 by Shelley Tanaka. Reprinted by permission of Hyperion Books for Children.

Page 346m: From *Bud, Not Buddy* by Christopher Paul Curtis. Copyright © 1999 by Christopher Paul Curtis. Reprinted by permission of Random House Children's Books, a division of Random House, Inc.

Page 364m: Adaptation of "The Making of the Lord of the Rings" by Katherine Murray, *OWL* Magazine, December 2001. Reprinted by permission of Bayard Press Canada Inc.

Artists

Greg Newbold: cover, page i

Photographs

Every effort has been made to secure permission and provide appropriate credit for photographic material. The publisher deeply regrets any omission and pledges to correct errors called to its attention in subsequent editions.

Unless otherwise acknowledged, all photographs are the property of Scott Foresman, a division of Pearson Education.

Photo locators denoted as follows: Top (T), Center (C), Bottom (B), Left (L), Right (R), Background (Bkgd)

42M Getty Images; 111L Brand X Pictures/Getty Images; 160J Digital Wisdom, Inc.; 228I Getty Images; 288M Getty Images; 315L Getty Images; 316M Getty Images; 388K Brand X Pictures; 392M Getty Images; 412M (T) © Comstock Inc, (Bkgd) Getty Images; 436M ©Dover Publications; 457L Getty Images; 476K Getty Images; 484M ©Image Source Limited; 512M Getty Images; 535L ©Royalty-Free/Corbis; 536M Hemera Technologies; 560M Getty Images; 634M Brand X Pictures; 654M Getty Images; 674M ©Dover Publications; 762M Brand X Pictures